PUBLICATIONS OF THE UNIVERSITY OF MANCHESTER

No CCXXXVII

HISTORICAL SERIES No. LXIX

SAINT BERNARD OF CLAIRVAUX

PORTRAIT OF ST. BERNARD

SAINT BERNARD OF CLAIRVAUX

BY

WATKIN WILLIAMS

NEC ENIM OPERA NOSTRA TRANSEUNT
UT VIDENTUR; SED TEMPORALIA
QUAEQUE VELUT AETERNITATIS
SEMINA JACIUNTUR

MANCHESTER UNIVERSITY PRESS

1935

Published by the University of Manchester at
THE UNIVERSITY PRESS (H. M. McKechnie, M.A., Secretary)
8-10 Wright Street, MANCHESTER, 15

PRINTED IN GREAT BRITAIN BY
THE ABERDEEN UNIVERSITY PRESS LIMITED
ABERDEEN, SCOTLAND

CISTERCIENSIBVS
SIVE NOTIS SIVE IGNOTIS
QVI NOSTRIS TEMPORIBVS
VETERA RENOVARE
NOVA CONDERE
INDEFESSE STVDENT
SANCTI BERNARDI
SCHOLARIS HVMILLIMVS

PREFACE

LOOKING back to one's first lessons in European history of the Middle Ages one seeks in vain for any reference to our subject. The Cistercians came to England; the Second Crusade was fought and lost; with momentous results Eleanor of Aquitaine married Henry Plantagenet. But nowhere evident in the picture did one find an Abbot of Clairvaux.

There was, of course, Milman's *History of Latin Christianity*, but that did not come one's way in childhood—fortunately, we may think, for surely—in spite of the recognition of him as " at once the leading and the governing head of Christendom," as "blessed with an amazing native power and greatness " (iv. 301 sq., ed. 1872)—the St. Bernard whom the dean portrays does not always escape the charge of travesty, to say nothing of inaccuracies which can scarcely be regarded as minor, such as the note (iv. 309) to the effect that " the second book (of the *Life*) bears the name of Bernard, Abbot of Beauvale " !   There was a pleasant translation of Neander's *Der heilige Bernhard und sein Zeitalter* published by Matilda Wrench in 1843, but one never heard of it.   In the early sixties Charles Kingsley was lecturing at Cambridge on *The Monk a Civilizer* and committed himself to the following statement as to monks in general and as to St. Bernard in particular: " You never get in their writings anything of that manly calmness, which we so deservedly honour, and at which we all aim for ourselves.   They are bombastic; excited; perpetually mistaking virulence for strength, putting us in mind for ever of the allocutions of the Popes.   Read the writings of one of the best of monks, and of men, who ever lived, the great St. Bernard, and you will be painfully struck by this hysterical element " (*The Roman and the Teuton*, 241, ed. 1889). In 1863 appeared Cotter Morison's *Life and Times of St. Bernard* and served well to correct this false impression. Later still, in 1890, Eales's *St. Bernard, Abbot of Clairvaux*, was published in the series known as *The Fathers for English Readers* ; and in 1893 Storrs's *Bernard of Clairvaux : The Times, The Man and His Work* was published in New York. This last careful study, in spite of the fact that it did—and did generously—somewhat belated justice to its subject, probably failed to arouse amongst British readers the interest which it deserved. At last, in 1899, came Marion Crawford's *Via Crucis*, a story of the Second Crusade, which, allowing for the exaggeration and the lack of perspective common to most settings of history in romance, in some degree succeeded in depicting the wilfulness of Queen Eleanor, the weakness of Louis le Jeune and the weird fanaticism of Arnald of Brescia over against the gracious and compelling presence of one whom it well described as " almost the world's physician in his day " (Chap. XIII. *ad init.*). No serious estimate of St. Bernard has, however, for sympathetic discernment, surpassed that of Dr. G. G. Coulton, published in 1923, in the first volume of his *Five Centuries of Religion*. More recently Dom Ailbe Luddy of Mount Melleray Abbey has published an interesting work entitled *Life and Teaching of St. Bernard* (Dublin, 1927), which deals fully with the theology of the saint and provides extensive passages translated from his treatises and from his correspondence.

But, alas, even now the quite intelligent public schoolboy's first association with St. Bernard is that of dogs ! Perhaps, if in dull moments during a sermon he has scanned his hymn-book, he may have some vague notion of a Bernard who wrote *Jerusalem the golden*, or—surely right this time ! —he may proclaim with assurance that it is the *Jesus, the very thought is sweet* to which St. Bernard owes his fame.

The other day one read in a venerable *Quarterly* words of a distinguished writer to the effect that " the time of which St. Bernard wrote his *Hora novissima, tempora pessima* " could scarcely have been a golden age. Thus such knowledge of the saint as may be the possession even of a really educated man is sometimes sufficiently confused. Not very long ago, too, one of our great journals contained a leading article on the proverb *Love me, love my dog*, confidently ascribing its authorship—as do some popular collections—to the genius of St. Bernard of Clairvaux, whereas he explicitly quotes it as "a common saying" (*In Fest. S. Michael. Sermo*, I. 3).

This last slip is perhaps excusable, but not so either the gaping *lacuna* of his absence from the history of the XIIth century, as it has for long been told to the young, or the prevailing impressions that he benevolently bred life-saving dogs and that he wrote one — certainly very beautiful — hymn.

To the late Abbé Elphège Vacandard, who loved England and rejoiced to bear the Christian name of one of her martyred archbishops, is mainly due the writing of this little book. Without his encouragement and guidance it would have been impossible. And—perhaps happily—on a field which he has harvested there has been little left for the gleaner ; rarely has it been necessary to do more than to draw upon the resources of his well-stored garner in the endeavour to build up some representation of the character of our subject as he played his part in Europe during at least the second quarter of the XIIth century. His personality as it told upon his contemporaries, this is what determines its message to us to-day. What was he ? Like many another he was a man of noble birth, blessed by the possession of good and pious parents who gave careful attention to the education of his character and to the cultivation of his mind. But, by whatever means shaped, the material was in each case exceptional. He was a shaft receptive of the finest polish, a gem apt for clear-cutting to the sharpest edge. His courage was, it would seem, indomitable ; his humility, whenever he recognized the claim of authority to be a just one, was profound. His accurate precision in distinguishing personal from official rights, his consistency in acting upon such distinction, were the more remarkable when we consider that his emotions were almost tempestuous. His soul was as transparent as his body was frail. The mistakes which men made—to their own undoing—in their dealings with him are to be explained, surely, by the fact that they interpreted him as they did themselves, rather than by any skilful diplomacy, any trained *finesse*, on his part. His simplicity disarmed them. It is idle work drawing the sword upon an angel ; the very violence of the thrust will bring a man to his knees. At any rate in his personal presence such characters as William of Poitiers, Roger of Sicily, Conrad of Hohenstaufen and Eleanor of Aquitaine were respectful and even submissive.

It may be contended that the portrait of him which has come down to us was drawn by his professed adherents. But his professed opponents also drew him, and we cannot fail to recognize the same person in what they offer us. The St. Bernard of Abélard and of Berengarius of Poitiers is fundamentally the St. Bernard of William of St. Thierry and of Geoffrey. Neither the discerning thinker whose grievance against him was acute, nor the ready lampooner who sought in him material for his wit, has succeeded in presenting us with a character which is not substantially that of the *Vitae* written by his friends. The same might be said of others who had opportunities of estimating his influence, such as John of Salisbury and Otto of Freising. The former in particular, judicially minded and sensitive to every breath of the spirit of the times, conveys to us the impression of a personality, not only outstanding but in its self-consistency grave and well-assured. Of Otto it may be said that the very admission which he makes of St. Bernard's credulity, so far from disturbing us, gives a touch of reality to the rest of the portrait (cf. p. 290 *infra*).

Primarily St. Bernard was neither a philosopher, nor a theologian, nor a statesman, but a mystic. It was in and through prayer, the bed-rock of mysticism, that the call came to him first to the religious life, then to be a master both intensively and extensively in its school and finally, by a pressure of circumstances which irked him and imposed upon him heavy correspondence, frequent interviews and incessant journeyings, to fulfil the function of a prophet to the Christendom of his day.

Happily, in addition to a considerable record of his doings, there has come down to us much of what he wrote—with the exception of his letters, probably a large proportion. By means of the latter we may learn something of the content of his prophetic message, whether addressed to clergy or to laity, to religious or to seculars. We have said that he was not primarily either a philosopher, or a theologian, or a statesman. Yet he concerned himself with all three callings ; for he handled with a surpassing touch, firm or delicate, as the case might demand, the moral problems which confronted each of them. It was rarely of his own motion that he wrote. For the most part men asked it of him. It was at the request of Godfrey de la Roche that he wrote *De Gradibus Humilitatis et Superbiae,* his first known treatise ; he was moved to write the *Apologia* by William of St. Thierry ; the *Sermones in Cantica Canticorum* would probably have been lost to us but for the solicitation of Bernard de Portis, the Carthusian monk of Portes-en-Bugey. So lowly was his self-esteem that he would leave it to the judgement of this comparatively obscure friend as to whether he should continue to commit to writing these precious reflections (*Epp.* CLIII., CLIV.).

The Church has sometimes been reproached with unwarrantable intervention in the political or in the social sphere. Was St. Bernard's influence open to such reproach ? There have been perhaps few instances of one man playing so important a part over, speaking relatively, so large an area of Western civilization. We could wish that we had more of his correspondence ; what is extant, however, sufficiently illustrates the restraint which he put upon himself. In the great treatise *De Consideratione* addressed to Eugenius III he speaks of the Pope's life as a life of *actio,* manifold and bewildering, and warns him of the danger, only too human as it is, of exceeding the limits proper to such *actio. Quid fines alienos invaditis ? Quid falcem vestram in alienam messem extenditis (De Consid.,* I. vi. 7) ? At least he knew the risk involved on this score in the tenure of any ecclesiastical office ; and we may believe that neither in body nor in spirit did he ever leave his cloister save only to fulfil the function of a *rector animarum.* History tells us, surely, that when he made enemies he made them of men who resented the enlightenment of their consciences, who shrank from seeing themselves as they really were.

His emotions, we have remarked, were almost tempestuous ; this fact constituted at once his most salient limitation

and the fine point of the goad with which he drove men.
Not often was he more deeply moved than when he wrote
his letter to Robert of Châtillon on the occasion of the latter's
seduction from Clairvaux to Cluny ; and it is in this very
letter that we find perhaps his most frank confession of his
limitation in this respect. *Fuerit certe meae culpae quod
discessisti. Delicato quippe adolescentulo austerus exstiteram,
et tenerum durus nimis inhumane tractavi* (*Ep.* I. 2).

And yet was he really lacking in sympathy with our
common frailty ? Most of us probably would have preferred
a prolonged stay at Cluny rather than at Clairvaux. How
attractive would have been the flavour of dishes seasoned
with choice spices imported from overseas or from the East !
How inviting the little beds spread with their dainty Ratisbon
coverlets of warm red or scarlet (Petr. Ven. *Statuta Congr.
Cluniac.* xi. and xviii., *P.L.* CLXXXIX.) !

Nay, it was but the entire correctness of his sense of values
which accounted for the sharpness of his tongue. " We needs
must love the highest when we see it " ; and he would have
men see that they might love. By nature he was no dour
puritan ; nor indeed by grace.

But let us look at him at his most human, the torrent of
his natural affection rushing uncontrolled. It is the death
of his brother Gerard ; and his passionate lament pours itself
forth in the midst of a sermon on the Song of Songs (XXVI.),
as it were in an atmosphere of mystic contemplation. Earth
touches heaven, and is sanctified by the contact. *Quousque
enim dissimulo,* he exclaims, *et ignis, quem intra meipsum
abscondo, triste pectus adurit, interiora depascitur ?* . . .
*Subtracto siquidem illo, per quem mea in Domino studia ut-
cunque libera esse solebant, simul et cor meum dereliquit me.* He
has restrained himself hitherto, but no longer is it possible.
*Sed feci vim animo, ac dissimulavi usque huc ; ne affectus
quidem vincere videretur. Denique plorantibus aliis, ego
(ut advertere potuistis) siccis oculis secutus sum invisum funus,
siccis oculis steti ad tumulum, quousque cuncta peracta sunt
exequiarum solemnia.* Later he breaks forth passionately in
language which reveals the tension of feeling. *Amarissima
separatio et quam non posset omnino efficere nisi mors ! Quando
enim me vivus vivum desereres ? Omnino opus mortis, hor-*

rendum divortium. Quis enim tam suavi vinculo mutui nostri non pepercisset amoris, nisi totius suavitatis inimica mors ? . . . Vivo ut vivens moriar : et hoc dixerim vitam ? Quam mitius me privares, O austera mors, vitae usu quam fructu !

All this is very human. And history is nothing if not human, the record of the action and reaction of personalities, which we only really understand when we have seen them comporting themselves in domestic crises. In St. Bernard's life there is no scene over which we may be tempted to draw a veil ; indeed it is doubtful whether there was any moment of it at which he was not too luminously transparent to be the subject of such treatment ; but then there must be no moment of it which we allow ourselves to reckon as of no account. This marvellous complex of mysticism, emotionalism and leadership is indeed worth knowing *teres atque rotundus ;* if only it be that we can, in our imperfect way, represent him so.

There is no doubt but that, socially and politically, St. Bernard's conscience was in advance of the standard prevailing among his contemporaries. How far this was due to a certain tenderness of sentiment it may be difficult to say ; but it is in large measure to be explained by its superior enlightenment. He understood, for example, the prophetic utterances as to the Jews in a sense not common in his day. Persecution generally as a method of conversion was not merely repulsive to him on the ground of its cruelty, but on psychological grounds he regarded it as futile. Whatever the civil arm might do to protect public morals by repressive measures, it was not by such measures that good Christians would be made. This was the line which he took in the matter of the sectaries in the Rhineland and in Languedoc. Arnald of Brescia was deserving of expulsion, first from Italy and then from France, not as a heretic, but as a menace to the peace of the commonwealth (cf. pp. 322 sqq. *infra*). It were well to remember that freedom of thought is something different from freedom of public speech, that toleration or suppression is to be justified mainly by circumstances ; and moreover that, should we fail to recognize in St. Bernard—a man possessed by the conviction : *Porro unum est necessarium* —a superabundance of what Matthew Arnold has described as the "*spontaneity of consciousness*, which tends continually to enlarge our whole law of doing" (*Culture and Anarchy*, 105, ed. 1897), it should be no matter for surprise. We are perhaps a little surprised to find him advising the extermination of the pagan hordes who threatened the flank of the Crusading armies, and doubtless for the moment he was not entirely true to his principle of abstention from interference in military affairs ; but quite possibly, allowing that it was an issue of war which was involved, he was not altogether wrong.

The tenderness of sentiment, the enlightened state of conscience, which marked St. Bernard are specially noticeable, as we should expect, in the records of works which his biographers class as miraculous. The earliest account which we have of any such work, the story of the cure of Josbert de la Ferté, is sufficiently typical to illustrate this (Gaufr. *Fragm., Codex Aureaevall.*, 25 sqq. Cf. pp. 219 sq. *infra*). But in any crisis of his life we are always aware of it ; this poise of double-edged emotional force and keen-sighted outlook of conscience, which goes so far to explain why men hailed him as a " man of God." And when we remember that in the background of it lay that indefinable magnetic gift which we call leadership, motived, chastened and corrected by intense mystic contemplation, we can perhaps understand why men did him more than lip-service.

Nor was it solely in respect of great affairs in Church or in state that he would demand such service. Even so late as the year 1152, when his thoughts would have been turning in the direction of his end, he would urge the claims of common honesty in small matters—so small, indeed, that we may be surprised that he should have been concerned with them— as not long afterwards at Metz he would urge at great cost of pain and labour the claims of humanity on a large scale (cf. pp. 358 sq. *infra*). Thus we have a little letter in which he appeals to Henry, Count of Champagne, son and successor of his old friend Theobald, to see that some pigs, belonging to the Austin Canons of St. Vorles at Châtillon-sur-Seine, which have been stolen are restored to their rightful owners (*Ep.* CCLXXIX.) ! It was just that scrupulous attention to every detail in which a principle is at stake which goes to make the genius of a prophet.

Never with him was there any eluding of " the choice of
tints. . . . Life's business being just the terrible choice."
Never was his mind at rest so long as there was any doubt
as to the tint to choose. A moral problem in solution—and
no more—was in his view uncongenial, even dangerous.

It is typical of the impression of his conscientious self-
scrutiny which prevailed among his friends that it is recorded
that after his missionary journey in Languedoc he was gravely
perturbed as to the true explanation of the many wonders
which he had recently wrought. Such things, he argued,
are either signs of great holiness or they are done by those
*qui virtutes multas in nomine Domini operantur, et a Domino
ignorantur.* After discussing the question with *viri spirituales*
he finally concluded that these marvellous cures *non ad
sanctitatem unius sed ad multorum spectare salutem . . . nec
ad meam fieri commendationem sed ad commonitionem potius
aliorum* (*Vita Prima*, III. vii. 20). It would appear as
though he were interpreting his acts of charity in the terms
of the highest degree of love, a subject of which he treats in
the *De Diligendo Deo* (X. 27)—seeking to lose himself, whether
meritorious or the reverse, in his instrumentality, indeed not
to be conscious of himself at all (*omnino non sentire seipsum*)
but *totus pergere in Deum ;* and from such a state as that to
respond to the claims of *fraterna charitas* whenever they
might arise. It is a remarkable illustration of the bearing
of his contemplative upon his active life, of mysticism upon
morals.

And indeed, although St. Bernard may not have been
primarily a philosopher, his intimate knowledge of human
nature and the scientific *netteté* of his analysis both of its
motives and of its actions, reinforced by his keen pastoral
zeal, made him a moralist of a very high order. In his treatise
De Gratia et Libero Arbitrio, written at a date shortly before
the year 1128 and sent to Cardinal Haimeric in response to
a request for some of his works (*Ep.* LII.), we have a carefully
and exhaustively reasoned statement of *libertas a necessitate*
as being the inalienable possession and the distinctive characteristic of man during his period of probation ; a statement
which had expressly in view the needs of plain people of
his day, let us say, of the ὀρεκτικὸς νοῦς as it found

itself frequently hindered rather than helped by the meta-
physics of the schools. Doubtless St. Bernard had read both
St. Augustine and St. Anselm on this subject, but his manner
of treatment while, it may be, no less scientific than is that
of either of them, would seem to be at closer grip with life
in the concrete. Here, as sometimes elsewhere, he reminds
us of Dr. Johnson. The present writer once gave to a friend,
a learned scientist and a Fellow of the Royal Society, a copy
of his modest English edition of this great work (*St. Bernard:
Concerning Grace and Free Will*) ; the reader's verdict was :
" I never really understood before what free will means."

Perhaps one of St. Bernard's most charming characteristics was his genius for friendship. Its most intimate type
we recognize in early days—in the case of Hugh of Mâcon
or Hugues de Vitry (cf. pp. 11 sq. *infra*). Later we trace
the same type in the case of William of St. Thierry. With
him it was the very soul of leadership ; the men of such
different ages as were Gaudry de Touillon and Robert de
Châtillon, who gathered around him at Châtillon-sur-Seine
to prepare themselves for the great step of seeking admission
to Cîteaux, met as friends under the roof of a friend. Fiery
temperaments like that of Roger of Sicily were reduced to
meekness by the persuasiveness of friendship ; weak, vacillating temperaments like that of Louis le Jeune were strengthened and steadied by the confidence of friendship. We
cannot fail to find in the genius of friendship one of the most
salient features of his correspondence.

Often the plainness of his speech and the severity of his
rebukes gave offence, but usually in the end the conviction
prevailed that, accordingly to his lights, he had dealt faithfully ; and, even as his long-standing friendship with Peter
the Venerable did not founder in " the storm of Langres "
(Petr. Vener. *Epp. Lib.* III. xvii. Cf. p. 163 *infra*), so too
did the time come when the " ancient enmities " between
himself and Abélard were " appeased " (*op. cit.*, IV. iv.
Cf. p. 312 *infra*), and a friendship formed, tardy doubtless,
but surely on St. Bernard's side none the less genuine for
the very difficulties which made it such ; a friendship which
we may think to have been a miracle of grace, seeing that
habet vera amicitia nonnunquam objurgationem, adulationem

nunquam (*Ep.* CCXLIII.) ; yet for the working of which miracle the divine influence would have found ready response from the will of one whose consistent desire it was : *Mihi contingat semper beare amicos terrendo salubriter, non adulando fallaciter* (*Ep.* IX.).

This, however, was scarcely the distinctively temperamental type of friendship which was proper to St. Bernard. The latter demanded a David—or rather many Davids, for it was not exclusive ; nor, on the other hand, was it jealous or *exigeant*. It was perhaps something of that feature of the *anima naturaliter Christiana* which we may trace in another great Burgundian monk of centuries later, Henri Dominique Lacordaire. It may be well illustrated by a letter written about the year 1143 to Peter the Venerable in which, excusing himself for plain speaking on a purely personal matter, he remarks : *Sed hoc dixi, ne quid clausum in mente retinerem quod ore non promerem, quod id vera recuset amicitia* (*Ep.* CCXXVIII.).

Cor ad cor loquitur ; the words aptly suggest the nature of the raw material of which, as it were in the workshop of mystic contemplation, was wrought this as many another great prophetic personality which, taking humanity as it found it, has sped it on its journey to the City of God.

It is difficult for me adequately to express my gratitude to the many friends who have with such unstinted generosity come to my aid. To begin with the illustrations. But for the helpful intervention of Monseigneur René Moissenet, Maître de Chapelle of St. Bénigne, and the sympathetic interest of the Conservateur of the Musée at Dijon and of Dom Tiburz Hümpfner, Secretary to the Abbot General of the Cistercians of the Strict Observance, the frontispiece would not have been possible. The map of Cistercian houses in France is the work of Dom Alexis Presse, Abbot of Tamié, and is reproduced by his kind permission. My wife I have to thank for her beautiful sketches and my son for his excellent photographs, all of these being work done upon the spot during family pilgrimages made in five successive summers to places hallowed by the memory of St. Bernard. For the Mediaeval plan of Rome I have to thank Dr. H. H. E.

Craster, Bodley's Librarian, and Dom André Wilmart, the latter of whom took infinite pains to obtain for me a satisfactory reproduction of the MS. at the Vatican. The plan of Rome taken from *Le Chiese di Roma nel medio evo*, intended to serve as a key to the older plan, appears by the generous leave of the author, Professor Cristiano Huelsen, and his publisher, Signor Leo S. Olschki of Florence. In the selection of it I was greatly helped by Mr. S. B. R. Sampson.

Again and again my friends the Abbot of Tamié, Mons. L. Morel-Payen, Librarian of Troyes, and Mons. Ch. Oursel, Librarian of Dijon, have patiently submitted themselves to my *questionnaires* greatly to the furtherance of my researches; and their readiness to place at my disposal precious MSS. and *incunabula* in their charge has enabled me to speak of many points at first hand. The Appendix *Literaria* owes more than I can express to the helpful suggestions of Professor Edward Bensly; to Mr. F. J. E. Raby and to Mr. Reginald Vaux I am indebted for advice as to the hymns attributed to St. Bernard, and to the Reverend G. B. Vaux for reading what has been said of St. Bernard as a Classical scholar. For guidance in any path of philosophy which I may have made bold to tread I would thank a beloved and venerated master, the late Professor J. A. Stewart. To many others I am grateful for valuable information; to Mons. Henri Omont and his *adjoints*—in particular Mons. Ph. Lauer—at the Bibliothèque Nationale; to Mons. A. Perrault-Dabot of the Monuments Historiques, Mons. G. Collon, Librarian of Tours, Mons. G. Jeanton of Tournus, formerly President of the Academy of Mâcon, Mons. P. Claudon, Archivist of the Côte-d'or, Mons. Jacquet of St. Marcel-lès-Châlon, Commandant Henri Charrier of Dijon, Mons. René Louis of Auxerre, Mons. A. Vittenet of Vitteaux, the Société des Bollandistes at Brussels, Professor A. Hamilton Thompson and the Keeper of Western MSS. in the Bodleian.

The Benedictines of Downside Abbey have given me much help; my friend Dom Adrian Morey especially, who has taken the greatest possible pains in reading the entire book in proof. Nor should I forget the inspiring encouragement and the sound advice of Professor E. F. Jacob, Professor James Tait and Mr. H. M. McKechnie, Secretary of the University Press. To all of these and to others whom to my shame I may have overlooked, I would say : Thank you *de plein cœur.*

An effort has been made to provide in the *Indices* something more than mere lists of names ; rather to distinguish homonymous persons and places, and to supplement at discretion the information given in the text.

The great collections of the *Monumenta Germaniae Historica,* the *Recueil des Historiens des Gaules et de la France,* the *Patrologia Latina* of Migne and the *Rolls Series* are cited as *M.G.H., R.H.G.F., P.L.* and *R.S.* respectively. *Gallia Christiana* is cited as *Gall. Christ.* Amongst other authorities to which reference is frequently made may be mentioned the *Regesta Romanorum Pontificum* of P. Jaffé, the *Concilia Generalia* of Ph. Labbe and G. Cossart, the *Sacrorum Conciliorum Nova et Amplissima Collectio* of J. D. Mansi, the *Cisterciensium seu verius Ecclesiasticorum Annalium Quatuor Tomi* of Angelo Manriquez, the *Fasciculus Sanctorum Ordinis Cisterciensis* of Chrysostom Henriquez, the *Italia Sacra* of Ferdinando Ughelli, the *Coronica general de la orden de San Benito* of Antonio Yepes, *España Sagrada,* the more familiar *Monasticon Anglicanum* and finally the *Originum Cisterciensium Tomus I* of Leopold Janauschek, the first part of a great work, alas, unfinished, but sufficiently complete to provide an exhaustive conspectus of every ancient Cistercian foundation, with the exception of one in Sicily or in Apulia unlocated and unnamed (cf. pp. 70 sqq. *infra*). The learned monk of Zwettl published it at Vienna in 1877.

And there remains to be acknowledged my debt to the illustrious Congrégation de St. Maur for such works as the *Annales Ordinis S. Benedicti,* the *Acta Sanctorum Ordinis S. Benedicti,* the *Spicilegium,* the *Thesaurus Novus Anecdotorum* and the *Veterum Scriptorum et Monumentorum Amplissima Collectio ;* for all of which, for *Gallia Christiana* and for the *R.H.G.F.* it was responsible, as the names of Mabillon, Massuet, Martène, Durand, d'Achery, Ruinart, de Ste. Marthe (*Sammarthanus*), Bouquet and Brial may remind us. Beaunier's *Recueil Historique, Chronologique, et Topographiques, des Archevêchez, Evêchez, Abbayes et Prieurez de France,* cited as *Recueil des Abbayes de France,* is a mine of information ; and the anonymous *Voyage littéraire de deux religieux Bénédictins de la Congrégation de Saint Maur* of Martène and Durand, with its delightful illustrations and its fascinating account of many of the sacred places of Mediaeval France, as they were three-quarters of a century or more before the Revolution had despoiled them, is a book the facsimile reproduction of which would be a contribution to *belles-lettres*.

It is to be hoped that here and there a reader may be found who is sufficiently interested to seek to familiarize himself with the pages of some of these works, most of which are on the shelves of our larger libraries ; it is everything to trace the story to its sources. He may even examine for himself at Dijon or at Troyes a few of such MSS. of Cîteaux or of Clairvaux as happily remain to us. I can confidently promise him the cordial welcome of their courteous custodians. But in these days of revived Cistercian life it is open to him to do yet more ; to wander in the broad alleys of Cîteaux once again trodden by the feet of sons of St. Bernard, or to spend a week at Tamié, hear the old Cistercian chant, see the old Cistercian Rite and turn the folios of the *Codex Aureaevallensis*. And Clairvaux ! What will he say of it, should he find himself there ? *Nunc igitur consurge Domine Deus in requiem tuam, tu et arca fortitudinis tuae.* In an atmosphere of great natural beauty and of venerable historical association, which neither the presence of a prison-house nor the lapse of time has availed to destroy, he will—in some degree, surely, enter into the spirit of the prayer.

WATKIN WILLIAMS.

SYNOPSIS OF CONTENTS

CHAPTER I

CHAPTER II

CHAPTER III

CHAPTER IV

CHAPTER V

CHAPTER VI

CHAPTER VII

The Healing of the Schism in Germany and in Italy . 134–158

CHAPTER IX

LOUIS LE GROS

Louis le Jeune

CHAPTER XI

c

CHAPTER XII

CHAPTER XIII

The Theology of the Schools . . . .

Abélard

GILBERT DE LA PORRÉE

CHAPTER XIV

CHAPTER XV

APPENDICES

INDICES

LIST OF ILLUSTRATIONS

* All illustrations marked by an asterisk are from original paintings by Mrs. Watkin Williams.

FONTAINES-LÈS-DIJON

CHAPTER I

CHILDHOOD AND VOCATION

FONTAINES-LÈS-DIJON, the name of which is to be explained by the springs at the foot of its acclivity, is the accepted birth-place of St. Bernard. It crowns a steep hill standing about a thousand feet above sea-level, two miles North by West of the old capital of Burgundy, a position from which, on a clear day, Mont Blanc may be descried on the distant horizon to the S.E.[1] In the XIth century there would have existed inside its double enclosure the great quadrangular *logis*, the dwelling of the seigneurial family, with on the ground-floor the rooms reserved for guests and for the sick. What is left to-day of the original structure of the *castellum* is probably not much more than the foundations together with considerable portions of three walls, namely, the two longer exterior walls on the East and West and the wall at right angles to them which bisects equally the interior. It was, we may believe, in a room on the ground-floor reserved for the sick, which since so early as the middle of the XVIth century has been used as an oratory under the name of " la chapelle monsieur saint Bernard," that the saint was born.[2] At first it would seem to have been under the charge of the *curé* of the parish until in 1613 the Feuillants, reformed Cistercians even stricter in their observance than the Trappists founded about a century later than themselves, obtained possession of the *château* and established in it a priory of their congregation which remained until the Revolution.[3] Happily in course of time it reverted to its sacred use ; it is now in the reverent custody of the Missionaires de St. Bernard, who settled there in 1880.

In spite of this well-established tradition a claim has been put in for Châtillon-sur-Seine as having been the birth-place of St. Bernard.[4] It is, however, scarcely tenable, being founded solely upon a reading in Recension A of the First Book of the *Vita Prima* corrected by Geoffrey in Recension B. It is true that St. Bernard's family possessed a house at Châtillon-sur-Seine, and that perhaps some fourteen

[1] Gaufr. *Fragm.*, *Cod. Aureaevall.* 2 ; Meglinger. *Iter Cisterc.*, 13, *P.L.* CLXXXV. 1565 sqq.

[2] Chomton, *Saint Bernard et le château de Fontaines-lès-Dijon*, I. 36 sqq.

[3] *Archives de la Côte d'Or*, H 996, f. 2 ; Court-épée, *Descript. du duché de Bourgogne*, II. 389.

[4] Lejeune, *Re-cherches sur le lieu de naissance de saint Bernard.*

I

of his early years were spent there ; but this fact carries little weight against the overwhelming documentary evidence to the contrary. Let us turn for a moment to this evidence. The First Book of the *Vita Prima* is the work of William of St. Thierry. In its Recension A it reads : " Bernard was born at Châtillon, a town of Burgundy " ; in Recension B Geoffrey corrected this to : " Bernard was born in Burgundy at Fontaines, the town of his father." [1] Curiously enough one MS. of outstanding authority for the text of St. Bernard's works, Douai 372, which dates from about 1175 and came from the Benedictine Abbey of Anchin, where it was written by the scribe Siger,[2] in which, however, the *Vita* is classified under Recension A, actually reads not " Châtillon " but " Fontaines," thus indicating a very early origin for the Fontaines-lès-Dijon tradition. William's interest in Châtillon-sur-Seine as not only the place of St. Bernard's education but also the scene of certain memorable events which preceded his admission to Cîteaux may have been so absorbing as to account for the mistake about his birthplace. Moreover, as representing the ancient stock of the Chevaliers de Châtillon, Tescelin, St. Bernard's father, was of greater importance than he was as Seigneur de Fontaines.[3] However this may be, none of the other biographers refer to Châtillon-sur-Seine in this connection. The *Vita Secunda* of Alan of Auxerre reads *verbatim* with Recension B of the *Vita Prima*.[4] The *Fragmenta* of Geoffrey, commonly called the *Vita Tertia*, make no reference at all to the birthplace. The *Vita Quarta* of John the Hermit, a writer who obtained much of his information on family matters from an exceptionally reliable source, namely, St. Bernard's cousin, Robert of Châtillon,[5] reads : " The most blessed Bernard then was born of noble stock in the country of Langres (*in pago Lingonensi*) at Fontaines, the town of his father." [6] We may notice one other suggestion which has been offered ; it deserves no more than a mere mention. There are at least two places in Burgundy bearing the name of Fontaines. Why prefer Fontaines-lès-Dijon, say, to Fontaines-en-Duesmois, not very far from Montbard ? The answer is simple. The former alone could be described as " the town of Bernard's father " and the *castrum* of Tescelin " overlooking Dijon " ;[7] to say nothing of the fact that the circumstances of his mother's death point unmistakably to Fontaines-lès-Dijon as distinctively the home of the family.[8]

Recension B of Geoffrey's record of the last days of St. Bernard states him to have passed away " after fulfilling

[1] *Vita Prima,* I. i. 1.

[2] Cf. *Speculum,* April, 1933.

[3] Gaufr. *Fragm.,* loc. cit.

[4] *Vita Sec.,* i. 1.

[5] *Vita Quarta,* i. 5.

[6] *Vita Quarta,* i. 1.

[7] Gaufr. *Fragm.,* loc. cit. ; Jobin, Saint Bernard et sa famille, 501 sq.

[8] P. 7 infra.

about sixty-three years." [1] We may conclude that this is a correction by Geoffrey of the words "sixty-four" found in such MSS. of Recension A as Munich 2613 and Berlin 334.[2] Alan of Auxerre uses precisely the same language in his record in the *Vita Secunda* and goes on to say that "all this happened in the same year as that in which the blessed Pope Eugenius III died . . . the one thousand, one hundred and fifty-third year after the Incarnation." [3] Thus there would seem to be good reason for assigning the birth of St. Bernard to the year 1090.[4]

The parentage of St. Bernard offers a genealogical study of some interest. It was exhaustively discussed in the XVIIth century by the learned Jesuit Chifflet, and in more recent days it has been discussed by Jobin and by Chomton.[5] Tescelin, his father, bore a name derived from the Gothic root *thiud*, meaning *people*, as found in *Dieterich* and in *Theodorich*, joined to the suffix *eling* by the suffix *isch*—which appears once again later in the family-tree as borne by his great-grandson, and curiously enough also with the added *sobriquet* of *Sorus*, the Sorel. The primitive form of the name would have been something like *Theodischeling*.[6] Unfortunately the name of neither of St. Bernard's paternal grandparents can be stated with any certainty. That Tescelin was noble is not to be doubted, if for no other reason than that he was related to Josbert de la Ferté, Vicomte de Dijon, Seneschal of Hugh of Champagne.[7] To concur with Chifflet in the suggestion that his mother was possibly Eve de Châtillon, otherwise Eve de Grancey, who after her first husband's death married Fulke d'Aigremont, also called Fulke de Sarceau, is probably the utmost that can be conceded.[8] The Abbé Chaume, in an article published in 1928, gives a pedigree of Tescelin in which he appears as hypothetically a son of Tescelin Rufus of Châtillon.[9]

With regard to St. Bernard's mother Aleth we are on a firmer foundation. The *Vita Quarta* explicitly states her to have been the daughter of Bernard of Montbard and of the stock of the Dukes of Burgundy.[10] Bernard was probably the founder of the Seigneurie de Montbard. Various names borne by his descendants lead us to believe that he was connected with the ancient family of the Counts of Tonnerre; [11] if this is the case it would have been through her father that Aleth was of the ducal line. Her mother Homberge is stated in *Gallia Christiania*, on the authority of the Chronicle of Sens, to have been Homberge des Riceys ; [12] but of this we may not be sure.

[1] *Vita Prima*, V ii. 15.

[2] Waitz, *M.G.H.* XXVI. 120.

[3] *Vita Sec.*, xxxi. 88 sq.

[4] Vacandard, *Vie de saint Bernard*, I. i. 1 note, éd. 1910.

[5] Chifflet, *S. Bern. Clar. Ab. Gen. Illustr.*, *P.L.* CLXXXV. 1199 sqq. ; Jobin, *S. Bernard et sa famille*, *passim* ; Chomton, *op. cit.*, II.

[6] Bourlier, *ap.* Chomton, *op. cit.*, II. 38 sq.

[7] *Vita Prima*, I. ix. 43.

[8] Williams, *Studies in St. Bernard of Clairvaux*, 41 sqq.

[9] Chaume, *Les origines fam. de saint Bernard, St. Bernard et son temps*, I. 85.

[10] Gaufr. *Fragm. loc. cit.* ; *Vita Quarta*, i. 1.

[11] Chifflet, *op. cit.*, 411 ; Petit, *Hist. des ducs de Bourgogne de la race Capétienne*, IV. 455 sqq.

[12] *Chron. Senon.*, *Gall. Christ.*, IV. 729.

Of the six other children of Bernard and Homberge the eldest surviving at his father's death, namely, Raynard Seigneur de Montbard, was the chief founder of Fontenay ; [1] Gaudry Seigneur de Touillon, a place some five miles North by East of Montbard, became a monk of Cîteaux,[2] and Milo, a *frère convers* of the same house ; [3] the younger daughter, who probably bore the name of Diana, is doubtfully said to have married Otto of Châtillon and to have been by him the mother of Robert of Châtillon,[4] to whose seduction from Clairvaux we shall refer later. Of the brothers and sisters of Tescelin the Sorel we can say nothing certain ; the conjecture has been ventured that one of the former was the above-named Otto of Châtillon.

The character of Tescelin stands out in the biographies as that of a man of probity and of piety ; out of his abundant substance open-handed to the needy ; highly esteemed by his overlord, the Duke of Burgundy, both for his counsel and for his valour.[5]

Aleth de Montbard gives us the impression of having been no ordinary personality. Her father had taken steps to have her well educated from an early age, having in view for her the life of a religious. But " the providence of God disposed of her otherwise," for, when at the age of fifteen years she was sought in marriage by Tescelin, Bernard was persuaded that " he could not rightly refuse to him her hand." [6] The records both of William and of John the Hermit, the latter, as we should expect, with the fulness of detail supplied by Robert of Châtillon—reveal to us charming traits of character ; a dignified fidelity to her husband's wishes, a domestic rule in the fear of God, a devotion to works of mercy, an education of her children with wise discipline. Robert was evidently much impressed by the manner of her ministrations to the poor and to the sick ; with her own hands she prepared their food, cleaned their utensils and did everything for them which usually is left to menials to perform.[7]

The children born to Tescelin and Aleth were seven in number, Guy, Gerard, Bernard, Homberge or Hombeline, Andrew, Bartholomew and Nivard, each of whom was dedicated to God by the mother's hands so soon as possible after birth, with the exception of Bernard, in whose case the dedication was made later with special solemnity.[8] This may perhaps be explained in some measure by the fact that before his birth Aleth dreamed that she was carrying in her womb a white dog-pup, tawny on the back, who barked furiously. This disturbing experience—easily accountable, it may be

Mabill. *Admon.* in *Libr. de Vita S. Bern.*, VIII. ; *Gall. Christ.*, IV. 492.

[2] *Vita Prima*, I. ii. 10 ; ix. 43 and 45.

[3] Chifflet, *op. cit.*, 540.

[4] *Vita Quarta*, i. 5 ; Chifflet, *op. cit.*, 643 ; Jobin, *op. cit.*, xxiii.

[5] Gaufr. *Fragm.*, *loc. cit.* ; *Vita Quarta*, i. 1.

[6] *Vita Quarta*, i. 1.

[7] *Vita Prima*, I. i. 1 ; *Vita Quarta*, i. 5.

[8] *Vita Prima*, I. i. 1 ; *Vita Quarta*, i. 3.

thought, if we remember Tescelin the Sorel—she subsequently communicated to a monk, who reassured her by the prediction that she should have a child who would prove a faithful watchdog of the Church and a saving healer of the wounds of men.[1] Aleth was evidently conscious that a peculiar destiny was reserved for Bernard ; he was the Samuel among her offspring. Like the rest of the children he was hardly nurtured, accustomed to simple fare and to plain living as one whose calling would be in the desert rather than in kings' houses.[2]

At Châtillon-sur-Seine Tescelin had a family-house standing on the Southern slope of the hill which is crowned by the *castellum* and by the Church of St. Vorles, a considerable portion of the cellars of which still remains and was by the kindness of the present occupier visited by the writer in 1927. To this house, about the year 1098—momentous as that of the foundation of Cîteaux—Aleth removed herself and Bernard, together doubtless with such of the other children as were born, in order that he might profit by the teaching of the Canons Secular of St. Vorles, into whose house was subsequently introduced, by the agency of St. Bernard, the Rule of St. Augustine.[3] Châtillon was in those days a famous educational centre ; its reputation lived on for at least another hundred years, for William of Armorica celebrates it as " the father of distinguished sons . . . and the teacher of great men." [4] Of Bernard's culture we shall speak later ; suffice it to say here that William of St. Thierry lays stress upon his precocious natural aptitude for learning, as well as upon his consciousness that the end set before him was to know God by means of the Sacred Scriptures rather than any literary or scientific facility for its own sake.[5]

The picture which the same writer gives us of his character in those early days is particularly striking. " In worldly affairs he was a mere child, loving to be alone, shunning publicity, remarkably thoughtful, obedient and submissive to his parents ; kind and gracious to all-comers, ingenuous and quiet at home, seldom out of doors, modest beyond belief ; never caring to talk much, but his heart given to God that so he might preserve his childhood's purity." [6] What hidden fires kindled from the altar lay beneath this grave and gentle presentment, withal so transparent that, we may well believe, they could not fail to have been recognized at any rate by a mother's eye ! In Geoffrey's portrait, drawn in later years, we trace the same features, matured by sad and difficult experience, but still determined by the ultimate factor in their

[1] Gaufr. *Fragm.* Cod. *Aureaevall.* 6 sq.; *Vita Prima*, I. i. 2 ; cf. Gaufr. Ab. Claraevall. *Sermo de S. Bern.*, 17.

[2] *Vita Prima*, I. i. 1.

[3] *Vita Prima*, I. i. 3 ; Gaufr. *Fragm.*, MS. *cit.*, 5 sq.; *Gall. Christ.*, IV. 770.

[4] Guill. Brit. Armor. *Philipp.*, I. 591, *R.H.G.F.* XVII. 130.

[5] *Vita Prima, loc. cit.*

[6] *Vita Prima, loc. cit.*

Vita Prima,
II. i. 1.

analysis, a " heart given to God." [1] To this we shall recur at the proper place.

Two stories recorded by William may be mentioned as illustrative alike of the conditions of the time and of the young Bernard's reaction to them. As the boy lay in bed one day, suffering from severe headache, he was aroused by the entrance of a little old woman who came to cure him by her incantations ; she succeeded but quite otherwise than as she expected, for he suddenly leapt from his bed with an angry exclamation and expelled her from the room ! William would give us to understand that the little patient's zeal was rewarded ; when she had gone " he felt himself entirely free from pain." [2]

[2] *Vita Prima,*
I. ii. 4.

The other story, told also by Alan of Auxerre, is that when one Vigil of Christmas he was awaiting Nocturns in the Church of St. Vorles there was some little delay and he fell asleep. Suddenly there was revealed to him the mystery of Bethlehem, Mary and the Holy Child " coming forth as a bridegroom from his chamber," " of form more beautiful than the sons of men." He was persuaded and he believed to the last that it was the very hour of the Lord's nativity. In any case it was an experience which confirmed his faith, sowed in him the seeds of mystic contemplation and became the incentive of his works upon the Incarnation.[3] In the *Fragmenta* Geoffrey, it should be said, describes the vision as having been vouchsafed to the boy " while he was still asleep in his father's house," and before he had been called by his mother to go to Nocturns.[4] He makes, however, no correction of this variant when constructing Recension B of the *Vita Prima* and it need scarcely give us much concern.

[3] *Vita Prima,*
I. ii. 4 ; *Vita
Secunda,* ii. 5.

[4] Gaufr. *Fragm.,*
MS. *cit.,* 6.

There can be no doubt as to St. Bernard's special devotion to our Lady and to her sacred maternity, and probably the tradition that he learned this first at Châtillon is well founded. There is a little chapel to which we descend by a few steps from the floor of the Northern transept of St. Vorles on its Eastern side, which has from at least the first quarter of the XVth century been associated with his memory. It is dedicated to Ste. Marie-du-Château and formerly contained an ancient image of the Blessed Virgin ; to it the tradition is that St. Bernard was wont to resort for prayer.[5]

[5] Gall. Christ.,
IV. 770 ; Chom-
ton, *op. cit.,* I.
155 sq.

It is not to be supposed that for all this gravity of spirit and of demeanour Bernard was other than a thorough boy ; the humour which from time to time sparkled spontaneously in the utterances of his later life is sufficient to dispel such a notion. Moreover, the envenomed and unfounded suggestion made by Berengarius of Poitiers during the controversy with Abélard, that in his youth he had been guilty of writing ribald rhymes, is in itself a testimony to some reputation for mirthfulness acquired in early days.[1] Amongst his school-fellows we might have recognized one who all his life remained closely associated with him, his kinsman Godfrey de la Roche-Vanneau, sometimes described as Godfrey de Châtillon; Alan of Auxerre writes of him as " having been brought up with the saint from early years."[2]

It was when St. Bernard " was passing from boyhood into youth . . . and her children having been faithfully brought up, she having done her duty by them, were beginning to go out into the world,"[3] that his mother died. The terms used alike by both biographers suggest that St. Bernard would have been of about sixteen or seventeen years of age. It was the custom of the family to migrate to Fontaines yearly for the long summer vacation, the great event of which was the celebration on 1st September of the Feast of St. Ambrosinian, patron of the village church, when Aleth would entertain generously the clergy of the neighbourhood. In this year, 1106 or 1107, she was possessed by the premonition, which she communicated to all around her, that she would not live to keep the feast. Alas, it was but too true, for on the eve she was struck by fatal fever. She insisted that there should be no interruption of the festivities ; and in the evening of 1st September, surrounded by her family, she passed away at the moment when the assembled ecclesiastics were singing the words : *Per passionem et crucem tuam libera eam, Domine*, and while she yet had strength to raise her hand to make the sacred sign.[4]

When the news reached the ears of Jarenton, the venerable Abbot of St. Bénigne-de-Dijon, he begged that her remains as those of a great saint might be buried in his basilica. Thither with much solemnity they were borne by the community, accompanied by respectful crowds, and found their resting-place on the lowest stage of William of Volpiano's *rotunda* at the foot of the Northern stairway and immediately to the left.[5] In 1250 they were translated to Clairvaux by Abbot Lexington.[6] Henceforth St. Bernard was out of tutelage, " beginning to live by his own rule and as responsible for himself."[7] How, we may ask, did he spend the next at least four years which intervened before he finally resolved to offer himself for the noviciate at Cîteaux ? The memory of his mother would, surely, constantly have been with him and her spiritual presence very near to him. He would some

[1] Bereng. Schol. *Apolog.*, Cousin *Petr. Abæl. Opp.* II. 771 sq.

[2] *Vita Sec., Prolog.*; Chomton, *op. cit.*, II. 58.

[3] *Vita Prima*, I ii. 5 ; *Vita Sec.* ii. 6.

[4] *Vita Prima*, I. ii. 5 ; *Vita Quarta*, i. 6.

[5] Chomton, *op. cit.*, I. 164 sq. ; *Monast. Gallic.*, Pl. 37.

[6] Flammeng, *Sépultures du choeur de l'église de Clairvaux*, V., P.L. CLXXXV. 1767 ; Henric. *Fasc. SS. Ord. Cist.*, II. xli. 4.

[7] *Vita Prima*, I. iii. 6.

years before have completed the education in grammar,
rhetoric and dialectic such as was considered necessary in
his day ; he would no longer have been *trivialis ;* he might
well have been at the end of his *quadrivium,* for he was an
apt scholar. It was an age of intellectual and literary revival generally ; France had not known the like since the
reign of Charlemagne. St. Bernard's taste in such matters
is unmistakable and its cultivation no less so. It is probable
that much of his knowledge of Classical and of post-Classical
literature in their various departments was acquired during
this period of four years. There is evidence that, at some stage
before his mind was seriously turned in the direction of
Cîteaux, the consideration of his further study in Germany

¹ Gaufr. *Fragm.*,
Cod. Aureaevall.
12 ; *Vita Prima,*
I. iii. 9.

was entertained by himself and encouraged by his brothers,[1]
who would doubtless have taken some pride in the budding
genius of the family. It is not to be supposed that any
objection was raised against St. Bernard's becoming a cleric
whether secular or regular ; scarcely otherwise could he have
found scope for his talents. But Cîteaux, known to be in
his thoughts, was another matter ; its very name was a
terror ; probably not a few of their friends among the young
Burgundian nobles had tried the life there and had felt it

² Petit, *op. cit.,*
I. 307.

to be impossible ; the situation was hopelessly unhealthy ; [2]
some ten years had elapsed since its foundation and it had
not as yet one daughter-house ; men respected Cistercian
sanctity but they shunned its almost, as it seemed, repulsive

³ *Vita Sec.,* iv.
14 ; *Chron.
Turon.,* Marten.
et Durand.
*Vet. Script. et
Mon. Ampl.
Coll.,* V. 1014.

⁴ *Exord. Parv.,*
VII.

⁵ *Exord. Parv.,*
XIV. ; Mans.
Concil., XX.
980 sq.

⁶ *Exord. Parv.,*
XVII.

severity ; extinction threatened the Order.[3] Robert of
Molesme, the founder and first abbot, after about one year
of rule, had been sent back by the Pope to his old monastery,
willingly accompanied by a certain number of monks " who
had no liking for the desert." [4] Alberic, his successor, had
perhaps done something ; he had obtained the *Privilegium
Romanum* from Paschal II under date 19th October, 1100,[5]
but little ostensible result was following. When on Alberic's
death in 1108 the Englishman, Stephen Harding, became abbot
there was no improvement ; matters rather grew worse ;
the Cistercians were " brought almost to the brink of despair
for lack of successors." [6] All this, of course, did but make
the prospect more attractive to a born knight-errant like St.
Bernard ; offered as a deterrent motive by his family, as
it naturally would have been, it had precisely the contrary
effect to that for which they hoped.

Meanwhile another force was active ; the influence of
his mother. The remembrance of her was such that " very
often he seemed to see her coming to him and complaining

reproachfully that it was not for the end of vain secular learning that she had educated him so carefully, that this was not the hope in which she had brought him up." [1] John the Hermit tells us of how Aleth appeared to her son Andrew from time to time " during a period of five years, as the history written by the servant of God, lord William, records," a remark which is probably a copyist's error, the reference being in fact to the appearances to St. Bernard recorded in the *Vita Prima* as above cited ; or it may be explained by the story told by Geoffrey in the *Fragmenta* of an occasion, reported also by William, upon which Andrew when in conversation with St. Bernard as to the vocation of them both suddenly cried out : " I see my mother." [2] We shall doubtless be correct in believing that during the five years 1107 to 1112 his mother was constantly present to the spiritual vision of St. Bernard, moving him to take such a step as he ultimately took. Immediately after referring to appearances made to Andrew—which, as we have suggested, should be read as made to St. Bernard—John the Hermit goes on to say that once " in the early stages of the discussion with his brothers concerning his vocation," presumably to be followed at Cîteaux, " his mother appeared to St. Bernard and said : ' Son Bernard, fear not, but play the man and fulfil to the end the work begun ; for it is God's work.' " [3]

It is probable that to this period belongs Geoffrey's portrait of St. Bernard. What strikes us in the character-sketch is forethought ; industry not only in study but in affairs, as of one " never less leisurely than when at leisure " ; cheerfulness under reproach ; modesty under praise—such modesty that when at some later date he found that the use of a hair shirt was bringing him a reputation for sanctity he at once discarded it—a graciousness of manner deriving from a graciousness of spirit. His colouring was fair ; his complexion transparent ; his height moderate ; his body spare, a fragile vessel for a precious treasure. Thus was he physically a bad subject for the severities of Cîteaux ; and in after years he suffered much, in particular from a severe gastric disorder which sometimes became so acute as to make it difficult for him to take his place in choir ; towards the end of his life it was only in cases of grave necessity that he was present at meetings of the community.[4]

And St. Bernard during the years of his later youth had good cause for hearkening to his mother's counsel to " play the man." The distinction both of his person and of his family would have exposed him to the dangers arising from

[1] *Vita Prima*, I iii. 9.

[2] Gaufr. *Fragm.*, Cod. Aureaevall. 18 ; *Vita Prima*, I. iii. 10.

[3] *Vita Quarta*, i. 8.

[4] *Vita Prima*, III. i. 1 ; I. viii. 39.

companionship with the young nobles of the day. His readiness to receive all-comers, the genius for friendship which was so marked a feature of his character ; these would have made him naturally sympathetic with his fellows of equal age and equal rank. Amongst them were some " whose morals unlike his own and whose stormy friendships beset the kindly youth with eager efforts to make him as themselves. Had their ways become sweet to him, needs must have been that what in this life was to him sweeter far, the love of chastity, would have become bitter." [1] With whatever skill and dignity he avoided successfully the snares deliberately set for him, the consciousness of the weakness of his own flesh remained with him and " he began to meditate flight." [2] The thought of Cîteaux, the " new plantation " which so many were declining " owing to the excessive austerity of its life of poverty," pressed itself upon him. For the seeker after God there were no terrors.[3]

It would seem that he made a confidant of his maternal uncle Gaudry, seigneur, as we remember, of a *castellum* called Touillon about five miles North by East of Montbard. Gaudry was a fine soldier, a man of honour and of influence, who subsequently bestowed his property of Touillon upon the Abbey of Fontenay.[4] He was the first of St. Bernard's family to throw in his lot with him. We may perhaps conjecture that what Aleth had been to St. Bernard as a mother that had she been to Gaudry as a sister. It was when Tescelin and three of his sons, Guy, Gerard and Andrew, the last still but a youth, were, in support of their overlord the Duke of Burgundy, laying siege to Grancey-le-Château that the crucial moment arrived.[5] It was about the autumn of 1111. Gaudry too was there ; and Bartholomew, the youngest son but one, probably not yet old enough to bear arms. Thither St. Bernard took his way, strangely dissentient as to his own vocation and as to theirs from all the rest.[6] As he rode along the rough and lonely road, about half-way between Châtillon and Grancey he came upon a church into which he turned aside to pray. When he remounted to continue his journey his mind was quite clear as to his vocation ; his resolve to present himself at Cîteaux was irrevocably fixed.[7] On his arrival at Grancey he found that Gaudry had on that very day, displeased by some breach of faith on the part of his overlord, told the Duke of Burgundy that " henceforth the shield would no longer hang from his neck," a remark the meaning of which was correctly read by St. Bernard's brothers. Gaudry and his nephew at once obtained from Tescelin his

[1] *Vita Prima*, I. iii. 6.

[2] *Op. cit.*, I. iii. 6 sqq.

[3] *Op. cit.*, I. iii. 8.

[4] Chifflet, *op. cit.*, 644 sq.

[5] Petit, *op. cit.*, I. 307.

[6] *Vita Prima*, I. iii. 9.

[7] *Op. cit. loc. cit.*

approval of their common purpose and the great surrender began.[1] First Bartholomew, "not yet a soldier," and then Andrew, "the tyro," moved by the vision of his mother's face, became *conversi*, a term which was applied to recruits for the monastic life before it was applied to lay brethren.[2] Next Guy, the eldest brother, joined them on condition that he could obtain the free consent of his wife Elizabeth; ultimately this consent was given and, according to the custom of the day, Elizabeth herself became a nun at Jully-sous-Ravières, presumably taking with her their two children to be brought up there.[3] Gerard, who for some time remained quite obdurate, was at last, when a wounded prisoner, almost it would seem *ad succurrendum* converted—for he thought himself at death's door. " I am a monk, a monk of Cîteaux," he exclaimed in terror. He was not, however, therefore released. An interview with St. Bernard, which was granted him, confirmed his resolution and he subsequently recovered from his wound and effected his escape.[4] There remained of the brothers only Nivard the youngest, a mere child. Later when the whole company of St. Bernard's recruits left Fontaines-lès-Dijon for Cîteaux, Guy, seeing him playing with his fellows, remarked to him, records Geoffrey in the *Fragmenta* : " Why, Nivard, you will be able to play to your heart's content now ; you will be master of the whole property some day."   " Ah," replied the boy, " this is no blessed distribution that all of you should inherit heaven and I but a bit of earth."   And Nivard was told to bide his time and to attend to his lessons. In the end his importunity won consent and he too became " a monk of Cîteaux." [5]

By the 22nd of October, possibly a week later,[6] St. Bernard and his neophytes, including Gaudry, all his brothers—with the exception of Gerard, who did not escape from captivity until the following Lent,[7] and of Nivard—Godfrey de la Roche [8] and Robert de Châtillon [9] were assembled at Châtillon-sur-Seine. From time to time others, in spite of the opposition of their family or of their friends, joined themselves to the little band of *conversi*, caught by the prevailing enthusiasm,[10] amongst them Hugh of Mâcon or Hugues de Vitry, an intimate friend of St. Bernard although a few years his senior.

The story of how Hugh was won to the cause is told by Geoffrey in the *Fragmenta* and by William in the *Vita Prima*. At some date previous to the arrival of St. Bernard at Châtillon he visited Hugh either at Mâcon or at some place between Mâcon and Dijon. There was an impression that he was setting forth on a pilgrimage to Jerusalem and his brothers

[1] Gaufr. *Fragm.*, *Cod. Aureaevall.* 17.

[2] Du Cange, *Glossar.* s.v. Cf. p. 22 *infra*.

[3] Gaufr. *Fragm.*, *Cod. Aureaevall.* 20; *Vita Prima*, I. iii. 10; *Vita Sec.*, iii. 9.

[4] Gaufr. *Fragm.*, *Cod. Aureaevall.* 7 sqq. ; *Vita Prima*, I. iii. 11 ; *Vita Sec.*, iii. 10.

[5] Gaufr. *Fragm.*, *MS. cit.*, 21 sq.
[6] *Vita Prima*, I. iii. 13 ; Williams, *op. cit.*, 67.
[7] *Vita Prima*, I. iii. 12.
[8] *Op. cit.*, I. ix. 45.
[9] S. Bern. *Ep.* 1 (10) and *Not. Fus. ad loc.*
[10] *Vita Prima*, I. iii. 13 and 15.

raised objections. Pardonably enough he did not enlighten them, seeing that his journey was in the direction " not of the Jerusalem in which the Lord once was but where he now is." [1] Their meeting was affectionate and heart spoke to heart in the closest confidence. The machinations of the worldly ecclesiastics of Mâcon failed to separate the friends ; and Hugh's confession to St. Bernard of his longing to become a monk ultimately took effect in his joining the party assembled at Châtillon.[2] Hugh was a distinguished person both in the Church and in the world ; we shall hear of him again.[3]

Six months were spent at Châtillon, probably in the family-house of Tescelin, a period of preliminary testing the need of which was amply proved by the lapse of two of their number.[4] We are struck by the care taken by St. Bernard—so old a head on such young shoulders—to obviate the danger of hasty decisions, to ensure that the surrender of each was an act well-weighed and deliberately willed. It was no case of mass-conversion or of impulsive herd-instinct. At about the end of March or early in April, 1112, at any rate not later than the Easter of that year,[5] thirty of them in all set forth for Cîteaux, passing on their way through Fontaines-lès-Dijon, where they bade farewell to Tescelin, now orphaned of all his children save Hombeline and Nivard. " What am I to say," writes Geoffrey in the Fragmenta, " of the courage of that father who in one day saw departing from him six sons "—Geoffrey would, in anticipation, include Nivard— " and such sons, and yet not only did not grieve but rejoiced greatly ? One warning alone he gave ; that they should act with moderation. ' I know you,' he said, ' that rarely if ever are you able to temper your zeal.' " [6] The scene is too sacred for comment. Within a few days St. Bernard and the twenty-nine were knocking at the gate of Cîteaux.

And Cîteaux was, as we have seen,[7] tottering to its fall, sustained only by the inspiring faith of the English monk who was its abbot, Stephen of Sherborne. The accession of the recruits from Châtillon-sur-Seine marked the point of departure of a great expansion. " Thenceforth the Cistercians founded abbeys in various dioceses." [8] The first was La-Ferté in the diocese of Châlon-sur-Saône, on the river Grône about ten miles above its confluence with the Saône, founded on 18th May, 1113 ; [9] the second was Pontigny, destined to be the asylum in later years of St. Thomas of Canterbury, of St. Edmund Rich and of Stephen Langton and his suffragans, founded on 31st May, 1114, in the diocese

[1] Gaufr. Fragm., MS. cit., 13 sqq.

[2] Op. cit. loc. cit.; Vita Prima, I. ii. 13 sqq.

[3] Gall. Christ., XII. 291 ; vide pp. 13, 112, 187, 304 infra.

[4] Vita Prima, I. ii. 15 sq.

[5] Gaufr. Fragm., MS. cit., 10.

[6] Op. cit. MS. cit., 20 sq.

[7] P. 8 supra.

[8] Exord. Parv., XVIII.

[9] Janauschek, Orig. Cisterc., I. 4.

ST. VORLES, CHÂTILLON-SUR-SEINE

of Auxerre about twelve miles N.E. of that city. In this latter foundation Hugh of Mâcon took an important part ; not only was he—and let us note it as an indication of the quality of the men who followed St. Bernard to Cîteaux— one year after his profession chosen to be first abbot of the second colony settled by St. Stephen Harding, but he was probably in large measure responsible for the initiation of the scheme.[1]

Let us try to get a picture of St. Bernard during the early years of his monastic life. In the days of his noviciate men heard him asking himself from time to time : " Bernard, Bernard, for what purpose did you come here ? " It was " with the intention of dying to the hearts and to the memory of men ; with the hope of lying hidden and overlooked like a lost vessel." [2] In the result how far otherwise did it prove to be ! And yet the love which he won, the unforgettable impression which he made, the service which as a vessel chosen to exceptional honour he rendered to the Church and to the world, all these would have been impossible had he not first sought to lose himself. He may, perhaps, soon have forgotten his father's warning as to the danger of ex- cessive zeal. In any case he was not slack or resourceless in availing himself of means for avoiding occasions of sin. Faithful to the Rule of St. Benedict, he feared, it would seem, most of all the *in multiloquio peccatum*, for when visitors assailed him with conversation he would, under the cover of his hood, stop his ears with tow. Thus so much as an hour would elapse and no syllable would pass his lips save only an occasional word of exhortation.[3] It is unnecessary to speak here in detail of the severity of the Cistercian life ; some account of it has been elsewhere given by the present writer.[4] A century later neither fish, eggs, milk nor cheese were eaten in the Order.[5] There can be no doubt but that the *régime* left its mark upon the bodily health of St. Bernard ; he would have been the last person to entertain the notion of any modification of it to meet his own infirmity ; his ideal in such a matter was that of the monks of the Egyptian desert.[6] Strictly conforming, we may be sure, to the Rule in respect of bedding and of clothing, St. Bernard is recorded to have been fastidiously clean. " He took pleasure always in poverty of garb but never in dirtiness." [7] Manual labour, whether in the fields or in the forests or on buildings, was, of course, unfamiliar to these young men of noble birth ; in St. Bernard's case this disability was accentuated by bodily frailty ; he had not, as had most of his companions,

[1] Janauschek, *op. cit. loc. cit.*

[2] *Vita Prima,* I. iv. 19.

[3] *Vita Quarta,* ii. 1.

[4] Williams, *Studies in St. Bernard of Clairvaux,* 86 sqq. Cf. p. 26 *infra.*

[5] Jacob. de Vitr. *Hist. Orient. et Occid.,* XIV. 300.

[6] S. Bern. *Ep.* 1 (11).

[7] *Vita Prima,* III. ii. 5.

been trained in arms. When the work was beyond his powers he would take up some work less honourable but less strenuous. When he was told that he had better sit still and do nothing he would humbly pray for the necessary strength and skill. In the end, we are told, he became a very good harvester.[1] Sleep he regarded rather as waste of time than as refreshment of mind and body ; thus he trained himself to a watchfulness which seemed to be more than human.[2] His spiritual absorption was so deep that after a whole year spent in the *cella* of the novices he could not say whether there was a vaulted ceiling or not ; and, although he passed many hours in the church, he thought that there was only one window to its sanctuary, whereas there were three.[3] Similarly, food had no savour for him ; he never knew what he was eating ; his feeling was that it was rather tiresome to have to eat at all ![4] Nor did all this imply any touch of *singularitas* or sense of peculiar superiority, the fifth degree of pride, a vice which he would later so scathingly reprobate in the first treatise which he is known to have written.[5] He studiously recognized himself as a backward novice and others as far holier and more perfect than was he.[6] It may occur to us that this excessive spiritual absorption, this life abstracted from its surroundings, was a strange preparation for the career of a man who when he emerged upon the stage of his day would seem to have been aware of everything, whose notice nothing would seem to have escaped. How was this previous training calculated to quicken the power of observation ? But in fact it was rather a training in valuation than in observation, in the habit of estimating correctly the degree in which a thing matters and in the power of dealing with it accordingly. The things of which St. Bernard took no account were for the most part things of which no account need be taken. Things worth noting he rarely overlooked.

Much time would undoubtedly have been devoted by St. Bernard during his noviciate and during the two years immediately following to the study of the Bible and of the writings of the Latin Fathers. His attitude towards these authorities is recorded by William of St. Thierry. " More willingly and more frequently " than he engaged in manual labour " he read in their simple meaning and in their due order the Canonical Scriptures. He used to say that there were no words in which he understood them better than he did in their own ; and he testified that whatever of divine truth or of virtue shone from them had more meaning for

[1] *Vita Prima*, I. iv. 23 sq.

[2] *Op. cit.*, I. iv. 21.

[3] *Op. cit.*, I. iv. 20.

[4] *Op. cit.*, I. iv. 22 ; vii. 33.

[5] S. Bern. *De Grad. Hum. et Superb.*, XIV. ; Williams and Mills, *Select Treatises of St. Bernard.*

[6] *Vita Prima*, I. iv. 22.

him as it came directly from the fountain-head than as it reached him in the streams of exposition. However, he humbly read the holy and orthodox expositors and by no means claimed that his own interpretation of any passage equalled theirs, but merely submitted it as not unsuitable; and treading faithfully in their footsteps he himself often drank from the same fountain as had they." These words are found also in the *Vita Secunda* of Alan of Auxerre.[1] The text which would have been before him at Cîteaux was that of St. Stephen Harding's version, about half-completed in 1109. It was a Cistercian principle to secure so far as was possible uniformity of liturgical books, as witness the psalter brought by Abbot Robert from Molesme, the Dijon MS. 30 (12).[2] The Biblical quotations in one treatise of St. Bernard, the *De Conversione*, admittedly a small section of his writings, have been collated with St. Stephen's version, the Dijon MS. 12-15 (9 *bis*), and with the Clementine Vulgate of 1592. The variants prove to be, comparatively speaking, negligible, except for the fact that two quotations, one from 'Genesis iv. 7, the other from Proverbs xviii. 3, are translations of the Septuagint version. We may think that the Bible which would have remained with St. Bernard to the end of his life would have been that which he learned as a child when taught by his mother and by the Canons of St. Vorles. It would be interesting to know how these translations from the Greek are to be explained.[3] They illustrate the statement of his biographers as to his study of the Scriptures, to which we have referred. We may even recognize his quotation and treatment of alternative variants; for example, the *cellaria* of the Vulgate and the *cubiculum* of the *Vetus Itala* in the Song of Songs i. 3.[4]

In the work of preparing a collection of liturgical books St. Bernard would probably have taken no part. The earliest known MS. of this collection, Dijon 114 (82), dates from after the year 1170, although much earlier provisional drafts of it whether separately or as a whole must have existed. The antiphonary as well as other sections of the MS. are unfortunately lost, having disappeared before Abbot Jean de Cirey made his inventory of the library of Cîteaux in 1480-1482.[5] At some date before his death in 1134 St. Stephen sent monks to Metz to transcribe the antiphonary there which had a great reputation. This reputation the Cistercians quite wrongly disregarded and were of opinion that the antiphonary was " corrupt in chant and in letter . . . and all but entirely contemptible." We may presume that St. Bernard

[1] *Op. cit.*, I. iv. 24; *Vita Sec.*, x. 32.

[2] *P.L.* CLXVI. 1373 sqq.; Martin, *St. Étienne Hard. et les premiers recenseurs de la Vulg. Lat.*, *passim.* Cf. Othon Dncourneaux, *Les Orig. Cisterc.*, 67, note (1) and 139 sqq. (*Revue Mabillon*, 1932, 3).

[3] S. Bern. *De Convers.*, X. 21; XI. 23. Cf. *Ep.* 87 (3). *Vide Appendix* I.

[4] S. Bern. *In Cant. Cant.*, XXIII. 8; *Serm. de Divers.*, XCII. 1 sq.; *De Grad. Hum. et Superb.*, VII. 21.

[5] Dijon MS. 610 P.f. *olim* 358 (2).

had during his early days at Cîteaux acquired some aptitude for the ecclesiastical chant, for it was to him and to his cantors at Clairvaux that the preparation of a Cistercian antiphonary was entrusted. St. Bernard concurred with the general chapter which dealt with the matter in the opinion that the Metz antiphonary was to be rejected ; and if we had the particular lost section of the Dijon MS. we should probably know exactly what he preferred ; although his judgement was wrong, as the best authorities of the day will now tell us.[1] His views, however, as to the proper emotional effect of melody, as expressed in a letter to Guy, Abbot of Montier-Ramey, strike us as being entirely Platonic.[2]

Considering what the addition of St. Bernard and his recruits—twenty-nine in all, for Robert of Châtillon's noviciate was postponed on the ground of his youth [3]—to the ranks of the novices at Cîteaux meant, it is probable that the literary and kindred activities to which we have referred were powerfully stimulated from the year 1112 onwards. The relief of mind brought to the abbot and to the senior monks who for so long had seen their numbers lessening month by month ; the assurance that the Order had some future, given by the answer to prayer which this accession so marvellously illustrated ; the enthusiasm which animated the newcomers, from Gaudry, the tried soldier of long experience, to Robert, the mere boy ; all this would have been the incentive, not merely to extension in new foundations, but to the intensive work without which no extension is possible. The re-creation of the Order in 1112 was something greater than its creation in 1098 ; and of that re-creation St. Bernard was the author at the age of but twenty-two years.

[1] S. Bern. *Super Antiph. Cisterc. Ord. ad init.* ; *Dict. d'Arch. Chrét. et de Liturg.*, III. ii. 1807.
[2] *Ep.* 398.
[3] S. Bern. *Ep.* 1 (8).

GENEALOGIES

I

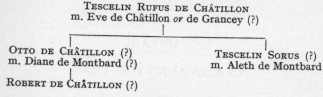

TESCELIN RUFUS DE CHÂTILLON
m. Eve de Châtillon *or* de Grancey (?)

OTTO DE CHÂTILLON (?)
m. Diane de Montbard (?)

ROBERT DE CHÂTILLON (?)

TESCELIN SORUS (?)
m. Aleth de Montbard

II

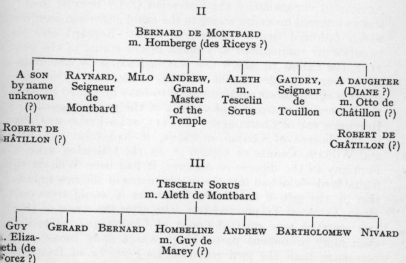

BERNARD DE MONTBARD
m. Homberge (des Riceys ?)

A SON by name unknown (?)

ROBERT DE HÂTILLON (?)

RAYNARD, Seigneur de Montbard

MILO

ANDREW, Grand Master of the Temple

ALETH m. Tescelin Sorus

GAUDRY, Seigneur de Touillon

A DAUGHTER (DIANE ?) m. Otto de Châtillon (?)

ROBERT DE CHÂTILLON (?)

III

TESCELIN SORUS
m. Aleth de Montbard

GUY . Eliza- eth (de ?orez ?)

GERARD   BERNARD   HOMBELINE m. Guy de Marey (?)   ANDREW   BARTHOLOMEW   NIVARD

The conjecture that Tescelin the Sorel was the son of Tescelin the Red is not at all improbable. Other conjectures, the probability of which it should be said varies in degree, are indicated by a note of interrogation in each case. It will be observed that account is taken of alternative opinions as to the parentage of Robert de Châtillon.

CHAPTER II

CLAIRVAUX, 1115–1124

ALTHOUGH expansion of the Cistercian Order became doubt-less an internal necessity owing to the rapid growth in numbers which followed upon the arrival of St. Bernard and his twenty-nine companions at Cîteaux in the spring of the year 1112, the extent to which this was facilitated by encourage-ment from outside should not be overlooked. The facts reveal a sympathetic understanding to have prevailed between the Cistercian pioneers and various of the great seigneurs of Burgundy and of Champagne. In 1113, at La-Ferté-sur-Grône in the diocese of Châlon-sur-Saône, it had been Savaricus and William, Counts of Châlon ;[1] in the following year, at Pontigny in the diocese of Auxerre, it had been William the feudal lord—who had met the requirements of the new founda-tion by the gift of land.[2] At Clairvaux it would seem that Hugh, Count of Troyes and Bar, who after the union of these two counties was entitled Count of Champagne, played an even more prominent part. Hugh was a more considerable personage than the lord either of La-Ferté or of Pontigny. In later years he fell much under the influence of St. Bernard, and the intimacy between the two men is illustrated by a charming letter, assigned by Mabillon to the year 1125, which the Abbot of Clairvaux wrote to Hugh upon the occasion of his entering the Order of the Temple and in which he grate-fully exclaims : " Can we forget your old love and the benefits which you so liberally conferred upon our house ? May God himself for love of whom you did it all never forget you ! "[3] We may well believe that Hugh was the prime mover in the matter and that it was at his solicitation that a band of monks, including amongst them St. Bernard's brothers, Gerard, Guy and Andrew, his uncle Gaudry, his kinsman Godfrey de la Roche[4] and his cousin Robert de Châtillon,[5] with St. Bernard as their abbot-elect, left the gate of Cîteaux in the June of 1115, numbering in accordance with Benedictine custom thirteen in all. There was some surprise, so William of St. Thierry tells us,[6] on the part of St. Bernard's companions,

[1] *Gall. Christ.,* IV. 1019.

[2] *Hist. Pontin. Monast.,*Marten. et Durand. *Thesaur. Nov. Anecdot.,* III. 1223.

[3] *Ep.* 31.

[4] Jobin, *Saint Bernard et sa famille,* 181 sqq.
[5] *Op.cit.,*XXIII. and 362.
[6] *Vita Prima,* I. v. 25.

18

"men of mature age, men of vigour alike in religion and in affairs," and some fear too, that St. Stephen had placed over them one " of such tender age, of such feeble physique, of such inexperience of the world." It was not the last occasion upon which St. Bernard's outward appearance would belie his true self. Taking their way laden with all the necessaries for the purpose of a new foundation, such as sacred vessels, vestments and books, their first recorded halt was at La-Ferté-sur-Aube where dwelt St. Bernard's kinsman Josbert de la Ferté.[1] Thence it was but a short three miles to the village of Ville-sous-Ferté, the home of another family related by blood to St. Bernard and to Godfrey de la Roche.[2] They were not far from their new home.

A valley, grim and forbidding at first sight, called of old the Vale of Absinth, watered by a little affluent of the Aube, opened out on the left bank of this river. William of St. Thierry portrays its dismal aspect and its evil repute— " a place of horror and vast solitude, a den of thieves." [3] Expanding to the East it narrowed Westward, dividing itself into two gorges to the N.W. and to the S.W. Down the latter ran the stream. And yet the valley well deserved the name which it has since borne in history for, although the woods were thick, and thicker still where on all sides but the S.E. they buried themselves in the gullies of the hills, the morning rays would have flooded it with light on days when France was herself—a " sunny land." St. Bernard knew himself to be in the domain of the Count of Troyes and here he elected to found his colony. The deed of gift printed in *Gallia Christiana* (IV. Instr. 155) and dated 1115 is taken from the Troyes MS. 2414, which is manifestly of a period later than the XIIth century. It is found in a XVIth century copy at the Archives de l'Aube (3H 321) and in an XVIIIth century collection of the *Acta* of Clairvaux (Troyes MS. 731). Geoffrey Felonie or Félénie, Josbert de la Ferté and Raynald de Perrecin are named in it as donors as well as Hugh of Troyes. It does not figure in the *Cartulary* of Clairvaux (Troyes MS. 730), itself a XVIth century copy. The original has not so far come to light.[4] Geoffrey, Josbert and Raynald were owners of lands in the vicinity of Clairvaux.

And at this point we touch upon a controversy. Precisely *where* was the selected site, the site of what, after a removal of which we shall speak later, was called the *Monasterium Vetus* ? There was an approach to the valley from the direction of Bar-sur-Aube which led over the hills on the N.W. through the village of Arconville. It was con-

[1] *Vita Prima*, I. ix. 43; Jobin, *Saint Bernard et sa famille*, XI.

[2] *Chron. Clare-vall.*; Jobin, *op. cit.*, XIII.

[3] *Vita Prima*, I. v. 25.

[4] d'Arbois de Jubainville, *Essai sur les sceaux des contes de Champagne*, 9 sq., éd. 1856; Prévost, *Recueil des Chartes et Bulles de Clairvaux (Analyses)*, éd. 1929.

tended by Philippe Guignard, a distinguished authority on Cistercian origins, in his article *Sur le Premier Emplacement de Clairvaux*,[1] that it was up this road at a place near Arconville now called the Fontaine-de-St. Bernard that the abbey first rose. His contention was based on the view that the traditional site could not have been open to the objections which were urged as necessitating the removal to which we have referred. When the abbey came to be rebuilt on a new site in 1136 the pressing considerations were that the old site was too far distant from the river, that it was not sufficiently level and that it was so confined as not to allow of cultivated fields and vineyards being laid out in its vicinity.[2] These objections, Guignard held, apply exactly to the Arconville site. Now it happens that we have a plan of the enclosure of the monastery which was prepared by Dom Nicolas Milley, Prior of Mores, in 1708.[3] This plan is one of a set of three of which at least 4600 imprints were taken from plates engraved at Clairvaux. Only two sets are now extant ; one is in the Bibliothèque Nationale, the other is in the Bibliothèque de la Ville at Troyes. On this plan we find the *Monasterium Vetus* ; but it is not in the position suggested by Guignard ; it is in the traditional position. It happens also that another Cistercian, Dom Joseph Meglinger, a monk of Wittenberg, visited Clairvaux in 1667 and has given us a very full and detailed description of the *Monasterium Vetus*, leaving no doubt but that he is referring to the original house built by St. Bernard.[4] An earlier authority still is an interesting book of 1517 entitled as *Voiaige de la royne de Sécile*, which tells the story of a journey made by the Queen of Sicily accompanied by the Comte and Comtesse de Guise from Joinville to Clairvaux.[5] Both these authorities, supported by Dom Milley's plan, confirm the view taken by Vacandard that what was traditionally called the Petit-Saint-Bernard, that is to say, the Westernmost portion of the present enclosure of the Maison Centrale de Détention, was the site of the original monastery. A visit to the locality itself would serve to establish the conviction that, considering the fact that in spite of the growth both in numbers and in importance the monks remained for twenty years where they first settled, the original site, wherever it may have been, was not at Arconville. As at Cîteaux so also at Clairvaux the initial difficulties in the way of providing bare necessaries were considerable ; indeed the records indicate that in the latter instance the pioneers were more dependent upon their own resources than they had been in the former.[6] Land which would yield its

[1] *P.L.* CLXXXV. 1697 sqq.

[2] *Vita Prima*, II. v. 29.

[3] *Vide* p. 396 *infra*.

[4] Meglinger. *Iter Cisterc. P.L.* CLXXXV. 1565 sqq.

[5] *Mémoires de la Soc. Académique du départ. de l'Aube*, XLIX. xxii. 3e série, 341 *n*. 3.

[6] *Vita Quarta*, ii. 2 and 4.

produce to labour was an imperative necessity. The Cistercian monk ate bread unpalatable enough, but he had to grow the grain and mill the meal whereof to bake it; and that meant first of all sufficient land to sow; nor would sufficient water to turn the mill be left out of account. St. Bernard may have been a poor harvester with his hands, but he was a good one with his head. We cannot suppose that with the wide choice which he was undoubtedly offered he overlooked all this in making his selection. On these various grounds then we do not hesitate to accept with Vacandard the traditional site.

There were, however, preliminaries, alike spiritual and ecclesiastical, which might not be delayed. St. Bernard had not yet been advanced to the priesthood; nor had he received the requisite episcopal blessing on his abbatial dignity. So soon as provision had been made for the shelter of the monks, for the fulfilment of the essential service of the *Opus Dei* and for the celebration of Mass, steps were taken for dealing with these preliminaries. The diocesan ordinary, Joceran, Bishop of Langres, was at the time absent, but on further consideration it came to mind that the diocese of Châlons-sur-Marne was ruled by a prelate of great distinction both in character and in intellect, William of Champeaux. He had been Archdeacon of Paris, and at his feet, when he presided over the cathedral school of Notre Dame, had sat Abélard. In 1108 he had founded the Abbey of St. Victor-de-Paris in which he became a canon regular; thence in 1113 he passed to the see of Châlons-sur-Marne. His association with St. Bernard, begun on the occasion of the latter's ordination as priest and his reception of the blessing on his abbatial rank, grew in intimacy as the years passed; dying in 1121 he is said to have been buried at Clairvaux in the habit of a Cistercian monk.[1] In due course went St. Bernard to Châlons accompanied by a monk, by name Elbode, seeking the priesthood and the blessing. Into the bishop's house entered a young man, modest and shrinking from the public gaze, pale and emaciated as one who had not long to live, followed by an older man, robust and well set up. The household marked the contrast; while some smiled, others expressed compassion and respect. " Which is the abbot? " it was asked. But William of Champeaux knew, and taking St. Bernard apart he came to recognize in course of prolonged converse that the coming of such a guest was no less than a divine visitation. Henceforth occasions of such converse were frequent, for " Clairvaux became for the bishop as a

[1] *Gall. Christ.,* IX. 877; Marten. et Durand. *Script. et Mon. Ampl. Coll.,* IX. 1023 n.

home and the bishop's house, nay, the entire city of Châlons, as a home for Clairvaux monks. Moreover, the Province of Rheims and the whole of Gaul were by William's means stirred to devout veneration of the man of God. Other men, moved by so great a bishop, learned to receive and to respect him as an angel of God." [1] William of Champeaux's premonition of the great future which lay before this unknown and humble monk was infectious, so the biographer would have us understand.

After the return of St. Bernard to Clairvaux building-operations and the laying out of the adjacent land would have claimed early attention. The monks were few in number ; nor as yet were there any *conversi*, a term applied by the Cistercians to the lay brethren who were admitted to the Order by licence of the diocesan, and upon whom devolved chiefly, but by no means exclusively, the manual services of the house.[2] In the early days of Benedictine history the term was applied to monks who had been *converted* to religion after their arrival at years of discretion, as distinct from those who having been received as *oblates* had been brought up (*nutriti*) in a monastery from a tender age. The *conversus* not being a choir monk was bearded and untonsured and probably from the first wore as now a brown habit ; but he was definitely professed and had a voice in the election of the abbot of his house. So soon as the pontificate of Eugenius III (1145-53) he was forbidden to marry if he returned to the world, a restriction suggestive of the necessity at the time of some strong deterrent from lapse into secular life.[3] About fifty years or more later the *Exordium Magnum*, the Vth and VIth *Distinctiones* of which were probably written at the beginning of the XIIIth century by a Clairvaux monk at Eberbach, a daughter of Clairvaux founded in the Rheingau in 1131, speaks of them as more numerous than the choir-monks.[4]

The plan of the *Monasterium Vetus* was on a very modest scale. Turning to Meglinger's invaluable description we read : " The church and the monks' dwelling-house are under one roof ; the refectory and the dormitory are separated by one flooring. On the ground-floor the unpaved refectory offered the bare earth to the tread of those most holy feet and was lit by few windows and they less than a palm in breadth. Adjoining the refectory is the kitchen, of closely restricted space. From the refectory a staircase leads to the dormitory which is of the same area as the refectory ; in it still remain a few of the sleeping-places formed of four planks "—we may presume

[1] *Vita Prima*, I. vii. 31.

[2] *Exord. Parv.*, XV. Cf. Othon Ducourneaux, *Les Orig. Cisterc.*, 95 sqq.

[3] S. Bern. *Ep.* 143, and Mabillon. *Nota ad loc.* Cf. Du Cange, *s.v.*

[4] *Exord. Magn. Cisterc.*, VI. ix., P.L. CLXXXV. 450.

these to have been of the nature of low pens—" to which an opening cut with the axe gave access. When I came to examine closely I found no trace of the monks having slept upon anything higher than the floor, with straw and dried leaves thrown into their sleeping-places. . . . At the top of the staircase leading from the refectory to the dormitory is the cell which the mellifluous father Bernard occupied. Next to this is another little cell, the dwelling for three months of St. Malachy "—surely Meglinger is in error as to the length of time [1]—" the spot which he ennobled by his most holy death." Shortly afterwards he adds : " From this (level) we descend to the church " ; from which statement, on referring to Milley's Plan I, we gather that the staircase rose from a point at which there were two doors, one admitting to the refectory, the other to the church ; this is confirmed by his description of the latter, as will shortly be seen. He takes reverent account of the details of St. Bernard's cell. " It is more like a prison than a cabinet." Little did the builders anticipate the strokes of statesmanship which in years not far distant would be dealt from that mean garret ! " It is covered by the bare roof, perhaps not open always to the rain but through which penetrate cold and heat and a thousand other plagues. A plank in case of rain or snow closes the window." The sleeping-place was at the head of the staircase already mentioned which appears to have intruded into the room at one corner, its top step forming in some way the abbot's bed, where lay, " to serve the purpose of a pillow, two logs smoothed by the axe " and " the girdle studded with nails and bits of iron which was found after his death next his bare flesh. The wall, hollowed in one place after the fashion of a chair, provided a seat raised a foot above the floor, but the cavity was so low that when sitting in it he could not raise his head. And this was the temple from which so momentous oracles were spoken to all quarters of the globe ! "

The church or oratory is plainly marked upon Milley's plan. It stood to the S.W. of the building above described and was entered by two doors in the East wall ; of these doors the Northernmost was at the foot of the staircase leading to the dormitory, thus, as was usual, facilitating attendance at Nocturns ; the other led into the open air. Meglinger does not fail to give us details of its state in his day. These details, with the exception of the decorative features which are certainly later, probably represent what existed from the first. The major altar, dedicated as in all Cistercian churches

[1] Cf. pp. 75 sq., 182 sq. *infra.*

to our Lady, was against the East wall, while " outside the choir or middle portion of the church were, on the right the

¹ Meglinger.
Iter Cisterc., §§
66-69.

altar of St. Laurence and on the left that of St. Benedict." ¹ A knowledge of Cistercian customs enables us to picture the bareness of the place. No colour brightened either walls or windows ; no lamp burned before any altar ; no glitter from the precious stuff of vestments or the gold of sacred vessels relieved the soft-toned white of the habits of the

² Consuetud.
Cisterc., XX.
and LXX,;
Guignard, Mon.
prim. de la règle
Cisterc.; Exord.
Parv., XVII.

choir-monks.² There were, of course, other buildings, such as a cellar and a grange, but even by the aid of Milley's plan it is impossible to identify them with any certainty. Of all this nothing, alas, remains to-day and, as we shall see, little of anything that ever was Clairvaux.

The admirable economy illustrated by these simple building operations did not, however, save the community from falling into grievous straits. It is probable that for some time their numbers were so small that, with the immediate work in hand of raising a roof over their heads, little opportunity was left for the heavy labour involved in clearing the land, in the main virgin-forest, for the purpose of cultivation. In any case we read that " more often than not they fed on beech-leaves. Their bread, like the prophet's of old, was made of barley, millet and vetch and was of such miserable quality that once a visiting monk, lamenting sadly their plight, secretly took away with him some of what had been set before him in the guest-house that he might show to everybody the marvel of men, and such men, living on

³ Vita Prima, I.
v. 25.

the like." ³ We may identify this visitor with a monk of Clémentinpré, of whom John the Hermit tells us. According to this writer the result was that, on his return to his own monastery, horses, mules and wagons were laden with more palatable food and despatched at once to Clairvaux, and thus a fellowship established between the two houses which extended to the habitual remembrance in prayer of each other's

⁴ Vita Quarta,
ii. 4.

dead.⁴ John, who obtained, we remember, a considerable amount of his information from St. Bernard's cousin, Robert of Châtillon, a monk who had personally experienced the difference between Cluniac and Cistercian fare, describes the penury of these early days as such that " their food was bread made not of oats—which they regarded as too costly— but of some sort of viler, nay, most vile mixture the ingredients of which were rather lumped together than blended. In summer their relish was the leaves of trees cooked, in winter roots." Their habits, he goes on to say, were " but most rarely repaired," and for scarcity of leather " their

shoes were held together by pieces of rope." The enthusiasm
of the ascetic does not account for all this. St. Bernard
himself possessed a considerable amount of this quality, but
he did not recklessly impose upon his sons the observance
of what it prompted in himself. In a condition of desperate
poverty he encouraged them to endure hardness. And need
was. For ere long, when they were reduced to the necessity
of going barefoot—a necessity met by the charity of an unnamed woman who brought them money to buy leather—
and had but one beast of burden, an ass which served the
abbot on his journeys and carried wood for their fires, they came
to St. Bernard and complained that they must return to
Cîteaux. In spite of his kind and gentle encouragement,
in spite of his exhortation to fear and to love God, they persisted in their resolve until, in response to St. Bernard's
prayer, money came in and they learned, as John the Hermit
puts it, that " they that fear God lack nothing." [1]

[1] *Vita Quarta,* ii. 5.

It is probably to this period of acute distress that we
should assign another incident recorded by the same biographer. That indispensable commodity salt was lacking.
" Take the ass, Gilbert, my son," bids the abbot, " and go to
market and buy us some salt." " But where is the money ? "
asks the astonished monk. " Believe me, my son," St.
Bernard replies, " I never knew the time when I had any gold
or any silver. There is One above who holds my purse and
my valuables in His own hands." " Well," remarks the other
with a smile, " if I go empty I shall return empty." However, reassured by the abbot's blessing, Gilbert sets out for the
market. On his way he meets a priest who, on learning his
errand, not only supplies him with salt from his own store,
but makes him a generous gift of money for the needs of the
house. [2]

[2] *Vita Quarta,* ii. 3.

In the *Fragmenta* of Geoffrey we find the story, repeated
by William of St. Thierry in the *Vita Prima,* of the woman
of Châtillon-sur-Seine who came to beg St. Bernard's prayers
for her sick husband, making an offering of precisely one
pound more than the sum of money which the cellarer, the
abbot's brother, Gerard, had but a few minutes earlier named
to St. Bernard as necessary in order to meet their immediate
requirements. [3]

[3] Gaufr. *Fragm.,* *MS.cit.,* 27 sqq.; *Vita Prima,* I. vi. 27.

Such records as these are, of course, common in the lives
of the saints. Here what strikes the reader is the serene
imperturbability of the chief actor. In the minds of the
rest would arise irresistibly the human question : " Master,
carest thou not that we perish ? " While from St. Bernard's

lips, in spirit if not in letter, fell in answer always the divine question : " How is it that ye have no faith ? "

In course of time, probably within the next two years, the community found themselves free from this distressing state ; but not therefore was their life an easy one. " Commonly the Cistercians take for food neither fish nor eggs nor milk nor cheese," writes, we know, Jacobus de Vitry in the XIIIth century,[1] and there is no reason for supposing that their diet in St. Bernard's day was at all more generous. " Let there be no white bread in our monasteries, not even on great feasts " ; " variety is to be avoided in the daily diet " ; " let no one in a monastery eat flesh or lard." [2] So we read in the Institutes of the General Chapter of 1152 ; proscriptions which testify to the fidelity of the Order to the spirit of the original *Consuetudines Cistercienses* of some years earlier. In these latter we find the injunction : " Let us use common herbs such as the earth yields." [3] Rich seasonings are prohibited ; " they certainly please the palate but they stimulate lust." Labour is the proper seasoning for the monk's table. " To an idler cabbage, beans, pulse and coarse bread are distasteful, but to a hard worker they are delicacies." So writes St. Bernard to Robert of Châtillon at Cluny.[4] The abbot himself was so far dead to the pleasures of the palate as for several days to have eaten unwittingly lard offered to him in mistake for butter, and once to have drunk oil supposing it to be water, saying when apprised of the fact that he noticed no difference for it allayed his thirst.[5]

No sooner had Clairvaux been firmly established in structure and in numbers than St. Bernard felt himself to be in a position to respond to an invitation from William of Champeaux, Bishop of Châlons-sur-Marne, to found a house in his diocese. The bishop had already, in 1116, obtained for this express purpose from Hugh Count of Vitry and others a grant of land in the Forest of Luis, held at the time by the Canons Regular of St. Corneil-de-Compiègne. The locality was in the Duchy of Bar (Bar-le-Duc) and about six miles from St. Dizier,[6] but the foundation was not actually effected until 10th October, 1118. The abbot of this house, Troisfontaines, which has the honourable distinction of being the first daughter of Clairvaux, was Roger, a man of noble birth whom, with others, St. Bernard had in 1116 enlisted at Châlons in the Cistercian Order.[7]

At this stage intervened, so inevitably that it might have been foreseen, an episode of some gravity. The severities

[1] Jacob. de Vitriac. *Hist. Orient. et Occid.*, XIV. 300.

[2] *Inst. Gen. Capit.*, XIV. and XXIV. ; Guignard, *Monum. prim. de la règle Cisterc.*

[3] *Consuet. Cisterc.*, LXIII. ; Guignard, *op. cit.*

[4] *Ep.* 1 (11 sq.).

[5] *Vita Prima*, I. vii. 33.

[6] *Gall. Christ.*, IX. 956 ; X. *Instr.*, 161 ; *Voyage littéraire de deux religieux Bénédictins*, II. 91.

[7] *Vita Prima*, I. xiii. 64 sq. ; Manric. *Annal. Cisterc.*, I., an. 1118, iii ; Beaunier, *Recueil des Abb. de France*, II. 594. ; Janauschek, *Orig. Cisterc.*, I. 6.

of the previous three years had not failed to take effect upon
a man who never spared his frail constitution. "Whether
by day or by night he was wont to pray standing, until his
knees, weakened by fasting, and his feet, swollen by labour,
could scarcely sustain the weight of his body." Alas, the
seeds were sown of that chronic gastric disorder which in-
creased with years,[1] the symptoms of it becoming in time   [1] Cf. p. 9 *supra.*
so distressing that special arrangements were made for his
convenience when in choir. In the end his condition became
such that " he was compelled to live by himself except upon
occasions when, for the purpose of conference or of exhortation
or of claustral discipline, it was his duty to consort with the
brethren." [2]   [2] *Vita Prima,*
And now already, almost immediately after the foundation   I. vii. 32,
of Troisfontaines, nothing but complete rest and good food   viii. 39.
stood between St. Bernard and irreparable collapse. But
where was the authority to enforce this imperative treatment ? Happily William of Champeaux arrived upon the
scene, realized the state of affairs and at once set off for
Cîteaux, where, on laying the matter before the general chapter, he was empowered with full discretion to take what steps
he thought best. St. Bernard was removed to a little cell
outside the cloister and beyond the precincts of the abbey.
There he remained for a whole year, probably 1118-19, out
of reach and out of hearing of all that concerned either the
Order or the house. It was not a particularly sumptuous
hospital, nor in his patient's estimate the physician in charge
of it particularly discreet. During his cure St. Bernard was
visited by William of St. Thierry, who describes the place
and tells us an amusing story about its guardian. " I found
him," writes William, " in his little hut, the sort of structure
that they put up for lepers at cross-roads." Meglinger goes
so far as to identify it with " a wooden cot like a shed for
sheltering cattle in the fields " which he saw in 1667.[3] As   [3] Meglinger.
for the physician, in reply to William's inquiry as to how he   *Iter Cisterc.,* § 61.
fared, the patient replied, " smiling in his generous way : ' Oh
I get on admirably. Here I am, after winning for myself
the obedience of reasonable men, reduced by the just judgement of God to the necessity of obeying an irrational brute
beast.' " [4] Doubtless like many saints he was a difficult   [4] *Vita Prima,*
patient. The writers of the *Voyage littéraire* also saw the   I. vii. 32 sq.
remains of this primitive hospital, which they note as being
behind the burying-place of visiting abbots who died at
Clairvaux. It contained, they tell us, no fire-place, a difficulty
which they report as having been overcome by arranging a

large perforated stone, underneath which was placed a lighted brazier all unknown to St. Bernard.[1] We think that sooner or later he must have discovered the ruse ; but perhaps the brethren threatened to invoke the authority of William of Champeaux!

During this period of enforced idleness the heart of St. Bernard would have been lightened by the reflection that within the walls of Clairvaux choice spirits were maturing for their future work. Amongst them may be mentioned Humbert, who in 1126 became the first Abbot of Igny in the diocese of Rheims, the fourth daughter of Clairvaux. Brought up from childhood in the Benedictine house of Chaise-Dieu— the impressive remains of which on their bleak plateau half-way between Ambert and Le-Puy may be familiar to travellers in Auvergne—about the year 1117 he sought admission to Clairvaux. Fifty years he lived in religion, the last thirty as a Cistercian.[2] Nor should we forget Raynald, the first Abbot of Foigny, a friend so intimate and so familiar that from him the titles " lord " and " father " fell painfully on St. Bernard's ears ; [3] nor Godfrey de la Roche, one of the original monks of Clairvaux, soon to become, in spite of his youth, the first Abbot of Fontenay. Godfrey, we have noticed, was St. Bernard's kinsman, certainly by affinity, perhaps also by consanguinity, but it is not known in what degree. The *Menologion Cisterciense* refers to him as one who " by his assiduity in prayer, by his obedience, by his frequent fasts, by his long watchings, by his zealous progress, emulated the mellifluous Bernard in virtue." [4] St. Bernard's confidence in his judgement was so great that about 1125, at his request, he wrote his first treatise, essentially a Benedictine study, *Of the Degrees of Humility and of Pride*. Not long after the year 1130 Godfrey laid aside the rule of Fontenay and returned to Clairvaux as prior, a step reasonably to be explained by the fact that he was the person best qualified to take charge of the abbey during St. Bernard's long periods of absence, which began to be frequent at about that date.[5] His responsibility as prior extended in these circumstances to such matters as the establishment of new colonies, for it was during St. Bernard's absence that, in 1135, Hautecombe, the eighteenth daughter of Clairvaux, was founded on the Lac-Bourget in Savoy.[6] It was probably in 1138 that he became Bishop of Langres, a see which he resigned in the winter of 1162-63 to return to Clairvaux, where he died in 1165.[7]

St. Bernard's return to public life was signalized by the foundation of Fontenay, the second daughter of Clairvaux,

[1] *Voyage littér-aire*, I. 99.

[2] S. Bern. *Sermo in Obit. Humb.*, 2; *Exord. Magn.*, III. 4 ; *Voyage litt.*, I. 87.
[3] *Ep.* 72.

[4] *Menol. Cisterc.*, 237.

[5] *Vita Prima*, II. v. 9, IV. i. 4 ; Jobin, *S. Bernard et sa famille*, 181 sqq.

[6] Manric. *Annal. Cisterc.*, I. ix. 301 n.
[7] *Chron. Clarevall.*, P.L. CLXXXV. 1247; Jobin, *op. cit.*, 279.

on 29th October, 1119.[1] It is remarkable as having been an event in which a leading part was played by St. Bernard's own family. Three of his mother's brothers were concerned in the matter. Raynard Seigneur of Montbard was donor of the land; Milo, still a humble *conversus*, and Gaudry, both monks of Clairvaux, are mentioned amongst "the first builders" of the abbey; and Godfrey de la Roche, we know, was its first abbot.[2] The site was a wooded valley about four miles from Montbard, then in the diocese of Autun; there the monks settled themselves in a little hermitage surrendered to them by a solitary named Martin.[3] Plancher speaks of this hermitage as in a wood called Chastelun or Chastelot belonging to the Abbey of Molesme, which in 1116, at the request of Stephen, Bishop of Autun, had granted it for a Cistercian colony. But the particular spot was not found to be commodious and in 1130, under the direction of Godfrey, the buildings, the remains of which still exist, began to be erected a little lower down the valley, presumably upon the land granted by Raynard of Montbard.[4] The great interest of the considerable remains of this structure is that they give us some idea of what Clairvaux was like when rebuilt about the year 1136, though not of the church itself as again rebuilt after St. Bernard's death in 1153.[5] The church of Fontenay was consecrated upon a great occasion in 1147 by Eugenius III, having been built by Everard, Bishop of Norwich, whose tomb still lies before the major altar.[6]

It was at about this time that other and nearer kinsmen of St. Bernard threw in their lot with him so far as to enter the Cistercian noviciate. Tescelin, already perhaps an old man of seventy, has his brief record in William of St. Thierry's narrative: "Left alone at home he went to his sons and joined himself to them; after remaining with them a short while he died in a good old age."[7] The "short while" we may put at two to three years. Manriquez dates his arrival at Clairvaux at 1117; Mabillon at 1119. Meglinger saw the tomb at Clairvaux in which he and his sons Bartholomew and Gerard were interred.[8] His youngest son Nivard had already, at the proper age, entered the noviciate at Cîteaux, and at the end of the year passed to Clairvaux.[9]

After the departure of Nivard from their common home Hombelline married; whom she married we cannot with certainty say. But, sole heiress of the family property, she found herself in the possession of great riches and indulged herself freely in luxury and in display. Having heard, however, of the reputation of Clairvaux, she was, as the chronicler

[1] *Vita Prima*, I. viii. 8; Manric. *Ann. Cisterc.*, I., an. 1118, iv; Beaunier, *Recueil des Abb. de France*, II. 410; Janauschek, *Orig. Cisterc.*, I. 8.

[2] *Vita Prima*, II. v. 29, IV. i. 4; *Gall. Christ.*, IV. 492; Chifflet, *De Illustr. Gen. S. Bern.*, 540.

[3] *Voyage litt.*, I. 149 sq.; Janauschek, *Orig. Cisterc.*, *loc. cit.*

[4] Plancher, *Hist. Gén. et Part. de Bourgogne*, I. 313; Jobin, *op. cit.*, 185.

[5] Oursel, *St. Bernard, Fontenay et l'architecture Cistercienne, Annales de Bourgogne*, I., an. 1929, 84 sqq.

[6] *Gall. Christ.*, IV. 492; *Voyage litt.*, I. 150.

[7] *Vita Prima*, I. vi. 30.

[8] Manric. *Annal. Cister.*, I. iii. 10; Marten. *Annal. Ord. Bened.*, VI. lxxiii. 12; Meglinger. *Iter Cisterc.*, § 61.

[9] Gaufr. *Fragm.*, MS. *cit.*, 22.

puts it, " moved by God to go and see her brothers. And when she came with imposing attendance and in superb apparel to visit that venerable brother of hers, he, loathing her and cursing her as the devil's snare set to catch souls, refused to go forth and see her. Hearing this she was confounded and, greatly put to shame that none of her brothers deigned to meet her and that Andrew, who had come to the gate, reprobated her as the filth of the gutter for the very splendour of her clothing—she wept and said : ' Although I am a sinner yet it is for such that Christ died. Because I am a sinner I need the counsel and the converse of the good. My brother may despise my flesh ; yet let not the servant of God despise my soul. Let him come ; let him command me ; whatsoever he orders I am prepared to do.' " St. Bernard came and thenceforth Hombeline lived a changed life.[1] Two years later, after, according to the custom of the day, mutual agreement with her husband, she entered the Benedictine nunnery of Jully-les-Nonnains—near Molesme and under the direction of that abbey—which was at the time ruled by her brother Guy's wife, Elizabeth, and of which Hombeline herself became prioress perhaps about the year 1130.[2]

The years 1120 and 1121 were of prophetic import for the Cistercian Order. The former saw the foundation on the 18th of October of Tiglieto or Tilet (*Tiletum*), the first daughter of La-Ferté-sur-Grône, so far South as the diocese of Aix in Liguria.[3] It was, however, the Northerly direction of the movement which was the more significant. The foundation of Foigny (*Fusniacum*), the third daughter of Clairvaux, in the diocese of Laon in Picardy on 11th July of 1121 may be said to have foreshadowed the expansion of the *Cisterciense Institutum* throughout the larger world of Benedictine Europe.[4] It was thus already so far entrenched as to be represented by eighteen houses, of which Tiglieto in the South and Foigny in the North may be regarded as the outposts. Foigny has, moreover, a special interest of its own as signalizing that mutual understanding between, on the one hand, St. Bernard and the Cistercians and, on the other hand, St. Norbert and the Premonstratensians, which was destined to prove so fruitful in the cause of monastic reform during the next half-century. St. Bernard would seem to have felt that Foigny was a valuable strategic position. For the purpose of establishing and personally supervising in their early days new foundations in Flanders and in districts yet more remote in a Northerly direction, such as the

[1] *Vita Prima,* I. vi. 30.

[2] Jobin, *op. cit.,* 135 sqq.

[3] Janauschek, *Orig. Cisterc.,* I. 9.

[4] *Op. cit.,* I. 10; *Gall. Christ.,* IX. 608 ; Manric. *op. cit.,* I., *an.* 1121, v; Beaunier, *Recueil des Abbayes de France,* II. 601 sq.

Rhineland, he frequently visited Foigny; he had a special regard for its monks, who were wont in later days to point with pride to the cell reserved for his occupation.[1] It was about the year 1120 that the invitation came to St. Bernard from Bartholomew de Vir, Bishop of Laon, to settle a colony of Cistercians in his diocese. In the first instance an offer was made of land upon which St. Norbert was at the time founding the *Caput Ordinis* of the Premonstratensians,[2] the story of which is told elsewhere.[3] This course has the appearance of having been, if not dishonourable, at least a little *gauche* on the part of Bartholomew; but in point of fact it proved to have the felicitous result of sealing the friendship between Cistercians and Premonstratensians, for St. Bernard refused the site offered, an act of generosity which would naturally bear fruit.[4]

Thereupon the Bishop of Laon offered land granted by the abbot of the Benedictine Abbey of St. Michel-en-Thiérache.[5] The locality was a thickly-wooded valley in the Pays-de-Thiérache, through which ran a river called the Aube, some five miles N.E. of Vervins in the direction of Hirson, and not far from the little town of Origny-en-Thiérache.[6] The bishop was a generous benefactor, making himself responsible not only for the building of the structure but also for additional gifts of land conveniently situated.[7] Twelve monks, under the rule of a certain Raynald as abbot, took possession on 11th July, 1121. Of Raynald it is recorded that he was a man highly esteemed by St. Bernard. Letters addressed to him by the Abbot of Clairvaux, four of which are extant and may be found in the Benedictine edition, reveal an intimacy between them which St. Bernard would hold to dispense Raynald, as we have seen, when addressing him, from the formality of such official titles as " lord " and " father," as well as the fact that the Abbot of Foigny was a man of considerable culture; indeed his correspondent rallies him pleasantly upon his devotion to Ovid.[8] The *Abbatum Series* found in the *History of Foigny*, written in 1670 by Prior Jean de Lanci, describes him as one " who from a tender age had been committed to monastic discipline "—probably he had been an oblate—as " a disciple of St. Bernard of Clairvaux specially dear to him on account of his gifts of mind," and as " trained by him in integrity of conduct and in zeal for religion." [9] It is plain that St. Bernard, realizing the importance of Foigny as a key-position and the peculiar responsibilities consequently laid upon its abbot, had selected for the post a man of outstanding distinction, for whose

[1] *Gall. Christ.,* IX. 628 sq.

[2] Beaunier, *op. cit.,* II. 603.

[3] Pp. 229 sqq. *infra.*

[4] *Gall. Christ., loc. cit.*

[5] Mabillon, in *S. Bern. Ep.* 72 *n.*

[6] Beaunier, *op. cit.,* II. 601 sq.

[7] *Gall. Christ., loc. cit.;* É. de Barthélemy, *Cartulaire de l'Abbaye de Foigny,* XVI. 10.

[8] *Epp.* 72 and 74. Cf. p. 28 *supra.*

[9] *Gall. Christ.,* IX. 629 sq.

character he could unhesitatingly vouch. When the colonists arrived they found probably little else than the site ; for a time they were compelled to use one and the same building both as a refectory and as a dormitory ; with their own hands they built a modest oratory, the precursor of the magnificent church consecrated in 1124. *Gallia Christiana* describes this as having been erected within three years and by the munificence of Bartholomew de Vir, a vast fane of 400 feet in length and 82 feet in breadth. Assuming the unit of measurement to be the Paris foot or *pied du roi* of 12·78912 English inches, we may form some impression of the area if we remember that Norwich Cathedral has a length of 407 feet and a nave-width of 72 feet. It was said to have been sufficiently spacious to accommodate at the time the greater part of the entire Order.[1] It was on the eve of the consecration that St. Bernard is recorded to have excommunicated the swarms of flies infesting the building, with the result that in the morning they were all dead.[2] For the first quarter of a century after its foundation Foigny proved to be a great centre of attraction ; there in 1150 or 1151 Bartholomew was himself professed a monk, and there Alexander, a prince of Scottish blood royal, spent his last days and died in the habit of a *conversus*.[3]

It was at a date a little earlier in the history of Clairvaux that there occurred an incident which involved St. Bernard in distressing controversy. Robert de Châtillon was the son either of Aleth's sister, Diane de Montbard, who married Othon or Otto de Châtillon Seigneur de Saffres ; or of a son of Bernard de Montbard, whose name has not transpired ; he was thus St. Bernard's cousin-german and not his nephew, as he has sometimes been called.[4] In childhood he had been promised or oblated to the Abbey of Cluny by his parents, who as was usual in the case of nobles made at the same time a gift of land to the community.[5] It was a vexed question as to whether he was an oblate in the strict sense of the term, that is to say, as having been offered according to the solemn rite prescribed in the Rule of St. Benedict [6]—or had merely been promised to religion. The *Exordium Magnum*, in the passage to which reference has been made, reads *promissus ;* Massuet uses the technical term *oblatus*.[7] The present writer has elsewhere given a short account of the custom of oblation [8]—as to which St. Bernard's own view was that the stronger claim in reason is possessed rather by what a man does " of himself knowingly and prudently " than by what is done " in behalf of him by another, himself knowing nothing of it."[9] It may be sufficient to say here that it

[1] *Gall. Christ.,* loc. cit.

[2] *Vita Prima,* I. xi. 52. Cf. p. 220 *infra.*

[3] *Gall. Christ.,* IX. 531 and 629; Manric. *op. cit., an.* 1121, v, 9; Piette, *Hist. de l'abbaye de Foigny,* 52 ; Janauschek, *Orig. Cisterc.* I. 10.

[4] *Vita Quarta,* i. 5 ; Jobin, *Saint Bernard et sa famille,* xxiii. and 362. Cf. p. 4 *supra.*

[5] *Exord. Magn.,* III. ix.

[6] *Reg. S.P. Bened.,* LIX.

[7] Massuet. *Annal. Bened.,* V. lxxii. (xcviii.), *an.* 1115.

[8] Williams, *Studies in St. Bernard of Clairvaux,* IV. 135 sqq.

[9] *Ep.* 382.

was open to various abuses, such as treating the monastery as a home for backward, or incorrigible, or deformed, or deficient boys; that there was considerable diversity of opinion as to the age at which oblates might be received; that at least two Popes, Clement III and Celestin III, laid down that they were not to be professed in religion against their will; that the Cluniacs took admirable precautions to guard against abuses of the system and the Carthusians in the *Statuta* drawn up by Guy, fifth Prior of the Greater Charterhouse, the friend and contemporary of St. Bernard, entirely forbade their reception. So much may be learnt from Martène's *Regula Commentata*, or Commentary on the Rule of St. Benedict.[1] St. Bernard claimed to have "by word and example begotten (Robert) to religion";[2] and in point of fact, when he and his companions set out for Cîteaux, Robert accompanied them, but was refused admission on the ground of his youth and bidden to wait for two years longer. Meanwhile he paid frequent visits to Cîteaux, apparently without let or hindrance on the part of the Cluniacs. In due course he returned to seek admission and entered into the Cistercian Order, as St. Bernard maintained, not from the Cluniac Order but from the world.[3] This would have been early in 1114. When in the following year St. Bernard led forth his colony to Clairvaux, Robert went with him.[4] Massuet held that he was professed at Cîteaux; Vacandard is disposed to think that his noviciate began at Cîteaux and was finished at Clairvaux;[5] certainly the tone of St. Bernard's Epistle I addressed to Robert gives some colour to the opinion that the Abbot of Clairvaux had professed him; the words above cited, "I have begotten you to religion," might indeed refer to this rather than to the fact that Robert had accompanied him to Cîteaux in 1112.

We may well suppose that after the comparative liberty of his Cluniac days—for he had certainly spent much time at Cluny—Robert found the discipline of Cîteaux a little irksome. However this may have been, it was nothing to the privations which he was called to endure during the early years of his life at Clairvaux. A brooding discontent, expressed perhaps to chosen intimates but of which St. Bernard was quite unaware, and in fact amounting to disloyalty to his abbot, arose and gained strength in his mind and was insidiously supported by the doubt as to whether he was not in conscience bound by the promise or the oblation, as the case might be, made to Cluny by his parents.[6] Doubtless something of the external effects of this discontent would

[1] Marten. *Reg. Comment.*, LIX., *P.L.* LXVI. 840 sqq. Cf. Udalric. *Antiq. Consuet. Cluniac. Monast.*, III. viii.
[2] *Ep.* I (10).
[3] *Ep.* I (8); Massuet. *Annal. Bened.*, *loc. cit.*
[4] *Exord. Magn.*, *loc. cit.*
[5] Massuet. *op. cit. loc. cit.*; Vacandard, *Vie de saint Bernard*, I. 89 sq. *éd.* 1910.
[6] *Exord. Magn.*, III. ix.

have been noticeable in his conduct, but St. Bernard would seem to have failed to appreciate the true explanation of his state, for he blames himself for harshness and lack of sympathy in his handling of the young monk.[1]

And for some years their grievance rankled in the minds of the Cluniacs, waiting watchfully for the opportunity of redressing it. The news of St. Bernard's illness and of his consequent seclusion from all affairs, whether of the Order or of his own monastery, during the year 1118-19, cannot have failed to reach them. Their opportunity had come. During his absence the Grand Prior, Bernard de Brancion, arrived at Clairvaux to interview Robert. St. Bernard refers to him as " presenting himself in sheep's clothing, being inwardly a ravening wolf." [2] The description is not inapt, for he introduced himself on the plea that he wished to encourage Robert and to confirm him in his vocation ; [3] the plea was, of course, equivocal. His manner of dealing with the " dainty soldier-boy " was sufficiently evident to the monks to enable them to report the whole story to St. Bernard as we have it reflected in the letter, Epistle I, which he wrote to Robert some years after he had yielded to the blandishments of the grand prior and returned to Cluny. Bernard de Brancion, of a great Burgundian family—the Château de Brancion still stands in its exclusive eminence about six miles West by South of Tournus—was somewhat of a fine gentleman with his contempt for manual labour. " What sort of religion is it," he asks, " to dig the ground, to fell timber, to cart manure ? " contrasting, doubtless for the benefit of his hearer, the rough and ready ways of Clairvaux with the stately refinements of his own great abbey. Somewhat too was he of an epicure. " To what end," he wonders, " did God create food if not that it might be eaten ? " Fasts, vigils, silence, menial service, all these are but folly. Quite a new gospel, as St. Bernard scornfully remarks. And so Robert turned his back upon the drab world of Clairvaux for the purple patch of Cluny, where on his arrival he found himself fêted and petted and spoiled to the top of his bent.[4]

Probably St. Bernard was not altogether unprepared for this foray. The Cluniacs would appear to have previously claimed Robert as an oblate of their house,[5] but without effect. The Abbot of Clairvaux had denied that the formal *petitio* of the parents prescribed by the Rule had ever been made ; although he would allow so much as that the child had been promised to Cluny. Oblation, we may notice, is to be distinguished as a formal act from a promise as an

[1] *Ep.* 1 (2).

[2] *Ep.* 1 (4).

[3] Massuet. *Annal. Bened.*, loc. cit.

[4] *Ep.* 1 (4, 5 and 13).

[5] *Exord. Magn.*, loc. cit.

informal expression of a purpose. As for the land actually given by the parents at the time when the promise was made, he would not dispute with the Cluniacs their claim to retain it ; he would simply point out that they had not retained the boy ; this last was the real issue, and on it they had surrendered, perhaps ten years ago, when Robert first applied to Cîteaux ; it could not reasonably be raised again at this late hour.[1]

This letter, we learn from Geoffrey, was not written until some years had elapsed after Robert's return to Cluny ; its words therefore, in spite of their seeming recklessness—in a sense they *were* reckless, for on a clear moral issue St. Bernard never beat about the bush—would have been weighed in all their implications ; moreover, there had been developments, and St. Bernard was in a position to tell the story of the machinations adopted by Abbot Pontius de Melgueil subsequently to the successful foray of his emissary. St. Bernard dictated it in a quiet spot in the open air outside the abbey-precincts, jealous lest its tenor should prematurely be revealed. His scribe was the monk William, afterwards first Abbot of Rievaulx. When heavy rain fell William would seek shelter but the abbot bade him write on. And, wonderful to relate, though both St. Bernard and the scribe were soaked the sheet remained dry. When, soon after he ceased to be his abbot's secretary, Geoffrey put together the *Corpus Epistolarum*, he gave, he tells us, the first place to this letter, written *in pluvia sine pluvia*, the spirit of which love had motived and the material of which love had preserved.[2]

Meanwhile, however, the Cluniacs had not been idle. They doubtless anticipated that the case would be referred to Rome, and with this in mind a successful attempt was made to obtain for Robert a dispensation from his Cistercian obedience. The dice was loaded ; for the Pope, Calixtus II, had been a Cluniac monk, elected to the Papal throne at Cluny itself after the death there of Gelasius II in 1119 ; the occasion had been memorable, for he had remained at the abbey until after the Epiphany of 1120, keeping great state and conferring as his parting gift the dignity of the *ex officio* cardinalate upon the Abbot of Cluny.[3]

St. Bernard's letter was a deliberate challenge, for he knew that, in addressing Robert, he was addressing all concerned. "A day of judgement, I tell you, will come when clean hearts will be worth more than crafty words and a good conscience than a full purse ; the judge in that day will neither be deceived by lies nor be bribed by gifts." So he writes ;

[1] *Ep.* 1 (8) and Mabill. *Not. ad loc.*

[2] Gaufr. *Fragm.*, *MS. cit.* 35 sq. ; *Vita Prima*, I. xi. 50.

[3] Martier et Quercetan, *Bibliotheca Cluniacensis*, 557 sqq.

scorning to insinuate he glories in the open charge. He would shame Robert by pointing out the deceit practised upon him : " Why is somebody cajoling you with an Apostolic dispensation when your conscience is bound by a divine verdict ? " [1] Vacandard thinks that the young monk never saw this letter ; [2] certainly it would have suited Abbot Pontius to intercept it. Probably, however, he did see it later, for the *Exordium Magnum* records that his heart was touched and his self-respect recovered.[3] This would have been in 1128, when, six years after he began to rule at Cluny, Peter the Venerable restored Robert to Clairvaux.[4]

It must be allowed that St. Bernard's temperament was rather administrative than legislative. It is to be doubted whether he possessed the peculiar gifts needed in order to be the successful framer of a system ; though his instinct as to the excellence of a system and as to whether that excellence was in any given case really effective was very keen. Moreover, his statesmanship, whether in a spacious or in a narrow sphere, was rather that of a prophet than that of a lawgiver. Indeed we may think that for him so far as concerned the religious life there was no Moses but St. Benedict ; although there might be many an Elijah whose vocation it was from time to time to interpret the Rule by the law of that charity, which to outrage is to eviscerate the Rule. On this point his mind was probably much nearer that of Peter the Venerable than is sometimes supposed ; it is one and the same charity which uses sometimes the method of *la fermeté*, at other times the method of *la persuasion*.[5]

Yet, when with the growth of the Cistercian Order in numbers and in importance there grew also the necessity for a Cistercian constitution, St. Bernard, his heart full of regret for the episode of Robert of Châtillon and his mind full of devices for the correction of conditions which made such an episode possible, could scarcely have failed to play some part in the framing of this constitution, although perhaps rather in the spirit than in the letter.

In 1100, two years after the foundation of Cîteaux, St. Alberic, the successor of St. Robert of Molesme, who had ruled but for a very brief space of time, took steps to obtain from Paschal II the *Privilegium Romanum* for Cîteaux in perpetuity.[6] But St. Alberic died in 1108 ; he did not live to see the " second spring " which was heralded by the arrival of St. Bernard and his companions in 1112.[7] It fell to his successor to take the steps ultimately necessitated by that eventful year. Calling to his counsels the Abbots of La-Ferté, Pontigny,

[1] *Ep.* I (7 and 9).

[2] Vacandard, *Vie de saint Bernard*, I. 98, *éd.* 1910.

[3] *Exord. Magn.*, III. 10.

[4] Petr. Vener. *Epist. Lib.* I. 35, *P.L.* CLXXXIX.

[5] René Bazin, *Millénaire de Cluny*, I. 17.

[6] *Exord. Parv.*, XIV. ; Mans. *Concil.*, XX. 980 sq.

[7] *Gall. Christ.*, IV. 984.

Clairvaux and Morimond and probably other abbots of the Order, St. Stephen Harding, whom the *Exordium Magnum* calls the " dux et signifer " of the valiant champions of Christ,[1] succeeded in producing three great documents which, although various in character, yet taken together may not unfittingly be described as the title-deeds of the Order, namely, the *Charta Charitatis*, the *Usus Antiquiores Ordinis Cisterciensis* or *Consuetudines Cistercienses* and the *Exordium Cœnobii et Ordinis Cisterciensis*, commonly called the *Exordium Parvum*.[2] Although Migne does not allow that St. Stephen was solely responsible for the *Charta*, speaking of him as " the chief . . . but not the only author "—founding his opinion doubtless upon the language of the *Prologus*: " The lord Abbot Stephen and his brethren have ordained "— nevertheless, however many may have had a hand in it— John of Paris speaks of twenty abbots in addition to St. Stephen [3]—the impression left after reading the treatise is that of a single dominant personality, gracious indeed but strong, deliberative, even legislative. Less detailed in its enactments than either the *Consuetudines* or the *Exordium*, it however, as it were once for all, reveals the proper quality of the reform initiated at Cîteaux and defines for the Cistercians their type in the great Benedictine brotherhood, a type still evidently traceable to-day.[4] As regards its name, St. Stephen " wished it to be suitably so called as being throughout its whole series fragrant of charity alone, in such a way that it does not seek as its own any end other than the payment of the one debt due, namely, that of loving one another." [5]

It should be said that, distinctive as that type may have been, yet even apart from the consideration of fidelity to the Rule in such matters as clothing, food, sleep and the recitation of the Divine Office—matters for the most part dealt with in the *Consuetudines*—the legislation of St. Stephen did but voice an appeal to the essential principles of Benedictine government as contemplated by the founder. As has been elsewhere observed [6] the contrast has sometimes been instituted between these principles as democratic and the principles adopted in later days, perhaps most noticeably at Cluny, as monarchic. But we may doubt whether this is true to fact. Cluny, it may be, represented a monarchy or at least a close oligarchy which became increasingly autocratic in its governmental methods, the last result, we may think, which would have commended itself to the mind of St. Benedict. It cannot, however, be supposed that a democratic system would have been any more acceptable in

[1] *Exord. Magn.*, VI.

[2] Guignard, *Monum. primit. de la règle Cisterc.*, 59 sqq., *P.L.* CLXVI. 1377 sqq., 1501 sqq.

[3] *P.L.* CLXXXIX. 122, *n.* 44. Cf. Bibl. Nat. MS. Lat. 4346, *infr. cit., ed. cit.*, p. 7.

[4] Vacandard, *Vie de saint Bernard*, I. 99, éd. 1910.

[5] *Exord. Cisterc. cum summa Cart. Carit.*, Bibl. Nat. MS. Lat. 4346, ed. Hümpfner, 1932. Cf. *Chart. Char. Prolog. ad. fin.*

[6] *Dublin Review*, Oct., 1928, 260 sq.

his sight.   Early Benedictine monachism, if we are to judge of it either from the language of the Rule as expressive of the intentions of the founder or from the primitive historical records preserved, for example, in the *Annals* of Mabillon, was nothing if not domestic.[1] As compared with other monastic codes, the Rule of St. Benedict is, speaking generally, marked by a paternal, almost maternal, tenderness ; the abbot is enjoined to be careful when scouring off the rust not to break the frail vessel ; to avoid over-driving the flock ; so to temper his treatment of the weak that there may be no risk of their fleeing from his hand.[2] During the Xth and XIth centuries, to go no farther back, this domestic type had tended to become by imperceptible degrees less emphatic. We may rightly suppose that St. Benedict as a Roman had some sense of the necessity in any family of a *patria potestas* ; it is plain that he was alive to the danger of a monk's having no settled home with a definite claim upon him, of his being a mere tramp in religion (*gyrovagus*) ; with this danger he dealt in the very first chapter of the Rule ; and it was to obviate this that the vow of stability was demanded.[3]

Nor, on the other hand, is there any suggestion to be found in the Rule that the brethren, when called to take counsel with the abbot, are to impose the opinion of a majority on any plea of democratic right ; they may be invited individually to offer an opinion, but in the last resort, being as they are disciples, they are to obey their master, against whose authority no appeal is contemplated.[4] Thus in its original conception the Benedictine monastery was an autonomous family ruled by a father.

Naturally, however, as daughter-houses came to be founded in increasing numbers, the notion of an authority wider than that of the abbot over the sons of his own house gradually prevailed, being based, as it might almost seem, upon the patriarchal ideal.   The older foundations could not fail to be conscious of a claim upon at least the loyalty of the younger foundations lineally descended from themselves, and here and there great abbots of statesmanlike gifts would give expression to and secure recognition of this claim by statutory means.   Such a man may have been, even so early as the end of the VIIIth century, St. Benedict of Aniane,[5] Abbot of St. Savin some thirty miles East of Poitiers, whose spirit would still have lingered in the cloister of that house when St. Berno, founder and first Abbot of Cluny, was professed there a hundred years later.   The development of this process, which was essentially centralizing, is illustrated with increasing emphasis by the

[1] *Reg. S.P. Bened.*, II.

[2] *Reg. S.P. Bened.*, LXIV.

[3] *Reg. S.P. Bened.*, LVIII.

[4] *Op. cit.*, III.

[5] *Vita S. Bened. Anian., P.L.* CIII. 372 sqq.

history of Cluny. At the beginning of the XIIth century, the great abbey had existed for about two hundred years. From 1109 to 1122 it was ruled by Pontius de Melgueil, a peculiarly, even dangerously, masterful personality. We have had occasion in the case of Robert of Châtillon to recognize in him the evil genius of Cluniac government. The first abbot to wear *ex officio* the Sacred Purple, he was in 1122 compelled to abdicate and, after an attempt to reinstate himself during the absence of Peter the Venerable in 1125— an attempt successfully resisted by Bernard de Brancion, who, it will be remembered, had been his own grand prior— he died in disgrace at Rome on 29th December of the same year.[1] The autocratic character of the centralization of Cluniac Benedictinism may be illustrated by a prescription concerning the observance of the Feast of All Saints through- out the Order to be found in the *Statuta* of Pontius. This prescription makes two assumptions ; the first is that it is itself irreformable ; the second is that of the solidarity of every house of the Order down to the smallest *cella*.[2] It may be allowed that these *Statuta* do associate the *Capitulum Cluniacense* as concurring with Pontius ; but the *Praeceptiones Piae* of the same abbot, also issued to the whole congregation, are issued in his name alone.[3] This is typical of the way in which, at a time when feudalism in France was developing in a monarchic direction, a system of centralization grew which might nowhere be found so firmly consolidated as in the Cluniac Order, possessed as it had been almost from the first of a glamour peculiar to itself.

It is not to be denied that, as Dr. Coulton has pointed out,[4] a vast organization such as the Benedictines had now become necessitated a strict visitatorial system ; visitation, therefore, would naturally be a corollary of reform. And so strongly did the idea of an authority more extensive than that of the individual abbot over his own subjects prevail that, in the constitution of the Cistercians as framed by St. Stephen and his assistants, we look in vain for anything like full recognition of the autonomy of the individual abbey. On the other hand, we notice that the term *Major Ecclesia* is applied at least to Cîteaux and to the four other foundations, the abbots of which had taken counsel with St. Stephen ; and more, that the title *Major Abbas* appears to be borne by the abbots of all mother houses in relation to their filia- tions.[5] Yet there is no suggestion of a monarchy of the Abbot of Cîteaux as such, by virtue of which he rules the Order as we find Pontius de Melgueil ruling at Cluny. The

[1] *Gall. Christ.,* IV. 1134 sqq. ; Jean de Virey, *l'Abbaye de Cluny,* 103 sqq.

[2] *Pont. Ab. Statuta, P.L. CLXVI.* 840.

[3] *P.L. CLXVI.* 841.

[4] Coulton, *Five Centuries of Religion,* II. 197 sqq. and *passim.*

[5] *Chart. Charit.,* IV. 18 ; V. 23.

annual visitation of his daughter-houses by a *Major Abbas*, which may be undertaken either personally or by a deputy, the abbot of another house of the same filiation, is something quite *familiar* in the strict sense of this term ; he visits them because he founded them ; they are his offspring ; and should they receive his visitation more than once a year, it is presumed that they will be the more pleased.[1] Who, it may be asked, is to visit the *Majores Ecclesiae* and above all Cîteaux itself, which is described as *Mater Ordinis ?* [2] As regards Cîteaux it is provided that it is to be visited annually by the Abbots of La-Ferté, Pontigny, Clairvaux and Morimond upon such a day as these latter shall themselves appoint, exclusive of that of the general chapter of the Order. And the *Charta* does not overlook the possibility of delinquency on the part of the Abbot of Cîteaux, for the correction of which it provides. In such unhappy case it will be the duty of the four other houses named above to admonish him, if need be four times, to amend his ways and the ways of his subjects ; and, in the event of his obduracy, to take steps for his deposition by the general chapter, or, should it be necessary to act before the general chapter is held, by an assembly of all the abbots of the filiation of Cîteaux together with some other Cistercian abbots as assessors, and, further, for the appointment of a successor approved by the monks of Cîteaux.[3] As regards the four other dominant houses, probably it is contemplated that strictly they are subject to visitation by the Abbot of Cîteaux only, although naturally he would be received with special honour in any house of the Order ; in either case he is to be regarded as *locum tenens* of the abbot of the house.[4] Here we get an interesting sidelight. It is laid down that, although for the time being *locum tenens* of the abbot, he is, unless the abbot be absent and thus unable to preside at table in the guest-house, to take his meals with the brethren in the refectory.[5] Now it is in accordance with the Rule that the abbot should preside at table in the guest-house ; [6] it is an entirely Benedictine custom ; yet we find William of Malmesbury mentioning it as the one point as regards which the Cistercian abbot does not live after the same fashion as his brethren the abbots of Black Monks : " The abbot makes no concessions to himself that he does not make to others ; he is everywhere with the brethren, everywhere taking charge of his flock, with this one exception, namely, that he is not with them at meals because his table is always laid with the travellers and the poor." [7] So far had the Black Monks in this

[1] *Op. cit.*, II. 8.

[2] *Op. cit.*, II. 4.

[3] *Op. cit.*, V. 27. Cf. Bibl. Nat. MS. *Lat.* 4346, *ed. cit.*, p. 9.

[4] *Op. cit.*, II. 4.

[5] *Op. cit.*, II. 4.

[6] *Reg. S.P. Bened.*, LVI.

[7] *De Gest. Reg. Angl.*, IV. 36, *De Cisterciensibus. R.S.* Cf. Ludovic. I. *Capit. Monach.*, Can. 27, *P.L.* XCVII. 385.

respect ignored the Rule that a writer, contemporary with St. Bernard, could refer to its observance as noticeable. In regard of the statutory visitation made by the Abbot of Cîteaux, he is forbidden to deal with any matter concerning the house which he visits against the will either of the abbot or of the brethren.[1] Plainly this is a very strict limitation and it indicates, surely, the anxiety of St. Stephen to avoid anything like the autocracy which had developed at Cluny.

It must be allowed that such a constitution as the *Charta Charitatis* establishes could in its letter be applicable only to a comparatively small congregation. As the Order grew it was inevitable that modification should result. Modification being the thin end of a wedge, the problem is how to prevent the thick end from becoming a change, not merely in the letter of a constitution but in its spirit. Official language expresses sentiment and it secures the recognition of sentiment ; and the recognition hardens sentiment in such a way as to justify yet stronger official language of a similar tenor. We realize this when some sixty years later, in 1178, in the *De Miraculis* of Herbert of Torres, we find the high-sounding title *Pater Universalis Totius Ordinis* applied to the Abbot of Cîteaux.[2] Again, as the Order reached out to what were in those days the ends of the earth, it was only by means of some measure of centralization that its identity, the very distinctive characteristics of its reforming spirit, could be preserved and it was only by means of regular visitation reaching the utmost limits of its expansion that any falsity to type could be detected and corrected. At the period in which St. Bernard lived " the bond which united all the Cistercian houses to the *abbaye mère* was purely that of brotherly love " ;[3] thus it is wont to be with an infant society and the *Cisterciense Institutum* was still such, although it was revivifying in the Benedictine Order the spirit of the Rule with a success and on a scale which have, perhaps, never been equalled. The problem for St. Stephen and his brother-abbots was to embody this spirit in a form sufficiently elastic to ensure its permanence as the dominant factor in the life of a great organism, which was growing rapidly by the absorption of national elements in many lands.

It has been told before [4] but it may be well to recall the story of the endorsement of the *Charta*, the constitutional treatise, and the *Usus*, the administrative treatise—the *Exordium Parvum* being the historical apology for the other two—by the Apostolic See. Calixtus II was still at Cluny

[1] *Chart. Charit.*, II. 6.

[2] *De Mirac. Libri Tres*, II. xxv. Cf. *Chron. Clare-vall. an.* 1178 ; *Gall. Christ.*, IV. 843.

[3] Vacandard, *op. cit.*, I. 101, éd. 1910.

[4] *Dublin Review*, Oct., 1928, 258 sq.

[1] Hugon. Monach. Cluniac. *Ep. ad Dom. Pont. Ab. Cluniac. ap. Biblioth. Cluniac.*, 557 sqq.; Guignard, *op. cit.*, XXX.

[2] Mabillon. *Annal. Bened.*, II. xx. (xlix.), an. 722, 64; *Gall. Christ.*, IV. 441.

[3] Jaffé, *Regest.*, 6795; *Exord. Magn.*, XXIII.; Manric. *Annal. Cistere.*, I., an. 1119, vii, 115.

[4] P. 35 *supra*.

[5] *Exord. Magn.*, III. ix. ; Massuet. *Annal. Bened.*, V. lxxii. (xcviii.), an. 1115, 605.

[6] *Chart. Char. Prolog.* Cf. Othon Ducourneaux, *op. cit.*, 83 sq.

[7] Petr. Ven. *Epp.*, Lib. I. 28, *P.L.* CLXXXIX. 138.

at the end of December in 1119.[1] While there he had occasion to visit Saulieu, the old capital of the Morvan, the occasion being the consecration of the new church of the Abbey of St. Andoche in that town, a Benedictine house founded before the year 722.[2] Here it was that, on 23rd December, the bull was dated ratifying the two Cistercian documents in question, which it describes as respectively the *Constitutio* and the *Capitula*.[3] To the circumstances of the Pope's being in Gaul we have already referred.[4]

Manriquez, in his *Cistercian Annals*, deals fully with the petition made by St. Stephen for this ratification, remarking that the statement of the *Exordium Parvum* that it was sent to Rome is to be understood in the sense that "ubi Papa, ibi Roma." It is noteworthy that the prohibition contained in the bull as to the reception of a Cistercian monk into any strange abbey without regular commendation was, in spirit at least, contravened by the seduction of Robert of Châtillon from Clairvaux by Abbot Pontius, the approval of which was by some means or another obtained from Calixtus by the Cluniacs almost at this very moment.[5] As regards the control exercised by ordinaries over the religious houses in their dioceses, the Cistercians in seeking to fortify themselves by Papal bull make no pretence to exemption therefrom. On the contrary, the *Charta* expressly provides that no house of the Order may be founded without the authority of the diocesan ordinary,[6] a provision which was in itself something of a challenge to Cluny, the houses of which congregation were privileged by independence of all save Papal episcopacy, a privilege of which Peter the Venerable would boast in a letter to St. Bernard: " It is our glory to have the Pope as our one and only most exalted bishop ; to him alone as such we render specific obedience." [7]

Thus it was that the Cistercians by a constitution framed some twenty-one years after the foundation of Cîteaux, having as it were come of age, called in question the hegemony as an exponent of the spirit of St. Benedict of that earlier and illustrious Benedictine congregation which during the previous two centuries had done so much for monastic reform both in France and beyond its borders. It has seemed to be necessary to give some account of the original constitution of the Order because there can be no doubt but that, framed as it was coincidently with the rise of St. Bernard's great influence, it both represented his spirit and in a measure controlled the monastic policy of his whole life.

CHAPTER III

THE EXPANSION OF CLAIRVAUX, 1125–36

It was not long after the foundation of Foigny in 1121 when, on 14th September of the same year, Le-Loroux or l'Oratoire (*Oratorium*), the ninth daughter of Cîteaux, was founded in the county and diocese of Anjou about three leagues from Saumur.[1] Then there followed as it were a moment of suspense ; a brief moment, for before another decade had elapsed thirty-one new houses were enrolled in the Order, of which ten were in districts where German was spoken while two, Waverley and Tintern, were in England.

The exceptional severity of the winter of 1124-25 resulted in a famine which prevailed throughout Burgundy and its neighbouring districts, and by reason of which Clairvaux suffered great privation ; nevertheless, the monks of their penury rose to the occasion with magnificent generosity.[2] It was not unusual in those days for a parish church to keep a roll of the poor for whose sustenance it made itself responsible.[3] John the Hermit tells us that St. Bernard on the occasion of this famine adopted a similar plan at Clairvaux, placing upon his roll the names of no less than two thousand needy folk. " The abbot and his brethren," we read, " took counsel and agreed to receive under their seal "—*sub signaculo*, thus formally attesting their roll—" two thousand persons." [4] The figures may be questioned ; for all St. Bernard's faith, he never undertook to make bread out of stones. Vacandard thinks the chronicler to be guilty of exaggeration, reliable as he was in regard of the details of St. Bernard's early life. He wrote about the year 1181. The *Life of St. Norbert* had appeared before 1164 and in it the Premonstratensians are recorded to have succoured five hundred of the poor.[5] Was John led to speak at random by his zeal for the credit of Clairvaux ? However this may be, 1125-26 was a very lean year in the district, full of anxiety for St. Bernard as to how to make both ends meet and scarcely likely to present a favourable occasion for the planting of a new colony. Yet

[1] *Gall. Christ.*, XIV. 726 ; Janauschek, *Orig. Cisterc.*, I. 10.

[2] *Vita Prima*, I. x. 47 ; *M.G.H.*, IV. 449.

[3] Imbart de la Tour, *De Eccles. Rustic.*, 69 sq.

[4] *Vita Quarta*, ii. 6.

[5] *Vita S. Norb.*, P.L. CLXX. 1257 sqq.; Madelaine, *Hist. de Saint Norbert*, 11 and 296.

43

in 1126 the site was accepted and the charter signed of the great Abbey of Igny in the diocese of Rheims by the benefaction of Raynald, metropolitan of the province.[1] The locality was a wild, unbroken country, thickly-wooded, about halfway between Rheims and Fère-en-Tardenois and some ten miles South by East of Fismes. The first abbot was Humbert, one of those religious who had left the houses of their profession for the stricter discipline of the Cistercians.[2] There was, however, something wanting to him. For nine years he had been at Clairvaux; the previous twenty years beginning with his childhood had been spent as a Black Monk at La-Chaise-Dieu. When in 1138 he wished to resign his abbacy, to lay down a heavy burden for a lighter, he incurred the grave displeasure of St. Bernard who wrote to him from Italy that he was breaking down the hedge of God's vineyard and exposing the fruit of it to the danger of being trodden underfoot. " I am surprised," he remonstrates, " that you should think that the course of which you have written to me "—his contemplated resignation [3]—" is a good way to prepare for death "—Humbert had evidently urged this plea—" and that you are not afraid to wish to die in such a state of scandal and under the anathema of our lord the Pope. And then, if it was so necessary (for you to resign) could no other time have been chosen than when I am detained by the needs of the universal Church, so that I am unable to go to the aid of that unfortunate church which you are imperilling? I beseech you, by him who was crucified for you, spare to torture further those who are already sufficiently afflicted." [4] It is to be presumed that fuller information modified St. Bernard's attitude of mind and that no Papal anathema was launched, for Humbert retired to Clairvaux, where he died in 1148, the Abbot of Clairvaux preaching a funeral sermon in which he apostrophized him as a man after his own heart.[5] He was succeeded at Igny as abbot by Guerricus, another Clairvaux monk, who had succeeded him at Clairvaux as prior.

Two years elapsed and then, it might almost seem, with growing momentum the great wave of expansion rolled on. On 7th September, 1128, was founded the fifth daughter of Clairvaux, Reigny in the diocese of Auxerre, with Stephen de Touci as its first abbot. The site was a pleasant plain bordering the right bank of the river Cure, about a mile and a half above Vermenton.[6] We next find the Clairvaux monks at Ourscamp on the Oise, another fair site, on the 10th of December in the following year. Here they were in the diocese

[1] *Gall. Christ.*, IX. 300, X. 37 sqq.; Manric. *op. cit.*, I., an. 1127, vi; Beaunier, *op. cit.*, II. 562 sq.; Janauschek, *op. cit.*, I. 14.

[2] Pp. 53 sqq. *infra*.

[3] Cf. Manric. *op. cit.*, I., an. 1138, ii, 3.

[4] *Ep.* 141.

[5] S. Bern. *In Obit. Dom. Humb. Serm.*, 4.

[6] *Gall. Christ.*, XII. 459; *Instr.*, 106 sq.; Janauschek, *op. cit.*, I. 15; Manric. *op. cit.*, I., *an.* 1128, vi; Beaunier, *op. cit.*, II. 844; Courtépée, *Descr. hist. et topo. du duché de Bourgogne*, VII. 44 sq.

of Noyon, strongly supported by its bishop and only ten miles from the great Benedictine Abbey of St. Corneille. Their first abbot was Galeran de Baudemont, formerly Abbot of Épernay.[1]

1131 was the first of the *anni mirabiles* of which Clairvaux would chronicle not a few before St. Bernard died. In four months no fewer than three foundations were effected. The Cistercians were installed at Cherlieu (*Carus-Locus*) in the diocese of Besançon on 17th June, in place of the Canons Regular of St. Augustine.[2] Geoffrey tells the graceful story of the healing by St. Bernard, on the occasion of a visit to inspect the locality, of a boy afflicted by uncontrollable chronic weeping. For days, we read, the boy would sob without intermission and inconsolable, his condition amounting to wasting disease. After confessing himself to the abbot during an interval of self-control he raised his face serenely for the kiss of peace and returned to his home happy and completely recovered.[3] The 7th July saw the foundation of Bonmont in the diocese of Geneva and in the Pays-de-Vaud,[4] and 14th September that of the illustrious Abbey of Eberbach in the diocese of Mainz on a beautiful site in the Rheingau, about two miles below that city on the Nassau bank of the river.[5]

Eberbach has special interest for the student of Cistercian origins, for here it was that the *Exordium Magnum* was finished probably during the first quarter of the XIIIth century, being in fact the natural expression, particularly in its Fifth and Sixth *Distinctiones*, of the exultant Cistercian enthusiasm of which Eberbach was at the time a focus. The place had had in its early days a somewhat chequered history. In 1116 Adelbert I, Count of Saarbrücken and Archbishop of Mainz, had founded there a house of Canons Regular of St. Augustine; but owing to the laxity of their life they were suppressed in the year 1131 and were replaced by a priory of Johannisberg (*Mons–S. Johannis*), a Benedictine abbey a few miles lower down the Rhine on the same bank.[6] In this very year, however, the site seems to have been bought for the Cistercians of Clairvaux [7] by Adelbert the diocesan, who put pressure upon the Benedictines of Johannisberg to evacuate the place on payment to them of fifty silver pounds, and invited St. Bernard to establish a colony from Clairvaux in their room.[8] The twelve monks who arrived were under the rule of Ruthard, evidently a person of some presence and distinction, well tested in the religious life; St. Bernard would doubtless have been alive to the possibilities involved

[1] *Gall. Christ.*, IX. 1129, X. 357; Manric. *op. cit.*, I., an. 1129, vii; Beaunier, *op. cit.*, II. 652; Janauschek, *op. cit.*, I. 17.

[2] *Gall. Christ.*, XV. 253; Manric. *op. cit.*, an. 1131, vi; Beaunier, *op. cit.*, I. 126; Janauschek, *op. cit.*, I. 19 sq.

[3] Gaufr. *Fragm.*, *MS. cit.*, 38 sq.; *Vita Prima*, I. xi. 53.

[4] *Gall. Christ.*, XVI. 467; Manric. *op. cit.*, I., *an.* 1131, vi; Beaunier,*op.cit.*, II. 1016 sq.; Janauschek, *op. cit.*, I. 20.

[5] *Gall. Christ.*, V. 654; Manric. *op. cit.*, I., *an.* 1131, x; Janauschek, *op. cit.*, I. 20 sq.

[6] *Gall. Christ.*, *loc. cit.*

[7] Gabriel. Bucelini, *Monasteriolog Germ.*, 23; *Germ. Sacr.*, II. 30; Janauschek, *loc. cit.*

[8] *Gall. Christ.*, V. 655.

[1] Gabriel. Bucelini, op. cit. loc. cit.

[2] Janauschek, loc. cit. ; Rossel, Eberbach, I. ; Vacandard, Vie de saint Bernard, I. 403, éd. 1920.

[3] Gall. Christ., IX. 473 ; Manric. op. cit., I., an. 1131, vi ; Beaunier, op. cit., II. 581 ; Janauschek, op. cit., I. 22 sq. ; Vacandard, op. cit. loc. cit., ed. cit.

[4] Cf. Vita S. Gosvin. Ab. Aquicinct., II. 19.

[5] Gall. Christ., III. 175 sq. ; Instr., 35 sq. ; Manric. op. cit., I., an. 1132, viii ; Beaunier, op. cit., I. 331 ; Janauschek, op. cit., I. 24 sq. ; Jobin, Saint Bernard et sa Famille, III. sq.

[6] Ep. 186.

[7] Manric. op. cit., I., an. 1131, vii.

in the venture of a foundation where others had failed. Six years later, in 1137, Adelbert died and was by his own request buried at Eberbach.[1] It should be said that Bucelini and *Germania Sacra* suggest other years than 1131 for the foundation, but the latter is accepted by Janauschek, Rossel and Vacandard.[2]

The following year, 1132, has perhaps even a greater interest for us than the preceding. Not only did Clairvaux settle four colonies in that year, but in that year it founded its first house in England, Rievaulx, and—at the moment so rich was its fecundity—on the very same day, 5th March, the Abbey of Longpont in the diocese of Soissons, about ten miles S.W. of the city of that name, the fine XIIIth century church of which would be consecrated in 1227 in the presence of St. Louis. Longpont is usually recorded as the tenth and Rievaulx as the eleventh daughter of Clairvaux. *Gallia Christiana* gives 3rd March as the date of both foundations but 5th March is preferred, as by Janauschek, so also by Vacandard who identifies the day as the Saturday before the Second Sunday in Lent.[3] Vaucelles, founded on 1st August of the same year in the diocese of Cambrai under peculiarly favourable auspices, was from its inception a comparatively wealthy abbey, being generously endowed by Hugh of Oisy, Seigneur de Crèvecoeur, Hugo de Mercorio.[4] The site was a valley very near the present road from Cambrai to St. Quentin, about eight miles from the former and not far North of the plateau of La-Terrière on " the Hindenburg Line " : the river Scheldt flowed within a short mile of the abbey, and Crèvecoeur, the home of its patron, lay about three miles to the N.E. The first Abbot of Vaucelles was an Englishman by name Raoul, and its first novice-master one whose charm we have already recognized, Nivard, St. Bernard's youngest brother.[5] St. Bernard himself conducted the band of settlers to Vaucelles where they were solemnly received by Hugh, his family and many of the neighbouring seigneurs, an event which illustrates the actively personal part which the Abbot of Clairvaux took wherever possible in new foundations, and of which we find a reminiscence in a letter written by him in 1140 to Hugh's son, Simon, begging him to confirm the donation of the Forest of Ligescourt made by his father to the writer for the needs of the abbey.[6]

Rievaulx was, as we have said, in these islands the first-begotten daughter of Clairvaux.[7] Waverley, founded by William Giffard, Bishop of Winchester, on 28th October, 1129, as the second daughter of l'Aumône (*Eleemosyna* al. *Cistercium-*

Minus) in the diocese of Chartres,[1] was the *première* Cistercian
abbey of England; but its claim was disputed by Furness
on the ground that Savigny, the latter's mother-house, founded
about the year 1105, settled its colony at Furness in 1127; [2]
the fact, however, being that Savigny was an abbey of Black
Monks which became Cistercian only in 1147.[2] Yet were we
to allow Cistercian seniority to *both* these houses, it is probable that in the XIIth century neither of them held the
pre-eminence which fell to the lot of Rievaulx; both of them
were during this period, as Aeldred, third Abbot of Rievaulx,
remarked of Waverley at an early stage, still comparatively
off the thoroughfare of life (*quasi in angulo*).[3] The founder
of Rievaulx, Walter Espec, was a notable figure in the North
of England. Under him it was that the barons and yeomen
of Yorkshire, rallying around the banners of St. Peter of York,
St. Wilfred of Ripon and St. John of Beverley, drove back
King David and his Scots at the Battle of the Standard in
1138. He was a man whose interests were on the side of
religion; for sixteen years earlier, in 1122, he had founded
a house of Canons Regular of St. Augustine at Kirkham,
some five miles S.W. of New Malton. In 1131 he offered
St. Bernard lands at Grif and Tilestone in the valley of the
Rye for the foundation of a daughter of Clairvaux. William
of Newburgh, in words which are probably none the less true
because borrowed from William of St. Thierry's description
of Clairvaux,[4] refers to the site as " a place of horror and of
vast solitude."[5] The charter of foundation may be found
in the *Cartularium Rievallense* published by the Surtees
Society with copious notes by Dr. T. C. Atkinson on the
boundaries of the land conveyed.[6] The ichnography of the
place lies outside our scope, but we may note that the knowledge of it has been considerably increased by excavations
made since Sir W. St. John Hope wrote his article in the
Victoria County History of the North Riding, of which excavations an account by Sir Charles Peers, late Chief Inspector
of Ancient Monuments, may be found in the *Antiquaries'*
Journal.[7] As first Abbot of Rievaulx an Englishman was
wisely chosen, William, the scribe of St. Bernard's famous
letter to Robert de Châtillon, one whose personality is the
more fascinating because so little is known of him. We may
perhaps read something of him writ large in Aeldred who,
after some two years' interval during which Abbot Maurice
ruled, succeeded him—probably in 1147, having previously
represented him at Rome in 1141 concerning the vexed question of the vacancy of the see of York, and been appointed

[1] Janauschek, *op. cit.*, I. 16 sq. ; Dugdale, *Mon. Angl.*, V. 237, ed. Caley.

[2] Janauschek, *op. cit.*, I. 95 sq.; Dugdale, *op. cit.*, VI. (2), 1102, ed. cit.

[3] S. Aeld. *Relatio de Stand.*, 184, R.S.

[4] *Vita Prima*, I. v. 25.

[5] Guill. Novoburg. *Historia*, I. 50. R.S.

[6] *Surtees Soc. Publ.*, LXXXIII. 16 sqq. 1887.

[7] *Journal of the Soc. of Antiquaries*, 1921.

¹ Gault. Daniel
Vita Aild., 67 ;
Powicke, *Bull.
John Rylands
Libr.*, 346 sq.
² Vol. LXXXVI.
2nd Ser. Vol.
xxxvi. 20 sqq.
1929.

by him on his return novice-master at Rievaulx.[1] We know
that he was locally canonized ; what is believed to be his
shrine is described and the problem of his canonization discussed by Sir Charles Peers in the *Archæological Journal.*[2]
At an early stage St. Bernard wrote commending the newcomers to King Henry I in a short letter dated by Mabillon
1132, which we may quote in full. " There is in your land
what is the spoil of your and my Lord ; spoil to the loss of
which he preferred death. As for me, I have taken steps
to pursue this spoil and to send of our soldiery men who
with a strong hand, if it displease you not, may claim it,
recover it and bring it home. Now therefore I have sent
in advance these scouts whom you see before you, in order
that they may explore the conditions skilfully and report
them faithfully. Aid them as the ambassadors of your Lord
and in so doing fulfil your service as his vassal. May he,
indeed, to his own honour, to your salvation, to the safety
and to the peace of your country, bring you in joy and in re-

³ *Ep.* 92.

nown unto a good and an untroubled end ! "[3] The traditional
notion of the Cistercian Order as a spiritual *militia* is interesting ; no less than is the use of such words as *praeda*,
disponere and *explorator* suggestive of a Cæsarian manner

⁴ Cf. Appendix.

on the part of the writer.[4]

The effect of this campaign of " the new knights of
Christ " and of their settlement upon the land granted by
Walter Espec was that from Rievaulx there at once radiated
an attractive force upon the religious of the North, such as
the Black Monks of St. Cuthbert of Durham and of St. Mary
of York, in particular upon the latter. The simplicity of
life and of worship, the strict and almost literal adherence
to the Rule, the scrupulous avoidance of the least suspicion
of simony, appealed to these Northerners and won the support of their metropolitan, Thurstan, Archbishop of York,
with the result that, as the inevitable sifting process took its
course, before many years had passed a grave crisis arose to
which we shall refer when telling of the foundation of Fountains
as a Cistercian house, which took place in 1134 or 1135.
Meanwhile one more foundation of 1132 remains to be recorded.

The zeal of the Cistercians for distant enterprise boiled
hotly in the third decade of the XIIth century ; too hotly,
as it might for a while seem even to the mind of St. Bernard.
Let us take an illustration of the extent to which the ten-
tacles were stretching. It is the year 1130, the last of the
decade. On the 8th day of September, in a valley about a

mile from Graz in the diocese of Seckau, Leopold Marquess of Styria is founding—posthumously by the hands of his widow, the Marchioness Sophia—the great Abbey of Runa or Reuna (*de-Runis*), the first daughter of Ebrach the fourth daughter of Morimond.[1] Such outposts were a long way from their central hold, from their *Caput Ordinis*, in those days; the journeying to the annual chapter general would have been tedious and difficult. St. Bernard may, perhaps, have feared lest the system should be too loosely knit or he may have recognized traces of the danger of a certain spirit of *wanderlust*, for we find him about a year earlier counselling Artald, Abbot of the Cistercian Abbey of Preuilly in the diocese of Sens, to abandon his project of founding a daughter-house in Spain and rather to arrange with the Abbot of Pontigny for a site in his possession near Villeneuve-l'Arch-evêque, which in fact was colonized from Preuilly as the Abbey of Vauluisant in 1129.[2] "I have heard," he writes, "that you wish to establish from your holy community an abbey in Spain. Now I am naturally wondering very much what reason there may be for this; what wisdom there may be in it; why it is that you want to exile your sons to such a distant place, involving thereby so great expense and so great labour in travelling and in building, when you may have near at hand a settlement already built and well prepared."[3] However, the time came when St. Bernard raised no objection to the crossing of the Pyrenees; and in 1132, on the invitation of Alphonso VII, King of Leon and of Castile IInd of the name, a colony from Clairvaux took over an abbey of Black Monks at Moreruela in Leon and in the diocese of Zamora which had lapsed to the Crown.[4]

The year 1133 was unfertile. St. Bernard was immersed in affairs. During the earlier part of the year he was still absent on his first visit to Rome whence, having achieved some success in the healing of the Papal Schism, he returned home at the end of June, only to find the Church in France scandalized by murderous contentions.[5] But the two suc-ceeding years were prolific. In 1134 were founded Himmerod in the diocese of Trèves on 9th March and Vauclair in that of Laon on 23rd May. The original settlement of what was eventually known as the Abbey of Himmerod was at Winterbach in the romantic valley of the Kyll, an affluent which reaches the left bank of the Moselle about four miles North of Trèves. Four years later, the locality proving to be incommodious, the monastery was transferred to the bank of the Salm which enters the Moselle on the same bank some

[1] Janauschek, *op. cit.*, I. 13 sq., 17 sq.; Wegele, *Mon. Eberac.*, 3 sqq.

[2] Javal, *l'Abbaye de Vauluisant, Saint Bernard et son Temps.*, I. 161 sqq.

[3] *Ep.* 75.

[4] Marten. *Annal. Bened.*, VI. 205; Man-ric. *op. cit.*, I., *an.* 1131, viii sq.; Janauschek, *op. cit.*, I. 23.

[5] *Epp.* 158-163. Cf. pp. 126 sqq. *infra.*

ten miles lower down; and there it acquired its name of Himmerod.[1] Vauclair is interesting from the fact that its first abbot was Henry Murdach who became third Abbot of Fountains in 1145 and in 1147 Archbishop of York. Its site was in the valley of Courmemblain, about halfway between Laon and Fismes, a locality now in the diocese of Soissons.[2]

A yet more momentous year was 1135. In spite of St. Bernard's absence in Germany and in Italy during the greater part of it, no less than five foundations were effected from Clairvaux, of which two were in districts so far remote from one another as Yorkshire and Lombardy. It may, however, be said that his visit to Italy after the Diet of Bamberg[3] contributed materially to the establishment of the Abbey of Chiaravalle-Milanese. It was on his long and busy journey home from the Council of Pisa—which council ended on the 6th of June in this year—that St. Bernard and Geoffrey, Bishop of Chartres, accredited by the company of the Papal Legates Cardinals Guy of Pisa and Matthew of Albano, went to Milan charged by the council with the duty of dealing with the state of affairs which had arisen out of the expulsion of the schismatic Archbishop Anselm. His arrival was the signal for a notable ovation.[4] His saintly reputation had in the month of May moved the Milanese to come out to meet him as he crossed the plains of Lombardy on his way to the opening of the council at Pisa; but St. Bernard, declining to enter the city, had passed on. There were, moreover, certain persons who appear to have sent to him special messengers named by St. Bernard " the very dear brethren Otto and Ambrosius," begging him to come to them at Milan. Of these persons he speaks in his letter of reply as *conversi*, evidently in the sense that they were postulants who would enter the Cistercian ranks. At first he was disposed to accompany these messengers to Milan; but on second thoughts he decided to proceed to Pisa, promising to return and forward their wishes.[5] This letter may belong to a date some months earlier than the period of St. Bernard's journey across Lombardy in May. Janauschek, evidently puzzled by records which give 22nd January, 1136, as the date of the foundation of the abbey, corrects the year to 1135. Vacandard follows the records giving 22nd July, 1135, surmising not unreasonably that the project was set on foot on 22nd January in that year and that Epistle CXXXIV refers to such initiatory steps.[6] In any case, by the generosity of the pious rich of the city, prominent amongst them being

---

[1] *Gall. Christ.*, XIII. 634; Manric. *op. cit.*, I., *an.* 1134, viii; Janauschek, *op. cit.*, I. 31.

[2] *Gall. Christ.*, IX. 633; X. 195; Dugdale, *Monast. Angl.*, V. 300 sqq.; Manric. *op. cit.*, I., *an.* 1134, viii; Beaunier, *op. cit.*, II. 602; Janauschek, *op. cit.*, I. 32.

[3] P. 142 *infra*.

[4] *Vita Prima*, II. ii. 9.

[5] *Ep.* 134.

[6] Vacandard, *Vie de saint Bernard*, I. 382, n. (3), *éd.* 1920.

one Guy, Captain of the East Gate, the walls of the twentieth daughter of Clairvaux, the first Cistercian foundation in Italy, rose that year near Rogoredo some few miles from Milan on the Pavia road.[1]

With the exception of that of Fountains the remaining four foundations were effected earlier in the year than was that of Chiaravalle-Milanese. It was probably at about the end of 1134 that St. Bernard travelled for the second time into Aquitaine on the mission of putting an end to the Papal Schism there, where alone in France the opponents of Innocent II, under the leadership of William X, Count of Poitiers and Duke of Aquitaine, held out against the lawful Pope.[2] With some difficulty the Abbot of Clairvaux succeeded in prevailing upon William to acknowledge Innocent—the dramatic episode of Parthenay belongs rather to the story of the Schism—and as an act of reparation the Count of Poitiers founded the Abbey of Grâce-Dieu, in the diocese of Saintes and in the province of Aunis, upon a site of which a colony from Clairvaux took possession on 25th March, 1135.[3]

This same journey of St. Bernard bore other fruit besides Grâce-Dieu. Jobin gives from the MSS. of the Church of Nantes the charter of foundation granted at the request of his mother Ermengarde by Conan III, Duke of Brittany, to the Abbey of Buzay on 28th June of 1135.[4] The charter refers to Ermengarde as having received the veil at the hands of St. Bernard in the Priory of Larrey near Dijon. Two letters, probably of an earlier date, are extant addressed by St. Bernard to Ermengarde, revealing a spiritual relationship quite unique so far as we know in his case where a woman was concerned,[5] a relationship quite accountable for the grant of the Isle of Caberon as a site for a daughter of Clairvaux. Nivard, St. Bernard's youngest brother, is named as the leader of the colonists, with the title of prior, and they are said to have been welcomed by the duke and his mother on 28th June, the Vigil of the Apostles. Janauschek's date, 16th June, is not supported by the charter.[6] Buzay was on the left bank of the Loire in the diocese of Nantes and about fifteen miles nearer the sea than that city. The arrangements for the foundation were made before St. Bernard's visit to Parthenay —possibly so early as the end of 1134; he would have left the neighbourhood on his journey to Bamberg, Pisa and Milan before Nivard—recalled from the Abbey of Vaucelles— and the Clairvaux monks arrived.[7] Matters, however, did not progress very favourably at Buzay. Conan was not quite so good as his word. Indeed, on a second visit to

[1] *Epp.* 132, 133; Manric. *op. cit.*, I., *an.* 1134, ii, *an.* 1135, ii. and ix.; Janauschek, *op. cit.*, I. 39; Ughelli, *Italia Sacra*, IV. 142.

[2] *Vita Prima*, II. vi. 32 sqq.

[3] *Gall. Christ.*, II. 1397; Manric. *op. cit.*, I., *an.* 1135, ix; Beaunier, *op. cit.*, I. 164 and 193; Janauschek, *op. cit.*, I. 34.

[4] Jobin, *Saint Bernard et sa Famille*, 578 sq.

[5] *Epp.* 116, 117.

[6] Manric. *op. cit.*, I., *an.* 1135, iv; Beaunier, *op. cit.*, II. 940; Janauschek, *op. cit.*, I. 35.

[7] *Vita Prima*, II. vi. 34.

Brittany St. Bernard found that not only had the duke failed to carry out his pledges, but he had recalled some of his benefactions. Practically there resulted a second foundation of the abbey, the charter of which frankly confesses the grave derelictions committed, confirms the earlier charter of 1135, and makes considerable additional donations. This charter, quoted in full by Jobin, may on internal evidence furnished by the names of witnesses be dated about 1145.[1] Ten whole years had, perhaps, elapsed during which Nivard, as to whom it is doubtful whether he was ever more than prior, would have borne the brunt of the battle. Nivard would appear to have been charged on several occasions with the delicate mission of watching over the interests, spiritual and material, of new foundations. If we are to identify him with the Nivard of St. Bernard's Epistles CCCI and CCCCLV as do some authorities, we find him in one and the same year, namely, 1147, at Espina or l'Épine in Spain and at Val-Richer or Soleuvre in Normandy, both of which houses were founded from Clairvaux probably in this year.[2]

In taking note of the foundation of Rievaulx we referred to the attraction which its Cistercian discipline exercised amongst the monks of the religious houses in its vicinity. This attraction was early at work. It was most strikingly illustrated in the case of the Benedictine Abbey of St. Mary of York. This house, originally peopled by monks from Whitby under Abbot Stephen, was founded in 1088 by Alan, son of Guy, Count of Brittany, and dedicated to St. Olaf, to which dedication William Rufus subsequently added the name of our Lady. Under Geoffrey, the third abbot, the discipline growing lax, some of the more zealous monks urged measures of reform.[3] At the end of two months, during which the reformers suffered considerable persecution, Geoffrey still proving unwilling to grant their request, they applied to the diocesan, Thurstan, Archbishop of York, who suggested a conference over which he should himself preside. When Thurstan arrived at the conference he found the ranks of the malcontent majority stiffened by the presence of visiting monks from Marmoutier and from Cluny; and not only so, but his archdeacon, the Dean of the Cathedral Chapter, the Prior of Gisburn and others who attended him, were excluded. A scene of indescribable disorder ensued, and finally Prior Richard, Gervase the Sub-Prior, the sacristan another Richard, in all thirteen monks, with difficulty escaped and followed the archbishop to his palace. It was impossible to leave matters as they were and Thurstan wrote

[1] Jobin, *op. cit.*, 590 sqq.

[2] *Gall. Christ.*, XI. 446, XIV. 749, 815, 861, 924, 1001 ; Jobin, *op. cit.*, 112 sqq. Cf. p. 84 *infra* and Marten. *Not. ad Ep.* 455.

[3] Horst. et Mabillon. *Not. Fusior in S. Bern. Ep.* 94.

to William de Corbeuil, Archbishop of Canterbury, a full account of the case. He has nothing but good to say of the reformers. They are men who "truly desire to obey the Gospel of Christ and the Rule of St. Benedict. The abbot and his monks ought at least to imitate the Egyptians and the Babylonians who allowed the Children of Israel to set out on their way to the land of promise. Laban, too, allowed Jacob, when he determined to flee secretly after suffering cruel persecution, to return to his country. Men, who leave a place where they have greater liberty to sin than not to sin, should be accounted not as guilty of desertion but as gifted with forethought." Finally he begs that they may be treated no worse than were the monks of Molesme by Hugh, Archbishop of Lyons, and by Pope Urban II in similar circumstances.[1]

From the *Annals of Waverley* and the *Chronicle of Peterborough* we learn that the monks of St. Mary of York were men living honestly, though far short of the requirements of the Rule, far short of the vow of their profession and of the perfection of Cistercian discipline; and that some of them when they heard of the strictness of the Cistercian Order were pricked in conscience, loathing their luke-warmness.[2] And plainly Thurstan was convinced of the entire sincerity of these seceders from York, for on 25th December, 1132, he settled them on some land near Ripon called Skeldale where, with but scanty shelter, they passed a winter in dire deprivation, living literally from hand to mouth. In spite of all, two only of the little band, Gervase the Sub-Prior and a monk by name Raoul, returned to York; the rest, after taking common counsel, "sent messengers to St. Bernard, declaring themselves to have chosen Clairvaux for their mother and himself for their father and to be ready in everything to follow his advice and to obey his orders."[3] Meanwhile the Abbot of St. Mary of York had anticipated them by a letter, in his reply to which St. Bernard disclaims at the outset all direct responsibility in the matter but presses two points; first that the reformers should have seceded in the face of such obstacles is some proof that their secession is "of God"; and secondly that it is quite plain that by not seceding they would have violated their consciences. His manner is probably designedly a little detached. The letter is a good illustration of St. Bernard's tact. The scene is a long way off; he would disabuse the mind of his correspondent of any notion that he is holding a brief for Clairvaux, rather than seeking to bring the persons interested in the

[1] *Inter S. Bern. Epist.*, 442 (Ed. Bened.); 490 *ap.* Migne.

[2] *Annal. Waverl.* and *Chron. Petroburg.*, Dugdale, *Monast. Anglic.*, V. 292 sq. Cf. William of Newburgh, *Hist.*, I. 49 sq. *R.S.*

[3] Dugdale, *op. cit.*, V. 286; *Cartae ad Font. Coen.*, VIII., X., XI., *ap. op. cit.*, V. 296 sq.

matter to view it judicially. Accordingly he proceeds to quote passages of St. Gregory, one from the *Pastoral Rule* [1] and the other from the *Homilies on Ezekiel*,[2] which implicitly and explicitly state the principle that a man who sets before himself a greater good and then does a lesser, sins. What such a man actually does, that is to say, the work in itself, may stand high in man's judgement ; but in God's eyes he himself has fallen very low because his choice has been lower than it might have been. In the light of this principle he would have the present burning question coolly judged. He has nothing more to say, except that to avoid offence he has perhaps spoken less strongly than he ought to have done.[3]

It would appear that Abbot Geoffrey was not entirely satisfied. He evidently felt the secession to be a reflection upon himself. That Gervase and Raoul had repented of their return to his abbey did not make matters any better for his wounded *amour propre*. St. Bernard in his reply to a second letter from the abbot deals less in generalities and comes to closer grips. Geoffrey, forsooth, counts it a grave misfortune that some of his monks should wish to live a stricter life ! He ought rather to go in fear for himself, for his sorrow is *the sorrow of the world* that *worketh death*. It is a failure in fatherly solicitude for him to grudge his sons their spiritual advancement. As for the two monks who have sought again the heights from which they rashly fell, the shame of their first failure is the measure of their renewed zeal and their past dishonour that of their present glory. The abbot may rest assured that the absolution granted in the first instance to all the seceders still covers these two monks, in spite of their return—certainly in God's judgement. Why, their return was, on St. Gregory's principle—again enunciated—apostasy ! Geoffrey would be well advised in saying nothing further about getting them excommunicated ; in any case St. Bernard declines to discuss the question, for he is not prepared to pass judgement upon the absent.[4] It was perhaps with the intention of strengthening the hands of the Archbishop of York, should any application be made to him to excommunicate Gervase and Raoul, that St. Bernard wrote to him in terms highly commendatory of the assistance given by him to the poor, meaning thereby the seceding religious.[5] Vacandard dates these Epistles XCIV, XCV and CCCXIII at about the May or the June of 1133 after St. Bernard's first journey to Italy. A letter written to Prior Richard, now by the suffrage of his reforming brethren first

[1] III. 28.
[2] *Hom.*, III.

[3] *Ep.* 94.

[4] *Ep.*, 313.

[5] *Ep.* 95.

Abbot of Fountains, he dates at 1133-34. This letter reveals the fact that St. Bernard had sent to Fountains some Clairvaux monks, in particular Geoffrey of Ainai, to give on the spot practical direction to the reforming spirit. Their report is that the hand of God is at work there. That most rare of all events, the bettering of the good, is occurring. Would that, St. Bernard exclaims, he might go and see it with his own eyes! Let them surpass mediocrity and avoid luke-warmness. He cannot write much, for the messenger waits, but Geoffrey of Ainai will do the rest.[1] The affiliation to Clairvaux had perhaps not yet been formally effected; but it cannot have been long delayed, 1134-35 being the date to which it is commonly assigned.[2] " And that place," writes William of Newburgh, " is called Fountains, where from thenceforth as from the fountains of the Saviour so many have drunk waters springing up unto eternal life." [3] William was born but a few years after the foundation of the abbey and spent his life as a Canon Regular of St. Augustine at New-borough, not so very far distant from the site.

One more foundation of this year remains to be noted. The early history of the Abbey of Hautecombe in the diocese of Geneva, now in that of Chambéry, on a romantic site bordering the Western shore of the Lac-du-Bourget at the foot of the Mont-du-Chat, is shrouded in some obscurity. Probably its original site was at a place on the opposite shore of the lake, in a " deep combe " where a few hermits had con-structed their rough dwellings at the beginning of the XIIth century. Whence they came cannot be stated with any certainty ; it has been suggested that it was from St. Jean-d'Aulps in the Chablais.[4] Subsequently they migrated to a place called Charay on the other side of the lake, bringing with them the name *Alta-Cumba*, and lived there as a com-munity according to the Cistercian reform from about the year 1125 until they were affiliated to Clairvaux as its eigh-teenth daughter on 14th June, 1135.[5] They are said to have received their site at Charay from Amadeus III, Count of Savoy, a prince who had fallen under Cistercian influence and proved himself to be a nursing father to the Order, as at Tamié on the *col* between Frontenex and Faverges and at St. Jean-d'Aulps.[7] Hautecombe was for centuries after its foundation the burial-place of the House of Savoy, of Boniface, Archbishop of Canterbury, and of his brother Peter amongst the rest. It is perhaps to be associated with Geoffrey of Auxerre, who is by some authorities identified both with Geoffrey, St. Bernard's notary and biographer,

[1] *Ep.* 96.

[2] Janauschek, *op. cit.*, I. 37. Cf. Manric. *Annal. Cisterc.*, I., *an.* 1132, viii.

[3] William of Newburgh, *Hist.*, I. 50. R.S.

[4] Pp. 60 sq. *infra.*

[5] *Gall. Christ.*, XV. 346, XVI. 479 ; Manric. *op. cit.*, I., *an.* 1135, ix ; Beaunier, *op. cit.*, II. 1016 ; Janauschek, *op. cit.*, I. 34 sq. Cf. Blanchard, *Hist. de l'Abbaye de Hautecombe.*

[6] Garin, *Hist. de l'Abbaye de Tamié*, 19.

[7] Janauschek, *op. cit.*, 41 sq.

and with the Geoffrey who was successively Abbot of Igny, of Clairvaux, of Fossanova and of Hautecombe.[1]

The Council of Pisa at which St. Bernard was present closed on 6th June, 1135, and after the council he was busily engaged in reconciling the Milanese to the Pope and to the Emperor.[2] It would have been the end of the year by the time that he was back at Clairvaux. Probably therefore it was early in 1136 that he was approached by the prior, Godfrey de la Roche, and other " venerable fathers " whose minds were seriously exercised as to the problem of housing the daily increasing numbers of brethren. These " foreseeing persons, anxious for the common welfare, strove to bring down for a while to the level of earthly things the man of God whose conversation was in heaven and pointed out to him what the needs of the house demanded. Accordingly they suggest that the locality in which they were settled was a strait place and inconvenient ; that, as their numbers were daily growing by the accession of newcomers, it was impossible to house them in the existing buildings ; indeed, that the church was scarcely large enough to contain even the professed monks alone. They proceed to say that they had considered a site lower down the valley with the convenience which it afforded by reason of the river flowing close below it ; that there is sufficient space there for all the requirements of the monastery, for meadows, farm, woodland and vineyards ; that, if the forest did not seem to provide sufficient enclosure, this could easily be supplied by walls of stone of which there was abundance on the spot." [3] St. Bernard was somewhat taken aback. We may think perhaps that he was a little weary, for the last six months or more had been full of hard and anxious work. And then to be greeted on his return home with a serious proposal for the *déplacement* of the entire establishment ! Did they realize, he questioned, the expense and the labour involved in erecting new stone buildings, to say nothing of—what they apparently contemplated—supplying running water to all the offices of the house ? Why, the world would think that they were millionaires—which they certainly are not—who did not know what to do with their money ! They must know perfectly well that they could not afford it. When they got halfway through people would be saying : " Here are fools who began to build and are not able to finish." But the prior and his supporters were not to be discouraged. If God had ceased to send them postulants there would be good reason against what they suggested ; but, as he has not done so, the only

[1] Chevalier, *Répert. des Sources Hist. du Moyen Âge, Bio-Bibl.*, I. 1701. Cf. Appendix.

[2] Jaffé, *Geschichte des Deutschen Reiches unter Lothar dem Sachsen*, 169, 239, 259; Hefele, *Hist. des Conc.*, trad. Delarc, VII. 222.

[3] *Vita Prima*, II. v. 29.

CLAIRVAUX

alternatives are either to rebuild on a more spacious site or to refuse any more postulants. Could the abbot doubt but that he who sends all these postulants will himself also provide for their housing? Would it not be lack of faith to be anxious about ways and means, and criminal to incur the risk of over-crowding? St. Bernard, rejoiced by their faith and by their charity, gave himself to much prayer, was rewarded by divine guidance [1] and acquiesced in their proposal.[2] William lays some stress upon the spaciousness and the loveliness of the new site, as well as upon the dignity and the size of the new buildings as compared with those of the *Monasterium Vetus*.[3]

The rumour of what was in hand reached the ears of Theobald of Champagne and of seigneurs and of bishops over a wide area. Ample resources were freely supplied for what noticeably Arnald of Bonneval in truly Benedictine phrase calls the *opus Dei*. The land was cleared and the timber felled and prepared for use; stones were quarried and the walls began to rise. It is probable that the monks and the *conversi* did much of the masonry and of the carpentry, but there was a great and notable piece of work for which their unaided efforts were insufficient. For this the services of skilled artisans, such as smiths, fullers, leather-dressers, cement-workers and others were employed, each provided with the special tools proper to his trade. The remarkable achievement contemplated and actually effected was no less than the utilization of the river Aube for the various needs of the abbey. Channels were constructed for conveying the running water to the mills; it was supplied by underground ducts to the kitchen and to all the offices; and finally its many distributed streams were made to meet again and return to the main current of the river; a fine feat of engineering from which we cannot withhold our admiration. The rapidity with which the entire structure of the monastery was completed is no less remarkable; and we are not surprised to learn that the new-born Clairvaux, after such an achievement, its soul alive and full of movement, gained ground and grew without delay.[4] William tells of the encouragement afforded to the work by divine revelations, and of the result as issuing in so many new foundations that the daughters of Clairvaux " on the nearer and on the further sides of Alps and seas filled many a desert spot," and he adds, " still are there daughters for which sites must daily be sought." [5] As regards the date at which the whole work was finished, the " in brevi " of Arnald of Bonneval suggests

[1] *Vita Prima,* I. xiii. 62.

[2] *Vita Prima,* II. v. 29 sq.

[3] *Vita Prima,* I. xiii. 62.

[4] *Vita Prima,* II. v. 31.

[5] *Vita Prima,* I. xiii. 62.

that it was an early one, and Vacandard is probably justified in speaking of it as " quelques années plus tard," later, that is to say, than 1136.[1] Although disused, the greater part of this structure remained until 1789, the year of the Revolution; but Vacandard, writing in 1885, speaks of nothing being left of it except the *chevet nord* of the church, which was very near the site of the little shelter in which St. Bernard spent his long rest-cure.[2] In 1927 the present writer failed to find even so much as this; and M. Morel-Payen, writing two years later, makes no mention of it.[3] It should be remembered that, at about the time of St. Bernard's death, the need of larger buildings was again felt, and that in the year 1154 these were taken in hand on a site about 240 metres East of the existing one.[4] While the abbacy was still vacant a monk, by name Laurence, was sent to Sicily, where he obtained from King William I a considerable sum of money for this purpose.[5] He brought back with him from Rome ten fine buffaloes, thus doing good service not only to the abbey but also to its neighbourhood. The work of building this third monastery advanced more slowly than was the case with its predecessor; it was not finished until 1178. The church, however, was consecrated in 1174, the year of St. Bernard's canonization; Henry II of England provided the means for roofing it with lead and was rewarded with the gift of a finger of St. Bernard, whose body was at the time translated, though but for a few years, for it was again translated when the buildings were finally completed in 1178.[6] Of these buildings there are left certain remains now put to the use of the Maison de Détention, namely, the *domus conversorum* as a saw-mill and the *cellarium* as a laundry. The latter is a fine vaulted room of seventy metres in length, with three naves separated by octagonal columns.[7] The scene is pathetic for the lover of St. Bernard. Admission is granted to visitors on application to the Préfet of the Department, but one should not accept the statement of one's very courteous conductor, an expert doubtless on matters of prison administration, if he should happen to remark that " tout ça est de St. Bernard "! The ichnography of the place may profitably be studied in such authorities as d'Arbois de Jubainville's *Études sur l'état intérieur des abbayes Cisterciennes et principalement de Clairvaux, au XIIᵉ et au XIIIᵉ siècles* (35 sqq.), Viollet-le-Duc's *Dictionnaire d'Architecture* (I. 265 sqq.) and Vacandard's *Le Premier Emplacement de Clairvaux* [8] cited above. Something too may be learnt from Dom Meglinger's *Iter Cisterciense* (70) and from Dom Milley's three plans of which we have

[1] Vacandard, *Mém. de la Société Académique de l'Aube,* XLIX. xxii., 3e série, 345.

[2] Vacandard, *op. cit.,* 348; *Vita Prima,* I. vii. 33 sq.

[3] Morel-Payen, *Troyes et l'Aube,* 278.

[4] Guignard, *Lettre à Montalembert, P.L.* CLXXXV. 1697 sqq.

[5] Herb. *De Miraculis,* II. 30, *P.L.* CLXXXV. 1341 sq.

[6] *Chron. Clarevall., R.H.G.F.* XIII. 713 and 715; Vacandard, *op. cit.,* 349.

[7] Morel-Payen, *Troyes et l'Aube, loc. cit.*

[8] *Mém. de la Société Académique de l'Aube, loc. cit.*

made use in dealing with the *Monasterium Vetus*, as well as from that very delightful work of the great Maurists Martène and Durand, *Voyage littéraire de deux religieux Bénédictins* (I. 186). Viollet-le-Duc, in his *Dictionnaire* (1853-69), expresses himself indebted to Harmand, the librarian of Troyes, and to Millet, the diocesan architect, and d'Arbois de Jubainville appears to give general approval to his work, including his two plans of the abbey reproduced in the Appendix together with Dom Milley's pre-Revolution plan of 1708, with which it may be compared. Vacandard gives the same measurement, 106 metres, of the length of the church as does Viollet-le-Duc. Flammeng's notes on the *Sépultures du choeur de l'église de Clairvaux* are summarized by Migne;[1] they contain a plan of the *abside* according with that of Viollet-le-Duc and indicating the positions of the tombs of St. Bernard and of St. Malachy of Armagh, the former immediately behind the major altar and West of the ambulatory, the latter next but one to St. Bernard's tomb and on the North of it. The tomb of Aleth of Montbard, to which her body was translated from the crypt of the *rotunda* of St. Bénigne-de-Dijon by Abbot Stephen Lexington in 1250, is not marked on the plan although it is described in the text ; and we know from Henriquez that it was before—*ex parte sinistra*, Flammeng tells us—the altar of St. Saviour, the central altar of the *abside* numbered V on Flammeng's plan, and therefore nearly due East of the tomb of her illustrious son.[2] A drawing of the abbey as it appeared in 1610 by J. Duviert is reproduced by Petit, in which the intention would appear to be to place in juxtaposition the three structures of 1115, 1136 and 1154-78.[3] A monograph on the ichnography of Clairvaux is a real need ; but it would seem to be impossible in the present state of things. It would presuppose work done on the site similar to what is being done at Cluny by Dr. Kenneth J. Conant for the Mediæval Academy of America. The existence of the convict-prison, alas, precludes anything of this kind.

[1] *P.L.* CLXXXV. 1765 sqq.

[2] Henric. *Fascic. SS. Ord. Cisterc.*, II. xli. 4.

[3] Petit, *Hist. des ducs de Bourgogne de la race Capétienne*, VIII. 208. Cf. Williams, *Studies in St. Bernard of Clairvaux*, Pl. 7.

CHAPTER IV

THE DAUGHTERS OF CLAIRVAUX, 1136–53

OF the three foundations effected in the year 1136 two were instances of succour brought by the Cistercians to the comparatively feeble religious life in houses of other Orders. The Abbey of Balerne owed its existence to some few monks, coming from either St. Étienne or St. Bénigne at Dijon, who settled there, if we are to accept Massuet's date, in 1097 ; [1] other authorities give 1107. Later, in 1135, it became Cistercian and the monks begged for an abbot to be sent from Clairvaux to rule them. This first Abbot of Balerne was Burchard, a man devoted to St. Bernard and a vigorous reformer. Janauschek gives 31st May, 1136, as the date of the foundation ; [2] and not long afterwards, probably in 1137, we find St. Bernard writing to Burchard in reply to various questions in general terms of encouragement, reminding him of the joy which follows the pangs of parturition and bidding him ascribe the credit of harvest to him who gives the increase. " This," he concludes, " is the answer which I give to your inquiries. When I come to you I will bear the burden of your necessities as my own." [3] It was too this Burchard who wrote a postscript to the First Book of the *Vita Prima*, presumably not long after the death of William of St. Thierry in 1147 or 1148, in which he refers to St. Bernard as " a second Benedict." [4] The site of Balerne—the buildings are, alas, a ruin—was in the diocese of Besançon about a mile and a half S.W. of Champagnole in the Jura, in a district now in the diocese of St. Claude.[5]

St. Jean-d'Aulps, in the diocese of Geneva, not far from Thonon in the Chablais, was a house with a similar history to that of Balerne. Its early days are of great interest ; for they reveal the fact that some eight years before St. Robert, St. Stephen and the rest of the Molesme reformers migrated to Cîteaux the spirit which prompted this momentous move was already alive amongst them. Two monks are said to have left Molesme in quest of more complete

[1] Massuet.
Annal. Bened.
V. 385.

[2] Janauschek,
op. cit., I. 41.

[3] *Ep.* 146.

[4] *Vita Prima*, I.,
*Subscript. Op.
Praeced.*

[5] *Gall. Christ.*,
XV. 247;
Manric. *Ann.
Cist.*, I., *an.* 1136,
vi; Beaunier,
*Recueil des
Abbayes de
France*, I. 125.

solitude about the year 1090 and to have settled at a place called Les-Harpes (al. *Vallis-Alpis*, Valperti). In 1094 St. Robert appointed a monk, by name Guy, as their first abbot, who in 1097 was succeeded by Garinus, under whom the new abbey was generously endowed by Amadeus III, Count of Savoy, and by others of his house. In 1120 Calixtus II dispensed the house from the jurisdiction of Molesme, and later, on 28th June, 1136, it was affiliated to Clairvaux.[1] Garinus appears to have ruled for about forty years, for we find a letter of St. Bernard, which Mabillon assigns to the year 1138, addressed to the "Alpensis Congregatio," in which the Abbot of Clairvaux deals with the election of a new abbot. He is unable to be present himself but he hopes to send Godfrey de la Roche, his prior, to represent him ; failing Prior Godfrey, some monks from Clairvaux will certainly be there to advise upon the occasion. By such representatives of St. Bernard they will be guided in the matter of the election, as well as by Garinus, their father, whom the new abbot is to succeed.[2] Garinus, abbot of his house, as we have seen, for at least forty years and at the time bishop-elect of Sion or Sitten in the upper valley of the Rhone, would have been a somewhat outstanding personality. William of St. Thierry records a visit of St. Bernard to St. Jean-d'Aulps, when a woman, from amongst the crowd assembled for the cure of their ailments, directly that she appeared before the saint collapsed under a sudden attack of her malady, but raised by his hand was at once completely restored.[3]

Not a little of the interest attaching to these early foundations of Clairvaux arises out of the fact that frequently they are in some way connected, either with a member of St. Bernard's own family, or with a person endeared to him by some common experience of sorrow or of joy. This is the case with Nerlac or Noirlac (*Niger-Lacus*), the third and last foundation of 1136, for its first abbot was Robert of Châtillon.[4] The name Noirlac—the story, be it said, is mere legend—is supposed to be derived from the fact that the son of the founder, Ebbo of Charenton, was drowned in the lake near by. Its old name was, however, *Domus-Dei* or *Domus-Dei-super-Carum*, for the river Cher flowed past its walls. The site in the archdiocese of Bourges was about four miles N.W. of St. Amand-Montrond,[5] and about halfway between Bourges and Moulins. Janauschek dates its foundation at 27th October, 1136,[6] holding the charter of 1150[7] to have been granted by Ebbo and his wife Agnes some years after the abbey was established, a not unusual proceeding. In this view he is

[1] Massuet. *Ann. Bened.*, V. 385; *Gall. Christ.*, IV. 730, XVI. 486 sq.; Manric. *Ann.Cist.*, I., an. 1136, vi; Beaunier, *op. cit.*, II. 1016 sq.; Aub. Mir. *Chron. Cisterc.*, 116; Janauschek, *op. cit.*, I. 41 sq.

[2] *Ep.* 142, and Mabill. *Not. Fus.*

[3] *Vita Prima*, I. xiv. 67.

[4] *Exord. Magn.*, III. 9 sq.

[5] *Voyage littéraire de deux religieux Bénédictins*, I. 38.

[6] Janauschek, *op. cit.*, I. 43; Manric. *op. cit.*, I., an. 1136, vi.

[7] *Gall. Christ.*, II. 195, *Instr.*, 64.

[1] Aub. Mir. *Chron. Cisterc.*, 95 ; Beaunier, *Recueil des Abbayes de France*, I. 246 sq.

[2] *Ep.* 378.

[3] Beaunier, *op. cit.*, II. 436.

[4] *Gall. Christ.*, IV. 833, *Instr.*, 165 sqq. ; Manric. *op. cit.*, I., *an.* 1136, vii.

[5] Janauschek, *op. cit.*, I. 44 sq.

[6] *Exord. Magn.*, VI. *ad fin.*

[7] Pp. 50 sq. *supra.*

supported by Aubertus Miraeus, Beaunier and other authorities against *Gallia Christiana*.[1] Before this charter was signed, however, the abbey, together with other Cistercian houses of the archdiocese of Bourges, was in some straits for lack of food, as we gather from a letter addressed to Suger by St. Bernard about 1149 in which he begs the benefaction of the royal bounty, Suger being at the time Vicegerent of Louis le Jeune, still absent on the Second Crusade.[2]

The year 1137 was marked by two foundations only. The first was that of Auberive (*Alba-Ripa*)[3] or, as Beaunier names it, Auberims, in Champagne, in the diocese of Langres at the foot of the Mont-Charnois and not far from the source of the Aube. It was founded and richly endowed by Guillencus, Bishop of Langres, under a charter granted in 1135,[4] but the date of the formal settlement from Clairvaux accepted by Janauschek is 4th February, 1137.[5] Its first abbot was a monk by name Raimbald ; his successor, Garnerius, a notable ecclesiastic, became in 1186 ninth Abbot of Clairvaux and in 1193 Bishop of Langres.[6]

Colomba, or Santa-Maria-della-Colomba, the second daughter of Clairvaux in Italy, was, like its elder sister Chiaravalle-Milanese founded rather more than a year earlier,[7] the fruit of St. Bernard's Italian journeyings in the cause of healing the Papal Schism. It owed its origin to a request made to St. Bernard by Hardwin (*Arduinus*), Bishop of Piacenza, and the clergy and people of the city that a colony from Clairvaux might be settled amongst them. With this request the Abbot of Clairvaux complied, and after his return home from Italy late in 1135 the monks were despatched. They arrived in 1136, as we infer from two charters granted in that year, one on 3rd April by the bishop, the other on 5th April by the city of Piacenza. The former refers to the site as a place which formerly bore the name of Careto but is now called Colomba ; the latter names it San-Michele and specifies it further as " in curia basilica ducis." Janauschek suggests that two sites were offered, that at Careto being ultimately selected. This accords with the tradition that the name Colomba is to be explained by the fact that while materials were being collected a dove made her nest at some little distance, namely, on the Careto site, from fragments of the timber lying ready for the work. The actual spot was in the diocese of Piacenza and about twelve miles or so from the cathedral city. The monastery was not formally in existence until 1137, for the bull of Innocent II which recognizes it is dated 7th February of that year and is addressed to St. Bernard, not to the first abbot, John, who entered upon his office on 3rd May, 1137.[1]

Under the year 1107 the Chronicle of St. Bertin tells the story of a hermit, by name Ligerius, who came from Berry and settled on the sea-dunes about a mile from Furnes in Flanders.[2] In course of time others were collected and a *cœnobium* was formed, to which in 1122 abbatial dignity was granted by John I, Bishop of Thérouanne (*Tarvenna*), a little city as it then was about ten miles South of St. Omer. Thérouanne was practically destroyed by Charles V in 1553 and is now a mere village, but its diocesan continuity is still represented by the see of Ypres. The monastery seems never to have become a house of Black Monks. In 1128 Ligerius moved it to a site in a neighbouring valley granted by Theodoric, Count of Flanders, and in 1138 his successor Fulk handed it over to Clairvaux. On 31st May in that year a colony from Clairvaux arrived at Les-Dunes with one Robert as its abbot.[3] This was the Robert, a man specially dear to St. Bernard and designated by him as his successor, who afterwards became second Abbot of Clairvaux.[4] About the year 1577 the abbey was so ruthlessly handled by the Calvinists, that it was beyond the power of the monks to restore it sufficiently to resist the combined forces of sea and sand. Horst refers to it as having been re-established at Bruges in his day by Abbot Bernard Campmans under the Apostolic authority of the Vicar-General for Belgium.[5] Janauschek explains that the monks were settled by an arrangement made with the Bishop of Bruges on 11th November, 1624, in quarters which had previously sheltered the refugees from Ter-Doest (*Thosa*), an abbey which had been founded—the only daughter of Les-Dunes—about halfway between Bruges and Zeebrugge in 1176.[6] It may be noted that the story of Les-Dunes affords an instance of a religious house seeking *proprio motu* to affiliate itself to the Cistercians, a fact which has a significance of its own. In Flanders, beginning during St. Bernard's lifetime and continuing on into the XIIIth century, peculiarly friendly relations, in marked contrast with the state of things too frequently prevailing elsewhere, existed between the Black Monks and the Abbeys of Cîteaux and Clairvaux. The Benedictines of Anchin, a great house famous for its school of scribes and of miniaturists, had, under Abbot Alvisus, a friend of St. Bernard [7] who became in 1131 Bishop of Arras, set the example of welcoming the Cistercian reformers as allies of their Order, and this example could not have failed to make itself felt with special force by an isolated non-Benedictine house such as was Les-Dunes.[8]

[1] Ughelli, *Ital. Sacra.*, II. 213 sq.; Janauschek, *op. cit.*, I. 45; Manric. *op. cit.*, I., *an.* 1135, i, *an.* 1137, v.

[2] *Iperii Chron. S. Bertin.*, *R.H.G.F.* XIII. 461, 470.

[3] Manric. *Annal. Cisterc.*, I., *an.* 1138, xiii; *Gall. Christ.*, V. 283 sq.

[4] Henric. *Fasc. SS. Ord. Cisterc.*, II. xli. 4; S. Bern. *Epp.* 324, 325.

[5] *Not. Fus. in* S. Bern. *Ep.* 324.

[6] Janauschek, *op. cit.*, 51 sq., 173.

[7] S. Bern. *Epp.* 65 and 395.

[8] *Auctar. Aquicinense*, *P.L.* CLX. 274; *Auctar. Affligemense*, *op. cit.*, 285 sq.

In marked contrast were the circumstances attending the foundation of La-Bénissons-Dieu, *Benedictio-Dei-in-Burgundia* as it came to be called in distinction from two other Cistercian houses of the same name, one in the County of Longford and in the diocese of Meath, the other in Gascony and in what was in the XIIth century the diocese of Comminges with its see at St. Bertrand-de-Comminges. It was founded in the same year as was Les-Dunes, in 1138, on 29th September, as the twenty-seventh daughter of Clairvaux, Louis le Jeune being the most notable of its founders. The site was in the diocese of Lyons four miles West of Pouilly-sous-Charlieu and about fifteen miles North of Roanne.[1] But it was too near the Benedictines of Savigny—not, be it observed, the house of that name which in 1147 became Cistercian ;[2] this latter was in Normandy, about twenty miles S.S.E. of Avranches— who regarded with considerable disfavour an invasion of *Monachi Grisei* into their neighbourhood, although indeed between them there stretched some forty miles across the mountains of the Beaujolais. It seems, however, that the newcomers from Clairvaux suffered sufficient annoyance to call for the intervention of St. Bernard, for in a letter dated by Mabillon at 1139, addressed to Fulk, whose recent election to the see of Lyons he and Godfrey, Bishop of Langres, had represented to the Pope as highly fitting,[3] he informs the archbishop of the state of affairs, invokes his aid and commends to him Alberic, the first Abbot of La-Bénisson-Dieu, of whom he writes : " I love him dearly as a mother loves her only son ; he who loves me will love him." The Cistercian colonists are, he urges, " poor men living among the poor. I particularly beg you to prevent the monks of Savigny from molesting them, for I consider that they are calumniating them quite unjustly."[4]

The foundation of one other, the twenty-eighth, daughter of Clairvaux, Alafoës or St. Christopher in Portugal and in the diocese of Vizeu fifty miles N.E. of Coimbra, may probably be ascribed to the year 1138, but certainly to a day unknown.[5] Alphonso I, King of Portugal, and a hermit by name John Zirita are recorded to have been concerned in it, the former to have made the grant of a site, and the latter to have brought other hermits whom he directed into a *cœnobium* affiliated to Clairvaux, of which he became the first abbot.[6] We shall hear of this John again in connection with the foundation of another daughter of Clairvaux in Portugal, St. John of Tarouca, in 1140. He was a remarkable man, enthusiastic, restless and possibly somewhat erratic,

[1] Manric. *Annal. Cisterc.*, I., an 1138, xv ; *Gall. Christ.*, II. 409, IV. 305 ; Beaunier, *op. cit.*, II. 396 ; Janauschek, *op. cit.*, 53.

[2] Pp. 81 sq. *infra.*

[3] S. Bern. *Epp.* 171 and 172.

[4] *Ep.* 173.

[5] Manric. *op. cit.*, I., an., 1123, i ; *España Sagr.*, XXI. 71 ; Janauschek, *op cit.*, 54 sq.

[6] Henric., *Fasc. SS. Ord. Cisterc.*, I. xix.

around whose personality has gathered a certain amount of legendary matter. We should like to hear the true story of his dealings with St. Bernard. The two letters addressed by the Abbot of Clairvaux, one to Alphonso and the other to John Zirita, to be found in the Benedictine edition are regarded by Mabillon as spurious.[1]

Two years elapsed before Clairvaux showed any sign of further expansion. But on 4th April, 1140, it settled its third Italian colony at Casamario in the diocese of Veroli in Campania. Casamario was a house of Black Monks, founded by some clergy of the cathedral church of Veroli in 1105, which having fallen into disorder sought to affiliate itself to Clairvaux.[2] It would, however, appear that when St. Bernard responded by sending monks who arrived in 1140, considerable opposition was encountered; a body of recalcitrants amongst the Black Monks remained for so long within the walls of Casamario, that it was not until after the return of Eugenius III to Rome from the Council of Rheims in 1148 that the Cistercians were finally placed in effective possession.[3]

A letter of St. Bernard written to Innocent II in or about the year 1135 calls attention to the prevalence at the time of a state of laxity—amongst the secular perhaps rather than the regular clergy—sufficiently scandalous to demand the intervention of the Pope. No diocese is specified with the exception of Troyes, and that would seem to be singled out because there a conscientious and active diocesan, Bishop Hatto, was putting to shame the negligence of his fellows by rebuking the insolence of his clergy. "Your servant," St. Bernard writes, "pleads the cause of him (*i.e.* the bishop) whose own fault consists entirely in the fact that he has rebuked the faults of the clergy."[4] Evidently he thought that Innocent might hear, or perhaps had already heard, some garbled story representing that the discord was really due to mismanagement on the part of the bishop. That the latter was a zealous reformer would account for the support of St. Bernard who would have met him, probably in some intimacy, at the Council of Pisa from which they had both but lately returned.[5] Some five years later Bishop Hatto invited St. Bernard to settle a colony in his diocese. A site was granted by the Abbot of St. Loup de-Troyes on the right bank of the little river Barse about ten miles East of Troyes, where a hamlet now bears the name of Larrivour but where, alas, there are left few traces of the ancient Abbey of l'Arrivour or *Ripatorium*, founded there from Clairvaux on 9th April,

[1] *Epp.* 421 and 422, and *Not. ad loc.*

[2] Ughelli, *Ital. Sacr.*, I. 1389; Manric. *Annal. Cisterc.*, I., an. 1140, x; Aub. Mir. *Chron. Cisterc.*, 116.

[3] *Casamariense Chartar.*, Janauschek, *op. cit.*, 58 sq.

[4] *Ep.* 152.

[5] Mabillon, *op. S. Bern. Ep. 23, Not. Fus.*

[1] Manric. *op. cit.*,
I., *an.* 1140, x;
Aub. Mir.
Chron. Cisterc.,
108; *Gall.
Christ.*, XII.
293 sqq., 597,
Instr., 260;
Beaunier, *op.
cit.*, II. 823 sq.;
Janauschek,
op. cit., 59.

1140.[1]   The first Abbot of l'Arrivour was Alan, the writer of the *Vita Secunda*. He ruled there until 1152 when he became Bishop of Auxerre. This dignity he resigned either in 1165 or in 1167 and retired to l'Arrivour, whence he frequently visited Clairvaux, dying there in 1181.[2]

[2] *Chron. Clare-
vallense, an.*
1165; *Chron.
Autissiodor.*,
M.G.H. XXVI.
239; Henric.
*Fasc. SS. Ord.
Cisterc.*, II. xli. 4.
[3] Manric. *op.
cit.*, I., *an.* 1140,
xi; Aub. Mir.
*Chron. Ord.
Cisterc.*, 101;
Henric. *Fasc.
SS. Ord. Cisterc.*,
I. iv. 28;
Beaunier, *op.
cit.*, I. 361.
[4] *Iperii Chron.
S. Bertin.*,
R.H.G.F.
XIII. 639.

The year 1140 proved to be very fruitful for Clairvaux. We have told the story of two foundations of this year; four, possibly five, more remain to be noted. Les-Dunes was less than two years old when in the same diocese as itself, that of Thérouanne, the sister Abbey of Clairmarais (*Clarus-Mariscus*) was founded on 26th April, 1140. Its origin is somewhat obscure. Aubertus Miraeus and others record its foundation from Les-Dunes in 1128 and its affiliation to Clairvaux so early as 1137.[3] Janauschek prefers to credit the account that, after Theodoric of Alsace, Count of Flanders, had returned from Jerusalem, he and his wife Sybil granted St. Bernard a site for an abbey among woods and marshes some three miles N.E. of St. Omer.[4] The name Clairmarais is said to have been adopted as expressive of a life of pure religion passed on these marshy lands. The first abbot was Geoffrey, Prior of Clairvaux. Here, too, as at Les-Dunes, we recognize the welcome accorded to the Cistercians by the Black Monks of Flanders. There are extant two letters addressed by St. Bernard about the year 1140 to the monks of St. Bertin, who at St. Omer were very near neighbours of Clairmarais. In one of these the Abbot of Clairvaux writes :

[5] *Ep.* 384.

" I ought to remember the benefits which you have conferred upon our brethren, nay, upon myself, and to thank you for them." [5] The other letter plainly implies that these same monks had been zealously devoting themselves to a more strict observance of the Rule of St. Benedict and encourages them to persevere, ending with the ejaculation : " May Christ have in his keeping your whole community, praying as ye are for us ! " [6] Even more explicit is an earlier letter

[6] *Ep.* 385.

written to Leonius, Abbot of St. Bertin. " What I may rightly trust you to do your charity has done in the sight of all men ; for when the opportunity came for revealing itself it could not remain hidden under a bushel. Most grateful am I for those offices of humanity which you have fulfilled to our brethren who dwell next door to you. What you do to them, you do to me ; nay, in doing it to them you do it still more to me." [7]

[7] *Ep.* 383.

Two points of special interest should not be omitted from any account of the early days of Clairmarais. When some years after its foundation it was compelled to migrate to a more convenient site close by, its necessities were met by a grant of land made by Stephen, King of England, there where what is left of it now stands. And when St. Thomas of Canterbury fled from another King of England in 1164 he found his arduous way to Clairmarais, the first Cistercian house to anger Henry II by the shelter afforded to the archbishop.

Of the foundation of the Abbey of St. John of Tarouca, so called from its proximity to the place of that name in the diocese of Lamego in Portugal, there are several contradictory records. What would seem to be common to them all is the statement that John Zirita and Alphonso I, both of whom had played so considerable a part in the foundation of Alafoës two years earlier in the same country, were actively concerned in it. As elucidated by Janauschek the facts emerge that in 1139, a year after the Clairvaux monks arrived at Alafoës, having had sufficient time to instruct the community there in the Cistercian *usus*, they were settled by John Zirita at a hermitage where under a charter dated on some day in June, 1140, they obtained from Alphonso a grant of land for the foundation of a house of their Order, the first abbot of which was a certain Boëmund.[1]

The origins of Whiteland (*Albalanda*) carry us back traditionally to the beginning of the VIIth century. Not long after the destruction of Bangor-Iscoed near Chester in 607 some of its few monks who escaped with their lives are said to have established a monastery in a thickly-wooded valley on the Carmarthenshire Taff—at a place now called Llangan, about sixteen miles West of Carmarthen—which received the name of Ty-Gwyn-ar-Taf, the White House on the Taff. Some authorities have associated with it as founder Rhys ap Tudor, Prince of South Wales in the days of the Conqueror. We shall, however, probably be correct in ascribing its foundation to Bernard, Bishop of St. David's from 1115-47, who invited monks from Clairvaux to settle in his diocese, the accepted date of the settlement being 16th September, 1140.[2] Little more of the abbey is left to-day than is sufficient to mark the site. The name of the first abbot known to us—in the main from Giraldus Cambrensis—is Peter.[3]

The fourth Italian daughter of Clairvaux, the second colony which in this same year, 1140, St. Bernard sent forth across the Alps, bore several names. Perhaps it was most familiarly known as *S. Anastasius-apud-Tres-Fontes*; but it was also known as *SS. Vincentius-et-Anastasius* sometimes with the qualification of *apud Tres Fontes* or the like, sometimes with

[1] Manric. *op. cit.*, I., *an.* 1119, iii; *España Sagr.*, XXI. 83; Janauschek, *op. cit.*, 61.

[2] Wharton, *Anglia Sacra*, II. 549, 649; Tanner, *Notit. Monast.*, *Caermarth.*, II. 701; Manric. *op. cit.*, I., *an.* 1140, x and xii, IV. *app.* 543; Janauschek, *op. cit.*, 61 sq.

[3] Girald. Cambr. *Opp. passim.*

that of *ad Aquas Salvias ;* finally it was also known as, in the vulgar tongue, San-Paolo-alle-Tre-Fontane. It stood on the road to Ostia, not far outside the Porta San Paolo, at the place where according to pious tradition the three fountains sprang, one at each bound of the severed head of the martyred apostle. So early as the pontificate of Anacletus I a little oratory had been built there, which in the days of Constantine the Great was replaced by a basilica dedicated to St. Vincent and St. Anastasius in which the relics of these martyrs were venerated. The date at which a monastery was first built there is un-certain ; but in the first quarter of the VIIth century there was a Benedictine occupation followed later by a Basilian ; last of all it became a Cluniac house. But in the earlier part of the XIIth century, such was the unhealthiness of the neighbouring *Aquae-Salviae,* it was entirely abandoned. About 1136 Innocent II took steps to restore its dilapidated structure, but it would appear to have remained unoccupied for some years longer. Meanwhile the Pope was interesting himself in another project. Amongst the letters of St. Bernard are found two, both of which were written in 1140 by Bernard Paganelli, the monk of Clairvaux who in 1145 was raised to the pontificate as Eugenius III.[1] The first is addressed to Innocent II. It is of the nature of a respectful complaint that when, in obedience to the Pope's command " through fire and water . . . in perils of robbers and of floods, in perils in cities and in solitudes . . . torn from the bosom of his own father (*sc.* St. Bernard)," he had arrived at the Abbey of Farfa, an illustrious house of Black Monks in the Sabina, he had learned not only that he was not wanted for the purpose for which he had been called there, but that Adenulph, the Abbot of Farfa, who had received him as a son, was greatly distressed by the turn which affairs had taken.[2] The second letter is addressed to the Abbot of Clairvaux. The writer dwells upon the delights of the house of his profession, and the more regretfully in that, as he thinks, it is in vain that he has sacrificed them. " How little did I understand," he writes, " when I was at Clairvaux that I was in an abode of pleasure amongst the trees of paradise ; thus it was that I made of no account that desirable country. What was it in me that so pleased you that you have made me a leader, a teacher to the nations, a prince over your own people ? "[3] This second letter is an interesting sidelight upon the character of the first Cistercian Pope, and so far it helps us to interpret the great treatise *Of Consideration* addressed to Bernard Paganelli in his pontifical capacity by the Abbot of Clairvaux

[1] P. 327 *infra.*

[2] *Inter S. Bern. Epp.* 343.

[3] *Ibid., Ep.* 344.

some nine years and more later. Let us take from the *Vita Prima* our account of the salient facts. " The Abbot of Farfa," we read, " had invited a colony of monks from Clairvaux with the intention of building for them a monastery ; but the Roman pontiff hindered the execution of his purpose, fetched them to himself and settled them elsewhere." [1] The monastery which Adenulph had in mind was not an entirely new house, but a house subject to himself by name San Salvatore about eight miles from Farfa, which he intended the Cistercians to reform ; the place to which the Pope actually transferred them was St. Anastasius.[2]

The Abbot of Farfa generously felt that some amends were due to Clairvaux. " Wherefore that distinguished and pious person, grieving greatly, deposited under deed a sum of money amounting to nearly six hundred silver marks, and coming to St. Bernard he offered this, begging that what had not been considered fitting in his own country, namely, the foundation of a new monastery, might now be effected on this side of the Alps (*i.e.* in France). The money was sought and, lo, it had entirely disappeared ! But the man of God when he heard the news said nothing more than ' Blessed be God who has spared us this burden, for,' he added, ' the men who have stolen it are thereby the more readily to be pardoned.' " And Geoffrey remarks, speaking out of the abundant experience of his master : " They are Romans, we know ; the amount seemed to them to be enormous and the temptation was strong." [3]

Considering the notorious insalubrity of the *Aquae-Salviae* it is quite probable that the Pope had had difficulty in finding monks who would run the risk of occupying the restored buildings of St. Anastasius. The arrival in Italy of men cast in the heroic mould of the sons of St. Bernard was therefore an opportunity not to be lost ; moreover, their reputation for husbandry would afford hope that by clearing and draining the land they would soon make the locality more salubrious. Bernard Paganelli had, however, no easy task in hand. But the Abbot of Clairvaux was at his back from the very first. One monk rebelled openly, and after some scandalous scenes left his brethren and went off to Rome in a mischief-making spirit.[4] The fever which had decimated the Cluniacs who had been the last occupants of the abbey broke out again, and the abbot requested leave from St. Bernard to have recourse to physicians outside the community and to make use of their remedies. The request was not granted. St. Bernard's reply is addressed to the brethren ; probably their

[1] *Vita Prima,* III. vii. 24 ; cf. *Vita Secunda,* xxiv. 66.

[2] Manric. *Annal. Cisterc.*, I., *an.* 1140, viii ; *Chron. Mont. Sereni, M.G.H. Script.*, XXIII. 146 ; Janauschek, *op. cit.*, L.

[3] *Vita Prima, loc. cit.*

[4] Dern. Pagan. *Ep. inter S. Bern. Epp.* 431. Ed. Bened.

abbot had reluctantly consented to raise the question, knowing how it was likely to be viewed. " The holy fathers our ancestors sought for damp and narrow valleys in which to found their monasteries, in order that monks being often ill and having death before their eyes might not feel themselves to be in possession of any certain lease of life." [1] In these terms would Fastredus, third Abbot of Clairvaux, in later days quote St. Bernard. Thus he is in the straits at St. Anastasius, although not uncompassionate, sufficiently firm. " Certainly," he writes, " it is sometimes permissible to take common herbs such as the poor use ; and on occasion this is what we actually do. But to buy drugs, to go in search of physicians, to swallow draughts, these courses are unbefitting religion (i.e. the monastic life) and contrary to simplicity of life ; above all they are incongruous both with the high character and with the integrity of our Order." [2] In this way was Bernard Paganelli serving his apprenticeship for the pontificate. Nor should we, without knowing more of the physicians of his day, condemn St. Bernard ; his own experience of their treatment had not been highly reassuring.[3] Indeed it may even be questioned whether in this matter of drugs and draughts he was not centuries in advance of his generation. In any case that his sons should run the risk of placing themselves in the hands of some " irrational brute beast " he could not for a moment approve. And so, strenuously enough, like many of its sister-houses, St. Anastasius began its Cistercian life ; to become there at the gate of the Holy City the nursing home of not a few cardinals, bishops and abbots who left their mark upon the history of the Church, amongst them not only Abbot Ferdinando Ughelli, the learned compiler of Italia Sacra, but also, as we know, its first abbot, Bernard Paganelli, the first Cistercian Pope.[4]

There remains to be noted one other daughter of Clairvaux, nameless,[5] and not even mentioned by Janauschek, which Vacandard ascribes to the year 1140. Roger, Duke of Sicily and Apulia, had in reward for the part which he was then playing in the Papal Schism been granted the title of King of Sicily by the Pseudo-Pope Anacletus in 1130, a title which in 1139 was confirmed by Innocent II when having fallen into his hands he could no otherwise effect his release than by recognizing officially the royalty of his captor.[6] St. Bernard, in a letter written to Lothair about the year 1135, had referred to Roger as " the Sicilian usurper " [7]—and justly, for he had usurped his dukedoms from his cousin William. The next year, writing to the Pisans in the same cause, he remarks

[1] Fastr. Ab. Claraevall. Ep. inter S. Bern. Epp. 491.

[2] S. Bern. Ep. 345.

[3] P. 27 supra,

[4] Aub. Mir. Chron. Cisterc., 104 and 116 ; Manric. Annal. Cisterc., I., an. 1140, viii ; Janauschek, op. cit., I. 62.
[5] Manric. op. cit., I., an. 1139, vii.

[6] Baron. Annales, ann. 1130 and 1139.
[7] Ep. 139.

with satisfaction : " At my instigation the constancy of Pisa
has not yielded to the malice of the tyrant of Sicily." [1]   The
evil repute of Roger was sufficiently notorious, for it is on
record that he wantonly desecrated the tomb of Duke Ranulph
at Bari in Apulia and treated his remains with disgusting
barbarity, as a climax to the infliction of nameless cruelties
upon the living.[2]

In the course of time, however, it became manifest that
something had happened to this savage brute. He had
succumbed to the fascination of the tamer ! " Far and wide
is bruited the fame of your munificence," writes St. Bernard
to Roger in 1139, adding the warning " use the discreet eye
and a hand open rather to the needy than to the greedy."
It would be well too that " he who sows blessings should also
reap blessings. Wherefore, I pray you, look favourably upon
the bearer of this letter whom, be sure, greed has not attracted but need has compelled to your royal presence. The
need, I mean, of his own brethren—and they are many in
number—not his own need ; the need of those by whom he
has been sent, namely, the faithful servants of God. Hear
patiently the tale of their sufferings ; hear and suffer with
them, for if you suffer with them you will also reign with them.
Let not the king despise a kingdom shared with such men ;
for theirs is the kingdom of heaven, who have despised the
life of this world. *Make to yourself friends of the mammon
of unrighteousness*, in order that when you lose your earthly
kingdom they may receive you into an eternal kingdom." [3]
Now what are we to understand by this ? Plainly the messenger is a monk ; doubtless a Clairvaux monk. He will
voice a need common to many ; doubtless to St. Bernard and
his sons. And significantly the sense in which the words
make to yourselves friends of the mammon of unrighteousness
are interpreted is precisely that in which they were interpreted by William the Pious, Duke of Aquitaine and Count
of Auvergne, when he was moved to found the Abbey of Cluny.
To bless the poor is to be blessed oneself ; religious are en-
duringly poor ; the wisest course is to bless them.[4] Such
was the characteristic sentiment of those centuries ; and it
is to be respected, not despised. We cannot doubt then but
that St. Bernard had begged for the foundation of a daughter
of Clairvaux either in Sicily or in Apulia. And the next letter
written by him to the King of Sicily confirms this. " Since
you seek me," he writes, " here I am, *I and the children whom
God has given me ;* for I learn that your humble servant
has so far found favour with your royal majesty that you

[1] *Ep.* 130.

[2] Otton. Frising.
Chron., VII. 23 ;
M.G.H. Script.,
XX. 261.

[3] *Ep.* 207.

[4] *Testament.
Will. Cognom.
Pii,* Marrier
et Querc .
*Biblioth
Cluniac.,* 2.

wish to see me. And who am I that I should disregard the
good pleasure of the king ? I hasten to him who has sought
me and, lo, here I am, not in mere weak bodily presence, the
presence in which Herod despised the Lord, but in my very
heart. Who shall separate me from that ? I shall follow it
wherever it may go ; and if it dwells at the ends of the earth
it will not be away from me." He means, of course, his
monks. " You have with you, O king, the light of my eyes,
my heart, my soul." [1] Invited to bring monks St. Bernard
had rather sent them and not come himself. All of himself,
however, that has not come is his " poor bit of a body " ; not
because his will has detained it, but necessity ; it was not
strong enough to follow the flight of his mind to Roger. He
is sending good seed-corn ; everything depends upon its being
sown in good ground. These monks are strangers and pilgrims ; and let the king remember that " it is not right that
they should have been sent for from afar to no purpose,
that, exiles from their own homes, they should wander upon
an unprofitable pilgrimage." If Roger allows his country to
be to them a " strange land " they will not be able to sing
the Lord's song in it.

The last letter suggests that all has gone well. " What
you asked for you have ; what you promised you have done,"
St. Bernard writes. Mention moreover is made of a certain
Bruno whom we may presume to have been the first abbot
of the new house. " We are sending to you master Bruno
who has been for many days my inseparable companion,
but is now the father of a multitude of souls which joy in
Christ, yet are lacking in this world's goods." It would seem
as though a Clairvaux colony was contemplated more numerous
than was normal ; and the letter ends with the reminder that
Roger's purse is heavier than the writer's.[2] Light is thrown
upon this by a letter which St. Bernard wrote at about this
date to the Abbot of Hautecombe, in which he asks the latter
to send a " reasonable and discreet messenger " to Montpellier
there to meet Roger's messengers who were coming to fetch
the daughter of Theobald, Count of Champagne, the betrothed
of Roger's son. If these messengers want to take back in
their ships only two monks as the " abbey "—which is what
we may infer that Roger, alarmed by the fear of being saddled
with a large number of colonists, now asked—St. Bernard
will not consent to this. Roger must receive not less than
the " whole abbey " (*tota abbatia*), which would mean not
less than twelve monks and an abbot ; or none at all.[3]

Reviewing the chronicle of foundations effected from

[1] *Ep.* 208.

[2] *Ep.* 209.

[3] *Ep.* 447. Cf.
p. 76 *infra*.

PONTIGNY

Clairvaux during the lifetime of St. Bernard, we shall be struck by the fact that the period with which we are now dealing was peculiarly prolific in settlements beyond the mountain barriers of the Pyrenees and the Alps. Of the twelve foundations of the years 1140 to 1142 inclusive exactly seven of them are in this category, and of these three were in Spain and one was in Portugal. If we take the view that Osera, the next daughter of Clairvaux, was affiliated to the Cistercians in 1141, then between some day in that year and 25th May, 1142, the three Spanish foundations followed one another in quick succession.

Osera (*Ursaria*) was a house of Black Monks in Galicia and in the diocese of Orense, about ten miles from the cathedral city of that name. Its existence arose out of a grant of a piece of land on the Mont Ursaria made in 1137 by Alphonso II, King of Castile, to some few wandering monks. Before many years had elapsed they invited monks from Clairvaux to teach them the Cistercian ways, and probably in 1141 they were affiliated to that house as its thirty-sixth daughter. Osera soon became an abbey of great repute and by the end of the century, repeatedly enriched by royal munificence, it had acquired the honourable title of the Escurial of Galicia or the Escurial of St. Bernard. How far its success may have been due in the early stages to the influence of John Zirita, it is difficult to say ; but certainly Cistercian, we might rather say Bernardine, enthusiasm was in those days at a high pitch in the North-Western corner of the Peninsula.[1]

At about this time the Bernardine monks secured their second foothold in the archdiocese of Bourges ; their first, we shall remember, was obtained at Nerlac in 1136.[2] La-Prée (*Pratea*) was situated on the right bank of the little river Arnon[3]—hence it was sometimes called La-Prée-sur-Arnon— about six miles from Issoudun and fifteen from Bourges. *Gallia Christiana* records that so early as 1128 Ralph, the feudal lord of Issoudun, submitted to St. Bernard the project of settling on his land a colony from Clairvaux, but that this was not finally effected until 28th October, 1147, a date which Janauschek accepts as that of the foundation of the house.[4] Against this, however, is the fact that in the *Fragmenta* of Geoffrey we read that Guy, St. Bernard's eldest brother, on his return with him from the country of Bourges, where he had been founding a new abbey, " fell ill of a severe fever at Pontigny and after a few days, on the night on which is celebrated the Feast of All Saints, passed worthily to join

[1] Manric. *Annal. Cisterc.*, I., an. 1140, xiii ; *España Sagr.*, XLI. 19 ; Janauschek, *op. cit.*, I. 63.

[2] Pp. 61 sq., *supra.*

[3] Manric. *op. cit.*, II., an. 1145, x ; Beaunier, *op. cit.*, I. 245 sq.

[4] *Gall. Christ.*, II. 207.

[1] Gaufr. *Fragm.*, *Codex Aureae-vall.*, 68, and *P.L.* CLXXXV. 528.

[2] Chifflet, *Genus Illustre S. Bern.*, *P.L.* CLXXXV. 1419. Cf. Jobin, *S. Bernard et sa famille*, 67.

[3] Gaufr. *Fragm.*, *loc. cit.*

[4] *Exord. Magn.*, V. 2; Janauschek, *op. cit.*, 86.

[5] Pp. 49 and 73 *supra.*

their company." [1] There can be no doubt but that this "new abbey" was La-Prée. Now Guy was apparently still alive in 1141, for his name occurs together with that of St. Bernard as witnessing a deed executed in that year; [2] but he died before the conflict between Louis le Jeune and Count Theobald of Champagne broke out in 1142.[3] Thus we may not be far astray in dating his death at 31st October, 1141, or possibly 1142, and the foundation of La-Prée a few days earlier. The first abbot of the house was, like its founder, named Ralph, a man of religious enthusiasm one would gather.[4]

Of the three foundations which with some degree of certainty may be ascribed to the year 1142 two were in Spain. In the case of each of these may be recognized the hand of that same Alphonso II, King of Castile, also VIIth King of Leon of the name, whose part in the foundation of Moreruela and of Osera has been recorded above.[5] He was, we may suppose, a man with a mission ; for in 1135 he had been crowned at Leon, with the high-sounding title of Emperor in Spain, to rule both the Christian and the Moslem peoples of Castile, Leon and Galicia. From a long distant past— Manriquez states from 782—there had stood near the Tambre, a river which runs into the sea about twenty miles S.E. of Cape Finisterre, and, it may be, thirty miles from Santiago de Compostella in the diocese of which it was—a religious house of both sexes by name Sobrado (*Superatum, al. Super-adum*). In course of time its power grew to the extent that it had under its authority no less than thirteen subject houses. Later, however, its great wealth became the spoil of its neighbours, and towards the end of the second quarter of the XIIth century it was reduced almost to extinction. The influence of Alphonso effected some restoration of its property, and on 14th February, 1142, it was handed over to a colony of Clairvaux monks under an abbot of the name of Peter.[6]

[6] Manric. *Annal. Cisterc.*, I., *an.* 1142, xii, IV. *app.* 544; *España Sagr.*, XVIII. 31; Janauschek, *op. cit.*, 67.

After an interval of little more than three months another daughter of Clairvaux was founded in Galicia on 25th May at a place then called Barcena, now La Barcia, in the diocese of Tuy, some six miles W.S.W. of Ribadavia. The origin of the Abbey of Melon (*De-Melone*) is ascribed to the VIIth century, and, although so early a date is historically doubtful, a monastery was already in existence in 1142 bearing the name of S. Maria-de-Barcena, the abbot of which, a certain Gerald, would appear to have been accepted by Martin, the leader of the Clairvaux colonists, as the first ruler of the re-constituted community. Here as at Sobrado the generosity of Alphonso entitles him to be regarded as the founder of the Cistercian house.[1]

Perhaps, however, the outstanding interest of the year 1142 is that on some day during its course there came into being the first Cistercian abbey of Ireland, and that at the instance of one who in the Calendar of Irish Saints occupies a position second only to that of St. Patrick; although it may be said, and said regretfully, that the great work of St. Malachy of Armagh deserves fuller recognition than outside a comparatively narrow circle of readers it has hitherto received. The story of the foundation of Mellifont (*Mellifons, al. Fons-Mellis, Manisther-Mhor*) takes us into the counsels of this veritable apostle, of whom St. Bernard wrote: "The first miracle and the greatest miracle that he ever wrought is in my judgement himself."[2] St. Malachy was about forty-five years of age when, on his way to Rome in 1139, he first visited Clairvaux, and made himself personally known to St. Bernard. At an earlier stage of his journey he had passed through York and had had some intercourse with, amongst others, Wallev or Waltheof, Prior of Kirkham, who subsequently became Abbot of Melrose. From him he would doubtless have heard something of the good effects wrought in the North of England by the Cistercians, to wit, the sons of St. Bernard at Rievaulx and at Fountains;[3] and when, continuing his way, he tarried awhile at Clairvaux, so deeply impressed was he that on his arrival at Rome he begged permission of the Pope to lay down his pastoral charge, and to live and die a Cistercian under the authority of St. Bernard. But this was not to be.[4] And so, if St. Malachy might not go and live at Clairvaux, Clairvaux, its spirit embodied in its colonists, might come and live in Ireland. The refusal of his request was more felicitous than would have been consent. Accordingly, visiting Clairvaux again on his way home, we find him saying to St. Bernard: "I pray you keep these with you for awhile in my place in order that they may afterwards teach us what they have learned from you," adding "thus will they be to us as a seed, and in this seed nations will be blessed, nations which have indeed of old heard of monks but have never seen a monk." "And," St. Bernard tells us, "leaving four of his companions he departed."[5] These four Irishmen were in due course professed at Clairvaux and later St. Malachy sent others for the same purpose. After what St. Bernard considered to be sufficient instruction had been given to them, one from amongst themselves was set over them as abbot, "the holy brother Christian"; a few

[1] Manric. *Annal. Cisterc.*, I., an. 1142, xi; *España Sagr.*, XXII. 24; Janauschek, *op. cit.*, 69.

[2] S. Bern. *Vita S. Malach.*, XIX. 43.

[3] *Op. cit.*, XV. 35 sq.

[4] *Op. cit.*, XVI. 38.

[5] *Op. cit.*, XVI. 39. Cf. p. 181 *infra.*

Clairvaux monks were added to them so as to make up the usual number of thirteen and they were sent on their way to St. Malachy.[1] This Christian, the first Abbot of Mellifont, was Christian O'Conarchy who in 1150 became Bishop of Lismore. The site upon which St. Malachy settled the Abbey of Mellifont was granted by Donough MacCorvoill or O'Carrol, Prince of Uriel, who is usually venerated as the founder. It was in the barony of Ferrard and in the diocese of Armagh, five miles from Drogheda in the County Louth and about a mile and a half from the left bank of the Boyne.[2] Something of the preliminaries we may learn from a letter addressed by St. Bernard to St. Malachy about the year 1140. " As regards your wish," he writes, " that two of the brethren should be sent to you in order to arrange beforehand about the site, after taking counsel with them we have thought best that they "— that is to say, the Irishmen—" should not yet be separated from one another until Christ is more fully formed in them, until they have been rightly taught how to fight the Lord's battle. Accordingly, when they have been trained in the school of the Holy Spirit and clothed with power from on high, then at length will they return, sons to a father, to sing the Lord's song no longer in a strange land but in their own." [3] Thus an additional interest arises out of the fact that here we see St. Bernard engaged in what he would have held to be his own proper work ; we note the firm handling of Celtic enthusiasm, the sympathetic tempering of hasty zeal, the steps taken to secure by means of the fellowship of Clairvaux monks the maintenance of the right tradition, and finally in true Benedictine spirit the reminder that the Lord's song, the *Opus Dei*, is the key to all solid success. Moreover, no more in Ireland than in Sicily [4] would he allow his sons to swarm otherwise than as was prescribed, that is to say, as a *tota abbatia* of an abbot and twelve monks.[5]

The *Exordium Magnum* tells us of a young monk, by name Gerard, a native of Utrecht or of Maëstricht (*Trajectum*), who on hearing that he was to form one of a colony intended to be settled very far afield came to St. Bernard in great distress of mind. " Grieving with less restraint than his fellows he thus addressed the man of God : ' Most blessed father, miserable boy that I am, I left my own home, spurning everything in this world which could prove desirable or lovable ; and for love of religion I came to you hoping to be counted worthy to enjoy the great sweetness of your presence, to be instructed by your teaching and by your example, to be aided by your merits and by your prayers and under the shadow

[1] *Op. cit.*, XVI. 39.

[2] Manric. *Annal. Cisterc.*, I., an. 1141, i; Dugdale, *Monast. Angl.*, VI. (2), 1132 sq. *ed. cit.*; Janauschek, *op. cit.*, 70.

[3] *Ep.* 341.

[4] P. 72 *supra*.

[5] *Consuetud. Cisterc.*, *Super Instituta*, XII.

of this fellowship of holy men to be protected against the whirlwind of temptation and the heat of youthful passion ; and, what I desire with all my heart, to await the last day buried amongst the sacred remains of our brethren in the cemetery here. And, lo, to-day you cast me out from your presence ; I lose the fellowship of this holy community ; and to crown these sorrows I am deprived of the burial for which I long.' " [1] We may ask what this means. It was no usual thing for a monk of Clairvaux, evidently devoted to his abbot, to complain of a task laid upon him even when it was that of a pioneer. But in those days the outlying world of North-Western Europe had its terrors. The Northmen, those wild sea-rovers from the unexplored regions beyond Saxonia whose passion for fighting had spurred them into the very heart of Burgundy—to say nothing of their exploits elsewhere—had left behind them at the beginning of the Xth century a memory of horrors which would still vibrate at the mention of their name. And now, when they were just awaking to the call to enter into the comity of Christian peoples, and Alvida, Queen of Sweden, begged St. Bernard to send monks to her land, " that mighty eagle of many wings and many feathers " would reassure his trembling sons on the eve of their departure no otherwise than by the question : " Is it not rather the will of God, which we are all bound to obey, than my own will that I am following in this matter ? " [2]

The monks set forth under Abbot Robert, and upon an unknown day in the month of June, 1143, a monastery was founded on the Eastern shore of Lake Wettern in East Gothland and in the diocese of Linçöping. The good work which had owed its inception to the petition of his wife was cordially supported by King Swerker, and in memory of her the new abbey was called Alfwastra (*Alvastra*). For four generations, beginning with that of Swerker, it served in Sweden, like its sister Hautecombe in Savoy, the purpose of a royal mausoleum. Its second abbot Stephen became in 1164 the first Archbishop of Upsala, being succeeded in this see on his death in 1185 by another monk of Alfwastra, John ; facts eloquent of the debt which the Christianity of Sweden owes to Clairvaux. The site at the modern Alfwastra, not far from the foot of the Omberg, may be identified by the not inconsiderable remains of the abbey-church.[3]

But this was not all. Closely associated with the foundation of Alfwastra was that of Nydala (*Nova-Vallis*), both being ascribed by Janauschek to the same month and year, June, 1143 ; the latter, however, claiming as its founder

[1] *Vita Prima,* VII. xxvii., *excerpt. ex Exord. Magn.*

[2] *Vita Prima, loc. cit.*

[3] Manric. *Annal. Cisterc.,* I., *an.* 1143, vii; Aub. Mir. *Chron. Cisterc.,* 107 ; Janauschek, *op. cit.,* 73 sq.

Gislo, Bishop of Linköping, in whose diocese it was situated near the Easternmost end of the little lake Roxen, about half-a-mile from Berg, S.E. of the point at which the East Göta canal enters the lake. It is still represented as a structure by the church of Vreta-Kloster.[1] Of Nydala the first abbot was Gerard, the timorous young monk of whom we read in the *Exordium Magnum ;*[2] there he ruled for forty years, winning the respect of kings and of princes, so that one powerful chieftain could say of him : " Whenever I feel Abbot Gerard to be looking at me I tremble as though the hidden thoughts and the secrets of my heart were open to his eyes." Thence too by his own wish was he taken all the long way to Clairvaux as his end drew near in order that, as St. Bernard had promised, he might die there and there await the last day. " And when the King of Sweden learned that he was dead he declared in his grief," we are told, " that his kingdom and his country were not worthy of such an honour as that so great a man should lie buried within their borders." [3]

The same year, 1143, found Clairvaux monks again on their way to Galicia, where on 1st June at a place called Meyra near Fuente Miñana (*Fons-Minii*) in the diocese of Lugo they settled on land which three years previously had been granted by Alphonso II to one of his vassals, by name Alvaro Rodriquez, who now bestowed it upon the Cistercians, Abbot Vitalis and his subjects.[4]

Quickly following upon the steps of their brethren in the direction of Spain, within a little over two months, on 3rd August another colony was founded—in the diocese of Montauban about twelve miles from that cathedral city and on the left bank of the Garonne. Belle-Perche (*Bella-Pertica*) had existed from the beginning of the XIIth century. It probably owed its foundation, partly to the family and to the neighbouring vassals of the Counts of Toulouse, then at the zenith of their power in Southern France, and partly to Blessed Gerald de Salis who was later responsible for the transference of several houses to the Cistercian Order, such as Cadouin in Périgord in 1119.[5] If it was originally conducted according to what Janauschek describes as the " peculiar institutions of Gerald," we can understand how before many years had elapsed it became a mere house of retreat for pious persons, both religious and secular, and entirely lost its strictly cœnobitic character. Like other of the foundations of Gerald it was ultimately affiliated to the Cistercians, being colonized by monks sent by St. Bernard under Abbot

[1] Manric. *Annal. Cisterc.*, I., *an.* 1143, vii ; Aub. Mir. *op. cit. loc. cit.* ; Janauschek, *op. cit.*, 74.

[2] P. 76 *supra.*

[3] *Vita Prima,* VII. xxvii., *excerpt. ex Exord. Magn.*

[4] Manric. *Annal. Cisterc.*, I., *an.* 1143, viii ; Henric. *Fasc. SS. Ord. Cisterc.*, I. 127 ; *España Sagr.*, XLI. 30 sqq. ; Janauschek, *op. cit.*, 75.

[5] *Gall. Christ.*, II. 1463, 1538 ; Janauschek, *op. cit.*, 7 sq.

Haimeric.[1] At Belle-Perche they would perhaps have received a legacy of Fontevrault traditions, severer in certain respects than the Benedictine, for Gerald had been an intimate of Robert of Arbrissel who founded the Order of Fontevrault in 1094.[2] There are grounds for the story that St. Bernard had himself visited Belle-Perche a few months before its affiliation to Clairvaux.[3]

Concerning the foundation of Belloc (*Bellus-Locus*) little is known. We cannot tell the name either of its founder or of its first abbot. It was in the diocese of Rodez in the Aveyron, in a beautiful valley about twenty miles N.W. of Albi, where there still exist considerable fine remains of the church. The accepted date of its foundation is 11th August, 1144.[4]

From 1143 to 1145 inclusive one foundation a year was effected from Clairvaux, all three of them in Languedoc. The fact that, as we shall see, Languedoc was at the time devastated by a form of Neo-Manicheism to such an extent that St. Bernard felt compelled to visit the neighbourhood in 1145 in order to counteract its effects, may in part explain this.[5] The third of these foundations remains to be noticed. Grand-Selve (*Grandis-Silva*) was in the diocese of Toulouse, about equidistant between that city and Montauban, near the left bank of the Garonne. And here again we recognize the hand both of Gerald de Salis and of the Count of Toulouse. In the year 1117 or 1118 a certain Oliver de Bessens and his wife Algarda would appear to have made Gerald the grant of part of what was then called the *Grandis Silva*, upon which, with the approval of Amelius, Count of Toulouse, he built a monastery subject to Cadouin, which from the first flourished abundantly. The Benedictine edition contains a letter of St. Bernard, which is ascribed by Mabillon to the year 1147, written to the people of Toulouse after his return to Clairvaux from a visit to their city and neighbourhood. In this he speaks of " our very dear brother and fellow-abbot, Bertrand of Grand-Selve " and of Grand-Selve as " our house by him lately handed over to us and to our Order, and specially united in fellowship with the Church of Clairvaux." [6] Thus Bertrand, the last abbot of the old foundation, had freely affiliated his house to Clairvaux and become the first abbot of the Cistercian foundation. Mabillon states the old foundation to have been Benedictine, and gives 1145 as the date of its affiliation to Clairvaux. There would seem to be no record of the day. Not a few of the succeeding abbots of Grand-Selve were distinguished men in Church and state; several of them

[1] Manric. *Annal. Cisterc.*, I., *an.* 1143, viii; Beaunier, *Recueil des Abbayes de France*, II. 869; Janauschek, *op. cit.*, 75 sq.

[2] William of Malmesbury, *Gest. Reg. Angl.*, V. 440; Janauschek, *op. cit.*, 8.

[3] *Gall. Christ.*, XIII., *Instr.*, 185 sq.

[4] Manric. *Annal. Cisterc.*, I., *an.* 1144, viii; *Gall. Christ.*, I. 267; Beaunier, *op. cit.*, I. 27; Janauschek, *op. cit.*, 79.

[5] Pp. 340 sqq. *infra.*

[6] *Ep.* 242, and Mabillon. *Not.ad loc*

became bishops and one, Odo of Châteauroux, was raised to the Sacred Purple.[1]

The following two years, 1146 and 1147, were marked each by a foundation in Belgium. The first was that of Villers (*Villarium*) in the diocese of Liège, halfway between Nivelles and Gembloux, some sixteen miles North of Charleroi and quite close to a little place now known as Villers-la-Ville.[2] There is no record of the name of any founder other than St. Bernard himself ; although we may suppose that according to his custom the Abbot of Clairvaux was responding to some local invitation in sending his monks to Brabant. Twice he visited it very early in its history, when travelling to and from the Rhineland in 1146-47.[3] It would seem that the original site proved to be unsuitable, chiefly owing to the lack of sufficient water and that, four or five years after the monks settled upon it on 1st June, 1146, the abbey was removed under the personal supervision of the Abbot of Clairvaux to its present site. The first abbot Laurence ruled but for a year, being desirous—to use St. Bernard's own phrase —*considerationi vacare*, and was succeeded by Abbot Gerard. Its roll of abbots was illustrious ; in particular we may mention Conrad, Count of Sayn in the Rhineland, who became successively Abbot of Clairvaux and of Cîteaux, and Cardinal Bishop of Porto in the second decade of the XIIIth century.[4]

To the year 1146 is ascribed also the foundation of Boxley in Kent and in the diocese of Canterbury. William of Ypres, Earl of Kent, who himself subsequently became a Black Monk at Laon, invited monks from Clairvaux who under Abbot Lambert settled on 28th October upon a site in his manor of Boxley about two miles N.E. of Maidstone.[5]

Seven miles West of Lisieux and in the diocese of Bayeux stand some XVIIth century buildings familiar in more recent years as the home of Guizot, the French statesman, all that is left of the Abbey of Val-Richer, the first colony of Clairvaux in Normandy. It was founded on 24th June, probably in the year 1147, in response to the invitation of a certain Robert Tesson. It should be noted that this was not the original *emplacement* of the house—we have seen similar early removals.[6] In the first instance the monks settled in the Val-de-Soleuvre not far from Vire, where Robert granted them a site ; the valley lay in the forest of Foupendant and in the direction of Torigny. That Nivard, St. Bernard's youngest brother, played, here as elsewhere,[7] an important part in the establishment of a colony we may conclude from the fact that another benefactor, William Sylvain, made his donation

[1] Manric. *Annal. Cisterc.*, II., *an.* 1147, xiv; Aub. Mir. *Chron. Cisterc.*, 120 ; Beaunier, *op. cit.*, II. 861 ; Janauschek, *op. cit.*, 81 sq.

[2] Manric. *op. cit.*, II., *an.* 1146, xiii ; *Hist. Villar. Monast.*, Marten. et Durandi, *Thesaur.Nov.Anecd.*, III. 1267.

[3] *Ex Martyr. Villar.*, XV., *Kal. Nov.*, P.L. CLXXXV.1827 ; *Vita Prima*, VI. xi. 36.

[4] Janauschek, *op. cit.*, 87.

[5] Manric. *op. cit.*, II., *an.* 1146, xii ; Dugdale, *Monast. Angl.*, V. 460 sq. *ed. cit.*; Leland, *Collect.*, VIII. 83 ; Tanner, *Notit. Monast., Kent*, VII. *note* m. ; Janauschek, *op. cit.*, 91.

[6] Pp. 29, 66 sq. *supra.*

[7] Pp. 51 sq. *supra.*

to Ste. Marie-de-Soleuvre into his hands ; [1] but there is no evidence that he was the first abbot—as we shall see, there is some question whether he was not six months later engaged upon the foundation of l'Épine in Spain.[2] The first abbot was Thomas, under whom the abbey was, with the approval of Philip, Bishop of Bayeux, removed to Val-Richer, a locality which although in the diocese of Lisieux was feudally subject to the *Ecclesia Bajocensis.* Soleuvre had proved to be intractable and sterile land upon which the monks were spending labour in vain.[3]

It is under this year, 1147, that there is chronicled an accession to the filiation of Clairvaux perhaps more notable in its effects than any known to us. When the great Abbey of Savigny in Normandy and in the diocese of Avranches, eleven miles S.W. of Mortain and some twenty miles S.E. of Mont-St. Michel,[4] became Cistercian on 17th September, 1147, it brought with it to its new allegiance all the houses of its filiation to the number of twenty-seven : being, on this side of the Channel, Furness, Neath, Quarr, Basingwerk, Combermere, Calder, Rushen in the Isle of Man, Swincshead, Stratford-Langthorne, Bildwas, Buckfast, Byland, St. Mary of Dublin and Coggeshall ; and in France amongst the remaining thirteen La-Trappe in the diocese of Sées in Normandy.[5] Savigny stood high in the opinion of St. Bernard. A letter written by him to the bishops in Aquitaine at an early stage of the Papal Schism, probably in the year 1132, warning them against trusting Gerard, Bishop of Angoulême, enumerates Savigny with approval amongst religious houses in Italy and in France which "firmly adhere to Innocent, sincerely support him, humbly obey him, faithfully recognize the true successor of the Apostles." [6]

Savigny was originally founded about 1105, on forest-land granted by Ralph de Fougères, as a house of Black Monks—by Vitalis de Mortain a Canon of the Collegiate Church of St. Evroult at Mortain, which owed its existence to the piety of Robert de Mortain, a companion of the Conqueror who was richly endowed by him in England. Vitalis fell under the influence of Robert of Arbrissel, the founder of Fontevrault, and subsequently gave himself to the life of a hermit. With such a man as its first abbot Savigny naturally set a strict, perhaps an ultra-Benedictine, standard of religion, and ultimately became the head of what Janauschek does not hesitate to describe as a congregation of its own. Under Serlo, the third abbot, its chapter general of 1147 obtained a bull from Eugenius III confirming the affiliation of the entire

[1] Horst. et Mabillon. *in S. Bern. Ep.* 301, *Not. Fus.* ; Jobin, *S. Bernard et sa famille,* 113.

[2] Pp. 83 sq. *infra.*

[3] Manric. *Annal. Cisterc.,* II., *an.* 1147, xiii, iv, *app.,* 550 ; *Gall. Christ.,* XI. 445 sq., *Instr.,* 81 ; Beaunier, *Recueil des Abbayes de France,* II. 720 ; Janauschek, *op. cit.,* 94.

[4] Manric. *op. cit.,* II., *an.* 1148; vii ; Beaunier, *op. cit.,* II. 733.

[5] Janauschek, *op. cit.,* 96 sqq.

[6] *Ep.* 126.

congregation to Clairvaux, which however was not effected without some opposition on the part of the English houses.[1] At Furness in particular Peter, the fourth abbot, voiced the discontent of the community by appearing personally at Rome before Eugenius III and successfully dissociating his abbey from the Congregation of Savigny in its affiliation to Clairvaux. However, on his way home he was intercepted, brought to Savigny, "there made a most excellent monk" and finally dispatched to Quarr as its fifth abbot.[2]

But this remarkable transfer of allegiance does not complete the list of Clairvaux's achievements in England and Wales during 1147. A day in that year, probably 23rd November, saw the foundation of Margam or Margan (*Marganense-Cœnobium*) in the diocese of Llandaff and in Glamorganshire, nine miles S.S.E. of Neath where already stood a daughter of Savigny. The abbey owed its origin to Robert, Earl of Gloucester, who died on 31st October of the same year and therefore, if we accept the first-named day as that of the arrival of the monks from Clairvaux under Abbot William, did not live to see the beginning of the good work which was completed by his son and successor, Earl William. A charter of 1349 quoted by Dugdale suggests that the endowment of the house owed also something to the liberality of the local chieftain, Morgan ap Caradoc.[3]

On 5th December, 1147, Clairvaux monks under Abbot Franc de Morvaux arrived at Aulne (*Alna*) on the Sambre, in the diocese of Liège, a place near Thuin about ten miles S.W. of Charleroi, so called from the abundance of its alder trees. Aulne had originally been dependent upon the Benedictine Abbey of Lobbes, founded in its close neighbourhood in the middle of the VIIth century; but so recently as 1144 it had become a house of Canons Regular of St. Augustine. The Third Part of the *Liber Miraculorum* opens with the story of St. Bernard's return to Clairvaux from Liège, after his travels in the Rhineland in the cause of the Second Crusade during the winter of 1146-47. He would have arrived at Liège about 18th January.[4] It was upon this occasion that, in response to the request of Henry, Bishop of Liège, who evidently was much impressed by St. Bernard's sanctity, he consented to send Clairvaux colonists to Aulne which thenceforth became Cistercian.[5] This was one of those cases in which the diocesan may seem to have acted high-handedly in favour of St. Bernard's sons; but the mere fact of the transference of Aulne to the Austin Canons three years earlier suggests that it was a house in which the Black Monks of

[1] *Gall. Christ.*, XI. 540 sqq., 552 sqq., *Instr.*, 110; Jaffé, *Regesta*, 9139; *Annal. Waverl. an.* 1147, *Rolls Series*, II. 232; Janauschek, *op. cit.*, 95 sq.

[2] *E Registr. de Furnese in Off. Ducat. Lancastr.*, Dugdale, *Monast. Angl.*, V. 246, *ed. cit.*

[3] *Annal. Margan. an.* 1147, *Annal. Monast.*, I. 14, *Rolls Series*; Tanner, *Notit. Monast.*, *Glamorgan*, VII., note n; Dugdale, *op. cit.*, V. 740 sqq.; Manric. *op. cit.*, II., *an.* 1147, xix; Janauschek, *op. cit.*, 107.

[4] *Vita Prima*, VI (*Pars* 3), xi. 35; Waitz, *M.G.H.* XXVI. 128 sqq.

[5] Manric. *Annal. Cisterc.*, II., *an.* 1147, xix; Martène, *Annal. Bened.*, VI. 408; *Gall. Christ.*, III. 1116; Janauschek, *op. cit.*, 108.

Lobbes had not of late been particularly successful; and now the canons in their turn may perhaps have done no better. Something of this kind would seem to have happened at Eberbach.[1]

It would have been also after St. Bernard's return to his own monastery in this same year, 1147, that upon a day unknown another daughter of Clairvaux, the Abbey of l'Épine (*Spina, al. Espina*), was founded in the kingdom of Leon and in the diocese of Palencia, about fifteen miles from Valladolid. Sancia or Sanche, sister of Alphonso II, Emperor in Spain, whose Bernardine enthusiasm we have already recognized in the foundation of Osera, of Sobrado and of Melon,[2] had, in the course of travels in France, Italy and Germany been impressed by the fervour and by the fidelity to Benedictine traditions exhibited by the Cistercians. She sought St. Bernard, who was at the time preaching the Second Crusade in Germany, and offered him as a site for a daughter of Clairvaux a property of her own, which bore the name of San Pedro de Espina. The deed of gift is dated 20th January, 1147,[3] when St. Bernard would have been at Liège. A monk to whom St. Bernard refers as "frater Nivardus" was sent with the colony in some responsible capacity—probably as novice-master; for the first abbot, whose name is doubtful, writing to St. Bernard, laments that "the brother," presumably Nivard, "who bears this letter is leaving us; he was very necessary to us, for he taught the novices and they were making good progress."[4] Antonio Yepes, the Spanish chronicler of the Benedictine Order, is sufficiently explicit upon the whole story. "The Infanta Sancia," he writes, "had a Cistercian monastery built in her palace," meaning probably in the *enclos* of her house, "and begged the holy man Nivard, brother of St. Bernard, to take charge of the construction; which he did, having the buildings modelled upon those of Clairvaux. After these were finished he returned to France to give an account to his holy brother of all that had happened; leaving Abbot Baldwin and his monks full of consolation and the good princess infinitely joyous at seeing her purposes happily fulfilled."[5] Now Yepes is positive upon two points; the name of the first abbot which is doubtful; and the consolation afforded by Nivard so abundantly as not to have been exhausted on his departure. As regards the former the chronicler is, as we have seen, wrong. He may be right as to the identity of Nivard. The present writer, if he may dare to feel in a small degree convinced where Vacandard was in doubt, suggests that this

[1] P. 45 *supra.*

[2] Pp. 73 sqq. *supra.* Cf. p. 49.

[3] *Ep.* 301; Manric. *Annal. Cisterc.*, II., an. 1147, xviii, IV., *app.* 550; *España Sagr.*, XXXVII. 197.

[4] *Ep.* 301; *Ep.* 373, *inter S. Bern. Epp.*

[5] Yepes, *Coronica Gen. de la orden de San Ben.*, VII. 328; Jobin, *S. Bernard et sa famille*, 116 sqq.

was the kind of work for which St. Bernard's *frater germanus* Nivard would seem to have possessed some special aptitude, as is evidenced by the part which he took in the foundation of Vaucelles, of Buzay and finally, in this year 1147, of Val-Richer;[1] and there would be nothing unreasonable in the supposition that a few months later than the foundation of Val-Richer he may have joined the Clairvaux colonists on their way to l'Épine. Moreover, in case that there had been another Nivard, we might expect St. Bernard to have described him unequivocally in his correspondence.[2]

Before two years had elapsed an unhappy controversy arose in Leon which of necessity involved St. Bernard. Ferdinand, the newly elected Abbot of Toldanos, a monastery of Black Monks, resented—as was thought, contumaciously— the subjection of his house to the great Abbey of Carrezeda[3] in the diocese of Astorga, founded by King Bermund II in 990 ; and took steps to affiliate his house to Clairvaux, being supported by the foundress of Toldanos, the Infanta Elvira, maternal aunt of Alphonso and of Sancia. Carrezeda, by the mediation of Sancia, invoked the authority of St. Bernard. The Abbot of Clairvaux maintained in reply that " nothing underhand had been done in the matter," that the monks of Toldanos " believed themselves freely to hold a place which had been founded in God's freedom and in subjection to no other monastery, as indeed their foundress maintained." The monks of Carrezeda were forgetting the words of Solomon : " Forbid not him who would do good ; if thou canst, do good thyself also."[4] St. Bernard, considering that the servants of God should not quarrel, would have Elvira arbitrate between the two houses with in the last resort a reference to the Bishops of Zamora and Astorga. In the end, however, when Carrezeda proved irreconcilable, the Abbot of Toldanos refrained from pressing his point. And—in 1203 Carrezeda became the seventeenth daughter of Cîteaux ! But Toldanos never was Cistercian.[5]

Alcobaça (*Alcobatia*) was the youngest of the three Lusitanian daughters of Clairvaux, the eldest having been the Abbey of Alafoës, founded in 1138.[6] The name was taken from two rivers, the Alcoa and the Baza, on the banks of which it stood about seven miles from the coast of the Atlantic and about forty miles N. by E. of Lisbon, its cathedral city. Lusitania was at that time ruled by its first king, Alphonso I of the House of Burgundy, son of that Henry of Burgundy who at the end of the XIth century married Theresa, the natural daughter of Alphonso VI of Castile, and received from

[1] Pp. 46, 51, 80 sq. *supra*.

[2] Aub. Mir. *Chron. Cisterc.*, 120 ; Janauschek, *op. cit.*, 108.

[3] Janauschek, *op. cit.*, LXVI and 209.

[4] Prov. iii. 27, *Vulg.*

[5] *Ep.* 301 and Horst. et Mabill. *Not. Fus. ad loc.*; *Ep.* 455 ; Manric. *Annal. Cisterc.*, II., *an.* 1148, viii.

[6] Pp. 64 sq. *supra*.

his father-in-law Lusitania in feudal tenure. Alphonso of Burgundy achieved the sovereign independence of Portugal, and had quite recently, in 1147, captured Lisbon from the Moors in a crusade in which he had been supported by the material aid of the English and by the spiritual aid of St. Bernard.[1] The correspondence dealing with this last point may be of doubtful authenticity, but it is not therefore historically valueless as evidence, considering the relation between the royal houses of Castile and Portugal and the interest taken by Alphonso, Emperor in Spain, in St. Bernard's work and in the expansion of the *Cisterciense Institutum* as represented by the daughters of Clairvaux in the North-West of the Peninsula. Not unnaturally the foundation of Alcobaça would be a thankoffering for the success achieved against the Moslem hosts at Lisbon.[2] February 2nd, 1148, is the date accepted by Janauschek, in spite of a chronology confused by the existence of a deed of gift granted by Alphonso to St. Bernard so late as 8th April, 1153, the solution offered by the learned historian, supported by Vacandard, being that this latter was a charter confirmatory of a *fait accompli*. Similarly are we uncertain as to the name of the first abbot ; it was either Randolph or Martin ; on this point Janauschek suggests that he was binominal. In later years Alcobaça became an abbey of very great importance by reason both of its wealth and of its numbers ; sometimes so many as nine hundred monks were found within its walls.[3]

The Abbey of Cambron (*Camberona*) is noteworthy as having had as its first abbot Fastredus, subsequently third Abbot of Clairvaux and for one short year, 1162-63, eighth Abbot of Cîteaux, a man whom as occupant of this last dignity Herbert of Torres describes—it is the first known occurrence of this high-sounding title—as " Universal Father of the whole Order," lamenting that " for their sins he had been so soon taken from them " ; a man, moreover, to whom we are indebted by one precious letter for several interesting reminiscences of St. Bernard.[4] Cambron, now called Cambron-Casteau, was founded by Anselm, a Canon Secular of the Church of Soignies, in the diocese of Cambrai and about five miles S.E. of Ath in Hainault ; and there Fastredus and his monks were settled by St. Bernard in person on 1st August, 1148.[5]

About a mile and a half outside Lille, on the road to Béthune, stand the remains of Loos (*Laus-Beatae-Mariae*), the foundation of which in the diocese of Tournai is ascribed to Theodoric, Count of Flanders, and his wife Sybil. Although negotiations in the matter had probably been in hand so early

[1] Osbern, *De Expugnatione Lyxbonensi*, ed. Stubbs ; cf. *Speculum*, VII. i. Jan., 1932.

[2] *Ep.* 470, *inter S. Bern. Epp.* ; *Ep.* 463 and *Not. ad loc., P.L.*

[3] Manric. *Annal. Cisterc.*, II., *an.* 1147, xvii, *app.* 3 sqq. ; Henric. *Fasc. SS. Ord. Cisterc.*, I. 102 ; Aub. Mir. *Chron. Cisterc.*, 114 ; Janauschek, *op. cit.*, 110.

[4] *Chron. Clarevall., an.* 1157 ; Herb. *De Mirac.*, II. 25 ; *Inter S. Bern. Epp.*, 491. Cf. p. 78 *supra*.

[5] Manric. *Annal. Cisterc.*, II., *an.* 1148, xvi ; *Gall. Christ.*, III. 171 sq. ; Beaunier, *op. cit.*, I. 330 ; Janauschek, *op. cit.*, 113.

as 1146, it was not until 15th December, 1148, that Abbot John and the Clairvaux monks made their solemn entry and took formal possession of the completed structure.[1]

At Longuay (*Longum-Vadum*), founded on 4th March of the next year, 1149, the Clairvaux colony was in the diocese of Langres in Champagne, over which had ruled since 1138 St. Bernard's kinsman, Godfrey de la Roche, first Abbot of Fontenay and subsequently third Prior of Clairvaux, a man devoted to the house which he had helped to found and to which he retired in 1161, four or five years before his death there.[2] In 1102 a pious man by name Christian and his two nephews, Guy and Hugh, had established a hospital for the sick at Longuay, over which Christian presided with the title of prior and which some years later, probably about 1136, became a house of Canons Regular of St. Augustine. Godfrey, a firm administrator, finding the discipline gravely relaxed, with the full approval of Eugenius III, his kinsman in religion, handed it over to Clairvaux. The first abbot known to us is Guy, who ruled from 1158.[3]

We have already had proof of the cordial relations prevailing between St. Bernard and Hatto, Bishop of Troyes, which resulted in the foundation of l'Arrivour in 1140.[4] These relations were a legacy to Hatto's successor, Henry, by whom they were fully maintained. Geoffrey records a visit of the Abbot of Clairvaux to Troyes, upon the occasion of which in the episcopal palace and in the presence of Henry and of Godfrey, Bishop of Langres, he restored to health a girl suffering apparently from spinal curvature.[5]

To 4th March, 1149, is ascribed the foundation of Boulancourt (*Bullencuria*) in Champagne and in the diocese of Troyes, the fifty-eighth daughter of Clairvaux; its site was in the parish of Longeville, about twenty-five miles E. by S. of the cathedral city. A letter which dates itself 1152, written by the Bishop of Troyes to St. Bernard and his lawful successors as Abbots of Clairvaux, gives the story of Boulancourt and confirms the rights of the Cistercians already acquired there. " In our diocese," we read, " there was a certain house of canons by name Boulancourt having an abbot, canons, lay brethren and women all vowed to holiness of life which, when discipline had entirely disappeared from it, excess was reigning, decency had departed, and I was invoked by the inhabitants of that house who could no longer endure the state of things or amend it themselves, I personally visited. There I was earnestly besought by the abbot and by all the canons, lay brethren and women to grant in perpetuity to

[1] Manric. *op. cit.*, II., *an.* 1149, x; Aub. Mir. *Opp. Dipl. et Hist.*, I. 698; *Gall. Christ.*, III. 303; Janauschek, *op. cit.*, 116.

[2] *Chron. Clarevall., an.* 1161; *Gall. Christ.*, IV. 492; Jobin, *S. Bernard et sa famille*, 226 sqq.

[3] Manric. *Annal. Cisterc.*, II., *an.* 1149, ix; *Gall. Christ.*, IV. 837, *Instr.*, 172; Beaunier, *op. cit.*, II. 443; Janauschek, *op. cit.*, 118.

[4] P. 65 *supra*.

[5] *Vita Prima*, IV. vii. 41.

God and to the Order of Cîteaux, in particular to the venerable
father and house of Clairvaux, to be by them reformed and
held according to the use of the Order, both the house and all
its possessions which they could no longer maintain themselves." [1]   Thus the monastery of these Canons Regular of
St. Augustine, who had originally come to Boulancourt from
the Abbey of St. Pierre-du-Mont at Metz about the year
1095, was surrendered by them to the bishop, who installed
in their place a Clairvaux colony under Abbot Gerard.[2]

   Herbert of Torres tells us of a certain Gonnarius Tetrarch
of Torres, one of the four districts into which Sardinia was
divided during the Pisan period, who on his return from a
pilgrimage to the shrine of St. Martin at Tours delayed a
while at Clairvaux. There in converse with St. Bernard
he revealed to the abbot something of his spiritual state
and was invited to enter into the life of religion. However,
to this he would not consent; and St. Bernard, in whose
view free consent was in such a matter of first importance,
sent him on his way home with the parting words: " Rest
assured that we shall see you back again here from Sardinia."
And the spark smouldered in Gonnar's heart, to be blown
into fierce flame by St. Bernard's death in 1153, when at
the age of forty, a strong and active man, he presented himself
at Clairvaux, begged to be professed, and lived there a good
monk for five and twenty years.[3] Probably Herbert knew
him well, for he was himself a monk of Clairvaux under
Abbot Fastredus, who ruled from 1157 to 1162; not only so
but he would later, when about 1180 he became Archbishop
of Torres, the modern Porto Torres in the Gulf of Asinara,
have learned something of Gonnar's reputation in the country
of his origin. But during the period of three or four years
immediately preceding his noviciate Gonnar saw the Cistercian
life lived at his own door. After his visit to St. Bernard he
seems to have made a pilgrimage to the Holy Places, and
on his return to have begged that a Clairvaux colony might
settle upon his own land at a place called, from its abundant
springs, Cabuabbas (*Caput-Aquae*); but also known from some
association with the archdiocese of Torres as *Turres-Sardiniae*,
although it was actually in the diocese of Bosa. The day
of the foundation was 5th March; the year is a little doubtful;
Vacandard gives 1149 with reserve; Janauschek accepts
1150. Nothing is known of the name of any Abbot of
Cabuabbas.[4]

   Fontmorigny (*Fons-Morigniaci*), near Montfaucon on the
left bank of the Loire and in the diocese of Bourges, mentioned

[1] Inter. S. Bern. Epp. 439. Ed. Bened.

[2] Manric. Annal. Cisterc., II., an. 1149, ix; Gall. Christ., XII. 604 sq., Instr., 268; Beaunier, Recueil des Abbayes de France, II. 824 sq.; Janaus- chek, op. cit., 118.

[3] Herb. De Mirac., II. 23.

[4] Manric. Annal. Cisterc., II., an. 1149, ix; Janauschek, op. cit., 119.

in a letter written by Eugenius III to Peter, Archbishop of
Bourges, and dated 15th March, 1146, confirming to Fontmorigny its possessions, is stated by Beaunier to have been
a house of Black Monks.   The Cistercians of Clairvaux under
Abbot Gilbert entered into possession of it on 1st May, 1149,
on the invitation of the feudal lord of Montfaucon.[1]

Of Aube-Pierres (*Albae-Petrae*), which was in the diocese
of Limoges and in the district of the Creuse not far from
Argenton, where Clairvaux monks settled not six weeks later,
on 10th June, there is no record either of the founder or of
the first abbot.[2]

The foundation of five daughters in little over three months,
that is to say, between 4th March and 10th June, 1149, two
of them so far distant one from the other as is Troyes in the
North from Sardinia in the South, and three of them on two
successive days, suggests the storm-tactics, the rapid movement, the *frappez fort, frappez vite* of a great campaigner.
Doubtless it was exhausting ; in any case there followed a
lull of two years and it was not until an uncertain day in 1151
that Clairvaux effected another settlement, and that its first
and only daughter in Denmark.   Our thoughts turn naturally to Eskil, Archbishop of Lund, whom our English Pope,
Hadrian IV, made Primate in 1154 ; an honour, however,
transferred to the see of Upsala in 1163.   Esrom, this Danish
abbey, was on the lake of that name in the North-Eastern
corner of the Island of Zealand and in the diocese of Roskild,
the old capital of Denmark.   But let us refresh ourselves for
a moment after the tedium of a bare chronicle and recall
the story of Eskil.   The interpretation of it is in large measure
to be found in the fact that in 1178, towards the end of a long
and active life, he became a monk at Clairvaux, where he
died three years later.[3]   This we may be sure was no mere
profession *ad succurrendum ;* except in so far as that a man
of so deep humility would in the retrospect have lamented
every hour spent, as he would conceive, idly in the past.
Such is the way of saints ! Geoffrey records a visit paid
by Eskil to Clairvaux through great perils and at great ex-
penditure both of labour and of money, motived by the desire
to know personally the man of God whom he already knew
in his sons dwelling in the monastery at Esrom.   The monks
at Clairvaux were not less edified by Eskil's spirit and behaviour than was he by theirs.   When on his departure he
would take with him some bread blessed by St. Bernard,
the saint would have him dispense with the re-baking customary in the case of bread intended to be carried across

[1] Manric. *Annal.
Cisterc.*, II., *an.*
1149, ix ; *Gall.
Christ.*, II. 198 ;
Beaunier,
*Recueil des
Abbayes de
France*, I. 244 ;
Janauschek, *op.
cit.*, 115.

[2] Manric. *op.
cit.*, II., *loc. cit.* ;
Gall. Christ., II.
644 ; Beaunier,
op. cit., I. 298
sq. ; Janaus-
chek, *op. cit.*,
115 sq.

[3] *Chron. Clare-
vall.*, ann. 1178,
1181.

the sea, assuring him that the blessing alone would preserve it sound ; and such it was three years later when Geoffrey and others last heard of it from the archbishop himself. The chronicler proceeds to relate upon the testimony of the same witness a miracle of healing wrought in later days, by means of relics of St. Bernard brought by Eskil from Clairvaux,[1] upon a monk of Esrom who was apparently epileptic. On the occasion of this visit of the archbishop Geoffrey was himself a monk at Clairvaux, and was sufficiently impressed by the devotion of Eskil to St. Bernard as to preface either the Third Book [2]—the first which he wrote— of the *Vita Prima* or the Fifth [3] by a letter of dedication addressed to Eskil. It was doubtless also on the occasion of this visit that Eskil confided to St. Bernard his longing to be professed at Clairvaux. " Of that secret thought which has so ardently arisen in your heart," he writes to Eskil in 1152, " your William (the bearer of the letter) will speak to you on my behalf ; your William, I say, and specially yours in the bowels of Jesus Christ. He has heard my words and you, when you hear him on this matter, will hear me." [4] It is not improbable that the question of Eskil's profession had been referred to the Pope, for we find St. Bernard writing to Eugenius III in or about the same year 1152 : " We would remind you of the affairs of the Archbishop of Lund. Supposing that there be no longer any reason for delay, there remains no reason why whatever may be the right course should not be taken." [5] As we have seen, it was not for another twenty-five years or more that Eskil was professed. We note St. Bernard's guarded words ; he is doubtless fearful lest his wishes should pervert his judgement in the matter. With Eskil in the settlement at Esrom was associated Henry, first Abbot of Varnhem in West Gothland, the first daughter of Alfwastra, so recently as 1150 founded like its motherhouse by King Swerker and Queen Alvida.[6] The site would seem to have been part of the legal patrimony of Eskil. As regards the day upon which the Clairvaux monks under Abbot Folmar entered into possession, Janauschek speaks with uncertainty ; but Vacandard, following the greater number of authorities, gives 11th February. A bull of Eugenius III under date 29th December, 1151,[7] is addressed to William, Abbot of Esrom, who may have been the " your William " of St. Bernard's letter to Eskil.[8] We may, perhaps, assume that for some reason Folmar's tenure of the abbacy was of short duration.[9]

In the old province of Maine and in the diocese of Laval,

[1] *Vita Prima,*
IV. iv. 25 sqq.

[2] Mabillon. *ex Baluz. Miscell.,* V. 453.
[3] Waitz, *M.G.H.* XXVI. 93, *ex Paris MS.* 7561.

[4] *Ep.* 390.

[5] *Ep.* 280.

[6] Janauschek, *op. cit.,* 120.

[7] Jaffé, *Regesta,* 9502.
[8] *Ep.* 390.
[9] Manric. *Annal. Cisterc.,* II., *an.* 1151, xiii; Aub. Mir. *Chron. Cisterc.,* 160 ; Janauschek, *op. cit.,* 136 sq.

anciently that of Le-Mans, about three miles West of the cathedral city and about two miles East of Le-Genest stand the remains of the Abbey of Clermont (*Clarus-Mons*).   It owed its foundation to Guy, Sieur de Laval, upon whose land Clairvaux monks settled on 17th May, 1152. The identity of its first abbot is somewhat doubtful ; he may have been Philip, a monk of Bonneval, whether of Bonneval in Dauphiné or of Bonneval in Poitou is not recorded—who in 1179 became Bishop of Rennes.[1]

[1] Manric. *Annal. Cisterc.*, II., an. 1152, vi ; *Gall. Christ.*, XIV. 527 ; Beaunier, *op. cit.*, II. 912 ; Janauschek, *op. cit.*, 131.

Twenty years had now elapsed since Clairvaux had established its first house in Spain at Moreruela in the diocese of Zamora. The two daughters of Moreruela, Nogales and Aquiar, were as yet unborn ;[2] meanwhile Moreruela was gaining good repute which would bring to it a foster-child. At the little village of Paleas in Leon, in the diocese of Zamora between that city and Salamanca, Martin, surnamed the Cid, a holy priest of Zamora, had built a guest-house with an oratory served by himself and like-minded friends.   In course of time, deeply impressed by the Cistercian life as lived at Moreruela, Martin, with the approval of the Bishop of Zamora, sought to submit himself and his companions to Clairvaux, whence some four monks arrived in March, 1137. To Martin, his brethren and these Cistercian monks occupying the guest-house at Paleas, Alphonso, Emperor in Spain, granted under date 4th October of the same year two derelict farms on the outskirts of Zamora, on the understanding that the aforesaid guest-house should become a regularly constituted Cistercian monastery.   We must assume that the four monks were sent by St. Bernard simply to investigate.   Apparently for some time Alphonso's condition was not fulfilled ; the newcomers did not coalesce with Martin and his friends ; nor was any monastery with a duly appointed abbot founded.[3] Quite what happened between March, 1137, and 28th June, 1152—the date accepted by Janauschek as that of the foundation proper, we do not know ; nor can we name the first abbot. The old site at Paleas was abandoned, owing to its unhealthiness and its general unsuitability, in favour of a place which later bore the name of Valparayso (*Vallis-Paradisi*), but was probably originally called from a spring near by Bellofonte (*Bellus-Fons*).[4]

[2] Janauschek, *op. cit.*, 152 sq.

[3] Yepes, *Coron. Gen. de la ord. de S. Ben.*, VII. 284.

Moureilles (*Moroliae*) was originally a house of Black Monks founded in the Vendée and in the diocese of Poitiers at the beginning of the XIIth century by the feudal lords of Triayze about six miles S.E. of Luçon and about fifteen miles N.W. of La-Rochelle, in the present day its cathedral

[4] *España Sagr.*, XVII. 87 ; Manric. *Annal. Cisterc.*, I., an. 1137, iv ; Aub. Mir. *Chron. Cisterc.*, 113 ; Janauschek, *op. cit.*, 131 sq.

city. Its first abbot was Michael Meschin ; under its third abbot it freely accepted the Cistercian *usus* and was affiliated to Clairvaux on 8th September, 1152.[1]

St. Bernard writes in 1152 to Peter, Abbot of Montier-la-Celle : " We grant and confirm to you and to your house the bakery at Troyes which used to belong to our monastery of Mores "[2] in the diocese of Langres. This arrangement, sufficiently convenient to the ancient Abbey of La-Celle which stood in the outskirts of Troyes, would probably have arisen out of the affiliation of Mores to Clairvaux, which happened, as did that of Moureilles, on 8th September of this year, 1152. Its affiliation may be fittingly recorded by quoting a letter addressed to St. Bernard in 1152 by Samson, Archbishop of Rheims. " Consenting with due anxiety in the matter to the petitions of your holiness, we laboured much and long with the Abbot and Canons of Blessed Denis in order to obtain from them a grant to us of the monastery of Mores with all its appurtenances for the purpose of establishing there an abbey of the Clairvaux Order. This with very great difficulty we have succeeded in doing. In the result by divine favour they have at last granted the monastery to us together with all its appurtenances, on condition that it be made a house of the Clairvaux Order. Accordingly we yield and grant it to yourself and to the holy congregation of Clairvaux, in order that an abbey of the Clairvaux Order may be founded there without further delay."[3] The three-fold repetition of the description *Claraevallensis Ordo* is noteworthy as a stage in the direction of the later description of the Cistercians generally as Bernardines. The first Abbot of Mores was Gerard, to whom we owe the story of St. Bernard's visit paid in spirit to the weary monks at Nocturns that he might stimulate their devotion.[4] The second was Menard, who tells us of how he found St. Bernard in church prostrate before the Crucifix, the sacred figure embracing the man of God ; and of how, fearful of intruding upon him at so sublime a moment, he departed silently and unobserved.[5] The third abbot was Herbert of Torres.[6]

It is within a year of St. Bernard's death. We cannot but feel drawn towards the great, strong, and most lovable personality, at once so humble and so fearless ; a personality steeped in the supernatural and therefore self-reproachful ; suffering increasingly, we may believe, from distressing gastric trouble which no physician of his day was competent to alleviate ; conscious, doubtless, that his time was short. " Death which for the young lies in ambush, for the old

[1] Manric. *Annal. Cisterc.*, II., an. 1152, vi ; *Gall. Christ.*, II. 1396 ; Beaunier, *op. cit.*, I. 193 ; Janauschek, *op. cit.*, 132 sq.

[2] *Ep.* 419.

[3] *Inter S. Bern. Epp.* 438. Ed. Bened.

[4] *Vita Prima*, IV. i. 3.

[5] Herbert. *De Mirac.*, II. 19 ; *Exord. Magn.*, IV. 3.

[6] Manric. *Annal. Cisterc.*, II., an. 1153, xvii ; *Gall. Christ.*, IV. 842 ; Beaunier, *op. cit.*, II. 443 sq. ; Janauschek, *op. cit.*, 135.

[1] S. Bern. *De Convers.*, VIII. 16.

sits ever at the gate." [1] So he had urged some thirteen years ago in the Schools of Paris. Death would indeed bring that rest for which the soul longs ; but meanwhile Christ calls the soul to toil on to the end. So he would remind himself,

[2] S. Bern. *In. Cant. Cant.*, XLVII. 5.

as more than once he had reminded others.[2]

We like to think that, before he passed away on 20th August, 1153, Clairvaux bore two more daughters. Janauschek does not hesitate to ascribe them to this period of little over eleven months ; Vacandard would seem to be somewhat doubtful. One was in Spain, the other in France. Monte-de-Ramo (*Mons-Rami*) like the greater number of Clairvaux's Spanish daughters was in Galicia. It lay in the diocese of Orense, about five miles from that city. It is by some authorities said to have been founded by Raymond, Count of Galicia, and therefore to have been called Monte de Ramon ; but the more reliable account is that it owed its origin to Theresa, natural daughter of Alphonso VI of Castile and wife of Henry

[3] P. 84 *supra.*

of Burgundy, Count of Portugal,[3] who in 1124 granted land for the foundation of a house of Black Monks called S. Juan-de-Monte-Ramo, the *vocable* of which was changed to S. Maria-de-Monte-Ramo on its affiliation to Clairvaux. Of its own motion it seems to have become Cistercian on 30th March, 1153. The first abbot of the newly affiliated house is said to have borne the name of William. An interest attaches to the fact that Chrysostom Henriquez, the XVIIth century writer of the *Fasciculus SS. Ordinis Cisterciensis*, of the *Lilia Cistercii*, a history of the nunneries of the Order and of their constitution, of the *Regula, Constitutiones et Privilegia Ordinis Cisterciensis* and of the *Menologion Cister-*

[4] Manric. *Annal. Cisterc.*, II., an. 1153, xvi ; *España Sagr.*, XVII. 26 sqq. ; Janauschek, *op. cit.*, 134.

ciense, was professed at Monte-de-Ramo.[4]

The other foundation of this year was effected on 13th August, precisely a week before St. Bernard died. La-Peyrouse (*Petrosa*) was in the Dordogne and in the diocese of Périgueux, near the village of St. Jean-de-Côle about five miles N.W. of Thiviers. The name of its first abbot was

[5] Manric. *Annal. Cisterc.*, II., an. 1153, xvii ; *Gall. Christ.*, II. 1505 ; Beaunier, *op. cit.*, I. 210 ; Janauschek, *op. cit.*, 134 sq.

Roger, but there is no reliable tradition as to its founder.[5]

Sixty-eight foundations ! It is a great record for thirty-eight years ; and, when we come to add to it the rest of the houses founded in the line of Clairvaux, it is greater still, for the number amounts to one hundred and fifty-nine, as compared with a total of three hundred and thirty-nine Cistercian houses, not including Clairvaux itself, founded during the same period of time. The year in which the Clairvaux stock was most prolific was significantly enough 1147, when St. Bernard was deeply engrossed in the affairs of the Second Crusade ; in that year out of a total of fifty Cistercian foundations, thirty-nine were in the Clairvaux line. The figures are eloquent of the results achieved by monks professed by St. Bernard and by his sons. And when he and his companions entered Cîteaux in 1112 the Cistercian Order was sterile ! [1]

In some cases it has been a little difficult to obtain historical and topographical information in such detail as might be desired ; in others it has been sufficiently easy. In no case, however, should it be impossible for the reader who happened to be, say, in Sweden or in Spain to identify, as he might well wish to do, the *sacra loca*. Here and there we trace plainly the footsteps of St. Bernard himself but, alas, nowhere in these islands. We should like to be able on the spot to picture him in converse with the faithful William at Rievaulx or with the apostolic Malachy at Mellifont ; but it is denied us. Great traveller though he was, he seems never to have crossed the Channel. At a few places there are associations with great historical personages, and consequently with the tendencies which are represented by them ; the reader will not fail to recognize these and, it is to be hoped, enjoy them. We may instance Becket at Clairmarais. Sidelights fall upon less generally known but not therefore less attractive men and movements, such as John Zirita and Alphonso, Emperor in Spain, and their influence upon the foundations in Galicia, and Robert of Arbrissel and the part played by his Order of Fontevrault at Belle-Perche and at Savigny. Thus we learn to appreciate the nexus between Clairvaux, that is to say, its spirit as embodied in St. Bernard and transmitted by him to his sons, and the movement of supernaturalism, of the ideal of the *Civitas Dei*, reacting against the materialism alike of strict monarchy and of constitutional feudalism as evidenced by the contest for predominance characteristic of the times, in which both these forces were so fiercely and frequently so unscrupulously engaged.

[1] *Chron. Turon.*, Mart. et Dur. *Vet. Script. et Mon.Ampl.Coll.*, V. 1014.

SUMMARY OF THE DAUGHTER–HOUSES OF CLAIRVAUX FOUNDED DURING THE LIFE–TIME OF ST. BERNARD

BELGIUM

Villers, 1146, p. 80.   Aulne, 1147, p. 82.

BRITISH ISLES

Rievaulx, 1132, p. 46.   Whiteland, 1140, p. 67. Boxley, 1146, p. 80.
Fountains, 1134-5, p.52. Mellifont, 1142, p. 75. Margam, 1147, p. 82.

DENMARK

Esrom, 1151, p. 88.

FRANCE

Troisfontaines, 1118, p. 26.	La-Bénissons-Dieu, 1138, p. 64.
Fontenay, 1119, p. 28.	L'Arrivour, 1140, p. 65.
Foigny, 1121, p. 30.	Clairmarais, 1140, p. 66.
Igny, 1126, p. 44.	La-Prée, 1141 or 1142, p. 73.
Reigny, 1128, p. 44.	Belle-Perche, 1143, p. 78.
Ourscamp, 1129, p. 44.	Belloc, 1144, p. 79.
Cherlieu, 1131, p. 45.	Grand-Selve, 1145, p. 79.
Bonmont, 1131, p. 45.	Val-Richer. cir. 1147, p. 80.
Longpont, 1132, p. 46.	Savigny, 1147, p. 81.
Vaucelles, 1132, p. 46.	Cambron, 1148, p. 85.
Vauclair, 1134, p. 50.	Loos, 1148, p. 85.
Grâce-Dieu, 1135, p. 51.	Longuay, 1149, p. 86.
Buzay, 1135, p. 51.	Boulancourt, 1149, p. 86.
Hautecombe, 1135, p. 55.	Fontmorigny, 1149, p. 87.
Balerne, 1136, p. 60.	Aube-Pierres, 1149, p. 88.
St. Jean-d'Aulps, 1136, p. 60.	Clermont, 1152, p. 90.
Nerlac, 1136, p. 61.	Moureilles, 1152, p. 90.
Auberive, 1137, p. 62.	Mores, 1152, p. 91.
Les-Dunes, 1138, p. 63.	La-Peyrouse, 1153, p. 92.

GERMANY

Eberbach, 1131, p. 45.   Himmerod, 1134, p. 49.

ITALY

Chiaravalle-Milanese, 1135, p. 50.
Colomba, 1137, p. 62.
Casamario, 1140, p. 65.
San-Paolo-alle-tre-Fontane, 1140, p. 67.

PORTUGAL

Alafoës, 1138, p. 64.   Tarouca, 1140, p. 67.   Alcobaça, 1148, p. 84.

SARDINIA

Cabuabbas, 1149 or 1150, p. 87.

SICILY

Name unknown, *cir.* 1140, p. 70.

SPAIN

Moreruela, 1132, p. 49.

Osera, *cir.* 1141, p.73.

Sobrado, 1142, p. 74.

Melon, 1142, p. 74.

Meyra, 1143, p. 78.

Espina, 1147, p. 83.

Valparayso, *cir.* 1152, p. 90.

Monte-de-Ramo, 1153, p. 92.

SWEDEN

Alfwastra, 1143, p. 77.

Nydala, 1143, p. 77.

CHAPTER V

THE SCHISM IN THE PAPACY

THE story of how the Papal Schism originated is recorded in its main outline by Anselm of Gembloux in his *Continuatio* of the Chronicles of Sigebert of Gembloux under the year 1130. "Lambert, who is also Pope Honorius, died"—this was on the night of 13th-14th February—"The peace of the Roman Church is interrupted, for two persons quarrel for the right to occupy the Apostolic See, one a certain Gregory"—that is to say, Innocent II—"and the other Peter Leonis, a Roman by birth and a monk of Cluny. Gregory, with the consent of certain of the cardinals, claims for himself the right to be elected which was conferred upon him by Pope Honorius during his life-time ; Peter, boasting of his high birth, seizes the Castle of St. Angelo and proceeds to the violence of slaughter, rapine and incendiarism. . . . Gregory, fearing Peter's power, escapes by the Porta San Paolo and by way of Spoleto crosses the sea and at length lands at St. Egidius." This suggests that he went for some reason to Spoleto after leaving Rome. In October " he subsequently journeys into Burgundy, is received at Cluny and meets with a friendly welcome from all in France. Next, Lothair, King of Germany, influenced by certain of his own bishops, graciously receives an embassy sent by the French on behalf of Gregory, and pledges himself by oath to support his cause." [1] St. Egidius is St. Gilles-les-Boucheries, about ten miles West of Arles, from which the sea has since receded, the usual port for pilgrims in the XIIth century ; it was here that an earlier exile from Rome, Gelasius II, had landed in 1118. [2]

Was this the beginning of that general persecution which St. Norbert had foretold two years before in 1128 ? [3] Was it in the category of those " divine secrets," the knowledge of which was revealed to one whose judgement and foresight St. Bernard so highly valued ? [4] In any case there were perhaps signs that a process of dissolution was imminent throughout Western Christendom ; a relaxing of the grip which held the

[1] Sigeb. Gemblac. *Chron.* Anselm. *Contin., P.L.* CLX. 254.

[2] P. 35 *supra*.

[3] S. Bern. *Ep.* 56 ; cf. pp. 232 sq. *infra*.

[4] S. Bern. *Ep.* 8.

parts together in consentient movement; a creeping paralysis, as it were, which indicated some lesion of the central, the controlling force. Or was it rather that a dual personality, mutually antagonistic, as it had almost imperceptibly grown to be, represented on the one hand by the Empire and on the other by the Papacy, was in possession of the body of Christendom, which it was gradually destroying as such, a fact which later might well explain the failure of the Second Crusade? Even in the previous century Gregory VII may have recognized this danger, and his policy have been framed to meet and to correct it.

The year 1130 was, however, an epoch in the life of St. Bernard. Hitherto his interest had in the main centred in things concerning directly his own and other religious orders, and indirectly various diocesan churches as they were affected either by their own internal irregularities or by the external usurpation of their rights by the Crown or by the feudality. Hitherto, moreover, and in part consequently, his dealings had been rather with individuals, approving the honourable and reprobating the dishonourable as the case might be; dealings of the nature of an influence working frequently behind the scenes in the background of public life. The great imperial conception of the Church had not as yet forced itself upon his attention to such a degree as to bring him out upon the world-stage as its international apostle. The Schism in the Papacy was the occasion of this epoch. Henceforth he would still pray: "Come then, Lord Jesu, and remove the scandals from thy kingdom which is my soul, in order that thou, as is fitting, mayest reign in it"; [1] but hence- [1] *De Laud. Mar. Virg.*, IV. 2. forth, as never before, the coming of the kingdom on earth would acquire for him a richer and a fuller meaning, akin to that vouchsafed to John in Patmos, as of an allegiance transferred exclusively to Christ in the person of his Vicar by every potentate in his official capacity as such who names his name. [2] Thus, at the moment at which the Cardinal [2] *De Divers. Serm.*, II. 3. Deacon Gregory of Sant' Angelo, now Pope Innocent II, landed at St. Gilles, a fugitive from his Apostolic See, there became conscious in St. Bernard what M. Georges Goyau felicitously describes as a "subconscient chrétien"; [3] an [3] Goyau, *Saint Bernard*, 76. experience which it was given to his magnetic personality to reproduce in the shape of a fresh orientation of the soul of Christian Europe.

A decree issued by Nicholas II in 1059 had laid down the due procedure to be followed in elections to the Papacy. "The Cardinal Bishops," we read, "shall in the first instance

deal with the matter of the election with the most careful
consideration, then associate with themselves the Cardinal
Clerks, and finally demand the agreement of the rest of the
clergy and that of the people "—undoubtedly of the local
Roman Church—" safeguarding the respect due to the
Emperor Henry "—that is to say, Henry IV—" and to his
successors." [1] The intention of this decree would seem to
be to vest the election in the Cardinal Bishops absolutely,
instructing them, however, to report the result of their deliberations first to the other members of the Sacred College,
and then to the clergy and people of Rome, acting throughout
in such a manner as might seem to them consonant with
the respect properly to be paid to the imperial authority.
There is no suggestion of any veto upon their decision ; nor
indeed should we reasonably expect to find such. In course
of no very long time the text of the decree became corrupt,
a result effected mainly in the imperial interest but partly,
doubtless, in the interests of the Cardinal Clerks. In any
case the omission in certain copies of the word *episcopi* lent
some plausibility to the plea that the right of the Cardinal
Bishops in the matter of Papal elections was not exclusive
of that of the other members of the Sacred College. The
right in question had not been challenged before ; but that
it was not by any means *ex animo* accepted explains in some
degree the disaster of 1130.

There was, however, much more than this to be held
accountable for the Papal Schism. Rome was a city of
factions ; and amongst the contending forces none were more
bitterly antagonistic one to the other than were the two great
families of the Pierleoni and the Frangipani.[2] Their rivalry
was acute within the *Curia*, where at the time of which we
write the Pierleoni were represented by Peter who had been
raised to the Sacred Purple as Cardinal Deacon of St. Cosmas
and St. Damian by Paschal II in 1116, and subsequently styled
Cardinal Priest of St. Calixtus by Calixtus II in 1120. He
early began to manœuvre with a view to securing his election
to the Apostolic See. " Peter Leonis for a long time past
had, as is plain from many proofs, striven to reach that
dignity, avaricious and ambitious man that he was." [3] So
we learn from Hubert of Lucca ; and it would not be difficult
to confirm his testimony from other contemporary writers,
such as, for example, Peter the Venerable, an irreproachable
witness, who in a letter addressed to Giles, Bishop of Tusculum,
could speak of Peter as a man guilty of " ambition, cupidity,
sacrilege, simony, perjury . . . and yet worse." [4] According

[1] *Liber Pontific.,*
II., *ed.*
Duchesne, 280.

[2] *Liber Pontific.,*
II., *ed.*
Duchesne, 380.

[3] Hub. Luc. *Ep.
ad Norb. Arch.
Magd., P.L.*
CLXXIX. 40
sqq.

[4] Petr. Ven.
Epp., Lib. II. 4.

to the Chronicle of Maurigny Peter's father was a Jew, another Peter, who on his conversion was honoured by being baptized by that excellent Pope Leo IX and by receiving his name. A man of considerable parts, he soon came to possess great influence both in the city and in the *Curia*, and on the occasion of seditious disturbances arising out of the question of investitures he was placed by the Pope in authority over the defences of Rome, and in particular over the Castle of St. Angelo or *Turris Crescentii*. He was thus the founder of the rich and powerful family of the Pierleoni ; not particularly ancient, however, in 1130. His son, Peter, a person of literary tastes, studied at Paris and elsewhere in France and ultimately became a monk at Cluny whence, on the advice of his father, Paschal II recalled him to Rome.[1]

There was one member of the *Curia* who was keenly alive to the ambitious machinations of Peter, namely, Haimeric, Chancellor of the Holy See, a man trusted and respected by St. Bernard and much in his counsels.[2] It was between Haimeric and Peter that " the battle of the tiaras " would seem to have been really waged. It is a little difficult to arrive at what exactly happened in the early stages. The account given by Anselm of Gembloux is no more than a record of external and obvious facts. It would appear, however, that, when it became plain that Honorius II was dying, Haimeric had him removed to the Monastery of St. Andrew on the Coelian Hill, not far from the strongholds of the Frangipani in the Coliseum and on the Palatine Hill. There the cardinals assembled to await his death. The Chronicle of Maurigny records that, " as some say too hastily, they invested Gregory with the pontifical *insignia*. This, they state, was done by favour of dispensation in order that they might frustrate the hope of a certain Peter who seemed to be aspiring to the Papacy in a mere worldly fashion." [3] This, if true, was of course quite irregular on the part of the cardinals in question. The Pope was still alive ; canonically his successor could not be elected until an interval of three days had elapsed after his death. We may, perhaps, connect this account with Anselm of Gembloux's reference to " the right conferred upon him (Gregory) by Pope Honorius during his lifetime " ; [4] or it may be derived from a source representing the influence of the Pierleoni, namely, a letter written to Didacus, Archbishop of Compostella,[5] the authorship of which is uncertain ; possibly it was the work of Pandulph of Pisa, a notorious partizan of the Pierleoni.[6] Suger in his *Life of Louis le Gros* speaks of the " older and wiser men of the

[1] *Chron. Mauriniac.*, II., *P.L.* CLXXX. 157 sq.

[2] P. 203 *infra.*

[3] *Chron. Mauriniac., loc. cit.*

[4] P. 98 *supra.*

[5] Watterich, *Pontif. Rom. Vitae*, II. 187 sq.
[6] *Liber Pontific.*, ed. cit., II. xxxvi.

Church of Rome" agreeing that, in order to avoid tumult,
"the election should take place nowhere else than in the
Church of St. Mark, and not otherwise than by common
consent." The cardinals whom he designates as *assiduitate
et familiaritate propinquiores Apostolici*, he tells us, did not
as yet dare formally to assemble, but before the death of
Honorius had been published elected Gregory ; while, on
the other hand, those who favoured Peter invited others,
assembled as agreed at the Titular Church of San Marco—
now incorporated in the XVth century Palazzo Venezia—
and, so soon as the death of Honorius was known, elected
Peter "by the common consent of many bishops, cardinals,
clergy and Roman nobles." [1]

[1] Suger. *Vita
Ludov. Grossi,
an.* 1130, *P.L.*
CLXXXVI.
1330.

Plainly, on a point of order, the supporters of Peter were
when they elected him as Anacletus II in a strong position ;
they had observed the agreed terms and their vote had been
unanimous. Further, it had been a felicitous opportunity
for the Cardinal Priests and the Cardinal Deacons to avail
themselves for the first time of the electoral right to which
they laid claim. From the letter to Didacus above-mentioned,
perhaps a tainted source, we learn that the electors numbered
twenty-four cardinals, of whom two only were Cardinal Bishops,
and included as well as the Bishops of Segni and Sutri,
various clergy of lower degree, arch-priests and others, and
the *élite* of the nobility of Rome.

Meanwhile what was Haimeric doing ? He too was
sufficiently aware of the danger of tumult. The steps taken
by him and his party may be described as reported in his
letter to St. Norbert, then Archbishop of Magdeburg, by
Hubert, Bishop of Lucca, whom Vacandard places first
amongst the authorities. He represents, it will be observed,
the supporters of Gregory as less timorous than does Suger.
"When the cardinals were assembled in the Monastery of
St. Andrew the Apostle it was resolved by them that the
election of the pontiff should be deputed to a commission
of eight persons, two being Cardinal Bishops, William of
Palestrina and Conrad of the Sabina, three being Cardinal
Priests, Peter of Pisa, Peter the Red and Peter Leonis, three
being Cardinal Deacons, Gregory of Sant' Angelo, Jonathan
and the Chancellor Haimeric, so that, should the lord Pope
Honorius who was then *in articulo mortis* die, the person
elected by them unanimously or by the wiser part of them
should by them all be accepted as lord and Roman Pontiff." [2]

[2] Hub. Luc. *op.
cit., loc. cit.*

It was doubtless a well-intentioned move on the part of
Haimeric to secure for Peter Leonis a place on this commis-

sion. But, failing unanimity, how was the question of the *pars sanior* to be decided? St. Bernard, writing in 1132 to the bishops of Aquitaine, speaks of it as decided by the "dignity of the electors," whether Cardinal Bishops, Priests or Deacons, as persons more deeply interested than the rest in the election of the Supreme Pontiff [1]—which might well do no more than take the question a step farther back! Apart from this, the proposal would seem to have been constitutional and calculated to guard against external pressure. William of Palestrina evidently took a leading part, for Hubert proceeds to say that he " together with the rest decreed that should anyone oppose an election so made he would be under anathema ; and should anyone attempt to elect another pontiff, what he might do would be taken as not done and he himself no longer allowed to hold office in the Church ; this decree Peter Leonis confirmed by word of mouth, saying that they ought not to doubt whether he would not be an occasion of scandal to the Church, seeing that he would rather be drowned than that scandal should arise on his account." [2]

When the cardinals reassembled, as had been arranged, next day, Peter Leonis and Jonathan—presumably also Peter of Pisa—were absent. " That carrion bird," writes Hubert of the first-named, " was either drowned or glutted with flesh." As a matter of fact he was engaged in collecting his adherents, fully prepared to face any anathema which might be launched against him. Some suspicion arose from the secrecy of Haimeric. Was the Pope alive or dead ? " Unless Honorius, whom they believed to be now dead, had shown himself to the people at the window . . . the herald of Antichrist," Peter—St. Norbert would recognize the reference to his prophecy—" would have declared himself before his time." Realizing that the Church was in danger from the storm already blowing up, " the men whose hearts God had touched . . . when on the sixth day from the beginning of Lent Honorius was taken to his fathers, after celebrating his obsequies under such conditions as place and time allowed, yet in quite due form, considering that a disturbance was imminent," took action.

" From amongst the eight persons chosen to be electors, William of Palestrina, Conrad of the Sabina, Peter the Red and the Chancellor Haimeric," in conjunction with other cardinals of various ranks evidently not members of the commission of eight, " elected as Supreme Pontiff the fifth of them, Gregory Cardinal Deacon of Sant' Angelo, though unwilling and in every way protesting ; Peter of Pisa, the

[1] *Ep.* 126 (13).

[2] Hub. Luc. *op. cit., loc. cit.*

[1] Hub. Luc. *op.
cit., loc. cit.*

sixth, and Jonathan, the seventh, holding with Peter Leonis, the eighth." [1] Honorius was dead, but he had not been three days dead, for it was the early morning of 14th February; his remains, however, had *pro forma* been temporarily entombed. Here we get some details from the letter addressed afterwards to Lothair by the cardinals and bishops of the Roman Church in the interest of Gregory. The cardinals left the Monastery of St. Andrew, taking with them the body of Honorius, and proceeded, first to the Lateran Basilica where Gregory received the reverential devotion of a vast crowd of the faithful and then to the Palladium, a monastery standing in those days upon the Palatine Hill—its site now marked by the Church of Sta. Maria Pallara or San Sebastiano—where he was invested with the Papal *insignia*, the distinctive feature of which was the red mantle or *pluviale*

[2] *Ep. Card. et
Episc. S. Rom.
Eccl. ad Lothar.*,
Mans. *Concil.*,
XXI. 432 sq. ;
Liber Pontific.,
ed. cit., II. 306.

rubrum.[2] All this was over at about nine o'clock in the morning.

At mid-day Peter Leonis, "with his conspirators and kinsmen and others plainly in his pay, quickly made his way to the Church of St. Mark near the fortified palace of his brethren, indecently donned the *cappa rubra* and usurped the fictitious *insignia* of the pontificate." [3] The act of investure was performed, so Hubert of Lucca tells us, by Peter, Bishop of Porto. The letter to Didacus, Archbishop of Compostella,[4] however, records that Peter Leonis himself opened the proceedings by proposing for election one of the Cardinal Priests ; if this is true it was a mere ruse, for the candidate in question immediately proposed Peter who, according to the same writer, was unanimously elected and acclaimed Pope as Anacletus II. If we make due allowance for the language of the letter to Lothair as that of men indignant at the support given by their brethren to an entirely unworthy candidate, the two accounts are not necessarily inconsistent.

[3] *Ep. Card. et.
Episc. cit.*

[4] P. 99 *supra.*

On the following day, 15th February, Anacletus made it plain that he would appeal to the arbitrament of civil war. " Trusting in the multitude of his riches, in the power of his family and in the strength of his armed forces, he attacked the quarters of the Frangipani to which Innocent and his brethren," that is to say, the cardinals of his party, " had retired. But his hopes were disappointed, for little harm was done, and his satellites returned to him having suffered considerable losses. Thereupon, in anger and indignation, he rode with a very great following to the Basilica of St. Peter, and took possession of it by violence," making booty of such treasures as would serve his purpose, amongst others of the golden crucifix—and destroying the rest " like a sacrilegious bandit." Boso, whom we quote, would know what he was talking about, for as chamberlain to Hadrian IV he was charged with the duty of repairing these ravages. His greed not yet glutted, Anacletus proceeded to commit similar depredations in other churches, enriched with the spoil of which he bought the support of almost every family of note in Rome, with the exception of the Frangipani and the Corsi ; even the former did not long remain faithful to Innocent, for we find that by the beginning of April he had quitted their quarters for safer shelter in the Trastevere amongst his own kin. However, in 1133—such was the fickleness of the Roman nobility—when Lothair brought Innocent back to the city they rallied to his side.[1]

A little later, and on the same day, namely, 23rd February, the two Popes were consecrated, Innocent by the Cardinal Bishop of Ostia in Haimeric's titular church of S. Maria Novella, and Anacletus in the Basilica of St. Peter by Peter, Bishop of Porto.[2] The appeal was now to universal Christendom. An Apostolic Legate, Gerard Cardinal Priest, had already left Rome on 18th February with two letters from Innocent, addressed, one to Lothair and the other to the German people ; the former an invitation to come to Rome in order that he may there receive " the fulness of honour and dignity," that is to say, the imperial crown from the Apostolic See, and at the same time subdue " the enemies of the Church and of the Empire " ; the latter a confirmation of what had been written to Lothair.[3] This was followed up by the letter from the cardinals and bishops of the Romans quoted above.[4] Thus, as we cannot doubt but that St. Norbert would have acquainted him with the purport of the letter received by himself from Hubert of Lucca, Lothair would have been well informed as to the state of affairs as represented by the friends of Innocent.

By this time Rome was no longer safe for Innocent. " When he was so beset on all sides that no one could without risk of life approach his presence, he made arrangements to leave the city and cross the sea to Gaul. Accordingly he and all the brethren who held with him, except Conrad of the Sabina, whom he appointed to stay and represent him in the city, embarked in two galleys, surmounted the difficulty of passing the mouth of the Tiber and by divine help made a prosperous voyage to Pisa." Here the details seem to vary a little from those given by Anselm of Gembloux.[5] " During

[1] Boson. *Vita Innoc.*, II., *Lib. Pontific., ed. cit.*, II. 380 sq. Cf. p. 123 *infra*.

[2] Jaffé, *Regest. Pontif. Rom., an.* 1130, 7404.

[3] Mans. *Concil.*, XXI. 429 sq.

[4] P. 102 *supra*.

[5] P. 96 *supra*.

his short stay at Pisa he arranged by the Lord's assistance a truce between the Pisans and the Genoese who were then engaged in fierce warfare. This having been duly concluded, he again embarked and voyaging by way of Genoa arrived safely at St. Gilles." [1]

Meanwhile Lothair had made no sign of intervening on either side. Anacletus also had approached him and his people. He had written letters on the same day, 24th February, both to Lothair and his queen, and to the prelates, the lesser clergy and the laity of Germany and Saxony. Lothair he had begged " to love his mother the Roman Church, and comformably with the power given him by the Lord to pay her honour." The ecclesiastics and the laity he had told that " our brother cardinals, deprived of the solace of a pastor, had with a wonderful and stupendous unanimity on the part of clergy and of people elected us to the supreme dignity of the pontificate " ; upon them also he had called to pay their wonted respect to the Roman Church. Significantly enough, in neither letter does he refer explicitly to any opposition raised to his election, confining himself to a reference to a " sinister rumour " which may have reached Germany and to the pious reflection that he had " lately experienced how inscrutable are the judgements of God, how unsearchable are his ways." [2]

However, Anacletus had no intention of letting his powder get damp while he was waiting upon Providence in the person of Lothair. There was a potentate nearer home ; a man, moreover, of better mettle for his purpose. Robert of Sicily had married his sister ; [3] he would strengthen his position by making a duke into a king. And so he did, receiving in payment the recognition of himself as Pope. [4]

It has been necessary to tell at some length the story of these two elections, in order to show what was really at stake, and thus to justify the line taken in the matter by St. Bernard. As will have been observed, considerable reliance was placed by the party of Innocent upon the fact that he had been elected by the *pars sanior*. The expression occurs in the letter written by Hubert of Lucca to St. Norbert ; its use by St. Bernard [5] may perhaps be explained by information which had reached him from the Archbishop of Magdeburg, of whose judgement, we know, he thought most highly. Boso in his *Life of Innocent II* amplifies it with some emphasis into *melior et sanior pars*. Suger in his *Life of Louis le Gros* speaks of *Romanae Ecclesiae majores et sapientiores* in this connection. On the other hand, it was doubtless

[1] Boson. *op. cit.*, II. 381 ; cf. *Vita Prima*, II. i. 2.

[2] *Anacl. Antipap. Epist. et Privil.*, P.L. CLXXIX. 689 sqq.

[3] Order. Vital. *Hist. Eccl.*, XIII. 5, *P.L.* CLXXXVIII. 938.

[4] Jaffé, *Regest.*, an. 1130, 8411 ; Baron. *Annal.*, an. 1130, lii.

[5] *Ep.* 126 (13).

ST. GERMAIN, AUXERRE

urged by the party of Anacletus that strict constitutional right was on their side ; although such a claim might well have been stultified not only by the fact that they, no otherwise than their opponents, had proceeded to the election within something like twelve hours after the death of Honorius, and before he had been more than merely temporarily entombed, but also by the fact that they had taken measures of quite outrageous violence and bribery in order to crush Innocent and his friends and to render his election futile. For Haimeric a moral issue was at stake, namely, whether a man whose character inspired no confidence was to be the next occupant of the See of Peter ; he could not divest himself of responsibility in the matter, and he was prepared to meet this issue by taking the risk of violating constitutional procedure. For him the *spirit* of the constitution was first, and the rest nowhere. Moreover, he might well have felt that the credit of the constitution would suffer grave damage if men were justified in saying : *summum jus, summa injuria.* He doubtless knew that if he took this view he would have the support of St. Bernard. In a word, he staked his all upon the *pars sanior*, not merely amongst the cardinals but throughout Christendom.

By force of arms, then, Anacletus was master in Rome, but nowhere else either by material or by moral means. Letters addressed by him to Didacus, Archbishop of Compostella, on 16th April, to Cluny, to Gerard, Bishop of Angoulême, to various bishops in Aquitaine on 1st May were of little avail.[1] Indeed he begged hard ; but he stayed at home. In France Innocent passed on through the Vivarais to Cluny, and thence by way of Roanne to Clermont in Auvergne. There he held his first council, and there messengers from Lothair probably met him. Boso records— although, as Duchesne remarks, his itinerary is a little doubtful—that thence he proceeded first to Orleans, near where, in the Abbey of St. Benoît-sur-Loire, he received Louis le Gros, and then to Chartres where he received Henry I of England, whom St. Bernard had persuaded to approach him with respect. To this we refer later.[2] Before Innocent had left Rome messengers had been despatched to Gaul to apprise the bishops of what had happened, and to exhort them to condemn the schismatics and to rally to the cause of unity as represented by himself ;[3] but loyal though the Gallican Church was to the Apostolic See, they were cautious in coming to a decision and it was not until the Council of Étampes had met—probably at the end of August or early

[1] *P.L.* CLXXIX. 696 sqq.

[2] P. 109 *infra.*

[3] *Vita Prima,* II. i. 3 sq. Cf. William of Malmesbury, *Hist. Novell.,* I. 5. *P.L.* CLXXIX. 1398 sq.

in September—that they felt themselves to be sufficiently in possession of the facts to enable them openly and as a body to support Innocent. The writer of the Second Book of the *Vita Prima* would seem to attribute their hesitation to the high character of their judicial minds.[1]

It was at the Council of Étampes that St. Bernard's influence first began to be widely felt. The council was convoked by Louis, and the presence of the Abbot of Clairvaux was specially invited both by the king and by the leading prelates of France. " Fearful and trembling he came, knowing well the dangerous state of things and how weighty was the matter. But God comforted him on the way, revealing to him in a vision of the night the mighty Church singing the divine praises in perfect concord ; wherefore he had hope that peace would assuredly be the issue." When fasting and praying he took his seat with the rest, king, bishops and princes were of one mind in desiring that " God's servant should be charged with God's business, and that the decision should depend entirely upon his judgement." [2]

This expression of confidence in St. Bernard was that of " archbishops, bishops, abbots and religious," amongst whom were the Archbishops of Rheims, Sens and Bourges, and Suger, Abbot of St. Denis. The last named was subsequently sent by Louis to greet Innocent at Cluny, where Peter the Venerable and his sons had recognized him as Pope in spite of the fact that Anacletus had been a member of their *conventus*. The question at the council turned, Suger tells us, " rather upon the character of the person elected than upon the election itself." [3] Thus, we see, Haimeric's view of the matter was entirely adopted. It is not difficult to conjecture the line which St. Bernard would have taken. It may well be illustrated by a letter written by him a little later, probably in 1131, to Hildebert, Archbishop of Tours, urging him to support Innocent—his hesitation was due to a rupture between himself and Louis [4]—which characteristically expresses his sentiments. Anacletus is " the abomination of desolation standing in the holy place, to gain possession of which it set fire to the sanctuary of God. It persecutes Innocent and with him all innocence. . . . His election by the best men, the approval of the greater number and, what is yet more effectual—the witness borne to his own high character, commend Innocent in the opinion of all, confirm his pontificate." He presses the point that Innocent had left Rome in obedience to the divine precept : *If they persecute you in one city flee to another*, as St. Paul had done

[1] *Vita Prima,* II. i. 3.

[2] *Vita Prima, loc. cit.*

[3] Suger. *Vita Ludov. Grossi,* P.L. CLXXXVI. 1331.

[4] Luchaire, *Instit. Monarch. de la France,* II. 79 sq.

at Damascus.   He was not afraid to face death, but he knew   [1] *Ep.* 124.
what his life represented, and gave place to wrath.[1]   We
seem to hear St. Bernard urging these and the like pleas
at Étampes.   In the result ". one voice speaking for all proposed that Innocent should be received by all as the Supreme
Pontiff ; and all alike ratified this, singing in the customary
manner   the   divine   praises "—meaning   perhaps that the
council chanted *Te Deum*—" and, promising obedience, all
alike subscribed to the election of Innocent." [2]   [2] *Vita Prima,*
    It is unlikely that the points of canon law, concerning   II. i. 3.
either unanimity of election or the rights of the Cardinal
Clerks, came under discussion at the council.   As we have
seen, Suger, who was himself present, records that the question
was rather *de persona* than *de electione*.   Innocent, in a letter
to Lothair dated on 11th May, had stated that the cardinals
had " against his wish and in spite of his refusal unanimously
elected him." [3]   On the other hand, Anacletus had reported,   [3] Mans. *Concil.,*
in the letter to the prelates, lesser clergy and laity of Germany   XXI. 428.
and Saxony above quoted, the " wonderful and stupendous
unanimity " of clergy and people in approving his election ; [4]   [4] P. 104 *supra.*
and the tenor of the letter to Didacus, Archbishop of Com-
postella, was to the same effect.[5]   In fact, against their op-   [5] Watterich,
ponents' plea of *pars sanior*, which perhaps they derided,   *Pontif. Rom.*
being, as they were, supporters of the claim of the Cardinal   *Vitae,* II. 189.
Clerks, as *pars senilior* !—the party of Anacletus insisted
strongly upon the unanimity of his election.[6]   The evidence   [6] William of
was thus on the point of unanimity entirely contradictory.   Malmesbury,
How far the council realized this it is difficult to say ; no   *Hist. Novell.,* I.
account, however, seems to have been taken of it.   Were the   5, *P.L. loc. cit.*
question at the time in St. Bernard's mind as at all one with
which it was necessary for the council to deal, he may well
have been guided by the opinion expressed in a letter written,
probably in 1131, to Geoffrey du Loroux, that Innocent's
election was won " by the number as well as by the merit
of the electors." [7]   Boso records the names of nineteen cardi-   [7] *Ep.* 125 ; cf.
nals who supported Innocent, of whom four were Cardinal   *Ep.* 124.
Bishops.[8]   The Vatican MS. 3762 of the *Liber Pontificalis*   [8] Boson. *Vita*
of Pierre-Guillaume states that Anacletus " was elected by   *Innoc.* II., *loc.*
the fewer number of cardinals," [9] whereas the letter to Didacus   *cit.*
mentions twenty-four.[10]   If in the treatise *Of Consideration*   [9] *Liber Pontif.,*
St. Bernard is referring to the claims of the Cardinal Clerks,[11]   ed. Duchesne,
it is plain that he regarded them as presumptuous and un-   II. 449.
founded, and he might therefore have been expected to treat   [10] P. 99 *supra.*
them as unworthy of his attention when proclaiming himself   [11] S. Bern. *De*
unequivocally for Innocent at the Council of Étampes.   But   *Consid.,* IV. v.
                                                            16.

we can scarcely doubt but that in his view, as in Haimeric's, all such considerations were, in the face of what was really at stake in the crisis, namely, the scandal of the election to the Apostolic See of a man whose success was due to terrorism and corruption, of quite secondary importance. Indeed he might reasonably have held that the election of Anacletus was by canon law invalidated by the use of bribery and *force majeure*, in spite of all that could be pleaded or even proved otherwise as to the regularity of its procedure. " It is not by reason of his good life or of his virtues that he attained his dignity, or that he holds it ; he usurped it by force, by fire, by bribery," he wrote in 1132 to the bishops of Aquitaine.[1] It is plain too from the same letter that when he wrote it another point of canon law had not escaped his notice. " It holds good by the authentic decree of the Church that after a first election a second should not be held. Therefore, when the first election had been held, that which was subsequently held was not a second election but no election at all " ;[2] meaning of course that the electors of Anacletus had omitted the first constitutional step of proving that the election of Innocent was null and void, and that by failing to do so they had invalidated their procedure. Whether he dealt with this point at Étampes we do not know. But we must admire the promptitude of Haimeric in taking the earliest possible opportunity for electing Innocent, and investing him in the *insignia* of his predecessors ;[3] though we may none the less regret that this latter function had not taken place in the Vatican Basilica. On a point of constitutional procedure it might conceivably have been urged that enthronement at St. John Lateran represented no more than tenure of the diocesan episcopate of Rome, whereas enthronement at St. Peter's represented tenure of the Papacy.[4]

The action of the Council of Étampes was practically decisive so far as France was concerned ; and when Suger arrived at Cluny to greet Innocent, he was able to report to him the allegiance both of the king and of by far the larger proportion of the episcopate. Next to St. Bernard, Peter the Venerable was the Pope's best friend in France, and in the atmosphere of the great abbey and of its good and kindly abbot he would have enjoyed the refreshment which he had so hardly earned, rewarding his hosts by the consecration of their splendid basilica.[5] From Cluny the Pope's way lay to Clermont in Auvergne, where at his first council, held on 18th November, he launched an anathema against Anacletus,[6] and where messengers from Lothair seem to have reached

[1] *Ep.* 126 (8).

[2] *Op. cit., loc. cit.*

[3] P. 102 *supra.*

[4] *M.G.H. Leg.,* II. 126 ; *Liber. Pontific. ed. cit.,* II. 306, *n.* 4.

[5] Order. Vital. *Hist. Eccl.,* XIII. 9, *P.L* CLXXXVIII. 933.

[6] Mans. *Concil.,* XXI. 437 sqq.

him. At Saint-Benoît-sur-Loire near Orleans he was, as we have seen, met by Louis le Gros accompanied by the queen and their children, who paid him homage as Supreme Pontiff.[1]

And what of England? There to some extent the dice were loaded against Innocent, for Peter Leonis had been Apostolic Legate in that country, where he had succeeded in making himself generally acceptable.[2] From Orleans the Pope was conducted by Geoffrey, Bishop of Chartres, to that city, where Henry Beauclerk, in spite of strong pressure to the contrary put upon him by the English bishops, made his submission to him.[3] This result was entirely due to the influence of St. Bernard, brought to bear in a personal interview with Henry held somewhere within his own territory. The king seems to have had considerable scruples. Arnald of Bonneval reports the interview. " Of what are you afraid ? " asks the abbot. " Are you afraid of sinning by obeying Innocent ? Just consider for how many other sins you have to answer to God. Leave this one to me ; I will answer for it." [4]

The messengers from Lothair who met Innocent at Clermont on 18th November would have brought pleasant news. " A council of sixteen bishops was assembled by the king," namely, Lothair, " at Würzburg in the month of October, at which the Archbishop of Ravenna, Legate of the Apostolic See, was present, and at which Gregory who is also Innocent was chosen and confirmed as Pope by King Lothair and by all present." [5] In this, surely, we may recognize the hand of St. Norbert. At last, then, Lothair had made a move and Innocent would have been encouraged to turn his steps towards Germany. Accordingly in the following year he made his way to Liège, where he was honourably received by Lothair, his queen, many petty princes and German prelates, and where on 1st April, 1131, a council was held attended by these distinguished persons, at which the number of archbishops and bishops present amounted to twenty-five—possibly to thirty-two—and of abbots to fifty-three.[6]

Amongst these last was happily St. Bernard ; for a critical moment arrived. A cloud overshadowed the serenity of the scene when Lothair, yielding to ill-advised counsels, sought to make a condition of his support the restitution to himself and to his successors of the right of investiture with the cross and ring. The Abbot of Clairvaux, however—probably no one else could have done it—saved the situation by stoutly resisting " the importunate and wicked demand of the choleric and angry king." [7] " The Romans trembled and grew pale, thinking

[1] Suger. *Vita Ludov. Grossi*, *P.L.* CLXXXVI. 1331.

[2] Eadmer, *Historia Novor.*, VI, *P.L.* CLIX. 519 sq.

[3] P. 105 *supra.*

[4] *Vita Prima*, II. i. 4.

[5] *Annal. Magdeburg.*, an. 1130, *ap. M.G.H. Script.*, XVI. 183.

[6] *Annal. Magdeburg.*, an. 1131 ; Boson. *op. cit.*, 381 ; Anselm. Gemblac. *op. cit.*, *P.L.* CLX. 254 sq.

[7] *Ep.* 150.

that they had fallen into a greater danger at Liège than that which they had escaped at Rome." The issue looked like disaster. But St. Bernard was no defeatist. He had no notion of standing by inactive while the Concordat of Worms, which in 1122 Calixtus II had won from Henry V, a greater man than Lothair, was being torn into shreds. "The holy abbot opposed himself like a wall. Boldly resisting the king, with surprising freedom he rebuked him for his spiteful suggestion and by his amazing authority restrained him from his purpose." [1]   The incident well illustrates the low cunning, the vacillating weakness, the ungovernable temper in high places with which St Bernard was frequently confronted, and the fearless, downright fashion in which he dealt with them. The presence of a man who knew his own mind and could enforce his will contributed to the felicitous conclusion of the council. "As on the triumphal way at Rome," Innocent ascended to the Church of St. Lambert, celebrated Mass and crowned Lothair and his consort.[2]   Thence he returned to France and spent Holy Week and Easter at St. Denis.[3]   By the 9th of May he was at Rouen, for a *privilegium* granted to the Abbey of St. Denis is dated there on that day. That his faithful chancellor was at his side during all these wanderings is indicated by the words found in the letters and privileges, "by the hand of Haimeric." [4]   At Rouen he again met Henry of England, who assured him that he would not lightly abandon the purpose of supporting him which he had declared five months ago at Chartres, and clinched his bargain not only by gifts from himself, but by moving his courtiers, and even the Jews, to a similar generosity.[5]   St. Bernard was at Rouen at the time, we gather. A few days later the Pope was at Beauvais ; [6] and not long afterwards we find him at Compiègne and then at Crépy-en-Valois on his way to Auxerre, where he remained for some two months ; the first document given at Auxerre during these months bears date 26th July, and the last 24th September.[7]   From this place undoubtedly it was that he set forth to pay his memorable visit to Clairvaux.

It was the Clairvaux of the first *emplacement* in which St. Bernard entertained his distinguished guest ; bare, mean and incommodious enough would it have seemed in comparison with Cluny, the splendid church of which the Pope had consecrated in October of the previous year. It was his own wish to pay this visit ; and "most affectionately was he received, with no noisy outburst of jubilation but with restrained melody of respect. The bishops wept ; the Supreme Pontiff himself wept ; and all admired the gravity of the community,

[1] *Vita Prima,* II. i. 5.

[2] Anselm. Gemblac. *op. cit., loc. cit.*
[3] Suger. *Vita Ludov. Grossi, P.L.* CLXXXVI. 1331.
[4] Innoc. II Pap. *Epp. et Privil., P.L.* CLXXIX. 93 sq.

[5] William of Malmesbury, *Hist. Novell.,* I. 5, *P.L. loc. cit.*
[6] Innoc. II Pap., *op. cit.,* 96 sq.

[7] Innoc. II Pap., *op. cit.,* 99 sqq.

that at a moment of such festive joy the eyes of all were fixed upon the ground and nowhere strayed in wandering curiosity, but rather that with fallen lids they saw nothing, only were seen of all their guests. Nought there did a Roman see to move his greed ; the look of things was not inviting. They saw in the church but bare walls. . . . All rejoiced in the Lord and kept festivity in virtues not in victuals. . . . If a piece of fish was found it was placed before the lord Pope ; the community enjoyed the look of it and not the taste." Arnald says nothing of the feelings of the guests, beyond recording that the cardinals were favourably impressed by the behaviour of the monks in choir.[1]

Innocent had doubtless more than once found it difficult to tear himself away from the embraces of the Gallican Church, so devoted were its sons to his person and to his interests ; but France was not entire Christendom. St. Bernard, however, he would not allow to be separated from him ; and, when he repaired to Rheims for the council which he had " convoked from five kingdoms," St. Bernard accompanied him, and there not only associated with the cardinals in his counsels, but conferred with him in private.[2] It was during the course of this council, which opened on 18th October, that the Pope consecrated Louis le Jeune, his brother Philip being now defunct, as his father's successor ; a step taken on the advice of Suger and others, including St. Bernard, in view of the anxiety lest the king, whose tenure of life was precarious, should suddenly be called to his account.[3] The " five kingdoms " represented at the council would presumably have been France, Germany, Aquitaine, England and Spain, all of which are mentioned by Suger. In January of the same year, 1131, Innocent had visited the Abbey of Maurigny on the river Juine, not far from Étampes, where he is said to have met Abélard and to have consecrated an altar in honour of St. Laurence.[4] It is noteworthy that the Chronicle of Maurigny, in its Second and most valuable Book,[5] provides us with a fairly full and certainly interesting account of the proceedings of the Council of Rheims, so far as they concern us. On the opening day, Saturday, 18th October, Louis presented himself, accompanied by Raoul of Vermandois and many other nobles, ascended the daïs, kissed the Pope's feet and knelt in prayer for the soul of his departed son. In touching terms Innocent addressed him, comforting him in his bereavement, reminding him that he is God's vicegerent in his own sphere, and concluding with the appeal : " It is your duty to comfort us, strangers as we are, exiles from our

[1] *Vita Prima,* II. i. 6 sq.

[2] *Vita Prima,* II. i. 5 ; Boson. *op. cit., loc. cit.*; Jaffé, *Regesta,* I. 850 sqq.

[3] Suger. *Vita Ludov. Grossi, op. cit.,* 1332 sq.

[4] *Chron. Mauriniac., R.H.G.F.* XII. 80.

[5] *R.H.G.F.* XII. *Préf.,* iv. 5.

home, whom you were the first of all to receive honourably into your kingdom, to greet with befitting homage, to overwhelm with benefits. May God, my lord King, grant you in return everlasting reward in that city of which are spoken glorious things." The Pope then rose from his seat, began the *Paternoster*, which, " as Christian custom requires," was said in silence, absolved the soul of the departed Philip and charged the assembled archbishops, bishops and abbots to attend the consecration of Louis le Jeune on the following day. At an early hour of Sunday " the young lad of ten years old, more or less," was anointed with the holy oil of St. Remigius amidst such surroundings as many said that they had never seen the like in France. After the Pope had resumed his seat at the council the same day, letters were presented from Lothair by the hand of St. Norbert, from Henry of England by the hand of Hugh, Archbishop of Rouen, from Alphonso Ist of Aragon and Alphonso IInd of Castile by the hands of bishops of their kingdoms and—what was specially gratifying—from the monks of the Greater Charterhouse by the hand of Hugh, Abbot of Pontigny, all assuring Innocent of their obedience to his will and of their devotion to his cause.[1] It was a great day for St. Bernard, for St. Norbert and—let us not forget the faithful single-minded chancellor, who had been constant at his master's side from the early morning of the day on which he left the Monastery of St. Andrew for the Lateran Basilica, and with whom had rested almost undivided responsibility throughout—a great day for Haimeric too.

But, as we shall see, even in the West the battle was not yet won, to say nothing of the East. In France Gerard, Bishop of Angoulême, had " not up to the present ceased to curse David " with something like " the fury of a Shimei "; and one great metropolitan, Hildebert of Tours, was still allowing his complications with Louis to tie his hands.[2] St. Bernard, in his letter to Geoffrey du Loroux, might count David I amongst faithful adherents ;[3] but so long as Anacletus was alive Scotland as a whole was by no means " the land o' the leal." We find Innocent writing from Paris on 22nd April, probably in the year 1131, to William, Archbishop of Canterbury, his Apostolic Legate, enjoining him to call to amendment and, if necessary, to excommunicate, John, Bishop of Glasgow, who had " lifted up his heel against his mother the holy Church of Rome and of York, and had not feared to lead whomsoever he could into the error of schism."[4] This John we gather to have been a disturbing element, radiating disaffection amongst his brethren and moving them

[1] *Chron. Mauriniac.*, II., *op. cit.*, 162 sq.

[2] S. Bern. *Ep.* 124 ; cf. p. 106 *supra.*

[3] *Ep.* 125 ; cf. p. 107 *supra.*

[4] Innoc. II Pap. *Epp. et Privil., P.L.* CLXXIX. 90.

to rebel against the authority of their metropolitan Thomas of York, and thus indirectly against the authority of the Pope whom Thomas recognized. On 29th November of the same year Innocent wrote two letters from Auxerre ; one to John himself, reminding him that both Calixtus II and Honorius II had been obliged to rebuke him for disobedience to his metropolitan, the same Thomas of York, charging him with breach of faith in thus renewing his evil courses, and sternly bidding him to amend them ; the other letter, on the same matter and in similar terms, was addressed to all the Scottish bishops.[1] Evidently the Papal Schism was an opportunity for a fresh outbreak of insubordination North of the Tweed ; none the less was the outbreak itself an opportunity, of which Innocent promptly availed himself, of letting it be understood, on the principle of *ubi Papa, ibi Roma*, who it was that sat in Peter's Chair.

In the East there was, we may conclude, no very decisive movement in favour of Innocent ; otherwise it would have been impossible for Anacletus to claim, in a letter written about the year 1130 to some correspondent unnamed, that "the whole Eastern Church, the Churches of Jerusalem, Antioch and Constantinople are with us, visit us, and maintain friendly intercourse with us " ; on the face of it an exaggeration, but doubtless having some slender foundation of truth.[2] On the other hand, on 2nd February, 1132, Innocent wrote to Louis le Gros from Cluny saying : " We have received letters of obedience and submission from our brethren, William, Patriarch of Jerusalem, and Asquitillus, Bishop of Bethlehem."[3] If either evidence is circumstantial, it is surely the latter ; but in truth the line of communication with the East was far less secure for any occupant of the Apostolic See than it was with the remotest diocese in the West.

[1] *Op. cit.,* 115 sq.

[2] Anacl. Antipap. *Epp. et Priv., P.L.* CLXXIX. 718 ; Baron. *Annal., an.* 1131, *n.* v.

[3] Innoc. Pap. *Epp. et Priv., P.L.* CLXXIX. 119 ; Mans. *Concil.,* XXI. 401.

CHAPTER VI

THE HEALING OF THE SCHISM IN FRANCE

ST. BERNARD, foretold before his birth as the dog who " by the healing medicine of his tongue would cure the wounds of many souls," [1] had done much in various directions ; but in Aquitaine the sore was still open. Here, as so often elsewhere, the explanation is to be found in the character of one man. Gerard, Bishop of Angoulême, was on many grounds an outstanding personality ; nor was he himself unaware of the fact. " Diotrephes who loves to have the pre-eminence " is St. Bernard's description of him in a letter addressed probably in 1132 to the bishops of Aquitaine.[2] Ordericus Vitalis could speak of him as " a very learned man, of great reputation and influence in the Roman Senate," [3] that is to say, the *Curia*, referring doubtless to the fact that under four successive Popes, beginning with Paschal II and ending with Honorius II, he had filled the office of Apostolic Legate in Aquitaine. A Norman by birth, he had occupied the see of Angoulême for over forty-three years when he died in 1136.[4] Certainly ambitious and—although a good canonist—suspected of simony in the exercise of his office,[5] we may think that he had come to regard himself as possessed of a vested right in the legateship. He was a fearless man ; for when William, Count of Poitiers, of whom we shall presently hear more, was living in adultery, Gerard without hesitation " rebuked and excommunicated him and ordered him to put away his unlawful love " ; although the count was, as we learn from William of Malmesbury, a very violent person.[6] A perusal of the pages of William's *Gesta Regum Anglorum* which deal with this period would suggest that it was owing to the high credit in which Gerard stood at Rome, combined with his masterful and self-satisfied character, that the difficulties in Aquitaine arose. For instance, at the Lateran Council in 1112 he seems to have dominated the proceedings, insisting successfully that the *privilegium*—which he facetiously qualified as *pravilegium*—extorted from Paschal II by Henry V to the detriment of

[1] *Vita Prima*, I. i. 2 ; cf. p. 5 *supra*.

[2] *Ep.* 126 (1).

[3] Order. Vital. *Hist. Eccl.*, XIII. 12, *P.L.* CLXXXVIII. 954.

[4] *Op. cit., loc. cit.*

[5] *Vita Prima*, II. vi. 32.

[6] William of Malmesbury, *Gest. Reg. Angl.*, V. 439, *P.L.* CLXXIX. 1384 sq.

much that Gregory VII had achieved, should be entirely revoked.[1]

Anacletus, of course, knew all about Gerard, alike his strength and his weakness, and saw in him an instrument useful for his purpose. Obviously the first thing to do was to confirm him in his legateship. This he did in a flattering letter dated 1st May, 1130, in which he addressed him as " a son beloved above all others, whom for his uprightness now long proved our holy mother the Roman Church has chosen out and specially honoured." The bearer of the letter was presumably a Cardinal Deacon by name Gregory, who was charged to tell Gerard all about " the scandal which had arisen in the Roman Church ; so that your love for us may be able to reject lying reports and cleave undoubtingly to the true testimony." [2] But Gerard was not so simple as all that ; he knew Anacletus quite as well as Anacletus knew him. He desired above all things to retain the legateship ; but he would prefer to hold it from a better Pope than Anacletus, provided it was the winning Pope ; this he thought Innocent to be. Accordingly, " he is the first, or amongst the first, to write to Pope Innocent ; his request is for the legateship ; it is not granted. He is indignant ; he recoils from him ; he goes over to another ; and now he boasts that he is *his* legate." [3] This is St. Bernard's terse description of what happened. Innocent too knew Gerard ; *non tali auxilio !* We may imagine the fury of the Bishop of Angoulême. Can we not recognize here the hand of Haimeric ? [4] The honour was conferred upon Geoffrey, Bishop of Chartres, an intimate of St. Bernard, and " a man of great qualities " ; the same who had conducted Innocent from Orleans to Chartres for his meeting with Henry Beauclerk.[5]

But Gerard's " snake-like cunning " did not fail him. He knew how much Anacletus needed him, and how little therefore it mattered that he had in the first instance refused the legateship at his hand ; moreover, Anacletus would conjecture that he was now personally embittered against his rival Innocent. Without delay Gerard sent a humble word begging the office, swearing allegiance and pledging himself to bring others, great feudal lords and whom he could, to swear the same. The consent of Anacletus was promptly given and two Cardinal Bishops, Giles of Tusculum and Peter of Porto, were despatched ostensibly to confer the dignity upon Gerard, but in reality to assist him in stirring up disaffection against Innocent.[6] Anacletus was generous in the bestowal of his favours ; for the scope of Gerard's legateship was extended so

[1] *Op. cit.*, V. 427 sq. ; Boson. *op. cit.* 369 sq.

[2] Anacl. Antipap. *Epp. et Priv., P.L.* CLXXIX. 698.

[3] S. Bern. *Ep.* 126 (2).

[4] S. Bern. *Ep.* 126 (1).

[5] *Vita Prima*, II. i. 4, II. vi. 34, III. vi. 18 ; *Vita Secunda*, xxi. 56. Cf. p. 109 *supra*.

[6] *Vita Prima*, II. vi. 32.

as to include France and Burgundy as well as Aquitaine. " He can, if he likes, add the Medes and the Persians and the midst of the coasts of Decapolis," writes St. Bernard in derision.[1]

[1] *Ep.* 126 (4).

In the second volume of his *Spicilegium* d'Achery published a contemporary invective against Gerard, written by Arnolph, then Archdeacon of Sées and afterwards Bishop of Lisieux, which, allowing for its somewhat violent partizanship, is a valuable source of information as to the methods employed by the legate of Anacletus for poisoning minds, in particular in the monasteries, against Innocent.[2] But Gerard's great objective was to control the authority of William X, Count of Poitiers and Duke of Aquitaine, in the interests of Anacletus. We have already noticed that in a good cause he had had some success in handling this licentious and violent but rather weak potentate.[3] St. Bernard fully recognized the danger latent in this quarter. He does not approach William directly ; but by means of a letter addressed to him by Hugh, Duke of Burgundy, for the terms of which he was, we may be sure, himself responsible. This letter is dated by Mabillon about the year 1132, and a reference in it shows it to have been written after Roger of Sicily had bought his royalty ;[4] indeed, a considerable point is made of the fact that the party of Anacletus " includes the Duke of Apulia alone among princes, and that because he was got hold of by the ridiculous bribe of a crown to which he has no title."[5] When, however, this proved to be ineffectual, early in 1132 St. Bernard, accompanied by Joslen, Bishop of Soissons, at the bidding of Innocent undertook a personal visit to the Count at Poitiers, with the result that, " contrary to the expectation of many, he had the happiness of bringing back with him the peace of the Church and the joy of the whole earth."[6] But Gerard was not yet beaten to the ground.

[2] Dach. *Spicil.*, II. 336 sqq. (*nov. ed.* I. 152 sqq.) ; *R.H.G.F.* XIV. 249 sqq.

[3] P. 114 *supra*.

[4] P. 104 *supra*.

[5] *Inter S. Bern. Epp.* 127.

[6] *Ep.* 128 ; *Vita Prima*, II. vi. 36.

We infer that, so unstable and so reckless was the count— no sooner had St. Bernard passed beyond the walls of Poitiers than disturbances broke out in the city, and, headed by the dean and other dignitaries, the followers of Gerard, not content with refusing to acknowledge Innocent, laid violent hands upon his adherents, even venting their rage upon an inanimate object like the altar in the cathedral at which St. Bernard when with them had said Mass.[7] So much popular feeling having been moved to the satisfaction of Gerard, the time was now ripe for him to deprive in an entirely uncanonical fashion, as of course he knew, first Poitiers and then Limoges of their diocesans and to substitute creatures of his own.

[9] *Vita Prima*, II. vi. 36.

"Now," writes St. Bernard, in a letter to the bishops of Aquitaine already quoted, "the legate makes bishops amongst you for his Pope, so that he himself may not be the only bishop whom his Pope has. He does not supply successors to the dead, he imposes usurpers to replace the living, relying upon the power of his tyrant, using as his occasion the wickedness of princes who persecute with unrighteous hatred the bishops of their states." [1] At Poitiers William the bishop, "an honourable man," "was violently expelled, condemned by Gerard and his assistant (*sc.* the count) simply because he denied the claims of Peter (*sc.* Anacletus). They then found an ambitious fellow, noble by birth but ignoble in credit, whom, in order that they might gain both him and his family to their cause, they elected with the consent of some of the clergy, and upon whom they laid profane hands." This man was Peter of Châtellerault.[2] "Another monster like this they intruded at Limoges, a certain Randolph, Abbot of Le-Dorat," a monastery about thirty-five miles North by West of that city. Arnald does not hesitate to accuse Gerard of buying with money the support of the Count of Poitiers.[3] This grave violation on the part of William of Aquitaine of pledges, which but a few months ago he had given personally to the Abbot of Clairvaux and to Joslen of Soissons, at once brings St. Bernard to the front again. He writes to William, this time himself, in terms brief but incisive. He has been doing all he could to promote the well-being and the honour of the count in full reliance upon the fidelity of William's pledges. And now! To whose evil counsels is this *volte-face* due? "He shall suffer the penalty for it, whoever he may be. Would that they were cut off who disturb you! Return, I beg of you, lest you too—which God forbid!—be cut off with them. Return, I say, and recall your friends to peace with you and the clergy to the Church." [4] He would have the count realize that in being advised by Gerard he is not only depriving dioceses of their rightful pastors, but himself of his real friends. The visit paid to William at Poitiers having taken place early in 1132, this letter would probably have been written not many months later in the same year, for events were moving rapidly; Gerard was a fast as well as a furious fighter.

It was perhaps at this stage that St. Bernard wrote what was of the nature of an encyclical letter to the bishops of Aquitaine.[5] In a brilliant apostrophe addressed to Gerard he ridicules unsparingly his ambitious vanity. " So then we are to conclude that Rome cannot have a Pope unless you are

[1] *Ep.* 126 (3).

[2] Dach. *Spicil.* (*nov. ed.*), I. 160; *R.H.G.F.* XIV. 259.

[3] *Vita Prima*, II. vi. 33.

[4] *Ep.* 128.

[5] Cf. p. 101 *supra.*

legate ? How do you happen to have this privilege in the Church of God ? Who gave you this prerogative in the heritage of Christ ? It cannot be said, can it, that you possess the sanctuary of God by hereditary right ? So long as you could have any hope of obtaining the favour of Innocent by that shameless and impudent request which you made to him, you wrote of him as a saint and as Pope. How is it that now you accuse him of being a schismatic ? Did his sanctity and his Papacy vanish with that vain hope of yours ? It is astonishing that within so brief a space of time sweet and bitter water should come from the same fount ! Yesterday it was : ' Catholic,' ' Holy,' ' Supreme Pontiff ' ; to-day it is : ' bad man,' ' schismatic,' ' riotous fellow.' Yesterday it was : ' the Holy Father Innocent ' ; to-day it is just : ' Gregory, Cardinal Deacon of Sant' Angelo.' " [1] However, the bishops do not need much telling about him. " You have," St. Bernard writes, " certainly learnt by your own experience what a savage, cunning enemy has risen up against you." [2] And for the present the Abbot of Clairvaux was obliged to leave it at that. But his words were not without effect, for when shortly afterwards the see of Bordeaux fell vacant and Gerard proposed to occupy it himself, the Bishops of Saintes, Périgueux and Poitiers addressed themselves to their metropolitan, Vulgrin, Archbishop of Bourges, begging him to nullify such an election. [3] Although the count had not yet formally made his submission to Innocent, the cause of Anacletus was now practically doomed in Aquitaine.

We shall remember that, as we know from his correspondence, [4] Innocent had made Auxerre—Auxerre, with its " quiet curve of river below," its " expression peaceful rather than radiant "—his headquarters during the months of August and September in 1131. Soon after the middle of October he had proceeded to Rheims. The Council of Rheims, which opened on 18th October, had not been the end of " the battle of the tiaras," but so far as concerned France it had brought victory within sight ; and on no reasonable grounds did it seem necessary for Innocent to remain any longer North of the Alps. However, his return journey was sufficiently leisurely. He was in Paris at Martinmas ; and then from 28th November to 30th December such of his letters as are extant are dated at Auxerre. On 18th January, 1132, we find him at Autun. None of the correspondence of this period gives any impression of a writer doubtful of his position, harried or otherwise perturbed. The letters for the most part deal with matters of ordinary occurrence, matters quite un-

[1] *Ep.* 126 (4).

[2] *Ep.* 126 (14).

[3] *Gall. Christ.*, II. 49.

[4] P. 110 *supra*.

connected with the Schism. For example, on 28th November, 1131, he had written from Auxerre to Héloïse, Abbess of Le-Paraclet, confirming her house in the possession of its property on condition of a small annual tribute to the Lateran Palace. In this, as in other letters having a contractual character, we read " by the hand of Haimeric." At Candlemas the Pope writes from Cluny to Louis le Gros in terms of great friendliness, telling him of his safe arrival there, and sending greetings to " our beloved daughter Queen Adelaide " and to " our most loving son King Louis," that is to say, Louis le Jeune, and to the rest of the boys. The time spent at Auxerre, briefly interrupted by the visits to Clairvaux, to Rheims and to Paris, had been a rest-cure ; the strain of conflict was in considerable measure relaxed and its effects were passing away.[1]

Until the middle of February Innocent remained at Cluny, whence he journeyed by way of Lyons, Vienne and Valence to Avignon, as though making for the sea at St. Gilles. He would seem, however, to have decided in the end to cross the Alps, and on 30th March he was at Gap. On 10th April he kept Easter at Asti, where six days later he wrote to Walter, Archbishop of Ravenna, doubtless with some sense of relief and gratitude : " *Transalpinati sumus!* "[2] At the end of May he was at Piacenza, where, alas, disillusionment awaited him. Here on 13th June he held his fourth council, summoning to it the bishops and other prelates of Lombardy, of the Province of Ravenna and of the March of Ancona.[3] The *Acta* of this council have unfortunately disappeared, but the correspondence of Innocent during the succeeding few weeks reveals paternal dealings, accepted in a filial spirit, not only with the Church of Piacenza but with those of Novara, Bergamo, Brescia, Lucca and Aquileia, as well as with religious houses in several of these cities.[4] Nevertheless the Pope, one conjectures, was a little restless. He was expecting the arrival of Lothair with an army which would at least impress the people of Italy and police the Holy City in his interests.[5] From 14th July to 4th November he seems to have moved about between Cremona, Brescia and Modena, avoiding Milan, where feeling was hostile both to himself and to Lothair who had a rival of his own with whom to reckon, Conrad of Hohenstaufen. On the last-named day Innocent was again at Piacenza, a little to the East of which, at Roncaglia, he met Lothair a few days later. But with what mean array had the king at last arrived ! He had no choice in the matter, so Otto of Freising tells us ; the troubles in his own kingdom restricted his resources available for the

[1] Innoc. II Pap. *Epp. et Priv., P.L.* CLXXIX. 114 sqq.

[2] *Op. cit.*. 136.

[3] Boson. *op. cit.*, 381 ; Jaffé, *Regest.*, I. 856 sq.

[4] Innoc. II Pap. *Epp. et Priv., P.L.* CLXXIX. 139 sqq. ; Jaffé, *op. cit.*, 857 sq.

[5] Boson. *op. cit.*, *loc. cit.*

¹ Otton. Frising.
Chron., VII. 18,
M.G.H. Script.,
XX. 257.

² Ep. 139.

³ Boson. op. cit.,
loc. cit.

⁴ Otton. Frising.
op. cit., loc. cit.

⁵ Mans. Concil.,
XXI. 410 sq.

⁶ Boson. op. cit.,
loc. cit.; Jaffé,
Regest., 7605
sqq.

⁷ P. 118 supra.

⁸ Pp. 46 sqq.
supra.

⁹ P. 104 supra.

service of the Pope.[1] St. Bernard, writing to him about the year 1135, could speak gratefully of his "fearful and laborious journey," regarding it as only by special divine favour that "before so diminutive a host the earth trembled and was still."[2]

The people of the Lombard plains were not impressed by the "general conference upon the state of the Church and of the Empire" held in their midst by the respective chiefs of each.[3] Lothair with his queen and a few lords spiritual and temporal, escorted by some fifteen hundred fighting men, was in their eyes "ridiculous and despicable."[4] It is to be feared that certainly at this stage the material arm was of little avail to the spiritual, even that the poverty of its external trappings tended to discount the value of such moral support as the personal presence of Lothair might otherwise have afforded. Nevertheless Innocent, his spirit undaunted, continued to advance. We can trace him at Bologna on 13th December[5] on his way to Pisa, where after crossing the Apennines he arrived about the middle of January, 1133.[6]

Where, meanwhile, was St. Bernard? Perhaps the last occasion upon which Innocent had seen him was in Paris at the Martinmas of 1131.[7] But the Abbot of Clairvaux, we know, had not been idle during the interval. The year 1132 had been for him a period of hard campaigning, so far successful as that, although William, Count of Poitiers, had as yet made no formal submission to Innocent, Gerard of Augoulême, whose tool he was, had now little credit left to his account in Aquitaine. And further, in that same year four daughters of Clairvaux had been founded, Longpont, Vaucelles, Moreruela, and above all, Rievaulx, every one of which was a stronghold for the cause of the rightful Pope.[8] So then St. Bernard well might now be recalled to the presence of Innocent. And, indeed, the situation in Italy was critical. The peace made by the instrumentality of the Pope between the Pisans and the Genoese in February, 1130,[9] had proved to be but patchwork. The rivalry between these two maritime powers was of age-long standing, complicated by ecclesiastical jealousies in Corsica and in Sardinia, which islands were choice bones of contention for the sea-dogs of the littoral. Innocent, recognizing with considerable acumen, not only that the ecclesiastical problem was as so frequently in those days fundamental, but that the solution of it belonged properly to his own sphere, placed the sees in Sardinia and all except three of the sees in Corsica under the metropolitanate of the Archbishop of Pisa ; at the same time conciliating the Genoese by separating them from the Province of Milan, granting their city metropolitan rank and assigning to it the remaining three sees in Corsica as its suffragans.[1] In this skilful arrangement it is more probable than not that St. Bernard had a hand. The importance of it lay in the fact that, the forces of Roger of Sicily, alike by land and by sea, being at the disposal of Anacletus, concerted action on the part of the Pisans and the Genoese was for Innocent the key to success. The Genoese perhaps constituted the more difficult element of the two ; and it was thought well that St. Bernard should visit them, in order if possible by his personal intervention to bring about a better state of things. This visit was paid early in 1133, probably in February. A letter written to them about a year later reveals the phenomenal success which attended his efforts. " The Church in its sore straits, the Church whose messenger I was, proved very soon that my visit to you last year was by no means fruitless. . . . Oh, those joyous days, alas, too few ! I shall never forget them. . . . I brought a message of peace, and when I found the sons of peace my peace rested upon them. I had gone forth to sow seed, not my own seed but God's seed ; and when the good seed fell on good ground, it brought forth fruit a hundredfold ; yea, seasonable fruit. The yield came quickly because the need was great." [2]

We feel at once that with the arrival of St. Bernard in Italy there arrives the driving force. Next it is the Pisans' turn to feel and to respond to its urge. In a letter written to them at about the same date we read : " Pisa has become Rome ; and of all the cities of the earth, it is raised to the level of the Apostolic See. This did not happen by chance or by the counsel of man ; rather by divine providence, by God's good favour ; God who loves them that love him and who said to his anointed Innocent : ' Dwell at Pisa and blessing I will bless it. Here will I dwell, for I have a delight therein.' " How well he knows the method of approach to the wills of these sturdy fighters with their stiff backs, their independent spirit. " At my suggestion," he goes on to say, " the steadfastness of Pisa yields no whit to the malice of the tyrant of Sicily ; it neither quails at threats, nor is corrupted by bribes, nor is deceived by craft." [3] This was precisely the result desired, and St. Bernard had achieved it. Genoa and Pisa were of one heart and of one mind ; and Roger, Anacletus's toy-king, was the laughing-stock of them both.

Innocent's *privilegium* addressed to Syrus, Bishop of Genoa, raising him to the dignity of a metropolitan and bestowing upon him the *pallium*, was dated at Grosseto on

[1] Boson. *op. cit.*, 381 sq. ; Innoc. II Pap. *Epp. et Priv., P.L.* CLXXIX. 174 sqq.

[2] *Ep.* 129.

[3] *Ep.* 130.

19th March ; and apparently during the course of the next few days terms of peace between the Genoese and the Pisans were formally concluded at Corneto.[1]   Shortly afterwards the Pope and Lothair held a conference at Calcinaja, a place East of Pisa on the right bank of the Arno, whence they advanced to Viterbo.   There is some evidence that here they were met by St. Norbert, and that discussions took place on a matter in which Anacletus had made a cunning move.[2]   " There are still some people," writes St. Bernard in his encyclical letter to the bishops of Aquitaine, " who, I know not with what contentious importunity and importunate contentiousness, protest that the question should be submitted to the judgement of the world, and maintain that everybody should receive the same sentence as a mere handful like themselves."   This meant that Anacletus was conscious that his cause was now irretrievably losing ground, and wanted both parties to be judged in the wrong.   The snare was too clumsily set to deceive St. Bernard.   He was the last man to allow the question to be re-opened after, as he held, Rome had spoken. " This," he replies, " is the business of the Universal Church, not of an individual.   You are calumniating your own mother —per impossibile, of course—and thus you are digging a pit into which you will fall yourselves, making a noose to catch yourselves so that you will not be able to return to the bosom of that mother.   However, a man who wishes to break with a friend is never at a loss for an opportunity.   Let that be ! You do not suppose, do you (I speak as a man), that God is going to change his mind, to revoke his sentence, to assemble a council from the ends of the earth ? "[3]   What sort of judges would such a council of the world be, he wonders. Partizans, of course, who do not meet in a judicial but in a litigious spirit.

As Innocent and Lothair approach Rome the sense of their lack of sufficient material force weighs upon them.   St. Bernard appeals to Henry Beauclerk, reminding him of his adhesion to the Pope pledged at Chartres in January, 1131 : " We are making God our friend by the justice of our cause ; we are scaring the enemy by our soldierly array ; but for this latter purpose, necessary as it is, we yet lack adequate means. You will know well enough what it is that is wanted to put the crown upon your splendid and gratifying reception of our lord Pope Innocent."[4]   There followed, on 30th April, somewhere near the Church of Sant' Agnese Fuori on the Via Nomentana, an encouraging episode.   They were met and welcomed by a considerable number of great Roman nobles,

[1] Innoc. II Pap. *Epp. et Priv., P.L. loc. cit.* ; Jaffé, *Regest.*, 7613, 7890.

[2] *Vita Norb. Ep. Magd., M.G.H. Script.*, XII. 701 sq.

[3] *Ep.* 126 (11 sq.).

[4] *Ep.* 138.

including the Frangipani,[1] headed by Theobald, Prefect of the
City, Innocent proceeding to the Lateran Palace and Lothair
pitching his camp upon the Aventine Hill. Meanwhile the
Genoese and the Pisans from the sea took possession of
Civitá Vecchia and—supposing that we read *Marmorata* and
not *Maritima*, a suggested emendation—would seem to have
penetrated up the Tiber, and established themselves on the
left bank between the Monte Testaccio and the Aventine,
quite close to Lothair's camp.[2]

But this was not an occupation of Rome. The Pierleoni
were sheltered in their own quarters, the Theatre of Marcellus,
which they had long ago converted into an almost impregnable
fortress at the foot of the Tarpeian Rock, commanding the
approach to the Trastevere by the bridges of the Isola San
Bartolomeo. Innocent was cut off from the Vatican Basilica
on this side. It is probable that neither Lothair, nor any
other stranger to the city, was prepared for the slaughter
involved in an attempt to fight a way round higher up the
river ; their adversaries, adepts at street-warfare, knew every
inch of the ground. And Anacletus did not move. He did
not, however, abandon his scheme of some arrangement with
Lothair which would annul the election both of himself and
of Innocent. After entrusting Peter, Bishop of Porto, with full
authority to negotiate in the matter, he seems to have gone
back upon his word, to the great displeasure of Lothair, who
publicly stigmatized him as a traitor, faithless to God and to
man.[3]

There can be little doubt but that Lothair was growing
impatient ; he was beginning to realize that he was something
like stalemated. The summer heat was approaching ; his
queen, Richinza, was with him ; his own affairs awaited
attention at home ; in particular he had yet to reckon with
his rival, Conrad of Hohenstaufen. As regards this last point,
if he returned to Germany as crowned Emperor, his expedition
would not have been entirely fruitless. But there was no
access to the Vatican Basilica, the proper place for such a
ceremony. On the advice of St. Norbert the Lateran Basilica
was chosen to serve the purpose, and there on 4th June
Innocent placed the imperial crown upon his head [4] on the
express condition that he observed the concordat as to investitures, made at Worms in 1122 and confirmed by himself
unwillingly enough at Liège on 1st April, 1131.[5]

Shortly afterwards St. Bernard left Rome for Clairvaux ;
not, we may be sure, despairing of the issue, but his sojourn
in the city would have revealed to him the local conditions as

[1] Cf. p. 103 *supra.*

[2] Boson. *op. cit.*, 382.

[3] Lothar. III *Constit., M.G.H. Leg.*, IV. (1), 167.

[4] Boson. *op. cit., loc. cit.*

[5] *Vita Norb. Archiep. Magd., M.G.H. Script.*, XII. 701 sq. Cf. pp. 109 sq. *supra.*

¹ S. Bern. *De Consid.*, IV. ii. 2.

he had not known them before. This " people, savage and intractable up to this very day," ¹ could not be handled like the rest of the world. Innocent's presence during the past six weeks, supported by Lothair now crowned Emperor and by the Genoese and the Pisans ; the welcome accorded by the Prefect of the City and other leading notables ; all this had been of value as a demonstration in force. Moreover, his duties at Clairvaux would claim his personal attention ; and above all, the position in Aquitaine was not yet sufficiently secure so long as the Count of Poitiers was not formally and irrevocably committed to the cause of Innocent ; for Gerard of Angoulême might well be expected to maintain his grip upon that weak prince unto the very last. Meanwhile the Pierleoni might for the while be left to exhaust their strength on the spot upon the Genoese, or the Pisans, or whom they would. As a fact Lothair lingered on until August when, in

² Jaffé, *Geschichte cit.*, 135 sq. ; Boson. *op. cit.*, 382.
³ Anacl. Antipap. *Epp. et Priv., P.L.* CLXXIX. 723.

view of the fevers of the season ² and, if we may believe Anacletus, " compelled by divine aid co-operating (with the Pierleoni) to retire in shame and ignominy and with great slaughter of his followers," ³ he set out for Freising in Bavaria. The Pierleoni being thus left free to patrol the city after their fashion, which meant death to anyone not of their party, no other course remained open to Innocent than a second time to take to flight ; and therefore in September, " lest his presence should add to the fury of that savage beast,

⁴ *Vita Prima,* II. ii. 8.

he returned again to Pisa " ⁴ by sea.

During St. Bernard's absence a disturbing incident bearing directly upon the Schism had occurred in a great city of France. The see of Tours had by the death of Hildebert in

⁵ *Gall. Christ.,* XIV. 81 sq.

February or March, 1133, fallen vacant.⁵ What followed was probably due to the fact that Hildebert had hesitated up to and beyond the last moment to declare himself for Innocent. Geoffrey, Count of Tours, with a high hand expelled the chapter from the city, precisely for what reason it is difficult to say. When they met, elsewhere than in their own cathedral, to elect a successor to the vacancy, two parties revealed themselves. One party, the other protesting, elected entirely uncanonically a young monk of Fontaines-les-Blanches, a Benedictine abbey in the neighbourhood, by name Philip, nephew of Hildebert's predecessor Gilbert. Now Philip was well known to St. Bernard as an admirable monk. After his election, however, he went off incontinent to Anacletus, who confirmed the action of the electors, ordained him priest,

⁶ Horst. et Picard. *Not. in S. Bern. Ep.* 151.

for he was no farther advanced than the diaconate, and consecrated him bishop.⁶ When this news reached St. Bernard at Viterbo in April he was greatly distressed. He at once writes to Philip, who is still at Rome. He evidently fears lest, surrounded as he is by the partizans of the antipope, Philip may be tempted to ridicule the writer's grief. In terms of affection and touching simplicity he reminds him that the grief is more than personal. " I am telling you of the Church's grief," he writes, " the Church who cherished you in her bosom as a budding lily flourishing with heavenly gifts. Who would not then have acclaimed you as a youth of good hope, of excellent disposition ? Alas, the fairest colour changes ! Oh, of how great a hope is France defrauded, France who begat you and nourished you ! " We note here with interest, and perhaps with some surprise, the unmistakable reminiscence of the *Heautontimorumenos* of Terence (*quanta de spe decidi*, II. iii. 9, IV. viii. ɴ), one of very many proofs of St. Bernard's Classical culture.[1] " Please," he adds, " reply and tell me, whatever it may be, just what you think of my remarks, so that I may know what to do ; I mean, whether to grieve more or to grieve less for you." [2]

[1] *Appendix.*

[2] *Ep.* 151.

But Philip made no answer ; he returned to Tours and took possession of the see. The better-advised party in the chapter thereupon elected a certain Hugh, who was consecrated at Le-Mans by the suffragans of the province. Such evident disfavour proved all too sufficiently the hopelessness of Philip's case, and he fled from Tours taking with him—to his shame be it said—the valuables both of his office and of the cathedral treasury ; we think that he must have sadly deteriorated during his short stay in Rome from the " youth of good hope," as St. Bernard knew him. Hugh's reception in the city was not entirely cordial—for Philip had also learnt in Rome how to win credit with the populace—but by 1st July he would seem to have been established firmly enough to exercise the jurisdiction of the see.[3]

But this was not the end of the matter. Innocent, when the election of Hugh was submitted for his approbation, quite rightly felt that it was impossible for him to act upon what was really an *ex parte* statement, and entrusted St. Bernard with Apostolic authority to institute an inquiry and adjudicate between the two claimants to the see. The Abbot of Clairvaux convoked both parties at Blois, which was neutral ground. The Chapter of Tours, the suffragans of the province and the abbots of the diocese were present in support of Hugh ; on the other side were the partizans of Philip. St. Bernard had personally, but ineffectually, invited Philip, whom he had met a few days earlier at Cambrai. Although in such case his

[3] Horst. et Picard. *Not.,* *loc. cit.* ; *Gall. Christ.,* XIV. 83.

presence was not material, his supporters objected that it was, and tried to bring about the postponement of the question on the ground of his absence.   When they were over-ruled they left the assembly, insisting upon a direct appeal to Rome—the old abuse—in spite of St. Bernard's Apostolic credentials. In the result Philip's election was nullified by St. Bernard. Hugh's election, as having taken place elsewhere than at Tours—probably at Le-Mans, where he was consecrated— being of doubtful regularity, was referred to the Pope.   St. Bernard's letter to Innocent, covering the formal report of the proceedings, indicates that Philip and his supporters may be expected to endeavour to corrupt the authorities at Rome. " The spirit of Gilbert," he writes, " has revived, they say, in Philip, his nephew after the flesh and the inheritor of his ambition. . . . Already once or twice this despiser of the Apostolic mandate has sought to evade justice by deceit, and now again he none the less presents himself with brazen face before the bar of equity.   To whom is it not quite plain that here is a man who, simply despairing of the justice of his cause, intends to use the resources of mammon against the

¹ *Ep.* 150 ; cf.
Ep. 431.

tower of strength ? " ¹   He would put the Pope upon his guard, and at the same time delicately remind him of his duty. As the Vicar of Christ he is the *turris fortitudinis a facie inimici* (Ps. lx. 4) ;   this implication is lost by translation.   However, Philip took good care to keep out of Innocent's way. Anacletus, his Pope, solaced him with the Archbishopric of Taranto, where doubtless Roger of Sicily would have protected his interests for the time.   His later history strikingly illustrates St. Bernard's care for the one lost sheep.   In 1139 he was degraded by Innocent, and as a simple deacon became a monk at Clairvaux, where he was prior at the time when the

² S. Bern. *Ep.*
257; Mabill.
ad loc.

saint who had sought and saved him died.²

A double incident, ghastly in its tragic details, occurred not long afterwards to tear the heart of the Abbot of Clairvaux ; no less than two murders in the ranks of the higher clergy. Murders were at any time only too possible in those days ; but such as these reflect strongly the lack of discipline, the spirit of disorder which inevitably ran riot during the Papal Schism.   Yet they played their part in its healing, for they served to reveal the moral recklessness, the social anarchy inherent in a state of things which might otherwise have seemed to be no more than the extension of the perennial Roman faction-fighting over a rather larger area than was usual.

We know that St. Bernard some four years earlier, about

1129, had played an important part in the reformation of the Chapter of Notre-Dame-de-Paris, strongly supporting the Bishop Stephen of Senlis in the introduction of the Canons Regular of St. Victor; a result which was achieved in the teeth of the opposition of Louis le Gros.[1] Thomas, the Prior of St. Victor, had for long borne the brunt of the odium attaching to this proceeding. The enemies of reform in meanly striking at him struck indirectly at St. Bernard and Stephen, in whose intimate counsels he was. A man of irreproachable probity himself, the abuse which appears to have displeased him most was the venality with which the Archdeacon of Paris, a certain Theobald Notier, discharged his office; for so-called justice in the archidiaconal court high fees had to be paid which weighed heavily upon the clergy. To remedy this abuse Thomas of St. Victor proposed wise administrative reforms. St. Bernard, in a letter to Innocent, tells him of the effects of this. " When he (Theobald) found himself opposed by blessed Thomas, a lover and defender of justice, because of the illegal exactions which on the score of his archidiaconate it had for some time quite improperly been allowed him to lay upon the clergy, he hated him so much that he was wont to threaten that he would murder him. Let him say, if he can, what else could have happened than that his nephews should in the end have laid impious hands upon this saint of the Lord."[2]

Stephen of Senlis reports the tragedy to the Pope. " A religious, Master Thomas Prior of St. Victor, obeying the law of charity, on a journey which piety had called him to undertake, engaged upon a holy work in the company of holy men on the Lord's day, was on my breast and in my arms by ungodly men cruelly brained, obedient unto death. . . . For the calamity which I suffer to smite your paternal heart it is sufficient, I think, that I tell you the simple facts."[3] Stephen was on his way back to Paris after paying an official visit to a convent of nuns at Chelles, and it was, significantly enough, close to the *castellum* of Stephen de Garlande at Gournay-sur-Marne that the murder was committed. The company, unarmed out of respect for the sanctity of the day—it was Sunday, 20th August—included, in addition to the Bishop of Paris and Thomas, several notable religious and secular clergy. The miscreants, Theobald Notier's nephews, were so desperate that they threatened the bishop himself with the sword if he did not go on his way without more ado. Instead of returning to Paris Stephen betook himself to Clairvaux, whence he wrote to the Apostolic Legate Geoffrey, Bishop of Chartres, begging him to come to him there. This letter supplies us

[1] Pp. 197 sqq. *infra.*

[2] *Ep.* 158.

[3] *Inter* S. Bern. *Epp.* 159.

[1] Steph. Paris. Episc. *Ep. ap.* Horst. et Picard. *Not. in S. Bern. Ep.* 158.

with a graphic description of what took place.[1] The letter to Innocent cited above was probably written at the same time and at the same place ; both letters would, in such case, have been submitted to St. Bernard.

The latter, fully convinced on the point, took immediate steps to ensure that the responsibility was laid upon the real culprit. Knowing that the Archdeacon of Paris was capable of disowning his agents, and anticipating that at the earliest opportunity he would try to disarm justice by personally exculpating himself in the presence of Innocent, he writes to the Pope. " This man asks : ' Did I kill him ? ' ' No ; you did not do the actual deed yourself. Your people did it, and they did it on your account. Whether it was also done by your means, let God consider and judge. If you are excusable, you whose teeth are spears and arrows, whose tongue is a sharp sword—then the Jews are not to be blamed for the death of Christ, for they were very careful to keep their own hands off him.' " [2] St. Bernard was not the less insistent because he had probably already heard of the other murder. That Innocent may know what manner of man he is, he fiercely apostrophizes Theobald : " You villain, do you think that the seat of supreme equity is a cave of robbers or a den of lions ? " Has he the effrontery to betake himself to the Apostolic See dripping with his brother's gore, licking his chops as a whelp returning to the dam after a foray ? " If he seeks a place for repentance, that is not to be denied him ; but if all he asks is a hearing of his case, I pray you let it be the kind of hearing that Moses gave to the worshippers of the calf, or that Phineas gave to the fornicating Israelite, or Matathias to the devil-worshippers ; or, to propose for your example one of your predecessors, the kind of hearing that Ananias and Sapphira got from blessed Peter."

[2] *Ep.* 158.

The other murder was that of Archibald, Sub-Dean of Orleans. It was the climax of a long period of unrest. In his letter to Innocent, covering the report of the proceedings taken at Blois against Philip the intruder at Tours, St. Bernard refers to " the disturbers of the Church of Orleans." [3] Several letters published by d'Achery in the third volume of his *Spicilegium*, in particular a letter written by Archibald himself to Henry, Archbishop of Sens, tell us who was the instigator of this disturbance.[4] A certain John had apparently usurped the Archdeaconry of Orleans during the vacancy of the see. When Archibald and others opposed this irregularity, they suffered grave injuries, including the spoiling of their goods. Reading between the lines we infer that they were

[3] *Ep.* 150.

[4] Dach. *Spicil.,* III., 488 sq. (*nov. ed.*).

made the victims of mob-law. The church itself was polluted by blood and many other sacrileges, and the whole state of affairs reflected gravely, so it was urged, upon the authority of the Pope. Geoffrey, Bishop of Chartres, also wrote to the Archbishop of Sens to the same effect. It is not improbable that John looked to Louis le Gros for some countenance in his intrusion. However, the matter was reported to Innocent and he commissioned Geoffrey and Stephen of Senlis, Bishop of Paris, to deal with it. The rescript makes it plain that the Pope had as yet no news of the murder. It is dated at Piacenza on 5th November.[1] Two months later, on 8th January, 1134—other years are suggested but we incline to follow Luchaire—he was aware of what had happened, for another rescript is addressed at Pisa on that day to the same persons, instructing them to bring the murderers to repentance, with a view to their being absolved from excommunication on making satisfaction to the relatives of their victim and to the Church of Orleans, which owing to the scandal given had been laid under an interdict. The rescript tells us that a certain Geoffrey, presumably the ringleader, had presented himself before the *Curia* at Pisa, and sworn to make satisfaction and to do his utmost to bring his fellows to the same mind.[2] No mention is made of John the real offender. It would seem that St. Bernard was not very well satisfied. He writes to the Pope in terms which indicate that the murder of Archibald had preceded that of Thomas of St. Victor; and evidently he knew something of the presence of the ringleader Geoffrey at Pisa ; indeed, he implies that if John was not there himself, he may be suspected of having made Geoffrey his stalking-horse. " The blood of Archibald Sub-Dean of Orleans has gained force (in its cry for vengeance). For, lo and alas, as the prophet says (Hos. iv. 2), *blood has mingled with blood* and united cries to you therefore the more urgently from France. . . . If, I say, the vigour of the Church spares John and Theobald Notier . . . who does not see what will follow ? To how many of the clergy will not the impunity of these men, against right and against law as it is, bring promotion gained by fear and not by merit ? "[3] The course of events in this case is a little difficult to unravel ; and we cannot say precisely how the matter ended.

The Pope, perhaps more fully informed in this instance, took stronger measures against the murderers of Thomas of St. Victor. On 16th November, 1133, he writes from Pisa to the Archbishops of Rheims and Sens and the suffragans of their provinces. " What profit is it to France," he asks,

[1] Mans. *Concil.*, XXI. 401.

[2] Dach. *Spic.*, III. 493 sq. (*nov. ed.*) ; cf. Horst. et Picard. *Not. in S. Bern. Ep.* 150.

[3] *Ep.* 161.

"that it should not be defiled by horrible monstrosities "—
meaning such schismatics as Anacletus and his partizans—
"or polluted by heresy, if it is befouled by the bloodshed of
holy priests ? " He is astonished that under the rule of his
"very dear, illustrious and glorious son Louis," whose duty it
is to punish murder, such a crime should have been attempted.
The utmost penalties both of ecclesiastical and of criminal
law must be meted out in such a case. The results of impunity
would be disastrous. At the peril of their souls his corre
spondents will overlook any material facts. Canon law will
instruct them how to act. Finally, they should see that the
body of the victim, a man who lived and died in obedience to
his bishop, receives burial with the highest honours in his own
church.[1] It is noticeable that Innocent is displeased by the
dangerous and reprehensible laxity shown in dealing with the
murder of Archibald. "If," he writes, "your zeal for vengeance had burned more fiercely against its fellow and similar
crime, this more recent outrage, its repetition, would not have
been committed."

We shall remember that Stephen of Senlis had written
from Clairvaux a letter to the Apostolic Legate, Geoffrey of
Chartres, fully reporting what had happened at Gournay-sur-
Marne.[2] Before the end of the year a council convoked by
Geoffrey and the Archbishops of Rheims and Sens assembled
at Jouarre, an Abbey of Black Monks near La-Ferté-sous-
Jouarre on the Marne between Meaux and Château-Thierry.
Amongst those present were the Archbishops of Rouen and
Tours, Theobald of Champagne and the Count of Nevers,
William II.[3] It would seem that the metropolitans were
not particularly moved to take such strong measures as the
circumstances demanded. The absence of Louis from the
council was noticeable, and the impression may have prevailed that he was at least a little indifferent as to whether
such ecclesiastics as Archibald of Orleans or Thomas of St.
Victor were alive or not. The language of Innocent's letter to
the Archbishops of Rheims and Sens above cited suggests no
less.[4] The sound moral pressure came from the religious
present, in particular from St. Bernard and Peter the Venerable, backed by a letter addressed to the council by Hugh,
Bishop of Grenoble, and Guy, Prior of the Greater Charterhouse, men always to be found on the right side.[5] But even
thus the murderers of Thomas were so indulgently treated
that the Abbot of Cluny wrote to Innocent begging him to
impose heavier penalties ; [6] and with some effect, for the Pope
deprived Theobald Notier and his accomplices of all ecclesias-

[1] Dach. *Spic.*,
III. 493 (*nov.
ed.*) ; Jaffé,
Regest., 7636.

[2] Pp. 127 sq.
supra.

[3] Hug.Gratian.
Episc. et
Guidon. Major.
Carth. Prior.
Epist. ap. Horst.
et Picard. *Not.
Fus. in S. Bern.
Ep.* 158.

[4] P. 129 *supra.*

[5] Horst. et
Picard. *Not. Cit.*

[6] Petr. Ven.
Epp. Lib. I. 17.

tical benefices and laid under interdict any place to which they might betake themselves until they had done adequate penance.[1]

As regards John and the murderers of Archibald of Orleans the issue, as has been observed, is a little difficult to discover.[2] Nothing seems to have been said about them at Jouarre ; and the personal pleading of their ringleader Geoffrey before the *Curia* at Pisa must be concluded to have had some measure of success. In any case, neither prompt nor summary justice was exacted, for, possibly so long as nearly two years afterwards, in 1135, St. Bernard writes to ask Innocent : " How long is that poor Church of Orleans going to make its vain appeal to the heart of the father of orphans, of the judge of the widow ? "[3] It was not until a new bishop, Elias, was at last enthroned in 1136 that the distracted diocese knew peace.[4]

Gerard of Angoulême, excommunicate, disowned by the suffragans and by the greater number of the faithful of the province, was however now in material possession of the see of Bordeaux, to which he had never been promoted by any pretence of election. He had the misfortune to spend, by way of an interlude, some little time in ward at the hands of Aymar, Seigneur of Archiac, a kinsman of the Bishop of Saintes, from which only the intervention of the Count of Poitiers delivered him, a fact which made it abundantly plain that once this prince was really delivered from the influence of Gerard, the day was won in Aquitaine.[5]

Accordingly, towards the end of the year 1134, Geoffrey of Chartres, as Apostolic Legate, called upon St. Bernard again to visit Aquitaine.[6] It was at about the time when the Abbot of Clairvaux was engaged in negotiations for the foundation of the Abbey of Buzay on the Loire, near Nantes, which involved personal interviews with Conan III, Duke of Brittany, and his mother, Ermengarde.[7]

William of Poitiers and Aquitaine was a difficult personality, elusive in his movements, evasive in his engagements ; a man of feeble will yet obstinate in unexpressed reservations ; who lived loosely and thought muddle-headedly ; just the wrong sort of ruler ; a ready tool for the hand of an accomplished schemer. Upon this occasion he had to face the strong combination of two men who acted with quite engaging simplicity ; for Geoffrey accompanied St. Bernard. At last he would perhaps be called to account by entirely honest and disinterested dealing.

As for Gerard, he did not relish an interview with such men. Indeed, as Arnald of Bonneval tells us, he " was

[1] Mans. *Concil.*, XXI. 450.

[2] P. 129 *supra*.

[3] *Ep.* 156.
[4] *Gall. Christ.*, VIII. 1448.

[5] Arnulph. Sagiens., Dach. *op. cit., loc. cit.* ; *R.H.G.F.* XIV. 259, *note (a)*.
[6] *Vita Prima*, I. vi. 34.

[7] Pp. 51 sq. *supra*.

beginning to lose countenance in the presence of his fellows and, fearing lest charges should be brought against him which he could not refute, he was wont to avoid public assemblies." [1] In such a state of mind he would scarcely encourage William to meet St. Bernard and the legate. Fortunately wiser counsels prevailed. Better men than Gerard urged upon William with success " that he should not decline colloquy with such illustrious persons ; for it might be that, after he had conferred with them, what now was thought to be difficult would be easy and what now seemed to be impossible would by some sudden stroke be made possible." From all quarters these men of goodwill amongst his followers assembled at Parthenay, and disclosed to the count their sense of shame that on this side of the Alps Aquitaine alone persisted in schism outside the Church ; outside the ark, and thus by the just judgement of God in peril from the waters of the flood. Finally, they reminded him of the men who perished in the gainsaying of Korah, insisting that never at any time has God failed to punish such wickedness. And William, as was to be expected, temporizes. He is prepared to obey Innocent as rightful Pope ; but as for the bishops whom he has expelled,[2] nothing will induce him to restore them ; they have unpardonably offended him ; moreover he has sworn—the common subterfuge !—that he will never receive them to peace. We gather from Arnald that William received representatives in the Château de Parthenay, and that for a day or two there were comings and goings of these between himself and the rest of his good angels outside. It was probably not until the count proved quite intractable that St. Bernard intervened with " more effective weapons." And what were these ?

Adjoining the château was the Church of Notre-Dame-de-la-Couldre which served as its chapel. It was the hour of Mass, and St. Bernard, followed by a vast crowd, entered and proceeded to the altar ; the Count of Poitiers, excommunicate in the midst of his own people, controlled as it were by some magnetic force, followed too, but stayed his steps at the narthex. After the *pax* St. Bernard placed the Sacred Host upon the paten and bearing it reverently in his hands, his countenance transfigured, his manner that of a judge not of a suppliant, passed outside the great door. Addressing the Duke of Aquitaine he says : " We have petitioned you and you have spurned us ; in the recent council the servants of God at your footstool you have treated with contempt. Lo, here has come forth to you the Virgin's Son, the head and lord of that Church which you persecute. Your judge is present, in whose name every knee in heaven, on earth, below the earth is bowed. Do you spurn him? Do you treat him with the contempt with which you treat his servants?" In the deep silence of tears and prayers men waited. William trembled, grew rigid and fell upon the ground. The soldiers lifted him, but he fell again speechless, listless, foaming at the mouth; groaning, "as it were," Arnald very reasonably remarks, "in epilepsy." St. Bernard approached nearer, touched him with his foot and bade him rise. "The Bishop of Poitiers," he says, "whom you drove from his church is here. Go and be reconciled to him; pledge yourself to him in the kiss of peace and restore him to his see. Then, making satisfaction to God, render to him glory for contempt. Throughout your dominions recall the divided and discordant to the unity of love. Submit to Innocent as Pope; and even as every church obeys him, so do you too obey so great a pontiff, God's elect."[1]

Whatever explanation of this remarkable scene we may be disposed to offer, it is memorable as having given the deathblow to the Schism in that part of Gaul where it died hardest. William became a changed man. He did exactly what St. Bernard at Mass that morning at Parthenay had told him to do. And he did more. As an act of reparation he founded in the diocese of Saintes the Abbey of Grâce-Dieu, where Clairvaux monks were in possession so early as on Lady Day of the following year, 1135.[2] Two years later, on Good Friday, 1137, he died on pilgrimage to Compostella.[3] Gerard, alas, "alone persisted in his evil ways," writes the chronicler, and proceeds to tell a gruesome story of his dying suddenly and unshriven; of the hasty burial of his remains by his nephews, and of their subsequent exhumation as unfit for holy ground by Geoffrey the Apostolic Legate.[4] Another and pleasanter version of his end is that he died protesting "that, if against the will of God he had in ignorance (of that will) espoused the cause of Peter Leonis, he confessed himself and repented";[5] a statement with a reservation which, it will be allowed, takes from its candour. But if we are to believe even so much as the general tenor of the authorities, from on the one side Arnolph of Sées—from whom Arnald probably derived his impression—to the writer of the Angoulême *Historia* on the other, his was a character difficult to read. What Gerard actually did is sufficiently evident and quite indisputable; but from the first he played obstinately and a little clumsily a losing game. A man of long and varied experience in ecclesiastical politics, the trusted agent of four successive Popes, *qu'allait-il faire dans cette galère?* That is the enigma.

[1] *Vita Prima*, II. vi. 37 sq.

[2] Pp. 51 sq. *supra.*

[3] Ord. Vital. *Hist. Eccl.*, XIII. 13, *P.L.* CLXXXVIII. 955 sq.

[4] *Vita Prima*, II. vi. 39; cf. p. 157 *infra.*

[5] *Hist. Pont. et Comit. Engol.*, R.H.G.F. XII. 397.

CHAPTER VII

THE HEALING OF THE SCHISM IN GERMANY AND IN ITALY

WILLIAM OF POITIERS had been a tool in the hand of a cunning master. Roger of Sicily was no man's tool. In Aquitaine the ambition has been Gerard's ; an ambition in the main ecclesiastical in its character which had in view the maintenance of himself as almost independent arbiter, responsible no more than nominally to the authority of a weak and distant senate of which he should be the proconsul without term of years. For material means to this end he looked to the Count of Poitiers, a prince probably of no ambitions. Roger of Sicily, on the other hand, quite frankly sought territorial aggrandizement, Mediterranean empire. The Genoese and the Pisans alike stood in his way ; and that they should play a leading part in the restoration of Innocent to Rome, at the price of expelling Anacletus who had given him royal dignity, was detrimental to his cherished schemes. These were the chief factors in the problem as yet unsolved South of the Alps.

After that great day at Parthenay St. Bernard, impatient of absence from his cloister, returned to Clairvaux, where for a while he lived in a little hut of woven pea-stalks a life of contemplation, favoured, so Arnald records, by the visitations of the divine Bridegroom ; a period during which it is probable that the *Sermons on the Song of Songs* began to take shape.[1] Here he would have remained from late in the year 1134 until about March, 1135. Meanwhile Roger had been consolidating his power in the South of Italy with some success, indirectly serving the purposes of Anacletus by closing the peninsula to Innocent beyond Pisa ;[2] he was now turning his attention to effecting a rupture of that strong combination of the Genoese and the Pisans which threatened the realization of his aims.

It was inevitable that rumours of these portentous movements should reach St. Bernard in his seclusion, and it is probable that it was at this time that he wrote the letter to the Genoese above quoted.[3] From it we learn both the extent of the danger and how St. Bernard would have it met. " Do

[1] *Vita Prima,* II. vi. 40 ; cf. p. 229 *infra.*

[2] Falc. Benevent. *Chron., an.* 1134, Murator. *Rer. Ital. Script.,* V. 119.

[3] Pp. 121 sq. *supra.*

now," he urges, " keep faith with your Pisan brethren, with
our lord the Pope ; maintain your loyalty to the king "—
that is to say, Lothair—" and your own self-respect. For
this is profitable, and it is fitting and what justice demands.
I have heard that messengers from Duke Roger have been
with you ; what they brought and what they took away I
know not. But for my part I confess that, to quote the poet,
timeo Danaos et dona ferentes. If by chance any one of you
(which God forbid) be found to do so foul a deed as to stretch
out his hand to filthy lucre, mark him henceforth as an enemy
of your name, a traitor to his fellow citizens who barters your
common honour and honesty." Similarly deserving of reprobation is anyone found to be going about secretly stirring up
disaffection. Evidently Roger's agents were active amongst
them ; and St. Bernard would put them on their honour not
to repeat their old evil deeds, but rather to expiate them by
righteousness. They are a warlike race ? Well ; "if you like
to go out to battle ; if it delights you to try your strength and
to prove your valour, let it not be against your friends and
neighbours ; when it would become you better to win vic-
tories over the enemies of the Church and—let me add—to
defend your own state against the invasion of the Sicilians.
Truly, if you win from them you will win more honourably,
and what you win you will more justly hold. The God of
peace and love be ever with you all. Amen." [1] Let us not ^[1] *Ep.* 129.
be offended by the words of blessing thus following immedi-
ately upon the unmistakable appeal to their fighting spirit.
It was a question not of peace or war, but of war in a righteous
or an unrighteous cause ; so, we may be sure, St. Bernard
felt.

Very soon afterwards was written the letter to the Pisans
also quoted above.[2] The fact that in it he commends to them [2] *Ep.* 130 ; cf.
Engelbert, Marquess of Friuli and Duke of Carinthia,[3] " a   pp. 121 sq. *supra*.
brave, active and, unless I am mistaken, faithful young man   [3] Mabillon. *Not.*
sent to the assistance of the lord Pope and his friends,"   *in St. Bern. Ep.*
indicates that St. Bernard had at the time left Clairvaux for   130.
the Diet of Bamberg, which opened on 17th March, 1135.
The language of the letter is that of a man who puts confidence in the valour and in the integrity of his correspondents.
It may be doubted whether the same confidence prevailed
generally amongst the friends of Innocent, whether at Pisa or
in Germany. The mission of St. Bernard to the latter country
is stated by Geoffrey to have been undertaken for the specific
purpose of arranging the imperial affairs of state, which were
critical. " When the servant of Christ entered Germany he

hastened to the neighbourhood of Mainz in order to restore peace between King Lothair and the nephews of his predecessor, the Emperor Henry, namely, Conrad, who afterwards succeeded Lothair in the kingdom, and Frederick, the father of the Frederick who was elected after Conrad and now reigns." [1] We may well suppose that Innocent was not really secure at Pisa, and that he therefore sent St. Bernard to do what could be done to effect a united front in Germany which might again turn upon Italy with some prospect of success against the adherents of Anacletus. The later mission of Engelbert was a reassuring earnest of what might be hoped to follow in the early future. After having been honourably received at Mainz by the Archbishop Henry, and after having gained a recruit for Clairvaux in the person of a distinguished ecclesiastic by name Mascellinus whom the archbishop had deputed to welcome him to the city, St. Bernard passed on into Franconia.[2]

Lothair had had some success against the Hohenstaufen during the autumn of 1134. Conrad and Frederick had fled from Ulm, and Swabia lay at the mercy of the Emperor ; but to create a desert is not to make peace. The two princes still roamed the land like bandits at large. Ultimately Frederick, the more tractable of the brothers, sued for peace. At the intervention of his kinswoman, the Empress Richinza, this was granted on conditions ; but one condition imposed, namely, that himself and Conrad should present themselves as humble suppliants at the Diet of Bamberg in the spring of 1135, galled the pride of the Hohenstaufen. Conrad remained for the time obdurate ; at last in the following September, at Mülhausen, he made his formal submission ; so far as Frederick was concerned it was only the persuasion of St. Bernard which saved the situation.[3] The Abbot of Clairvaux's mission had as its ultimate object the peace of the Church, and as an essential preliminary the peace of the Empire ; doubtless it was therefore under his influence that at the Diet of Bamberg Lothair proposed, acceptably to the princes present, another Italian campaign. It was not, however, until shortly before Christmas in 1135 that Lothair could write to Innocent : " Now that both (brothers) have been vanquished alike by the material and by the spiritual sword—for Frederick at Bamberg and Conrad at the very next diet earned our good graces— both are bound by their oath to us to serve the Church. But we did not take them into favour otherwise than with this reservation and on this condition, namely, that they should receive full absolution from no one but from your paternity alone." At the end of the letter he reassures Innocent as to

[1] Vita Prima, IV. iii. 14 ; cf. Otton. Frising. Chron., VII. 19, M.G.H. Script., XX. 257.

[2] Vita Prima, loc. cit.

[3] Annal. Magdeburg., an. 1134, M.G.H. Script., XVI. 185.

the proposed expedition to Italy. " I want to tell you this. We shall celebrate the Lord's birthday at Spires when we shall assemble the princes and discuss the Roman expedition. I beg of you to send your legate and a letter to this diet in order that by these means under grave penalties, let them be what they may, you may warn the archbishops and the abbots to serve a cause which is both yours and ours." [1] We must admire the generosity which marked Lothair's treatment of the Hohenstaufen, in particular of Conrad, who for seven long years had resisted his authority. In the circumstances it was sound policy ; to have allowed even the least plausible grievance to rankle would have been fatal. That it commended itself to St. Bernard we cannot doubt ; the spirit generated by his presence at Bamberg would not have expired six months later when Conrad made his submission at Mülhausen.

Whether St. Bernard returned to Clairvaux when he left Bamberg or made his way directly to Italy we do not know. The bull of Innocent convoking the Council of Pisa had been promulgated on 8th November, 1134.[2] It is probable that St. Bernard would so soon as possible have turned his attention to the necessity that it should have full effect where such effect was most difficult to secure, namely, in Italy. A letter, which Mabillon assigns to the year 1134, written by him to Louis le Gros reveals the fact that his correspondent was by no means favourably disposed towards the project of the council. His opposition seems to have been so serious that we may think that, had St. Bernard been in France, he would have sought a personal interview with the king. It is not easy to understand what precisely was the latter's frame of mind. Was he jealous of Lothair ? Or was he pandering to the indolence of the prelates of his kingdom, when he forbade them to attend the council at Pisa on the ground that it would be too hot ? But surely Henry the Wild Boar, Stephen of Senlis and Geoffrey of Chartres were not the kind of men who would take account of so trifling a cost ! The most probable explanation is that Innocent had in some way inadvertently offended his *amour propre*. Let us hear what St. Bernard says : " Why, my lord King, is your anger moved against God's elect, whom moreover your highness received into your kingdom and chose out to be a father to yourself, and even a Samuel to your son ? "—referring to the consecration of Louis le Jeune at Rheims in 1131—" Your royal indignation is armed not against strangers but against yourself and against your own. . . . A council is being assembled. What is there in this detrimental to your royal honour, to the advantage of

[1] Marten. et Durand. *Vet. Script. et Mon. Ampl. Coll.*, I. 753 sq.

[2] Mans. *Concil.*, XXI. 488.

your kingdom ? . . . It would be a different matter were it not that every one, who is not so hard-hearted as to pay no attention to the straits of our mother Church, knows that at the present moment an assembly of bishops is a necessity. But they say : ' The heat is too excessive ' ; as though our bodies were made of ice ! Or is it that our hearts are frozen and that there is no one who, as the prophet says, is *grieved for the affliction of Joseph ?* It cannot be this. Now I, who of your subjects am least in dignity though not in fidelity, tell you that it is inexpedient for you to hinder so great and so necessary a good work." He would state his reasons more fully were it not that he knows that " to a wise man a word is sufficient." And now follows what is probably the true explanation of the difficulty. " If, however, the rigour of Apostolic authority has done anything which your highness may regard as an offence to your high dignity, your faithful servants present at the council will do their best endeavours to have it either revoked or tempered suitably to the honour due to you." [1] Whatever may have been its cause, Louis's wrath was sufficiently assuaged and the French contingent at the council was proportionately large, including the Archbishops of Rheims, Sens and Bourges, the Bishop of Chartres and sixteen abbots, amongst them Peter the Venerable. [2]

The month of May, 1135, found St. Bernard on the plains of Lombardy. Anselm of Pusterla, Archbishop of Milan, had long held out both for Anacletus and for Conrad of Hohenstaufen, The situation in the city was thus, as elsewhere, complicated by imperial considerations. Certain of the cathedral chapter took the other side, and did not spare their criticism of Anselm. When he proceeded to excommunicate them they, on the ground that he had himself been excommunicated by his suffragans, appealed to the civil power. After a turbulent scene had been enacted and much strong language used, the authorities of the city decided to hand the case over to the suffragans of the province. The arrival of these prelates accompanied by a large following of monks, amongst whom we seem to recognize Cistercians from the description of their habits, was, owing to Anselm's inflammatory language, but provocative of further violence. The archbishop would appear to have escaped with his life, first to his palace and then to the more secure asylum of the Church of St. Ambrose. The excitement having abated and some *pourparlers* having taken place between Anselm and the authorities, the former agreed to submit himself to the tribunal of his suffragans, excepting only the question of his loyalty to Conrad—the very

[1] *Ep.* 255.

[2] Petr. Ven. *Epp., Lib.* I. 27.

last exception which the Milanese would allow ! Ultimately, popular feeling having declared itself unmistakably in cries of " Away with the archbishop ! ", Anselm escaped from the city and his functions were for the time deputed to the Bishop of Alba.[1]

All this happened during the Lent of 1135, not very long before St. Bernard arrived in the neighbourhood. In recording the foundation of the Abbey of Chiaravalle-Milanese on 22nd July of this year we referred to the despatch of messengers from the city to invite a visit from St. Bernard, a request to which he felt unable to accede.[2] Assuming Anselm to have already left Milan, there was no immediate need for St. Bernard's presence there ; whereas his early arrival at Pisa was of paramount importance. The council opened on 30th May, and closed on 6th June.[3] The attendance would have been disappointing, for there were, it seems, but fifty-six bishops present, all of whom came either from France or from Italy ; the credit of England was perhaps saved by the Archbishop of Rouen.[4] Arnald roughly but, as he intimates, sufficiently summarizes its work. " It consisted in the excommunication of Peter and the degrading of his supporters ; and "—he adds, writing very soon after St. Bernard's death in 1153—" this sentence holds good to-day." [5] In the context he records the great respect paid to St. Bernard who, although he was absent from no session and did not fail to make himself felt in every sentence passed and in every definition laid down, yet never looked for deference to be shown to him or arrogated to himself superior wisdom.

There was, however, one matter with which the council dealt, namely, the unsatisfactory state of the Church of Milan, to which Arnald refers but indirectly, remarking that the Milanese "had earnestly petitioned that the Abbot of Clairvaux might be sent to them." [6] The Bishop of Alba, charged with the administration of the diocese on the flight of Anselm, could not leave things as they were. Accompanied by the archdeacon and other higher clergy, he therefore presented himself before the council and begged that Innocent would canonically regularize the deposition of Anselm, a request to which he willingly enough acceded on their taking oath of fidelity to himself as lawful Pope. The stroke was bold, for the populace of the city was still inflammable. Anselm had left behind him many friends, and it needed a persuasive voice in order to gain the goodwill of men who well might feel that they had been made the victims of a *coup d'état*. St. Bernard, obviously marked out for such a task and specially sought for

[1] Ludolph. de S. Paul. *Hist. Mediolan.*, *M.G.H. Script.*, XX. 45 sqq.

[2] Pp. 50 sq. *supra.*

[3] Jaffé, *Regest.*, 7695, 7700 ; Mans. *Concil.*, XXI. 487 sq.

[4] Order. Vital. *Hist. Eccl.*, XIII. 7, *P.L.* CLXXXVIII. 941 sq.

[5] *Vita Prima*, II. ii. 8.

[6] *Vita Prima*, II. ii. 9.

by the Milanese of better mind, desired to have at his side Geoffrey of Chartres " whose integrity and sincerity he had often proved." After the council was closed therefore he and Geoffrey set out for Milan together with the Cardinals Guy of Pisa and Matthew of Albano as Apostolic Legates *a latere*.[1] His reception was a veritable ovation. When having crossed the Apennines his approach was known, there came out of the city to a distance of some seven miles " nobles and lowly born, knights and foot-men, burghers and poor, streaming from their homes in separate companies to greet the man of God. All alike were delighted to gaze upon him ; they who could hear his voice accounted themselves most fortunate. Multitudes kissed his feet ; and although it pleased him ill, yet did he not reason with or forbid men prostrate in devotion to his person. When they could they even plucked threads and tore strips from his garments as remedies for the sick, judging that whatever he had touched or used was thereby sanctified." [2] Thus slowly and through the crowd he reached the city ; and when in public they treated of the business which had brought him and the cardinals amongst them, the Milanese were ready in everything to do his will. Arnald records various cures wrought by St. Bernard during his sojourn in the city. One took place on the third day after his arrival when he was celebrating Mass in the Church of St. Ambrose. The subject was a young girl described as " vexed by a violent onslaught of the devil," who was brought to him while the clerks were singing and he was seated at the *sedilia*. It would appear that St. Bernard took the chalice, and wine having been poured into it over his fingers with which he moistened her lips, the evil spirit left her.[3] Another case is recorded in remarkable detail. It was that of a boy vexed for three years by the devil, whose state, according to his bearer, was worsened when he entered a church or was signed with the cross or was sprinkled with holy water, or heard the gospel read, or assisted at the holy mysteries. St. Bernard gently laid his staff upon the child's neck, and his brother Gerard, with a touch of the family scepticism to which we shall refer later,[4] in order to test the truth of the story signed unperceived his back with the cross. When the patient, who before had lain apparently senseless on the ground, began to groan distressfully, he was placed upon St. Bernard's bed. His condition was aggravated ; he rolled off on to the ground again ; he bit his attendant ; he tore the hair of those who approached him ; he could scarcely be controlled at all. However, he was again placed upon the bed. When St. Bernard and the brethren prostrated them-

[1] Ludolph. de S. Paul. *Hist. Mediolan.*, M.G.H. Script., loc. cit. ; *Vita Prima*, loc. cit.

[2] *Vita Prima*, loc. cit.

[3] *Vita Prima*, II. ii. 11.

[4] P. 220 *infra*.

selves in prayer, the chaff on the bed began to burn and the
evil spirit burning too cried aloud in pain. St. Bernard
ordered holy water to be poured into the mouth, but the child
closed it firmly ; a wedge was inserted between his teeth, and
the water trickled down his throat. The effect was immediate ;
the devil left him ; and the child, arising calm and perfectly
restored, embraced his restorer, exclaiming " Thank God, I am
well." [1] No wonder that when such stories were bruited
about through the whole of Italy men said that a great prophet
had arisen. And here let us remind ourselves of two points.
First, Arnald was keenly alive to the danger of credulity on
the part of a chronicler ; next, he was insistent upon St.
Bernard's dread and distrust of the reputation of a thaumaturge. In the *Preface* to his record he writes : " If I have
carelessly mixed bitter colocynth in the pottage Elisha, I
hope, will season it with meal ; and my desire to do what I am
told "—that is to say, to tell the plain story of St. Bernard's
life from the date at which William of St. Thierry had left off
—" will excuse the abundance of my folly." [2] Of St. Bernard
he remarks : " He never exalted himself, he never strutted
proudly in the midst of his wonders but, thinking humbly of
himself, he believed himself to be not the author but the
agent of the venerable works which he wrought ; and, although
he stood supreme in the judgement of all men, in his own
judgement he stood very low indeed." [3] His miracles were,
in fact, the natural expression of his wisdom of speech and of
his probity of conduct, as both of these were wrought in him
by God.

In such a favourable atmosphere as was thus created
St. Bernard sought, while it still prevailed, to secure a lasting
peace. The destinies of the Church and of the Empire, that
two-fold polity each department of which in its proper sphere
was sacred in his eyes, might well seem to await their determination at the *fiat* of these Lombard folk, proud and intractable yet impressionable to a degree which would have made a
man less balanced in his judgement, less sure of his convictions
than was St. Bernard, tremble for the future. The Abbot of
Clairvaux, however, appreciated, as perhaps did no one else
in Europe, the value of establishing upon a firm footing a right
relation between the spiritual and the material forces of
Christendom. He recognized, moreover, that neither at Rome
nor at any city North of the Alps was to be found the centre
of gravity of this great structure, but at Milan alone ; Milan
which had not ceased to be the Milan of St. Ambrose and
Theodosius. Lothair had evidently pressed the point that the

[1] *Vita Prima,*
II. iii. 16 sq.

[2] *Vita Prima,* II.
Praef.

[3] *Op. cit.,* II. iv.
25.

rejection of Conrad by the Milanese should be the condition of their reconciliation to Innocent. His motives were doubtless upon no very high plane ; but St. Bernard, interpreting the Pope's mind, regarded his policy as sound, and we find him writing later to the Emperor : " The Milanese were not received into the favour of the lord Pope and into the unity of the Church until having explicitly abjured Conrad they had openly accepted our Lothair as their king and ruler, and with the whole world confessed him as the Augustus, the Emperor of the Romans, and according to the counsel and mandate of the lord Pope vowed on the most holy gospel that they would make worthy satisfaction to you for the injury done." He proceeds to urge that Lothair should give thanks to God that this good result has been attained without bloodshed ; that when the Milanese, through Innocent, " the mediator of their reconciliation," beg for his clemency they should find him placable and well-disposed, for in such case they are likely to be stable in their present purpose and to pay him due service and honour. Finally, knowing well the man with whom he has to deal, he remarks : " It is not fitting that your faithful servants who labour for your honour should be confounded in your sight as they will be if, having in reliance upon your benignity held out hopes of pardon, when they come to ask for it they find you (which God forbid !) inexorable." [1] The occasion of the oath of obedience alike to Innocent and to Lothair to which St. Bernard refers was a solemn Mass of thanksgiving celebrated by him in the Church of St. Ambrose.[2] The position was further consolidated by the foundation of the Abbey of Chiaravalle-Milanese, the twentieth daughter of Clairvaux, on 22nd July, as it were an army of spiritual and peaceful occupation left upon the spot.[3]

But St. Bernard had not yet finished his work at Milan. Fully conscious of the value of atmosphere, almost Platonic in his insistence upon the influence of art upon character, the magnificence of the churches of the city seemed in his view to be calculated to enervate the spiritual vigour both of priests and of people. He would recall, as he had done some ten years ago in the *Apologia* addressed to William of St. Thierry, the words of Persius : " Tell me, ye pontiffs, what doth gold in the sanctuary ? " [4] Ignoring, however, the distinction which in that context he had made between what is fitting in a cathedral and what is fitting in a monastic church, he required the Milanese to strip their shrines of the great wealth of ornament which was their traditional glory.[5] It was a bold stroke, but it was entirely successful ; so much so that it did

[1] *Ep.* 137.

[2] Ludolph. de S. Paul. *Hist. Mediolan., M.G.H. Script., loc. cit.*

[3] Pp. 50 sq. *supra.*

[4] S. Bern. *Apol. ad Guill. S. Theod.,* XII. 28 ; Pers. *Sat.,* II ; cf. Appendix.

[5] Ludolph. de S. Paul. *Hist. Mediolan., M.G.H. Script., loc. cit.*

but enhance his reputation for sanctity and attach the populace the more faithfully to his person. The Pope had canonically regularized the deposition of Anselm, but the archiepiscopal see still remained vacant. They in their generation
would repeat the story of St. Ambrose, and shout their
" Bernard, archbishop." " How many churches," writes
Arnald, " destitute of pastors have chosen him for their
bishop ! The Church of Langres ; the Church of Châlons
(-sur-Marne) ; in Italy the city of Genoa and Milan, the
metropolis of Liguria, desired him as shepherd and as master.
Rheims, the noblest city of France, the capital of Lower
Belgium, sought to be ruled by him. All these invitations he
disregarded ; the honours offered did not appeal to his soul ;
neither were his footsteps turned in the direction of glory, nor
did the bishop's ring and mitre delight him more than the
rake and hoe." [1] When the crowd of clergy and people sought
St. Bernard at the Church of St. Laurence where he was
lodged, his reply was that on the morrow he would mount his
horse and, giving the beast free rein, did it take him away
from their city God himself would have answered in the
negative their request.[2] The route chosen was the road to
Pavia,[3] a city with which the Milanese were not upon the best
of terms. Indeed, it was only at St. Bernard's persuasion
that they had recently released sick prisoners of war taken
not from Pavia alone but from Cremona and from Piacenza.[4]
The response to the friendly gestures mediated by St. Bernard
was not in every case a ready one. Cremona, whither St.
Bernard proceeded after leaving Pavia,[5] proved difficult to
handle. " The Cremonese," he writes to Innocent, " have
hardened their hearts ; their good fortune is ruining them.
They despise the Milanese and their self-confidence betrays
them. Putting their trust in horses and in chariots, they
disappointed my hope and frustrated my labour. I was
leaving them in sorrow when, lo, there arrived from you no
little consolation ; so that although tribulations for Christ's
sake abound, yet there abound also consolations through
him." [6] This consolation was the news of the Pope's safety
and of the success so far vouchsafed to his cause. The rest of
the letter refers to a matter which had brought St. Bernard
much anxiety.

Robald, Bishop of Alba, who had provisionally administered the diocese of Milan since the deposition of Anselm, was,
shortly after St. Bernard's departure, elected archbishop on
the understanding that he should still retain the see of Alba,
a little city in Piedmont.[7] This had met with the approval of

[1] Vita Prima, II. iv. 26.

[2] Ludolph. de S. Paul. Hist. Mediolan., M.G.H. Script., loc. cit.

[3] Vita Prima, II. iv. 21.

[4] Ludolph. de S. Paul. Hist. Mediolan., M.G.H. Script., loc. cit.

[5] Vita Prima, II. iv. 21.

[6] Ep. 314.

[7] Ludolph. de S. Paul. Hist. Mediolan., M.G.H. Script., loc. cit. ; cf. Catal. Archiepp. Mediolan., M.G.H. VIII. 105.

Innocent ; indeed, as St. Bernard points out, the Church of
Milan had received many proofs of the Supreme Pontiff's
good-will. " God deals favourably with you ; the Roman
Church does no less. He is to you a father and she a mother.
Truly, what is there which she ought to have done and has
not done ? When you asked for distinguished persons to be
sent to you from the *Curia*,"—referring to the mission of
Cardinals Guy of Pisa and Matthew of Albano [1]—" it was done.
When you asked that what you had unanimously resolved as
to the election of your venerable father "—Robald of Alba—
" should be confirmed, it was done. When you wished that
what save in grave necessity is forbidden by the sacred canons,
namely, that a bishop should hold an archbishopric in plurality
should be granted in your case, it was granted." [2] Here we
must observe that the original is a little difficult. The words
in Mabillon's text are : *translationem episcopi in archiepisco-
patum*, which speak of what was an everyday occurrence ;
episcopi should perhaps be emended to *episcopii*. Reading
thus, on the face of it the suggestion is that the see of Milan
had been degraded from metropolitan to suffragan rank, and
that the revocation of that sentence was the favour in question.[3]
But what authority is there for holding that such a degradation
ever took place ? The raising of the see of Genoa to metropolitan rank [4] had not involved the degradation of Milan
therefrom, although at the time the see of Bobbio had been
transferred from the latter province to the former.[5] Again,
allowing that the degradation did then take place, for the
Pope to revoke it could scarcely be described as " forbidden
by the sacred canons." Whereas, plurality, such as was
Robald's occupancy of the sees of Milan and Alba, " save in
grave necessity " might not unreasonably be so described.

But what had happened to cause St. Bernard so much
anxiety was really this. The Milanese, we gather, enamoured
of their supposed liberties, had questioned the supreme
authority of the Apostolic See, and were unwilling that
Robald should take the customary oath of subordination to
the Pope. St. Bernard reasons with them. " Fulness of
power," he writes, " over all the churches of the world has by
a singular prerogative been granted to the Apostolic See. . . .
If by chance anyone attempts to resist its authority, it is
prompt to avenge all disobedience. You have proved this "
—in the case of Anselm, it is to be supposed—" What did
your disobedience profit you, and the backsliding to which
you were so ill-advised by your false prophets ? " [6] The
archbishop would appear to have been willing enough to take

[1] P. 140 *supra.*

[2] *Ep.* 131.

[3] Mabillon. *Not.
in loc.* ; Horst.
Not. Fus. in loc.

[4] Pp. 120 sq.
supra.

[5] Boson. *op. cit.*,
381.

[6] *Ep.* 131.

the oath, the requisite condition for the reception of the *pallium*,[1] but found his course violently obstructed by the popular feeling. " What is he to do ? " asks St. Bernard of Innocent. " He wishes to obey and, lo, beasts of Ephesus gnash their teeth upon him ! " [2] The quandary in which the Milanese are placing Robald is reflected in a passage of the letter written to them above quoted, in which he seems to be addressing the archbishop individually. " If anyone says to thee : ' To obey is in a measure the right thing, in a measure it is not,' considering that thou hast experienced in thyself the fulness of Apostolic power and the integrity of Apostolic authority, is not such a man either himself seduced or trying to seduce thee ? Do what I tell thee to do ; for I am not seducing thee. Be turned rather to humility and to meekness, for God gives grace to the humble and the meek shall inherit the earth." [3]

Anselm had unsuccessfully endeavoured to reach Anacletus at Rome ; [4] and there can be little doubt but that his partizans left behind at Milan were responsible for this recrudescence of schismatic spirit. The question put to Innocent in St. Bernard's letter presently quoted suggests that in his difficulty Robald had turned for guidance to the Abbot of Clairvaux. But it would seem that no less was needed than the personal presence of St. Bernard in the city.[5] Innocent had wearied of the vacillation alike of the archbishop and of his people, and was meditating strong measures. St. Bernard pleads with him. " Call to mind, kind lord, the words which your own Lord spoke : *Lo, these three years do I come seeking fruit of this fig-tree and find none.* But you have waited scarcely three months, and you are already sharpening the axe's edge. If you had endured three years' delay we might rightly ask for yet a fourth from a faithful follower of his lord. Therefore we too say : *Let it alone for this year also.*" [6] And so St. Bernard turns again to his spade-work in the Lord's garden at Milan. Happily, his labour proved to be so far fruitful as that Robald's difficulties were removed, and he was able to present himself at Pisa and take the oath of fidelity to Innocent as Supreme Pontiff. Nothing further was heard of the supposed ecclesiastical liberties of the Milanese.[7]

We are disposed to think that St. Bernard's visit to Cremona had already taken place, so that soon after leaving Milan he would have crossed the Alps on his way home, Greeted respectfully on his journey by the shepherds and herdsmen of the Jura, who returning to their rude dwellings told with joy the story of how they had received the blessing

[1] Duchesne, *Lib. Pontific.*, II. 294.

[2] *Ep.* 314.

[3] *Ep.* 131.

[4] Ludolph. de S. Paul. *Hist. Mediolan.*, *M.G.H. Script.*, *loc. cit.*

[5] *Vita Prima* II. iv. 24.

[6] *Ep.* 314.

[7] Ludolph. de S. Paul. *Hist. Mediolan.*, *M.G.H. Script loc. cit.*

then at Spires, the necessity of prompt and vigorous measures ; a contention supported by Robert of Capua, who was also present. St. Bernard does not delay to write to the Emperor in the same sense. " Blessed be God who has chosen you and raised up a horn of salvation for us to the praise and glory of his name, to the restoration of the imperial honour, to the succour of his Church in an evil day, finally to the working of salvation at this present time in the midst of the earth." The implication is that the existing disorder is bad for the Empire, bad for the Church and bad for the world generally ; and —he puts this first—bad because it gives a false impression of the divine providence. St. Bernard's language is never mere haphazard verbiage. " It was by the working of God's power that you concluded so prosperously the laborious and difficult journey which you undertook before for the peace of your kingdom and for the freedom of the Church. At Rome you then attained most gloriously the height of imperial dignity " —meaning his coronation as Emperor—" and, what is more, you attained it by the aid of no great material force, just in order that the greatness of your mind and of your faith might be more plainly manifest. But if the earth trembled before an insignificant little army like that, what sort of terror are we to expect to possess the hearts of our enemies when the king goes forth with a mighty arm ? While it is not for me to be stirring up strife, I am quite certain that it is the duty of an advocate of the Church to ward off the fury of schismatics who attack it ; and that it is the duty of the Emperor to vindicate his crown against the Sicilian usurper. For even as it is undeniable that it is an injury to Christ for the spawn of a Jew to have usurped the See of Peter ; so is it beyond doubt that a man who makes himself a king in Sicily injures the Emperor." [1]

[1] *Ep.* 139.

And Lothair came. In September he reached Lombardy by way of the Brenner, and with the able assistance of his son-in-law, Henry the Proud, Duke of Bavaria, had such good success that by the month of May, 1137, he was in undisputed control of the country so far South as Reggio on the West and as Bari on the East.[2] At Viterbo in the Patrimony of St. Peter, where Innocent was from at least 26th March to 8th April, 1137,[3] an unpleasant misunderstanding arose between him and the Duke of Bavaria who, after reducing the city, levied a heavy tribute which, in spite of the Pope's objection that the place was properly within his own civil jurisdiction, he insisted upon paying into his war-chest.[4] St. Bernard was perhaps present upon the occasion, for it was at Viterbo that his

[2] Bernhardi, *op. cit.*, 668 sqq.

[3] Innoc. Pap. *Epist. et Priv.*, *P.L.* CLXXIX. 323 sqq.

[4] *Annalista Saxo, M.G.H. Script.*, VI. 773.

youngest brother, Gerard, who accompanied him, was brought to death's door by grave sickness. The touching lament made for this beloved kinsman when he did come to die at Clairvaux a year later recalls gratefully the mercy which spared him " to be restored alive to his friends " in their common home.[1] By the 7th of May Henry, in pursuit of his plan of campaign, which was apparently to encircle Rome in isolation from the rest of Italy, had arrived at the foot of Monte Cassino, Innocent still accompanying him.[2] The abbot, a young man by the name of Raynald but two months elected, was a supporter of Anacletus. To the proposal that Innocent should confirm his election on the condition of his renouncing the cause of the antipope, he returned an obstinate refusal. The Duke of Bavaria soon learned the futility of attempting to reduce by force of arms so impregnable a stronghold, and as the result of negotiations the Abbot of Monte Cassino, evidently doubtful of the ultimate success of Roger of Sicily, was persuaded—not, it should be noted, to acknowledge Innocent as Pope, but to accept the necessity of submission to Henry ; and the imperial flag was hoisted on the abbey-church.[3] The Duke of Bavaria was a stronger character than was Lothair, and his high-handed manner was by no means acceptable to the Pope. He had all the determination of Roger combined with a better-balanced judgement ; but his interest was quite frankly to promote the supremacy of the Empire ; so far as Innocent had the same interest—and no farther—he was in Henry's eyes the rightful Pope.

Leaving Monte Cassino, the duke turned his attention to re-establishing the authority of Robert of Capua, and that end having been satisfactorily achieved, he arrived at Bari on 30th May, 1137, where Innocent met Lothair.[4] Probably it was some relief to him to be set free from the sole tutelage of Henry ! By the middle of September the whole of Southern Italy had submitted to the imperial forces.[5] But to what did this amount ? In the first place, it was not particularly pleasing to Innocent that Lothair should found upon it a claim to the suzerainty of Campania and of Apulia which the Pope regarded as his own, a right which even Roger of Sicily had recognized. It was a matter in which Ranulph of Alife, whose vassalage was involved, was of two minds ; he actually swore allegiance both to the Pope and to the Emperor, a proceeding calculated rather in the end to increase the difficulty than to relieve it.[6] What St. Bernard thought of the matter it is hard to say. Probably he was not well informed as to the constitutional rights of the case. The statement

[1] S. Bern. *In Cant. Cant.*, XXVI. 14 ; *Vita Prima*, III. vii. 21.

[2] *Annal. Casinens.*, *M.G.H. Script.*, XIX. 307, 309.

[3] *Chron. Casinens.*, IV., *M.G.H.* VII. 817.

[4] *Annalista Saxo*, *M.G.H. Script.*, VI. 773 sq.

[5] Bernhardi, *op. cit.*, 711 sqq.

[6] Otton. Frising. *Chron.*, VII. 20, *M.G.H. Script.*, XX. 258.

made in his letter to Lothair to the effect that it was " the duty of the Emperor to vindicate his crown against the Sicilian usurper " was a little unfortunate, and might easily have been quoted to the detriment of Innocent in this particular.[1] And then, over the roofs of Monte Cassino floated the imperial standard ! Innocent, however, had not confirmed the election of the youthful abbot, the avowed adherent of Anacletus. There were, too, within the walls of the abbey others who held of the same schismatic party, notably the learned librarian, one Peter, from whose *Chronicon Casinense* much of our information is derived. He it was whom unfortunately Lothair instructed to investigate the rights of the case. Peter, though learned, was unscrupulous ; falsified diplomas were produced which deceived all concerned on the Pope's side, and Innocent had no alternative other than to withdraw his claim of suzerainty.[2] We may assume that Lothair himself was not privy to the fraud, which was perpetrated not in his interest but solely in that of the antipope. But on the question of spiritual jurisdiction Innocent, supported by the cardinals and by St. Bernard, held out firmly. He demanded that Abbot Raynald and his monks should pledge him their allegiance and disown Anacletus. After negotiations lasting from the 6th to the 18th of July, 1137, Innocent in the end gained his point ; but whether by an oversight at the time, or more probably owing to his unwillingness to exact too much at once, he had not dealt with the matter of Raynald's election.[3] However, it was not forgotten altogether, and about two months later the Cardinals Haimeric and Gerard, together with St. Bernard, were despatched to Monte Cassino for the purpose of settling it. Lothair promptly intervened, declaring that as he was feudal suzerain of the abbey this proceeding was *ultra vires*. It was the old problem of investiture with the cross and ring revived. But the firmness of Innocent's representatives would appear to have cowed the Emperor, for on the threat to suspend ecclesiastics of all ranks who approved the imperial intervention he withdrew his claim, and Raynald was thereupon deposed as unfit to occupy the abbatial chair. The *Chronicon Casinense* makes it plain that St. Bernard's authority carried great weight in all these proceedings.[4] Raynald was replaced by Wibald, Abbot of Stavelot, a sufficiently eligible person, be it said, and elected ostensibly by the free vote of the monks—but in reality Lothair's nominee. Innocent had no other course open to him than to ratify this.[5]

Lothair, a victim to sinister presentiments which deprived

[1] *Ep.* 139. Cf. p. 148 *supra*.

[2] Bernhardi, *op. cit.*, 728 sqq.

[3] Bernhardi, *op. cit., loc. cit.*

[4] *Chron. Casinens.*, IV. 122, *P.L.* CLXXIII. 963 sq.

[5] *Chron. Casinens., op. cit.* 965.

him of the capacity of putting the top-stone upon any work which he took in hand, was now on the point of leaving Italy. There was only one man, it would seem, who could be counted upon to get to grips with Roger of Sicily, to grasp the nettle, to see the thing through. At Farfa early in October St. Bernard was bidden to retrace his steps to Apulia, and beard the lion in his den. " At the most urgent request of the Emperor, on the order of the Apostolic See, moved by the prayers of the Church and of secular princes, sad and unwilling, weak and in feeble health—to tell the truth, bearing about in fear the pale shadow of death, we drag our steps to Apulia." [1] So he writes to his sons at Clairvaux. There is no doubt but that he was very ill, and that the strength of his affection made him shrink from the possibility of never seeing them in the flesh again. " Sick and pressed for time," he goes on to say, " the words which I dictate are broken by sobbing, as the scribe can testify, our beloved brother Baldwin, whom the Church has called to a different office and to a different dignity." Baldwin, the first Cistercian cardinal, had been raised to the Sacred Purple by Innocent at Clermont in 1130. [2] About a month earlier, in a letter written to the abbots of the Order assembled at Cîteaux, he had asked them too as he would ask his own sons to pray that he might be spared to return home. " I speak as a man because of my infirmity ; I long that death may be delayed until I am restored to you, so that I may not die elsewhere than in your midst." [3] Not for a moment shall we suspect St. Bernard of being self-centred ; the burden of both letters is the expression of his anxiety for the Church, of his deep sense of the need of the prayers of his correspondents in his arduous task.

No sooner was Lothair's back turned than, as was to be expected, Roger fell upon Campania with savage ferocity. The atrocities of his Saracen forces baffle description. The reply to a timorous suggestion of peace on the part of the Abbot of Monte Cassino was that if the Sicilian caught him he would hang him on the spot. Ranulph of Alife alone made any show of resistance to his terrible father-in-law. [4]

And now St. Bernard, the man of tender heart and of ready tears, with an intrepidity which came of the resolution to die abroad in honour rather than at home in shame, makes his way to the presence of Roger. The opposing forces faced one another on the plains behind Salerno. Arnald tells the story of what happened. " When he had found the king in camp he stayed him for many days, warning him in the words : ' If you fight you will leave the field beaten and in disorder.'

[1] *Ep.* 14

[2] Mabillon. *Not.*, *ad loc.*

[3] *Ep.* 145.

[4] *Chron. Cas-inens.*, IV. 126, *op. cit.*, 970 sqq.

But when at the last moment the king's army had been greatly increased, not knowing that the event of war does not stand in numbers, he disdained to listen any longer to the holy man's talk of peace. Thereupon St. Bernard exhorted earnestly Duke Ranulph and the Catholic host, and promised them victory and triumph, even as he had promised defeat to the king. When he had gone his way to the next village, and was standing in prayer, suddenly are heard the shouts of men in flight and in pursuit. And truly, near by, Ranulph was following up the routed army of the king. . . . Yet not even by this disaster inflicted upon him from on high was the king's mind corrected." It was 30th October, 1137.[1]

St. Bernard did not hesitate to follow Roger up to Salerno where he took shelter, and with some success urged him squarely to face the dilemma presented by the Schism. The king proposed a discussion between chosen advocates of the opposing parties. Early in December St. Bernard, Cardinals Haimeric, Gerard and Guy of Castello, the latter subsequently Celestin II, on the one side, and on the other Peter of Pisa and the Cardinals Matthew and Gregory, appeared before Roger at Salerno. The conference lasted eight days, four being allotted to each party, and the advocates of Anacletus having the first word. The real clash of arms was between St. Bernard and Peter.[2] " I know," remarks the Abbot of Clairvaux, " that you are a wise and learned man, Peter. Would that a party more discreet "—*sanior pars ;* we shall remember the emphasis laid throughout upon this aspect of the case—" and of better credit had obtained your services ! Would that a juster and happier cause could have your advocacy ! Then doubtless no eloquence could withstand your reasonable contentions. As for ourselves, rustic fellows as we are, more often wont to handle the mattock than to plead in court, were it not that the faith is at stake we should maintain the silence which is enjoined upon us "—he is probably thinking of the Sixth Chapter of the Rule of St. Benedict— " But now charity compels us to speak because that robe of the Lord which at his passion neither the Gentile nor the Jew dared to tear, Peter Leonis with the approval of the Jew his master tears and divides. There is one faith, one Lord, one baptism. We know neither two Lords, nor twin faiths, nor two baptisms. To go back to old days ; in the time of the flood there was one ark. In this eight souls escaped the flood ; the rest perished ; all who were not in the ark perished. No one doubts but that this ark was a type of the Church. Of late men have built a second ark ; and there being two arks,

[1] *Vita Prima,* II. vii. 44 sq. ; Romoald. *Annales, M.G.H. Script.,* XIX. 423.

[2] Falcon. Benevent. *Chron.,* Murator. *Rer. Ital. Script.,* V. 125 ; *P.L.* CLXXIII. 1243 sq.

one is of necessity a counterfeit doomed to be lost at sea."[1] He proceeds to argue that, supposing Anacletus's ark to be the true ark, then—the ark of Innocent in which, sitting as it were with millstones tied to their necks, are the peoples of the East and of the West, of France, of Germany, of Spain and of England; the monks of Camaldoli, of the Chartreuse, of Grandmont, of Cîteaux and of Prémontré; innumerable others, both monks and nuns; bishops, abbots and secular princes[2]—with all this human freight must the ark of Innocent sink to the bottom of the sea. Roger of Sicily? Oh! He is safe enough as sole passenger on the ark of Anacletus. Is it conceivable that the whole world is going to perish simply to satisfy the ambition of Peter Leonis?

To this magnetic appeal all present save only Roger responded. A strange insensibility, not merely to the higher emotions but even to the appeal of reason, was characteristic of this man, as obtuse as he was headstrong. Peter of Pisa would seem to have been scared. With adroit generosity St. Bernard took him by the hand and, both rising to their feet, thus addressed him: " We will enter into what, believe me, is the safer ark "; and in due course Peter in the Abbot of Clairvaux's presence made his submission to Innocent at Rome.[3]

The true explanation of Roger's obstinacy is that he was hankering after Cassino and Benevento, the Patrimony of Peter in Campania.[4] On the score that he was too dull-witted to follow the reasonings of learned men, and that further elucidation was necessary before he could rightly detach himself from the cause of Anacletus, he invited representatives of Innocent to another conference, this time in Sicily. Accordingly, Cardinal Guy followed him to Palermo, where, as might have been expected, the disputants did no more than beat the air. Probably had the cardinal been empowered by Innocent to confirm Roger's royalty—as doubtless the crafty Norman hoped—the result would have been very different.[5]

Innocent meanwhile had been in Rome since the end of October; for on 1st November, 1137, the word *Romae* begins to replace *in territorio Romano* in his correspondence.[6] Thither went St. Bernard, bringing with him his captive cardinal, Peter of Pisa, and others whose adherence he had won.[7] Whatever may have happened later,[8] Peter's submission was at the time accepted, and shortly afterwards, in January, 1138, we find his curial subscription to a bull of Innocent.[9] The beginning of the end came at last when, on 25th January, Anacletus

[1] *Vita Prima*, II. vii. 45.

[2] Cf. S. Bern., *Ep.* 126.

[3] *Vita Prima*, II. vii. 46.

[4] *Op. cit., loc. cit.*

[5] Falcon. Benevent. *Chron.*, Murator. *Rer. Ital. Script., loc. cit.*

[6] Innoc. Pap. *Epist. et Priv.*, P.L. CLXXIX. 335 sqq.

[7] *Vita Prima, loc. cit.*

[8] S. Bern. *Ep.* 213.

[9] Innoc. Pap. *Epist. et Priv., op. cit.,* 344.

[1] Duchesne, *Lib. Pontific.*, II. 383.

[2] Innoc. Pap. *Epist. et Priv.*, *op. cit.*, 350.

passed to his account; [1] still in possession of the Lateran, for it was not apparently until 21st March that Innocent began to date his correspondence there. [2] St. Bernard writes to Peter the Venerable : " Thanks be to God who has given victory to the Church and has crowned and completed her labours. Our sorrow is turned into joy and our mourning into the music of the lute. The winter has passed ; the rains have abated ; flowers have appeared in our land ; the time of lopping has come ; the useless branch, the rotten limb, has been cut off. He, that wicked one I mean who made Israel to sin, has been swallowed up by death and gone down into

[3] *Ep.* 147.

the belly of hell." [3] Can we wonder at the strength of his language ? To St. Bernard Anacletus was Judas, the betrayer of his master. The harm which he had done to Christendom during eight long years was incalculable. No complaining word is said of the lamentable fact that all this while he had

[4] *Reg. S. P. Ben.*, I.

compelled the writer to be a *monachus gyrovagus* [4]—in a sacred cause, be it said, but all unwillingly—over the face of the earth. What may indeed fill us with wonder is that St. Bernard should be able on his return to Clairvaux to resume at once and with calm recollection his *Sermons on the Song of Songs.* " The mad fury of the lion (*leonina rabies*, with reference to Peter Leonis) is stilled ; wickedness has come to an end ; the Church is at peace," he remarks ; that peace which had ever been the possession of his own heart and the purpose

[5] *In Cant. Cant. Serm.*, XXIV. 1.

of his toilsome wanderings. [5] Arnald tells us that Anacletus was vouchsafed three days in which to repent, but that abusing the divine long-suffering he died impenitent, and was buried

[6] *Vita Prima*, II. vii. 47 ; Boso, Duchesne, *op. cit.*, II. 383.

[7] Order. Vital. *Hist. Eccl.*, XIII. 17, *P.L. loc. cit.*

in an unknown tomb. [6] Ordericus Vitalis, on the other hand, speaks of his death as sudden. [7]

The malcontents, however, probably incited by letters or emissaries from Roger of Sicily, proposed to maintain the Schism in being. About the middle of March they elected another antipope, Gregory, Cardinal Priest of the Title of the Holy Apostles, who took the name of Victor IV. His reign was not of long duration. The persuasion of St. Bernard had detached from him the leaders of his party, the family of the Pierleoni ; and on their defection all opposition broke down. " The ridiculous pontiff himself," under cover of night, betook himself to St. Bernard and placed himself entirely in his hands. The Abbot of Clairvaux—what an hour of justifiable triumph ! —led him repentant to Innocent. 29th May, the Octave of Pentecost, 1138, was a great day in the Vatican Basilica, for then it was that " all the people of Peter Leonis humbled themselves at the feet of our lord the Pope, and as his liegemen

Gerard of Angoulême died, and to the exhumation of his remains by the Apostolic Legate, Geoffrey of Chartres.[1] This was doubtless motived by the same spirit of reprisal which is accountable for the treatment meted out to Peter and others at Rome ; for in obedience to the Lateran Council Geoffrey saw to it that every altar consecrated by the Bishop of Angoulême was razed to the ground. His unfortunate kinsmen were deprived of every ecclesiastical dignity which they enjoyed.[2] It was not only somewhat ungenerous and, as we have seen, scarcely honourable to wreak vengeance upon Peter of Pisa, but it was comparatively easy ; no less easy was it to victimize the family and to asperse the memory of Gerard of Angoulême. But there was another old enemy whom it was quite impossible to treat in this high-handed fashion.

Roger of Sicily, we are given to understand, had duly recognized Innocent as " father and lord " ; but this by no means meant that he had relinquished his claim to feudal suzerainty over those districts of Southern Italy which formed part of the Patrimony of Peter. That the Lateran Council of April, 1139, should have launched against him its excommunication was but to stimulate him to renewed self-assertion. Ranulph of Alife had passed away shortly before the council came to an end. The occasion was felicitous for Roger, and on 25th May he landed at Salerno with the declared intention of annexing the Duchy of Apulia and so much of Southern Italy besides as he could make his prey. Robert of Capua, relying upon the Pope's moral support, at once took the field against him.[3] Innocent materialized his support to the extent of betaking himself with the entire *Curia* to San Germano—the mediæval name for the town of Cassino—where he arrived before hostilities broke out, and whence he sent an embassy to Roger. On one condition, and on one only, would the Sicilian acknowledge the disputed Papal suzerainty, namely, the annexation of Southern Italy, including the Duchies of Apulia and Capua, to his kingdom. But Innocent refused to abandon Robert in his extremity, and such forces as were at his disposal, combined with those of the Duke of Capua, advanced to the attack of the Castello di Galluzzo, a stronghold some ten miles South of San Germano occupied by the enemy. A fatal move ! They were enveloped by Roger, only Robert and a few others escaping capture. Himself and the cardinals thus in durance vile, the Pope found no course open to him other than on 25th July to revoke the excommunication of Roger, to confirm him in his royal dignity

[1] P. 133 *supra.*

[2] *Vita Prima,* II. vi. 39; *Chron. Mauriniac.,* II., *P.L.* CLXXX.

[3] Falcon. Benevent. *Chron., Murator. Rer. Ital. Script.,* V. 126 sqq. ; Order. Vital. *Hist. Eccl.,* I. 29, *P.L. op. cit.*

and to invest his two sons with the Duchies of Apulia and Capua respectively, for which fiefs the King of Sicily undertook to make an annual payment in token of his homage.[1]

This was the Treaty of Miniano. Its significance was that by sheer virile force the old sea-roving Norman type, as represented by Roger, had not only successfully established itself in what was substantially sovereign royalty over a considerable area of Mediterranean coastland, and that at the very gates of the capital city of Christendom—the feudal homage pledged to the Apostolic See being little more than a negligible factor—but also won for itself a place in the European concert on equal terms with powers the highest in dignity and the oldest in history. A reflection of the displeasure felt by the Emperor Conrad III at this result may perhaps be recognized in a short letter addressed to him by St. Bernard, in which allusion is made to " a complaint thought fit to be brought as to the invasion of the imperial authority." [2] But it is probable that the Abbot of Clairvaux did not consider himself called upon to intervene, provided that, as was at least formally the case, the rights of the Apostolic See were duly secured ; nor could he have felt otherwise than that, after the long absences and the exacting negotiations occasioned by the Schism, his duty was now at home. It was, however, given to him by firmness and by fair dealing in some measure to tame the savagery of " the tyrant of Sicily." Not only did he, as it would seem, raise no objection to the marriage of the latter's son, Roger III, Duke of Apulia, to Elizabeth, third daughter of Theobald of Champagne [3]—an alliance by means of which the king sought to consolidate his status amongst the princes—but, as we record in another connection,[4] he successfully effected, about the year 1140, the foundation of a daughter of Clairvaux either in Apulia or in the island of Sicily itself.[5] Indeed, so friendly and so secure an *entente* was established between these two men—arresting assurance as it was in that age of the ultimate dominance of moral force—perhaps the strongest characters of their generation, that apparently Roger not only sent ships to France to convey the Clairvaux monks to his dominions, but left to their judgement the selection of a site.[6] To St. Bernard's stipulation as to their number being no less than a *tota abbatia* we have already referred.[7]

[1] Falcon. Benevent. *Chron.*, *op. cit.*, V. 128 sq. ; Order. Vital. *op. cit.*, *loc. cit.* ; Jaffé, *Regest.*, 8043.

[2] *Ep.* 183 ; cf. pp. 148, 150 *supra*.

[3] S. Bern. *Ep.* 447.

[4] Pp. 70 sqq. *supra*.

[5] S. Bern. *Epp.* 207 sqq.

[6] S. Bern. *Ep.* 447.

[7] P. 72 *supra*.

CHAPTER VIII

EPISCOPAL IDEALS

WE have seen that when St. Bernard left Rome on the Friday after the Octave of Pentecost in 1138 it was with high credit attaching to his name. He was hailed as *Pater Patriæ ;* and we know something of the degree in which it was due to him that the Church had emerged from a prolonged crisis which had shaken its very foundations.[1] Fresh anxiety awaited him. [1] P. 155 *supra.* " You know," he wrote later in the same year to the bishops and cardinals of the Roman *Curia,* " how—if it is fitting that I should mention it—I was with you in evil days, coming and going to and fro the king's realm, standing by you and supporting you in your trials to an extent that, my bodily strength well-nigh exhausted, I was scarcely able, when God had restored peace to the Church, to return to my own country. . . . And lo, when I did return I found tribulation and grief. I have called upon the name of the Lord, and it has not profited me ; I have called upon yours and it has availed me nothing. For indeed the mighty gods of the earth have arisen with great power, to wit, the Archbishop of Lyons and the Abbot of Cluny. These, trusting in their own strength and boasting in the multitude of their riches, have drawn near and set themselves against me ; and not against me only, but against all the servants of God ; against you amongst the rest ; against themselves, against God, against all justice, and against all honour." [2]

[2] *Ep.* 168.

The anxiety in question arose out of an election to the see of Langres, St. Bernard's own diocese. It was moreover complicated in the sequel by the interests of a monk of Clairvaux, his kinsman Godfrey de la Roche. Before St. Bernard had last left Rome the Archbishop of Lyons, Robert, Dean of Langres, and Ulric, canon of the same church, had arrived there for the purpose of obtaining from Innocent II for themselves and for the chapter leave to take steps to fill the vacancy ; which leave was granted on the express condition that they should act " upon the advice of religious

¹ S. Bern. *Ep.* 164.

persons " in making the election.[1] This condition, as a
matter of usual procedure in episcopal elections, was shortly
afterwards formally confirmed by the Lateran Council of

² Labbe, *Concil.,* X. 1009.

1139.[2] The precise sense in which the term *religiosi* is to be
understood in this connection has been disputed. Are the
abbots of the monasteries in the diocese intended or, more
generally, men of sound faith and exemplary piety ?   Judging
from a letter addressed to the Pope by St. Bernard in which
he writes : " Let the charge of electing a man pleasing to
God be laid, I beg, upon persons who are beyond suspicion,

³ *Ep.* 169.

who seek not their own ends but those of Jesus Christ," [3] we
infer the latter to be here the true meaning of the word
" religious."   This would appear to be confirmed by the fact
that, writing in 1144 to the clergy of the archdiocese of Sens,
St. Bernard remarks : " What is to be looked for is the advice
of the suffragan bishops, the approval of religious men in the
episcopate, and that what is of common interest should be

⁴ *Ep.* 202.

handled by all in common." [4]   Even supposing the reference
in this latter instance to be to bishops who have been in the
cloister, there is no suggestion of any obligation to consult
the representatives of religious houses in the diocese as such.

To return to the story.   The Archbishop of Lyons and his
party charged with their instructions from the Pope left
Rome, being followed shortly afterwards by St. Bernard.   No
sooner had the Abbot of Clairvaux crossed the Alps than, as
he wrote to Innocent, he was met by " not a few religious
persons "—it would be like him to use the equivocal term in
irony—who informed him that the day had been fixed for the
consecration of the Bishop-Elect of Langres, of whom they
could say nothing good.   Indeed, St. Bernard refrains from
mentioning the discreditable details which had reached his
unwilling ears.   At once he decided, on the advice of these
" religious persons," to go to Lyons in order to prevent if

⁵ *Ep.* 164.

possible this nefarious arrangement from taking effect.[5]   The
chosen prelate was a Cluniac monk whose identity is doubtful.

⁶ Petr. Ven. *Epp. Lib.* II. 28; Horst. et Mabillon. *Not. Fus. in S. Bern. Ep.* 164.

He may have been Alberic, formerly Grand Prior of Cluny and
at the time Abbot of Vézelay.[6]   In any case he was strongly
supported by Peter the Venerable, as well as by the Archbishop of Lyons, another Peter, and by Odo, son of Hugh II

⁷ S. Bern. *Epp.* 164 and 167.

Duke of Burgundy.[7]   Knowing that investiture with the
regalia should precede investiture with the spiritualities, a

⁸ Pp. 205 sq. *infra.*

point upon which the king was sensitive,[8] Peter the Venerable
duly presented the bishop-elect to Louis at Le-Puy-en-Velay

⁹ Petr. Ven. *Epp. Lib.* I. 29; S. Bern. *Ep.* 164.

in the early autumn.[9]   Not long afterwards he was consecrated by the archbishop, assisted by the Bishops of Autun

and Mâcon, as St. Bernard reports to Innocent.[1] Matters [1] Ep. 166.
were thus being carried with a high hand, for the electors had,
in fact, been the metropolitan, the Dean of Langres and the
aforesaid canon, Ulric. A gross indignity was inflicted upon
the Church of Langres, the motive of which it is a little difficult
to detect. Why should Peter the Venerable have so flag-
rantly lent himself to the violation of canonical right ? As
regards the moral objection to the elect urged by St. Bernard
in the strongest terms—" Shame forbids me to repeat what
common fame reports of him, nay, I should say the notorious
infamy of the man " [2]—Peter retorted that this was nothing [2] Ep. 167.
but Cistercian prejudice.[3] Was his attitude a protest against [3] Petr. Ven.
partizanship ? However this may have been, *etsi bene saltat*, Epp. Lib. I. 29.
extra chorum saltat, for it was entirely without bearing upon
the constitutional question of the status of the electors.
Ultimately he suffered humiliating defeat.

St. Bernard did not delay in ensuring an appeal to Rome.
Reference has been made to his letters addressed to the Pope
and to the Roman *Curia*. In another letter to the Pope he
mentions the principal appellants, Pontius, Archdeacon of
Langres, Bonami, canon of the same church, Falk, Dean of
Lyons, and two Clairvaux monks, Bruno and Geoffrey.[4] A [4] Ep. 164.
letter written to the dean associates with these Guy, Treasurer
of the Church of Lyons.[5] The opposition was more than [5] Ep. 165.
merely local, and the more forcible as shared by members of
the metropolitan chapter, in particular by Falk, a man of
some character, who subsequently became Archbishop of
Lyons. It is characteristic of St. Bernard that the moral,
one might almost rather say, the practical aspect of the affair
assumed in his view large proportions. What had been done
seemed to him to be not merely wrong, but highly impolitic.
In spite of Peter the Venerable's contention that the bishop
was of blameless character, he continued to insist to the
contrary. " O pious mother Church of Lyons, what a spouse,
nay, what a monster have you given to your daughter !
What indeed ? Am I to call such a thing as this an honourable wedlock, a chaste bed ? . . . You have elected and
consecrated a bishop as one would not choose a bailiff or a
rent-collector." [6] So he writes to Falk and Guy. [6] Ep. 165.

However, Rome was a long way off and the unfitness of
the Cluniac for the episcopate on moral grounds might be
difficult to prove. St. Bernard knew well enough the dangers
attending appeals on such grounds, the uncertainty as to how
the *Curia* might dispose of conflicting evidence.[7] On the [7] Pp. 254 sq.
canonical point his position was impregnable. The Arch- *infra*.

bishop of Lyons had plainly acted *ultra vires;* moreover, he had flatly disregarded the instruction which he, the Dean of Langres and the Canon Ulric had received from the Pope.[1] The immediate and vital consideration was to ensure that the appellants were suitably represented. St. Bernard would appear to have taken upon himself the selection of such persons as were to present the case at Rome. To denude the Church of Langres of its chapter would be, he tells the Pope, to expose it to the risk of plunder and pillage. Accordingly, having enjoined upon the chapter the necessity of maintaining a united front at home while their appeal was in course, he despatched to represent them from among themselves the Canon Bonami together with the Archdeacon of Langres and Herbert, Abbot of St. Étienne-de-Dijon.[2]

All that we know of the appeal is that it was successful, and that the Cluniac monk never became Bishop of Langres. But the sequel was startling in many quarters ; to St. Bernard it was profoundly disconcerting. The delegates, whoever they may have been, appointed to fill the vacant see nominated the Abbot of Clairvaux.[3] In this, as he had done in other instances,[4] he steadfastly refused to accede to the proposal. He was not, however, to be dispensed entirely from searchings of heart in this matter. If Clairvaux was not to lose its abbot, it must lose its prior ; if it was not to be St. Bernard, it must be his *alter ego,* " the staff of his tottering footsteps," " the light of his eyes," his very " right arm." [5] The choice next fell upon Godfrey de la Roche. As we have suggested, St. Bernard was at first displeased. Further consideration, however, would appear to have reconciled him to the selection. He could not but have felt that it was a recognition of his own episcopal ideals, and that these were well represented by Godfrey. And after all, was it right that he should again disregard the authority of the Apostolic See in the persons of its delegates ? " What has happened to our Godfrey at Langres "—where the formal election by the chapter would have taken place— " has been contrary to the expectation and intention of the bishops (*sc.* of France) and contrary to my own. But there is One who in a certain fashion wins the consent of the unwilling, and compels even the opposition of human wills to serve his own ends." [6] So he wrote to Louis le Jeune in a letter which sought to bring the king to reason in the matter of the investiture of Godfrey. The situation was delicate, for the *regalia* had already been bestowed upon the Cluniac monk. Louis had doubtless to face the risk of offending Peter the Venerable who had been prominent in the cause of his monk ; and there

[1] Pp. 159 sq. *supra.*

[2] *Ep.* 169.

[3] *Vita Prima,* I. xiv. 69.
[4] P. 143 *supra.*

[5] S. Bern. *Ep.* 170.

[6] *Ep.* 170.

was the further risk that to annul the investiture recently granted at Le-Puy might reflect upon his royal dignity generally throughout France, and specially in the diocese of Langres. An earlier request of St. Bernard had not, we infer, met with a flat refusal ; but the delay was sufficient to be damaging in its effects. " I thank your clemency," he now writes, "for the kind response with which you have honoured me. But, indeed, the delay terrifies me, seeing as I do the temporalities of the see exposed to plunder and to pillage. These temporalities are yours ; this being so, we plainly recognize and we deplore the dishonour done to your royalty—dishonour which you rightly bid us to dread—if there is no one to protect them." [1] [1] *Ep.* 170. Here St. Bernard is appealing to an experience common enough, alas, in those days. The election, he urges, has been duly made, and the elect is a faithful man ; " as he would not be were he willing to hold what is yours at other hands than yours. He has not so much as offered to touch the temporalities ; he has not yet entered your city ; he has not taken a single step in the matter, although the invitation of clergy and people, the affliction of the oppressed and the wishes of good men have most vehemently prompted him in this direction. This being so, there is need, as you see, that your plans be matured not only for the sake of your own credit, but for the sake of our necessities. And unless by the present messengers your serenity makes a favourable reply to the expectant people who are your people you will—a most undesirable end —stir up against you the hearts now devoted to you of many pious folk and, as I fear, inflict no small damage on your own *regalia* attached to this church." [2] The letter, we feel, was [2] *Ep.* 170. skilfully drafted, respectful, wise and firm. Peter the Venerable took his defeat in a generous spirit ; his love for St. Bernard did not founder in " the storm of Langres." [3] Louis [3] Petr. Ven. did not much longer delay the investiture of Godfrey, who *Epp. Lib.* III. seems to have been consecrated in October, 1138. [4] Consider- 17. ing the tangle of affairs and the slowness of communication in [4] *Gall. Christ.,* those days, it says much for St. Bernard's tactful driving- IV., *Instr.,* 170. force that the matter had been satisfactorily settled within a period of some eight months.

In France the XIIth century was marked by the coming to birth of that sturdy bantling, social liberty Its cries were heard, naturally enough, first of all in the great cities where the industrial populations began to form themselves into corporations, and in course of time these corporations for their mutual self-protection, at the price often of violence and disorder, cohered into communes. We can easily understand that this result was in the eyes of potentates and prelates a menace to seigneurial rights. It was not, however, regarded with the same disfavour by the king, constituting, as it did, a restraint upon the powers of the subordinate feudality. At Rheims the *bourgeoisie*, whose interest it always was to take when possible peaceful means, saw its opportunity in the vacancy of the see occasioned by the death of Archbishop Raynald on 13th January, 1138,[1] and obtained from Louis le Jeune on pecuniary terms authority to establish in the city a commune with a mayor at its head. It may, perhaps, be supposed that Louis was the more willing to grant this concession, as hoping to find in it a means of limiting the powers of Theobald of Champagne. Such a commune already existed at Laon, not very far distant. It was specified that the Commune of Rheims was to be similarly constituted, in particular that the rights of the archbishopric and of the other ecclesiastical institutions of the city were to be duly safeguarded.[2] The king's favour was peculiarly acceptable, for the reason that there was prevalent among the people the tradition that the civil and criminal jurisdiction in the city had, in the old days of St. Rémi and for many subsequent generations, been in the hands of aldermen popularly elected, and that the existing *ex officio* jurisdiction of the archbishop was a usurpation of these ancient rights.[3] It should, however, be said that the proposed Commune of Rheims was in one material respect not constituted on the lines of that of Laon. The latter had been established upon the basis of a common understanding between the bishop and the townsfolk.[4] At Rheims it was established *sede vacante* over the heads of all future occupants of the see. The new archbishop would take office on terms unknown to his predecessors for some centuries past, and in the definition of which he had had no voice. The *regalia*, of which the rights in question had hitherto formed a constituent part, were still in the hands of Louis, and to him the chapter appealed. The king, consistently as he believed with the limitations of his recent grant, wrote to the mayor and commune charging them to respect the long-established seigneuries of the churches of Rheims, in particular those of the cathedral and St. Rémi.[5] This order was ignored. The commune took its stand upon the constitution of Laon, ground which had been prepared for it by the equivocal wording of the royal charter. Communal justice replaced ecclesiastical justice and resistance on the part of the cathedral chapter and of the Abbey of St. Rémi was suppressed by force, their men-at-arms being committed to prison.[6] Thus

[1] *Gall. Christ.,* IX. 84.

[2] Ludov. VII. *Ep., R.H.G.F.* XVI. 5.

[3] Joann. Sares. *Ep., op. cit.,* XVI. 568 ; cf. *Ep.* cccxxi, *Materials for Hist. of Archbp. Th. Becket,* VI. 225, *R.S.*

[4] Guibert. *De Vita Sua,* III. 7, *P.L.* CLVI. 922.

[5] Ludov. VII. *Ep., R.H.G.F.* XVI. 5.

[6] *Op. cit.,* XVI. 5 and 6.

to the evils attendant upon the long vacancy of the see were added the terrors of revolution.

It was the same year, 1138, as that in which St. Bernard was so intimately concerned with the episcopal crisis in his own diocese of Langres ; [1] nevertheless, he found time to bestow upon the task of allaying this trouble also. It was plain to him that the distressing situation was really due to the delay in filling the see. " The Church of Rheims," he wrote to the Pope, " is falling into ruin ; the glorious city is given over to shame ; passers-by cry aloud that there is no sorrow like its sorrow. Fightings without ; fears within. Nay indeed, fightings within ; for its own sons fight against it, and it has no father to set it free from strife. Its only hope is that Innocent may wipe the tears from its cheeks. How long, my lord, is it to be left uncovered by the shield of your protection ? How long is it to be trodden under foot and find none to lift it up ? " [2] Louis would seem to have been the great difficulty. St. Bernard knew him well, and one conjectures that he recognized in the delay the desire to give the Commune of Rheims time to establish itself, so that when the new archbishop received the *regalia* they would come to him shorn of the civil and criminal jurisdiction of a feudal lordship ; he would thus be compelled to accept the *fait accompli*. Moreover, the existence of the commune would strengthen the king's hand against Theobald of Champagne. But a commune without civil and criminal jurisdiction would be no commune at all. St. Bernard's way of putting it to Innocent was this : " The king has humiliated himself ; his indignation "—against the commune for its forcible usurpation of jurisdiction—" has now abated." In fact, to use a vulgar phrase, Louis had climbed down ; on second thoughts he decided that it was worth his while to sacrifice his dignity. " What course then is open," asks St. Bernard, " except for the Apostolic hand to succour the afflicted church and bring remedies and dressings to its wounds ? I believe, therefore, that the step to be taken is to hasten the election, so that the popular insolence may not scatter to the winds what there is left ; its fury must be resisted with a high hand." He is confident that once the election has been duly made, by the divine favour all else to be desired will follow.[3]

Unfortunately the Pope, doubtless with the best intentions, took steps which did but prolong the delay. He forbad the electors to assemble before Louis had taken his advice on the whole matter ; and further, he required that the associations or corporations which had been guilty of the excesses reported

[1] S. Bern. *Ep.* 170 ; cf. pp. 159 sqq. *supra.*

[2] *Ep.* 318.

[3] *Ep.* 318.

[1] Innoc. II.
Pap. Ep.,
R.H.G.F. XV.
394.

to him should be broken up.[1] Possibly St. Bernard had spoken in too strong terms ; although he had not asked for the suppression of the commune, only that its abuses should be corrected. Possibly the Pope was jealous of the ecclesiastical rights at stake. On both these points his judgement might well have been influenced, not only by his own local experience at Rome, but by the general trend of events in Italy. Not many months later Arnald of Brescia would be condemned at the Lateran Council of 1139. However, Louis was not prepared to take the extreme step of revoking his grant of a commune ; he contented himself with instructing that the civil and criminal jurisdiction should be restored to

[2] Ludov. VII.
Ep., R.H.G.F.
XVI. 5 sq.

the ecclesiastical authorities.[2] Finally the Apostolic Legate, Geoffrey, Bishop of Chartres, and the Bishops of Auxerre, Soissons and Arras were commissioned by Innocent to supervise the election to the vacant see. The choice of the chapter fell, as it had at Langres, upon St. Bernard ; and again he protested. Pressed by the king in terms sufficiently flattering and reassuring, hailed by all as the one man who for his wisdom and his holiness might be trusted to rule the Church of Rheims, to mollify and to restrain the commune and to bring peace to the city, he yet held out firmly against the proposal. " My monastic habit leads to the supposition that I am fit to fulfil these high functions ; but the habit does not make a man holy, although it may convey the impression of holiness. No

[3] S. Bern. Ep.
449.
[4] Gall. Christ.,
IX. 84 sqq.
[5] Ep. 210.

one knows me better than I know myself." [3] He was not to be moved. Without further delay the chapter elected Samson de Mauvoisin, Archdeacon of Chartres,[4] " a man of outstanding merit," [5] as St. Bernard shortly afterwards described him to the Pope, a man of whom after some seven years' testing as

[6] Ep. 247.

occupant of the see he would write to Eugenius III as one " whose praise is in the Church." [6] This latter testimony means much, for it was no light task to which Samson set himself. Neither the king nor the commune would have been particularly pleased that juridical authority in the city and in its neighbourhood remained as it had been before the vacancy occurred—in the hands of the Church. And in fact the archbishop had not long entered upon his duties before efforts were made to place difficulties in his way. The malcontents in the city would seem to have gathered around a suspended priest, whom they forcibly provided with an altar at

[7] Menol. S.
Symphor., an.
1140, R.H.G.F.
XVI. 5.

the Church of St. Symphorian on All Saints' Day, 1140.[7] This open defiance of authority strictly ecclesiastical was a climax which left Samson no alternative other than to invoke the secular arm. Louis probably did something to support the

CLOISTER OF FONTENAY

archbishop, but it was Theobald of Champagne who stood stoutly by him.   William of St. Thierry, who knew his Rheims, writing very shortly after the event, tells us that St. Bernard, accompanied by Joslen, Bishop of Soissons, hastened to the scene, and in the archiepiscopal palace addressed a large body representative both of the clergy and of the citizens, upon whom he urged peace.[1]   Within a period of three weeks the disturbance was sufficiently quelled for the desecrated Church of St. Symphorian to be reconsecrated with great solemnity,[2] and for the people of Rheims to accept without resistance what must have been a somewhat distressing penalty, namely, the entire suppression of the commune.[3]   Some few years later St. Bernard was involved in a prolonged conflict of a somewhat similar character, which for us in England has an interest of its own.

After Louis le Jeune and the Crusaders had left St. Denis about the second week in June, 1147,[4] Eugenius III remained for some time in France.   He was at Auxerre from 14th July until 6th September,[5] at about which date he went to Cîteaux,[6] in order to attend the general chapter at which Savigny and its daughters were affiliated to the Order.[7]   On his way back to Auxerre the Pope consecrated, on 21st September, in the presence of ten cardinals, eight bishops and many abbots, St. Bernard amongst the rest, the church which Everard, Bishop of Norwich, had built for the Abbey of Fontenay.[8] Later in the year, accompanied by St. Bernard and by a great following of cardinals, he travelled, passing through Verdun,[9] to Trèves; where he arrived on 30th November.[10]

An open sore had long been draining the strength of the Church in the Province of York.   Archbishop Thurstan had died in February, 1141, and the election of his successor still remained of doubtful regularity.   The story is told by John, Prior of the Augustinian house of Hexham, a practically contemporary chronicler who wrote a continuation of Symeon of Durham's *De Gestis Regum Anglorum* from the year 1129 to the year 1154.   John records that after the death of Thurstan the Chapter of York spent a whole year in fruitless discussion, and then finally, under persuasion from the Apostolic Legate, Henry of Blois, Bishop of Winchester, elected a relative of King Stephen, Henry, Abbot of Caen.   However, nothing came of this, because when the legate required him to resign his abbacy Henry appears to have refused   The legate was the king's brother, but his desire to see his kinsman metropolitan of the province did not induce him to dispense him in this matter of plurality.   In January the chapter elected by a sufficient

[1] *Vita Prima*, I. xiv. 67.

[2] *Menol. S. Symphor.*, an. 1140, *R.H.G.F. loc. cit.*

[3] *Annal. Rem. et Colon.*, an. 1140, *M.G.H.* XVI. 733.

[4] Pp. 281 sq. *infra.*

[5] Jaffé, *Regest.*, 9094 sqq.

[6] *Op. cit.*, 9132 sqq.

[7] *Op. cit.*, 9139 ; cf. pp. 81 sq. *supra.*

[8] *Gall. Christ.*, IV. 492.

[9] Jaffé, *Regest.*, II. 20 ; *Vita Prima*, IV. iv. 21.

[10] Jaffé, *Regest.*, 9182 sqq. ; *Cont. Gest. Trevir., M.G.H.* XXIV. 378.

[1] *Vita S. Will., Hist. of the Church of York and its Archbps.,* II. 270 ; Stubbs, *Chron., op. cit.,* II. 390. *R.S.*

majority William FitzHerbert, their treasurer, who also was of the blood royal, being a son of Emma, the king's sister.[1] This election was suspected of being simoniacal, and Walter, Archdeacon of London, set out to interview the king and on behalf of himself and other archdeacons protest against it. On his way he was intercepted by the Earl of Yorkshire and imprisoned in Bytham Castle. Meanwhile, the archbishop-elect was conducted to Stephen at Lincoln, and there confirmed in all the temporalities of the see.[2]

[2] Joann. Hagust. *Hist.,* Symeon of Durham, II. 306 sq., *R.S.*

It would appear that St. Bernard at an early stage became aware that William was appealing to the Pope, for he writes to Innocent II : " The Archbishop of York is approaching you—a man of whom I have more than once written to your holiness, a man who instead of choosing God for his helper has trusted in the multitude of his riches. His cause is weak and feeble and, as I learn from the testimony of truthful witnesses, from the sole of his foot to the crown of his head there is no soundness in him. What does it mean ? Why does a man who has no justice on his side betake himself to the judge who searches out unrighteousness, to the guardian of equity ? Does he think that he can pervert justice at the Roman *Curia* as he has done in England ? . . . He approaches you with the support of many whom he has won over by his importunity and by his money. . . . Now what in a case like this will the Vicar of Peter do, if not what Peter did in the case of one who thought that the gift of God was to be bought

[3] S. Bern. *Ep.* 346.

with money ? " [3] This move on the part of the archbishop-elect probably followed an appeal which was lodged against the Apostolic Legate's decision in his favour by William Abbot of Rievaulx, Richard Abbot of Fountains, Cuthbert Prior of Gisburn, and Waltheof Prior of Kirkham, amongst others, on the ground that the archbishop-elect " had canvassed the electors to this honour by pecuniary guarantees." [4] The

[4] Joann. Hagust. *op. cit.,* 311.

appellants, together with the Archdeacon of London and William, the Cantor of York, were cited to Rome to appear before the Pope face to face with the archbishop-elect and his supporters on the Third Sunday in Lent, 1143. Two points came before the *Curia ;* the question as to the pressure put upon the chapter by William, Earl of Yorkshire, in order to compel it to elect the royal nominee, and the question of simony. St. Bernard, while holding the latter to be the more serious by no means accounts the former as negligible. Writing to Celestin II, who ascended the pontifical throne later in the same year, he speaks of the indignity which the appellants would unjustly suffer if they were required " to render obedience to and to accept the sacraments from a man who had been twice thrust upon them, first by the king and "—what amounted to the same thing in this case—" then by the Apostolic Legate." [1]   He saw plainly that it was a flagrant abuse of royal influence common enough in his day but none the less utterly offensive to him, and he stood firmly for the electoral freedom of the chapter.   The archbishop-elect was given to understand that if the Dean of York was prepared to swear that compliance with royal precept had not been forced upon the chapter by the Earl of Yorkshire and if he himself would swear that he had not used bribery as a means to his election, his consecration would be sanctioned.[2]   This amounted to leaving the matter very much in the hands of one man, William of St. Barbe, Dean of York.   Liberty, John of Hexham tells us, was granted to the persons concerned to substitute another witness of approved character in place of the dean. The explanation of this grant is that the latter had been to Rome in order apparently to ensure the validity of his own election to the see of Durham, to which on his return he was consecrated by the Apostolic Legate Henry and nine other prelates in Winchester Cathedral on the Octave of the Feast of St. John Baptist.   While at Rome he had obtained a letter from Celestin empowering the legate to substitute in the matter of the oath above-mentioned other witnesses than himself.   It is not quite clear why he sought this dispensation, but so soon as the news that it had been granted reached by some side wind the ears of St. Bernard, his suspicion was at once aroused.   The whole proceeding had been conducted in secrecy behind the backs of the appellants, and its tendency was to evacuate of its solid value the oath in question. Possibly the dean felt that he could not honestly take the oath ; on the other hand, to have flatly refused to do so would have been to make an enemy of one who to all appearances would be his near neighbour and his metropolitan.   Probably the party which supported the archbishop-elect were anxious to get a damaging witness out of the way.   Plainly, however, this second Papal rescript represented, as compared with the original stipulation, a material change of front.   " What am I to say," wrote St. Bernard to the Roman *Curia*, " of the secret and in truth "—may we so translate *tenebrosas* ?— " shady letter which this William boasts himself to have obtained ?   Would that he had received it from the princes of darkness and not from Apostolic princes ! . . . What am I to say to you if a scandal like this does not scorch you, a scandal which offends not little children but "—applying the terms to

[1] *Ep.* 235.

[2] Joann. Hagust. *op. cit.* 313 ; S. Bern. *Ep.* 236.

moral adultness—" great and perfect men ? " However, some atonement is yet possible. " Supposing that this man (the archbishop-elect) has received sacrilegious consecration " it is still open to the *Curia* to redeem its character, for, he writes, " it will be a much more glorious thing for you to cast down Simon Magus from his seat than it would have been for you to forbid him to attempt to take it." [1] When William of Durham returned from Rome in September he was summoned to appear before the Apostolic Legate at Winchester, where, on the ground of complications in his own diocese, he excused himself from testifying on oath to the canonical validity of the archiepiscopal election. In his place were appointed Ralph, Bishop of the Orkneys, Severin, Abbot of St. Mary of York, and Benedict, Abbot of Whitby, all of whom swore to the freedom from royal control with which the chapter had proceeded in the matter ; and on 26th September in Winchester Cathedral, to the great joy of his friends, William the Treasurer was consecrated Archbishop of York by the Apostolic Legate Henry, the diocesan bishop, his own uncle.[2] We may remind ourselves that both Archbishop William FitzHerbert and Henry of Caen, upon whom the chapter's choice had first fallen, were of the royal family. It is not difficult to detect the legate's desire to find an occupant for the Northern metropolitan see who would forward his own ambitious schemes. Were Henry of Blois to succeed in raising Winchester to the status of a metropolitanate—an end at which he aimed—he hoped that two of the three English provinces would be ruled by members of the royal house, and York with himself possessed of legatine authority become a mere appanage of Winchester. In order to be quite fair to the archbishop, it should be said there were some who in spite of the charges attaching to his election could speak well of him. Such was the anonymous writer who, certainly no later than the XIIIth century, telling the story of his life, even implied that after the irregular fashion not uncommon in those days he had been raised by local veneration to the altars of the Church.[3] Again, we read in the XVth century *Chronicle* doubtfully ascribed to John Brompton, Abbot of Jervaulx [4]—a Cistercian house, be it noted, not very far distant from York—that " when Archbishop Thurstan died the canons elected Blessed William, treasurer of the same church, on the grounds both of his high moral character and of his outstanding fitness for the post." It is true, however, that the chronicler adds that " this William, sprung of the illustrious family to which King Stephen belonged, had been

[1] *Ep.* 236.

[2] Joann.Hagust. *op. cit.*, 315.

[3] *Vita S. Will.*, Hist. of the Church of York and its Archbps., II. 270 sqq., *R.S.*

[4] Cf. Hunt, *John Brompton, Dict. Nat. Biogr.*

marked out by his high birth ; for he was the son of the most potent Count Herbert," going on to say that " his jealousy of power and his uncontrollable love of domination " led to difficulties which ultimately resulted in an appeal to the Apostolic See.[1] Writing some three hundred years after the event, this authority was able to give a more dispassionate account than that which had reached St. Bernard when the fray was at its hottest. However untrustworthy on certain points, in this case his testimony, together with that of the anonymous writer of the *Life*, may perhaps be cited as helping us to form a correct estimate of the character of one who, whatever his merits, proved to be a veritable stormy petrel to the Church in England.

[1] Joann. Bromt. *Chron.*, Twysden, *Decem Script.*, 1028 sq.

And the consecration of the archbishop raised at once a storm of indignation in his province. Grave suspicion prevailed as to the straight dealing of the legate. The letter from Rome, on the authority of which the Dean of York had been dispensed from swearing to the canonical integrity of the election, was the weak point in the case. No one appeared to have seen it. The substitution of other witnesses than the witness most likely, as having been present, to know the facts —the very witness whom William had himself selected—this had an evil look. " A man who in order to escape condemnation," writes St. Bernard to Celestin II, " appealed of his own free choice to the testimony of William the Dean, when this testimony fails him how has he not on his own admission lost his case ? How has he not by his own sentence pronounced himself guilty ? "[2] He presses upon the Pope that it is his plain duty to see that the orders of his predecessor are carried out. " Who does not know that the case of the Church of York was decided by him ? Would that nobody knew what sort of effect has been given to a decision pronounced by so great a man ! . . . How does the matter stand ? William the Dean has not taken the oath required—and the other William is a bishop ! . . . Unless I am much mistaken, his suffragans will resign their sees rather than pay allegiance to this idol ; this is what will happen unless your authority intervenes with a strong hand."[3] To the *Curia* he writes : " You know quite well that the sentence went forth from the lord Pope Innocent of excellent memory, with the approval of yourselves and of the entire Roman *Curia*, that the election, I should say, intrusion of William of York was to be held null and void unless the other William, then dean, should refute on oath the charge brought against him."[4] It would appear from reading the authorities cited that the more serious charge of simony

[2] *Ep.* 235.

[3] *Ep.* 235.

[4] *Ep.* 236.

was bound up with the charge of intrusion so inextricably, that the heads of several religious houses in the diocese felt themselves unable to remain at their posts. Robert, Prior of Hexham, had immediately on hearing of the election migrated to Clairvaux where he became a Cistercian monk.[1] William, the saintly Abbot of Rievaulx, experienced later distressing heart-searchings on the point, which were allayed only by the assurance of his beloved master that while the election of the archbishop may have been uncanonical, his consecration was valid. " I can say with certainty," St. Bernard writes, " that neither the injustice nor the sin is yours. You have done what you could ; and now, as Augustine has it,[2] another man's wrong-doing does not stain your conscience, seeing that you have not consented to it in your heart but rebuked it with your tongue. . . . For the rest, be of good cheer, and set your mind at ease. Know that in Orders and in the other sacraments he who baptizes and consecrates is Christ the Lord, the high priest of our souls. . . . Moreover, we should have to leave this world entirely if we wished to avoid all the wicked men from whom the Church suffers." [3] Although he had thought well almost to threaten the Pope with such a possibility, we cannot suppose that St. Bernard would have regarded a general exodus of the best men in the province otherwise than as a disaster ; so far as the Cistercian abbots are concerned, there is evidence that he did what he could to prevent it.

It is probable that at this stage a change took place in Celestin's attitude towards the Bishop of Winchester, Henry of Blois, the villain of the piece ; a change which, if it did not settle the dispute, at any rate delayed a settlement adverse to the true interests of the Church. John of Hexham records that the Pope was " an adherent of the House of Anjou, and intended to strengthen its hands in its efforts to weaken the power of King Stephen " ; and that " for this reason he became an enemy of Henry of Winchester." The result was that the latter's legatine authority was revoked. In the same year (1144) Celestin died, and Henry at once made his way to Rome, delaying for a while at Cluny, of which house he had been a monk. At Rome, although he found some favour with Lucius II, he did not succeed in recovering the office of Apostolic Legate.[4] This was conferred upon Hincmar, Cardinal Bishop of Frascati (*Tusculum*), who was despatched to England with the *pallium*. William of York, a man, as John of Hexham remarks, " who had always been nursed in luxury and riches," secure as he supposed himself to

[1] Joann. Hagust. *op. cit.*, 311.

[2] S. Aug. *De Verb. Domini Serm.*, XVIII.

[3] *Ep.* 353.

[4] Joann. Hagust. *op. cit.*, 315 sq.

be, was occupied with trifles, and failed to meet the cardinal, thereby making no very favourable impression upon that august person.[1] Apparently the legate had passed through Clairvaux on his way, for St. Bernard writes to the Abbot of Rievaulx: " I made what suggestion I could to the lord Bishop of Tusculum, who is charged with legatine authority in England, and he gave me his faithful promise that, unless he did something still better for us, he would at least see that the *pallium* which he brought with him was not granted to the archbishop unless William the Dean, now a bishop, swore the required oath." [2] Meanwhile an anxious moment arrived. Richard, Abbot of Fountains, died late in 1144 or early in 1145. The party of reform, for so we may describe it, lost a strong supporter. But St. Bernard took care that it found a stronger in his successor, Henry Murdach, Abbot of Vauclair, who had been professed at Clairvaux ; himself an Englishman, and thus the more competent to deal with the situation.[3] Whatever may have been elicited by the inquiry instituted by Hincmar, we know that it was in large measure due to Henry Murdach that the Cardinal Legate returned to Rome with the *pallium* unbestowed soon after the death of Lucius II in 1145.[4] We may remark in passing that the so brief pontificates of Celestin and Lucius were scarcely favourable to a speedy settlement of the matter in dispute.

Lucius was succeeded by Eugenius III, the first Cistercian Pope, in whose election Cardinal Hincmar would have taken part after he arrived in Rome. St. Bernard's first letter to his own son in religion is a word of joyful warning, such as we might expect to find him writing, a preface as it were to the great treatise *Of Consideration*. His second is a direct appeal to the Apostolic See once and for all to put an end to this crying scandal. The Church in the Province of York, the Church throughout the world ; above all the Cistercians in their English outposts, fighting against heavy odds for the maintenance of a self-respecting and clean-handed episcopate, all were looking hopefully to the central Apostolic authority at Rome. " I am importunate," writes St. Bernard to the Pope, " but I have my excuse. It is the Apostolic office of Eugenius. Men are saying that now it is I who am Pope, and not yourself. On all sides they assail me with their affairs ; amongst them are friends whose right I cannot gainsay, not merely without scandal but without sin. And there is another excuse no less valid. Time after time the pen is being used against this idol of York ; and the repetition of its

[1] Joann. Hagust. *op. cit.*, 317.

[2] *Ep.* 360.

[3] S. Bern. *Epp.* 320 and 321.

[4] Joann. Hagust. *op. cit.*, 318.

attack is necessary simply because, often as this weapon has been directed against it, not yet has the idol been transfixed through and through. . . . He who is in the place of Peter can at one blow fell Ananias and Simon Magus. To put it more plainly, it is the acknowledged prerogative of the Roman Pontiff alone by his peremptory sentence to depose bishops, for the simple reason that while many are called to take charge of parts of the Church he has authority over the whole." [1]
In a later letter to the Pope he presses the point again almost ruthlessly : " What particular steps should be taken in order to cast down this man—and there appear to me to be various alternatives—it is not for me to dictate to your wisdom. I do not trouble myself as to the direction in which the unfruitful tree falls, provided that it does fall." He points significantly to the fact that " there is extant a letter (of the late Dean of York) to the Apostolic Legate in which he plainly states that the intrusion (of William FitzHerbert) was manifest, and that he never was properly elected. Thus, then, the defender whom the latter had prepared for himself he has to accept as his accuser." [2] It was a matter of common knowledge that what the dean would not swear to formally he would allow in a letter which presumably he did not intend to be quoted. At the moment all that the Pope did was to suspend the archbishop until William the Dean had sworn the formal oath required by Innocent II. Meanwhile the armed retainers of some of the archbishop's kinsmen pillaged the property of Henry Murdach and of the monks of Fountains. [3] Doubtless they would have killed the abbot had they succeeded in getting him into their hands, for blood was very hot. Finally, the dean's letter to Henry of Blois was accepted as sufficient condemnation of the archbishop and, as we learn from Gervase of Canterbury, the Benedictine chronicler who wrote some fifty years later, the Pope formally deposed him at a council held in Paris during the spring of 1147, and ordered a new election ; [4] a rescript to this effect was sent to William, Bishop of Durham, and the Chapter of York, directing that the matter should be dealt with before forty days had elapsed after the receipt of his instructions. [5] But partizanship would die hard. After the six long years which had elapsed since 1141, the Pope's decision did but seem to give it a fresh objective. The Chapter of York assembled in the Priory of St. Martin at Richmond, where the majority elected Henry Murdach ; the rest present, who favoured the deposed archbishop, [6] elected a certain Master Hilary, who had been an unsuccessful candidate in 1142, and was probably an

[1] Ep. 239.

[2] Ep. 240.

[3] Joann. Hagust. op. cit., 318 sq.

[4] Gervas. Dorobern. Chron., I. 134 sq., R.S.; Jaffé, Regest., II. 41 sqq.
[5] Joann. Hagust. op. cit., 320.

[6] Roger de Hoveden, Annales, I. 198. R.S.

ecclesiastic attached to the household of Henry of Blois ; these latter had no intention of handing over the see to a Cistercian, least of all to one who had been a monk of Clairvaux. The majority, who had been strongly supported by the Bishop of Durham, recently promoted from the Deanery of York, by the Bishop of Carlisle, by the Cantor of York and by the archdeacons, concurred in the proposal that Henry Murdach should at once go to Trèves, where Eugenius then was, and where he was consecrated by the Supreme Pontiff on the Octave of the Feast of St. Andrew, the Second Sunday of Advent.[1] The malcontent minority were in some degree propitiated by the fact that Eugenius appointed their candidate Hilary to the vacant see of Chichester.[2]

But there remained another whose displeasure had been provoked, King Stephen. That in the end his kinsman had been deposed was by no means gratifying to the family ambition which his brother, Henry of Blois, all of whose machinations had now been defeated, would not have failed to stimulate. Moreover, his throne had never been particularly secure, and, however injudicious it may have been to reveal the fact, it was perhaps not unnatural that the entire loyalty of the new archbishop should have been a little suspect in his eyes. Again, an archbishop who had been a monk of Clairvaux, consecrated by a Pope who had been professed in the same cloister, might be expected to display something of that unpleasant independence which made the name of St. Bernard a terror to weak and wilful princes. In any case, as we learn from William Little, the Augustinian Canon of Newburgh who wrote a *History* of England, beginning with the Norman invasion and ending with the year 1197—Stephen was not content with the customary oath of allegiance taken on the reception of the temporalities of a see but, perhaps remembering, too, that Henry had unusually already been consecrated, demanded of him what would appear to have been a special oath of fidelity to his person before he invested him with the *regalia*.[3] An *impasse* resulted ; Henry refused to comply, and the king refused to withdraw his demand. The former soon found the partizans of the deposed archbishop to be so truculent that his only course seemed to be to lay the city of York under an interdict. Count Eustace, the king's eldest son, arrived upon the spot, and proceeded to encourage by force of arms the violation of the interdict—a measure to which doubtless Stephen was privy. Nameless horrors followed this armed intervention, and the king, terrified by the lengths which his irresponsible agents were allowing matters to reach, finally

[1] Cf. p. 167 *supra.*

[2] Joann. Hagust. *op. cit.*, 320 sq.

[3] William of Newburgh, *Hist.*, I. xvii, I. 56, *R.S.*

granted the *regalia* to the archbishop, but only " after a lapse of several years," probably—we may say—in 1149.[1]

It had been a long campaign of stone-walling, the kind of warfare in which St. Bernard was now a proved veteran. But, although his eyes had never been off the front, he had viewed it from a distance. His correspondence which deals with it is addressed to the Pope and to the *Curia ;* no letters have come down to us such as in analogous circumstances he had written to Louis le Jeune and to prelates and to princes in France. What information reached him came chiefly from Cistercian sources, true no doubt in point of fact, but inevitably coloured by the sense of terror which would have possessed men colonizing a land as yet strange and unknown for the most part to their leaders, if not to their rank and file ; a land the laws and customs of which differed in certain material respects from those of the Continental countries with which they were more familiar ; a land, moreover, the civil ruler of which was but loosely propped upon his throne. Yet in the main they were right in their contention ; on more counts than one the election of William FitzHerbert was uncanonical. Nor were his pastoral qualifications for the episcopate entirely satisfactory, although, as we have seen,[2] it may be doubted whether he was quite the scoundrel which the Cistercians and their friends in their reports to St. Bernard made him out to be. Indeed, John of Hexham goes so far as to describe him as " neither murmuring nor complaining during the whole period of his humiliation, but as, conscious of his integrity, enduring patiently in the silence of his heart." [3]

We read in the work commonly called the *Annals of the Four Masters*, under the year 1134, that Imar O'Hegan " died at Rome on his pilgrimage." [4] This was that Imar, an anchorite " of most austere life, an inexorable castigator of his own body, dwelling in a cell near the church " of the city of Armagh, to whom, as St. Bernard tells us, St. Malachy repaired as a young man in order to be further instructed in that form of life which Imar himself so strictly observed.[5] It is to the *Life of St. Malachy*, written by St. Bernard, that we owe almost everything that is known of the great Irish bishop, who may be said to have saved by his reforming zeal the Christianity of his country from the extinction which threatened it in the XIIth century. That the Abbot of Clairvaux should have found time to write his *Life* is sufficient evidence of the high esteem in which he held him as an exponent of episcopal ideals.

Malachy O'Margair was born of noble and Christian

[1] William of Newburgh, *op. cit., loc. cit., ed. cit.*

[2] Pp. 170 sq. *supra ;* cf. Tout, *William Fitz-Herbert, Dict. Nat. Biogr.*

[3] Joann. Hagust. *op. cit.,* 320.

[4] *Annals of the Kingdom of Ireland by the Four Masters, an.* 1134, *ed.* O'Donovan, II. 1047.

[5] S. Bern. *De Vita S. Malach.,* II. 4.

parents at Armagh about the year 1095. Although he came of a stock which St. Bernard does not hesitate to describe as barbarian, he was well educated; a lettered youth who "derived no more injury from his savage lineage than do the fishes of the sea from their native brine." [1] Others besides himself who gathered round the cell of Imar became possessed by the spirit of reform. But Malachy was wise beyond his years and before long, encouraged both by his diocesan and by Imar, he received the diaconate. At the age of only twenty-five years he was promoted to the priesthood. For these infringements of canon law, which as then current required a minimum age of twenty-five for the diaconate and thirty for the priesthood, St. Bernard regards "the zeal of the ordainer and the merits of the ordained" as reasonably accountable. Not content with having so early advanced Malachy to the priesthood, the Archbishop of Armagh proceeded to use him as his coadjutor, first of all in the work of eradicating superstition, which was appallingly prevalent, and then in that of introducing "the customs of the Holy Roman Church" in regard both of discipline and of worship. St. Bernard records the distressing conditions with which Malachy was called to deal, and with which he dealt with some success. Men supposed to be Christians "were either ignorant or negligent of the very salutary use of confession, of the Sacrament of Confirmation, of the marriage-contract." [2]

The ecclesiastical constitution existing in Ireland at the time was responsible for much of this reversion to what amounted to little less than practical paganism. Originally it had been established by St. Patrick after his arrival in Ireland in 432. Based upon the system with which he had been familiar in Gaul, in particular at Auxerre, where St. German the diocesan had been his master, it gradually adapted itself to the tribal conditions of a country in its state of social development very different from Gaul. There was only one province, that of Armagh, and during the life-time of St. Patrick the suffragans strictly so called were all either appointed or approved by himself. [3] Sees were not multiplied unnecessarily but, where tribal considerations demanded such a course, ecclesiastics of rank below the episcopate would seem to have been appointed to rule districts from the tribal centres. We can understand how out of this would have arisen a kind of prescriptive right, according to which the ecclesiastical rule of these districts sometimes came to be regarded as hereditary in the family of the chieftain, even when the supreme ruler was not a priest but a bishop. Side by side with this another

[1] S. Bern. *op. cit.*, I. 1.

[2] *Op. cit.*, III. 6 sq.

[3] Ryan, *Irish Monasticism*, 84 sqq.

12

development was in course. Although St. Patrick founded a church which was primarily episcopal and clerical in its government, yet monasteries played so important and so increasingly predominant a part in its life that in VIth century Ireland jurisdiction was almost entirely in monastic hands, whether the heads of houses were bishops or only priests. Thus "the essential connection between the episcopal order and ecclesiastical government bade fair to be lost to view."[1]

We can understand how under such conditions, which constituted not so much an *imperium in imperio* as a disruptive clanship on the one hand and an accentuated congregationalism on the other, not only might the valuable corrective of a central authority which was alike the guardian of the *norma fidei* and the interpreter of the moral code be ignored altogether, but the sense of what the Christian religion really means become almost entirely lost. And something like this St. Malachy found to be the case, as we have it on the testimony of St. Bernard. The eight consecutive predecessors of Celsus—the archbishop who ordained St. Malachy —in the see of Armagh had been married laymen; the best to be said of them was that they had been *literati*. "The result was," St. Bernard writes, "that throughout the whole of Ireland there spread that laxity of ecclesiastical discipline, that weakening of corrective authority, that voidance of religion of which I have already spoken; so that everywhere savage barbarism replaced Christian kindness, nay, a veritable paganism was propagated in the name of Christ."[2]

As coadjutor to Archbishop Celsus Malachy set himself vigorously to the task of reform, "promulgating laws full of justice, moderation and equity, but at the same time establishing in all churches the sanctions and decrees of the holy fathers, in particular the customs of the Holy Roman Church,"[3] for nowhere, not even in the metropolitan city, were the canonical hours sung. It is noteworthy how fundamental this obligation of the *Opus Dei* was felt to be. After a short time of refreshment spent at Lismore with the Bishop Malchus, on the invitation of his maternal uncle, the Abbot of Bangor in the County Down, and under the direction of his old master Imar, he proceeded to reform both spiritually and materially that great house which had recently been almost destroyed by pirates.[4] In 1124, when still under thirty years of age, Malachy, elected Bishop of Connor,[5] received consecration at the hands of the Archbishop of Armagh. No sooner had he, with great diffidence, entered upon his duties than he discovered that he had been called to rule "not men but beasts.

[1] *Op. cit.*, 189 sq.

[2] S. Bern. *De Vita S. Malach.*, X. 19.

[3] *Op. cit.*, III. 7.

[4] *Op. cit.*, VI. 12 sqq.

[5] *Annals of the Four Masters, an.* 1124, *ed. cit.*, II. 1019.

Nowhere had he known such barbarism ; nowhere had he found such moral obliquity, such deadly customs, such impiety, such savage laws, such stiffneckedness, such uncleanness of living ; men Christian in name, pagan in fact." [1] On foot and accompanied by a body of his own disciples, who never left his side, Malachy systematically visited his diocese, meeting more often than not with contumely and rough handling, suffering from hunger, fatigue and nakedness ; yet in the end he " overcame evil with good. Why should he not have done so ? He persevered in knocking, and according to the promise in due time the door was opened to him." Barbarous customs were replaced by Roman laws ; churches were re-built, clergy ordained, the sacraments duly administered and devoutly frequented, and above all concubinage sanctified by Christian marriage-rites.[2] His salutary efforts were, however, unfortunately interrupted by revolution ; the city of Connor was destroyed and Malachy was compelled to flee to Munster, where, aided by the generosity of the King Cormac, he founded the Abbey of Ibrach in the County Kerry, in which himself and a hundred and twenty brethren took shelter.[3] Shortly afterwards the Archbishop of Armagh fell mortally ill. On his death-bed he executed a deed appointing Malachy his successor. Doubtless he sought to set a precedent which might help to break down the vicious system of an hereditary episcopate. But, alas, this was but a bequest of factional strife, to some extent facilitated by Malachy's unwillingness to take up the burden of the metropolitanate. First of all a certain Maurice seized and, " supported by the civil power " —which probably meant the interest of the ruling chieftain— " for five years occupied the see, not as a bishop but as a tyrant." [4] On his death one Nigel—" Nigellus quidam, immo vere nigerrimus," remarks St. Bernard in his inimitable manner [5]—intruded himself ; but his behaviour proved to be so discreditable that the king, the bishops and the faithful laity cast him out ; and finally Malachy, now at the age of thirty-seven, entered Armagh as Primate of all Ireland and metropolitan. This would seem to have been in the year 1132.[6] It was but for so long a time as enabled him to restore discipline, to reform morals and to establish peace that Malachy occupied the chair of St. Patrick. Within three years he resigned in favour of Gelasius, a good man of his own selection. The see of Connor had originally been separate from that of Down ; the tenure of both sees in plurality was an abuse which he now corrected by leaving the Bishop of Connor in possession and by himself taking the see of Down.

[1] S. Bern. *De Vita S. Malach.*, VIII. 16.

[2] *Op. cit.*, VIII. 17.

[3] *Op. cit.*, IX. 18.

[4] *Op. cit.*, X. 20.

[5] Cf. Appendix I.

[6] *Op. cit.*, XI. 22, XII. 24 ; *Annals of the Four Masters*, an. 1132. ed. *cit.*, II. 1041.

¹ Ryan, *Irish Monasticism,* 170 sqq.

In the spirit of primitive Irish custom, especially in the diocese of Armagh,[1] Malachy constituted the episcopal household at Down as a monastery of regular clergy, and " again girded himself as a new recruit of Christ for spiritual warfare, again put on the strong armour of God ; clothed himself with the humility of holy poverty, with the rigour of cœnobitic discipline ; found time for contemplation ; was instant in prayer ; all of which, however, he had more zeal to undertake than he had strength to fulfil." Yet did he not live the life of a recluse. Not only was his own diocese industriously administered, but " he went forth sowing his good seed ; managing the affairs of the Church and issuing his decrees with full ecclesiastical authority like an apostle. And when all men saw the signs and wonders which he wrought, none asked him : ' By what power do you do this ? ' for where the spirit of the Lord is there is liberty." [2]

² S. Bern. *op. cit.,* XIV. 31 sq.

Thus the Church in Ireland was, in fact, ruled by one man, who was not the occupant of the primatial see. The state of things was, moreover, irregular on other grounds. The *pallium* had never during the whole course of the history of the Irish Church been conferred upon any of its prelates. Archbishop Celsus had raised the see of Cashel to the rank of a metropolitanate—the formal recognition of an arrangement already made by Murtagh O'Brien, King of Munster— but he had, strangely enough as it may seem, quite definitely reserved its subordination to his own see of Armagh. Finally, the see of Dublin was not ecclesiastically in Ireland at all ; its bishop was a suffragan of the Province of Canterbury ; the last survival of the tradition that the primacy conferred by Gregory the Great upon St. Augustine extended to the whole of the British Isles.[3] We are not surprised, therefore, that in 1139 Malachy decided to go to Rome in order to lay the whole matter before Innocent II.[4] Crossing to Scotland, he first made his way to York, where he met amongst other ecclesiastics, Waltheof, Prior of Kirkham, subsequently Abbot of Melrose ; thence, having there heard doubtless great accounts of the Cistercians of Rievaulx and of Fountains, he proceeded to Clairvaux to visit the abbot of the mother-house of whose daughters in Yorkshire he had received so favourable an impression.[5]

³ Gougaud, *Les Chrétientés Celtiques,* 358 sqq., éd. 1911.
⁴ *Op. cit.,* XV. 33.

⁵ *Op. cit.,* XV. 36, XVI. 37.

St. Bernard's delight at meeting Malachy was only tempered by the sense of his own unworthiness of such a friendship. " Sinner though I be," he writes, " from that moment I found favour in his eyes and thenceforward to the end of his life I was esteemed by him as at the first." And the satisfaction was mutual ; for no sooner had Malachy arrived at Rome than he sought permission from the Pope to pass the remainder of his days as a monk at Clairvaux. But this, he learned, was not to be, and he proceeded to lay before Innocent the considerations which had originally moved him to approach his throne. He had but to tell his story to attentive and sympathetic ears. The initial step taken was to appoint him Apostolic Legate for the whole of Ireland in place of Gilbert, Bishop of Limerick—the first to hold this office in Ireland—an old man now past his powers for such a post, but who, be it said, had in his day done yeoman service for sound discipline throughout the Irish Church.[1] As regards the pallium, that demanded some solemnity of procedure. Malachy had begged that the metropolitanate of Cashel established by Archbishop Celsus might be confirmed by the Pope, and the pallium conferred upon the occupants both of that see and of the see of Armagh. The metropolitanate of Cashel was duly confirmed ; while so far as concerned the pallium the Pope required that a council of the bishops, clergy and leading laymen of Ireland should be convened, at which the question might be discussed. If as the result suitable persons were by common consent appointed to petition for the pallium, he would confer it according to the tenor of their request.[2] After a month's stay in Rome Malachy returned to Ireland, paying a second visit to Clairvaux on his way. Here, as we record elsewhere,[3] he left four of his companions in order that they might be professed Cistercian monks and form the nucleus for a foundation in Ireland.[4] After crossing the Scottish border he was honourably entertained for awhile by King David I, and finally landed at Bangor, perhaps early in 1140.[5] Here he availed himself of the opportunity of rebuilding in stone the ancient monastery and of quickening the religious fervour of its brethren. But these conservative people were ill-pleased by this novel construction. " Good sir," one asked, " what is the use in our country of strange buildings such as these ? We are Irish, not French. What is this folly ? What need of this extravagance, this proud display ? How can the poor and needy like yourself do a work of such expense ? Who will ever see it finished ? "[6] However, as St. Bernard tells us, " God's servant found in God's purse what he had not in his own " ; he shared " a common purse with God."[7] Not only was Bangor rebuilt, but such an era of sound construction was initiated that, during the ten years which elapsed between the foundation of Mellifont in 1142 and St. Bernard's writing of the Life of St. Malachy, the walls of seven Cistercian

[1] Gillebert. De Statu Ecclesiae, P.L. CLIX. 995 sqq.

[2] Op. cit., XVI. 37 sqq.

[3] P. 75 supra.

[4] Op. cit., XVI. 39.

[5] Op. cit., XVII. 40, XVIII. 42.

[6] Op. cit., XXVIII. 61.

[7] Op. cit., XXVIII. 63.

houses arose to testify to the excellence of this strange French style ! [1] Of the foundation of Mellifont we speak elsewhere. [2]

Giraldus Cambrensis records that the reproach was brought against Malachy that by giving himself too exclusively to the contemplative life, he neglected the crying needs of contemporary Ireland. [3] We shall, however, probably feel that his work needs no vindication. It is only a view superficial and short-sighted which—to take one consideration alone—can ignore the fact that the advent of the Cistercians to Ireland on the invitation of St. Malachy meant that a civilizing force was introduced into the country, and a true sense of values spiritual and material created, the like of which had in its history seldom been known before. We may add that for Irish monasteries it meant for the first time the formal observance of the Rule of St. Benedict. [4]

The steps which the Pope had indicated as necessarily preliminary to the grant of the *pallium* were long and unaccountably delayed. After a lapse of nine years it was resolved at a council of fifteen bishops and two hundred priests, held at Patrick's Island near Skerries in the Co. Dublin in 1148, that Malachy should go " a second time to Rome to confer with the successor of Peter." [5] Conscious that he was nearing his latter end, sad at heart that Ireland still lacked the Papal favour symbolized by the *pallium*, hoping, too, that his old longing to die at Clairvaux might even yet be fulfilled, Malachy took his departure. That the Apostolic See was occupied by a Cistercian of Clairvaux doubtless gave no little confidence both to himself and to his friends, over whose heads there brooded, nevertheless, the mournful anticipation of his death in a distant land. Albeit cheered on his way by visits paid to King David of Scotland and to his friends the monks of Gisburn, he found on reaching the South-Eastern coast of England that, owing to some unexplained misunderstanding between the Pope and King Stephen, his embarkation was forbidden. The unfortunate delay involved meant that he missed Eugenius in France, where he had been presiding at the Council of Rheims, [6] for the Pope had already reached the neighbourhood of Pisa on his way back to Rome. [7]

It would have been about the middle of October when Malachy arrived at Clairvaux. It was not for long that he was to remain there ! He was approaching nearly a celestial city of which Rome is but the terrestrial shadow. " How festive but how few were the days which then I spent with you ! " exclaims St. Bernard. " To us all how joyful, how affable, how incredibly acceptable a guest he was ! " On the

[1] *Op. cit.*, XVI. 39, XXIX. 64.

[2] Pp. 75 sq. *supra*.

[3] Gir. Cambr. *Topogr. Hibern.*, III. 28, Camden, *Anglica a Vet. Scripta*, 746.

[4] Gougaud, *Les Chrétientés Celtiques*, 364 sq., *éd.* 1911.

[5] *Annals of the Four Masters*, *an.* 1148, ed. cit., II. 1083 sqq.

[6] Pp. 314 sqq. *infra*.

[7] S. Bern. *De Vita S. Malach.*, XXX. 67 sqq. ; Jaffé, *Regest.*, II. 59 sq.

Feast of St. Luke, 18th October, after celebrating Mass,
smitten by fever he took to his bed.   St. Bernard could
express the sympathy evoked only by writing : " And all of
us fell sick with him."   Tenderly nursed, he gently protested :
" There is no need for this ; but what you order I will do for
love of you."   Urged not to despair of life, he replied : " He
who of his mercy has brought me to the place which I sought
will not deny me the end which I desired.   For my body here
is its rest ; for my soul the Lord will provide who is the
saviour of them that hope in him." [1]   He insisted on rising
from his bed and on descending to the little church of the
Monasterium Vetus just below his cell, there to receive
Extreme Unction and Holy Viaticum.   " Who could believe
that he was a dying man ?   Only himself and God could
know that." [2]   On the Eve of All Saints the fever increased
and then subsided in refreshing sweat.   Calling St. Bernard
and others to his side he prayed : " O God, keep them in thy
name, and not them only, but all who by my word and by
my ministry have given themselves to thy service."   About
midnight on 1st-2nd November " the psalms and hymns and
spiritual songs " for those in their last agony, recited by the
whole community and by many abbots who were present,
were interrupted by the passing of Malachy in his fifty-fourth
year.[3]   " Malachias, i.e. Maelmaedhog Ua Morgair, Archbishop of the Chair of Patrick, chief head of the West of
Europe, legate of the successor of Peter, the only head whom
the Irish and the foreigners obeyed, chief paragon of wisdom
and of piety, a brilliant lamp which illumined territories and
churches by preaching and good works, faithful shepherd of
the Church in general . . . after the fifty-fourth year of his
age resigned his spirit to heaven on the second day of November
. . . and was buried in the monastery of St. Bernard at
Clarvallis in France with honour and veneration." [4]   The
discrepancy between St. Bernard's words " in his fifty-fourth
year " and the statement of the *Annals of the Four Masters*
leads us to date Malachy's birth at *about* 1095.   He was
buried the same day *in aquilonari latere* [5] of the new church.
We should probably understand by this the North transept ;
for the position of his tomb on the Northerly side of the choir
next but one to that of St. Bernard, as found on the plan
provided by Migne, based upon researches made in the XVIth
century by William Flammeng, a Canon of Langres who
spent his declining years at Clairvaux, is that in the later
church consecrated in 1174.[6]

We have lingered over the story ; partly for its own sake,

[1] *Op. cit.*, XXXI. 70 sqq.

[2] *Op. cit.*, XXXI. 71.

[3] *Op. cit.*, XXXI. 73 sq.

[4] *Annals of the Four Masters*, an. 1148, ed. cit., II. 1085.

[5] *Vita Prima*, V. iii. 24 ; S. Bern. *De Vita S. Malach.*, XXXI. 75 ; cf. Gir. Cambr. *De Lib. a se Script.*, I. 416, R.S.

[6] *P.L.* CLXXXV. 1765 sqq. ; cf. p. 59 *supra*.

as being that of an entirely selfless character ; of a self simply unconscious of the high value which it possesses, given unreservedly to the service of others.   As we remark elsewhere, St. Malachy's greatness has never received the homage due to it.   But there are other grounds upon which the story claims our attention.   In the first place, we get to know St. Bernard better by the perusal of his *Life of St. Malachy*. In Malachy his conception of saintliness stands out objectified in strong relief.   Geoffrey tells us that, when saying Mass for the soul of Malachy on the day following his death, he substituted at the *postcommunio* for the collect for the departed that for a canonized bishop, and devoutly kissed the remains of one whom he recognized as already raised to the altars of the Church.[1]   Both word and act alike were significant. St. Bernard, perhaps, knew few men better than he knew Malachy ;   and in his relations with Malachy we recognize, not merely his conception of true saintliness, but his superlative gift of eliciting the expression of the genuine self of another—provided that sufficient opportunity of intimacy existed, and that there was anything worth eliciting.   For St. Bernard Malachy's miracles were essentially one with the miracle which God had wrought in him in his interior being. " In my judgement," he writes, " his first and greatest miracle was himself." [2]

Then, as a bishop in his own proper vocation, St. Bernard venerated him, as he would have venerated Carlo Borromeo or Félix Dupanloup had he known either of them.   The test was the example of the apostles.   Malachy was " a true heir of the apostles."   Like Paul, he nourished his body only in order that he might the better preach the gospel, while others " feed themselves and do not preach the gospel at all, or preach it in order that they may feed better.   Other bishops think themselves happy if they enlarge their borders ;   Malachy gloried in enlarging his charity.   They gather into their barns and fill their vats that they may load their tables ;   Malachy collected into deserts and into solitudes stock for heaven. Although they receive tithes and first fruits and offerings, nay, in addition to this by the bounty of rulers taxes and tribute-money and who knows how much more ?—nevertheless they are full of anxiety as to meat and drink ;   Malachy, with none of these resources, yet enriched many from the storehouse of faith. . . .   As for the people, they do not even recognize their existence ;   Malachy educated them.   Potentates and tyrants they honour ;   Malachy chastized them.   O apostolic man, whom such and so many signs of apostleship ennoble ! " [3]   It

[1] *Vita Prima,* IV. iv. 21.

[2] S. Bern. *De Vita S. Malach.,* XIX. 43.

[3] *Op. cit.,* XIX. 44.

is a grave indictment of contemporary episcopacy, which in its scope we can, it is to be feared, scarcely limit to Ireland. There is much in the indictment which suggests that St. Bernard is not speaking merely on hearsay. Some critics will doubtless seek to discount it as they seek to discount other evidence which he offered, as for example in the *Apology to William of St. Thierry*, the strictures of which it is not difficult to justify from the letters of Peter the Venerable himself. It has to be remembered, however, that St. Bernard never blamed his fellows for failing to " grasp " ideals, provided that their " reach " was directed towards them. All that he would ask would be : " What's a heaven for ? " And his method was, when he found a concrete embodiment, so far as might be in this world, of an ideal—as here of an ideal bishop—to place it in a good light and then in the same light to let men see the rest. His *mise en scène* was always dramatic, but that was just because it was so spontaneous ; the focussing merely of sufficiently familiar and indisputable *data*, which otherwise could never either have spoken their moral warning or have revealed their true historical actuality. The *Life* was written in response to the request of Congan, Abbot of Innislonagh, the mouth-piece of the Cistercians of Ireland. Much of the record is based upon information supplied by Congan, and St. Bernard was careful to insist that what he was offering was not an encomium but a faithful statement of facts.[1] Eulogy was reserved rather for his two sermons on St. Malachy preached at celebrations of the anniversary of his death, in the second of which he explicitly invokes him as a saint in glory. " Who," he asks, in his letter of tender condolence addressed to the monks of Ireland, " would dare to suppose that, now that Malachy is a saint, he can be of less service to, or love the less, his own sons ? "[2]

It was in 1145 that Henry, brother of Louis le Jeune, had been by St. Bernard professed a monk at Clairvaux. Four years later, in 1149, the see of Beauvais fell vacant by the death of Odo III, and the Chapter, clergy and faithful of Beauvais elected Henry to fill it. St. Bernard, writing to Peter the Venerable in 1149 from Cîteaux, where he was present at the chapter general, conveys to him the special salutation of " the Bishop-Elect of Beauvais "[3] in terms which accord with the fact that Peter had advised acceptance of the see on the part of Henry, who had apparently at first been somewhat reluctant.[4] The early days of Henry's episcopate supplied sufficient explanation of such reluctance. The zealous young Cistercian found himself at once confronted by an abuse of

[1] *Op. cit., Praefat.*

[2] *Ep.* 374 (2).

[3] *Ep.* 389.

[4] Petr. Ven. *Epp. Lib.* V. viii and ix.

long standing. The great feudal lords of the diocese had been accustomed to levy heavy pecuniary charges upon their bishop as the condition of their protection of his rights, an impost which bore the name of *beneficia denariorum*.[1] The weight of these charges, in effect a kind of black-mail, did not tend to decrease. Henry from the first flatly refused to pay them, a proceeding which was naturally strongly resented by those who had profited by them. The seigneurs succeeded in enlisting the king on their side, while Henry was supported by his other brother, Robert of Dreux, a man who would not hesitate to counsel or to take strong measures of resistance.[2] The situation became critical. "Added to other difficulties which lie in our way," writes St. Bernard to the Pope, "is the fact that the Bishop of Beauvais and his brother the king are not of one mind in the matter."[3] The city of Beauvais and its neighbourhood were indeed exposed to the danger of war, and it was mainly due to Suger, who felt keenly the impropriety of a bishop "daring to lift up his foot against the Crown," that it was in the end averted.[4] St. Bernard's reference to a report that Robert of Dreux "had done something outrageous or had persuaded the bishop to do so" leads us to suspect that the count was of no real assistance in the solution of the difficulty.[5] Suger's final word—alas, it was one of the last occasions of his intervention in any public affair of importance, for he died on 12th January, 1151—was that the best course would be to invite the Pope to take action.[6] Meanwhile, Eugenius III had probably already heard of the strong stand taken by the Bishop of Beauvais and of the opposition with which he had met. There was some question as to whether Henry should personally lay his case before the Pope; but St. Bernard delayed this course, on the ground that at the time it would involve an absence so long as to be dangerous to the interests of his diocese.[7] However, in his letters to Eugenius he does not hesitate to appeal both to their common brotherhood as monks of Clairvaux, and to the persuasive spectacle of this "devout youth" so full of disinterested zeal for the welfare of his diocese.[8] In the end Henry found a favourable opportunity for his journey to Rome.[9] The result proved advantageous to his case, for Eugenius issued bulls to the Archbishop of Rouen, his metropolitan, to Louis le Jeune, to St. Bernard and to the Bishop of Auxerre, all dated 25th February, 1151, which effected a reconciliation between Henry and his brother the king, and disposed of the claims of the seigneury to the entire satisfaction of the former.[10] In the earlier half of October, 1151, died Hugh of Mâcon,

[1] Jaffé, *Regest.*, 9451 sqq.

[2] S. Bern. *Ep.* 307.

[3] *Ep.* 305.

[4] Joann. Sares. *Hist. Pontific.*, XXXV. 70 sq. ed. Poole.

[5] *Ep.* 307.

[6] Joann. Sares. *Hist. Pontific.*, *loc. cit., ed. cit.*

[7] *Ep.* 305.

[8] *Epp.* 305 and 278.

[9] Jaffé, *Regest.*, 9451 sqq., 9456 sqq.

[10] *Op. cit.*, 9452 sqq.

Hugues de Vitry, the fifty-fourth Bishop of Auxerre, a see which he had occupied since 1136, when he ceased to be first Abbot of Pontigny.[1] He had been, we shall remember, the friend of St. Bernard's youth.[2] His last days were harassed by intrigue. It would seem that when not fully in possession of his faculties he had been persuaded by a certain Stephen, a deacon who was probably a member of his household, to execute a deed bequeathing to " his nephew, a mere boy, a feckless fellow, almost everything which he possessed for the upkeep of the episcopal establishment." Scarcely anything at all was left either to the poor or to the churches of the diocese. That Hugh of Mâcon, who is no stranger to us, should have acted in this way had he known what he was doing is inconceivable ; it would have been sheer nepotism and a scandal to all who might hear of it. There were some who said that he knew nothing at all about it, and that Stephen had written exactly what he liked, and even sealed it with the episcopal signet. " And this is quite credible," writes St. Bernard, in a letter addressed to Eugenius III after Hugh's death, from which we learn much of the story.[3] After securing his legacy—with a hand sufficiently generous to himself, for, " an insult to all religious sentiment," no spare coins were overlooked as a small addition to seven churches and much land—the youth set out for Rome in order to obtain Apostolic confirmation of his rights. Thinking that his equipage for so long a journey was not suitably furnished by the episcopal stables, he annexed the horses of the monastery before he left. Although there is no record of the issue of his journey— unless we are to identify him with the Geoffrey of the second election [4]—there can be no doubt as to what it was. " You will show true piety to the uncle if you treat the nephew like anything but a father ! " is St. Bernard's advice to Eugenius.[5]

Meanwhile, the election to the vacant see took its course. A candidate whose name does not transpire was chosen by eleven priests, nine deacons and a number of clergy in minor orders. And now there intervened the hand of William IV, Count of Nevers. The count was a believer in the principle *divide et impera ;* he had tried to act upon it before.[6] " Remember," writes St. Bernard to the Pope, " what happened at Nevers, and see whether by similar art, nay, rather by similar fraud, and by the same instigator a second election has not, as they say, been planned in this case also, so that already one candidate having been chosen both may be rejected and thus, in the end, they may craftily introduce a third—anybody whom they like," in plain, the nominee of the

[1] *Gall. Christ.,* XII. 291 ; *R.H.G.F.* XIII. 303.
[2] Pp. 11 sq. *supra.*
[3] *Ep.* 276.
[4] P. 188 *infra ;* cf. S. Bern. *De Consid.,* III. ii. 11.
[5] *Ep.* 276.
[6] S. Bern. *Ep.* 276.

¹ *Ep.* 275.

Count of Nevers.¹ With characteristic boldness St. Bernard's proposal was that Eugenius should cut the knot. " I have said," he writes, " and I say it again : ' Remember what happened at Nevers.' Sometimes the course most consistent with order is to set aside the usual order. Right-minded men recognize that your keys are, one the key of discretion, the other that of power " ; meaning that the Pope has the power at his discretion to appoint bishops directly, and that the present is an occasion, albeit exceptional, upon which he

² *Ep.* 276.

should exercise his discretion and do so.² In Epistle CCLXXV after warning him, as we have seen, against the Count of Nevers, St. Bernard goes on to tell the Pope exactly what had happened with regard to the second election, for he had sent a monk from Clairvaux to inquire into the whole matter. He

³ Cf. p. 187
supra.

found that another candidate, by name Geoffrey,³ had been elected by the cantor, the archdeacon, the treasurer, Hugh a priest and brother of Geoffrey, and Stephen, the deacon above mentioned who had acted so unscrupulously about the bishop's will.

Eugenius hesitated to take the extreme measures suggested by St. Bernard, and appointed a commission of three persons, one of whom was St. Bernard, with power to supervise the election in normal canonical order. The Abbot of Clairvaux submitted the name of Alan, who subsequently wrote the *Vita*

⁴ *Gall. Christ.,*
XII. 293 sqq.,
598. Cf. p. 66
supra.

Secunda, at the time Abbot of l'Arrivour, a Cistercian house ; ⁴ but it was acceptable to one only of the other commissioners, and the matter was again referred to the Pope, whose pronouncement in favour of Alan raised the malign suggestion that he was the tool of St. Bernard. The latter was, of course, indignant ; less on his own account than on that of Eugenius. " Have I ever sought," he asks the Pope, " to rule churches, to dispose of bishoprics, to create bishops ? A suitable instrument for such a purpose ! An ant, forsooth, drawing

⁵ *Ep.* 280.

a waggon ! " ⁵ This was doubtless a belated piece of obstruction on the part of the Count of Nevers—" a man who certainly does not tread in his father's footsteps ; but rather obstructs this as he does every good work," writes St. Bernard.⁶

⁶ *Op. cit.*

In the end, Alan was duly elected.

But there was another difficulty to be confronted. The correspondence of St. Bernard reveals that in any election to a vacant see there were five distinct rights which required to be respected. That of the king to grant *congé d'élire*, what

⁷ *Ep.* 282.
⁸ *Epp.* 202 and
275.

St. Bernard calls " favor Regis " ; ⁷ that of the clergy of the diocese to choose a candidate ; ⁸ that of the metropolitan, his comprovincials, and the abbots of the diocese, together with the Apostolic Legate, to intervene in case of dispute ;[1] that of the Pope as final arbiter in any such dispute ;[2] and that of the king to confer the temporalities or *regalia*.[3] Apparently in the case with which we are now concerned Louis had granted his *favor* for the election, but had contended that it held for the first election only. Alan had been elected at the third. " Neither reason nor custom supports this," writes St. Bernard to him. " Tell me, if you remember, how many times in the recent election at Soissons the clergy assembled to elect disagreed, and went away again having done nothing ? Yet I do not think that it was just so many times that they renewed their request for the leave to elect, which you had deigned once for all to grant them."[4] He did not expect that the king would continue to sadden the Church of Auxerre and himself, the writer, as he had never done before. Nor did he.

The story of this election in all its aspects well illustrates the dangers to which, with a king like Louis and seigneurs like William of Nevers, the Gallican Church was exposed, and suggests the chaos which but for St. Bernard might frequently have been its fate.

[1] *Epp.* 164 and 202.
[2] *Epp.* 276 sq. and 280.
[3] *Epp.* 170 and 282.
[4] *Ep.* 282.

CHAPTER IX

THE CROWN AND THE FEUDALITY

Louis le Gros

THE XIIth century was over a large area of Western Europe a period of struggle between the Church and the civil power. On the part of the former it might even seem that there was some evidence of the, perhaps conscious, effort to reap the fruits of Canossa as a tribute to the genius of Gregory VII. Professor Augustin Fliche of Montpellier, in his interesting monograph *On the Influence of Gregory VII and of the Gregorian Ideas on the Thought of St. Bernard*, has sought to find in the treatise *Of Consideration* addressed to Eugenius III, as well as in other works of the same writer, traces of the extent to which the conception of what Montalembert would later describe as " libre église en libre état " had taken possession of the mind [1] of the great prophet-statesman of that day. Monsieur Fliche has claimed to recognize the profound influence exercised upon St. Bernard by the *Registrum* of Gregory VII. However this may be, certainly dramatic episodes were now and then emphasizing this ideal. It had been responsible for the persecution of St. Anselm, and it would account for the martyrdom of St. Thomas of Canterbury, whom the Cistercians were so valiantly to protect, as may sufficiently be learnt from the correspondence of John of Salisbury and of others in the third quarter of the century.[2] It developed forcible characters ; it played its part in St. Bernard's case. In France the struggle was not one between the Church and monarchism as such ; for Suger, whose jealousy for the Church's rights was beyond suspicion, was an ardent monarchist, and after the accession of Louis le Jeune in 1137, viewing with anxiety and with distrust the growing power of such a noble as Theobald of Champagne, set himself actively—and, we may believe, on grounds of sound policy—in opposition to the efforts of the feudality to consolidate itself against the monarchy, and that in spite of Theobald's relation to the Abbot of Clairvaux as

[1] *Ap. S. Bern. et son Temps,* I. xiii. ; cf. Fliche, *La Réforme Grégorienne,* II. 224 sq., 389 sq.

[2] *Ap. Materials for the Hist. of Archbp. Th. Becket, R.S.*

friend and patron.[1] Theobald, fourth Count of Blois and second Count of Champagne, was, as the son of Stephen of Blois and Adela, daughter of the Conqueror, nearly related to the royal house of England. When his uncle Hugh entered the Order of the Temple in 1125, Theobald acquired from him feudal rights over the County of Champagne which, added to those which he already possessed as Count of Blois, made him the accepted head of the feudality of France and a serious rival to the king. The contemporary writer of the *Life of Suger*, an anonymous monk of St. Denis, refers to him as a *cultor religionis*—meaning presumably that he was well-disposed towards monasticism, for he had himself only been dissuaded from the religious life by the advice of St. Norbert [2] —who " was wont to honour Suger in every way and to put him forward as his advocate with the Kings of France." [3] Plainly it needed statesmanship to maintain the balance of power ; but Suger could always rely upon the judgement and intrepidity of St. Bernard to support him in any efforts to ensure, whether against the monarchy or against the feudality, the freedom of the Church and respect for its authority in its own proper spheres of faith and morals.

Before the arrival during the reign of Louis le Jeune of certain grave crises in which St. Bernard and Suger acted upon the whole unanimously, the Abbot of Clairvaux had sometimes taken resolute and independent steps in matters in which he felt it to be his duty to intervene. A letter addressed by St. Bernard to Theobald of Champagne about the year 1127 may be regarded as typical.[4] The Apostolic Legate, Matthew of Albano, and various bishops were, it appears, at the time assembling for the council held at Troyes in 1128. After speaking with some plainness of a case of high-handed dealing with a religious house on the part of the count's officials and of two cases, one of excessive severity, the other of great brutality, both of which are brought home more nearly to the count himself, St. Bernard concludes by warning him to honour the members of the council, to respect its deliberations and to support its decrees, and further—as a last word, an *aculeus in fine*—to look to it that he pays proper homage to the Bishop of Langres for a fief which he holds of that see. " Receive," he writes, " as is fitting, with more abundant honour him who is both our bishop and yours ; and pay him reverently and humbly due homage for the fief which you hold of him." Theobald, we think, must have been presuming upon his newly acquired dignity as Count of Champagne. These words of warning follow, as has been

[1] *Vita Prima*, II. viii. 52, IV. iii. 12.

[2] d'Arbois de Jubainville, *Hist. des ducs et des comtes de Champagne*, II. 260 sqq.

[3] *Vita Suger*. I. x, P.L. CLXX. 1257 sqq.

[4] *Ep.* 39.

said, three specific representations. The rough handling of the Canons Regular of Lariscourt in the diocese of Châlons-sur-Marne by the count's soldiers and officials had encouraged the neighbours of this religious house to adopt a similar treatment of the monks ; the wife of one of Theobald's men who had suffered penalties, possibly just but certainly very severe, had begged St. Bernard's intercession that they might in some degree be remitted ; and then there was a distressingly bad case of cruelty for which Theobald could scarcely be held otherwise than directly responsible.

We take this last incident first. " A man who had been vanquished in a duel has been by your express order deprived of his eyes by the Provost of Bar-sur-Aube. And, as though it were not enough for him to lose both his duel and his eyes, all his possessions have been confiscated by your officials. If you please, it is only right that by your favour these should be restored to him so that he may be able to support his miserable life. I may add that the iniquity of a father ought not to be charged to his innocent children, and they thus prevented from inheriting their home—if indeed there be any ! " We may well regret that more of such frank and fearless prophecies against injustice in high places have not come down to us. A man who speaks like this does not, be sure, do it once only.

Vacandard has pointed out that significantly St. Bernard did not go so far as to express disapproval of the duel in itself as a prevailing custom of the day. From so early as the IXth century the Popes had forbidden ecclesiastics to appeal to the arbitrament of single combat accepted by proxy in the persons of their lay champions ; but the prohibition had been in large measure a dead letter. Abélard could tell of religious houses which compelled their retainers to fight duels in their causes.[1] But Abélard was a gentle soul ; albeit the son of a father trained in arms,[2] his mental attitude was so modern that he would probably have regarded such a test as derogatory to the honour of truth in any form. In St. Bernard's veins ran blood of a different blend ; to the warrior-stock of which he came the *jus duelli* counted for something ;[3] its honour was maintained no less by fighting than by fighting fairly. That he was, however, inspired by a keen sense, both of justice and of mercy, is shown by another incident in which Theobald was concerned.

They were the days immediately following the Council of Troyes.[4] A certain man, by name Humbert, had by the count's order been exiled and deprived of wife, children, property and friends.[5] Whatever the precise character of his

[1] Abael. *De S. Joh. Bapt. Sermo*, Cousin, *Opp.* I. 572. Cf. *Downside Review*, Jan. 1935, 88 sqq.

[2] P. 291 *infra*.

[3] Renati Choppini, *De Domanio*, III. xxvi. 583. Cf. *e reg.* S. Bern. *Ep.* 376 and Mabillon. *Not. ad loc.*

[4] *Ep.* 56.

[5] *Ep.* 35.

offence may have been, St. Bernard makes it plain in a letter
to Theobald that in his view there has been some miscarriage
of justice, that Humbert has not been proved to be an offender
to the extent supposed. " In a case in which the crime is not
certainly known to have been committed or is capable of
being excused it is your duty not merely not to refuse to
show mercy, but most gladly to seize the opportunity of doing
so." [1]   The pleas urged, namely, the benefit of the doubt for
the accused and extenuating circumstances reveal a judicial
mind. That St. Bernard was not altogether unsuccessful in
his advocacy we infer from the words of another letter.
" Thank you for the favour which in this matter I have
found in your eyes, in that you have deigned to accept
Humbert's true defence of himself, and have most justly
rejected the false accusation made against him." [2] St.
Bernard had not relied entirely upon his own resources, for he
had enlisted the interest both of Geoffrey of Chartres [3] and of
an abbot Hugh Farsitus. [4] The identity of this Hugh is a
little doubtful ; the most probable suggestion would seem to
be that he was the person mentioned by Abélard in the same
connection with St. Norbert in the sermon above cited, who
later became second Abbot of Prémontré. [5]

Perhaps the most remarkable instance of St. Bernard's
power of imposing his will upon the Count of Champagne, and
that in a matter of considerable publicity, is to be found in an
account of the conversion of a condemned criminal which we
read in the *Book of the Miracles* of Herbert of Torres, whence
probably it found its way into the *Exordium Magnum*. [6]
Manriquez, in his *Annals*, assigns the event to the year 1146 ;
the place was probably Troyes. On his way to visit Theobald
on affairs of state St. Bernard met this man being led forth to
execution. " I will hang this murderer myself," remarks the
abbot, taking the rope from the hands of the executioners.
Naturally, on hearing this strange piece of news, the count
hurries out to meet him and remonstrates with him for seeking
to deprive the gallows of so suitable a prey, the very devil
himself personified. Evidently Theobald has some nervous
suspicion of St. Bernard's intentions. " I know all about
him, most excellent sir," replies the abbot, " the worst of
scoundrels, well deserving the worst of punishments. But do
not suppose that I am going to let a fellow like this go scot-
free ; I am going to hand him over to executioners who will
inflict upon him penalties so much the more deserved as they
will be enduring. You had decreed that he should be made
away with by a short punishment, by instantaneous death.

[1] *Ep.* 37.

[2] *Ep.* 38.

[3] *Ep.* 56.

[4] *Ep.* 35.

[5] Abael. *op. cit.*, Cousin, *Opp.* I. 590 ; Horst. et Mabill. *Not. Fus. in S. Bern. Sermo.*, 35.

[6] *De Mirac.*, II. xv ; *Exord. Magn.*, II. xv.

You would have him hang dead upon the gibbet for one day or perhaps for many. I propose that for many years he shall hang alive, suffering the penalty of continual crucifixion." Theobald was speechless; and St. Bernard, on the spot clothing the man in his own tunic and cutting his hair, took him away to Clairvaux, where he lived in religion for thirty years, personally known by the name of Constantius to Herbert of Torres, who tells the story.

Reference will be made later to the support given by St. Bernard to Suger's endeavours to protect the clergy against the wanton reprisals taken upon them by Louis le Gros after his defeat in the matter of investitures at the Council of Rheims in 1119.[1] The last ten years of this monarch's reign could not have failed to be full of difficulty for St. Bernard. The respect with which he was on all hands regarded as a champion, alike of the rights of the Church and of high principles in statecraft, was growing *pari passu* with the frequently violent and vindictive encroachments of Louis. The fact that the monarchist sympathies of Suger were shared by St. Bernard did not make the difficulty any less; on the contrary, it tended to increase it. The reign of Louis may be described as a long military epopee, most of the outstanding incidents in which were occasions when a strong-willed man sought to stretch his feudal rights to the breaking point, and then by force of arms to save them from actual breaking. To such a man his vassals' vassals (*vasalli vasallorum*)[2] were his own vassals not merely indirectly but directly, entirely regardless of the rights of their immediate overlords. Indeed, it may be questioned whether the king did not seek to bring about such an attenuated feudalism as was established by William of Normandy in England at the Conquest. Something of this tendency we shall recognize later in the case of Louis le Jeune.

Nor was it only in respect of feudal rights proper that Louis was, perhaps advisedly, indifferent to accepted procedure. A family by name de Garlande had, since 1112, possessed to an unusual degree the confidence of the king. There were four brothers; from the year named until 1127 one or other of them, sometimes more, might be found in occupation of high office at court. Stephen, the brother with whom we are concerned, who came to court as a very young man at a time when his eldest brother Anseau was high seneschal, had not to wait long after his arrival before the chancellorship was conferred upon him. We may continue in the words of the *Chronicon Mauriniacense*,[3] the Annals of the Abbey of Maurigny, a contemporary document. This

[1] P. 223 *infra.*

[2] Renati Choppini, *op. cit.,* III. iv. 377.

[3] *Chron. Mauriniac.,* II, R.H.G.F. XII. 76.

abbey was on the river Juine, a little below Étampes. Of the three volumes of the *Chronicon* the IInd is perhaps the most valuable record.[1] " When William, brother of the seneschal Anseau died "—William had succeeded Anseau in this office —" Stephen, their brother, was made seneschal of the royal palace "—this was in 1120. " In past generations it was an unheard of thing that a man who was a deacon should be in military command next only to the king "—the office of seneschal carried with it this command. " This man was active in affairs, well-endowed with worldly wisdom, possessed both of large ecclesiastical revenues and of close intimacy with the king ; indeed, so close that it was said that he ruled the king rather than served him. In our time, so far as temporal success goes, he surpassed all other mortals." The chronicler goes on to tell of how in the end Stephen overreached himself. " Swollen with pride and forgetful of his proper place, he frequently made himself objectionable to Queen Adela, so that, he increasingly becoming hated and the king displeased, he was deprived of his honours and banished from court." Thus in 1127 his ascendancy over Louis le Gros abruptly ceased, never to be resumed in the same proportion.[2]

 This long-lived scandal had not failed to disquiet St Bernard. For him the special offence was the fact that this dainty soldier, this worldly place-hunter who had the king's ear and helped himself out of the king's purse, was not merely a deacon but Archdeacon of Notre-Dame and Dean of Orleans to boot. It must have been upon the very eve of Stephen's fall from high estate that St. Bernard, in the same letter [3] to Suger in which he expressed his joy at the reform of St. Denis, gave vent to his indignation. " Whose heart is not outraged, whose tongue does not complain at least in secret, that in defiance of the Gospel-precept a deacon should at once be serving God and mammon ? That this man should be so highly exalted by ecclesiastical honours as to be inferior not even to bishops, and so loaded with military honours as to take precedence of dukes ? I ask : What is this monstrosity which wants to look like both a clerk and a soldier, and is neither the one nor the other ? " The service done by him at court is nothing less than the preference of the cup of devils before the cup of the Lord. Canon law forbids pluralism. Here is a pluralist so unblushing as to take no account of his various ecclesiastical titles, so long as he can parade his civil honours and his military state ! Here is a man " who confuses his offices ; a man so delicately nurtured as to love, on

[1] *R.H.G.F.* XII. *Praef.*, V. iv. 68 and 76.

[2] Suger. *Vita Ludov. Grossi*, *P.L.* CLXXXVI. 1329 and *n.* ; cf. *ed. ejusd. ap. Les classiques de l'histoire de France.*

[3] *Ep.* 78.

the one hand, rather the display than the discipline of warfare, and, on the other hand, rather the gains than the godliness of religion ! " In a single question, St. Bernard strikes both at Louis and at his favourite. " What king," he asks, " ever set over his army a cleric with no stomach for fighting, and not rather one of the bravest of his soldiers ? "

We do not know for certain whether the king ever had any knowledge of this letter, but it is scarcely to be doubted but that some inkling of it reached him. St. Bernard probably intended that Suger should lay to heart its words both for his own sake and for the sake of France. The Abbot of St. Denis was already a great power in the state ; let him look to it that he was not supplanted ! The moment was favourable for him to assert himself, and the occasion demanded no less. St. Bernard counted much upon the zeal of a neophyte who had but lately set his own house in order, and might be expected to be looking for a new field of work. It was scarcely any fear of the royal displeasure which restrained him from addressing Louis directly ; we prefer to think that it was fidelity to Suger and confidence in his regenerated judgement.

In dealing with the subject of St. Bernard as a monastic reformer we shall quote a letter in which he describes a religious house at Laon as having been at a time not far remote " a brothel of Venus." [1] He is referring to the Abbey of St. John in that city, a royal foundation which had for some years been causing grave anxiety to the bishop, Bartholomew de Vir. We may tell the story in the words of the chronicler Hermann.[2] " Not only had the ancient fervour of the religious life grown cold in this monastery and the external possessions of the house diminished, but very evil reports concerning the nuns were noised abroad. On this account, the same bishop "—Bartholomew de Vir—" being very greatly distressed (for he found them to be frequently promising amendment in response to his warnings, but never giving effect to their promises) on the advice and by the authority of the lord Pope Innocent, of the lord Raynald, Archbishop of Rheims, as well as of Louis King of the French to whom this monastery properly belonged, turned all these nuns without exception out of the house. Then in their stead he placed there as abbot the monk Dom Drogo, Prior of St. Nicaise of Rheims, and with him a sufficient number of monks taken from various monasteries." There is here a little confusion. A council was held at Arras in 1128 attended by the king himself, by the Archbishop of Rheims, by the Bishops of Laon, Arras, Soissons and by the rest of the suffragans of the

[1] *Ep.* 48 ; cf. p. 225 *infra*.

[2] Herman. *De Mirac.*, III. 22 ; Horst. et Mabill. *Not. Fus. in S. Bern. Ep.* 48.

province, as well as by several abbots, including St. Bernard. At this council the reform of the abbey as stated was decreed and later formally confirmed by Louis le Gros [1] and, after he ascended the papal throne in 1130, by Innocent II through his legate, Matthew of Albano.[2] In this instance, albeit that a royal foundation was concerned, St. Bernard and his friend Bartholomew de Vir encountered no difficulty on the part of the king. Probably, judging from St. Bernard's language, the state of affairs was too scandalous to admit of any doubt as to the right method of procedure.

About this time arrived a crisis more obscure in its causes and more extensive in its effects than the last described. Baronius in his *Annals* notes under the year 1127 that the bishops of the Province of Sens were strongly moved to a stricter observance of their duties by the example of the Cistercians, and above all by the spoken and written exhortation of St. Bernard. Amongst these bishops he mentions first Stephen of Senlis, Bishop of Paris, associating with him Suger, who at that time had ruled St. Denis for five years. Plainly the spirit of reform was strongly represented in the capital and in its near neighbourhood. We find in the *Spicilegium* of d'Achery a letter addressed to Stephen by a friend whose name does not transpire, throwing light upon the state of affairs.[3] Louis is represented as despoiling the bishop and his friends of their property ; this persecution is said to have been stirred up by certain of the clergy, notably the dean and the archdeacons, and to amount to more than a merely personal matter, for it infringed the liberties of the Church ; the suggestion is offered that the aid of the Archbishop of Sens and of his suffragans should be enlisted " in order that as sharers in your rights they may succour you against all comers, and if necessary go with you to Rome." Stephen appears to have attempted to reform the Chapter of Notre-Dame. The king had at first approved of his action, but on the appeal of the chapter to him as their protector he had withdrawn his approval. The royal prohibition of reform was not, however, to be accepted without resistance. The Bishop of Paris was fully conscious of the canonical strength of his position, and gave evidence of this fact in some fashion— what, we do not know—which irritated the king. He was deprived of his *regalia*, a move which he promptly countered by laying the diocese under an interdict. Unfortunately this strong measure only resulted in violence on the part of his enemies ; driven from Paris to save his life, he fled for refuge to the Archbishop of Sens ; whereupon his goods and those of

[1] *Gall. Christ.,* X. 192.

[2] Mans. *Concil.,* XXI. 372; Horst. et Mabill. *Not. Fus. in S. Bern. Ep.* 48.

[3] Dach. *Spicileg.,* III. 102.

his friends were spoiled. So much we infer from the letter above cited ; further evidence to the same effect is given by Luchaire in his *Annals of the Life and Reign of Louis le Gros*.[1]

[1] Luchaire, *Louis le Gros*, 424 sqq. ; cf. eund., *Instit. monarch. de la France*, II. 266 sqq.

It was impossible that St. Bernard could be an indifferent spectator of this outrage, especially when he considered that the king was bound to the Cistercians by a bond of brotherhood freely accepted some years before, which not only gave the Order the right but imposed upon it the duty of intervening in such a case. A letter was therefore addressed to Louis in terms sufficiently respectful but firm and quite explicit, for which St. Bernard was probably responsible, in the name of St. Stephen Harding, Abbot of Cîteaux, and of the entire body of Cistercian abbots and brethren.[2] After

[2] *S. Bern. Ep.* 45.

pointing out that the king, who had solicited their prayers, was making them a poor return by persecuting the bride of that heavenly Bridegroom to whom those prayers were addressed, forgetful of the words " he that despiseth you despiseth me," the letter proceeds : " We take steps therefore to draw your attention to these things boldly, but in all kindness for your own sake ; warning you and supplicating you in the name of that friendship and fraternity which you have deigned to share with us, but have lately grievously wounded by not ceasing ere this from your evil behaviour. Moreover, if we are not counted worthy to be heard, but rather to be despised, we your brothers and your friends who daily pray for you, for your children and for your kingdom—you will soon learn that our poor succour to its utmost of its power cannot fail the Church of God and his servant, we mean the venerable father, our friend the Bishop of Paris, who, seeking our humble efforts on his behalf against you, has asked of us a letter to the lord Pope." Before, however, taking this step, the Cistercians offered to meet the king in conference wherever he might appoint, with the express proviso that the case being still unjudged the king should restore to the bishop the *regalia*, the temporal rights of which he had been deprived.[3] Mabillon dates this letter in the year

[3] Cf. Gratian. *Decret., P.L.* CLXXXII. 152, *note* (150).

1127 ; but it is more probable that it was not written until 1129. The offer made in it was never formally accepted. The dice were heavily loaded against St. Bernard and his friends, as we shall see. The reforms proposed at Notre-Dame consisted in nothing less than the transformation of the chapter by the introduction of the Canons Regular of St. Victor. Stephen de Garlande had only recently been discredited ; in the earlier stages of the controversy his influence had been felt in support of the chapter, and it would be natural to expect that in underhand ways he would still continue to lend it to the same cause, if only in retaliation upon the party which had brought about his fall. It appears that an interview took place between the king and certain bishops and abbots, amongst them the Archbishop of Sens, St. Bernard and his old friend, Hugh of Mâcon, Abbot of Pontigny, at which the advocates of the Bishop of Paris, in spite of their humble attitude were roughly received and summarily dismissed. It was upon the morrow of this interview that, according to a passage in the *Vita Prima*—confirmed by the *Fragmenta* but suppressed by Geoffrey, it should be noted, in his Recension B—St. Bernard warned Louis that on the night before it had been revealed to him that the penalty of his royal contumacy would be the death of his eldest son Philip.[1] The king was unmoved. His obduracy may be explained.

The suggestion of an appeal to Rome had an effect quite different from that for which the Cistercians had hoped. Directly Louis became aware of it he resolved to anticipate his opponents by appealing himself behind their backs. Like a bolt from the blue the news reached St. Bernard and his friends that Honorius II had raised the interdict. The Abbot of Clairvaux at once protested in a short but incisive letter to the Pope.[2] He regrets that grave necessity should have brought the Cistercians out of their claustral seclusion into the glare of publicity. He insists that just when the king's anger has been overcome by the humility, or more truly by the firmness, of the bishops the authority of the Supreme Pontiff has intervened to cast down firmness and to exalt pride. Louis, whose surreptitious appeal to Rome was the expression of his sense of instability, had before the interdict was raised shown signs of yielding. " We know," writes St. Bernard, " that, as is perfectly clear from your letter, it was because you had been told a lying tale that you ordered this so just and so necessary an interdict to be raised. But shall not iniquity, now that its lie has been unmasked, be made to feel that it has deceived itself and not your high majesty ? And yet there is one thing at which we do marvel, and that is how it came about that the cause was judged *ex parte* and a verdict given against an absent person." St. Bernard would not presume to dictate to the Pope how the real offender is to be punished and pity to be shown to the innocent ; " on this matter," he remarks, " most kind father, consult your own heart." Another letter,[3] written to the Pope in the name of Geoffrey, Bishop of Chartres, relates something of Louis's

[1] Gaufr. *Fragm.*, *Codex Aureaevall.*, 37 sq. ; cf. *P.L.* CLXXXV. 526 ; *Vita Prima*, IV. ii. 11 ; Suger. *Vita Lud.* *Grossi*, XXI, an. 1131, *P.L.* CLXXXVI.

[2] *Ep.* 46.

[3] *Ep.* 47.

interview with the metropolitan and suffragans of the Province of Sens and with others, in particular how the king, after having consented to restore the *regalia* to the Bishop of Paris, suddenly, on the arrival of the Papal letter raising the interdict, recalled his consent.   Both Luchaire and Vacandard find difficulty in disentangling the threads of this long tale of struggle.   Precisely how it ended we do not know.   Stephen, on the mediation of Matthew of Albano the Apostolic Legate, and advised by the Bishop of Chartres, under the protection of a safe conduct presented himself before Louis.   In the absence of any trustworthy record of their interview we may assume that they made peace together.   The ill-feeling pro-voked died hard in Paris.   We read of the Prior of St. Victor, a friend and intimate of Stephen, having been murdered by the nephews of the Archdeacon of Paris in the very arms of the bishop.[1]

[1] *R.H.G.F.* XV. 334 sqq., 381 sq. Cf. pp. 127 sqq. *supra.*

Not yet, however, were the Cistercians allowed to retire to their " claustral seclusion " from the thick of the fight ; not yet had Louis le Gros finished with the unfortunate Province of Sens.   The occupant of the Papal throne was no Hildebrand to draw the teeth and talons of a tiger who had tasted blood. The metropolitan, Henry the Wild Boar, Archbishop of Sens, was a man who not many years before at the instigation of St. Bernard had ceased to be a courtier, and had become a pastor of souls.   So much so, that it was by means of a letter addressed to him, which acquired the dignity of a treatise, that St. Bernard sought to reach the ears of the episcopate in general.   We refer to the treatise *Concerning the Behaviour and the Office of Bishops.*   This letter was written about the year 1126.   Almost on its first page we read : " Quite recently news of you has reached us more pleasant than was wont to be, and that by the chance of no uncertain rumour, but by the trustworthy mouth of the venerable Bishop of Meaux "— Burchard, Henry's suffragan—" When asked of your state, with a cheerful countenance and with full confidence he replied : ' I think that the good man is now going to submit himself for the future to the counsels of the Bishop of Chartres ' "— Geoffrey, who was entirely in St. Bernard's interest—" This answer of his I received as gladly as I was sure that the counsels given you would be most faithful." [2]   Henry was, then, a neophyte in the party of reform.   Within about a year he was called upon to play his part in the affair of Stephen of Senlis.   We have seen how well and how unflinchingly he played it.   The particular plea upon which he was now him-self attacked was that of simony.   It is not improbable that

[2] *De Mor. et Offic. Episc.,* I. 2.

this had been a vice of his unregenerate days. St. Bernard, defending him in a letter to Cardinal Haimeric, Chancellor of the Apostolic See, refers to a malicious search for proofs of simony by men who would find if they could the polluting corpses of dead vices under the swaddling clothes of new-born virtues.[1] We are almost entirely dependent upon St. Bernard's correspondence for the history of this case.[2] Mabillon dates these letters 1128; perhaps, however, assuming the contest between the king and Stephen of Senlis not to have ended before 1129 at the earliest, they should be dated a year or two later. The first letter to the Pope[3] is a grave denunciation of Louis's conduct. The king is not so much persecuting the bishops—St. Bernard represents it as part of a studied policy —as he is in their persons persecuting zeal for righteousness, piety of life and religion itself. Men who formerly, when living worldly lives, were honoured, trusted and familiar, are, now that they are devoting themselves to their sacred calling, and bringing credit to their ministry, treated as enemies. A case in point is that of the Bishop of Paris. But let it be well noted, although smitten he was not crushed. And now the Archbishop of Sens is the object of attack in order that when the metropolitan has been beaten to his knees, the suffragans may be subdued. Why, it is another Herod! A Herod, forsooth, who is not perturbed about a Christ in the manger, but envies a Christ exalted with power in the Church! The king has absolutely nothing to allege against the archbishop; all that he wants to do is to break his spirit. If St. Bernard is deceived or deceiving, let him be examined before the Pope. Indeed, that is his earnest wish, his humble prayer. To take the case before the king's judgement-seat and to accept his verdict is, alas, nothing else than to deliver a man over to the will of his enemies. In his second letter[4] to Honorius, the notion of Louis as another Herod is maintained. The Pope is Joseph, the "just man." Let him see what can be done for the mother (the Church) and the child (the archbishop) in the Province of Sens. St. Bernard concludes by insisting that it is patent beyond question that the king is seeking to persecute revived religion in the person of the archbishop, who before he became its promoter incurred no displeasure at all. And St. Bernard, we feel, was right. He and his cause had their enemies and those enemies had the ear of a man who, as Luchaire points out, saw that the success of this new reform would have the direct effect of limiting his power over the lands of the Church, and consequently of diminishing his revenues. "The whole of his reign," continues that writer,

[1] S. Bern. Ep. 51.

[2] Epp. 49-51.

[3] Ep. 49.

[4] Ep. 50.

" was devoted to husbanding the strength of the royal authority and increasing the material resources of the Crown." [1]   Two influences and two only hindered him : the Papal power and the irrepressibly rising tide of religion represented by St. Bernard and the Cistercians—who brought that power into play.   We may conclude that the matter ended in a way sufficiently satisfactory to the archbishop.   Indeed, so firmly did his authority become established that his zeal would sometimes outrun his discretion ; for about ten years later we find St. Bernard writing to remonstrate with him sharply for unjust harshness in deposing one of his archdeacons. [2]

This continual intervention in affairs inevitably tended to create in the minds of many considerable displeasure detrimental to the Abbot of Clairvaux.   It was less the part which he played in great national crises, which might seem to be reasonable and convincing, than his interference, unjustifiable it was sometimes thought, in local questions.   We infer this from a letter [3] written by him to Haimeric in 1129.   We have already referred to this letter ; we shall do so again later. [4] Here the point is the charges made against St. Bernard on the ground of his being a busybody in other men's matters which are not his own proper concern.   The letter, we notice, was evidently intended to be submitted to the College of Cardinals.   Probably it was a vindication of his conduct in answer to a rebuke administered by Haimeric in a letter now lost ; the opening words suggest no less.   " Is it then so, that for the poor and needy to speak the truth begets hatred, and that not even misery itself can escape envy ?   Should I complain or should I glory that by speaking the truth I am become an enemy ?   Is it because I speak what is true or because I do what is right ? "   The first charge with which he deals is that of unwarrantable interference in the affairs of the diocese of Verdun.   Henry, Bishop of Verdun, was suspected of corrupt administration of the funds of the Church. Being on terms of some intimacy with St. Bernard, he consulted him in the matter.   St. Bernard's advice was that in order to avoid public scandal he should resign his see.   This he consented to do and, the case having been referred by the Pope to his legate, Matthew Bishop of Albano, a council was held at Châlons-sur-Marne in 1129, at which his resignation was accepted. [5]   The plea urged against St. Bernard was not supported by the facts.   All that he had done was, when asked for his advice by one of the parties concerned who was his personal friend, to give it ; and it was taken.   Well might he protest : " Neither am I moved by shameful vituperation,

[1] Luchaire, *Inst. monarch. de la France,* II. 269.

[2] *Ep.* 182.

[3] *Ep.* 48.
[4] Pp. 196 *supra,* 225 *infra.*

[5] Dach. *Spicileg.,* XII. 311.

nor do I accept undeserved praise ; I have nothing to do with happenings of which I am not the author." [1] He had not removed this prelate from his charge ; by leave of the Apostolic Legate he had removed himself, wisely no doubt, but willingly. Yet it must be allowed that, from the average point of view of established authorities in Church and state, St. Bernard might well appear to be a troublesome if not a dangerous person. The Papal *Curia* would naturally be besieged with the exaggerated reports of persons whose motives would range, from jealousy and from tenacity of vested interests at the one extreme, to dislike of innovation and to conscientious conservatism at the other. The language of the Abbot of Clairvaux was not measured by any other standard than that of the truth ; the truth, it may be claimed, always spoken in love. His fearlessness and frankness, combined with the quite evident strength of his personal affection and of his loyalty to high office, would have presented an enigma ; the cogency of his reasoning, which at times seemed almost ironically to disclaim its rights at the footstool of authority, would have disquieted the minds of men who had had no experience of his like. In fact, a prophet had arisen and the world, much even of the best of it, was not yet quite sure whether he would bless or curse. It was early days, and early days are days of difficulty. The halcyon days, we know, would come when the Church would have emerged from the Papal Schism, and Eugenius III, the first Cistercian Pope, would occupy the chair of Peter, and a great Abbot of Cluny, Peter the Venerable, would have learned to know and to love St. Bernard, and Suger's keen appreciation of his single-mindedness and of his good judgement would bear fruit at the royal court of France. Meanwhile the Cistercians had in Haimeric, that Southerner from Castres in Aquitaine, who was made Chancellor of the Apostolic See in 1126, a friend who, all through the long years of his cardinalate from 1121 to 1141, was loyal. His intimacy with St. Bernard grew closer as time passed. He would beg the abbot's prayers and seek his guidance.[2] He was, we may believe, frequently his correspondent ; fourteen letters written to him by St. Bernard are extant in the Benedictine edition. To him was addressed the great mystical treatise *Concerning Loving God.* To his own sons at Clairvaux St. Bernard could write from Italy in 1137 : " Pray for the lord Chancellor who is to me as a mother ; and for the lord Luke, for the lord Chrysogonus and for master Ivo, who prove themselves to be to us as our own mother's sons." [3] All of these cardinals we can identify ; [4] to one, Ivo,

[1] *Ep.* 48 (2).

[2] S. Bern. *De Dilig. Deo, Praef.*

[3] *Ep.* 144.
[4] Mabillon. *Not. ad loc.*

¹ *Ep.* 193.

who had been a Canon Regular of St. Victor of Paris, St. Bernard would write three years later in the matter of Abélard.¹ In the Sacred College, then, Haimeric had by that time taught his " brothers " to befriend his friend.

Louis le Jeune

We shall have occasion to notice Suger's success in establishing at the Council of Rheims in 1119 the distinction between investiture with the cross and ring, that is to say, with the spiritualities of a see, and investiture with the sceptre, that is to say, with its temporalities or *regalia*.² By a confusion of thought the holding of temporalities has sometimes been described as the expression of ecclesiastical feudality. It should, however, be remembered that, in the strict sense of the term, there was no such thing as ecclesiastical feudality.³ And this for one essential reason ; the fact that the dignity of a bishop or of an abbot, as the case might be, was not hereditary. The development of the feudal system did not in theory, however often in practice, result in making the bishopric or the abbacy a strictly feudal tenure. This was an aspect upon which the Hildebrandine party, wherever its influence was strong, laid jealous emphasis—but scarcely with success—claiming that temporalities were held in free and not in feudal tenure, albeit that in case of the vacancy of a see, due either to death or to translation, the temporalities reverted *ipso facto* to the Crown. Plainly this reversion had its advantages ; the revenues were not exposed to the risk of seizure by the lay seigneurs ; they were protected by the royal safeguard. An instance of the explicit assurance of such a safeguard may be quoted from the *Bibliotheca Cluniacensis*.⁴ It was given in 1119 by Louis le Gros to the Abbey of Cluny in the following terms : " We decree and grant and promise that we and our successors, Kings of France, are bound to maintain, protect and guard as our own property the abbots who may rule at any time and their successors and the monastery of Cluny and its aforesaid priories. . . ." The meaning is unmistakable. What applied to a great, perhaps exceptionally privileged, abbey applied equally to a diocesan see. But such rights of protection not only were monarchic in their tendency—the acceptance of this safeguard against the invasions of the Counts of Châlon put an end to the political independence of Cluny—but lent themselves too readily to gross abuse. A case in point, to which we refer again later,⁵ was the occupation of the episcopal palace at Châlons-sur-

² P. 223 *infra*.

³ Luchaire, *Inst. monarch. de la France*, II. 55 sq.

⁴ Marrier et Quercetan, *Biblioth. Cluniac.*, 576.

⁵ Pp. 212 sq. *infra*.

Marne in 1143 by Robert of Dreux, brother of Louis le Jeune, which led St. Bernard to write in strong terms to the king in whose name it was done.   He reminds him that he is " preventing their pastor from being set over the sheep of Christ at Châlons and, contrary to what is just and right, allowing his brother with his soldiers, archers and crossbowmen to be billed in the bishop's house." [1]   Rightly, the Crown had taken possession *sede vacante ;* but it appeared to be arbitrarily retaining possession as it were *jure spolii.* St. Bernard felt this to be unjustifiable and offensive, as well as detrimental to the spiritual interest of the diocese.   How, we may ask, was it to be explained ?   Was the condition still one of *sede vacante* when St. Bernard wrote ?   We may assume that it was not ; or he would have been urging—a thing which we can scarcely suppose—an invalid plea.   The accepted formalities required that investiture with the *regalia* should precede investiture with the spiritualities.[2] We find Suger, a staunch friend of St. Bernard, making this claim seven years later during his regency.   The see of Chartres is vacant, and he sends to the chapter a letter in which we read : [3] " Seeing that by the obligation of our office it is our duty to attend diligently to the affairs of the kingdom and to maintain its rights, we commend to your favour the bearers of this letter as our representatives to receive and keep the *regalia* on behalf of our lord the king ; begging you as faithful subjects to aid them faithfully in all that is fitting, until such time as the divine mercy may, according to the usual order, console with a suitable successor your so great church orphaned of so glorious a pastor."   Undoubtedly we have here the claim of the Crown to resume the temporalities and to hold them until in the " usual order " *congé d'élire* or *eligendi licentia,* election and royal approbation have followed—but no longer. And this investiture with the *regalia* preceded the consecration of the bishop.

In 1140 the see of Poitiers was vacant.   The chapter proceeded to elect a certain Grimoard, Abbot of Alleux.   There is no evidence to show that the election was made otherwise than in due order ; but the metropolitan Geoffrey du Loroux, a man of learning and attainments, proceeded to consecrate the elect before he had been invested with the *regalia.* Louis le Jeune at once annulled the election.   The explanation of this unfortunate occurrence is to be found in certain privileges granted by the king to the Province of Bordeaux, which in his view the metropolitan had exceeded. When Louis married Eleanor of Aquitaine she brought to France a great

[1] *Ep.* 221.

[2] Luchaire, *op. cit.,* II. 82.

[3] Suger. *Ep.* 14, *P.L.* CLXXXVI.

dowry. On the day that Poitou and Aquitaine would pass to Henry Plantagenet, Louis would perhaps wish that it had been less. But at the time he made, as it were, a thank-offering for it in the shape of a grant to the bishops and abbots of the Province of Bordeaux. He would no longer require the revenues of sees and of abbacies to be paid to him during vacancies, nor expect homage or oaths of allegiance on election to vacancies ; but he did not renounce a quite distinct right, that, namely, of investiture with the *regalia*.[1] This was a distinction which for some reason the Archbishop of Bordeaux failed to appreciate. He was under the impression that in his province the king had by one stroke surrendered his right as ultimate owner of the temporalities ; whereas he had merely without prejudice suspended in certain respects his exercise of that right, protecting himself in each case by requiring the formality of investiture. Consequently, Grimoard having been canonically elected, Geoffrey, in all good faith, consecrated him Bishop of Poitiers. Louis, as we have seen, at once refused to recognize him, and even forbade him to enter his cathedral city. St. Bernard complained to Joslen, Bishop of Soissons, a man much in the king's counsels, that the royal step had been rash and ill-advised. " The kingdom and its rulers," he wrote, " suffer injury if the king's business is in the full light of day done impetuously, and is not allowed to take its course rather circumspectly than in headlong fashion. I am glad, very glad, that the king trusts you and confides in you." He recognizes that the real victim of the king's displeasure is the archbishop. " Why does my lord the king," he asks, " seek to bring against the Archbishop of Bordeaux charges which are unfounded ? Is this done by your advice ? Far from you be such advice and from me such a suspicion ! But, in a word, what is the wrong that he has done ? Is it that in the exercise of his canonical right he has consecrated a person elected by the equal approval, vote and voice of the people of Poitiers ? Is it that he has not taken out of the mouths of the hungry, out of the laps of the churches of Poitiers, what a dying man has bequeathed to them ? "[2] Here, of course, St. Bernard uses hyperbolical language, and designedly ; for the king could neither legally nor honourably make any pecuniary claim on the estate of the defunct. He is certainly right in urging that Louis had acted with jealous precipitancy and without sufficient inquiry as to the *bona fides* of the archbishop ; and, with a reminder of the danger " paries cum proximus ardet," he warns the bishops to look to their roofs ! In the following year, the matter was settled by the investiture of Grimoard with the *regalia*.[3]

[1] *R.H.G.F.* XVI. 2 ; Luchaire, *Instit. monarch.,* II. 77 sqq.

[2] *Ep.* 342.

[3] *R.H.G.F.* XII. 408.

As Louis le Gros had been the victim of the evil influence of Stephen de Garlande, so did not his son escape that of a courtier whose ambition was no less and whose cunning, considering that he had no such support from the tradition of family service as had Stephen, was perhaps greater. Cadurce was a native of Berry, a province which at the opening of the XIIth century had come into the possession of the Crown of France. The greed of this man was enormous. When Louis set forth on the Second Crusade the most troublesome person whom he left to the management of his regent Suger was this turbulent Berrichon who, with the added dignity of the royal chancellorship which he had obtained in 1140, was Archdeacon of Bourges and of Châteauroux and Abbot of St. Sulpice.[1] Shortly after he became chancellor, the archbishopric of Bourges falling vacant, he at once marked it as his prey and anticipated opposition—for his rapacity was by no means favourable to his popularity—by pressing his suit upon the king. Louis announced that the election by the chapter should be quite free, but at the same time excluded the candidate most likely to be acceptable to the electors. This was Peter de la Châtre (*Castrensis*, of Castres) or Pierre Aimeri. William of Nangis in his *Chronicle* under the year 1142 states explicitly : " King Louis had granted to the Church of Bourges liberty to elect any bishop whom it wished, except the said Peter ; and he had sworn publicly that so long as he himself lived he should not be archbishop." [2] Peter, Matthew Paris tells us, was a nephew of Cardinal Haimeric, Chancellor of the Apostolic See,[3] and when in spite of the royal prohibition he was elected, he found himself strongly entrenched. " He set out for Rome, and was consecrated by Pope Innocent, who said that the king was a child who ought to be properly taught and restrained from acquiring these bad habits, adding that it was no liberty at all that an exception like this should be made by princes, unless it could be proved before an ecclesiastical judge that a man was not fit to be elected." [4] Matthew Paris records that Peter was consecrated at Paris by Pope Eugenius, which can scarcely be correct.[5] As for Cadurce, him the Pope pronounced to be an improper person to hold any benefice in the Church. When, despatched by Innocent II to take possession of his see, Peter returned to France, Louis proved himself to be as good as his oath, and excluded him from the city of Bourges. However, Theobald, Count of Champagne, was prepared to shelter him in his territory, and thither he went.[6] The Pope, too, could use the weapon of exclusion, spiritual but none the less dread ; he laid under

[1] *Op. cit.*, XII. 86 sq. ; Luchaire, *op. cit.*, I. 188, 193, 203.

[2] Guill. Nang. *Chron. an.* mcxlii, *R.H.G.F.* XV. 359 ; cf. Radulfi de Diceto, *Imag. Hist.*, *R.H.G.F.* XIII. 183 ; *Gall. Christ.*, II. 51.

[3] Matt. Par. *Chron. Maj.*, II. 179, *R.S.*

[4] Guill. Nang. *Chron. an.* mcxlii, *ap. op. cit., loc. cit.*

[5] Matt. Par. *op. cit., loc. cit.*

[6] *R.H.G.F.* XII 86 ; Combes, *L'Abbé Suger,* 90 sqq.

an interdict every place in France down to the smallest village where the king might be found. To the dispassionate onlooker even at this distance of time the situation appears critical. To St. Bernard it was infinitely distressing. The tension between Louis and Theobald was severe. About 1143 St. Bernard concludes a letter to the Pope by saying : " I do not dare to write to you of the imminent perils of the Church, of the grave schism which we fear and of the many troubles which we are now enduring. But I have written to certain holy bishops of your *Curia ;* you will learn from them, if you so wish, what I have written." [1] He is evidently anxious that a petition made by Louis for the raising of the interdict should be granted. For this he had pleaded in the letter to the cardinals, Alberic, Bishop of Ostia, Stephen, Bishop of Palestrina, Hincmar, Bishop of Tusculum, and the Chancellor Gerard.[2] The Church is only now recovering from the Papal Schism, the *rabies leonina* as he is wont to term it ; and it is again threatened by disaster of the same kind if not of the same magnitude. " For two things," he writes, " we do not excuse the king. He swore unlawfully, and he kept his oath unjustly. He did not wish to keep it, but he was ashamed to break it. As you well know, it is shameful for a man of Frankish stock to break his oath, however ill done it may have been to swear it publicly ; yet no wise man can doubt but that illicit oaths ought not to be kept. However, we do not claim that even this "—that is to say, the keeping by the king of his illicit oath—" can be excused. And, indeed, we have not undertaken so much to make excuses, as to beg pardon. It is for you to consider whether his anger, or his youth, or his rank, can to any extent at all excuse him. It can, if you decree that mercy is to triumph over judgement, taking into account that he is both a king and a youth, and thus he be spared this time on the understanding that he does not presume to do any such thing again. I should say : Let him be spared if possible, provided that the liberty of the Church is in all respects secured and the reverence due to the archbishop safeguarded, a man whom Apostolic hands have consecrated. This is what the king himself humbly begs ; this is what the whole of our all too sadly stricken Church in France suppliantly entreats."

Louis, then, seemed to contemplate yielding on the question of the investiture of Peter de la Châtre ; but before he actually did so much happened of which the story must be told. Several seigneurs had contracted or proposed to contract matrimony with members of the family of Theobald or

Champagne. This tendency Louis viewed with suspicion, and declared the alliances in question to be matrimonially null, on the ground that feudally they required the consent of himself as suzerain.[1] A test case arose. Raoul, Count of Vermandois and the king's seneschal, was married to a niece of Theobald, by name Leonora. He now wished to marry Queen Eleanor's sister, Petronilla. In this project he was, as might be expected, supported by the king. The claims of royal suzerainty were, however, not considered strong enough to offer any prospect of success, and the plea was made that the bar of consanguinity existed between Raoul and Leonora. This plea, on being submitted to the Bishops of Tournai, Senlis and Laon—the last being Bartholomew de Vir—was upheld. The matter reached the Pope's ears, with the result that in 1142 a council was held at Lagny near Paris over which the Apostolic Legate, Cardinal Ivo, presided and at which the Count of Vermandois was excommunicated, his lands laid under an interdict and the three bishops suspended.[2] The interesting thing is that the marriage of Raoul and Petronilla was afterwards at the Council of Rheims in 1148 declared valid! [3] Meanwhile, however, Theobald was triumphant and the king furious. St. Bernard was entirely on Theobald's side in the matter. In a letter to Innocent II, dated by Mabillon 1142,[4] he speaks of the three bishops as " audacious men who in opposition to God have not feared to separate those who have been joined together by God ; nay, more, who have added sin to sin by joining together those who ought not to be joined together." On the general question of Louis's interference in the matrimonial affairs of his feudatories, he would later be found pressing the point that the king is throwing stones from a glass house. With amazing frankness he would write in 1143 to the Cardinal Stephen, Bishop of Palestrina : [5] " With what face does a man "—meaning the king—" highly concern himself to prescribe to other people about consanguinity, who is himself openly living with a woman who is his cousin in the third degree of consanguinity ? " Here the precise fact is that Queen Eleanor was a great grand-daughter of Aldearde, wife's sister to Humbert II of Maurienne, the maternal aunt of Adela, the king's mother.[6] In the earlier letter [7] he asserts the true explanation of the quarrel to be the fact that at the Pope's command Theobald had received the Archbishop of Bourges into his territory. He has no faith in the king's profession of regret for his conduct to the archbishop ; in any case his regret has had no lasting result. We can scarcely think that St. Bernard was mistaken, for Louis had invaded Theobald's

[1] S. Bern. *Ep.* 222 ; Combes, *L'Abbé Suger,* 97 sqq.

[2] Labbe, *Concil. Append.,* X. 582 ; Dach. *Spicileg.,* XII. 480.

[3] Joann. Sares. *Hist. Pontific.,* VI. 13 sqq., *ed.* Poole.

[4] *Ep.* 216.

[5] *Ep.* 224 (4).

[6] Horst. et Mabill. *Not. Fus. in S. Bern.* *Ep.* 224, and Migne, *P.L. Not. ad loc.*

[7] *Ep.* 216.

14

dominions, laid waste wide stretches of country, interfered with the clergy, disposed of ecclesiastical benefices, and finally crowned his terrors by taking by storm a little place called Vitry, about twenty miles S.E. of Châlons-sur-Marne, where such excesses were committed by his soldiery that the whole town was razed to the ground by fire, about fifteen hundred people being taken or burnt alive ; in the church the victims of fire numbered some hundreds.[1]   Vitry-le-Brûlé, as it was thenceforth named, became a dreadful memory for Louis.

[1] R.H.G.F. XII. 116, XIII. 272.

It is probable that the king began to realize that the curses of his people were being added to the censures of the Church.   It might, too, be better to have the Count of Champagne as a friend than as a foe, supported as Theobald was by St. Bernard.   Accordingly, he offered to evacuate the territory occupied, provided that the count would secure the raising of the interdict laid upon the lands of Raoul of Vermandois.   In this the mediation of St. Bernard was necessary. The Pope would attend to no one else.   But the Abbot of Clairvaux saw at once that Theobald's acceptance of these terms did not imply any pledge to supplicate for the recognition of the marriage between Raoul and Petronilla.   For the moment Theobald had the better of the bargain.   Fully conscious of this, St. Bernard for the imperative sake of peace would have the tale of woe and disorder ended at once upon the terms offered by Louis.   He writes to the Pope in a letter,[2] dated by Mabillon 1142, that Theobald the most devoted son of his holiness, the defender of the Church's liberty, had no other course open to him than, in order to prevent the devastation of the country and the disaster of a kingdom divided against itself, to undertake on oath to do his utmost to get the interdict raised ; that he had been urged to take this course by faithful and wise counsellors who declared that " this could be done by you "—that is to say, the Pope—" quite easily and without any detriment to the credit of the Church, seeing that the power would rest with you without a word to reimpose and irrevocably confirm the sentence, perfectly just as it was, and thus artifice be defeated by artifice, peace forthwith restored and the man who boasts in his evil deeds and is strong in unrighteousness gain nothing thereby."   Certainly this is the wisdom of the serpent !   The question at issue as to Raoul's marriage with Petronilla, the queen's sister, was ostensibly left unsettled ; the very offence which had called for the interdict was ignored.   Meanwhile, however, internecine strife would cease and the interdict would still be a weapon in the Pope's armoury should he see fit to use it, and more, a weapon

[2] Ep. 217.

which if used again it would be in his power never to recall until the offence which it was used to correct had been corrected. In writing to the king St. Bernard magnified the generosity of Theobald by pointing out that he had made no difficulty about the absolution of the Count of Vermandois [1] [1] *Ep.* 220. —implied by the raising of the interdict—"albeit, as you know," he says, "it is not a matter of justice" that he should be absolved; meaning that the interdict was justly deserved so far as the count was concerned; and that the offence for which it was imposed remained still uncorrected. However the interdict was raised and the treaty of peace signed, for the king by Suger and by Joslen, Bishop of Soissons, for Theobald by Hugh, Bishop of Auxerre, and by St. Bernard; and Louis, in the end, restored the County of Vitry, the occupied territory, to the Count of Champagne. But from a letter written by St. Bernard to Suger and Joslen in 1142 [2] we infer that [2] *Ep.* 222. some difficulty was encountered in inducing Louis to give effect to the treaty. A letter from the king, probably written in reply to St. Bernard's *Epistle* CCXX, is quoted for the information of the two royal delegates. Louis speaks of Count Raoul as having been fooled, and of his case as having been simply deferred. St. Bernard replies that Theobald had done what he undertook to do; and points out, as he had pointed out to the Pope, that it is an instance of a man falling into the pit which he had dug for another. The royal delegates are bound to see that the king fulfils the undertakings which he gave by their lips.

Surprise has been expressed that St. Bernard and the Pope should have lent themselves to such a method of restoring peace. We venture to think that, although, as being not unlikely to leave a sense of resentment in the minds of Louis and Raoul, it may not have been highly politic, it was yet entirely honest. If the king and Raoul had required at the time a recognition of the latter's matrimonial claims, they should have said so. St. Bernard evidently thought that they deliberately said nothing about them, intending afterwards to put in the plea that their validity was implicitly recognized by the raising of the interdict. They had asked to be dispensed from punishment, and they had thought that such dispensation carried with it acquittal of crime. They had forgotten the truth of the saying: *Nulla poena, quanta poena!* But St. Bernard detected the workings of the king's mind; he was obsessed by the idea that his suzerainty entitled him to dictate the matrimonial alliances of his vassals. Theobald had done precisely what he had pledged himself to do; and

Louis was in honour bound to do the same or else, as St. Bernard puts it to him, he would " add sin to sin."

Apparently it was after all these happenings that the king was at last brought to yield upon the question of the election of Peter de la Châtre to the see of Bourges. As we have ¹ *Epp.* 218, 219. learned from two letters already quoted,[1] addressed by him in 1143, one to the Pope and the other to certain cardinals, St. Bernard had pleaded hard in support of Louis's petition for the raising of the interdict laid upon any place where his presence might be found. The royal method of recalling a hasty and unjust oath was more than laconic ; it was scarcely self-respecting. Nothing whatever was said upon the point, but Macarius, Abbot of Maurigny, was despatched to Rome, armed with the king's authority to accept any terms what-
² *Chron. Maur-*   ever as the condition of the raising of the interdict.[2] Alas,
iniac., R.H.G.F.   his mission failed of success ! In spite of the influence of the
XII. 87.   cardinals, presumably the same as were addressed by St. Bernard in *Epistle* CCXIX—in his cause, " he returned home, having neither by prayers nor by presents obtained the favour
³ *Chron. Maur-*   of reconciliation."[3]
iniac., loc. cit.   And now the Pope insisted upon a separation between Raoul and Petronilla, under penalty of another interdict were he disobeyed. The whole question was re-opened and Louis, probably realizing by this time that he had fallen into a pit, made it plain that he would appeal to the arbitrament of war. Well might a contemporary chronicler record that " Western France, having lost its king, suffered under his son, Louis, who now reigns, owing to the war between him and Theobald of Blois such hazards of plunder and of fire that, unless it had lately found peace by the merits, prayers and counsels of the monks who dwelt in the land, it might be thought that it
⁴ Otton. Frising. would have been utterly destroyed."[4] Theobald turned his
Chron., VII.   attention to the strengthening of his position by matrimonial
xxi., Hofmeis-   alliances, proposing to marry his eldest son, Henry, to Lauretta,
ter, *Script. Rer.* the daughter of the Count of Flanders, and one of his daughters
Germ.   to the Count of Soissons, projects of which the king had
⁵ S. Bern. *Ep.* apparently already heard,[5] thus flaunting his independence in
222.   the face of his suzerain. Nor was Louis inactive ; he was notably animated against the Church. The sees of Paris and
⁶ *Gall. Christ.,* Châlons-sur-Marne fell vacant, probably in the year 1143.[6]
VII. 64, IX.   Guy of Montaigu, elected to the latter see, the king refused to
881.   invest with the *regalia*. Meanwhile the revenues of both sees were accumulating for his war-chest. Under his brother,
⁷ Cf. pp. 204 sq. Robert of Dreux, marauding bands of soldiery plundered
supra.   the episcopal domains of Châlons-sur-Marne.[7] Nor did the

Cathedral of Rheims or the Abbeys of St. Rémi, St. Nicaise and St. Thierry-lès-Reims escape their greedy grasp. Of all this St. Bernard complained bitterly in the letter to Cardinal Stephen, Bishop of Palestrina, already cited.[1] To the king's best counsellors, Suger and Joslen, it would have been a time of grave anxiety. They would seem, however, to have been impotent to counteract what we may conjecture to have been the evil genius which swayed Louis's will, namely, Queen Eleanor, whose purpose of maintaining as valid the alliance between her sister, Petronilla, and Raoul of Vermandois would naturally be served by the king's insistence upon his feudal suzerainty. There is some evidence that surprise was felt and reproach expressed on the score of Suger's failure to mend matters, for we find St. Bernard writing to him later [2]— Mabillon dates the letter so late as 1150 : " I wish it never to enter into your mind that I in any degree believed that it was by your advice or with your consent that the things which we lament are happening," words which, a little unaccountable if written so late as Mabillon suggests, evidently reflect and rebut charges made against the Abbot of St. Denis. Nevertheless, it would be unlike St. Bernard not to favour more strenuous measures than were actually taken. " I thought and—not to offend you—I still think that it is by no means sufficient for you," that is to say himself and Suger, " not to be the authors of the breach of peace unless you are using all your efforts to restrain the people who are such, whatever may be their rank, and laying your curses upon their counsel and their company." [3] So he wrote to Joslen in 1143.

Meanwhile, events did not prosper with Theobald. Geoffrey, in the Fourth Book of the *Vita Prima*, gives a piteous picture of his plight.[4] The passage in question represents Recension B. It opens with the statement that not less marvellously than mercifully did the divine aid deliver this most pious prince from the great trials which beset him. It describes this friend of the poor and of all the servants of God, in particular of St. Bernard, as the victim of a conspiracy on the part of the king and of other powerful neighbours, despairing of escape. Certain bishops and various leading men, including St. Bernard, are represented as meeting to discuss the state of affairs. It is agreed that the Count of Champagne is entirely in the king's power, and that only God can deliver him ; but that, alas, as yet the divine arm has not been raised to smite his foe. Theobald is being beset by his neighbours on all sides ; the few supporters whom he has are falling away ; even his own vassals are losing heart ; every one is seeking to

[1] *Ep.* 224 ; *vide* p. 209 *supra ;* cf. *Ep.* 221.

[2] *Ep.* 381.

[3] *Ep.* 223.

[4] *Vita Prima,* IV. iii. 12.

attach himself to the winning side. Subsequently, and not improbably as deputed by the persons who had attended this meeting, Godfrey de la Roche, Bishop of Langres, sought St. Bernard's opinion, asking him whether he had received any divine guidance in the matter. The Abbot of Clairvaux is sensible of nothing but sorrow upon sorrow ; nevertheless, he is prepared to foretell that within five months peace will come. And, so the writer tells us, on the last day of the fifth month peace did come, in response to the fervent prayers and in reward of the indefatigable exertions of St. Bernard, to the devout but sorely tried Theobald.[1] The story of this stage of the conflict is told also by Arnald of Bonneval [2] in terms which, so far as they go, are consistent with what we learn from Geoffrey.

Vacandard thinks this meeting recorded by Geoffrey to have taken place at some time during the first half of the winter of 1143-44. Innocent II had died on 24th September, 1143.[3] St. Bernard saw his opportunity, and at once wrote to his successor, Celestin II, in touching terms. "What Count Theobald supplicates is what I also supplicate ; indeed, he is a son of peace. He has the zeal for peace, but it is of you that we entreat the effect of peace. Your Apostolate is the debtor of peace ; the position which you occupy is the seat of peace. All men love peace ; few deserve it. Forsooth, your servant protests himself to be amongst the lovers of peace ; whether he is amongst those who deserve it is for you to judge. One thing, however, even if we do not deserve peace, the necessity of the bride of Christ, that is, the Church requires it ; the friend of the Bridegroom will not surely make her sad." [4] And the king and Theobald availed themselves of the same opportunity. Without delay the Pope wrote to the Bishop of Arras, intimating that he wished to deal with the question of the marriages proposed for the Count of Champagne's son and daughter, which Louis regarded as infringing his right of suzerainty.[5] When the king's emissaries were presented to the Pope, he rose from his chair and, blessing France, withdrew the interdict visited upon his obstinacy in the matter of Peter de la Châtre.[6] But there still were storm-clouds in the sky. A conference was held at Corbeil, over which the king presided. Unfortunately, Joslen, Bishop of Soissons who, as we have seen, exercised some authority over Louis, was not present at it. "I confess," wrote St. Bernard to Joslen, "that we wanted your help and your presence." [7] However, the Abbot of Clairvaux was supported by the intimate friend of his youth, Hugh of Mâcon, now Bishop of Auxerre, and

[1] Gaufr. *Fragm.*, *Codex Aureae-vall.*, 69 sq.
[2] *Vita Prima*, II. viii. 54 sq.

[3] Boson. *Vita Innocent. Sec.*, Watterich, *Pontif. Roman. Vitae*, II. 179.

[4] *Ep.* 358.

[5] *R.H.G.F.* XV. 409 ; Jaffé, *Regest.* 5979.

[6] *R.H.G.F.* XII. 871.

[7] *Ep.* 225.

probably by Suger. The king appears to have lost his temper and in high dudgeon to have abruptly left the scene. St. Bernard and Hugh did not hesitate to tell him what they thought of his behaviour and what their next step would be. " You know," they wrote, " the way, the unreasonable way, we take leave to say, in which you left us on that occasion." [1] The particular remarks at which Louis had taken umbrage were evidently some which insinuated that his own counsellors were compelling him to stand out in the sight of all as the head and fount of the prevailing evil ; whereas men ought to fear him as the defender of the innocent, and to feel the weight of his hand as the avenger of wrong. His *amour propre* revolted at the suggestion that to his own detriment he was being thrust by his advisers, probably not excluding the queen, into the forefront of the fray. In this same letter, he was informed by his correspondents that they had sent to him Andrew of Baudemont, the procurator of the Count of Champagne, [2] " in order that by word of mouth he may explain our proposals and report to us whatever answer you see fit to give. If you persist, which God forbid, in refusing good counsels, we are innocent of your blood. God will not any longer allow his Church to be trodden under foot by you or by yours." This letter had the effect of bringing the king to consent to another conference. It is significant that at this conference, held at St. Denis [3] in the late spring or early summer of 1144, it was made abundantly evident that, as we have hinted, it was Eleanor of Aquitaine who was ultimately responsible for the *intransigeance* of her royal husband ; for she was present upon the occasion, and put herself forward to advocate the cause of her sister, Petronilla, and Raoul of Vermandois. Then it was probably that St. Bernard so rebuked her for abusing her influence that she was subsequently moved to confide to him the fact of her sterility, and to beg him to pray that she might have a child. The chronicler records that the Abbot of Clairvaux required as the condition of his prayers that she should amend her ways as the king's evil genius, that Louis himself pressed him to grant her request, and that at about the same time in the following year a child was born.[4] This would have been their eldest daughter, Mary.

Thus, in the end came peace ; and it came upon terms which taken as a whole commended themselves to St. Bernard. In him the common sense of France, to say nothing of its religious instinct, had found its exponent. Louis himself and his queen, wayward and uncertain as they both were in sympathy, in emotion, in aim and in directive force, were

[1] *Ep.* 226 ; cf. Combes, *L'Abbé Suger,* 105 sqq.

[2] *Cf.* Suger. *Vita Ludov. Grossi, R.H.G.F.* XII. 35 (301).

[3] S. Bern. *Ep.* 225.

[4] *Gaufr. Fragm., Codex Aureaevall.,* 70 sq. ; *Vita Prima,* IV. iii. 18.

beginning to feel the strength of that will which, in a fragile framework as it was, could lift no arm to smite or to restrain, yet willed peace, and simply because it willed peace won peace. Over the king's head hung like some sword of Damocles the memory of Vitry-le-Brûlé, the memory of a past which might at any time transform itself into the retribution of a dreadful present. Theobald, a far nobler type, receptive of more truly spiritual impressions, conscious at times, as we know, of a void which religion alone could fill, endowed with something of the reckless generosity of a child, would have doubted, at any rate in St. Bernard's presence, whether it was all worth while, or indeed, quite right. Both parties, too, were doubtless war-weary.

Celestin II was perhaps less uncompromising in his requirements, less unguarded in his speech, than had been his predecessor, a man who had fought his way to the Papal throne through a long period of schism characterized by the vindictive scheming, the faction-fighting, the ruthless terrorism which had so often shown themselves to be congenial alike to the great families and to the populace of Rome, and which on this occasion had invaded the very *penetralia* of the Church.

For the last time Louis withdrew his forces from the occupied territory of the Count of Champagne. Theobald said no more of the matrimonial alliances proposed for his children. One marked success certainly the king could later claim ; as we have seen, the marriage between Raoul of Vermandois and Petronilla was in 1148 pronounced valid.[1] Meanwhile, influenced by St. Bernard, he consented to acknowledge Peter de la Châtre as Archbishop of Bourges, and promised to atone for the violation of his rash oath by a pilgrimage to Jerusalem.[2]

There are two incidents which occurred almost within two years of the death of St. Bernard, and with regard to which he played some part. It may be well to refer to them here. Amongst the vassals of Louis le Jeune were two whose family connections and personal characters combined to place them in a position of considerable independence. These were Geoffrey Plantagenet, Count of Anjou, and his son the Duke of Normandy who subsequently succeeded to the throne of England as Henry II. Some difficulty arose between Geoffrey and one of his vassals, Gerald of Montreuil-Bellay, a fief about fifteen miles South of Saumur which has the interest of having been in the XVth century held by the Harcourts. The petty warfare ensuing resulted in the capture of Gerald and in the imprisonment of himself, his wife and

[1] Joann. Sares. *Hist. Pontifical.*, VI. 13 sqq., *ed.* Poole ; cf. p. 209 *supra*.

[2] Radulfi de Diceto, *Imag. Hist., R.H.G.F.* XIII. 183 ; cf. *op. cit.*, XII. 116.

children. Louis thereupon made preparation to intervene in favour of Gerald by force of arms ; and the encounter between the Count of Anjou and his son Henry on the one hand and their supreme overlord on the other was only delayed by a sudden illness which prevented the king from taking the field. Happily Louis rose from his sick-bed somewhat mollified, and consented to negotiate with Geoffrey.[1] The Fourth Book of the *Vita Prima* records the circumstances in a passage which the biographer has erased in his Recension B, possibly because he was doubtful whether Geoffrey's death within fifteen days of a threatening prophecy which fell from St. Bernard's lips was an authentic statement of fact. Geoffrey did die suddenly on 7th September, 1151,[2] and there is no reason for doubting the record of the *Vita Prima* that St. Bernard, together with various bishops and feudal potentates, was present at the negotiations, comforted Gerard in his distress and rebuked the Count of Anjou for his ruthless severity.[3] There is nothing in the account given by Robert of Torigny, Abbot of Mont-St. Michel, which would seem to be inconsistent with this. In any case Geoffrey agreed to grant liberty to Gerald and to his family on condition that the stronghold of Montreuil-Bellay was not re-fortified. Moreover the Duke of Normandy yielded a point which had probably accounted for much in the quarrel ; he did, what to the sore irritation of Louis he had not yet done, namely, fealty for his duchy.

We now come to the second of the two incidents. The negotiations above-mentioned took place at Paris shortly after the king's recovery from illness and probably in August, 1151. Whether the intrigue between Henry Plantagenet and Eleanor of Aquitaine, Queen of France, then and there matured or only began, it may be difficult to say ; but their presence was mutually perilous. Robert of Torigny refers to their union as " either sudden or premeditated " ;[4] a statement which leaves us in doubt as to what preceded it. What hand had St. Bernard in the divorce which followed the infidelity of Queen Eleanor ? We have already referred to the fact that some eight years earlier, in 1143, he had in a letter to Stephen, Cardinal Bishop of Palestrina,[5] recognized in terms of some asperity the bar of consanguinity existing between Louis and Eleanor.[6] That the council held in 1152 at Beaugency on the Loire about sixteen miles S.W. of Orleans, which pronounced the queen's divorce, was unaware of St. Bernard's opinion thus expressed is improbable. Robert of Torigny states that " they were divorced by the authority

[1] Robert. de Torign. *Chron.*, ed. Howlett, *R.S.* 159 sqq.

[2] Robert. de Torign. *Chron.*, ed. cit., 163.

[3] *Vita Prima*, IV. iii. 13.

[4] Robert. de Torign. *Chron.*, ed. cit., 165.

[5] *Ep.* 224.

[6] P. 209 *supra*.

of the Church (*Christianitatis*) at Beaugency on oath taken"—
presumably by themselves—"before the archbishops and
bishops that they were consanguineous." [1] Whether St.
Bernard brought any pressure to bear upon Louis is another
question. It has been maintained that he did; [2] but it is
disputed by Vacandard on the ground that it is suggested
by no strictly contemporary authority, its only support being
found in a statement cited by Brial from a MS. of the third
quarter of the XIIth century, the *provenance* of which is the
Abbey of Anchin in Flanders [3]—a house of Black Monks which
at the time held St. Bernard in high veneration ; a fact which
might either vouch for the accuracy of the MS., or on the
other hand account for its exaggeration of the part played
by the Abbot of Clairvaux in the divorce. Balancing the
probabilities there would seem to be nothing unreasonable
in thinking that, given the impediment of consanguinity,
St. Bernard might well have regarded the infidelity of Eleanor
as a call to Louis to dissolve the union which existed between
them, and have pointed this out to the king. After all the
authority in question does no more than record concisely that
" by the advice of the lord Bernard, Abbot of Clairvaux, he
put away his wife." And, indeed, seeing that she took with
her the smiling lands and the fair cities of Aquitaine, some
persuasion may have been necessary.

[1] Robert. de Torign. *Chron.*, ed. cit., 164.
[2] Luchaire, *Instit. monarch. de la France*, II. 281, *note* 2.

[3] *R.H.G.F.* XIV. 21 ; cf. *op. cit.*, XII. 231, *note* (*b*).

CHAPTER X

MONASTIC IDEALS

It was about the year 1122 and not long after the foundation of Foigny, an event which had brought him into close relation with Bartholomew de Vir, Bishop of Laon, and with St. Norbert, first Abbot of Prémontré, that St. Bernard's reputation as a monastic reformer began to assume considerable proportions. Foigny was an outpost of the Cistercian movement beyond the borders of Champagne, the thin end of that great wedge of penetration to the North-East which he was destined to drive home so hard before he died. There can be no doubt but that this reputation was in large measure due to St. Bernard's noticeable success as a wonder-worker. We are not concerned with the nature of the phenomena which the historians of his life class as miraculous. It is sufficient for our purpose to accept them as phenomena. The first recorded case of the kind is that of the cure of St. Bernard's own kinsman, Josbert de la Ferté, Viscount of Dijon. We are not told that the patient's life was indefinitely prolonged, but rather that he was restored to a condition in which it was reasonably possible for him to make his peace with God before he died, an end much to be desired, for Josbert had been a robber of the Church and of the poor. La-Ferté was quite near Clairvaux but, alas, St. Bernard was absent at the time when Josbert was smitten down by a paralytic stroke and entirely deprived of the power of speech. It being plain that he was dying his son, Josbert the Younger, and his friends at once sent a messenger to fetch the Abbot of Clairvaux. On his arrival three days later he found the sick man in the state described. Although deeply moved by the distress of the patient and of his family, St. Bernard nevertheless with almost brutal frankness goes straight to the point. "You know," he says, "as well as I do how this man has laid a heavy hand upon the Church, how he has oppressed the poor, how he has offended God! Well; let his heirs undertake to repair his injustice and he will recover his speech, confess

219

himself and receive the sacraments." Readily is the undertaking given; but the Clairvaux monks at the bedside, Guy and Gaudry, St. Bernard's brother and uncle, are terrified by the rashness of the abbot's pledge. " Trouble not yourselves," he replies to their objections, " God can easily do what you so difficultly believe," and passes to the church to say his Mass. Scarcely has he finished when the news reaches him that Josbert has recovered his speech and is asking to see him. The sick man ratifies the undertaking of his son, penitently confesses himself, receives the sacraments, gives generous alms, arranges his temporal affairs and dies like a good Christian two or three days afterwards, retaining his speech to the last.[1] As regards the date of this event we may assume that it was earlier than the consecration of the church of Foigny in 1124, recorded by William of St. Thierry a little later in the *Vita Prima*, when St. Bernard excommunicated over-night innumerable invading flies with such success that they were all dead in the morning; and " the cursing of the flies of Foigny " became a common saying in the neighbourhood.[2]

[1] Gaufr. *Fragm.*, Codex Aureaevall.,25 sqq.; *Vita Prima*, I. ix. 43; *Vita Secunda*, xi. 36.

[2] *Vita Prima*, I. xi. 52.

Not long afterwards with two Clairvaux monks, the same Guy above-mentioned and Godfrey de la Roche, St. Bernard was passing through Château-Landon, a place about halfway between Nemours and Montargis where was the ancient Abbey of St. Séverin. A youth suffering from a fistula in his foot exposed his wound and begged to be healed. St. Bernard signed the wound with the cross, and on their return after a few days it was found to be in a perfectly healthy condition. But Guy refused to accept the *post hoc ergo propter hoc*, and with the freedom of a near relative rebuked the abbot for his presumption.[3] It is noticeable that both these recorded phenomena occurred in a comparatively sceptical atmosphere created by members of St. Bernard's own family.

[3] *Vita Prima*, I. ix. 45.

His uncle Gaudry, however, at about the same time fell grievously ill, and in his anguish sang a different song from that which had been heard from him at the bedside of Josbert de la Ferté. He begged St. Bernard to do for him what he had done for others. The Abbot of Clairvaux, always apt to indulge in harmless pleasantry, rallied him upon his inconsistency; but in the end laid his hands upon him with prayer and the fever left him.[4]

[4] *Vita Prima*, I. x. 46.

Yet the reputation of a wonder-worker was not acceptable to St. Bernard. It was growing and, as he keenly felt, growing painfully to himself. At last he protests. To Peter, Cardinal Deacon and *legatus a latere* of the Apostolic See, he writes about

the year 1127 : " I am positively too much ashamed to take
any pleasure, when I find that what is reverenced or loved in
me is not what I really am, but merely what I am supposed
to be.   For in fact I am not loved at all when I am loved in
this fashion, but something in me—I know not what—which is
not myself is loved in place of me.   And yet, to speak the
truth, I do know what it is ; it is absolutely nothing at all.
Without doubt what is supposed to exist and does not exist
is just that—nothing at all.   Moreover, when what does
not exist but is merely supposed to exist is loved it is not real
love.   The wonder of it, nay, the pity of it is that men should
be able to love like that." [1]   Thus in his own characteris- [1] *Ep.* 18.
tically trenchant way he would make such admirers look
foolish, sentimental, even insincere.   On another occasion,
in a sermon preached on St. Martin's Day, we find him remarking with some contempt that while the divine word
has beatitudes for the poor in spirit, the meek, the mourners
and the like, it has none for the wonder-workers.[2]   Naturally [2] *Serm. in Fest.*
enough, in spite of himself, the vehemence of his disavowal *S. Mart. Episc.,*
did but increase his reputation.   Revealing the depth of his 16.
humility, it served to strengthen the conviction established
by his miracles that he was a " man of God " like one of the
prophets of the Old Covenant ; indeed the title is not in-
frequently given to him by his biographers.

Amongst those who fell under the influence of his reforming
zeal were two men, one already playing a great part and destined to play a greater in the France of his day and generation,
the other if less famous yet honoured in a very high degree
by a friendship which was perhaps quite like no other that
St. Bernard shared.   Let us take the lesser first.

William of St. Thierry, born of noble stock at Liège, was
educated at Rheims, where he was professed a monk in the
Abbey of St. Nicasius.   In 1120 he became Abbot of St.
Thierry near Rheims.[3]   The fact that at his instigation, Black [3] Horst. et Mabil-
Monk of a Cluniac abbey though he was, St. Bernard in 1125 lon. *Not. Fus. in*
wrote the *Apology* with its severe castigation of monastic *S. Bern. Ep.* 85.
abuses is sufficient evidence that in the matter of reform they
were both of one heart and of one mind.[4]   Such was his in- [4] Mabillon,
timacy with St. Bernard that, as we know, he was invited by *Admon. in S.*
the monks of Clairvaux to write the *Life* of their abbot,[5] *Bern. Apol.,* III.
and that moved by him St. Bernard wrote no less than two [5] *Vita Prima,* I.
important treatises, that *Concerning Grace and Free Will* *Praefat.*
shortly before 1128 [6] and that *Concerning the Errors of Abélard* [6] *De Grat. et Lib.*
in 1140.[7]   Nor must we forget that it is probably to William *Arb., Praefat.*
that we owe in large measure the incentive which later led [7] Guill. Ab. *Ep.*
                                                               inter S. Bern.
                                                               Ep. 326.

1 *Vita Prima,* I. xii. 59.

to the composition of the *Sermons on the Song of Songs.*[1] Perhaps the Abbot of St. Thierry's zeal was not always according to knowledge—sometimes the disciple fails rightly to interpret the teaching of the master—for about the year 1130 he appears to have fallen victim to what in these days we should call an inferiority-complex. He had shown symptoms of this when some few years earlier, himself in ill-health, he

2 *Vita Prima,* *loc. cit.*

had visited St. Bernard in his sickness.[2] The idea seems to have taken possession of him that he ought to strip himself of his abbatial dignity and enter Clairvaux as a simple monk. Hitherto as the abbot of a house of Black Monks he had promoted reform by the exercise of authority ; surely he could better promote it by placing himself under the authority of another ! And under whose authority if not that of the great Cistercian ? But St. Bernard would not hear of this. " My advice to you," he writes, " is to hold fast the position which you now occupy ; remain where you are and study to be of profit to those whom you rule ; do not run away from the duty of a ruler when you are able to be of profit by fulfilling it. Woe to you indeed if you rule and do not profit your subjects ! But more grievous woe to you if, because you are afraid to

3 *Ep.* 86.

rule, you run away from the duty of profiting them." [3] William however failed to respond to this treatment ; nor would St. Bernard yield. About five years later we find the

4 *Gall. Christ.,* IX. 187.

Abbot of St. Thierry a Cistercian monk at Signy,[4] an abbey in the diocese of Rheims and in the district of the Ardennes, founded in 1134 ; there he wrote the first book of the *Vita Prima* and gave himself to that close study of theology which enabled him to play his part in the controversy with Abélard ;

5 Mabillon. *Ad-mon. in Libr. de Vita et Gest. S. Bern.,* I. sq. ; Janauschek, *Orig. Cisterc.,* I. 34.

there too he died about the year 1148.[5] He was an interesting personality, about whom we should like to know more. That he was very intimate with St. Bernard and sought earnestly to forward his projects of monastic reform is certain ; but it is equally certain that at one crucial moment—crucial because hitherto William had been a reformer inside the fellowship of Black Monks and not outside it as a Cistercian—he declined to follow the course which St. Bernard indicated to him as imperative. We turn to the story of another Benedictine abbot who, it can scarcely be doubted, was led by the influence of St. Bernard to set in order his own house, and that one of the greatest abbeys of France.

Born about the year 1081 the origin of Suger is shrouded in obscurity. At the age of twelve he was placed at school in the Royal Abbey of St. Denis, but there is no reliable record of his parentage. His father is supposed to have been a certain Elinard and one of his brothers to have been Alvisus Bishop of Arras.[1] Considering the fact that the names Sigurius, or Sigerius, and Alvisus were in the XIIth century both common in Southern Flanders it is not improbable that he was of Flemish extraction.[2] If the surmise as to his relation to Alvisus who became Bishop of Arras in 1131 is correct, we recognize at once an already existing link with St. Bernard. This Alvisus had been successively a monk of St. Bertin at St. Omer, Prior of St. Vedast of Arras and Abbot of Anchin. The Flemish monasteries welcomed cordially the Cistercian reform and Alvisus was a devoted admirer of St. Bernard.[3] When he became Bishop of Arras he established an assiduous commerce between the religious houses of his diocese and the Abbeys of Cîteaux and Clairvaux, in spite of the fact that the Abbey of Anchin over which he had ruled was a Cluniac house. There are extant two letters addressed to him by St. Bernard.[4]

At St. Denis Suger had as a fellow-pupil the heir to the throne, the son of Philip I afterwards known as Louis le Gros. He became Abbot of St. Denis in 1122 and simultaneously the chief minister of Louis le Gros.[5] His capacity for statesmanship had already revealed itself, and in such a way as to be not particularly pleasing to the king. His appointment to high office in the state is therefore the more remarkable. In 1119 he had persuaded Calixtus II to hold a council at Rheims,[6] and succeeded in establishing the distinction between investiture with the cross and the ring as spiritual and that with the sceptre as temporal, consistently with which distinction the former was the office of the Pope and the latter that of the king. Considering what " the battle of investitures " meant in those days this was no small achievement.[7] But the king smarted under the defeat ; and in the same year he began to deprive the clergy of their benefices in order to confer them upon men who had fought for him in the English war which followed the dispute about the succession to the Duchy of Normandy. Suger secretly sought the aid of St. Bernard, and the Abbot of Clairvaux intervened on behalf of the clergy with some success.[8] This was perhaps the first occasion of co-operation between the two men. Thenceforth in monastic reform, in affairs of state and in ecclesiastical policy it was close and frequent, and only came to an end when in 1151 Suger died, some two years before St. Bernard.

So far as monastic reform was concerned no religious house stood in greater need of it than St. Denis. Abélard

[1] Suger. *Ep.* 22, *P.L.* CLXXXVI. ; Combes, *l'Abbé Suger*, 6 sqq. ; *Hist. Litt. de la France*, XII. 361.

[2] *Gall. Christ.*, VII. 368.

[3] Dijon MS. 130; *Chron. Acquicinct.*, *P.L.* CLX. 314.

[4] *Epp.* 65 and 395. and Horst. et Mabillon. *Not. Fus. ad loc.*

[5] Suger. *Vita Lud. Grossi*, *P.L.* CLXXXVI. 1315 sqq.

[6] Suger. *Vita Lud. Grossi*, *P.L.* CLXXXVI. 1312 ; Mabill. *Acta SS. Bened.* II., *Praef.*, *Saec.* iii. 41.

[7] Combes, *L'Abbé Suger*, 55 sqq. ; Suger. *Epp.* 19 and 20, *P.L.* CLXXXVI.

[8] Combes op. cit. 80 sq.

[1] Abael. *Hist. Calam.*, 9 sq. ; Cousin, *Opp.*, I. 19 sqq. ; cf. p. 295 *infra*.

had stigmatized the laxity prevailing there under Abbot Adam, Suger's predecessor.[1] As Vacandard has suggested, it is not impossible that the new Abbot of St. Denis recognized his own portrait in the *Apologia* and was ashamed. In any case St. Bernard's letter, addressed to him in 1127 congratulating him upon the success of the measures which he had taken to establish a more becoming simplicity in his own life and in that of his subjects, gives ground for the belief that Suger had undergone nothing less than a personal conversion. " Who is it," St. Bernard asks, " that has set before you such perfection ? As for me, I confess that although I was longing for so great results I was not expecting them. Who indeed would have believed that, if I may say so, at a sudden bound you would have reached such heights of virtue, such sublimity of merit ? " So edifying are the internal conditions of the great abbey as compared with what they have been that he exclaims : " I might call myself blessed to have lived, not to see such things—for I am far away—but even to hear of them. But you, brethren "—addressing, as it were, the entire community—" are far more blessed, for to you it has been given

[2] *Ep.* 78.

actually to take part in them."[2] It is a long letter, sufficiently long to set forth in some detail the contrast between the old abuses and the new reforms, between a life in which doubtless Cæsar had received his due—but at the price of defrauding God, and a life of sacred song in which martyrs take pleasure and angels join their voices.

A year or two later Suger turned his attention to the Abbey of Argenteuil, some seven miles from Paris, on the road to Mantes, a Carlovingian house of the IXth century where Héloïse was professed.[3] The Abbey of St. Denis appears

[3] Suger. *De Rebus in Admin. sua Gestis*, III., *P.L.* CLXXXVI.

to have had some proprietary rights in the place which made it easier for Suger to disperse the lax nuns—Héloïse going to Le-Paraclet near Nogent-sur-Seine—and to introduce monks from his own abbey. A letter to Suger, written by St. Bernard about the year 1147 during the former's regency, refers to the extent of his responsibilities as that of one " to whom is known to be entrusted the care of all the churches," and expresses the conviction that the writer can count upon him

[4] *Ep.* 369.

to do some service to the Abbey of St. Victor.[4]

Thus plainly the zeal of Suger was not exhausted by the reform of his own Abbey of St. Denis. On the Mont-Ste. Geneviève or ancient Mons Locutitius a little way outside the walls South of Paris, the site of the modern Pantheon, stood a house of canons secular dedicated to the Blessed Apostles Peter and Paul, usually, however, called the Abbey

of Ste. Geneviève or the Abbey of the Mount.[1] Its state is
described by Stephen, Bishop of Tournai—formerly its abbot
—as at the time one of "threatening ruin, exposed as it
was to many risks owing to the hideous condition not of its
walls but of its morals." It was the year 1147; Louis le
Jeune was absent on the Second Crusade and Suger was Vice-
Gerent of the Kingdom, with full powers of government.[2]
Acting with the approval of the Cistercian Pope, Eugenius
III, the Abbot of St. Denis introduced into the house the Rule
of St. Augustine. St. Bernard strengthened his hand by two
letters of congratulation, one already cited,[3] but warning him
in the second that the Abbot of Ste. Geneviève, a certain Odo,
was a somewhat pusillanimous person whose courage would
need to be sustained.[4]

Doubtless other religious houses besides the famous Abbeys
of Cluny, St. Thierry-lès-Reims and St. Denis experienced
searchings of heart as the great diatribe of the *Apologia* became more widely known. In several cases St. Bernard
suffered odium on the ground that he had acted with too high
a hand. Amongst these we may instance that of St. Sepulchre,
outside the walls of Cambrai. In 1129, defending himself
against charges of unwarrantable interference, he writes to
Cardinal Haimeric, Chancellor of the Apostolic See, his friend
at Rome : "What is it in me that has displeased you ? Is it
that at Cambrai that open enemy of his own monastery,
Fulbert (the expelled abbot), has been forced to give place
to Parvin (the newly elected abbot), who on the testimony of
all men is a faithful servant and a prudent man ? Or is it
indeed that at Laon [5] a sanctuary of God which was a brothel
of Venus has been restored to its proper use ? For which of
these things do you, I will not say, throw stones at me, but
tear me to pieces ? " In this letter St. Bernard addresses
himself to the *Curia* in the person of Haimeric, as is made
plain not only by the terms " your brethren "—*fratres* being
a common title for the College of Cardinals—but by the concluding words : " I do not think that, even if I keep myself in
the background and say nothing in my defence, the complaints
of these monasteries against me will cease so long as in my
absence the Roman *Curia* continues to prejudge the case at its
mere discretion." Evidently the charges had been formulated
and presented in a way which roused the Pauline independence
characteristic of St. Bernard.[6]

Similarly the year before, in connection with reforms at
the Abbey of Pouthières in the diocese of Langres, he appears
to have fallen under reproach for invoking the secular arm in

---

[1] S. Bern. *Epp.*
369 and 370,
and Horst. et
Mabillon. *Not.*
Fus. ad loc.

[2] *Vita Suger.*
III. 1, *P.L.*
CLXX.

[3] *Ep.* 369.

[4] *Ep.* 370.

[5] Pp. 196 sq.
supra.

[6] *Ep.* 48, and
Horst. et Mabil-
lon. *Not. Fus.*
ad loc.

the person of the Count of Nevers, the successor of the founder. Writing to Abbot Gerard he categorically denies the charge of having made any accusation against him to the count. "When I sent a letter to this prince on behalf of your monastery I considered that in so doing I was acting in your interest, not against it. In fact I had heard that it was with your approval, even on your suggestion, that he proposed to come and visit you in order to discover the truth of the report that grave disorders existed in your house, and at whose door they lay, so that what was found to be wrong might by his zeal and care be corrected on the spot." [1] During the five years or more following the writing of the *Apologia* St. Bernard seems to have been constantly active in translating its precepts into practice. The breadth of his view is shown by the fact that he did not everywhere seek to introduce his own Cistercians into monasteries of Black Monks or of canons regular, but rather to incite the existing communities to be faithful to their own principles, and only where this failed to aggregate them to the Order of Cîteaux. In this sense he was no party-man. Thus was it in 1129 at St. Nicolas-aux-Bois in the diocese of Laon, an abbey of which at the time William of St. Thierry's brother Simon was abbot. The point at issue in this case is interesting. There was then only one religious order in which it was strictly regular for monks to take charge of parishes with the cure of the souls of secular persons, and that, as we shall see, was the Premonstratensian. Simon had in the legitimate exercise of his authority handed over to the Bishop of Arras certain parishes, *altaria* as they were termed, hitherto served by his monks, with the result that he was made to suffer from his own subjects what St. Bernard does not hesitate to describe as "persecution for righteousness's sake." The cause seems to have been taken to Rome, and Innocent II to have appointed Samson, Archbishop of Rheims, and Joslen, Bishop of Soissons, as arbiters. The persecution was sufficiently severe to compel Abbot Simon to leave his abbey ; but in the end his monks brought him back, preferring rather to lose their parishes than to lose their abbot. So we learn from a letter addressed to the Pope by the Archbishop of Rheims.[2] St. Bernard's letter addressed on the occasion to the abbot himself is remarkable for its conciliatory tone. He would have his correspondent not forget that "while it is the way of the ungodly to resist strongly the counsels of the godly, yet it is not always contrary to godliness to deny the few godly their desires, however just and holy they may be, when there are many who oppose them " ; and

[1] *Ep.* 81. Cf. Migne, *P.L. Not. ad loc.*

[2] Horst. et Mabillon. *Not. Fus. in Ep.* 83.

he instances the case of Samuel who against his own better
judgement anointed Saul. Thus the abbot would be wise
not to compel his weaker subjects against their will to a stricter
life, for they had been professed as Cluniacs—but rather to
use gentle persuasion ; and, on the other hand, to urge the more
zealous to show charitable condescension towards the weaker,
so far as without sin it was possible, and to maintain their
own stricter way of life, provided no scandal was given, or
in the last resort to betake themselves to another monastery
in which they would find brethren living more strictly.[1] [1] *Ep.* 83.
This advice coming from St. Bernard may seem a little surprising, but it is not really inconsistent with his teaching in
the treatise *Concerning Precept and Dispensation* ; [2] moreover [2] *De Praecepto et*
the conditions were doubtless recognized to be unusual. *Dispens.,* XVI.
46 sqq.

A courageous and successful attempt was made about the
year 1130 to introduce amongst the monasteries of Black
Monks in the Province of Rheims the Cistercian custom of
holding annual general chapters. The first of these was held
at Soissons in the Abbey of St. Médard, a Cluniac house
ruled by Geoffrey, afterwards Bishop of Châlons-sur-Marne.
Abbot Geoffrey was a man held in high esteem by Peter the
Venerable who wrote of him as having been " the first to
disseminate, promote and advance the divine Order of Cluny
throughout the whole of France," and as having driven the
devil from his lair in many a monastic dormitory.[3] Horst [3] *Petr. Ven.*
and Mabillon regard this chapter as definitely the outcome of *Epp. Lib.,* II.
the *Apology* and as one of the first, if not the first, of its kind xliii, *P.L.*
ever held by the Black Monks.[4] Certainly the occasion CLXXXIX.
was critical ; and St. Bernard did not fail to rise to it. He 265.
opens his formal letter to the assembled abbots with the words : [4] *Horst. et*
" I am annoyed that I am prevented by my occupations *Mabillon. Not.*
from being personally present with you ; however neither *Fus. in Ep.* 91.
space nor the cares of business can prevent me from being
present with you in spirit, nor indeed from praying for you and
from rejoicing with you and refreshing my spirit with you."
Warning them to pay no attention to men who suggest that
there is such a thing as over-much righteousness, or that all
is well so long as they are no worse than their fathers were,
men who call good evil and evil good, he falls into the singular
as though addressing each abbot by himself. " Thou must
either ascend or descend ; if thou art merely standing still
where thou now art, thou art falling." Then going straight
to the point he urges them boldly to disregard the " traditions
of men," meaning thereby those relaxations of the Rule of
St. Benedict which had wrought havoc in the Order.[5] This [5] *Ep.* 91.

general chapter had the effect of setting a standard, in so far as that Innocent II prescribed that henceforth general chapters of Black Monks should be held annually.[1]

[1] Horst. et Mabillon., *loc. cit.*

THE CARTHUSIANS

It must not be forgotten that besides the Benedictines, the Cistercians and the canons regular there were other orders which in the XIIth century played their part in the religious life, notably the Carthusians. What was St. Bernard's relation to the monastery of the Greater Charterhouse, founded in 1084 by St. Bruno, a German of Cologne, amidst the rocky fastnesses of Dauphiné, the locality so graphically described by Balzac in *Le médecin de campagne*? In St. Bernard's day the house was ruled by Guy, the fifth prior and the first compiler of the Statutes of the Order. A feature of the Carthusian Rule was its mixed character; the monks of the Order lived a life partly cœnobitic and partly eremitic. Its severity was scarcely less than that of the Cistercians, whether in food, sleep, clothing or manual labour. In all this there was a sympathetic point of contact with St. Bernard, and when about the year 1125 Prior Guy and his brethren invited him to write to them upon the subject of perfect love he was deeply moved. His reply was a letter interesting from the fact that the greater part of it was afterwards embodied in his treatise *Of Loving God*.[2] A little later, probably in the same year, he writes again, lamenting that although he had been not far from their neighbourhood he had not visited them, using language sufficiently familiar in his correspondence: " My business made me angry, for it meant not that I neglected you, but simply that I could not go and see you." [3] How often does he bewail his immersion in affairs! However, in due course they met face to face. Prior Guy died in 1137, but at some time before that date St. Bernard undertook a journey to Dauphiné in order to visit Hugh, Bishop of Grenoble, and the Carthusians. It was upon this occasion that, travelling for a whole day along the shore of the Lake of Geneva, he was, as it would seem, so rapt in contemplation as to have no recollection afterwards of having seen any lake at all.[4] His meeting with Bishop Hugh recalled to his biographer that between the Queen of Sheba and Solomon, except that in this case each, as he " fell upon his knees and in such posture exchanged the kiss of peace, found in the other far more than fame had told." [5] At the Greater Charterhouse the impression made upon Guy and his monks was that what they knew of

[2] *Ep.* 11.

[3] *Ep.* 12.

[4] *Vita Prima,* III. ii. 4 ; *Vita Secunda,* xvi. 45.

[5] *Vita Prima,* III. ii. 3.

St. Bernard from his letters was confirmed by his presence in the flesh. One thing alone for a moment disturbed them, the magnificence of his mount—borrowed from an uncle, a Cluniac monk domiciled in a priory near Clairvaux; but the explanation given only served as further evidence of his holy indifference to all earthly things as such. He had not noticed the caparison.[1] He would with equal satisfaction have ridden a sutler's mule! Probably no religious atmosphere outside his own Order of Cîteaux so commended itself to St. Bernard as that which prevailed amongst the Carthusians, unless it were the atmosphere of Prémontré under the rule of St. Norbert as its abbot ; for it was at the pressing solicitation of a certain Bernard, monk of the Chartreuse-des-Portes-en-Bugey near Ambérieu, and after submitting to him in some shape the earlier portion of his work, that in 1135 he was persuaded to write his *Sermons on the Song of Songs*.[2] Can we doubt but that by means of these wonderful studies, classical in the literature of their subject, the mystical life found responsive cultivation in the houses of the Carthusian Order ?

[1] *Op. cit.*, III. ii. 4; *Vita Secunda*, xvi. 45.

[2] *Epp.* 153 and 154 ; cf. Williams, *Mysticism of St. Bernard of Clairvaux*, 24 sq.

THE PREMONSTRATENSIANS

There are two religious orders both dating from the third decade of the XIIth century with the foundation of which St. Bernard was very closely concerned, namely, the Premonstratensians or Norbertines—who were in England commonly called the White Canons—and the Templars. It is interesting to remember that, when about the year 1120 Bartholomew de Vir, Bishop of Laon, invited St. Bernard to settle a Cistercian colony from Clairvaux in his diocese, the site which he originally offered was land upon which St. Norbert, the founder of the Premonstratensians, was actually establishing his mother-house of Prémontré, but which St. Bernard formally refused, an act of generosity which he was later compelled in self-defence to recall to the memory of Hugh, the second Abbot of Prémontré.[3] Ultimately the colony was settled at Foigny near Vervins in the Thiérache on 11th July, 1121, as the third daughter of Clairvaux.[4] The community of religious sentiment between St. Bernard and St. Norbert is sufficiently evidenced by the fact that it was to these two men that Bartholomew de Vir looked to promote as pioneers his projects of monastic reform.

[3] *Ep.* 253.

[4] Pp. 30 sq *supra*.

St. Norbert was born at Xanten, not far from Cleves in the diocese of Cologne, in 1080. He was therefore St. Bernard's senior by ten years. Of noble parentage, his early years were pleasantly spent in the courts of princes, and he was an acceptable person to great men such as the Emperor Henry V. This however was not regarded as an obstacle to his being meanwhile a canon of the College of St. Victor at Xanten. Later, by a reaction to which nothing in the case of St. Bernard corresponded, he sought the priesthood and was in 1115 ordained deacon and priest on the same day. In the following year, resigning all his dignities and benefices and giving to the poor all his possessions except ten marks and a she-mule, he set out with two lay companions on a long journey through Gaul in search of recruits for his campaign. At St. Gilles near Arles he found Gelasius II, recently exiled from Rome, making his way painfully to his death-bed at Cluny. From him he obtained a faculty to preach, confirmed in 1119 at Rheims by his successor Calixtus II. At least three adherents he lost by death, but gained a very staunch one in Hugh, subsequently second Abbot of Prémontré. Calixtus II did more for him than confirm his faculty; he commended him to Bartholomew de Vir, the very Bishop of Laon who was so strong a supporter of St. Bernard.[1]

There was in a suburb of Laon a house of canons secular dedicated to St. Martin which had fallen into disorder both spiritual and material. The first use which Bartholomew de Vir made of St. Norbert was to place him at the head of this house; but, alas, so wayward and hard-hearted were its members that the saint could do nothing to amend them, and was in despair preparing to turn to some more hopeful sphere of work. The Bishop of Laon, most unwilling to lose him, thereupon bought from the Abbey of St. Vincent-de-Laon a piece of land called *Praemonstratum*, about three leagues from the city and in the Forest of Coucy or the *Silva Vedogia* (de Voas).[2] It was, like the Forest of Cîteaux, a wild, damp and not very accessible spot, lying in a valley below the Massif-de-St. Gobain, famous in the Great War. Here on Christmas Day, 1121, forty or so religious were professed canons regular.[3] The name Prémontré has been taken to mean *praemonstratum*, or even *pratum monstratum*, in the sense of the piece of land indicated by divine revelation; but the place already bore the name when the abbey was founded, and good authorities such as *Gallia Christiana* give no credit to the story.[4] Three years later, in 1124, St. Martin-de-Laon was handed over to Prémontré by the Bishop of Laon, amongst the signatories to the deed of gift being St. Bernard and Raynald, first Abbot of Foigny, who had been a monk of Clairvaux and was honoured by the confidence and affection of St. Bernard in a high degree.[5]

[1] *Vita S. Norb.*, I. 3, II. 9, IV. 23, VII. 37, *P.L.* CLXX. 1257 sqq.; Aub. Mir. *Ord. Praemonstr. Chron.*, 14 sqq.

[2] *Gall. Christ.*, IX. 642 sq.; Beaunier, *Recueil des Abbayes de France*, II. 603.

[3] *Vita S. Norb.*, VII. 38 sq., *P.L. loc. cit.*; Gasquet, *The English Premonstr., Transactions, R.H.S. New Series*, XVII. 1 sq.

[4] *Gall. Christ.*, *loc. cit.*

[5] *Gall. Christ.*, IX., 662, X. 191 sq.; cf. pp. 28, 31 *supra.*

There can be little doubt of St. Bernard's influence upon early Premonstratensian development. Aubertus Miraeus writes : " Not only was he responsible for the foundation of very many monasteries of his own Order but, what is more remarkable, he was an outstanding figure in the promotion and in the increase of the Premonstratensian Order. We may instance the illustrious Abbey of Tongerloo in Brabant which is only too proud to proclaim that it owes its origin and its liberty in large measure to him. Listen to the diploma of Burchard, Bishop of Cambrai : " and he proceeds to quote the diploma in which the names of the two petitioners for the " liberty granted " to Tongerloo, as a house founded for " brethren of the Premonstratensian Order living under the Rule of Blessed Augustine," are Waltman, Abbot of Antwerp, and Bernard, Abbot of Clairvaux.[1]

But, apart from such explicit evidence as that of the two documents to which reference has been made, there is in the Premonstratensian customs some suggestion of Cistercian influence, influence which would naturally be explained by the part taken by St. Bernard in the foundation of the Order. Let us illustrate this point. Jacques de Vitry, writing in the XIIIth century, tells us that " the canons and lay brethren abstain entirely from flesh-meat except in case of illness. From the Feast of the Holy Cross until Easter, after the manner of the Cistercians, two dishes only are served in the refectory." The word here used is *pulmentum* and cannot mean a meal, for the Cistercians during the period in question ate only one meal daily. " They do not wear," he proceeds to say, " shirts but use sheepskin," that is to say, their inner garment was not of linen or of wool but of pelt ; " they sleep clothed in white tunics and shod with strong shoes. Their cloaks are of white undyed wool." As regards the employment of their time he tells us that " at fixed hours during certain seasons they go out to manual labour." So far they associated themselves with the Cistercian effort to restore the literal observance of the Rule of St. Benedict ; but it should be observed that they differed fundamentally from the Benedictines and indeed from all other religious orders of their day [2] by the fact that " in their own persons they undertook parochial duties and the cure of the souls of seculars." Not only, however, did they in the ways indicated support the Cistercian reform, but in their external appearance they must have looked very like Cistercians. Their choice of such a site as Prémontré recalls the Cistercian ideal of a *cœnobium in deserto ;* in fact the charter securing St. Martin-de-Laon to Prémontré refers

[1] Aub. Mir. *Chron. Cisterc. Ord.*, 90 sq.

[2] Coulton, *Five Centuries of Religion,* II. 148; cf. Cuthbert, *Dublin Review,* Oct., 1931, 287.

[1] Jacob. de Vitriac. *Hist. Occident.*, 322 sqq.

to St. Norbert as having " established the eremitic life under canonical profession," thus it would seem setting a comparatively new standard for canons regular.[1]

Again, the rapid early expansion of the Order would suggest a healthy rivalry with the *Monachi Grisei*, as the Cistercians came to be called in distinction from the Black Monks of other Benedictine houses. Aubertus Miraeus tells of three foundations in addition to that of Prémontré effected in 1121, of another in 1126 and of three more in 1128.[2] In England the first foundation effected was at Newhouse or Newsham near Brocklesby in Lincolnshire in 1143, and from it sprang Alnwick in Northumberland in 1147, St. Agatha at Easby near Richmond in Yorkshire in 1152, Welbeck in 1153, Barlings, six miles North-East of Lincoln, in 1154, and in the same year Sulby or Welford, six miles South-West of Market Harborough.[3] This growth is, we shall allow, remarkable ; and considering the expansion from Clairvaux in the same country—beginning with the foundation of Rievaulx in 1132 and ending with that of Margam in 1147— during the immediately preceding quarter of a century is it difficult to detect the Bernardine stimulus behind it all ? St. Bernard's attention was never more closely concentrated upon the promotion of reformed monasticism than it was during the period extending from 1147 to his death in 1153. In the year 1149 from Clairvaux itself alone five colonies were settled.[4]

[2] Aub. Mir. *Ord. Praemonstr. Chron.*, 229 sqq.

[3] Gaudens, *Life of S. Norbert,* 172 sq. ; Gasquet, *Collect. Anglo-Praemonstr.*, I. vii. sqq.; *Registr. Praemonstr.*, MS. Ashmole, 1519.

[4] Pp. 86 sqq. *supra.*

But perhaps the motive force of St. Bernard's support lay even deeper than we have suggested, namely, in his appreciation of the high value of St. Norbert's apostolate and of his spiritual fitness to fulfil it. Writing in 1131 to Bruno, recently elected to the see of Cologne, who had consulted him on the question of his acceptance of such a charge, after giving his own view St. Bernard concludes : " But you have one whom you can consult face to face, the lord Norbert, a man so much the more capable of revealing to you the divine secrets as he is well-known to be nearer to God than I am." [5] Again, writing in 1128 to Geoffrey, Bishop of Chartres, who had asked him whether there was any truth in the rumour that St. Norbert was contemplating a pilgrimage to Jerusalem, St. Bernard replies : " When a few days ago I drank deeply from that heavenly reed " (*fistula*, a word of sacred connotation as associated with the sacramental chalice) " his mouth I heard nothing of such a purpose." At the same time he does not hesitate to express his disagreement with St. Norbert's anticipation of the near advent of Antichrist ; a subject

[5] *Ep.* 8.

which they had discussed on the occasion, apparently with
the result that St. Bernard had persuaded the Abbot of
Prémontré to modify his view so far as to say that he expected
to see before he died a general persecution, terms reasonably
descriptive of the Papal Schism which began two years later
in 1130.[1] The letter of 1131 above quoted indicates some   [1] *Ep.* 56.
conviction on the part of St. Bernard that St. Norbert had
insight into " the divine secrets."

But no less appreciative was St. Bernard of the Order itself
than he was of its founder.   When in 1139 some difficulty
arose concerning the right of the Premonstratensians to occupy
the Abbey of St. Paul-de-Verdun he could commend them to
Innocent II as " canons of good fame and of good life." [2]   [2] *Ep.* 178.
Similarly he wrote to Queen Melisande of Jerusalem of those
of them on pilgrimage to the Holy City in 1142, that they were
in need of no other commendation than their own merits.
" They will be found to be, unless I am mistaken, men of
wisdom, fervent in spirit, patient in tribulation, powerful
in deed and in word. . . . Receive them as you would Christ,
for whose sake they are pilgrims " ; [3] and it was by his gift that   [3] *Ep.* 355.
the Premonstratensian Order came into possession, not only
of the site of St. Samuel at Jerusalem, but also of a thousand
gold crowns wherewith to build a house, both of these bounties
granted by King Baldwin to the Cistercians.[4]   [4] *Ep.* 253.

Here and there the Premonstratensians were establishing
themselves in religious houses which had deservedly fallen
into disrepute, as in 1140 at Beaulieu,[5] an Abbey of Augustinian   [5] *Ep.* 253.
Canons in the diocese of Troyes, and as a few years earlier, in
1136, at the Benedictine Abbey of St. Paul-de-Verdun.   In
both these cases the hand, the supporting arm, of St. Bernard
was at their service.   At St. Paul-de-Verdun it is doubtful
whether without his countenance they would not have been
routed for, as we have seen, it was St. Bernard who when the
security of their tenure was gravely questioned could give
powerful testimony at the Papal *Curia* to the excellence of
their work, in the end winning the day for them despite the
opposition of the Abbot of Cluny, no less a person than his own
respected friend Peter the Venerable.[6] The same generous   [6] Petr. Ven.
sympathy which had impelled him to yield to St. Norbert   *Epp. Lib.*, II. xi,
the site of Prémontré later led him to endow the Order with   *P.L.*
the site of Sept-Fontaines at Clermont in the diocese of   CLXXXIX. 200
Langres.[7]   sq.

The concurrent rapid expansion of Cistercians and Premon-   [7] *Ep.* 253. Cf.
stratensians throughout the North of France prompted the   *Gall. Christ.*, IV.
establishment in 1142 of a friendly pact recorded by Manriquez,   853.

according to which no abbey of either Order was to be founded within two leagues of any abbey of the other, nor any grange within one league.[1] The original MS. of this pact still exists in the Archives of the Haute-Marne at Chaumont.[2] About the year 1150 some misunderstanding unfortunately arose. St. Bernard had admitted as monks at Clairvaux two Premonstratensians by name Robert and Fromund. He was further accused of having by force prevented the building of a nunnery —on the Continent the Premonstratensians frequently established houses of canonesses—by the Abbey of Basse-Fontaine, a Premonstratensian house in the diocese of Troyes founded in 1143 by Walter II Count of Brienne.[3] And there were other grievances which it is unnecessary to take into account. Hugh, the Abbot of Prémontré, wrote somewhat bitterly. St. Bernard's reply is a valuable authority for the relations between the two Orders, and it is an able vindication of his own conduct, tempered by a touching appeal for unity. He justifies his handling of the matters in dispute by reference both to the Papal authority which had supported him and to the pact which he had strictly observed. But he has no notion of a rupture of their friendship. " I shall cleave unto you," he writes, " in spite of you ; I shall cleave unto you in spite of myself. Of old I bound myself to you by a strong chain, charity unfeigned, charity that *never faileth*. . . . My soul is sad that on any pretext whatever I should have offended you. It will still be sad until your forgiveness has refreshed it. If you delay I shall go and lie at your gate, knocking persistently, soliciting in season and out of season until I either deserve or extort your blessing. Half the winter has already passed, and I am still waiting deprived of my garment."[4] How charming is the concluding allusion ! He is waiting for their charity to cover his sins. It is needless to add that by this letter the bond between the two Orders was reforged never to be broken again during the life-time of St. Bernard.

THE TEMPLARS

The origin of Hugh de Payns, the founder of the Order of the Temple, the Poor Knights of Christ and of the Temple of Solomon, as they are described in their Rule, has been a matter for dispute. Some authorities have assigned to him, although born in or near Troyes in Champagne, a Neapolitan origin. Others have traced him to the Haute-Provence, the land *par excellence* of chivalry, where his family is said to have

[1] Manric. *Annal. Cisterc.*, I. 432 sq.
[2] *Fonds Chapelle aux Planches*, 7.

[3] Morel-Payen, *Troyes et l'Aube*, 256.

[4] *Ep.* 253.

Knights Templars

possessed the Seigneury of Argental together with various properties in the Lyonnais and in neighbouring districts. Others have thought to find his birthplace at a château in the Vivarais where the highlands of Auvergne decline below Montélimar to the valley of the Rhone.[1] Be this as it may, he was uniformly called " de Payns "; the first house of the Order was established at Payns or Payens—now pronounced *Pains*—a village about eight miles North of Troyes, and the council at which the Order received its formal sanction was held at Troyes.

We shall probably not be wrong in supposing that the Maison de Payns—the Templars spoke of their houses as *maisons* or *maisons du Temple*—received its domain from the family of the first Grand Master and that this family had the legal right to bestow it.[2] 1070 is the accepted date of the birth of Hugh de Payns; when he died in 1136[3] St. Bernard was forty-six years old and the Church in France was just emerging from the distresses of the Papal Schism.[4] Hugh is recorded to have had one son, Theobald de Payns, who became in 1139 Abbot of Ste. Colombe-de-Sens[5] and after St. Bernard's great appeal at Vézelay in 1146 joined the Second Crusade. This is all that is known of his family. As regards himself we find the name of a Hugo de Paenciis or de Péanz mentioned as that of a witness to various deeds executed in Champagne at the end of the XIth century,[6] but he is not to be recognized with any certainty until about the year 1119, when he associated himself with Geoffrey de St. Omer and a few other knights unnamed who, as well as himself, had perhaps taken part in the First Crusade—for the protection of the pilgrims by safeguarding the roads, by maintaining access to the wells and by generally policing the holy places and the approach to them from the coast. Baldwin II, King of the Latin Kingdom of Jerusalem, appreciating the value of their service, granted them a house on Mount Moriah near the Temple of Solomon; hence the title which they bore. At an early date they appear to have professed themselves religious, taking the three vows of poverty, chastity and obedience at the hands of the Patriarch of Jerusalem.[7] For nine years after 1119 little was heard of them, except for the mention of Hugh de Payns by the title Master of the Temple in a privilege granted by Baldwin II in 1125,[8] until Hugh with five companions made his way to France in 1128 in order doubtless to seek recruits, for the Order at the time numbered no more than nine members;[9] indeed the only recorded adherent—a notable one—during the period 1119-

[1] Pétel, *La commanderie de Payns et ses dépendances*, III. sqq.

[2] de Curzon, *La maison du Temple de Paris*, 14.

[3] *Obit. du Temple de Reims*, ap. de Barthélemy, *Doc. Inéd.*, IV. 321.

[4] Pétel, *op. cit.*, III.

[5] *Gall. Christ.*, XII. 149.

[6] Lalore, *Cart. de l'Abbaye de S. Loup*, 13, *Cart. de Montiéramey*, 24.

[7] William of Tyre, *Hist.*, XII. 7, *P.L.* CC; Jacob. de Vitriac. *Hist. Orient.*, 116; Maillard de Chambure, *Règle et statuts secrets des Templiers*, 41 sqq.; de Curzon, *La Règle du Temple*, 12 sqq.

[8] *Fontes Rer. Austriac.*, Ser. xii. 94.

[9] Pétel, *op. cit.*, I.; Maillard de Chambure, *op. cit.*, *Règle*, § 2.

1128 was Hugh, Count of Champagne, whom St. Bernard congratulated upon the occasion in an interesting letter which betrayed—generously enough, as we might expect—his regrets that the count had not found his vocation rather at Clairvaux than in the Maison du Temple.[1]

The emergence of the Order from its obscurity brought to the light of day a fact of social and political significance. A new idea destructive of feudalism had been realized, and realized under essentially monastic conditions, namely, the establishment of a regular armed force not mercenary, yet entirely independent of all external control so far as any religious order rightly could be. This would not of course have been generally recognized at the time, but it contained within itself infinite possibilities both of good and of evil as later history would show. Meanwhile it was plain to Hugh de Payns that recruitment would be forwarded by anything like ecclesiastical approbation, and we find him presenting himself with his five companions, Roland, Geoffrey, both of unspecified origin, a certain Geoffrey Bissot, Payen de Mont-didier and Archibald de St. Amant, at the Council of Troyes in 1128.[2] Considering the part played by St. Bernard, his presence at the council, his hand in the framing of the Rule and his subsequent writing of the treatise *In Praise of the New Warfare*, it is reasonable to conjecture that his guidance had been sought and followed by the Order in this matter of sup-plicating the sanction of the Church. Matthew, Bishop of Albano and Apostolic Legate of Honorius II, presided at the council, supported by amongst others Henry, Archbishop of Sens, a man, we know, much under St. Bernard's influence, Raynald, Archbishop of Rheims, the Abbots Stephen Harding of Cîteaux and Hugh of Pontigny—the latter being Hugh of Mâcon, a friend of St. Bernard, we shall remember, from early days—the Abbots of Troisfontaines and of Molesme and Theobald, Count of Champagne.[3] The Cistercians present were very much upon their own ground, and in sufficient force to make the vote of the remaining members—for the most part suffragans of the Provinces of Rheims and Sens—almost a negligible quantity. The six petitioners evidently gave some details of the Rule which they already observed. It was, in spite of Dugdale's opinion to the contrary, in type rather Benedictine than Augustinian ; such at any rate is what is now known as the Rule of the Temple, and it is un-likely that what was approved at the council differed materially from that which had stood the test of nine years' service.[4]

The Latin text of the Rule is given by Labbe and Cossart

[1] *Ep.* 31 ; d'Arbois de Jubainville, *Hist. des ducs et comtes de Cham-pagne,* II. 140 sq.

[2] *Règle des Tem-pliers,* § 2, Mail-lard de Cham-bure, *op. cit.*

[3] *R.H.G.F.* XIV. 231 sqq. ; Mail-lard de Cham-bure, *op. cit.*, *loc. cit.*

[4] Schoonebeck, *Hist. des Ordres Mil.,* I. 241.

in their *Concilia* from a late XIIth century MS. of the Bibliothèque de St. Victor now in the Bibliothèque Nationale at Paris, where it is catalogued *fonds latin* 15045 ;[1] de Curzon gives also a French text based upon three MS., one in the Archives of the Côte d'Or at Dijon,[2] another in the Bibliothèque Nationale at Paris and a third in the Corsini Library at Rome. Vacandard doubted whether the Latin text in question is *verbatim* the text approved at the Council of Troyes, but, however this may be, there can be no reason for doubting that in the main it received its sanction at the council and that under the direct influence of St. Bernard.[3]   To this last fact, namely, the influence of St. Bernard, points the not infrequent issue of the *Regula Pauperum Commilitonum Christi Templique Salomonis* with such an official Cistercian document as the *Exordium Parvum*, with the *Menologion Cisterciense* of Henriquez and with the *Chronicon Cisterciensis Ordinis* of Aubertus Miraeus ; further, significantly enough, the treatise *In Praise of the New Warfare* is found in this very XIIth century MS. of the Rule.

In the prologue to the Latin text of the Rule the scribe states explicitly : " I, John Michael, have been counted worthy to write by divine grace the present document at the order of the council and of Bernard, the venerable Abbot of Clairvaux, to whom this work " (i.e. of framing the Rule) " was fittingly entrusted." There are here and there in the text traces of sympathy with the Cistercian manner, as, for example, the preference of white garments for men who have turned their backs upon a life of darkness in order that so clothed " they may make profession of being reconciled to their maker by their pure and white life. For what is whiteness but untainted chastity ? "[4]   They are, unless in grave necessity, to sleep each in his separate bed clothed in their undergarments, with a light continually burning until the morning.[5] Boys are not to be admitted to the Order, " for it is better that they should not be vowed in childhood at all than that, when they grow to manhood, they should violate the Rule and withdraw."[6]   These indications may seem to the general reader to be slight, but by one familiar with the Cistercian treatment of the Rule of St. Benedict and of the monastic problems of the XIIth century they are unmistakable.   It should be remembered, however, that the Rule provides for a class of married members, as well as for a class somewhat corresponding to the tertiaries of the mendicant Orders of a later day.[7]   In this latter class were afterwards enrolled even popes and kings ; but the strictness of its requirements is shown by the fact

[1] Labb. et Cossart., *Concil.*, X. 923 sqq.

[2] H 111 MS. (*Maison de Voulaines*).

[3] de Curzon, *La Règle du Temple*, 12 sqq.

[4] § 17. *De qualitate et modo vestimenti.*

[5] § 21. *Quot et quales panni in lecto sunt necessarii.*

[6] § 14. *Ut pueri, quamdiu sunt parvi, non accipiantur inter fratres Templi.*

[7] § 69. *Quomodo fratres conjugati habeantur.*

that Philip the Fair was refused admission to it so late as about the beginning of the XIVth century, a time when it might have been supposed to be in the interest of the Order to conciliate him, for he was persecuting it with characteristic savagery.[1] Certain additions to the Rule, chiefly concerning internal organization, were made in 1135 at the Council of Pisa which was attended by St. Bernard.[2] Presumably their spirit is embodied in the XIIth century Latin text. In any case they do not minimize the extent of St. Bernard's influence; rather the contrary.

Immediately after the Council of Troyes Hugh de Payns travelled throughout France and England, returning to Jerusalem in 1129.[3] Thenceforth the Order grew rapidly in numbers. Dying, as we have seen, in 1136, the first Grand Master took no part in the Second Crusade, but the knights were well represented in the great army which left Paris for the East under Louis le Jeune a few days after Pentecost in 1147.

It remains to take some account of St. Bernard's treatise *In Praise of the New Warfare*, addressed formally to Hugh de Payns but plainly intended to be an exhortation to the whole Order. The precise date at which it was written is not known, but internal evidence reveals that the Templars were at the time a famous and numerous body. " What is happening at Jerusalem is known throughout the world. The isles and the nations from afar hear of it. The story is bruited from East to West like a torrent bringing glory to the Gentiles, and a rush of waters making glad the city of God." In this " so great a multitude of men " it is a matter for congratulation that there are so few evil livers.[4] It was of course written before the death of Hugh de Payns in 1136; Mabillon was disposed to date it not earlier than the year 1132.[5] The treatise is to some extent of the nature of an apology. Good reasons had to be offered as to why it was right for the Church to give the sanction of a religious order to an organization ostensibly militant, in days in which too frequently the means taken to satisfy " the love of vainglory and the greed for any kind of earthly possession "[6] brought a blush to Christian cheeks. Evidently the Grand Master was pressing for such an apology from a man whose judgement was beyond dispute. " Once, twice and thrice, beloved Hugh, you have asked me to write a word of exhortation to yourself and to your fellow-knights "[7] are the opening words of the treatise. Hugh de Payns had not explicitly asked for an apology; and St. Bernard does not explicitly write one, simply because to pro-

[1] Maillard de Chambure, *op. cit.*, 139.

[2] French text, §§ 79-121 ; Maillard de Chambure, *op. cit.*

[3] *Auctar. Roberti de Monte, an.* 1128, *P.L.* CLX. 443.

[4] *De Laude Nov. Milit.*, V. 10.

[5] Mabillon. *Admon. in op. cit.*, III.

[6] *Op. cit.*, II. 3.

[7] *Op. cit., Prolog.*

claim the ideal of the Order, to measure the nearness of its
approach thereto and to urge yet closer approximation constitute the most powerful of apologies.   It is a new kind of
military service, we learn, hitherto unheard of, the service
of men armed against spiritual wickedness in high places,
There is a twofold conflict involved in which while the body is
clad in mail the spirit is protected by the breastplate of faith.
A man who falls in other warfare may die *in* the Lord ;
he who falls in this warfare dies not only *in* the Lord but
for the Lord.[1]   When he inflicts death upon the wicked it is   [1] *Op. cit.*, I. 1.
an act not of homicide but, " so to say, of malicide." [2]   The   [2] *Op. cit.*, III. 4.
Baptist did not forbid the Roman soldiers their military
service ;   he implicitly approved it by telling them to be
content with their pay.[3]   *A fortiori* men are not forbidden   [3] *Op. cit.*, III. 5.
a military service which they follow by divine vocation,
called as they are to imitate our Lord himself who forcibly
cleansed the Temple, " his sacred hand armed not indeed with
a sword but with a scourge " ; and the presence of the infidel
to-day is far greater desecration than was that of the trader
of old.[4]   So St. Bernard urges.   He came, we know, of an   [4] *Op. cit.*, V. 9.
ancient fighting stock ;   it was not in him to fear either man
or devil ;   but the son of Tescelin the Sorel would sanction no
drawing of the sword in other than a righteous cause.   " That
we may put to shame those whose service is done plainly
not to God but to the devil, let us speak briefly of the behaviour
and of the manner of life of the knights of Christ, of how they
conduct themselves in battle or when at home, in order that
it may be shown how different is the service of God from that
of the world." [5]   There are two essentials, discipline and   [5] *Op. cit.*, IV. 7.
obedience.   The latter covers in minute detail all times and
all places.   The Templar is never off duty ;   rather is he ever
alert to follow the least suggestion of the will of his superior.
In the matter of discipline he is an ascetic.   Neither in food
nor in clothing nor in conversation nor in sexual intercourse is
he less restrained than a religious should be.   Without property of his own he lives in a house common to the Order ;
without a will of his own his necessities are determined by
the will of the Grand Master.[6]
  [6] *Op. cit., loc. cit.*

About one third of the treatise sets forth and extols the
ideal of the New Warfare ;   the remainder is an allegorical
treatment of the sacred places of the Gospel, of their names
and of their history, spiritually applied to the everyday life
of the Templar.   Thus Bethany is " the house of obedience,
the home of Mary and of Martha in which Lazarus was raised
from the dead ; where surely we have a figure of the two lives "

—St. Bernard means probably the active and the contemplative
—"and of the clemency of God towards sinners; where too the
virtue of obedience together with the fruits of repentance are
commented to us."[1] If one were asked what it is in the psychological constitution of the faithful and consistent Templar
to which St. Bernard looks as his safeguard, one would probably say that it is the conviction that there is only one evil,
and that is sin, for "the soul cannot be separated from God
in any other way than by sinning."[2] If the Order was a
religious order it was in very large measure because St. Bernard
was in a sense its first novice-master. The treatise represents
the means which he took to ensure, so far as he was able, the
permanence of the atmosphere of religion in what we have
described as the concrete realization of an idea, new alike in
the social and in the political world, and thus to protect
it against the possibilities of evil inherent in itself.

THE GILBERTINES.

There was another religious order to the foundation of
which St. Bernard contributed directly as well as indirectly.
The Gilbertines possess for us special interest from the fact
that, with the exception of one Scottish house, a double foundation effected about the year 1221 at Dalmulin, on the North
bank of the river Ayr and a short distance N.E. of the town of
that name, which had but a short lease of life—some seventeen years perhaps—from their origin to their end they were
English.[3] At some date between 1131 and 1139 Gilbert, son
of Sir Joslen of Sempringham, who was charged with the
cure of souls in the place, a village about three miles E.S.E.
of Folkingham in Lincolnshire, on discovering that not a
few women of the locality wished to give themselves to the
religious life, obtained from Gilbert of Gaunt, afterwards Earl
of Lincoln, a grant of land for a priory. It was probably at
about the time of Gilbert's visit to Cîteaux in 1147, to which
reference will presently be made, that double foundations of
monks and nuns developed in the Order. After Gilbert's
death in 1189 they gradually disappeared and the Order
eventually consisted of separate houses of canons living according to an extended form of the Augustinian Rule, and of nuns
who observed the Rule of St. Benedict as interpreted at
Cîteaux.[4] The Prior-General or Master might be the prior, or
a canon, of any house; but the annual chapter general was
always held at Sempringham. In 1147 Gilbert, apparently
anxious that the Order should be placed upon an irreproachably
constitutional basis and doubtless also favourably impressed

[1] *Op. cit.*, XIII. 31.

[2] *Op. cit.*, XI. 19.

[3] Edwards, *The Gilbertines in Scotland*, III. 7 sqq.; Hamilton Thompson, *Cambr. Med. Hist.*, V. 682.

[4] *Vita S. Gilb.*, Dugdale, *Monast. Angl.*, VI (2), xii. *ed.* Caley; Gasquet, *Engl. Monast. Life*, 229.

by the life lived in the Cistercian abbeys of England, in particular at Rievaulx, the abbot of which house—probably William —was known to him, made a journey to Cîteaux where Eugenius III was at the time present for the chapter general. His request then made that the Cistercians should undertake the direction of the Order was not granted, on the ground that " it was not permitted to them to rule over monks, and certainly not over nuns, of another Order than their own." Apparently his proposal had been somewhat different from that of normal aggregation to Cîteaux. The Pope was, however, so favourably impressed by Gilbert that he formally entrusted to him the government of the entire Order,[1] to which the Privilegium Romanum was granted in 1148. St. Malachy is said to have been at the time at Cîteaux and Gilbert to have had much familiar conversation with him as well as with St. Bernard.[2] As regards St. Malachy, the chronology is a little difficult, for the *Annals of the Four Masters* give 1148 as the date of his second visit to France ;[3] but the statement in the *Life of St. Gilbert* points to some meeting between the two men having taken place there. As regards St. Bernard, William of Newburgh records that Gilbert, distrusting his own inexperience, " decided to go and consult a man distinguished for his wisdom and for his holiness, namely, St. Bernard, Abbot of Clairvaux ; and, instructed by his revered judgement and confirmed thereby in his purpose, no less zealously than confidently persevered in his pious work."[4] When we come to examine the Institutions of the Order, drawn up in the first person by Gilbert himself—as it would seem— we recognize the spirit of Cistercian severity generally, as well as specific characteristics which recall Cistercian uses. For example, provision is made for something like *conversi*, a matter as to which Gilbert states that he consulted " the first Abbot of Rievaulx," William, scribe of the letter to Robert of Châtillon. They are referred to as *mercenarii* or *mercenariae* as the case may be ; but it is made plain that they are not mere hired servants but monks or nuns, a " religious habit " being worn by the *mercenarii* " such as the Cistercian brethren wear."[5] We cannot doubt but that St. Bernard's share in the compilation of these *Institutions* was considerable, and that his influence upon the Order would have been felt whether directly or indirectly from 1147 onwards until the year of his death. Nor should we fail to note that the prohibition of the ecclesiastical chant issued by Gilbert to the nuns of the Order,[6] to which it is probable that John of Salisbury refers,[7] is much in the Cistercian spirit.[8]

16

[1] *Vita S. Gilb.,* op. cit., VI. (2), xi, *Institut.,* II., op. cit., VI. (2), xxx.

[2] *Vita S. Gilb.,* op. cit., VI. (2), xii.

[3] Cf. p. 182 *supra.*

[4] William of Newburgh, *Hist.,* I. xvi.

[5] *Institut.,* I, Dugdale, *Monast. Angl.,* VI (2), xxix sq. ed. cit.

[6] *Institut. ad Monial. Ord. Pertin.,* XX, op. cit VI (2).

lxxx, ed. cit.

[7] Joann. Sares. *Policrat.,* I. vi, ed. Webb, I. 43.

[8] Cf. S. Bern. *Ep.* 398 ; Aelred. Rievall. Ab. *Speculum Charit.,* II. ii.

CHAPTER XI

THE APOSTOLIC SEE

" BUT if in certain cases he seems to have exceeded the due mean, a thing which it is not easy to avoid in matters involving much anxiety and difficult to handle, the value of his great achievements should excuse him ; work which redounds to the advantage of the Christian commonwealth rightly deserves no man's reprobation. For what more exacting, what more difficult task is there than utterly to eradicate the abuses of ecclesiastical investiture deeply rooted by long lapse of time and by the authority of many princes ? " So Mabillon justly questions of the work of Gregory VII.[1] And, in truth, the character of this great pontiff is perhaps only now in an age more sympathetic in its estimate of mediæval conditions beginning to be understood. The portrait of a harsh and overbearing ruler, obsessed with the sense of his almost personal autocracy, no longer hangs upon our walls. It is discredited by facts which escaped the notice of observers persuaded *a priori* that they were not there. The *Registrum* of Gregory is a record of the Pope's letters written between 1073 and 1083, amounting to three hundred and sixty-one ; in addition to which there are extant eighty-three written between 1073 and 1085, the year of his death, the last three of which are of doubtful authenticity.[2] Even a cursory perusal of this correspondence cannot fail to reveal the moderation of Gregory's dealings, whether in ecclesiastical affairs or in such civil affairs as were properly within his cognizance. The general tone adopted may well be illustrated by the opening words of a letter dated Rome, 2nd March, 1078. " Seeing," he writes, " that it is the custom of the Holy Roman Church, which by God's ordinance all unworthily we serve, to tolerate some things, some things even to cover up, guided rather by the rule of temperate discretion than by the rigour of canon law, it is with great pains that we have considered the cases of the bishops of France and of Burgundy who have been suspended or condemned by our legate Hugh, Bishop of Die." [3]

[1] Mabillon. *Acta SS. Bened.*, II. *Praef. Saec.* iii. 41.

[2] S. Greg. VII. Pont. Rom. *Registr., P.L.* CXLVIII. 285 sqq.

[3] *Op. cit.*, V. 17, an. 1078.

Lest it should be supposed that this suave preamble is but the velvet glove of an iron hand, let us investigate what follows. Six recalcitrant prelates are concerned, persons of no less importance than the Archbishops of Rheims, Besançon, Sens, Bordeaux and Tours and the Bishop of Chartres. We infer from the language of the rebukes administered the nature of the offences committed. The Archbishop of Rheims, we are given to understand, " had been accused on many charges ; and had withdrawn himself from the synods to which he had been summoned by Hugh, Bishop of Die, on the ground that the sentence passed upon him did not seem to be in accordance with the dignity and with the customary clemency of the Roman Church." The Pope, however, restores him to his office on certain conditions, which suggest, as has been said, the nature of his offences. It is to be clearly understood that the archbishop will not craftily or treacherously disregard the summons of an Apostolic emissary or of an Apostolic rescript, but will faithfully obey the decisions of the Roman Church ; that he will be prepared to answer Gregory or any of his successors on charges brought against him ; finally that he will deal honestly with the treasures, ornaments and lands of the Church of Rheims and not unrighteously alienate them. The fair treatment meted out to the other five prelates is remarkable. For example, the Archbishop of Tours is restored to his office " because he had no legal accusers " ; even the bishops who had accused him — presumably informally — failed to formulate their accusation ; moreover, his case has already been dealt with by Gregory's immediate predecessor, Alexander II, and is not to be re-opened unless on some fresh and definite accusation. It is plain that another legate is, or has been, appointed not to supersede but to act in concert with the Bishop of Die ; that they are together to proceed to Tours, to summon the suffragans, the rest of the clergy and the laity of the province and to admonish them in the name of Blessed Peter that their metropolitan is to be believed on the point of his election and that, understanding the charges against him to have failed, nothing more is to be heard of the matter. In tact the letter appears to be a model of administrative justice. Reading between the lines we recognize its fairness to the accused, to the legate and to all who had a right to be interested in the good government of the Church.

In the matter of Gregory's historic conflict with the Emperor, Henry IV, it is needless that we should enter into details. It is sufficient to note that fundamentally the point at issue was that which at the time constituted the outstanding problem for a reforming Pope, namely, the investitures. Long before he was elected to the pontificate he had appreciated the fact that weak and indifferent predecessors in that high and responsible office had allowed to stand unchallenged the view that the supernatural body corporate was no more than merely a *religio licita*, recognized on conditions imposed by the caprice of princes temporal, holding " of the world " and only on the basis of such tenure allowed to exist " in the world " at all. When, after the long siege of Rome, Gregory lay at the mercy of his enemy, and only by the intervention of Robert Guiscard, Duke of Apulia, escaped first to Monte Cassino, and then to Salerno where in 1085 he died,[1] the victory of Canossa would have seemed doubtless to be pyrrhic ; but in fact these tragic events proved to be the very fire from heaven consuming the accepted sacrifice ; men had to learn that " the freedom of the Church could not be secured otherwise than at the cost of the life and of the material credit of its defender." [2]

It is to Hugh, Abbot of Cluny, that Gregory reveals his inmost self ; and it is from letters written to the ruler of a house in the cloister of which " he had lived as a monk among monks," [3] that we learn how deeply conscious he was alike of his own weakness and of his dependence upon divine aid. " Feeble though we be," he writes in 1074, " yet alone and beyond our strength both of mind and of body we bear, in this most grave day, the heavy weight not only of spiritual but of secular affairs ; and daily we go in fear of falling beneath the burden, for by no means can we find in this world any helper to support it with us. Wherefore in the name of the Lord Almighty we beg of you (as we have done from the very day of our ordination) to call upon your brethren to pray continually to God for us ; for, unless by the intercession of them and of other faithful souls we obtain divine aid, we shall be unable to escape danger not only to ourselves, but also, what we fear much more, to the Church." [4] And again to the same Abbot Hugh he writes in 1078 : " But when the poor Jesus, my kind comforter, very God and very man, stretches out his hand, most sad and afflicted though I be, he brings me joy ; but when he sends me away I am much distressed ; in myself indeed I am always dying, but in him I sometimes live ; in my own strength I fail utterly." [5] This is the real Hildebrand.

It has been necessary to place Gregory VII in a fair light in order to estimate how far his principles and his practice are accountable for St. Bernard's ideal of papal government.

[1] *Acta Pontif.,*
P.L. CXLVIII.
112 sq., 127 sq.,
138 sqq.

[2] Guéranger,
Inst. Liturg., II.
450 sqq.

[3] Baron. *Annal.,*
an. 1049.
Cf. *e regione*
Brooke, *Cambr.*
Med. Hist., V.
52, *note* 1.

[4] S. Greg. VII.
Pont. Rom.
Registr., I. 62,
an. 1074.

[5] *Op. cit.,* V. 21,
an. 1078.

The fact that the Abbot of Clairvaux wrote for his old and well-beloved pupil, Eugenius III, a treatise setting forth this ideal is sufficient proof that the matter was very near his heart ; and when we remember that we are in a position to interpret it by reference to the history of his handling of the various points in dispute between rival Popes, between secular princes and ecclesiastical persons and between ecclesiastical persons themselves, upon occasions when he either was invited to intervene or believed it to be his duty to intervene on his own motion, we shall perhaps feel that the task is not so very difficult.   Professor Augustin Fliche, than whom no one is more competent to give an opinion upon the subject, finds nowhere in St. Bernard's writings any explicit reference to the *Registrum*.[1]   Setting aside the Sacred Scriptures in which plainly his works are steeped, St. Bernard's direct and explicit quotations of Christian writers are comparatively few and far between.   The matter is dealt with more fully in the Appendix under the head of *Literaria*.   In passing a word may be said about it here.   We are conscious of his great indebtedness, say, to St. Augustine and to St. Gregory the Great ; and now and then he will refer to them or quote their words, as in the treatise *Of Precept and Dispensation* he makes use of a passage from St. Augustine's letter to Armentarius,[2] and when writing to the Abbot of St. Mary of York he appeals to the *Pastoral Rule* and to the *Homilies on Ezekiel*.[3]   For Boëthius, the " Wise Man," as St. Bernard calls him, standing as it were in a class apart, he would seem to have high regard, quoting him twice in one chapter of a treatise into which he certainly put his whole soul.[4]   And it is an interesting feature of his writings that they reveal something of a pleasurable familiarity with such Classical authors as Cicero, Virgil, Horace, Ovid, Persius, Lucan and Statius. These reminiscences however might be represented as merely the graceful touches of a stylist whose native instinct has caught and stored the salient phrases of old writers and does not fail to use them aptly, rather than as revealing a mind which has made its own, perhaps almost unconsciously, the distinctive thought, the epoch-making message of a great master.   This latter we seem to recognize that with regard to Gregory St. Bernard has done.   That in the solution of all the urgent problems concerning the government of the Church with which St. Bernard was confronted, problems of investiture, of simony, of the alienation of ecclesiastical property, he acted as in similar circumstances Gregory would have acted we can scarcely doubt.   But were his basic

[1] Fliche, *L'influence de Grégoire VII et des idées Grégoriennes sur la pensée de S. Bernard, S. Bernard et son Temps,* I. 138.

[2] S. Bern. *De Praecept. et Disp.,* I. 2 ; S. Aug. *Ep. ad Arment.,* 127.

[3] *Ep.* 94.   *Vide* p. 54 *supra.* Cf. S. Bern. *De Consid.,* I. ix. 12.

[4] S. Bern. *De Convers.,* VIII. 13 sq.

principles those of Gregory?   Let us turn to the *Five Books on Consideration* for an answer to the question.   The treatise was written at intervals during the years 1149-53 ; it was perhaps finished not long before St. Bernard's death in 1153. It was the product of reflection upon the Universal Church in the breadth of its dimensions, as it appeared increasingly day by day *sub specie aeternitatis*.   An old man's vision, it was apocalyptic ; apocalyptic in an atmosphere of tender affection, for it is only to love that revelations are vouchsafed. He saw " our Eugenius " precisely as he had described him in 1145 in a letter to the cardinals remonstrating with them on his election ; he saw a " ragged fellow " in a position in which his duty called him " to direct princes, to command bishops and to dispose of kingdoms and empires " ; he saw a man, who had chosen for himself " the meanest office in the house of his God," chosen by others, as St. Bernard believed by little less than a miracle, to be " the master of the whole household."

¹ *Ep.* 237.

And this man was his own " son of tender age " ! [1]

With such a man both duty and inclination prompt him to be frank.   " If I know you," he writes, " you have not ceased to be poor in spirit because you have become the father of the poor.   A change has been made in your position, not in yourself ; my confidence is that your promotion has not changed your previous state, but has simply added to it." He was the same man that he had been, but charged with new duties.   " I am going to admonish you, not as a master but as a lover (*amans*).   I may seem to be out of my senses (*amens*), but only to one who does not love, who is not con-

² S. Bern. *De Consid., Prolog.*

scious of the power of love." [2]   The contrast between what Eugenius is personally and what he is officially is strongly emphasized.   " Reflect that you are a man, naked and poor and wretched and pitiable ; a man lamenting his existence, blushing at his nakedness, grieving that he was born, murmuring at what he has grown to be ; a man born for toil and not for honours ; a man born of a woman and therefore born in sin ; a man full of many miseries and therefore full of tears."   Presently he breaks off to point the paradox. " It is a salutary conjunction of ideas that you should consider that you are the Supreme Pontiff, and that none the less you should weigh well the fact that you not merely once were,

³ *Op. cit.,* II. ix. 18.

but still are the vilest dust." [3]

But what is Eugenius officially ?   A little earlier in the treatise he has been exculpating his conscience from charges brought against him on the score of the failure of the Second Crusade.   He would not answer for himself ; he would have the Pope answer for him " according to the wisdom and the power given him from on high." His present purpose is to submit to " his grandeur " the necessity of consideration, that is to say of " earnestness of mind in the investigation of truth." Here then is a case in point. " If great men ought to consider great matters, to whom is zeal for consideration more becoming than to him who has no equal upon earth ? " [1] And again a few pages later he writes : " Come, let us investigate somewhat more closely the question as to what it is that you are, the question, I mean, as to what the character is which for the time being you sustain in the Church of God. What are you ? The high priest, the supreme pontiff. You are the chief of bishops, the heir of the apostles ; in preference you are Abel, in steersmanship Noah, in patriarchate Abraham, in order Melchizedek, in dignity Aaron, in authority Moses, in judgement Samuel, in power Peter, in unction Christ. You it is to whom the keys have been handed ; you to whom the sheep have been entrusted. There are indeed other doorkeepers of heaven, other shepherds of the flocks ; but you have inherited the names of doorkeeper and shepherd in a sense more glorious, as it is more distinctive than have they. They have their flocks assigned to them, each his own flock. To you all the flocks have been entrusted as one flock to one shepherd. Nor are you the shepherd only of all the sheep, but also of all the shepherds. Do you ask me how I would prove this ? From the word of the Lord. For to which, I do not say of the bishops, but of the apostles were the whole of the sheep so absolutely and so inseparably entrusted ? *If you love me, Peter, feed my sheep.* What sheep ? The people of this or that city or district or kingdom ? *My sheep,* he said. To whom is it not plain that he did not designate any particular sheep, but assigned all sheep ? Where there is no exception, there is no distinction. And perchance the rest of the disciples were present when, giving this commission to one, he would commend to all unity in one flock and in one shepherd as it is written : *My dove is one, my fair, my perfect dove.* Where unity is, there is perfection." [2]

We have quoted at sufficient length to convey St. Bernard's meaning. This is his conception of the authority of the Apostolic See ; and it is entirely that of Gregory VII. He speaks from a conviction fortified by experience gained during the period of the Papal Schism. He had in a letter dated by Mabillon 1135 pressed this conviction upon the Milanese who wished to prevent their archbishop from taking the oath of fidelity to Innocent II.[3] " The fulness of authority

[1] *Op. cit.,* II. i. 4. II. ii. 5.

[2] *Op. cit.,* II. viii. 15.

[3] P. 144 *supra.*

over all the churches of the world has as a special prerogative been granted to the Apostolic See. He therefore who resists this power resists the ordinance of God. He (the Pope) can, if he judge fit, establish new bishoprics where they did not exist before. As regards such as do exist, he can lower the status of some and exalt that of others, as reason may dictate to him ; so that he may make archbishops of bishops and the converse, as may seem to him to be necessary. From the ends of the earth he can summon the highest ecclesiastical persons, whoever they may be, not once nor twice but so often as seems expedient to him. Moreover, he is ready to punish disobedience should anyone attempt to resist his will." [1] It may be remarked here that St. Bernard has no notion of the schismatic Greeks as being beyond the scope of the authority of the See of Peter. " They are," he writes to Eugenius, " by their obstinacy both with us and not with us ; joined in the faith but alienated by discord. Although in the matter of the faith itself they have strayed lamely away from the right path . . . your office it is to provide a remedy for this wound also." [2] He would imply that in spite of their claim to orthodoxy, up to a certain point a just claim, there are failings in this respect which it belongs to the Pope's Apostolic authority to correct.

Now these are precisely the principles which, in Gregory VII's handling of the cases of recalcitrant prelates in France and in Burgundy, we saw administratively at work.[3] Men are often willing to accept an authority with reservations which secure them against its invasion of some province or provinces in which they regard themselves as possessed of a sacred independence. In so doing they justify themselves by an appeal to conscience : " I ought not to grant so much as that." St. Bernard made no such reservations in his submission to the See of Peter. He was tenacious of nothing so firmly as of his right—because it was his duty—as a monk to " make himself a stranger to secular business," a course which St. Benedict held to be one of the " instruments of good works," paradoxically enough as it might seem to secular persons.[4] Yet he protested more than once in letters written to Cardinal Haimeric, Chancellor of the Apostolic See, his readiness to surrender even this at the bidding of the Pope, claiming freedom however to express strongly his sense of his own limitations. " I judge," he writes, " nothing to be safer for me than to obey the will of the lord Pope ; though would that he saw fit to consider my powers ! Would forsooth that he knew that I am incompetent to do these things "—to deal

with public affairs—" or at any rate how difficult it is for me
to do them ! " But he will not press the point of his unfitness.
" To a wise man I have said enough." [1]

It is important to notice that the authority which St.
Bernard recognizes as divinely sanctioned is that of the Pope,
by no means that of the *Curia*. Indeed he makes the distinction most forcibly. He will obey " the legate of the Apostolic
See," but, warning Haimeric that certain complaints are vocal,
he remarks : " I do not think that, even were I to keep quiet
and to say nothing, the murmuring of the churches would
cease unless the Roman *Curia* ceased to give judgement in
untried cases and in the absence of the accused, simply as its
members happen to wish." [2] He has a poor opinion of the
ecclesiastics who surround Eugenius, of the local Roman
clergy and of the people of Rome generally. It is just the
unique supernatural dignity of the pontifical office which
makes the existing state of things so terrible. " In the first
place," he writes, " those clergy who set a standard for the
clergy of the whole Church ought to be the best regulated
of all. Then, whatever is done wrongly in your presence
brings the greater disgrace upon you. It touches the honour
due to your holiness that those who stand before your presence
should be so well regulated, so well developed in character,
as to reflect the ideal, to present the norm, of all that is
honest and seemly. Above all, men should be found who are
apt for their particular duties, fit ministers of the sacraments,
solicitous for the proper instruction of the people, watchful
to maintain their own personal chastity." Thus he would
have the *Curia* consist of good and able men. Local conditions,
as St. Bernard can testify, make this difficult. " What,"
he exclaims, " am I to say of the populace ? It is the Roman
people ! I could neither more briefly nor yet more exactly
give you my opinion of your parishioners. What for centuries has been so notorious as the shamelessness and arrogance
of the Romans ? A race quarrelsome and turbulent ; a race
up to this very day untamed and intractable, that knows not
to submit save only when it is not strong enough to resist.
This is the misfortune ! And upon you falls the duty of dealing
with it. The fact is not to be disguised. Perhaps you are
laughing at me because you are persuaded that it is incurable "
—that is to say, Eugenius may think that he knows his Rome
better than does St. Bernard—" Now do not despair. What
is required of you is not to cure (*curatio*) this evil state, but to
take care (*cura*) of it. In a word, you have heard it said :
Take care of him—not *cure him* or *make him well*." [3]

[1] *Ep.* 52 ; cf. *Ep.* 48.

[2] *Ep.* 48.

[3] *Op. cit.*, IV. ii. 2.

All this is extraordinarily intimate and incisive. More-over it expresses the insight of a keen observer, of a sound judge of men. We might add that implicitly it raises the perennial question of the influence, for good or for ill, of the local element in the Roman *Curia*, a question, as St. Bernard makes clear, entirely distinct from that of the authority of the Supreme Pontiff. He fully recognizes the difficulty of reforming the *Curia*, and he indicates that this is so great because at the root of it is the further difficulty of reforming the people of Rome. This latter is not a thing that can be done out of hand ; the case must be watched and not allowed to get any worse than it is ; in this as in other matters he would

[1] *Op. cit.*, I. vi. 7. " counsel not what is heroic, but what is possible " ; [1] he is anxious lest Eugenius's zeal, of which he does not doubt, should outrun his discretion.

But his insistence upon the necessity of excluding from high office in the Church any who are not in every respect suitable is entirely Gregorian. In 1076 the clergy and the people of the diocese of Dol in Brittany had sent to Gregory a young man under the canonical age to be consecrated to their vacant see, then a metropolitanate, only to be told that the Pope would not hear of him but had substituted another, " a man prudent, good, distinguished for the excellence of his conduct and worthy of all reverence," with the added warning that, " as they wish for the favour of Blessed Peter the Apostle and of us his unworthy servant, they are to show to him (the

[2] S. Greg. VII, Pont. Rom. *Registr.*, IV. 4, *an.* 1076, *P.L.* CXLVIII. person consecrated) all obedience as to a father and a ruler." [2] St. Bernard's touchstone is just this—character. He would have Eugenius begin by using it to test the prelates who are coadjutors at his own side, his *collaterales*. " They have no power except such as you assign or allow them. We come back to that (*sc.* that Eugenius is the fount of authority). Impute to yourself whatever you suffer from a man who without your authority can do nothing. It is your function to call to your side from any quarter and to associate with your-self after the example of Moses, elders, not young men ; men, I mean, who are mature in character rather than in years. Should not they be chosen from the whole world, who are to judge the whole world ? Surely a man does not obtain for himself such an office as this by asking for it ! There are things which unavoidably the importunity or the need of those who ask extorts from us. But that is when the things

[3] S. Bern. *De Consid.*, IV. iv. 9. are our own personal property." [3] Thus, St. Bernard urges, Eugenius should select from a wide area ; he should select with reference solely to character ; and, as he is selecting for

public office, he should ignore the personal considerations out of which the typical place-hunter makes capital. In a fine passage, too long to quote in full, he describes the kind of men which, " excluding the whole of this pestilent class," it will not afterwards repent him to have introduced into the *Curia*. They should be, he writes, illustrating in his characteristic manner from sacred history, " to kings as John, to the Egyptians as Moses, to fornicators as Phinehas, to idolaters as Elijah, to misers as Elisha, to liars as Peter, to blasphemers as Paul, to traffickers as Christ. Men who do not spurn the common folk, but teach them ; who do not caress the rich, but scare them ; who do not burden the poor, but cherish them ; who do not fear the threats of princes, but despise them.[1] Men whose entrance is not with tumult, nor their departure in anger ; who do not spoil churches, but rather better their state. Men who do not empty purses, but refresh hearts and punish crime ; who respect their own good name and do not envy that of others. Men who have both a zeal for prayer and the habit of prayer, and who in all events trust more in prayer than in their own diligence or toil. Men whose coming brings peace, whose going leaves regret ; whose speech is edification, whose life is righteousness, whose presence is a joy, whose memory is a blessing." [2] But we must not run on. It is all, we cannot but feel, quite masterly. Taken with what has been already quoted, it gives us St. Bernard's notion as to what manner of persons they ought to be who at the fountain-head of authority do the service of the Church. The extent to which venality prevailed amongst the Pope's *collaterales* of that day may be inferred from two outstanding cases of probity which St. Bernard quotes, those, namely, of the Legates Cardinal Martin at Florence and Geoffrey of Chartres in Aquitaine ; [3] to which, moreover, John of Salisbury refers in the *Policraticus*.[4]

So far we have suggested that St. Bernard's recognition of the Apostolic See as responsible officially for the good government of the Universal Church, both generally and in its constituent parts, is explicit in the treatise *Of Consideration*. It would not be difficult to show from the treatise *Of the Conduct and of the Office of Bishops* addressed to Henry, Archbishop of Sens, so early as 1126, that consistently with the doctrine of his great hand-book, as it may well be called, written for the guidance of Eugenius, he would seek to promote in every province and in every diocese the reforms initiated by Gregory VII in the preceding century. True son of St. Benedict that he was, he would remind every prelate that

[1] Cf. p. 184 *supra.*

[2] *Op. cit.,* IV. iv. 12.

[3] *Op. cit.,* IV. v. 13 sq.

[4] Joann. Sares. *Policrat.,* V. xv. *ed.* Webb., I. 348 sq.

¹ *Ep.* 368. Cf.
*Reg. S. P.
Bened.,* LXIV.

" grave is the condemnation of those who fill high office
(*praesunt*), if they do not strive to profit (*prodesse*) also." ¹

Here too is the same insistence upon the Papal prerogative.
There are men who would flatter the archbishop into the
assertion of an unfounded independence. " They are wont to
say to you : ' It is fitting that the church entrusted to your·
charge should grow in importance ; at least that it should
maintain the dignity which it possessed when you took it
in charge. Are you any feebler than was your predecessor ?
If the church '—meaning the metropolitan see of Sens—' does
not grow in importance by your means let it not lose thereby.'
Christ spoke and commanded and acted quite differently.
Render, he said, *to Caesar the things that are Caesar's, and to God
the things that are God's.* What he spoke with his lips he took
care presently to fulfil in his deeds. Creator of Caesar though
he was, he did not delay to pay tribute to Caesar ; he set you
an example in order that you should do likewise. But when
did he, who took care to show respect to secular authority,
refuse to pay the reverence due to the priests of God ?   Accordingly supposing that you are sedulous in your attention to
Caesar's successor, that is to say, to the king at his courts
and his councils, in his affairs civil and military, is it therefore
derogatory that you should show yourself to be towards
whomsoever may be the Vicar of Christ what of old has been
ordained in the churches ? "   St. Bernard would support
this last contention, as it would seem, by an *a fortiori* argument.
" But the apostle says : *It is of God that the powers that be
are ordained.* So the persons who would dissuade you from
this (supposed) ignominy "—that is to say from submission
to the Vicar of Christ—" will have seen what it is to resist the
ordinance of God."   He would imply that if they know their
Bible they will remember that the apostle, referring to no
higher authority than that of Caesar, goes on to say : *They who
resist shall receive to themselves condemnation.*   " It is forsooth
highly ignominious that the servant should be as his lord, or
the disciple as his master ! They suppose themselves to be
extremely deferential (*deferre*) to you in their efforts to put
you before (*praeferre*) Christ." ² The meaning is clear, the
more so for the flashes of irony which illuminate it.

² S. Bern. *De
Mor. et Offic.
Episc.,* VIII. 31.

It may be asked how we are to account for the grave disorders which, as the treatise *Of Consideration* suggests, prevailed in the Roman *Curia* apart from the low standard of
morals amongst the inhabitants of the place. The Gregorian
reforms had been effected mainly by the instrumentality of
a system of centralization " provided to meet a great need." ³

³ S. Bern. *De
Consid.,* III. ii.
6.

It will have been noticed that out of the six prelates with whose cases Gregory VII deals in his letter of 1078 [1] five were metro- [1] P. 243 *supra*. politans. The metropolitanate was an historical development, a matter of—doubtless justifiable—expediency, and consequently the exercise of its authority was the less restrained by accepted principles; in many cases the office of metropolitan would tend to become in large measure personal, its functions indefinite and its responsibility vague. When the Gregorian system of centralization dawned upon the delighted eyes of diocesans, naturally the relief which it offered by way of appeal to the Apostolic See was in many quarters cordially welcomed and frequently embraced. But in those days it was no easy matter for any man to cross the Alps at short notice, still less for a bishop to leave his diocese unshepherded for months at a time. Thus there developed apace and to considerable proportions the system of the *legatus a latere*. This was a well-employed functionary; for appeals arising out of every conceivable occasion of dissatisfaction on the part both of clergy and of laity tended to increase. There was no intermediate authority which could refuse to allow a case to be taken to the Pope's judgement-bar. Comprovincials came to learn that in many cases appeals proved to be more vexatious than was the caprice of metropolitans; and generally the impression grew that legates from the Apostolic See, sumptuously entertained in archiepiscopal and abbatial palaces and in great feudal castles, were not too ready to lend an ear to ecclesiastics of subordinate rank or to vassals of insignificant status. Moreover, the authority proper to the diocesan was being undermined. " The opinion here," writes St. Bernard to Innocent II in 1139, " of those who rule their people faithfully is that justice is perishing in the Church, that the keys are of no avail," that is to say, that the disciplinary function of the diocesan is annulled, " that episcopal authority is being treated with utter contempt, so long as no bishop is in a position to avenge promptly injuries done to God, or is allowed to punish illicit acts of any kind even in his own diocese. Cases are referred to you and to the Roman *Curia*. You reverse, so it is said, what has been rightly done; you confirm what has been wrongly done. Shameless and contentious people from among the clergy, even men expelled from monasteries, run off to you. On their return they boast and bluster to the effect that they have found protectors, when in fact they ought to have felt the punishment of an avenger." Phinehas did not hesitate most promptly and most justly to draw sword upon the offenders at Baal Peor. " Oh, but of course he was confounded and thrust away; he fell back when he found himself confronted by the shield of an Apostolic defender!" The result of the present state of things is, St. Bernard would have the Pope know, that "everywhere the bishops are despised and put to shame; and the fact that their right judgements meet with contempt derogates most gravely from your authority also."[1]

Thus in more ways than one the system had grown to be an abuse; metropolitans and suffragans alike groaned under it; the inferior clergy and religious were demoralized; the laity were scandalized. In fact the administration of justice in and by the Church was at best unstable and at worst corrupt. "There needs your close and your paternal consideration," St. Bernard writes to Eugenius, "lest what was provided to meet a great necessity become, by improper use, quite unprofitable. It seems to me that appeals may result in being positively pernicious, unless as a system they are used with the utmost moderation. They are addressed to you from every quarter of the globe. That of course is a tribute to your unique primacy. But you, if you are wise, will rejoice not in your primacy but in its good fruits. It was spoken to the apostles : *In this rejoice not, that the spirits are subject to you.* As I have said, appeals are addressed to you and would that the results were as fruitful for good as the appeals are necessary. Would that when the oppressed cried out the oppressor were made to suffer ; and that the ungodly did not proudly boast that the poor was consumed!" We pause for a moment to note the Psalm-language, never with St. Bernard a mere mannerism, but always expressive of deep emotion : *Dum superbit impius incenditur pauper.*[2] "In my opinion," he goes on to say, "a man ought to be made to suffer himself when he has brought an appeal without due cause. The principle fixed for you by the law of justice and of unchangeable divine equity, and if I mistake not by the very law which governs appeals, is that an appeal unlawfully brought may neither advantage the appellant nor damage the respondent. For why should a man (the respondent) be worn out on no good grounds at all? How just it is that a man (the appellant) who wants to injure his neighbour (by appealing) should injure himself! To have appealed without good grounds is to do a wrong; to have appealed wrongly and also with impunity is an encouragement to groundless appeals. Every appeal is wrong to which a man is not compelled because he cannot obtain justice. It is allowable to appeal, not in order to oppress others, but only if you are yourself oppressed."[3]

All this makes the state of things quite clear; and it is, we cannot but feel, very equitable. There were many appeals which both in themselves and in their issue were a miscarriage of justice; and things were in a vicious circle. The root of the matter was the unfitness of the *Curia* generally, as a body sitting at Rome, to be a court of appeal at all; the result of this unfitness was aggravated when a *legatus a latere* with plenary powers was deputed to hear appeals on the spot far away from the fount of supreme authority at Rome, which was ultimately the Pope himself. Eugenius must take in hand the reformation of the *Curia*. The Gregorian system of centralization was defeating its own ends.

In order to drive home his exhortation St. Bernard would give a few instances of what was happening. " A certain man publicly espoused a wife. The nuptial day arrived. All preparations had been made and many guests had been invited. When, lo and behold, a fellow who lusts after his neighbour's wife vociferates an appeal, asserting that the woman had been given to him and that he ought to have her. The bridegroom is stupefied; everybody is puzzled; the whole of the arrangements are upset; the priest does not dare to proceed; the guests go home, each to his own breakfast; the bride is compelled to refrain from the bridegroom's bed and board until the report comes from Rome. This happened at Paris, a great city of France, the king's seat. Again, in the same city a man who had espoused a wife fixed the marriage-day. Meanwhile some calumny arises, people saying that they ought not to be married. The case was referred to the judgement of the Church but without the least expectation of a sentence; the appeal was made without any grounds, without any serious charge being brought, merely for the purpose of vexatious delay. Well; the man, unwilling either to be at a loss over the arrangements made or to be deprived of the companionship of the woman he loved, treated with contempt or as a mere pretence the appeal made and proceeded to do what he had intended to do."

So much for the laity. Now St. Bernard cites a purely ecclesiastical case. " What about a recent piece of presumption on the part of a young man in the Church of Auxerre ? Forsooth, when the holy bishop died and the clergy wished as was customary to elect another, this man appealed and forbad the election to take place until he had been to the Holy City and come back again ! However he did not even act upon his own appeal; for, when no attention was paid to him as having appealed without any reason at all, he assembled to himself whom he could and on the third day after the election had been made by the other parties held an election on his own account." [1]

[1] *Op. cit.*, III. ii. 11. Cf. p. 187 *supra.*

These cases cited illustrate the kind of thing that is happening. St. Bernard calls it *usurpatio ;* it is the unjustifiable interruption of the course of law. He has earlier in the treatise inveighed against " the law's delays." " Cases which must come to your bar—and by no means all need do so—I should like customarily to be despatched with diligence, but with expedition." [2] This usurpation does not, it is true, originally represent any disrespect for the supreme authority of the Pope, quite the contrary ; but in effect it is bringing that authority into contempt. Contempt must be smothered unborn in the very womb of its mother, " which will happen if befitting punishment is measured out to usurpation." [3]

[2] *Op. cit.*, I. x. 13.

[3] *Op. cit.*, III. ii. 12.

The question may arise at this stage as to the extent to which St. Bernard anticipated with approval what in the XVIIth century came to be known as Gallicanism. To the present writer it would seem that the answer is : To no extent at all. It would have been possible for him, in face of the abuses persistently prevalent despite the Gregorian reforms, to conclude that the existing system had had its day ; that it was an anachronism ; that under the most favourable conditions, such as were those established by the great statesman-Pope, it had been tried and found wanting. What St. Bernard might have suggested to replace it is difficult to say. There was perhaps an element of loosely-knit federalism in many of the religious orders, but it is scarcely conceivable that he would have regarded anything like its adoption as a system of universal ecclesiastical government as other than a sacrilege. *As is the heavenly so are they that are heavenly.* The Church is ruled as are the angels.[4] Certainly what St. Bernard had himself suffered from the Roman *Curia* in the matter of Robert of Châtillon had been as iron entering into his soul, as we may gather from the bitterness of his cry : " There will come a day of judgement when clean hearts will avail more than cunning words, and a good conscience than a full purse ; then indeed the judge will neither be deceived by lies nor bought by bribes. Lord Jesu, to thy tribunal I appeal ; I reserve myself for thy judgement." [5] But the very fierceness of his indignation in this case, as generally, is in itself expressive of his deep sense of the sanctity of the authority central at Rome and supreme throughout the world, and of his horror at the degradation which it suffered from the traffic in justice.

[4] S. Bern. *In Cant. Cant.* XXVII. 7.

[5] *Ep.* 1 (7).

Reform of the abuses of an existing system was however scarcely the purpose of Gallicanism. The famous manifesto issued by the Assembly of Clergy in 1682, and so strongly supported by Bossuet in his *Défense de la Déclaration*, was rather the language of a medley of instincts, national and political, seeking to realize themselves in the circumscription of the authority of the Apostolic See within such limits as might arbitrarily be determined by the state, than of the righteous indignation of men zealous for the honour of the house of God. And this leads us to consider briefly St. Bernard's notion of the authority of the Pope over secular princes.

We have noticed that St. Bernard speaks of the " ragged fellow " whom the cardinals had chosen to occupy St. Peter's Chair as called by his duty " to direct princes . . . and to dispose of kingdoms and of empires." This conception is entirely Gregorian. We find Gregory VII writing in 1080 to William the Conqueror: " The good favour of God has provided that mankind should be ruled by two offices, the Apostolic dignity and the royal. Yet the Christian religion functions according to a distinction between these offices as the greater and the lesser, in such a way that the royal dignity may be directed and superintended by the Apostolic dignity." [1] And this is consistently St. Bernard's view of the matter.

He would urge that the Pope is the heir of the apostles whose " sound went forth into all lands and their words unto the ends of the world." But what this inheritance implies, whether in his own case or in that of the apostles, he would have Eugenius consider seriously. " I do not think it to be unqualified; it would rather seem to me that what has been given to you is administration, not possession. Christ by right of creation and by merit of redemption is the possessor. Yield to him possession and lordship ; do you take charge of administration. That is your part ; do not stretch out your hand to anything more." [2] Later he refers to the two swords. " He who denies you your sword does not seem to me to pay sufficient attention to the Lord's words : *Put up thy sword into its sheath.* It is your sword, certainly at your command, yet not to be drawn by your hand. Otherwise if it did not belong to you when the apostles said : *Lord, here are two swords,* the Lord would have said, not : *It is enough,* but : *It is too many.* Therefore the Church has two swords, the spiritual and the material ; the latter is to be drawn for the Church but the former by the Church ; the former by the hand of the priest ; the latter by the hand of the soldier, albeit it is

[1] S. Greg. VII, Pont. Rom. *Registr.*, VII. 25, an. 1080, *P.L.* CXLVIII. Cf. Brooke, *Cambr. Med. Hist.*, V. 83 sq. ; Sturzo, *Papacy and Empire*, *Dublin Review*, July, 1934, 25 sqq.

[2] S. Bern. *De Consid.*, III. i. 1.

17

understood at the will of the priest and on the orders of the
Emperor." [1]   The same thought occurs in a letter written to
Eugenius in 1146. " Peter has two swords, one to be drawn
at his command, the other by his hand so often as is
necessary." [2]   It will be remembered that both passages
date from the period of the Second Crusade, but the notion
was not unfamiliar in the Middle Ages.   John of Salisbury
remarks in the *Policraticus* : " This sword (the material)
then the prince receives from the hand of the Church, for the
Church does not stain a sword with blood.   Yet even this is
her sword, but she uses it by the hand of the prince." [3]

While as a possibility the ultimate appeal may always be
to the arbitrament of the prince's sword, yet St. Bernard, in
advance of his times, would seek to exhaust all other resources
first.   For him the use of material force was a confession of
spiritual weakness.   " Although it may undoubtedly be better
that heretics should be restrained by the sword—his sword
I mean who bears it not in vain—rather than that many should
be led astray," yet such a course is but second best.   He may
admire the zeal of men who would apply to them such a test
as the ordeal by water, but indeed to punish them if they
refuse it is but to make them martyrs to their own wrong
belief.   " Faith is a matter of persuasion, not of compulsion." [4]
That the enforcement of the just claims of the Church, as
interpreted and supported by the Pope, was in his view the
first duty of the civil power is sufficiently shown by the part
which he played in the long struggles which marked the reigns
of Louis le Gros and Louis le Jeune, in the Papal Schism and
in the Second Crusade ; but he was too highly enlightened
a psychologist not to recognize that physical compulsion was
open to the danger of reaction from more quarters than one.
The propagation of heresy was perhaps in St. Bernard's day
sometimes a menace to the public peace ; in such circumstances
its prohibition was doubtless, as it would be in any day, a
justifiable measure.   Moreover, the public advocacy of sexual
practices, such as those of the Neo-Manichæans called *Textores*
reported to St. Bernard by Irwin, Provost of Steinfeld, to which
we refer later, was a thing which might not unreasonably
call for the intervention of the civil arm on the ground of its
being a menace to public morals. [5]   Nevertheless even in so
grave a case as this St. Bernard's advice may be summed up
in his interpretation of *the foxes that spoil the vines*.   " If
in the allegory we are to understand the churches to be the
vines and the heresy, or rather the heretics, to be the foxes,
then it is plainly intended that heretics are not to be got rid of

[1] *Op. cit.*, IV. iii.
7.

[2] *Ep.* 256.

[3] Joann. Sares.
Policrat., IV. iii.
ed. Webb, I. 239.

[4] S. Bern. *In
Cant. Cant.*
LXVI. 12.

[5] *Op. cit.*, LXV.
4, LXVI. 4 sqq. ;
Everv. Steinfeld.
Praepos. *Ep.
ad hoc.* Cf. pp.
333 sq. *infra*.

but made captives ; made captives, I mean, not by arms but
by reasoning which dispels their errors ; and so themselves
to be reconciled to the Catholic Church and recalled to the
true faith." [1]

    As regards the treatment meted out to the Jews by the
sword of the prince at the command of the Church his attitude
is similar.   Indeed he has for them a peculiarly tender feeling ;
perhaps he would remember what their rabbis had done to
help St. Stephen Harding in his revision of the Scriptures of
the Old Testament.   In any case, while no efforts should be
spared on the part of the Pope to win them to the Christian
Faith, it had to be recognized that there was something of
the nature of a divine purpose in the delay to their conversion.
" At some time or another the fulness of the Gentiles must
come." " This time has its limit which cannot be anticipated "
by the use of force.[2] The state of the Jews was indeed most
pitiable. " *The ox knows its master and the ass its master's
crib, but Israel did not know me ; it did not understood.* You
see, O Jews," he exclaims, " that I am more kindly disposed
towards you than was your own prophet. I have compared
you to the beasts; he placed you below the beasts." [3] In
what appears to be an encyclical letter addressed in 1146 to
certain clergy and Christian people concerned in the Second
Crusade [4] he writes : " The Jews ought not to be persecuted
or slain or even expelled. . . . If they are to be utterly ex-
terminated how are we to hope for their salvation, their conversion, which is promised in the end ? " If the Gentiles—
he is at the moment thinking of the Saracens—show violence
to the Christians, then " they who bear not the sword in vain
must oppose force to force. But it belongs to Christian
piety to beat down the proud and to spare the submissive,[5]
especially those to whom the law has been promised "—that
is to say, the old law fulfilled in the new—" whose are the
fathers and of whom is Christ according to the flesh, who is
blessed for ever." [6] Again, in the same year he writes to
Henry, Archbishop of Mainz : " Unless the Church had the
hope that these unbelievers (the Jews) would be brought to
believe it would seem to be superfluous and idle to pray for
them. But with the eye of piety it considers that God looks
favourably upon a man who renders good for evil and love
for hatred. What is the meaning of the words : *Slay them not*?
What is the meaning of : *When the fulness of the Gentiles shall
have come in, then all Israel shall be saved*? Or of : *When the
Lord builds up Jerusalem he will gather together the scattered
of Israel*? Do you propose to make the prophets liars and

[1] *Op. cit.*, LXIV. 8.

[2] S. Bern. *De Consid.*, III. i. 3 sq.

[3] S. Bern. *In Cant. Cant.* LX. 5.

[4] Cf. p. 268 *infra.*

[5] Virg. *Æn.*, VI. 854.

[6] *Ep.* 363. Cf. *Ep.* 365.

to make void all the treasures of the kindness and mercy of Jesus Christ ? You have not got to preach your own doctrine but the doctrine of the Father who sent you. However, I suppose that it is enough for you "—the monk Raoul—" to be as your master. He was a murderer from the beginning, a liar and the father of lies." [1]   This is how St. Bernard could talk of the anti-Semite of the hour, his righteous wrath once moved !

There are then two swords, one spiritual, the other material. The Pope controls the use of both ; he uses the former himself in administering the discipline of the Church alike to ecclesiastical and to secular persons, whatever their rank may be ; the latter he entrusts to secular authorities to be used in his behalf and at his discretion. Whether or not St. Bernard would have approved as well-judged—let us say—the course taken by Pius V in the case of Elizabeth, there can, we think, be no doubt but that he would have regarded it as within the competence of the Pope to take it. But he evidently accepted and urged the implication attached to the view which he took of the Papal authority. The Pope was not essentially, but only accidentally, a secular prince at all ; and it was of paramount importance that his official trappings, or rather the absence of such, should proclaim this fact. " Either deny that you are a shepherd to this people or show yourself publicly to be such," he writes to Eugenius. " You will not deny it ; lest he whose chair you occupy should deny that you are his heir. This is Peter, who knows nothing of going about at any time bedizened with jewels and silks, decked with gold, riding upon a white horse, escorted by soldiery, surrounded by attendants acclaiming him aloud. Yet he believed that he could quite sufficiently fulfil the saving precept *Feed my sheep* without these things. You are the successor of Peter, not of Constantine. I would say : Tolerate this sort of thing in the present circumstances, but do not exact it as due to your office." [2]

It must not be supposed that St. Bernard viewed the Papacy, its duties and its responsibilities, as one who would impose the discipline of Cistercian simplicity upon the whole Church. But, as we have suggested, he did regard them *sub specie aeternitatis*, and consequently urged what cannot better be described than as a becoming σεμνότης. In the advent of Eugenius to the pontificate he undoubtedly saw, and promptly availed himself of, the opportunity of implementing the Gregorian reforms in such a way as that they

[1] *Ep.* 365. Cf. pp. 266 *sq. infra.*

[2] S. Bern. *De Consid.*, IV. iii. 6.

should not be a mere passing phase.   Eugenius might well
be expected to lend himself to the task.   How could he fail
to respond to such an appeal as was voiced in St. Bernard's
first letter addressed to him as Pope ?   " Who will give me
to see before I die the Church of God as in the days of old,
when the apostles spread their nets to take not gold or silver
but the souls of men ? " [1]   [1] *Ep.* 238.

CHAPTER XII

THE SECOND CRUSADE.

St. Bernard's interest in the care and in the protection of the Holy Places is made sufficiently evident by the part which he took in the foundation of the Order of the Temple, the Poor Knights of Christ and of the Temple of Solomon, to give them their descriptive title—so early as the year 1128. We have, too, seen that he had in 1142 interested himself with Queen Melisande on behalf of some Premonstratensian Canons on pilgrimage to the Holy City, and that, probably at an earlier date, through his instrumentality the Order had entered into possession of the site of St. Samuel together with a sum of a thousand gold crowns for the building of a monastery.[1] In spite, however, of the wide extension throughout Europe both of the Cistercians in general, and of the daughters of Clairvaux in particular, St. Bernard would seem to have judged it imprudent to send his sons to Asia. Geoffrey tells us that his reasons were the dangers arising from " the attacks of pagans and the insalubrity of the climate." [2] We may well believe that they lay deeper than this. In the first place, so far as Jerusalem was concerned, the ground was since 1142 already occupied by the Premonstratensians ; [3] in the second place, he was, as we may recognize, keenly alive, certainly from the year 1128, to the danger of the excessive diffusion of his Order to the extremities of the earth ; it had to be quite plain to him that a remote foundation was entirely justifiable.[4] We may think that his decision not to settle a colony of his monks in Palestine was unfortunate ; for had a daughter of Clairvaux existed in that land in 1147 he would probably have accompanied the Crusading hosts, and the issue of the expedition might conceivably have been other than it was. Certain it is that if the situation could possibly have been saved, his personal presence and nothing else could have saved it.

There is no trace to be found in the treatise *In Praise of the New Warfare* of any anxiety on the part of St. Bernard as to the safety of the Holy Places under the adequate

[1] P. 233 *supra.*

[2] *Vita Prima,* III. vii. 22.

[3] Manric. *Annal. Cist.,* I. 432 sq. Cf. pp. 233 sq. *supra.*

[4] *Ep.* 75. Cf. pp. 48 sq. *supra.*

protection of the Templars; on the contrary, he writes to Hugh of Payns and his knights: " You are sufficient securely and faithfully to guard the heavenly charge entrusted to you, provided that in no degree do you ever presume upon your own prudence or bravery, but rely only upon the help of God." [1] Letters written by him between the years 1135 and 1143 breathe the same spirit of confidence. For instance a letter addressed to William, Patriarch of Jerusalem, in the former year refers to the Templars as " such strenuous champions of the Church." [2] But in the latter year Fulk of Anjou, King of Jerusalem, died [3] and the government of the Latin Kingdom passed into the hands of his widow Melisande, there to remain during the minority of the young king, her son Baldwin III, a boy of but twelve years. [4]

Alas! Melisande began badly by breaking the alliance made by Fulk with the powerful Emir of Damascus. The result was to expose the Latin Kingdom to the attacks of Zengi, the Emir of Mosul, into whose hands it had long been the policy of the Greek Emperors, in their jealousy of Western influence, to play. In 1144 Edessa, a Latin principality which was the bulwark of Jerusalem, fell a prey to Zengi. Antioch might be expected to be his next victim, and we hear from Otto of Freising of the Bishop of Gabula in Syria arriving at Rome, " complaining with tears of the danger in which the Church beyond the sea stood owing to the capture of Edessa, and desiring to cross the Alps in order to solicit help from the Kings of the Romans and the Franks." [5] The Chronicle of Maurigny speaks of similar embassies from Antioch and Jerusalem arriving at about the same time in France. [6]

Whatever may be said of Conrad III, Louis le Jeune's mind was already turned towards the Holy Places, " seeing that he had a secret wish to go to Jerusalem because his brother Philip, bound by a vow so to do, had been prevented by death from fulfilling it; " [7] this, together with the ineffaceable memory of Vitry-le-Brûlé and the recollection of his promise to expiate his rash oath in the matter of Peter de la Châtre and the archbishopric of Bourges, [8] disposed him favourably towards the Church of Jerusalem in its threatened peril. Odo de Diogilo tells the story of how the young king, at the time but twenty-five years of age, when assembled at Bourges with the bishops and civil potentates of his realm at the Christmas of 1145 for the purpose of his coronation, [9] then " first revealed the secret of his heart." He was at once supported by the Bishop of Langres, Godfrey de la Roche, St. Bernard's kinsman, a man much in the king's

[1] De Laude Nov. Mil., XIII. 31.

[2] Ep. 175. Cf. Epp. 289 and 392.

[3] William of Tyre, Hist., XV. ad fin., P.L. CC.

[4] S. Bern. Ep. 354.

[5] Otton. Frising. Chron., VII. xxxiii, Hofmeister, Script. Rer. German.

[6] Chron. Mauriniac., R.H.G.F. XII. 88.

[7] Otton. Frising. Gest. Frid. I Imp., I. xxxv., Waitz, Script. Rer. German.

[8] Pp. 210 and 216 supra.

[9] P. 268 infra.

counsels, who spoke "altogether as a bishop should of the plundering and oppression of the Christians and of the insolence of the pagans," urging the duty of all to undertake with their own king an expedition for the succour of their brethren and, as he put it, "of the King of them all." Louis himself exhibited a burning zeal in the cause and a becoming contempt for worldly considerations, the genuineness of which impressed men ; yet, in spite of the fact that many of those present were moved to tears, the seed sown was not harvested. The greater number held back.[1] Suger in particular regarded the proposal as unwise and endeavoured to persuade Louis to abandon it.[2] However, it was resolved to hold an assembly at Vézelay in the next Passiontide, when the matter would be more fully considered. Meanwhile Louis took the precaution of submitting his project to Eugenius III. The Pope's approval was unqualified. In words, to the king's mouth "sweeter than the honey-comb," he bade all obey the royal call, granted plenary indulgence to the Crusaders, promised his fatherly care of their wives and children and prescribed various details as to the conduct of the expedition. He expressed the wish personally to initiate the holy work, but regretted that he was prevented from doing so by his despot, the Roman people ! That charge he delegated to Bernard, the holy Abbot of Clairvaux. It may be remarked in passing that Otto of Freising's account states that St. Bernard was present at the assembly at Bourges, that the question of an expedition to the East was there submitted to him and that, holding himself to be incompetent to deal with it, he counselled its reference to Eugenius III ;[3] but there is no trace of this either in Odo de Diogilo's account or anywhere in the *Vitæ* of St. Bernard. We do know, however, that Louis had more than once consulted the Abbot of Clairvaux, and that the latter had declined to discuss the matter until "at length commanded by an Encyclical Letter of the Supreme Pontiff himself to lay it before peoples and princes, acting in this as the mouthpiece of the Roman Church."[4] Eugenius would appear to have issued two bulls, one on 1st December, 1145,[5] addressed to Louis, the princes and the rest of the faithful in Gaul, the other on 1st March, 1146,[6] addressed to the faithful of Gaul, calling them all to the Crusade, which latter is probably identical with the *generalis epistola* to which Geoffrey refers in the *Vita Prima*.[7]

Remembering St. Bernard's influence over the three principal actors in the prelude thus briefly outlined—to say nothing of his relations to the Premonstratensians and to

[1] Odon. de Diog. *De Ludovic.* VII *Profect. in Orient.*, I, *P.L.* CLXXXV.1207. Cf. S. Bern., *Ep.* 247.

[2] *Vita Suger.*, R.H.G.F. XII. 108.

[3] Otton. Frising. *Gest. Frid. I Imp.*, *loc. cit.*

[4] *Vita Prima*, III. iv. 9.

[5] Jaffé, *Reg.*, 6177.

[6] *Op. cit.*, 6218.

[7] Otton. Frising. *Gest. Frid. I Imp.*, I. xxxvi., Waitz, *op. cit.* ; Odon. de Diog. *op. cit.*, *loc. cit.* Cf. Vacandard, *Vie de saint Bernard*, II., 274 sqq., *notes*, éd. 1920.

VÉZELAY

the Templars—we may not be very far wrong in concluding, not only that he was the mainspring of the movement when it had once begun, but that its initiation was really due to him. Godfrey de la Roche, whom we should not leave out of account, Eugenius III, and, now at last in some degree, Louis, were all his spiritual children, informed by his mind and instinct with his ideals. When on Palm Sunday, 31st March, 1146, the great assembly took place at Vézelay, his dominating personality was overwhelming. Louis, radiant with satisfaction that "at length had dawned for him the day for which he longed . . . received" at St. Bernard's hand "the special cross sent to him by the Supreme Pontiff. Many chief men joined with him in taking the cross. And because within the town there was no room for the vast multitude, there was set up for the Abbot of Clairvaux in a field outside the walls a wooden platform from the height of which he might address the surrounding crowd. At this work he laboured so long as he remained in the town." [1] Odo's description of the scene is circumstantial as of an eye-witness.

[1] Odon. de Diog. *op cit., loc. cit.*

Otto of Freising speaks of "Louis, King of the Franks, there taking the cross from the afore-said abbot and pledging himself to the warfare beyond the sea, together with the Counts Theodoric of Flanders and Henry, son of Theobald of Blois, and other barons and nobles of his kingdom," adding that there were present at Vézelay upon the occasion potentates and illustrious persons from various provinces of Gaul. St. Bernard would appear to have prefaced his appeal by reading out the Papal bull of the previous December.[2] The Theobald to whom Otto refers as "of Blois" is to be identified with Theobald, Count of Champagne. Amongst others who then took the cross may be mentioned the queen, Eleanor of Aquitaine, the king's brother, Robert, Count of Dreux, and his uncle Amadeus III, Count of Maurienne, William, Count of Nevers, Archibald de Bourbon and Enguerrand de Coucy; and of prelates Godfrey de la Roche and Arnolph, Bishop of Lisieux.[3] "It was resolved that the expedition should set forth at that time next year, and all returned each to his own home with joy." [4]

[2] Otton. Frising. *op. cit.,* I. xxxvi. sq.

[3] *Chron. Mauriniac., R.H.G.F.* XII. 88.

[4] Odon. de Diog. *op. cit., loc. cit.*

There now remained the important work of kindling in good time the enthusiasm of princes and of peoples, not only in France but throughout the rest of Western Christendom. Louis despatched messengers to Roger of Sicily, who sent back representative nobles of his kingdom charged in his name to promise supplies of food and of ships and of all other necessaries for the expedition, and moreover to pledge the

personal service either of himself or of his son. To the Eastern
Emperor at Jerusalem, Manuel I, Louis likewise applied, receiving in answer a prolix and adulatory letter full of promises
of support, which as might have been expected were never
fulfilled. To the rulers of Germany and Hungary he represented the need in which the expedition would stand of facil-
ities in the matter of food and of transport, and not only
received from them satisfactory replies on these points but
from not a few of them the assurance that they would themselves take the cross.[1]

[1] Odon. de Diog. op. cit., P.L. CLXXXV. 1207 sq.

But more was needed than the approval of the Pope and
the promises of princes. In such an enterprise the popular
imagination counted for more than all else ; and to the popular
imagination the appeal must necessarily be of the nature of
a divine call, and moreover sufficiently emotional in its manner.
Nor to be effective must it be less than the prophetic cry of
a single arresting personality, as it were of a messenger from
on high whose credentials were unmistakable, whose impact
upon the wills of individuals was such as to render them the
common will of all. But such a prophet needed to be a man
balanced in his judgement and in full command of his own
emotions. Otto of Freising tells us of a certain monk, Raoul
by name, a zealous religious but scantily educated, who set
forth for the Rhineland and moved many thousands of people
at Cologne, Mainz, Worms, Spires, Strassburg and other cities
of the neighbourhood to take the cross, unfortunately encouraging them to massacre the Jews, which they proceeded
to do relentlessly. St. Bernard's indignation at once moved
him to denounce Raoul, who appears to have been a Cistercian,
and his enterprise to have been sanctioned by the personal
presence of the Abbot of Lobbes in Hainault.[2] The matter
was perhaps first brought to St. Bernard's notice by a letter
addressed to him by Henry, Archbishop of Mainz, who had
punished the persecutors, his action being supported by
Arnald, Archbishop of Cologne, who had given asylum in a
fortress, which then stood on the summit of the Wolkenburg
to the East of the Drachenfels, to many of the Jewish refugees.
His reply is sufficiently incisive. He has no time to write at
length but he will say this much—warning the archbishop
that in every good cause " scandal must arise "—that, as for
the fellow who has caused this scandal, he has arrived upon
the scene " sent neither by man nor by man's agency and
certainly not by God. . . . A fellow without heart and without
intelligence ! A fellow whose stupidity is set upon a candle-
stick that all men in the house may see it "—unfortunately,

[2] Otton. Frising. op. cit., I. xxxviii. sq.

we may remark, they had not done so—" Three charges most
fittingly lie at his door. He has usurped authority to preach ;
he has treated bishops with contempt ; he has incited to murder." [1] All this happened in the autumn of 1146. It was
a bad beginning, and St. Bernard would at once repudiate
the methods of this disreputable freelance. We may add
that his remarks to the Archbishop of Mainz lead us to doubt
whether this prelate had been quite so prompt in suppressing
the persecution as he might have been.

But sooner or later the Jewish problem with its attendant
difficulties must inevitably arise. Only a richly supplied
war-chest could suffice for the needs of an expedition to the
East on such a scale as was contemplated. Well aware of
this Louis took early steps to levy a war-tax upon his vassals,
upon the bishops and upon the religious houses. The ten-
tacles of this exaction reached the least considerable member
of the feudality and the poorest priory of every Order. [2] How
were the royal demands to be met ? We may well believe
that in many cases it was possible only by means of recourse
to the Jews. Even a great ecclesiastical magnate like the
Bishop of Langres found it necessary—though doubtless with
modified regret, seeing that he happened to be Godfrey de
la Roche—to pawn the treasures of his church. [3] The services
of the money-lender were thus indispensable. It is the story,
alas, of every great war. This difficulty was inevitable.
Christendom was increasingly, and to an alarming extent, in
the hands of the Jews. But what of another difficulty ?
Louis had not levied the war-tax at all upon these, the
richest subjects of his realm. Whether he regarded it as
ungenerous to compel them to contribute to a cause of which
their consciences disapproved, or whether he was sufficiently
astute as to avoid giving them any excuse for demanding
exorbitant rates of interest on their loans it is impossible
to say. In any case their exemption caused great offence.
" Why," in effect asked Peter the Venerable of the king,
" should not the Jews contribute more than anyone else
to the expenses of the holy war ? Robbers as they are,
this is the very occasion for compelling them to disgorge !
Sacrilegious blasphemers, this is the way in which to punish
their impiety ! " [4] The tone of this letter is not quite worthy
of the great Cluniac ; we may surmise that he was perhaps
still smarting under the memory of extortions arising out of
the grave financial straits in which he had found his abbey
on succeeding Hugh II as ninth abbot in 1122. [5] There is
no evidence to show that Louis yielded to the pressure, but

[1] *Ep.* 365. Cf.
Ep. 363 and pp.
259 sq. *supra.*

[2] Radulph. de
Diceto *Abbrev.
Chron.,
R.H.G.F.* XIII.
183 ; *Gall.
Christ.,* II,
Instr., 231 ;
*Inter. S. Bern.
Epp.* 484.
[3] *R.H.G.F.* XIV.
324.

[4] Petr. Vener.
Epp. Lib., IV.
xxxvi, *P.L.*
CLXXXIX.
369 sqq.
[5] Petr. Vener.
*Dispos. Rei
Famil., P.L.*
CLXXXIX.
1052 sqq.

[1] Jaffé, *Regest.*, 14345.

rather the contrary ; [1] it was a moment at which he was at his best both as a moralist and as a statesman.

To recur to St. Bernard's doings immediately subsequent to the great decision made at Vézelay. Odo de Diogilo speaks of him as, " his frail and scarcely living body hiding his vigorous spirit," passing swiftly throughout the land and quickly recruiting many for the service of the cross.[2] To Eugenius St. Bernard writes with commendable humility, ascribing his success entirely to the Apostolic mandate : " Cities and towns are empty. Scarcely is it possible now to find one man among seven women ; to such an extent everywhere are there widows whose husbands are still alive." [3] This passage is the concluding paragraph of a letter in which he had remonstrated with the Pope for suspending the use of the *pallium* by Samson, Archbishop of Rheims, on the ground that he had exceeded his rights by crowning Louis at Bourges on the previous Christmas Day. This action on the part of Eugenius reflected upon the king himself ; some heart-burning resulted and for a moment the cause of the Crusade was imperilled.[4] " It was certainly not a help that the Archbishop of Bourges "—the diocesan, and therefore affronted by the course taken by the Archbishop of Rheims— " should be the means of detracting from the honour of the king," writes St. Bernard.[5] Louis was evidently sensitive upon the point ; but we may assume that the Pope yielded to the persuasion of the Abbot of Clairvaux, for the incident was closed without further trouble.[6]

[2] Odon. de Diog. *op. cit.*, *P.L.* CLXXXV. 1207.

[3] *Ep.* 247.

[4] *Gall. Christ.*, IX. 86. Cf. p. 263 *supra*.

[5] *Ep.* 247.

[6] Jaffé, *Regest.*, 8896.

Time being limited and it being clear to him that his personal presence was demanded rather in Flanders, Belgium, North-Eastern France and the Rhineland than elsewhere, St. Bernard was compelled to deal with the Southern, Eastern and Western regions of Gaul by means of letters addressed to princes or to clergy or to people or, quite generally, to all three classes combined. We may mention a letter written to the Count and Barons of Brittany by his secretary Nicholas of Montier-Ramey,[7] which may probably be recognized as the draft of an encyclical letter written by himself, variously addressed in various MSS., in some to the Clergy and People of Eastern France, or to the Bishop, Clergy and People of Spires, or of Cologne, in others to the English People, in others again to Manfred, Bishop of Brescia.[8] We may perhaps assume that this encyclical letter was written after the visit of the monk Raoul to the Rhineland, for it strongly discourages anything like persecution of the Jews. There is little doubt but that it was the archetype of the written appeals to

[7] *Inter. S. Bern. Epp.* 467, *P.L.* (*Ed. Ben. Ep.* 426).

[8] *Ep.* 363 and Mabill. *Not. ad loc.*

which Otto of Freising refers as despatched by St. Bernard at this time, in which, eloquent as they were of his enthusiasm in the Crusading cause, the Abbot of Clairvaux was careful to found his denunciation of persecutors upon the authority of the Sacred Scriptures.[1]

St. Bernard's steps were first directed towards Flanders, the fatherland of Godfrey de Bouillon, accompanied by Baldwin of Châtillon, a Fleming whose family had won distinction in the First Crusade, by Geoffrey, his biographer, and by one of his own monks who bore the beloved name of his deceased brother Gerard. It is the autumn of 1146 and we find him present at a council of the Province of Rheims held at Arras, where he would have met his friend Alvisus, the diocesan bishop, formerly Abbot of Anchin.[2] Dom Pitra, to whose treatise on St. Bernard's journey in Flanders we are much indebted, suggests that he would not have failed to visit Boulogne, the great Abbey of Anchin, his own Cistercian foundations of Vaucelles, Les-Dunes and Clairmarais, as well as other places with which he had intimate relations and where his influence would be felt. There is evidence of his presence at the Abbey of St. Bertin[3] at St. Omer and at Ypres, at which latter place he met Theodoric of Alsace, Count of Flanders, who had taken the cross at Vézelay.[4] We can trace him at Bruges,[5] at Afflighem in Brabant, at Gembloux in Namur,[6] and on 18th October at Villers, his own daughter-house in that diocese,[7] whence he would seem to have passed to Liège and thence to Worms and to Mainz. Dom Pitra's *Documents sur un Voyage de S. Bernard en Flandres* is, allowing for minor inaccuracies, a valuable source of information as to the Abbot of Clairvaux's doings previous to the date at which the record of the *Liber Miraculorum* begins. It was first published in 1848 in the *Revue Catholique* of the University of Louvain (III., pp. 400 and 457) and was reprinted by Migne (*Patr. Lat.* CLXXXV. 1797 sqq.) in 1879.

The *Liber Miraculorum* is a work of great interest, to which further reference will be found in the Appendix.[8] Suffice it to say here that it is of the nature of a diary, consisting of the records made at the time by St. Bernard's fellow-travellers so far as its first two parts are concerned ; and that so far as its third and last part is concerned it is the report of Geoffrey, St. Bernard's biographer, an eye-witness throughout. To describe the first two parts as a diary is not to imply that there is an entry for every day, but rather that there is a continuous itinerary, supplied at intervals with dates. From Frankfort to Constance and from Constance to Spires the contributors

[1] Otton. Frising. *op. cit.,* I. xxxix.

[2] *Charta ex Archiv. Insulens.* (Lille), *P.L.* CLXXXV. 1823 sq.

[3] *Charta ex Chron. S. Bertin., op. cit.,* 1825.

[4] *Charta e Registr. S. Martin. Yprens., op. cit.,* 1826.

[5] *E Cartular. Abbat. de Eechout, op. cit.,* 1825 sq.

[6] *Ex Chron. Villar.,* Marten. et Durand. *Thes. Nov. Anecd.,* III. 1269.

[7] *Ex Martyr. Villar.* XV *Kal. Nov., op. cit.,* 1827.

[8] Appendix, II and III.

are Hermann, Bishop of Constance, and his chaplain Everard, Frewin, Abbot of Salmansweiler, and Baldwin, Abbot of Châtillon, Philip, Archdeacon of Liège, Alexander, Canon of Cologne, two unidentified ecclesiastics by name Otto and Frank and two Clairvaux monks, the above-mentioned Gerard and Geoffrey. From the second part, which records the journey from Spires to Liège, the names of Hermann, Frewin and Baldwin are absent ; an Everard contributes—probably not the chaplain, who had presumably accompanied his bishop when the latter and the two abbots parted from St. Bernard at Spires. Besides this Everard three other new figures appear upon the scene ; Dietrich, Abbot of Vieux-Camp, Irwin, Provost of Steinfeld [1] and a priest of the diocese of Constance by name Volkmar. Neither Alexander nor Otto nor Frank take any further part ; although, if we are to accept Vacandard's opinion,[2] they accompanied St. Bernard to Liège. The form of dialogue, according to which each speaker, as it were his note-book (*schedula*) in hand,[3] presents his matter, is a little quaint ; but we feel that step by step throughout freshly made impressions are being recorded. As we might expect from the title of the *Liber* considerable prominence is given to the miracles wrought by St. Bernard, valuable means as they doubtless were for enforcing his appeal ; the work has not failed, however, to gain an acknowledged place as Book VI of the *Vita Prima*.

We have seen that on 18th October, St. Bernard was at Villers.[4] Thence he reached Mainz by way of Liège and Worms. The *Liber* tells us that " on the First Sunday of Advent we crossed the border of the diocese of Constance " ;[5] this was on 1st December, about six weeks after the departure from Villers. At Liège Philip the archdeacon would presumably have joined himself to them. They were apparently at Worms during the early days of November, as we gather from Volkmar speaking at the beginning of the following January.[6] It was here that for the first time St. Bernard had an opportunity of dealing personally with the scandal caused by the monk Raoul. One valuable corrective of the evils occasioned by this dangerous fanatic [7]—which could not have failed to prejudice the cause of the Crusade—was to enlist the support and the direction of the supreme civil authority. Circumstances, alas, were not very favourable. Conrad III, the first Hohenstaufen Emperor, was involved in conflict with the Guelphs ; the disturbed state of the city of Rome—which, as we have seen, hampered Eugenius III [8]—and the growing ambition of Roger of Sicily made matters no easier

[1] Cf. p. 331 *infra*

[2] Vacandard, *Vie de saint Bernard*, I. xxviii, *éd.* 1920.

[3] *Vita Prima*, VI. v. 19.

[4] P. 269 *supra*.

[5] *Vita Prima*, VI. i. 1 sq.

[6] *Op. cit.*, VI. vii. 23.

[7] Otton. Frising. *Gesta Frid. I Imp.*, I. xl.

[8] P. 264 *supra*.

for him. Conditions such as these had their bearing upon the failure of the Crusade. The imperial position was not strong and St. Bernard's hopes, both that Conrad would exercise his authority in suppressing a disorderly fanaticism and that the appeal of a Holy War would consolidate the Empire, seemed likely to be disappointed. In the letter from which we have already quoted [1] addressed to the Bishop, Clergy and People of Spires amongst others he not only, as we have seen, denounces persecution of the Jews but he appeals to his readers to lay aside internecine strife. "Let that ancient—I do not call it warfare (*militia*), but malice (*malitia*), cease; a thing which has accustomed you to overthrow one another, to kill one another so that you are being utterly consumed one of another. What is this so terrible lust of destruction which excites you to transfix your neighbour's body with the sword, and at the same time perchance to destroy his soul?" [2] As he plainly saw this state of things was breaking up the Empire; but his warning, like that of many another prophet, fell upon the too heedless ears of princes. The people for their part yielded to his appeal, rather as its religious aspect touched their imagination than as its political aspect enlightened their mind. It was probably his consciousness of this that moved him to speak of the danger of forestalling the action of authority by taking up arms and advancing to the fray undisciplined and unled. Evidently it had been asserted that St. Bernard had usurped the function of a *generalissimo*. "If any man says that he has been commissioned by me it is untrue, even if he shows a letter of mine to that effect; you must reply that the letter is forged or falsified. It is necessary that real soldiers, men trained in the art of warfare, be chosen as commanders; that the army of the Lord take the field at one concerted time, acting as a united force, in order to be strong at all points and ready to resist attack from any quarter." [3] He would have them distrust the pushing fellow who loves to be authoritative. As for himself, let them remember the story of the First Crusade. St. Bernard has not forgotten it. He is no Peter the Hermit come to life again!

On his arrival at Mainz, probably about the second week in November, the Abbot of Clairvaux found that there was less need to kindle zeal than there was to correct the aberrations due to the fanaticism of the monk Raoul, whom however he persuaded to return to his monastery.[4] Indeed so hotheaded was the populace that his strictures upon the treatment meted out to the Jews, gratefully acknowledged as they were by the rabbis, provoked at first strong resentment

[1] P. 268 *supra*.

[2] *Ep.* 363.

[3] *Ep.* 363.

[4] Otton. Frising. *Gest. Frid. I Imp.*, I. xl.

¹ *Annal. Rodens.*
(Klosterrath),
M.G.H. XVI.
718.

which it needed all his skilful persuasion to appease.[1] Resolved to seek a personal interview with Conrad, St. Bernard
pressed on to Frankfort. He was, we gather, depressed in
spirit; for when Hermann, Bishop of Constance, who met him
there begged him to visit his diocese he raised as an objection
the amount of work which he had in hand, adding that he was
made sad and anxious by his long absence of nearly a year

² *Vita Prima,*
VI. i. I.

from Clairvaux, whither he was returning so soon as possible.[2]
The interview with the Emperor failed to relieve his mind.
Conrad would appear to have repelled his persuasion by the
blunt statement that " he had no intention of taking part
in the expedition "; upon which St. Bernard contented himself with the meek reply " that it was not for him further to

³ *Op. cit.,* VI. iv.
15.

importune his royal majesty." [3] Conrad perhaps felt himself
to be rebuked; for. when presently Hermann and others
renewed their request to St. Bernard to go to Constance, the
Emperor added his own; and the holy man, moved by the
fear of the Lord and by the sense that a great door was
open to him, acceded; and so " on the First Sunday of Advent

⁴ *Op. cit.,* VI. i. I.

we crossed the border of the diocese of Constance." [4] Thus
in spite of bitter disappointment St. Bernard had recovered
his spirits; his temperament was, we feel, prevailingly opti-
mistic; and his faith furnished him, even when things seemed
to be at their worst, with an amazing power of self-recovery.

At Kenzingen, then, in the diocese of Constance near Frei-
burg-im-Breisgau, they arrived on 1st December and " were

⁵ *Op. cit., loc.
cit.*

received with the greatest popular devotion," [5] passing on to
Freiburg on Tuesday, 3rd December. Here, seeing that the
rich as compared with the poor failed to respond to his appeal,
St. Bernard ordered that prayers should be offered for them
that their hearts might be touched, with the result that some

⁶ *Op. cit.,* VI. ii.
2 sq.

of the wealthiest and the worst of them took the cross.[6] Thence
their way lay through Krotzingen, Heitersheim and Stieng
to Basel, which they reached on the following Friday, St.
Bernard's credentials being attested at every stage by wonders

⁷ *Op. cit.,* VI. ii.
3 sqq.

of healing.[7] They would seem to have left Basel the next
day and, after a journey of about twenty-five miles which took
them through Rheinfelden, to have spent Sunday, 8th December,
at Schaffhausen. Everard from time to time refers to " the
soldiers of my lord," implying that the Bishop of Constance
was attended by his military escort. The excitement at Schaffhausen on Tuesday, 10th December, was such that St. Bernard
was obliged to remain in hiding, and it was not until the next

⁸ *Op. cit.,* VI. ii.
5 sqq.

day that he was able to show himself to the admiring crowds.[8]
On Thursday, 12th December, they entered the city of Constance,

where, Frewin tells us, " owing to the confusion few could see what happened." "None of us," adds Geoffrey, "dared to mingle with the crowd." However they were able to record their eye-witness of various miraculous cures, somewhat tumultuously acclaimed by much singing in the cathedral and by the clanging of bells.[1]

On Saturday, 14th December, the episcopal chapel was the scene of several cures, and not improbably on the same day St. Bernard left Constance for Winterthur, thence travelling back to Germany through Zürich, Rheinfelden and Basel. The Fourth Sunday of Advent, 22nd December, he spent at Strassburg.[2] On the following Tuesday, the Vigil of Christmas, he was at Spires, having made the journey by boat on the Rhine.[3] The *Liber* tells us little of the influence which he exercised otherwise than by means of his miracles of healing, but Geoffrey elsewhere emphasizes the perhaps no less miraculous effect of his words ;[4] and yet, be it remembered, they were spoken to hearers for the most part ignorant both of the Romance tongue and of the Latin familiar to the *literati ;* it would have been impossible for him to dispense with the services of an interpreter,[5] though it would have been unlike him not at times to have enforced his message by the use of what little German he knew. But in truth his success was the measure of what he was ; his eloquence was of the highest order, the eloquence of the heart. *Thy lips are like a thread of scarlet and thy mouth is comely.*[6] To behold him was enough.

St. Bernard found Conrad at Spires where a Diet of the Empire had been convoked for Christmas. The story recorded by Manriquez and repeated by Pien of his having concluded the *Salve, Regina* with the words *O clemens, o pia, o dulcis Virgo Maria,* prostrating himself three times before the image of our Lady in the cathedral, and of his having been saluted in response with the words *Salve, Bernarde,* may perhaps be regarded as apocryphal, for it is nowhere mentioned in the *Liber* or by any of the writers of the *Vitae.*[7] The triumph however which awaited him was substantial, if not immediate. His public preaching of the Crusade before the Emperor and the princes took little effect, in spite of what they would have learned of the enthusiastic popular response evoked on his recent journey. But on Friday, 27th December, he again sought an interview with Conrad, " approaching him with his wonted gentleness of manner "—" from whom he at length obtained this answer, that he would consider the matter and consult his advisers, and on the following day give his

[1] *Op. cit.,* VI. iii. 10.

[2] *Op. cit.,* VI. iii. 11 sqq.

[3] *Op. cit.,* VI. iv. 15.

[4] *Vita Prima,* III. iii. 7.

[5] Cæsar. Heist. *Dial. Mirac.,* I. xvi ; Manric. *Annal. Cisterc.,* II. *an.* 1146, ix. 5.

[6] *Song of Songs,* IV. 3.

[7] Manric. *Annal. Cisterc.,* II. *an.* 1146, x. ; *Acta Bolland.,* Aug. IV. die 20, *P.L.* CLXXXV. 874 sqq.

final decision. Then at Mass the Divine Spirit began to stir the spirit of the blessed father to speak, contrary to his custom when uninvited, for that the day ought not to pass without a sermon. What more? He spoke, and at the end of his sermon he addressed the Emperor not as a crowned head but quite freely as a man. He represented to him the future judgement and himself at the bar of Christ his King, who asks him : ' O man, what have I not done for thee that I ought to have done? ' " Reviewing the wealth and the dignity bestowed upon Conrad, St. Bernard moved him to exclaim with tears : " I do indeed acknowledge the benefactions of his divine grace ; henceforth with his aid I will not be found ungrateful ; seeing that you call upon me I am ready to serve him." Amid the acclamations which on all sides greeted the imperial words Conrad, his nephew Frederick Barbarossa and innumerable princes took the cross at St. Bernard's hand.[1] On the following day at an assembly called by the Emperor the Abbot of Clairvaux exhorted not only those who had pledged themselves to the Holy War, but all the inhabitants of the city. As he was leaving the place of meeting, hedged about by Conrad and the princes in order to protect him from the pressure of the crowd, he healed a lame boy who was brought to him. " This," he said, turning to Conrad, " is for your sake, that so you may know that God is truly with you and that he has accepted the work which you have begun." [2] One interesting piece of information we owe to Otto of Freising who himself, he tells us, took the cross the following February, probably at Ratisbon, together with others in response to an appeal made by Adam, first Abbot of Ebrach— interesting because it reveals the fact that St. Bernard's hope of a united Germany was at any rate at this early stage in some small degree realized. Welf, the Guelph leader, had even anticipated Conrad by enrolling himself among the Crusaders on Christmas Day, his example being shortly after- wards followed by Ladislas, King of Bohemia, by Odoacer, Marquess of Styria, and by Bernard, Count of Carinthia.[3]

On Friday, 3rd January, the little company, now as we have seen somewhat differently constituted, in particular lacking the Bishop of Constance and his escort,[4] left Spires ; [5] but not before a report based upon their *schedulae* had been despatched to Clairvaux addressed to the monk Henry, brother of Louis le Jeune, which report formed afterwards substan- tially the First Part of the *Liber Miraculorum.*[6] It was doubt- less intended to tell its story to the King of France. It is possible, though perhaps it would be tedious to the reader,

[1] *Vita Prima,* VI. iv. 15.

[2] *Op. cit.,* VI. v. 17.

[3] Otton. Frising. *Gesta Frid. I Imp.,* I. xlii.

[4] P. 270 *supra.*
[5] *Vita Prima,* VI. vii. 23.

[6] *Op.cit.,* VI. v. 20, vi. 22.

to trace St. Bernard's steps through Worms, Kreuznach, where he kept the Feast of the Epiphany, Pichenbach, a little village near Boppard, Coblenz and Remagen to Cologne, which he reached on Thursday, 9th January.[1]   Here on Saturday the throng was so great and the events so crowded that, as Geoffrey confesses, they were unable to make adequate notes.   St. Bernard decided not to show himself to the people on that day, but took the opportunity of addressing himself to the clergy, rebuking them with some effect for their un-Scriptural manner of life.[2]   When he did show himself in public, the cures which he wrought were so numerous and so arresting that the streets of the city continually re-echoed with wild cries caught by the attentive ear of Gerard and duly recorded : " Christ, uns gnade !   Kyrie, eleison !   Die Heiligen alle helffen uns ! " [3]

It was probably on Monday, 13th January, that, escorted awhile by the crowd, they left Cologne for the Benedictine Abbey of Brauweiler, a few miles distant on the road to Aix-la-Chapelle, where they spent the night ; going on the next day so far as to Jülich they would have arrived at Aix-la-Chapelle on Wednesday, 15th January.[4]   Thence they passed on to Maëstricht and presumably on Saturday, 18th January, reached Liège, where on Sunday St. Bernard spoke to an assembly of the clergy convoked—perhaps at the instigation of the archdeacon Philip—in the bishop's palace.[5]   At Liège another document was prepared and thence despatched to the clergy of Cologne, probably by the hands of Alexander, Canon of Cologne, reporting all that had happened since they left Spires on 3rd January.   This document forms substantially the Second Part of the *Liber*.[6]   There is MS. evidence for the belief that both the report sent to Henry, brother of Louis le Jeune, and that sent to the clergy of Cologne were prefaced, each by a covering letter for which the two Clairvaux monks Gerard and Geoffrey were in the main responsible.[7]

In spite of his longing to be at home again at Clairvaux St. Bernard's journey thither from Liège was by no means direct.   It is at this stage that Geoffrey, his biographer, makes himself alone responsible for the narrative.   At Liège appeared upon the scene another Philip, evidently a monk of Clairvaux— for Geoffrey refers to him as " our Philip " in distinction from the archdeacon—and probably a Liégois,[8] who may have been the Philip who later made the three documents into one *Liber* of Three Parts.[9]   Quite possibly there was some anxiety at Clairvaux concerning St. Bernard's frail health and Philip was sent to meet him at Liège, being chosen for that purpose as a native of the place.   The Sunday spent there was that

[1] *Op. cit.*, VI. vii. *passim*.

[2] *Op. cit.*, VI. vii. 25.

[3] *Op. cit.*, VI. viii. 28.

[4] *Op. cit.*, VI. ix. 30 sq.

[5] *Op. cit.*, VI. ix. 33.

[6] *Ep. Gaufr., op. cit.*, VI. x. 34.

[7] Waitz, *M.G.H.* XXVI. 122 sqq.

[8] *Op. cit.*, VI. xi. 35.

[9] Phil. de Clarevall. *Praefat.*, *P.L.*CLXXXV. 371 sq.

[1] *Vita Prima,* VI. xi. 35.

following the Octave of the Epiphany.[1] On Wednesday, 22nd January, the travellers left Huy on the Meuse. Nothing is said of their visit, although quite near to Huy was the Abbey of Neufmoûtier, founded by Peter the Hermit and where then his body lay. There is evidence in the language used at this stage, "we hastened," "he was hastening," that St. Bernard felt pressed ; moreover it is possible that, considering all things, he did not wish further to revive the memory of Peter and the First Crusade lest it should excite extrava-

[2] *Op. cit.,* VI. xi. 36 sq.

gantly the popular imagination.[2] On the same day, 22nd January, they reached the Abbey of Gembloux about twelve miles N.W. of Namur ; and on the following day St. Bernard

Canivez, *L'Ordre de Cîteaux en Belgique,* 86. Cf. p. 269 *supra.*
[4] *Op. cit., loc. cit.*

found himself again at Villers,[3] where he "visited his new plantation and comforted his pilgrim sons."[4] Their movements were rapid ; for they left Fontaine-l'Évêque on Friday, 24th January, and by way of Binche arrived at Mons the same day. We note that at Fontaine-l'Évêque Philip was among some of his own people, and also that at Mons he had friends in the place ; he would therefore have been of service to the

[5] *Op. cit.,* VI. xi. 37.

travellers.[5] At Mons they found the diocesan Nicholas, Bishop of Cambrai, with some of his clergy, and also many religious collected from all quarters, awaiting them with a welcome. On Saturday they were at Valenciennes, whence on Sunday,

[6] *Op. cit.,* VI. xi. 38.

26th January, they pushed on to Cambrai.[6] Here the crowd was so great that day that at one moment they had difficulty in preventing St. Bernard from being crushed, and in getting

[7] *Op. cit.,* VI. xii. 39.

him safely sheltered in the house of the canons regular.[7] His frail physique was no subject to be hustled, however amiably ! And he was in the fifty-seventh year of a very hard life. The following Tuesday night was passed at Vaucelles, a daughter-

[8] P. 46 *supra.*

house, we remember, of Clairvaux,[8] the delay there being explained by St. Bernard's "unwillingness to deprive his

[9] *Op. cit.* VI. xii 41.

sons of his paternal visitation and comfort."[9]

Their movement continued to be rapid. Leaving Vaucelles the next morning and bearing to the S.E., they probably halted for the night at Gomme and reached the Abbey of Hombleux on Thursday. On Friday, 31st January, they were

[10] *Op. cit., loc. cit.*
[11] Beaunier, *Recueil des Abbayes de France,* II. 599 ; *Gall. Christ.,* IX. 587. Cf. pp. 196 sq. *supra.*
[12] *Vita Prima,* VI. xii. 41.

at the Abbey of St. Jean-de-Laon.[10] What memories would its cloister have had for St. Bernard![11] Did Bartholomew de Vir greet him there ? Had he done so, Geoffrey, surely, would have told us. On Saturday they passed through Rheims on their way to Châlons-sur-Marne, which they reached the same day, 1st February.[12] Here were assembled Louis le Jeune, ambassadors both from Conrad and from Welf the Guelph leader, together with a considerable number of French and

German princes ; and here on Sunday they kept the Feast of the Purification. The express purpose of their assembly was to confer with St. Bernard concerning the expedition to Jerusalem. The conference lasted two days, during which the Abbot of Clairvaux steadfastly refused to yield to importunate requests to go forth to the people, placing the public good before the claims of individuals. The deliberations concluded, St. Bernard left Châlons-sur-Marne—where, we learn, he had met Godfrey de la Roche amongst other friends— probably late in the day on Tuesday, 4th February, and reached Donnemont, about twenty miles North-East of Troyes, the same evening. On Wednesday he travelled by way of Rosnay [1] and Brienne-le-Château to Bar-sur-Aube. The next day, after saying Mass in the Church of St. Nicholas, he ended his long wanderings by arriving home at Clairvaux, a short ten miles distant.[2] It was Thursday, 6th February.

There was not only the joy of being once again among his own sons, but that of bringing with him, " like the patriarch Jacob returning with two bands," no less than thirty postulants for the noviciate and the good news of nearly as many more to come later.[3] His time of refreshment was not, however, of very long duration, " a few days," [4] and that only secured by orders which he gave that sick persons should not be admitted to the monastery, thinking indeed rather of thus assuring the quiet of the brethren than his own. Evidently his reputation as a healer, which every step in his journey had enhanced, had gone before him to Clairvaux.

The assembly held at Châlons-sur-Marne at the beginning of the month was preliminary to another to be held on the Sunday in Septuagesima, 16th February, at Étampes.[5] Thither St. Bernard soon after he returned home set out, by way of Mondeville—a village which existed in those days near the site of Champignol-lès-Mondeville [6]—and Ville-sur-Arce, where he passed the night. Thence through Bourguignons, Fouchères and Vaudes he reached Troyes, probably on Wednesday, 12th February. Here he preached in the cathedral before a vast multitude, from whose thronging he was compelled to take shelter in the bishop's palace, where he performed many acts of healing. Later he renewed these works of mercy in the cathedral near the entrance to the chancel, in the presence of the Bishop, Henry, and of Godfrey de la Roche, Bishop of Langres, who seems frequently to have been with him at this time.[7] On Thursday, 13th February, passing through Prunay-Belleville he arrived at Trainel, and the next day by way of Bray at Montereau-faut-Yonne,

[1] Cf. op. cit., IV. vii. 41.

[2] Op. cit., VI. xiii. 42 sqq.

[3] Op. cit., VI. xiii. 44.
[4] Op. cit., VI. xiv. 45.

[5] Odon. de Diog. De Ludovic. VII Profect. in Orient., I, P.L. CLXXXV. 1208.
[6] Morel-Payen, Troyes et l'Aube, 257.

[7] Vita Prima, VI. xiv. 45 sqq.

where he found Theobald of Champagne and many others. Thence on Saturday, 15th February, crossing the river Loing at Moret-sur-Loing, he reached Étampes.[1]

[1] Op. cit., VI. xiv. 48 sq. Cf. op. cit., IV. vii. 42.

The assembly had been convoked by the King of France, who appears to have been desirous, " as was his wont," we are told, " that they who shared in the work should share also in the plans." It was generally expected that the presence of St. Bernard at the council would contribute to the unanimity of all. He had but recently returned from Germany where he had achieved remarkable results in this direction. The first day was spent in reading the letters sent, and in hearing the messengers who had come, from all quarters. On the following day, when the opinions expressed were under discussion, it was said by some who knew them that the Greeks were not to be trusted. Alas, the courage and the enthusiasm of Louis and his counsellors led them to disregard this warning, and to favour the project of marching the forces of the Crusaders overland through Greece, in spite of the fact that Roger of Sicily promised not only supplies but also ships for transport by sea. Probably this preliminary question of the route to be taken had been already discussed at Châlons-sur-Marne, and Louis and Conrad had there come to an understanding in favour of their combined forces taking the continental route through Greece. Roger may have been in some degree motived by ambition and by jealousy of the Germans and Greeks, but events proved that his judgement was sound ; as for the Greeks, he knew them better than did most people and was well acquainted with the fact that they did not want to strengthen Latin influence in the East, and that therefore their heart was not in the Crusade.[2] The rejection of their advice would appear to have given some umbrage to the Sicilians, for Odo tells us that " they left the assembly in annoyance." On the following day, Tuesday, 18th February, arose the serious question, concerning in the main France, as to what provision was to be made for the government of the kingdom during the absence of Louis. Its discussion was prefaced by the solemn invocation of the Holy Ghost— " Would," remarks Odo, " that the like had been done on the preceding day ! "—and by some words of spiritual exhortation from St. Bernard. The king wished to leave the matter to the judgement of the prelates and the princes, and would seem to have taken counsel apart with them. On their return to the assembly St. Bernard, with the words : " Lo, here are two swords ! It is enough," pointed to Suger and to William III, Count of Nevers. The proposal was acclaimed by all present,

[2] Odon. de Diog. op. cit., P.L. CLXXXV. 1208.

with the exception of the two nominees. The count pleaded his vow to become a Carthusian, a vow not long afterwards fulfilled. Suger, at first resisting with becoming modesty, partly overcome by the prayers of the king, bishops and nobles, but chiefly in obedience to orders later given by the Pope, subsequently consented to undertake sole charge of the vice-gerency. Before the assembly dispersed it was decided that the combined forces of the Crusaders should set forth at the following Pentecost from the city of Metz,[1] an intention which was never precisely fulfilled. It will be remembered that the date had been fixed for Easter by the French assembled at Vézelay ;[2] the agreed postponement to the later date of Pentecost made at Étampes was a concession to the Germans.[3]

Soon afterwards St. Bernard left Étampes and took his journey by way of Maisse, Milly and Moret-sur-Loing to Sens, where, conjecturally on Sunday, 23rd February, in the presence of the clergy collected together to greet him, he wrought several works of healing. Thence through Joigny he continued on his way to Auxerre. There, Geoffrey tells us, after as his first course paying a visit of devotion to the shrine of St. German he passed the night at the bishop's palace. It was probably on the morning of Tuesday, 25th February, that he left Auxerre by way of Chablis for Tonnerre, where he said Mass the following day ; and crossing the Armançon reached Molesme the same evening.[4] Here we pause for a moment to think of him, the prophet of his century, indefatigably making his way accompanied by a few monks, sometimes perhaps only by Geoffrey, along roads familiar to the traveller of to-day who loves him sufficiently to trace his footsteps, every morning saying his Mass and everywhere dispensing his gifts of healing and of encouragement. Eliminate the miraculous if we will, and we leave everything in the picture ; " his greatest miracle was himself." On Thursday, 27th February, St. Bernard was once again at Clairvaux, a long day's journey through the forests.[5]

But the situation was not yet entirely satisfactory in Germany. East of the Saxons and the Moravians and stretching up beyond the Elbe to the borders of the Danes were Slavonic tribes who caused anxiety, " neighbouring peoples given over to the uncleanness of idolatry."[6] Were the whole of the armed forces of Christian Europe on their way over land to Greece, these tribes might take them in flank ; and once that they had crossed the Hellespont, might seize the opportunity for an invasion of the West. There was doubtless good ground for this anxiety, for men know their

[1] *Op. cit.*, 1208 sq.; *Vita Suger.*, R.H.G.F. XII. 108.
[2] P. 265 *supra.*
[3] S. Bern. *Ep.* 458.

[4] *Vita Prima*, VI. xiv. 50, xv. 51 sq. Cf. IV. vii. 42 sq.

[5] *Op. cit.*, VI. xv. 53.

[6] Otton. Frising. *Gesta Frid. I Imp.*, I. xlii., ed. Waitz.

neighbours better than do other people. Might it not be well that the Saxons, the Moravians and the Danes should, as their share in the Crusade, guard these Eastern and North-Eastern frontiers? These were considerations to which Conrad was not indifferent, and to deal with them he summoned a Diet of the Empire to meet at Frankfort. It opened on 13th March.[1] Geoffrey provides no record of St. Bernard's journey thither but, referring to him as at Trèves on 27th March,[2] gives some details both in the *Liber* and in the Fourth Book of the *Vita Prima* of his return-journey to Clairvaux by way of Rethel, an abbey in the neighbourhood of Thionville, Metz and Toul.[3] St. Bernard's attitude towards the pagan neighbours who threatened the Eastern and North-Eastern borders of the Empire was sufficiently severe. There were to his mind but two alternatives, their conversion or their extermination. In view of their reputed implacability and of their menace both to the flank of the advancing army of Crusaders and to the vulnerable state of Western Europe which the expedition to Jerusalem must inevitably produce, the latter alternative alone would seem to be open. Anything like a compact with such enemies would prove no better than a snare. The diet was of this mind, and its decision was embodied in a letter addressed by St. Bernard to the people of Moravia in the name of the Emperor, the prelates and the princes.[4] Further, in the Pope's name the Saxons, Moravians and Danes were accorded by him the status of Crusaders; their distinctive responsibility being denoted by a special badge in the form of a cross surmounting an orb, thus : $\stackrel{+}{\mathrm{O}}$.[5] It was arranged that their forces should assemble at Magdeburg on the following Feast of the Apostles, 29th June. We may remark that the greater number of wonderful works recorded by Geoffrey in the Fourth Book of the *Vita Prima* were wrought during the travels, the story of which has been briefly told. If we remember this, we shall be in a position to estimate the driving force of St. Bernard's appeal in support of the Crusade by the outbursts of popular enthusiasm which everywhere greeted him, and nowhere more irrepressibly, one might almost say, more frantically, than in the Rhineland. As an instance we may cite the occasion upon which at Frankfort—probably during this very diet— Conrad, a tall and stalwart figure, was compelled to take him up in his arms like a child and carry him to a place of safety.[6]

Meanwhile Eugenius who, although at the time gravely preoccupied owing to the difficulties occasioned by the disaffection of the Roman populace, had about the midsummer

[1] Vacandard, *Vie de saint Bernard*, II. 305, *n.* 1, *éd.* 1920.
[2] *Vita Prima*, VI. xvi. 54.
[3] *Op. cit.*, IV. viii. 47 sqq., VI. xvi. 55 sqq., xvii. 58 sq.

[4] S. Bern. *Ep.* 457.

[5] Otton. Frising. *Gesta Frid. I Imp.*, I. xlii., *ed.* Waitz.

[6] *Vita Prima*, IV. v. 31.

of 1146 supported the King of France by writing to Manuel, the Eastern Emperor,[1] now—in spite of the fact that, perhaps displeased by Conrad's indifference to the revolt of the Pope's temporal subjects at Rome, he had called him to account for enlisting in the Crusade without reference to himself as Supreme Pontiff [2]—decided to cross the Alps and countenance the expedition by an interview with Louis le Jeune. This took place at Dijon.[3] Subsequently the Pope paid a visit to Clairvaux, where under the influence of St. Bernard on 10th April he issued a bull, confirming the steps recently taken at the Diet of Frankfort.[4]

The preparations were nearing accomplishment. Without attempting to estimate the numbers of the combined armies of Louis and Conrad, we may note that the forces of Saxons, Moravians and Northerners which took the field against the pagan Slavs amounted to about 100,000 men ; [5] that some 13,000 English, Flemings and other sea-faring folk embarked at Dartmouth with the idea of effecting a landing either in North Africa or in Palestine ; [6] that Alphonso I of the House of Burgundy was collecting an army to wrest Lisbon from the Moors,[7] a result actually achieved mainly by the aid of the expedition from Dartmouth ; [8] that the Piedmontese princes were ready to take service under the King of France ; and that, finally, Roger of Sicily, by whatever motives it might be that he was urged, would certainly not fail to make good display of the naval forces the superiority of which to all others was his characteristic boast. And when we have noted all this, we may well reflect upon the magnitude of the work of one man ; the one man whose will, now persuasively, now sternly, now perhaps a little angrily expressed, was responsible for it, the monk Bernard of Clairvaux ; who in becoming a monk had not mistaken his vocation, but rather who because he was a monk and a good monk was all else that he was.

In May, as a vanguard of the main host, a contingent of about 100,000 men left Bamberg under Conrad.[9] A little later the King of France was on his way. Odo de Diogilo describes the solemnities of his departure. It is probably the Wednesday after Pentecost, 11th June, and Louis " as was the custom of victorious kings " would beg of Blessed Denis the charge of the sacred oriflamme, and permission to go forth to war. His mother, the queen his wife, surrounded by other illustrious laity, Eugenius, Suger and his monks await him in the great basilica. He enters ; and " prostrating himself most humbly he adores his holy patron. The Pope

[1] R.H.G.F. XV. 440.

[2] Conrad. Ep., Jaffé, Biblioth. Rer. German., I. 111.

[3] Annal. S. Benign. Divion., R.H.G.F. XII. 411.

[4] Jaffé, Regest., 9017.

[5] Annal. Magd., M.G.H. XVI. 188.

[6] Stubbs, Chronicles of the Reign of Richard I, I. 144.

[7] Jaffé, Regest., 9017.

[8] Helmold., Chron. Slavorum, I. 62, M.G.H. Script., XXI. 58 ; Robert. Torign. Chron., ed. Howlett, 155 and 310. Rolls Series.

[9] Annal. Palidens. (Pöhlde), M.G.H. XVI. 82.

and the Abbot of St. Denis open the golden door of the shrine
and carefully take out the silver casket, so that when the king
has seen and kissed him whom his soul loves he may the
more joyfully depart.   Then, when he has received at the
hands of the Supreme Pontiff the oriflamme from where it
hangs above the altar, the pilgrim's scrip and the apostolic
blessing, he withdraws himself from the crowd to the dormitory
of the monks.   The thronging of the people, the presence of
his mother and his wife, breathless with tears and with emotion
of heart, forbid him to delay.   It were as foolish as it were
impossible to endeavour to describe the grief and sorrow of
the bystanders.   On the same day the king, accompanied
by a few of his friends, takes his meal with the brethren in
the refectory and, having embraced all, retires amid their
prayers and tears." [1]

The expedition to Jerusalem was, we know, a failure ;
a failure which amounted to an international disaster.   Quite
apart from its religious significance it had appealed to the
enterprise of the West, to its latent instinct of expansion.   In
those days the trend of civilization, then represented in the
main by Latin Christendom, had no outlet Westward ;   the
movement had no alternative but to retrace its steps and
gather up the fragments overlooked on the way, or consolidate
the position of various settlements left behind on its advance.
And, taking the wider view made possible by our knowledge
of later events, the Crusades were not entirely unfruitful ;
there were fragments lying about ungathered ;   characteristic
possessions of the Semitic races of the Nearer East which
ultimately found their way to the treasury of the West.   The
marvel is that in spite of repeated failures the undaunted
West, hindered rather than helped by the fickle Christian East,
again and again renewed the attack.   The Second Crusade,
which interests us solely so far as St. Bernard's responsibility
for it is concerned, demanded organization, military, political
and social, on a scale with which it was perhaps beyond the
powers of any man of those days to cope.   If we leave out of
account the armies charged with the protection of the Eastern
and North-Eastern German frontiers—of the possibly 200,000
men who marched under Louis and Conrad many were of
questionable, even of criminal character;   many more were
totally unfit for military service.   Otto of Freising records the
astonishment with which was greeted, as wrought " by the
hand of the Most High," the enlistment of "a vast multitude of thieves and robbers." [2]   The *Annals of Würzburg* tell
us of the crowd of serfs and countrymen inconsiderately

[1] Odon. de Diog. De Ludovic. VII Profect. in Orient., I, P.L. CLXXXV. 1209 sq.,

[2] Otton. Frising. Gesta Frid. I Imp., I. xlii., ed. cit.

allowed to take up arms in the cause.[1] There was, moreover, a great camp-following of women of high rank attended by their tire-maidens, which the presence of Queen Eleanor with the French army more than sanctioned.[2] Too much confidence had undoubtedly been placed in the good faith of Manuel, the Eastern Emperor; in the single-mindedness of Roger of Sicily.[3] The somewhat unfortunate intimacy between Raymond, Count of Antioch, and Queen Eleanor could not, it might be contended, have been foreseen; but the risk involved in the presence of women at the front should never have been undertaken.

The raising of the siege of Damascus in the late summer of 1148 wrought consternation in the West, and the obloquy at once fell upon St. Bernard; no less readily for the fact that there was an ill-founded suspicion of the loyalty of the Templars.[4] Resilient as ever, he faced it without blanching. His heart torn by the suggestion that the infidels were asking, and no wonder, *Where is now their God?* while he firmly holds that "every man's adequate and full exculpation is the testimony of his own conscience," yet if blame is to fall he would prefer that men should murmur against himself rather than against God. "It is well for me," he writes to Eugenius, "that he should use me as his shield. I willingly expose myself to the lying tongues of detractors and the envenomed darts of blasphemers, rather than that they should find their mark in him."[5] "If the children of Israel fell and perished because of their iniquity, are we to be surprised," he asks, "if the Crusaders sinning after the same fashion suffer the same disasters? Did the fate of Israel reflect upon the good faith of God's promises? Neither does the fate of these. For God's promises never preclude the exercise of his righteous judgement."[6] St. Bernard was, of course, unerringly correct in his explanation of the failure. The *morale* of the expedition was at fault. This weakness had revealed itself at an early stage. Other causes doubtless were responsible; but had the element of *morale* not been woefully lacking, they might have been counteracted. During the period of preparation he had uttered his warning against the danger of appointing unsuitable commanders;[7] but he would now allow no recriminations upon this score—to countenance them would be but further to weaken confidence. "Let not," he urges, "the sad and unexpected event"—he is probably referring to the retreat from Damascus—"be charged against the rashness of the commander."[8] If it is true to say that an army marches upon its stomach; it is no less true to say that it fights and

[1] *Annal. Herbipol., M.G.H.* XVI. 3.

[2] *Annal. Herbipol., op. cit., loc. cit.*

[3] Odon. de Diog. *op. cit., P.L.* CLXXXV. 1220 sqq.

[4] Joann. Sares. *Hist. Pontifical.,* XXV. 57 sqq., *ed.* Poole.

[5] *De Consid.,* II. i. 4.

[6] *Op. cit.,* II. i. 2.

[7] P. 271 *supra.*

[8] *Op. cit.,* II. i. 2.

fights to victory with its soul. We have learned that. May we not think that this great army of the East had left its soul behind—in the abbot's cell at Clairvaux ? May it not, too, have been that that irrepressible buoyancy, that almost incurable optimism, which characterized St. Bernard's outlook on any work which he regarded himself as undertaking in response to divine vocation, had led him to underrate the difficulties of the expedition ? He scarcely appreciated—in spite of past experience—the fatal weakness of Louis le Jeune, the cunning savagery of Roger of Sicily, the mutual animosity of Conrad and Welf. He knew little of Baldwin of Jerusalem beyond what he may have heard from the Templars, and almost nothing of Manuel and the Greeks ; he had perhaps no suspicion of their growing jealousy of Sicilian influence in the Mediterranean. But it may be asked : Was it his business to organize and direct the intelligence-department of the war ? Again, so far as purely military matters were concerned, such as the unity of command or the unfamiliarity of Western fighting-men with Saracen methods of warfare, these were considerations not for a monk, but for the professional soldier. He had expressly disclaimed such responsibilities, and urged the need of men trained in military service ; he had emphasized the importance of concerted action, of a force strongly knit in unity.[1] And this at a time when the fanaticism of Raoul was calculated to rake all sorts of unsuitable recruits into the ranks. He doubtless saw the dangers ahead on such scores as these ; and he uttered his warnings ; but he was not the recruiting sergeant or the enrolling officer. Whether he could have prevented the queen from accompanying Louis is perhaps doubtful ; it was certainly a bad example, and opened floodgates ; but she was a personality as masterful as she was baneful.

We are not concerned to tell in detail the story of the Crusade ; suffice it to say that as the months, nay, the years passed, disaster followed disaster. The Greeks—whose sincerity seems to have been doubted from the day when, in 1147, Louis accompanied by Godfrey de la Roche, Bishop of Langres, passed through Constantinople on his Eastward journey, and so lacking in frankness was his reception that men recalled the proverb : *Timeo Danaos et dona ferentes* [2]—managed to promote a sense of insecurity which culminated on the occasion of their attacking the ships conveying Louis and his queen from Palestine, and even capturing that on board of which was Eleanor, a misfortune which was retrieved only by the intervention of the Sicilian fleet.[3] Roger was now

[1] S. Bern. *Ep.* 363 (8) ; cf. p. 271 *supra.*

[2] Odon. de Diog. *op. cit.*, II, *P.L.* CLXXXV. 1211 sq.

[3] Joann. Sares. *Hist. Pontifical.*, XXVIII. 61, *ed.* Poole.

at open war with Manuel, who on his side sought to strengthen his position by an alliance with the Emperor Conrad. At home in France Suger, regarding the Second Crusade as ended in failure, would initiate another ; [1] but any such project was rendered futile by a new situation of a disruptive character. Conrad's *entente* with the Greeks was threatening a combined attack upon Roger, which would effectually prevent the Sicilians from taking part in another expedition to Palestine. The prevalent French opinion, voiced by Suger and supported by Peter the Venerable,[2] was that any new expedition should have as its first objective the punishment of the Greeks. St. Bernard, although probably untouched by the motive of taking vengeance upon Manuel, was keenly alive to the danger of a final rupture between Conrad and Roger in the West, and we infer that he wrote to both of them counselling peace.[3] But Conrad was obdurate,[4] and the Abbot of Clairvaux would seem to have said no more. It is improbable, we repeat, that he shared his countrymen's vindictive feeling towards the Greeks ; for him the long record of failure told the story rather of the chastisement of God than of the treachery of men. But, as we shall see, he was not indifferent as to the main purpose of the Crusade. Suger holding that, while for the time perhaps the Greeks must go scot-free, another attempt should be made to secure the Christian custody of the Holy Places, began by calling together a council at Laon in April, 1150, at which Louis presided. The general opinion was that the matter could not profitably be discussed in the absence of the prelates of the Church of France ; and another council at which they were present assembled at Chartres in May on the Third Sunday after Easter.[5] The matter had already been submitted to the Pope, but no reply had as yet been received. Eugenius was cautious. The attempt made to reconcile Conrad and Roger, in which St. Bernard had played a leading part,[6] had perhaps not been altogether according to his mind. The ambition of Roger, doubtless underestimated by St. Bernard, was a menace to the Patrimony of Peter and the glorification of Sicilian arms in the East would not, the Pope feared, improve matters [7] When the Papal rescript reached Suger it was a little disconcerting. Eugenius's reply, to put it bluntly, amounted to no more than : " Try again if you like ; but I am not very hopeful. I do not doubt the courage of your fighting-men or the devotion of your clergy ; and I give you my Apostolic blessing. Finally, see what your king says." [8] In plain words he would throw upon Louis the responsibility of a decision. This would not satisfy St. Bernard.

[1] *Vita Suger.* III, *R.H.G.F.* XII. 110 ; *Suger. Epp.* 143 and 146, *P.L.* CLXXXVI.

[2] Petr. Vener. *Epp. Lib.*, VI. 16, *P.L.* CLXXXIX. 424.

[3] Wibald. *Ep.* 225, *P.L.* CLXXXIX. 1311 sq.

[4] Conrad. *Ep. inter Wibald. Epp.* 188, *P.L.* CLXXXIX. 1284 sqq.

[5] Suger. *Ep.*, *R.H.G.F.* XV. 523.

[6] *Vide supra.*

[7] Wibald. *Ep.* 259, *P.L.* CLXXXIX. 1335 sq.

[8] Jaffé, *Regest.*, 9385.

That his old pupil should regard the question in this irresponsible and detached fashion was a reproach to his master and a reflection upon the See of Peter. " In a matter of such universal interest, of such grave importance, one must not act half-heartedly nor yet timidly," he writes to Eugenius. " Read what a philosopher says : *He is no brave man, whose spirit does not rise when things are at their worst.*[1] . . . Now is the time to use both swords, when the Lord is suffering. For Christ is renewing his passion there "—that is to say, at Jerusalem—" where he suffered once before. Who is to use them if not yourself ? Both swords are Peter's, one to be drawn at his command, the other by his hand. . . . I hold that now is the time, and now the need, to draw them both in defence of the Eastern Church. You ought not to be less zealous than was he whose seat you occupy. What is to be said of a man who possesses authority and refuses to exercise it ? . . . The successor of Peter will not be terrified by the losses of the earlier expedition ; he will rather set himself to the task of repairing them."

There was, however, another problem of paramount importance which had arisen and had, as was supposed, been solved at the Council of Chartres. It was now fully recognized that lack of *morale* had been the fundamental cause of the failure of the last expedition, and that the sole means of obviating this in future was the appointment of a man to the supreme and unified command whose conviction of the essential necessity of *morale* in all its aspects was unquestionable. As was almost inevitable the choice fell upon St. Bernard. In the letter to Eugenius quoted above he gives his own view of the matter. " You may rest assured not only that such a proposal was made contrary to my advice and to my wishes, and that I am still of the same mind with regard to it, but that to give it effect is quite beyond my powers so far as I am able to judge of them." He is evidently at a loss to explain this choice ; a born fighter and of soldier-stock, he does not doubt his own spirit, but he does gravely doubt his strength and his experience. " Who am I to dispose men in battle-array and to lead them forth against the enemy ? What is so alien from my profession, even if I had the necessary physique and the necessary training ? But it is not for me to instruct your wisdom. You know all this. I only beg of you in the name of that love which in a very special way you owe me that you will not sacrifice me to the will of man, but that, as is incumbent upon you above all others, you will take counsel of God and see to it that it is his will that is done upon earth as it is in heaven." [3]

[1] Senec. *Ep.* 22.

[2] *Ep.* 256.

[3] *Ep.* 256.

In spite of this appeal, so reasonable in its argument and so religious in its spirit, Eugenius in the end confirmed the decision of the Council of Chartres.[1] But the Cistercians ranged themselves in resistance [2] and, as we know, it never took effect. The mistake was surely that the proposal was not modified. St. Bernard was not a king, and for him to have been in supreme military command would have been, as he plainly indicated, *chose pour rire*, but—for him to have been at the front as prophet and as priest would have been of incalculable advantage. Strangely enough, no one seems to have thought of this, although it was precisely the office which he had filled with such singular success during the period of preparation. Had the possibility ever entered his mind? We do not know. All that can be said is that, had the proposal been made to him, he could not have rejected it on any of the grounds alleged in his letter to Eugenius, except that of physical disability. And would this have weighed with so courageous a spirit? Apart from his duty to his own sons at Clairvaux, what might have determined him would have been the feeling that he ought to remain in France and support Suger in the conduct of affairs at home.

In taking stock of the various influences responsible for the Second Crusade we cannot hesitate to allocate the first place to the personality of St. Bernard. This, surely, is a matter of common agreement. In a few words to review the chief actors. Louis le Jeune was in a sense St. Bernard's convert; he owed to him what he was as a Christian king; and in 1146 he was shown to be a man of piety and of religious principle, single-minded on the whole in the matter in hand, although perhaps not without some *arrière-pensée* towards the maintenance of the Latin Kingdom in Palestine as an outpost of France but—he was always distressingly weak-willed, never independent of the stronger will of his queen. Conrad from the first had, we feel, more than half an eye upon his interests in Germany and in Italy. Eugenius's great glory was his confidence in St. Bernard, firm in the early stages, although perhaps a little faltering towards the end, probably owing to the painful embarrassment occasioned him internally by the citizens of Rome and externally by Roger of Sicily, who throughout played the part of a typical Northman. Of Roger no more need be said. Suger stands out as primarily a great patriot and a faithful servant of Louis, zealous above all else for the honour of France. Of St. Bernard, once again, what shall we say? No one else worked so hard at what in modern phrase we should call spade-work, spade-work in what he

[1] Jaffé, *Regest.*, 9398.
[2] *Contin. Præmonstr.*, *M.G.H.* VI. 455.

regarded as his own proper field, the field of conscience and of duty, national and individual. No one's eye was throughout more single. No one stirred more deeply and directed more wisely the popular enthusiasm. With irresistible force he drove before him the sentiment of Christian Europe, until it found itself upon the horns of the great dilemma indicated by him in a letter to Suger written probably about the year 1149. " The Church in the East cries so piteously in its distress, that a man whose heart is not touched to its very core cannot claim to be a son of the Church at all." [1] If for the most part men chose pity and sonship, it was St. Bernard who brought it about. *Nam data sibi dicendi facultate, fere persuadebat semper desiderio suo.*[2]

[1] *Ep.* 380.

[2] Joann. Sares. *Hist. Pontifical.* IX. 21, *ed.* Poole.

CHAPTER XIII

THE THEOLOGY OF THE SCHOOLS

Abélard

It may be desirable, before referring to St. Bernard's relations with Abélard and with Gilbert de la Porrée, to say something about a problem which in the XIIth century was regarded as important, and was consequently eagerly discussed in the great schools of that day, the problem of universals. The disputants were divided into at least two parties ; we say " at least " because it is possible to recognize a third, to say nothing of variant modifications of each of them. The question at issue was this. Is, to take an example, man, the *genus* man, the universal, a *subsistens in se*, an object existing in itself, or are the only *subsistentia in se* individual men, the various *species* of the *genus*, the particulars, John, Henry, George and the rest ? Should we take the latter view and say that the *genus* man is no more than a mental concept, represented when we refer to it by a *nomen*, a mere *vox ?* The Nominalist answer was that man, the *genus*, the universal, was a concept derived inductively, and thus founded upon an empirical basis ; when we discuss this concept dialectically we give it a *nomen*. Realism, on the other hand, maintained that man, the *genus*, the universal, is more than a mere concept of the mind ; that it is, like the Platonic Ideas, an eternal objective *subsistens in se*, not contingently upon whether we form the mental concept of it but necessarily. Conceptualism, the third view, not so distinctly traceable as the other two, would seem to have been somewhat to the effect that man, the *genus*, is a mental concept, but that it is a concept truly *subsistens in se*, not eternally like the Platonic Ideas but in the mind of the thinker after it has been formed.

We recognize, on the one hand, affinities between Nominalism and Aristotelianism—between the doctrines of *universalia post rem* and *universalia in re*—and, on the other, affinities between Realism—the doctrine of *universalia ante rem* or *extra*

[1] Grote,
Aristot.,
(App. I), 555.

[2] Speculum,
V. i. 5,
Jan. 1930.

[3] Reade,
Cambr. Med.
Hist., V. 789
and 793.

[4] Sikes, Peter
Abailard, App.
II.

[5] Aristot.
Categor., V.
Οὐσία δέ ἐστιν ...
εἰρήσθω.

[6] Petr. Abael.
De Intellectibus,
Cousin, Opp., II.
750 sq. Cf.
notit., ibid., 761.

[7] Lasserre, Un
conflit religieux
au XIIe siècle,
47 sqq.
[8] Joann. Sares.
Metalog., II.
xvii., ed. Webb,
92 sq. Cf.
Webb, John of
Salisbury, 87.
[9] Joann. Sares.,
op. cit., II. x, ed.
cit., 77 sq.
[10] Otton.Frising.
Gest. Frid. I
Imp., I. xlix.,
Waitz, Script.
Rer. Germ.

rem—and Platonism.[1] As regards this last, it was an age marked generally by the growing influence of Neo-Platonism ; St. Anselm of Canterbury had derived through St. Augustine much of his philosophy from Plato ; such a work as the first part of the Timaeus in the translation and with the commentary of Chalcidius was to be found in the libraries of St. Bertin, Bec, Anchin, Canterbury and elsewhere ; [2] the channels through which the doctrine of Plato, its distinctive qualitas, reached the West before the middle of the XIIth century were numerous.[3] As regards Aristotle, the Western schools were already possessed of several of his works in their Latin versions,[4] such, for example, as the Categories, in which we find the Platonic Realism combated by a statement which in point of fact is rather Conceptualist than Nominalist.[5]

Applied to the doctrine of the Trinity the Nominalism of Roscelinus tended in the direction of tritheism ; the Realism of Gilbert de la Porrée in the direction of Sabellianism. Abélard perhaps took the view that universals are subsistentia, but only in so far as they are related to particulars.[6] It is possible, however, that he never seriously sought any third solution of the problem such as was offered by Conceptualism, for the reason that in advance of current thinkers he regarded it as never having been satisfactorily stated. He might well have held that genera are not names but things, and yet—that no thing is a subsistens in se.[7] John of Salisbury in the Metalogicon distinguishes Abélard's opinion as being to the effect that the universal is neither an intellectus, a mental concept, nor a mere vox, but a sermo, a stated proposition.[8] John had been Abélard's pupil at the Mont-Ste. Geneviève for about a year from 1136 to 1137.[9]

Otto of Freising prefaces his story of Abélard by remarking that a certain credulity characterized St. Bernard which, combined with his abhorrence of masters who, " relying upon their secular learning, founded themselves somewhat exclusively upon human reasoning," [10] led him to give ear too readily to any report of their doctrine which suggested its incompatibility with the Christian faith. Otto, let us note, became about the year 1136 Abbot of Morimond, a Cistercian house where he died in 1158, having returned thither on resigning the see of Freising in Bavaria ; he took part in the Second Crusade ; nothing points to his having been otherwise than favourably disposed towards St. Bernard. The result of this credulity was, he tells us, that " not long ago," that is to say not long before the year 1147, " at his (St. Bernard's) instigation Peter Abélard was silenced, first by the bishops of

Gaul and then by the Roman pontiff." Abélard, he goes on
to say, was a native of Brittany, " a land producing clergy of
acute and cultured intellects, but otherwise dull enough " ; [1]   [1] *Op. cit., loc. cit.*
in fact, great thinkers but feckless in affairs. A distinguished
French writer, the late Monsieur Pierre Lasserre, whose
fantasy is, we know, apt to be ingenious on the subject of the
gifted Breton, as witness his romance *Le secret d'Abélard*, has
founded upon these last words a theory. He affects to trace
in Abélard a temperamental type recognizable in other natives
of the same district; he instances de Chateaubriand, de la
Mennais and Renan. It is not to be denied that his theory
is attractive; nor is he incompetent to construct it; his
Jeunesse d'Ernest Renan, in which he discusses a religious crisis
of the XIXth century somewhat analogous to that with which
we are concerned, is sufficient proof to the contrary.[2] But   [2] Lasserre, *op.*
we may doubt whether his theory is accountable for so much   *cit.*, 69 sqq.
as he would have us believe it to be. It is true that Abélard
was conscious of two strains co-existing in himself. " As from
the nature of my country and of my race I was light in spirit,
so also from my disposition I was distinguished by a proneness
to literary pursuits." [3] But the *animo levitas* to which he   [3] Abael. *Epist.,*
here refers is, surely, something quite different from the   I. *al. Hist.*
stoliditas of Otto's statement ; as for the *ingenium*, it is some-   *Calam.,* I,
thing which Abélard attributes with a touch of pride to his   Cousin, *Opp.,* I.
own personality, which has surmounted the obstacles presented   3.
by his native stock—unless we are to restrict the sense of the
word *ingenium* so narrowly as to make one of the most
original of thinkers no more than the creature of his past.
That Abélard would rather seek to emphasize this triumph of
individual endeavour seems to follow from the fact that he
immediately proceeds to speak of his father as a man, possessed of but a smattering of education and brought up to the
calling of arms, who subsequently gave himself enthusiastically
to the pursuit of letters and encouraged his sons to do the
same. Minerva became for the family henceforth what Mars
for a long past traditionally had been. In the letter quoted
Abélard is telling to an anonymous friend—but we are tempted
to think that it was intended for the ear of Héloïse [4]—the   [4] Heloiss. *Ep.,*
story of his life, revealing himself as he was at first and as he   II., *ad init., op.*
came to be afterwards; and it may be well to note that   *cit.* I, 72.
learning, learning to the end of sound thinking, was his first
and his last love. Not that religion was left out of account—
religion was certainly in his blood, so far as such a thing can
be innate—but his faith was always a *fides quaerens intellectum ;*
he must always be able to give " a reason concerning the hope
that is in him." Of this we shall later say something.

Abélard was born in 1079 at Le-Pallet, about ten miles South of Nantes. His first master was Roscelinus, then teaching at Loches, the great Nominalist whose doctrine was condemned at the Council of Soissons in 1092 as savouring of tritheism. In later years he sat at the feet of Anselm of Laon, a man of the opposite school, for he had been a pupil at Bec of St. Anselm, the Realist opponent of Roscelinus. It was, however, when he had as his master William of Champeaux, under whom he studied dialectic in the episcopal school of Notre-Dame at Paris, that he first obtained notoriety. Otto writes of him as " so arrogant and so confident in his own opinion that he would scarcely humble himself to listen to his masters " ; [1] and he himself boasts in the letter above-mentioned that, although at first an acceptable pupil to William of Champeaux, " I afterwards proved myself very vexatious to him, when more often than not I attempted to refute his arguments and to reason against him and sometimes to show myself to be the better disputant of the two." [2] Abélard's eminence would seem to have aroused the displeasure of his fellow-pupils also, for he writes : " They were the more indignant with me in proportion to my youth and to the brevity of my studies." [3] Not improbably they were disgusted by the conceit and by the studied ridicule of a tyro, as well as offended by his thinly veiled contempt for anything like loose reasoning. In truth, young though he was, Abélard was aspiring to be a master. Accordingly, supported by " certain of the mighty of the land " against what he describes as " the secret machinations " of William of Champeaux, he first established himself at Melun. Subsequently he moved to Corbeil, near Paris, where owing to his excessive study his health broke down ; upon which he retired to Brittany for several years. On his recovery he returned to Paris, to find that William had recently, in 1108, founded the Abbey of St. Victor, of which he became a canon regular,[4] " with the intention, as was said, of increasing his reputation for piety, so that he might be promoted to the higher rank of the episcopate, which happened shortly afterwards when he was made Bishop of Châlons-sur-Marne." [5] As a matter of fact, it took five years for William's piety to mature sufficiently for the purpose, but the remark is a side-light upon the character of the writer. At Paris, now studying rhetoric under his old master, he " compelled him to destroy " his earlier doctrine of universals ; an amended theory being now propounded by him, to the effect that the *res* is in the particulars after such a fashion that it cannot be described as the same *res* essentially

[1] Otton. Frising. *op. cit., loc. cit.*

[2] Abael. *Ep.*, I. 2, Cousin, *Opp.* I. 4.

[3] *Op cit., loc. cit.*

[4] *Gall. Christ.*, IX. 877.

[5] Abael. *Ep.*, I. 2, *op. cit.*, I. 5.

(*essentialiter*), but only with a difference proper to each particular (*indifferenter*). It reads as if Abélard's dialectic rapier had driven William into an uncomfortable corner. In any case he seems to have gained *éclat* and attracted pupils.[1] Not long afterwards he was again at Melun for a short time. On his return to Paris he found that by the influence of William the Schools of St. Victor and Notre-Dame were closed to him as a master; and he was compelled to establish a school for himself on the Mont-Ste. Geneviève outside the city. This was entirely contrary to what in these days we should call professional *étiquette*; it savoured of charlatanry. It was an unwritten law that a man should not undertake a *magisterium sine magistro*, that is to say, that he should not begin to teach in public without the recognition and direction of some master of repute.[2] This Abélard could not obtain; nevertheless, from the day of its foundation in 1113, the year in which William of Champeaux was made Bishop of Châlons-sur-Marne, the School of Ste. Geneviève became a serious rival to the two older schools; perhaps in the end its fame eclipsed theirs. It would have been soon afterwards that Abélard betook himself to Laon, in order to see what theology he could learn there from Anselm. He speaks with supreme contempt of this old pupil of a greater Anselm; we should scarcely suppose him to have been worth Abélard's consideration, although, as we have seen,[3] Otto refers to him as his master. " Anyone who came to him with a question for solution went away more puzzled than ever. To listeners, indeed, he was wonderful to hear, but to questioners he was of no use at all. He had a marvellous command of words, but the sense was contemptible and devoid of reason. When he lit a fire he filled his house with smoke, but he made no illumination." In fact he was the barren fig tree of the gospel; the old oak to which Lucan compared Pompey, *magni nominis umbra*. " When I found this out I did not lie idle for many days under his shade!" However an amusing episode detained him longer than he anticipated. A certain pupil of Anselm asked him as a student in physics (in the contemporary sense of the term) what he thought of the study of sacred literature. His reply was that, so far as concerned the salvation of the soul, it was an excellent thing; but that he could not understand why, with the books themselves or at least the usual *glossae* at his disposal, an educated man wanted any master in the subject. Derisively asked whether he would himself illustrate the point, he acceded; an obscure passage of the prophet Ezekiel was selected, and the work of a *glossator*

[1] *Op. cit., loc. cit.*

[2] *Op. cit., loc. cit.,* Cousin, *Opp.,* I. 6. Cf. Abael. *Ep.* I. 8, Cousin, *op. cit.,* I. 18.

[3] P. 292 *supra.*

placed in his hands. Urged, as an inexperienced exponent of the Scriptures, to take his time, he indignantly remarked that it was a matter not of being used to it but of having the brains for it. In the end, he tells us, his hearers were well satisfied ; but Anselm was very jealous, and persecuted him for his proficiency in this subject as William had persecuted him for his proficiency in philosophy.[1] This was Abélard's abundant grievance, pouring itself without stint into the ear of the sympathetic Héloïse.[2] His early relations with this gifted daughter of the Montmorencis do not particularly concern us ; the story is sufficiently familiar. It should, however, be said that their sequel redounded to the credit of them both. The pathos of the mutual fidelity and solicitude revealed cannot fail to touch us. Abélard can surely be reproached for no *animo levitas* at any stage towards one who, from the time when at the age of about seventeen she became his pupil under the roof of her uncle, Fulbert Canon of Notre-Dame, never, it would seem, ceased to adore him as the embodiment of all that is inspired, honest and fearless in the art of a master. A testimony, most remarkable considering its *provenance*, to the character of Héloïse is to be found in a now rare book, entitled *La Vie de Pierre Abeillard, abbé de saint Gildas de Ruis, ordre de saint Benoist, et celle d'Héloïse, son épouse, première abbesse du Paraclet*, published anonymously at Paris in 1720 by Dom François-Armand Gervaise, Abbot of La-Trappe, together with a sympathetic estimate of the work of Abélard and a generous appreciation of the protection afforded to him by Peter the Venerable.[3]

On his return to Paris from Laon shortly afterwards Abélard completed and improved his *glossae* on Ezekiel. He was working, he confesses, in luxury of circumstances and in pride of mind when, albeit unwillingly, he was suddenly by divine grace deprived of both ; how he lost the former he does not tell us ; as regards the latter, he could recognize a dispensation of providence, for *knowledge puffeth up ;* his manuscript was destroyed by fire.[4] It was at about this time, the year 1117, that Héloïse became Abélard's pupil. Subsequently they fled to Brittany where, with Fulbert's consent, they were clandestinely married. Later she was professed a nun at the Abbey of Argenteuil near Paris, and Abélard himself became a monk of St. Denis.[5] Of this Otto writes : " Having on a certain sufficiently notorious occasion behaved himself improperly, he was made a monk in the monastery of St. Denis. There, giving himself by day and by night to reading and to thinking, his intellect grew keener and more learned than

[1] *Op. cit.*, I. 3, Cousin, *Opp.*, I. 7 sq.

[2] Heloiss. *Ep.*, II., *ad init., op. cit.*, I. 72.

[3] *Bibliothèque de Douai (Hist. de France*, P. in oct. 6780).

[4] *Op. cit.*, 4, Cousin, *Opp.*, I. 8 sq.

[5] *Op. cit.*, 7 and 8, Cousin, *Opp.*, I. 12 sqq.

ever." [1] Abélard describes the great abbey as a place of "most secular, and even disreputable living," and the abbot Adam, Suger's immediate predecessor, as one " whose conduct was the baser, and whose ill-fame was the more notorious, in proportion to his high prelacy over the rest. Indeed, frequently and vehemently rebuking both privately and publicly their uncleanness, I made myself so burdensome and so odious to them that they joyfully took occasion from the daily importunity of my pupils to send me away." [2]

It was now for the first time that he gave himself to the consideration of the fundamental doctrine of the Trinity. He wrote his treatise *Of the Divine Unity and Trinity* in response to the request of his pupils, who complained " that to use language which the understanding cannot follow was not what was wanted ; that nothing can be believed unless it is first understood ; that it is ridiculous for a man to set forth what neither himself nor those whom he would teach can understand ; that the Lord himself reproves such people as *blind leaders of the blind.*" [3] While it is probably true that this particular request was quite spontaneous, we cannot but think that it was the fruit of seed sown by Abélard himself. His teaching was essentially of the type which stimulates intellectual appetite ; and at last he was listening to the expression of that *fides quaerens intellectum* which he had generated in his pupils. And now indeed the gauntlet was thrown down, nay, rather flung in the face. What did it mean, this specious contradiction of the great *dictum* of St. Augustine, *fides praecedit intellectum,* this blasphemous negation of the Lord's promise to reveal truth to babes, this cruel voidance of the faith of simple souls ? [4] Henceforth whatever Abélard might write would always be suspect. And here it may be said that for Abélard intellect was the intellect of the scholar, of the philosopher ; it would seem that the reasoning faculty of the *rudis,* the serf, the seafarer, the man-at-arms did not fall within his vision at all. What was such a man to do ? Was he to conclude that faith was not for him because he was not possessed of the *ars disputandi* of a trained dialectician ? Or was he to accept Christian doctrine only in the sense in which it commended itself to this or to that master ? If he were to adopt the latter alternative, what would he be doing if not believing *without* understanding, taking for granted the validity of conclusions the premises of which were wholly unintelligible to him ? And why should he prefer the authority of an individual master to that of the Church ? *Securus judicat orbis terrarum.* In some such light as this the

[1] Otton. Frising. *op. cit., loc. cit.*

[2] Abael. *Ep.,* I. 8, Cousin, *Opp.,* I. 17.

[3] *Op. cit.,* 9, Cousin, *Opp.,* I. 18.

[4] Cf. S. Aug. *De Util. Cred.,* IX 21.

problem would have presented itself to a man like St. Bernard, a pastor of souls.

Looking back upon it all from a psychological point of view somewhat different from that of the XIIth century, it might seem to us that the interaction of faith and understanding was in a measure overlooked. In the first place, no act of faith, surely, whether it be that of the boor or of the philosopher is entirely devoid of intellectual content. Each understands—up to a point—what he is doing ; of each the reasoning faculty, such as it may be, is exercised. Because in the case of the philosopher the exercise of this faculty is exceptionally discerning, albeit limited, that is no valid pretext for straining to breaking-point the intellect of the boor. Alas, at that breaking-point faith goes ; and the search for understanding ends in despair of finding it. And again, the paradox offered by a *fides praecedens intellectum* and a *nihil creditum nisi primitus intellectum* may express the truth that the healthy soul is always adding to faith a knowledge which increases faith, only in each case a knowledge which is intelligible to it ; a knowledge which is unintelligible to a man is for him no knowledge at all. Truly we are sometimes disposed to think that the real obscurantist was not St. Bernard but Abélard himself.

It is an interesting question as to how far the use by Roscelinus, much after the fashion of the Greeks, of the term *substantia* for that which the Latins call *persona*,[1] is reflected in Abélard, and explains his condemnation at Soissons in 1121. However this may be, there is ground for supposing that the latter laid himself open to the charge, not only of dealing with the accepted dogma of the Trinity in a spirit of academic detachment, but of confusing the proper spheres of philosophy and theology. Not that he was ever a pure rationalist. " I do not want to be a philosopher at the price of being rejected by Paul ; nor yet an Aristotle at the price of being separated from Christ, for there is none other name under heaven whereby I can be saved. I adore Christ reigning at the Father's right hand. With the arms of faith I embrace him working divinely in that glorious virginal flesh which he received of the Holy Ghost." [2] So he wrote to Héloïse in the confession of faith which at the end of his life he addressed to her. It is impossible to regard this as the expression of a mere death-bed repentance, and not as the summary of a soul's long experience. Beneath all his combativeness in dispute, his zeal for sound reasoning simply as such, his frank intellectual pride, his naïve consciousness of his own mental

[1] Gilson, *La philosophie au moyen âge*, 40.

[2] Abael. *Ep. et Fid. Conf. ad Hel.*, Cousin, *Opp.*, I. 680.

superiority, there lay buried this hidden treasure. His last
written words known to us dig it up to the light of day.

The treatise *Of the Divine Unity and Trinity* met, he tells
us, with considerable approval, except on the part of his rivals.
The chief of these were Alberic, rector of the cathedral school
at Rheims, and Leutald or Lotulph of Novara, whom he
stigmatizes as " schemers of long standing " ; to both of them
Otto of Freising refers as " illustrious persons and masters of
repute." [1]   Both had been distinguished pupils of Anselm of
Laon.   Of Leutald we know little ; Alberic had at one time
been a fellow-pupil of Abélard in the school of William of
Champeaux ; he was *elected*, no more, Bishop of Châlons-sur-
Marne in 1126.[2]   Abélard's account of the circumstances in
which the Council of Soissons [3] was held five years earlier, in
1121, is a little laconic, and certainly disdainful.   He speaks of
William as well as of Anselm as already dead.   William's death
could have been but recent.[4]   " As both of these persons
(Alberic and Leutald) were masters in the schools at Rheims,
they urged their archbishop Ralph with frequent suggestions
that they should invite Conan, Bishop of Palestrina, then
Apostolic Legate in Gaul, and hold a little meeting at Soissons
by way of a council ; and that they should cite me to attend,
bringing with me the notorious book which I had written
concerning the Trinity.   And so it happened.   But before I
reached the place my two aforesaid rivals so defamed me both
to clergy and to laity, that on the day of my arrival the
populace almost stoned me and the few of my pupils who had
come with me, saying that I had spoken and written that there
are three Gods, which was precisely what they had been persuaded to believe." [5]   Abélard anticipated events by going
direct to the legate, and asking him to examine his book and
judge whether it contained anything contrary to the Catholic
Faith ; if it did, he was prepared to correct it or to make any
suitable satisfaction.   His request was refused, and he was
told to submit the book to the archbishop and to the rest of
his rivals in order that, as he puts it, " he might be judged by
his accusers."   And so the council was held, and after a brisk
battle of words, in which Abélard would appear to have been
the victor, hastened to its destined end, which was of course
his condemnation.   The legate, a more illiterate person than
he ought to have been—knowing less of philosophy and of
theology than did even the archbishop—was persuaded to
decide that there should be no further inquiry into the matter,
and that the book should be burnt.   At the next meeting of
the council Abélard was compelled to put it on the fire with

[1] Otton. Frising.
*Gest. Frid. I
Imp.*, I. xlix.,
Waitz, *op. cit.*

[2] S. Bern. *Ep.*
13 ; Mabill.
Not. ad loc.

[3] Otton. Frising.
op. cit., loc. cit.

[4] Marten. et
Durand. *Script.
et Mon. Ampl.
Coll.*, IX. 1023
sq. *not.* (6).

[5] Abael. *Ep.*, I. 9,
Cousin, *Opp.*, I.
18 sq.

his own hands, and was delivered over to the Abbot of St. Médard, who was present, " to be taken to his cloister like a prisoner." Throughout Geoffrey Bishop of Chartres, the only learned member of the council, had befriended Abélard.

It has been necessary to compress the story into a few words. It is told by the prisoner at the bar, and therefore his point of view prevails in it ; but it sparkles with just sufficiently restrained humour and with thinly veiled sarcasm and, in spite of the fact that at the end he speaks of himself as in tears, he would seem to have been quite satisfied with himself, as he usually was when he got the better of an opponent in an argument. Ultimately the legate sent him back to the Abbey of St. Denis to the company of men whose " infamous life and shameless behaviour " had, as we have seen, so revolted him before.[1] Happily, Abbot Adam was succeeded by Suger in 1122. An unacceptable member of the community, Abélard was not long to remain there ; least of all when he sought to prove on the authority of Bede—whom the monks rejected as " the most mendacious of writers," that their patron had been Bishop, not of Athens, but of Corinth. By the influence of Stephen de Garlande the royal seneschal [2] in the same year, 1122, he obtained his liberty, and betook himself to the territory of Theobald II, Count of Champagne, where, in a lonely spot previously known to him, a piece of land was given to him by sympathetic friends, and where, with the consent of the Bishop of Troyes, he built a little oratory of reeds and branches, which he dedicated first to the Holy Trinity and afterwards to the Paraclete. Here he " abode in the wilderness " with one cleric as his companion. The locality may easily be identified to-day about four miles S.E. of Nogent-sur-Seine by the crypt of the church of the Abbaye-du-Paraclet, to which we shall have occasion to refer later. Soon he was surrounded by pupils, and little huts were built in which they lived a life rivalling in its severity that of the early Cistercian pioneers.[3] It was at about this time, perhaps during the years 1123 to 1125, that Abélard first began to recognize the extent to which he had fallen under the displeasure of St. Bernard. His bodily presence was obscurely hidden, but his fame was growing daily. Many-voiced echo was telling of him to every ear. His old rivals, he tells us, despairing of their own powers, were beginning to enlist against him " new apostles to whom every one gave the utmost credence ; men, one of whom boasted that he had resuscitated the life of canons regular, the other that of monks." The reference to St. Norbert and St. Bernard is

[1] *Op. cit.,* 9 sq., Cousin, *Opp.,* I. 19 sqq.

[2] Pp. 194 sqq. *supra.*

[3] *Op. cit.,* 10 sq., Cousin, *Opp.,* I. 23 sqq.

unmistakable.   As regards the latter, we do well to recall
Otto of Freising's remarks concerning the readiness with which
he was prone to accept reports detrimental to the reputation
for orthodoxy of men who relied much upon their secular
learning and upon human reasoning.[1]   Abélard lamented
bitterly that both his life and his doctrine were so widely
aspersed by these two influential abbots that for fear of in-
curring their censure his old friends dissimulated any regard
which they had for him.   He was terrified to hear of any
council being held, expecting that its purpose was his public
condemnation.   So keenly did he feel his outlawry in spirit
from the Christian commonwealth that he even meditated
the plan of removing himself in body to some land of pagans
where, unsuspected of crime or of heresy, he might, on the
condition of paying his civil dues, quietly live to himself his
own Christian life.   But another way of escape offered itself.
He was in 1125 elected Abbot of St. Gildas-de-Rhuys, a house
of Black Monks on the coast of Brittany about three miles
South-West of Sarzeau and in the diocese of Vannes.   " I fell,"
he writes, " into the hands of Christians and monks far worse
and wilder than any pagans."   He soon proved himself quite
incapable of coping with the dissolute life of the community.
It was in 1129 that Suger took over the Abbey of Argenteuil
from the nuns of whom Héloïse was abbess, and introduced
his own monks from St. Denis.[2]   Abélard then left St. Gildas-
de-Rhuys and accompanied Héloïse to Le-Paraclet, where
under their combined direction the nucleus of a community
was formed and a house built of which all that now remains is
the XIIth century crypt above-mentioned.[3]   In 1131 occurred
the first recorded meeting between St. Bernard and Abélard.
It took place at the Abbey of Maurigny, on the occasion of the
benediction of an altar by Innocent II.[4]   And probably a few
years later St. Bernard visited Le-Paraclet.   With whatever
reception he may have met from the abbess and her nuns—
Abélard wrote to him that " rather as an angel than as a man
he had by his holy exhortations strengthened both her and
the sisters "[5]—the personal sentiments of Héloïse towards
one of the " pseudo-apostles " whose detractions were so
painful to Abélard would naturally not have been very cordial.[6]

In 1136 Abélard was again at Ste. Geneviève teaching, both
by his words and by his writings, with a reinvigorated independence of thought.   There appeared in succession the *Theologia
Christiana*, the *Introductio ad Theologiam*, the *Scito teipsum* and
the *Commentaria in Epistolam ad Romanos*.   The *Sic et Non*
was at about this time revised.[7]   Information as to these

[1] P. 290 *supra*.

[2] P. 224 *supra*.

[3] *Op. cit.*, 12 sq., Cousin, *Opp.*, I. 28 sqq.

[4] *Chron. Maur-iniac.*, *R.H.G.F.* XII. 80. Cf. p. 111 *supra*.

[5] Petr. Abael. *Ep. Div. Bern.*, Cousin, *Opp.*, I. 618.

[6] Heloiss. *Ep.*, II., *op. cit.*, I. 72.

[7] Rémusat, *Abélard*, I. 179.

activities reached St. Bernard by means of a letter addressed
to himself and to Geoffrey, Bishop of Chartres, by William,
formerly Abbot of St. Thierry, early in the year 1140. When
he finds the common faith dangerously corrupted, and no one,
not even those who ought to speak, making any protest,
William is gravely perturbed. " It is not," he writes, " a
question of small matters, but of belief in the Holy Trinity,
of the person of the mediator, of the mystery of our common
redemption. Peter Abélard is again teaching and writing
novelties ; his books are crossing the seas and overleaping the
Alps ; his new opinions concerning the faith are broadcast
throughout provinces and kingdoms, are frequently preached
and are maintained with such impunity that they are said to-
have authoritative support in the Roman *Curia*. . . . I can
tell you that this evil is still labouring to bring to the birth ;
unless it is prevented from doing so a snake will appear for

¹ *Inter S. Bern.* which a charmer will not easily be found." ¹ A copy of the
Epp. 326.   *Theologia Christiana* has recently been examined by William,
and he appends thirteen dangerous assertions culled from
Abélard's works, such as, for example, " that the Father is
plenary power, that the Son is a certain power, that the Holy
Spirit is no power at all ; that the Holy Spirit is not of the
substance of the Father and the Son as the Son is of the
substance of the Father ; . . . that Christ did not assume
flesh and suffer in order to set us free from the yoke of the
devil ; . . . that we do not derive from Adam the guilt of
original sin, but only the punishment." He has heard of
other works of the same writer, the *Sic et Non*, the *Scito teipsum*,
the doctrine of which may be as monstrous as their titles.
" God knows," he writes, " I have loved this man and I should
wish to love him still ; but in a case like this no one is my

² *Op. cit., loc. cit.* nearest relative, or my friend." ² As we gather from St.
Bernard's reply, William enclosed a brief tractate, a cursory
perusal of which suggested that it was well calculated to refute
this false doctrine. But St. Bernard must have time fully to
consider the matter. He proposes that after Easter they
should meet and confer upon it. Meanwhile, William will
please to be patient with his silence, " for," he writes, " of
most of these things, indeed of almost all of them, I have so

³ *Ep.* 327.   far known nothing." ³

It would appear that as the result of this interview it was
decided that St. Bernard should discuss the whole matter
personally with Abélard. Geoffrey reports the circumstances
as follows. St. Bernard, " wishing with his wonted goodness
and kindness of heart rather to correct his errors than to put

him (Abélard) to confusion, met him in private conference. Moreover, with such moderation and with such reason did he deal with him that, struck by remorse, he promised to correct everything in accordance with St. Bernard's judgement." [1] It is only fair to Abélard to draw attention to certain of his remarks bearing upon the general question in dispute. In the prologue to the *Introduction to Theology* he writes : " If in this work I have by my fault ranged outside the orbit of Catholic meaning or language, let it be pardoned to me in consideration of my intention ; I am always ready to make satisfaction for wrong statements, either by correcting them or by deleting them, whenever any of the faithful has established my error on rational or on Scriptural grounds." [2] Again, he had a keen sense and a profound abhorrence of the prevalence at the time of extravagant heresy which was leading the ignorant into detestable error. " Anyone may know," he remarks, " that there was never a heretic in old days who went to such extremes of folly as do certain of our contemporaries. Lately there was a layman Tanquelmus in Flanders and Peter, a priest, in Provence ; and many another could I instance. Tanquelmus, forsooth, worked himself up into such a state of madness as to have himself named the Son of God and invoked as such and even, as is reported, to have persuaded the deluded populace to build a church in his honour." [3] He was fully alive to the intellectual and emotional dangers which beset the uninstructed populace. Probably he would have held that these dangers justified a reasonable presentation to them of the common faith. But none the less he should have known that what was needed was not solid food but milk. His " detractors," as he called them, might very well have had doubts as to whether the *pabulum* for which he was inviting men to scramble was not too strong meat, not merely for the professed *rudis*, but for many an ecclesiastic who ought to be *literatus* and was not. In the passage immediately following the last quoted he expresses his disapproval of certain " masters in divine literature, who notably in these days occupy amongst us the seats of pestilence and go about, one in France, another in Burgundy, a third in Anjou, a fourth in Bourges, not only holding but teaching many things contrary to the Catholic Faith or to holy doctrine."

It would be beyond our scope to attempt any full discussion of the theological position of Abélard. We shall have something more to say about it, however, when we come to refer to St. Bernard's treatise *On the Errors of Abélard*. At the period immediately preceding the Council of Sens of the year

[1] *Vita Prima,* III. v. 13.

[2] Abael. *Introd. adTheol.Prolog.,* Cousin, *Opp.,* II. 3.

[3] Abael. *Introd. adTheol.,op.cit.,* II. 84. Cf. Turberville, *Cambr. Med. Hist.,* VI. 702.

1140 attention was concentrated upon the consideration of his doctrine of the Trinity. He appeared to teach that there are degrees of superiority and inferiority in the rank of the sacred persons ; degrees not in order of origin, but in fulness of godhead. This he stoutly denied. He definitely repudiated the language attributed to him by William of St. Thierry, namely, that " the Father is plenary power, the Son a certain power, and the Holy Spirit no power at all." " These words," he protests, in his *Apology*, " as is most right, I abhor and detest as not so much heretical as diabolical, and I condemn them and their author alike. If any man can find them in my writings I confess myself to be, not merely a heretic but an heresiarch." [1] But this latter was precisely what St. Bernard contended that he was.

We may perhaps explain this contradiction by the fact that Abélard maintained the existence of an esoteric knowledge of God ; to which the ordinary Christian was, and must remain, an entire stranger, for it was the prerogative of the philosopher alone. It was possessed even by the pagans of the past, who only lost it because " they did not humbly pay to God the due debt of worship neither gave thanks." [2] They failed " to recognize that this exceptional gift to them of a knowledge of God came by divine grace, and accordingly to praise him for it." [3] The extent to which " by the revelation of God the doctrine of the Trinity itself was known to them is plainly indicated by the Apostle Paul in the *Epistle to the Romans*, when he says : *That which may be known of God is manifest in them, for God manifested it unto them*." [4] Abélard is not referring to the common folk but to philosophers, as the opening words of the paragraph make evident : " Now after the witness of the prophets (of the Old Testament) it is permissible to submit that of philosophers." [5] He would recognize, as had the Alexandrian fathers, a Dispensation of Paganism, that men had been " trained in different covenants of the one Lord." [6] With St. Augustine he would find confirmation of Christian doctrine in the writings of the Greeks.[7] To his contemporaries, however, he would appear to claim for himself as a philosopher a special right, in virtue of a special gift, to penetrate unfettered in thought into Christian mysteries without in any way impinging upon the sphere of dogmatic theology or compromising his orthodoxy as a Catholic. It would conceivably be allowed that *quantum ad forum externum* he might be as free as he liked in thought, provided that he did not publish his vagaries. Abélard himself might perhaps be able to reconcile them with the accepted Catholic

[1] Abael. *Apol.*, Cousin, *Opp.*, II. 720.

[2] *Rom.* I. 21.

[3] Abael. *in Ep. ad Rom.*, Cousin, *Opp.*, II. 174.

[4] *Rom.* I. 19.

[5] Abael. *Introd. ad Theol.*, Cousin, *Opp.*, II. 28 sq.

[6] S. Clem. Alex. *Strom.*, VI. 5.

[7] E.g. S. August. *De Civ. Dei*, XI. 21, *ed.* Welldon, 488 sq.

formulae, but simple minds which on his own showing were not possessed of this special gift of dialectical *acumen* which he claimed could not fail to be scandalized by their publication ; to them they would appear to be nothing less than denial of the faith.   In this light, whatever he may have been in himself, towards others he was an heresiarch, dangerous in proportion to the attractiveness of his literary style, to the interest of his past history and to the large number of his pupils.

A letter addressed to Innocent II in this year, 1140, by the Apostolic Legate, Geoffrey of Chartres, and by the bishops of Gaul reveals the subsequent course of events.   The writers state that, as the result of reports which had reached him frequently and from many quarters, St. Bernard had read the *Theologia* and other works of Abélard ; that he had conferred with him privately and then, " as the gospel prescribes, in the presence of two or three witnesses " ; and that he had admonished him " in a quite amiable and friendly way " to restrain his hearers from meddling in such matters and to correct his books.   Abélard took this ill and made repeated requests to the legate and to the bishops to cite St. Bernard to appear before them at Sens on the Octave of Pentecost, when he would himself be present in order to prove and to defend the opinions to which the Abbot of Clairvaux had taken exception.[1]   At first St. Bernard declined to accede to this proposal.   When, however, he learned that in any case Abélard would be there, and moreover that he was collecting a body of his pupils to accompany him in order to hear a public disputation, to be as it were spectators of a joust of dialectic between himself and his opponent, he no longer hesitated.[2]   The bearing upon this of a recently discovered letter of Abélard should not be overlooked, as evidence of his desire to display himself before the council.[3]

Meanwhile Abélard was not without support ; some of it indeed of doubtful credit.   Arnald of Brescia, who had been his pupil at Ste. Geneviève about the year 1115,[4] stormy petrel that he was, would appear to have recently arrived in France expelled from Italy ; for St. Bernard in a letter to Innocent II, describes him as playing the armour-bearer to Abélard's Goliath.[5]   More serviceable to Abélard, and therefore the more dangerous to St. Bernard, was a certain Hyacinth who at the time had considerable influence in the *Curia*.   He was, perhaps, the Jacinctus Bobo who was afterwards made a cardinal by Lucius II.[6]   Abélard was boasting that his works were in the hands of the *Curia* and that he could count

[1] *Vita Prima,* III. v. 13.

[2] *Inter S. Bern. Epp.,* 337 ; S. Bern. *Ep.* 189.

[3] Sikes, *Peter Abailard,* 228 sq.

[4] P. 320 *infra.*

[5] *Epp.* 189 and 195.

[6] Mabill. *Not. in S.Bern.Ep.*189.

[1] S. Bern. *Epp.*
193 and 338.

[2] *Ep.* 189.

[3] *Ep.* 338.

disciples among the cardinals.[1] Of this Hyacinth St. Bernard
speaks in the same terms in two letters, in one to Innocent
II already cited[2] and in another to Cardinal Haimeric.
" Hyacinth," he writes, " made show of doing me a great
deal of harm ; but he did not succeed—not because he did
not wish, but because he was not able to do so." [3]   Hyacinth
was probably responsible for the favourable view of Abélard
taken by various members of the *Curia* to whom he had submitted certain of his works. With the support of the free
lance Arnald and of his friends in high office at Rome Abélard
would be in good heart for his encounter with St. Bernard.

That the Abbot of Clairvaux would gladly have been
spared this battle of words there can be no doubt. In the
first instance he had declined it, both because, as he told the
Pope, he was " but a child," whereas his adversary was a
trained gladiator in dialectic, " from early years a mighty
man of war " ; and because it seemed to him to be an indignity " that the *ratio* of the faith should be bandied about
in argument by the *ratiunculae* of men." Moreover, he objected to the controversy being made a personal matter.
Abélard's own writings were his sufficient accusation ; it was
not for St. Bernard but " for the bishops, whose proper

[4] *Ep.* 189.

office it is, to pronounce upon dogmatic questions." [4]   Similarly he had written to the bishops themselves, urging the
danger of precipitancy—Abélard was evidently spoiling for
the fray—and pressing upon them the fact that the cause

[5] *Ep.* 187.

was much more theirs than it was his.[5]   It was due to St.
Bernard's foresight that, when Abélard appeared before the
council, it was not to give a display of dialectic but to be
judged. In fact he had so far been out-witted.

On the eve of the Octave of Pentecost Henry the Wild
Boar, Archbishop of Sens, saw his city invaded by a vast
concourse of ecclesiastics. There arrived, with the exception
of the Bishops of Paris and Nevers, all his own suffragans,
amongst them Geoffrey, Bishop of Chartres, Apostolic Legate,
and Hugh of Mâçon, Bishop of Auxerre, the old friend who
in 1145 would successfully avail himself of St. Bernard's
services in a controversy concerning feudal rights with William,

[6] S. Bern. *Chart.*,
III, *P.L.*
CLXXXII. 717
sqq.

[7] Otton. Frising.
*Gesta Frid. I.
Imp.*, I. 1.,
Waitz, *op. cit.*

[8] *Vita Prima*,
III. v. 15. Cf.
p. 313 *infra*.

Count of Nevers.[6]   Thither too came Samson, Archbishop of
Rheims, with three of his suffragans, Geoffrey of Châlons-
sur-Marne, Alvisus of Arras and Joslen of Soissons ; [7]   Samson,
Alvisus and Joslen being prelates much in the confidence
of St. Bernard. Amongst the large number present might
have been recognized Gilbert de la Porrée, subsequently
Bishop of Poitiers.[8]   Nor did the king, Louis le Jeune, and

William, Count of Nevers, fail to attend; for the original purpose of the assembly had been the veneration of certain relics in the cathedral.[1]

Whether the *Sermon on Conversion*, variously entitled *ad clericos* and *ad scholares* in the MSS., was delivered at Paris before or after the council it is difficult to say. But St. Bernard, being in the neighbourhood on other business, only delivered it under pressure from the diocesan Stephen of Senlis, and it deals not with heresy but with morals, being, in fact, a dramatic analysis of the disordered conscience, followed by an unsparing rebuke of the laxity of conduct prevailing among the clergy and a powerful appeal on a very high oratorical level for honesty and for clean living. Incidentally it has the great interest of having gained twenty-three recruits for Clairvaux, amongst them Geoffrey, St. Bernard's biographer.[2]

It is impossible to regard the *Apologeticus*, or apology for Abélard, which Berengarius, a pupil of his of whom nothing certain is known,[3] addressed to St. Bernard otherwise than as a lampoon; indeed at the outset the writer warns us not to take too seriously anything which he may say " against the person of the man of God." Nevertheless he gives us some information which may reasonably be accepted as true. After the veneration of the relics in the cathedral at Sens St. Bernard preached to the people and commended Abélard to their prayers; " although," to quote Berengarius, " behind the scenes he was arranging to have him expelled from the Christian world." [4] The bishops and the rest of the council having supped, the *Theologia* and other works were produced, incriminating passages were read aloud; and, as Berengarius puts it, after their *nunc est bibendum* the hearers were in a fit state to punctuate their disapproval with a *pulsanda tellus* ! Allowing for the exaggerations of the lampooner, it is a little doubtful whether this preliminary meeting was equitable or even canonical, for in the result it meant that Abélard was condemned unheard; at least it was prejudicial to his fair hearing. The council proper was held in the cathedral on the next day, Sunday. St. Bernard commented on the *Theologia;* but Abélard declined to make any answer. The bishops in their letter to Innocent II record that he was given every opportunity, and assured of just judgement and of protection against personal injury.[5] This last remark suggests that he was in fear of an outbreak of popular violence such as had greeted him at Soissons.[6] Otto of Freising speaks as if his only utterance, which was an appeal to the

[1] Episc. Gall. *Ep. inter S. Bern. Epp.* 337.

[2] Gaufr. *Fragm.*, *Cod. Aureaevall.*, 64 sq.; *Vita Prima*, III, *Praef.* and IV. ii. 10; *Excerpt. ex Exord. Magn.*, xiii. 19 sq.

[3] *R.H.G.F.* XIV. 294.

[4] Bereng. Schol. *Apolog.*, Cousin, *Opp.*, II. 772.

[5] *Inter S. Bern. Epp.*, 337.

[6] P. 297 *supra*.

[1] Otton. Frising.
*Gesta Frid. I
Imp., loc. cit.,*
Waitz, *op. cit.*
Cf. *Vita Prima,*
III. v. 14.
[2] P. 304 *supra.*
[3] *Vita Prima,*
III. v. 15 ;
Bereng. Schol.
Apolog., Cousin,
Opp., II. 773.

[4] *Epp.* 189 and
338.

[5] *Inter S. Bern.
Epp.,* 337.

[6] *Inter S. Bern.
Epp.,* 337.

[7] *Inter S. Bern.
Epp.,* 191.

Apostolic See, was in some measure intended to ward off anything of the kind ; [1] but probably his strongest motive would have been the confidence that, by the instrumentality of Hyacinth and of his friends in the *Curia*, the ground had been prepared to his advantage at Rome.[2] The story ran that as Abélard left the council he remarked to Gilbert de la Porrée : " Look to your roof ; there is a fire next door." [3]

Abélard's unforeseen appeal was a skilful counter, and doubtless disconcerting. Had the council, which to all intents and purposes was canonically provincial, now any authority to pass sentence on him ? Hyacinth was present, and although according to St. Bernard he had expressed himself in not particularly respectful language towards the Pope and the *Curia*, it was perhaps part of his plan to claim that the matter was no longer in the hands of the council.[4] On the other hand, was the appeal—made, as it was, previously to any sentence of the council—canonically regular ? Had Abélard the right to deny the competence of the council to judge him ? [5] The bishops decided to pronounce no sentence upon his person, but to arrange in *capitula* certain statements from his writings which they held to be erroneous, and to submit them to the Pope under a covering letter from the Archbishop of Sens, the Bishop of Chartres, Apostolic Legate, and the Bishops of Orleans, Auxerre, Troyes and Meaux.[6] This letter was supported by another addressed to Innocent by the Archbishop of Rheims and his three suffragans present at Sens, Joslen of Soissons, Geoffrey of Châlons-sur-Marne and Alvisus of Arras.[7] It is probable that alike in motive and in matter both these letters owed much to St. Bernard. Finally the Abbot of Clairvaux himself wrote a letter to which reference has already more than once been made. He wrote with full consciousness of what was at stake, yet not without the expression of his deep sorrow that he should so soon again be called upon to engage in battle against the enemies of the Church. " In my folly I have but lately been promising myself rest, seeing that the leonine fury," meaning, of course, the schism of Anacletus, " has passed away and peace is restored to the Church. . . . We have escaped the lion but we have met the dragon, who lies in wait for us with a craft perchance not less dangerous than the loud roaring of that beast." What is so desperate, he tells Innocent, is the subtle attractiveness of the new teaching. The poison is everywhere as acceptable as honey. But it is a new gospel, a new faith, another foundation than that which is laid. " Virtue and vice are discussed on false moral principles ; the sacraments with no regard to the faith ; the mystery of the Holy Trinity is propounded neither simply nor soberly ; but everything is set forth perversely, everything unwontedly and otherwise than as we have received it." [1] For St. Bernard it meant unsettlement of mind, the questioning of the validity of grounds and of motives which for centuries had served to steady and to direct human conduct ; it was the putting into the melting-pot of divinely accredited and well-tested engines of defence against evil. On all these scores the arrival of Arnald of Brescia was a sinister enough omen ; and finally Hyacinth, a truculent fellow, was a disruptive force in the *Curia* itself ; Nicholas, the Clairvaux monk who bears the letter, would tell the Pope all about his behaviour at Sens.

Reference has been made to the *capitula* sent to Innocent by the Archbishop of Sens and his suffragans.[2] In the XVIIth century the learned Maurist Dom Orsin Durand found in the Vatican Library a MS. numbered 663, which contained fourteen *capitula* of the heresies of Abélard. Mabillon was of the opinion that these were the *capitula* which St. Bernard sent to the Pope under cover of his *Epistle CXC*, commonly known as the *Tractate on the Errors of Abélard*.[3] It is probable that they are identical with the *capitula* sent by the council and that, as we may think, St. Bernard was responsible for the drafting of them. The treatise may well have been despatched soon after the letter of the council, *Epistle CCCXXXVII*. A reference to it disposes us to doubt whether, had St. Bernard crossed swords with Abélard before the council as judges, he would have been routed so ignominiously as he seems to have feared. Less keen of intellect, he yet possessed forensic gifts wanting to his adversary. His reasoning was concrete, Johnsonian ; of a character likely to commend it at the bar of men who used their senses. There was occasionally something of the *argumentum ad baculum* about his manner, it would seem. Dealing with Abélard's teaching concerning the Trinity he remarks : " I am surprised that a man of intellectual force and somewhat learned, as he would have himself to be, can reconcile his belief that the Father, the Son and the Holy Spirit are consubstantial with the denial that the Holy Spirit proceeds from the substance of the Father and of the Son ; unless perhaps he would maintain that the Father and the Son proceed from the substance of the Holy Spirit, which is unheard of and not to be said. But if neither of these statements is true what, I ask, does consubstantiality mean ? " [4] Again

[1] *Ep.* 189 (2).

[2] P. 306 *supra*.

[3] *De Error. Abael.*, IX. 26.

[4] *Op. cit.*, I. 3.

on a kindred subject he writes : " To the Son, as has been said, he attributes wisdom ; not indeed wisdom without any qualification (*simpliciter*) but a certain wisdom which he defines in the deity as wisdom merely of discerning. Perhaps he is afraid of doing injury to the Father if he attributes as much to the Son as he does to him ; and so, because he does not dare to attribute to the Son the whole of wisdom, he attributes to him half of it." [1] Later in the treatise St. Bernard refers to Abélard's definition of faith as valuation (*aestimatio*), " as though it were permissible for a man to think or to say what he pleases, or as though the mysteries of our faith depended uncertainly upon vague and various opinions and were not rather founded upon certain truth." [2] The passage which St. Bernard has in mind occurs in the *Introduction to Theology* and runs as follows : " Faith is the judging (*existimatio*) of things which do not appear." [3] It is obviously a reminiscence of Hebrews xi. 1, *existimatio* being substituted for *argumentum*. We shall scarcely feel that the substitution is felicitous. And was it quite ingenuous on the part of a dialectician like Abélard to make it ? The remainder of the treatise deals for the most part with the doctrine of redemption. Broadly speaking Abélard's view may be stated to have been that it was not the devil who had made to man the promise of immortal life but God ; and that therefore no right of the devil had been violated by man's disobedience. And further, in his own words, " the devil acquired no right over man whom he led astray by leading him astray, unless perhaps, as we have said, by the leave of the Lord who handed him over to him as to a gaoler or to a torturer for punishment." [4] Let us state St. Bernard's view also in his own words. " This right of the devil over man, although it was not justly acquired but unjustly usurped, is yet justly allowed. Therefore man was justly held captive in such a way that the justice of it was founded, neither in what man had done, nor in what the devil had done, but in what God had done " ; perhaps the last clause were better rendered " in what God is." Where the real divergence was emphatic was as to what was effected by the passion. " We were justified," writes Abélard, " in the blood of Christ and reconciled to God because, by this singular favour shown towards us, namely, that his Son assumed our nature and in that nature persevered unto death in the work of teaching us both by word and by example, he bound us more closely to himself in love ; so that kindled by such bounty of divine favour love no longer fears to endure anything for his

[1] *Op. cit.*, III. 6.

[2] *Op. cit.*, IV. 9.

[3] Petr. Abael. *Introd. ad Theol.*, I, Cousin, *Opp.*, II. 5.

[4] Petr. Abael. *Comment. in Ep. ad Rom.*, II, Cousin, *Opp.*, II. 205.

[5] S. Bern. *De Error. Abael.*, V. 14.

sake." [1] " The efficacy of Christ's death is now quite definitely and explicitly explained by its subjective influence upon the mind of the sinner." [2] On the other hand, St. Bernard tells us that " the prince of this world came and found nothing in the Saviour ; and when nevertheless he laid hands upon the innocent, he most justly lost those whom he held in durance ; since he who owed nothing to death, receiving unjustly the penalty of death, justly set free both from the debt of death and from the dominion of the devil him who was guilty of death." [3] Thus, it would appear, for St. Bernard the dominant idea was that of objective satisfaction effected prior to any " subjective influence upon the mind of the sinner," although we shall have indeed misread him if we can suppose him to have ignored this latter. [4]

Before we lay down the treatise two fine passages may be quoted. " It was not the death itself which pleased him (the Father), but the will of him who freely died and by that death destroyed death, wrought salvation, restored innocence, triumphed over principalities and powers, spoiled hell, en-riched the citizens on high, brought about peace between heaven and earth, made all thing new." [5] And again : " God the Father did not demand the death of the Son, yet he ac-cepted it when offered ; what he thirsted for was not blood but salvation, for salvation was in the blood." [6]

St. Bernard was not content with refuting Abélard's doctrinal statements ; he found in his character material for animadversion. To him he was a kind of dual personality, almost uncanny in its workings. " He is," he writes to Cardinal Ivo, " a man inconsistent with himself ; inwardly he is Herod, outwardly he is John ; an entirely double-faced person having about him nothing of the monk except the name and the habit." [7] He warns Cardinal Guy of Castello, a former pupil of Abélard who in 1143 was raised to the pon-tificate as Celestin II, against a man " whose mouth is full of cursing, bitterness and guile." [8] We need not regard this as particularly uncharitable ; it was after the manner of the psalmist, in whose language he was steeped.

As the toils tightened Abélard struggled to free him-self. A pathetic figure, his health was beginning to fail and he was of two minds as to whether he should brazen it out to the bitter end or not. We know from Otto of Freising that he wrote a profession of his faith. [9] The text of it is for the greater part lost, but we may gather something of its matter and of its manner from a *Disputation* written in reply to it by an anonymous abbot ; it appears not only to

[1] Petr. Abael. *Comment. in Ep. ad Rom.*, II, Cousin, *Opp.*, II. 207.

[2] Rashdall, *The Idea of Atonement in Christian Theol.*, 358.

[3] S. Bern. *De Error. Abael.*, VI. 15.

[4] Rashdall, *op. cit.*, 438.

[5] *Op. cit.*, VIII. 21.

[6] *Op. cit.*, VIII. 22.

[7] *Ep.* 193.

[8] *Ep.* 192.

[9] Otton. Frising. *Gesta Frid. I Imp.*, *loc. cit.*, Waitz, *op. cit.*

have stated his own beliefs, but to have been unsparing in
its criticism of St. Bernard.[1] Its tone would have been quite
different from that of the *Confession* above-mentioned [2] addressed to Héloïse.

Ere long Abélard set out on a journey to Rome. On his
way he stopped at Cluny where the news of the Papal judgement probably reached him.[3] The rescript, dated 16th July,
1140, was addressed to the Archbishops of Sens and Rheims,
to their suffragans and to the Abbot of Clairvaux. The
sentence runs : " On the authority of the sacred canons
we have condemned all the perverse doctrine of the same
Peter, and we have imposed upon him as a heretic perpetual
silence. Moreover, all the followers and defenders of his error
we decree to be separated from the company of the faithful,
and to lie bound under excommunication." [4] To enforce the
meaning all the works of Abélard were publicly burnt in
the Vatican Basilica.[5] Another rescript of the same date
brought instructions that not only Abélard but also Arnald
of Brescia was to be incarcerated, each in a monastery convenient for the purpose.[6]

Rome had spoken ; *causa finita est.* Are we to declare
that the whole course of proceedings was scandalous ? On
the view which we have taken, which makes no claim to be
at all profound, such a protest seems scarcely reasonable.
We have, laying aside so far as is possible all *parti pris*, to
carry ourselves back into the XIIth century, and to try to
realize the state of the Western world in those days, intellectual and moral. If we decline to attempt the impossible,
as it may seem—then we must try to form some estimate
of the characters of the two chief actors in this tragedy.
Taking the rank and file, the overwhelming majority of
humanity, which of these two men, St. Bernard or Abélard,
understood his generation the better ? Above all, which of
them was the more fully alive to the dangers to which its
limitations exposed it ? Which again was the more enthusiastic for its well-being ? Which more evidently wore
the mantle of the prophet ? Just because of its rich en-
dowments humanity is at certain childlike, almost childish,
stages in its history the easy prey of charlatans. Not that
Abélard was such ; but, as we have seen,[7] he was well aware
of their prevalence. At such stages, of which the XIIth
century was perhaps one, what it needs is very plain instruction, both protective and directive. Then if ever is
it the man who fell among thieves. Whose finger, St.
Bernard's or Abélard's, was the more sensitive to the beat

[1] *Disput. Anon.
Abb.,* Tissier,
*Bibl. PP.
Cisterc.,* II. iv.
238 sqq., *P.L.*
CLXXX. 283
sqq.

[2] P. 296 *supra.*

[3] Petr. Ven.
Epp. IV. iv.,
P.L.
CLXXXIX.
305 sq.

[4] *Inter S. Bern.
Epp.* 194 ; Jaffé,
Regest., 8148.

[5] Gaufr. Ab.
Clarevall. *Ep. ad
Card. Alban.,*
14, *P.L.*
CLXXXV. 595
sq

[6] Jaffé, *Regest.,*
8149.

[7] P. 301 *supra.*

of the patient's pulse in his day ? St. Bernard's diagnosis we shall, it may be, think to have been at times almost inspired. He might not have been able to state his reasons with the skill of a trained dialectician like Abélard ; he may sometimes have been impatient of opposition ; he may even have been dictatorial in his manner; he was, as Abélard certainly felt, alarming by the magnetism of his personal attraction ; but he knew the patient and the patient was his first consideration. Let us, however, be fair to Abélard. Let us recognize in him the hero of criticism and of independence of thought, the fruition of whose services to intellect is not immediate—indeed immediately they may be disastrous in certain of their effects—but in the future. Nor had he long to wait, for his influence may be found in the writings of Hugh of St. Victor, of Peter Lombard and of John of Salisbury, to name no more than these.[1]

A contrast has been drawn of St. Bernard the loyalist with Abélard the rebel. But this, surely, is to anticipate the atmosphere of centuries later. Abélard was entirely loyal in his Roman allegiance. Fully conscious of this it was that he not merely appealed, but became a pilgrim, to the Apostolic See. He was not so much as cited to its bar ; and the Council of Sens deliberately left his person at liberty. There would seem to be no reason why in this instance we should reject the evidence of Berengarius, who tells us that " in his so many and so great straits Abélard fled as to a city of refuge to the tribunal of Rome. ' I am,' he said, ' a child of the Roman Church. I would have my case judged as was that of a heathen of old. I appeal to Cæsar.' "[2] Although he would not allow that his intentions had been other than irreproachable—" I have openly taught," he asserted, " what seemed to me to contribute to the maintenance of the faith and to the promotion of good morals "—he was yet prepared to correct anything to which exception was taken by the proper authority. And this he actually did, perhaps with a sad smile at the remembrance of St. Benedict's warning in the Rule, *in multiloquio non effugies peccatum.* He was a son of the Church ; what the Church received he received, and what the Church rejected he rejected.[3]

His pilgrimage, in more senses than one, reached its end elsewhere than at Rome. By permission of the Pope, granted on the request of Peter the Venerable that he should be admitted a Cluniac monk, he spent his days at Cluny in intercourse with the abbot and his monks and in such intellectual study as his sufferings, in particular a distressing

[1] Reade, *Philosophy in the Middle Ages, Cambridge Med. Hist.,* V. 803 sqq.

[2] Bereng. Schol. *Apolog.,* Cousin, *Opp.,* II. 775.

[3] Petr. Abael. *Apolog.,* Cousin, *Opp.,* II. 720.

affection of the skin, would allow. We can picture him sitting under the now secular lime tree, the *tilleul d'Abélard*, if we may believe it to be so old—and placidly reflecting upon an interview with St. Bernard at which, as he reported to Peter the Venerable, " their ancient enmities had been appeased." [1] This interview, which took place at Cîteaux, had been felicitously arranged by Abbot Raynald. Abélard's health grew worse at Cluny and Peter, with the hope of improving it, sent him to the Priory of St. Marcel, about two miles from Châlon-sur-Saône. There on 21st April, 1142, in the presence of the whole community he died a Christian death [2] at the age of sixty-three. After a brief period of interment in the chapel of the infirmary at St. Marcel his remains were granted by Peter to the Abbey of Le-Paraclet, whither they were secretly translated. It is interesting to note that, his father now dead, Héloïse begs the Abbot of Cluny to obtain from the Bishop of Paris or from some other bishop a prebend for their son Astralabius. She also prays for Abélard's absolution, duly signed and sealed by Peter, to be sent to her in order that it may be hung over his tomb.[3] After her own death in 1164 their remains lay side by side, until in 1800 they were taken to Paris and in 1817 reinterred at Père-Lachaise. And this was the fleshly dissolution of one whom Vacandard does not hesitate to describe as " the most illustrious forerunner of Peter Lombard and of St. Thomas Aquinas." [4] He himself, as Peter the Venerable wrote—the most homely line of a somewhat stilted encomium [5]—

Ad Christi veram transivit philosophiam.

The tablet now fixed on the South wall of the Church of St. Marcel was inscribed at some date between 1650 and

[1] Petr. Ven. *Epp. Lib.*, IV. iv., *P.L. loc. cit.*

[2] Petr. Ven. *Ep. ad Heloiss.*, Cousin, *Opp.*, I. 714 ; Otton. Frising. *Gesta Frid. I Imp.*, I. li., Waitz, *op. cit.*

[3] Heloiss. *Ep. ad Petr. Ven.*, Cousin, *Opp.*, I. 715.

[4] Vacandard, *Vie de saint Bernard*, II. 180, éd. 1920.

[5] *P.L.* CLXXXIX. 1022 sq.

HIC PRIMO JACUIT PETRUS ABELARDUS
FRANCUS ET MONACHUS CLUNIACENSIS
QUI OBIJT ANNO 1142
NUNC APUD MONIALES PARACLITENSES
IN TERRITORIO TRECASCENSI REQUIESCIT
VIR PIETATE INSIGNIS SCRIPTIS CLARISSIMUS
INGENIJ ACUMINE RATIONŪ PONDERE DICENDI ARTE
OMNI SCIENTIARUM GENERE NULLI SECUNDUS.

1736. It may have marked the cenotaph in the chapel of the infirmary and, when about the year 1675 under Alexander de Nagu de Varennes, who became prior in 1633, this building was destroyed, then have been removed to its present position. The cenotaph, which represented Abélard in his monastic habit, was itself removed to the same place at the same time ; but it no longer exists, having probably disappeared at the Revolution.[1]

GILBERT DE LA PORRÉE

Gilbert de la Porrée was born at Poitiers in the year 1076. Otto of Freising, under the date 1142, describes him as having " from youth to maturity given himself to the study of philosophy in different parts of Gaul," as having " both in name and in fact fulfilled the office of a master," as having " recently attained to the height of episcopal rank at Poitiers " [2] and, it is to be noted, as a man " whose habit it was, owing to the subtilty of his mind and to the keenness of his reasoning faculty, to state many propositions in a quite unusual way." [3] Otto would seem to be referring less to the matter than to the manner of his teaching, as that of one who took some pleasure in startling his hearers, who at any rate did not run in a groove ; John of Salisbury represents him as characteristically contemptuous of the folly of his age.[4] In the first instance he had learned from a certain Hilary who taught in Gilbert's native city of Poitiers. Subsequently his masters had been Bernard of Chartres and the two brothers Anselm and Raoul of Laon. It would probably have been from Bernard of Chartres that he derived his theory that universals, ideas in the Platonic sense, confer such a universality upon their particulars that, not singly but taken in their totality, these latter are themselves universals, being, however, in each case rather an *eidos* than an *idea*.[5] Thus man, the universal, is an *idea ;* on the other hand, man, the human race—not the particular man—is also a universal, but an *eidos*. Gilbert, Otto goes on to say, was a person who impressed people favourably by his gravity, but unfortunately when he began to teach he was so abstruse that even the most learned and highly cultivated intellects could with difficulty understand him.[6]

On the occasion of a diocesan synod held in 1146 Gilbert expressed himself in a sermon to the clergy so strangely, as it seemed to his hearers, that one of his archdeacons, Arnald who bore the *sobriquet* of " sober sides " (*qui non ridet*), openly reasoned with him and a joust of dialectic between

[1] *Gall. Christ.,* IV. 960 ; Court-épée, *Descr. hist. et topogr. du duché de Bourgogne,* V. 182 sq., *éd.* 1780 ; Perrault-Dabot, *Mém. de la Soc. d'hist. et d'archéol. de Châlon* (1929), 55.

[2] *Gall. Christ.,* II. 1178.

[3] Otton. Frising. *Gesta Frid. I Imp.,* I. xlviii., Waitz, *op. cit.,* 67 sq. Cf. Joann. Sares. *Hist. Pontifical.,* VIII. 17 sq., *ed.* Poole.

[4] Joann. Sares. *Metalog.,* I. v., *ed.* Webb, 16.

[5] Gilson, *La phil. au moyen âge,* 59 ; Reade, *Cambr. Med. Hist.,* V. 809 sq. Cf. Joann. Sares. *Metalog.,* II. xvii., *ed.* Webb, 91 sq.

[6] Otton. Frising. *op. cit.,* I. lii.

them ensued. The matter could not rest there, and Arnald and his brother archdeacon Calon decided to go to Rome and lay an appeal before the Apostolic See.[1] We rely for many of our details upon a letter written to the Cardinal Bishop of Albano, Albino by name, by Geoffrey, fourth Abbot of Clairvaux.[2] About forty years earlier Geoffrey had written a *Libellus contra Capitula Gilberti*, which also he had addressed to Cardinal Albino ; this got mislaid and was only brought to light again when he had already restated in the letter almost everything which was material.[3] Taken together the *Libellus* and the letter are valuable evidence ; moreover, they are generally supported by Otto of Freising.[4] Eugenius III, exiled from his city by revolution, was from some day in May, 1146, until the end of December in the same year at Viterbo.[5] Otto tells us that the two archdeacons met him at Siena on his way to France ; we gather that it was now early in 1147. His reply to their appeal was that on his arrival in France he would inform himself more fully, and deal with the matter accordingly. The appellants returned and after laying their case before St. Bernard enlisted his support.[6] The Pope had in view the council convened to meet at Paris the following Easter. His stay in this city lasted from 20th April to 7th June, 1147 ;[7] at some time between these two days the council was held ; on 21st April St. Bernard was in the immediate neighbourhood ;[8] and he was present at the council.[9] Gilbert was opposed, not only by St. Bernard but also by other distinguished authorities, such as Adam of Petit-Pont, Canon of Paris, "a subtle person," Hugh of Champfleuri, Chancellor of the King, and Hugh of Amiens, Archbishop of Rouen, who all three deposed to having heard damaging statements fall from his mouth.[10] The principal charge against him, derived rightly or wrongly from his commentary on the *De Trinitate* of Boëthius, would seem to have been that he taught "that the divinity is not God ; that there is in God a form or essence which is not God."[11] "This," writes Geoffrey, "was the origin of his wrong doctrine. He propounded that there is in God a form by which God exists, but which is not God ; just as humanity is the form of man, not what he is but that by which he is man."[12] To this we shall recur. After a discussion which lasted for several days, the Pope decided to postpone the matter for further consideration at a council to be held at Rheims on Mid-Lent Sunday, 21st March, in the following year, 1148. Eugenius was awaiting a favourable opportunity for his return to Rome, where the reaction of feeling following the

---

[1] *Op. cit., loc. cit.*

[2] Gaufr. Ab. Clar. *Ep. ad Alb. Card.*, 2, *P.L.* CLXXXV. 587 sqq.

[3] *Op. cit.*, 13.

[4] Gaufr. *Libell. contra Cap. Gilb.*, *P.L.* CLXXXV. 595 sqq.

[5] Jaffé, *Regest.*, 8923 sqq.

[6] Otton. Frising. *op. cit.*, I. xlviii.

[7] Jaffé, *Regest.*, 9024 sqq.

[8] *Gall. Christ.*, VIII. 613.

[9] Gaufr. *Ep.*, *loc. cit.*

[10] Otton. Frising. *op. cit.*, I. liii.

[11] Gaufr. *Ep.*, *loc. cit.* Cf. Mans. *Concil.*, XXI. 711.

[12] Gaufr. *Libell. De Cap. Primo ; Ep. ad Alb. Card.*, 4.

failure of the Second Crusade had added to the difficulties of his position.[1]

The Council of Paris had been formally dissolved; the Council of Rheims was a new council, upon the importance of which the authorities lay stress. Otto refers to it as "general," "universal"—although probably we should not regard the terms as technical; Geoffrey describes it as "a great council" at which were assembled "the bishops of four kingdoms, of Gaul, of Germany, of England and of Spain."[2] Gilbert presented himself, attended by the clergy of his household bearing a large collection of patristic and other works, not forgetting, we may be sure, those of the bishop's distinguished predecessor, St. Hilary, which he had studied deeply.[3] We should remember that Gilbert was a man of immense learning, possessed of one of the finest libraries of his day.[4] He had submitted his commentary, which the Pope had handed to Abbot Godeschalk of the Premonstratensian house of Mont-St. Éloi, instructing him to draw up a report upon it. Godeschalk accordingly attended with his report based upon various patristic authorities. One "mighty pillar of the Church," the Cardinal Legate Alberic, Bishop of Ostia, was, alas, missing; he had recently died, but not before he had learned in Aquitaine much concerning the character and the doctrine of Gilbert; had he been present the Bishop of Poitiers' self-assurance might have been less emphatic.[5]

Amongst the prelates present at the council were Gilbert's metropolitan Geoffrey du Loroux, Archbishop of Bordeaux, Joslen, Bishop of Soissons, and Suger, Abbot of St. Denis.[6] After much discussion, in which many joined but apparently few shone, for Gilbert was an accomplished fencer—and the Pope was beginning to weary of the prolonged and fruitless logomachy, St. Bernard put the trenchant question. "The origin of this scandal is," he remarks to Gilbert, "that many think that you believe and teach that the divine essence or nature, the divinity of God, his wisdom, goodness, greatness, is not God, but the form by which he is God. If you believe this, say so plainly or else deny it." The reply was prompt. "The form of God, the divinity by which he is God, is not itself God." "Now," says St. Bernard, "we have got what we have been looking for; let his confession of faith be written down." Gilbert raised no objection and formally attested his belief in writing. "Now do you write," he says, turning to the Abbot of Clairvaux, "that the divinity is God." Calmly St. Bernard replies: "Let it be written

[1] Otton. Frising. op. cit., I. lvi.; Balzani, Cambr. Med. Hist., V. 376 sq.

[2] Otton. Frising. op. cit., loc. cit.; Gaufr. Libell., 4, P.L. CLXXXV. 596.

[3] Gaufr. Ep. 4.

[4] Planctus Laurent., R.H.G.F. XIV. 380.

[5] Gaufr. Ep. 3. Cf. Joann. Sares. Hist. Pontifical., IX. 21, ed. Poole.

[6] Op. cit., loc. cit.

with an iron stile of adamantine point, or if you will engraved on flint, that the divine essence, form, nature, deity, goodness, wisdom, virtue, power, greatness, is truly God." [1] St. Bernard pressed the point that if the form of God is not God, it is something higher than God, seeing that from it God derives his being, founding himself upon such passages in the *De Trinitate* of St. Augustine as "God is great, not by partaking of greatness but by being himself greatness." [2]

Gilbert continued to produce his authorities, Greek as well as Latin, and the discussion, much of it probably unintelligible to the majority of those present, to take its course until Passiontide began. [3] We may recapitulate in the words of Geoffrey the statements charged against him. "I. That the divine essence, substance and nature which is called the divinity, goodness, wisdom, greatness of God and the like, is not God but the form by which he is God. II. That the three persons, Father, Son and Holy Spirit, are neither one God nor one substance nor one anything. III. That the three persons are three by their three unities, and are distinguished by three properties which are not the same as the persons themselves ; but that there are three eternal units, differing both from one another and from the divine substance. IV. That the divine nature was not incarnate nor did it assume human nature." [4] Whether this be a fair statement or not, there is little doubt but that the four articles are theologically associated. Gilbert contended that his view offered the only escape from the dilemma presented by the Arian doctrine of plurality of essences and the Sabellian doctrine of one essence which is one person ; and his view he based upon the distinction between the *subsistens*, God, and the *subsistentia* or *substantia qua est subsistens*, the divinity. Theodoret, he declared, had held that "whosoever understands the nature and the person to be the same, falls either into Arian division or into Sabellian confusion." Less plausible would seem to have been his contention that the *assumens* at the Incarnation was "that which is proper to the Son, not that which is proper to the Trinity " ; [5] although in making this statement he professed to found himself upon the VIth Council of Toledo. [6]

Finally the council was dissolved ; "we have heard," said the cardinals, "what has been put before us and now we will adjudicate upon the matter and define suitably." Thereupon St. Bernard, growing impatient of "the law's delays," promptly convened some ten archbishops and the

[1] *Op. cit.*, 4.

[2] *Op. cit.*, 5 ; S. Aug. *De Trin.*, V. x. (11).

[3] Otton. Frising. *op. cit.*, I. lviii.

[4] Gaufr. *Libell.*, *ad fin.*

[5] Otton. Frising. *op. cit., loc. cit.*

[6] Mans. *Concil.*, X. 662.

majority of bishops, abbots and masters available, and with them drew up a confession in four articles, denying explicitly the four statements ascribed to Gilbert.[1] This was submitted to the Pope and to the cardinals by the bishops, Hugh of Auxerre and Milo of Thérouanne, and by Suger, Abbot of St. Denis.[2] The cardinals were furious at such previous action. " What," they exclaimed, " have this abbot of yours and the Gallican Church been doing ? . . . Why, these Frenchmen, without our knowing anything about it, have presumed, forsooth, to write a creed for themselves ! " There was evidently some support for Gilbert in the ranks of the *Curia*; and perhaps some—certainly unfounded—suspicion that those same Frenchmen were contemplating in the last resort a separatist move.[3] However, at the orders of Eugenius St. Bernard explained that what was intended was not a formal *symbolum*, but an expression of belief analogous to that of Gilbert.[4] Nevertheless he had forced the pace, and he was reassured by the Pope's statement that the Roman Church in no way dissented from the terms which had been used in the confession. Shortly afterwards an assembly was held in a hall of the archiepiscopal palace which was called Tau, from its being built on the plan of the letter T. This is referred to by Geoffrey as an assembly of " the whole Church " ; whatever we are to understand by this, it was something different from the council which had already been dissolved. Its proceedings suggest that its status should be interpreted on the principle of *ubi Papa, ibi Roma*. The Pope himself unmistakably adopted a tone of supreme authority, and Gilbert was decidedly more submissive than he had been hitherto. When called upon to abjure freely the four articles charged against him, his reply was : " If you believe otherwise, so do I; if you state otherwise, so do I; if you write otherwise, so do I." Thereupon the Pope on his Apostolic authority and with the consent of all present condemned the articles, and gave strict injunctions that none should dare either to read or to transcribe Gilbert's commentary on the *De Trinitate* of Boëthius until the Roman Church had corrected it.[5] When Gilbert offered to correct it himself exactly as the Pope might wish, he was told : " This work of correction will not be entrusted to you." The matter was entirely reserved to the Apostolic See.[6] Thus Gilbert was reconciled to the Church, and returned to his diocese to find with some sense of satisfaction that he had been so thoroughly whitewashed as now to be quite acceptable to his archdeacons.[7]

[1] Gaufr. *Ep.* 7.

Cf. Joann. Sares. *Hist. Pontifical.*, VIII. 18 sqq. and XI. 25, ed. Poole.

[2] *Op. cit.*, 8.

[3] Joann. Sares. *Hist. Pontifical.*, IX. 21, ed. Poole.

[4] Otton. Frising. *op. cit.*, I. lx.

[5] Joann. Sares. *Hist. Pontifical.*, XI. 25 sq., ed. Poole.

[6] Gaufr. *Ep.* 8.

[7] Otton. Frising. *op. cit.*, I. lx.

To St. Bernard, however, the way in which it had all ended was by no means acceptable. In spite of the strong prejudice which, generated in the main by the action which he had taken against Abélard, possessed the minds of the cardinals to his disfavour,[1] the support of Eugenius had technically won for him the day ; yet he was evidently perturbed by the fact that the settlement remained no more than superficial, so long as Gilbert refused to allow that he had misinterpreted St. Hilary. Accordingly through John of Salisbury, Gilbert's pupil—who had been present at the council and whose testimony to its proceedings has a freshness and an impartiality peculiar to itself—he approached the Bishop of Poitiers and suggested a friendly conference. The latter, with some disdain for an adversary whom he regarded doubtless as unworthy of his steel, declined. The corrections of his commentary on the *De Trinitate* of Boëthius he had accepted ; but when he came to embody them, he made it plain by his remarks that he did so solely on the ground that he had caused scandal by the use of language, the orthodoxy of which ought to be sufficiently irreproachable in the eyes of men who know how to reason.[2] It is not probable that he ever really abandoned the position which he had taken. But he underrated St. Bernard's acumen. Addressing himself to Eugenius not long afterwards in answer to the question " What is God ? " the Abbot of Clairvaux writes : " I venture to put it to you that there is not anything by which God exists which is not God. How is not that which gives existence to God, supposing it not to be God, better than God ? But we contend that that better thing, namely, the divinity by which they say that God exists, is naught else than God. 'What?' they say, 'Do you deny that God possesses divinity ? ' No ; but what he possesses that he is." [3] We find him very near the end of his life again referring to the subject ; when, after repudiating Gilbert's perverse interpretation both of Boëthius and of Fulgentius, he exclaims : " God forbid that the Catholic Church should allow that there is, forsooth, a substance or anything else at all by which God exists and which is not God." [4]

Gilbert died in 1154 but he lived on in his works, in particular in his *Liber Sex Principiorum* which was in effect a completion of the *Categories* of Aristotle ; it found its commentators so late as the dawn of the Renaissance.[5] His theology, or rather his conception of theological *data*, was perhaps influenced by the peculiar character of his realism.

[1] Joann. Sares. *Hist. Pontifical.*, IX. 20 sq., ed. Poole.

[2] Joann. Sares. *op. cit.*, XII. 27 and XIII. 30, ed. cit.

[3] S. Bern. *De Consid.*, V. vii. 15.

[4] S. Bern. *In Cant. Cant.*, LXXX. 8.

[5] Gilson, *La phil. au moyen âge*, 58 sq.

[6] P. 313 *supra*.

It was, moreover, impossible for him to regard theological *data* when treated metaphysically as exempt from the treatment applied to any other *data*. He was probably incapable of doing so. If in his view the *subsistentia* humanity was not man the *subsistens*, then by no process of reasoning intelligible to him could the *subsistentia* divinity be proved to be God the *subsistens*. Perhaps we shall say that his opponents were equally incapable, and that in fact they cut rather than untied the knot. In any case shafts from the theological bow fell blunted by their impact against the mail of his logic. It was not that he held the formal teaching of the Church to be theologically untrue, but rather that he felt the matters with which he dealt to be no concern of theology proper. Let the theologians mind their business and he would mind his. In truth it was as yet too soon for the *synthesis ;* it awaited a St. Thomas of Aquino.

CHAPTER XIV

ARNALD OF BRESCIA AND HIS CONGENERS

TURNING from Abélard and Gilbert de la Porrée to Arnald of Brescia, we pass from an atmosphere of metaphysical to one mainly of moral interest ; moral in no restricted sense of the term, for it concerns both social and political life and the latter no less ecclesiastical than civil. Born a few years later than St. Bernard, Arnald was educated at Brescia either in a monastic or in an episcopal school. Early in life, after receiving the minor order of *lector*, he travelled to France, and became a pupil of Abélard on the Mont-Ste. Geneviève ; [1] he may have been amongst those to whom Abélard referred when he wrote that, on the day of his arrival at Soissons for the council of 1121, " the populace almost stoned me and the few of my pupils who had come with me." [2] He was a man apparently of irreproachable morals, indeed an ascetic. Even St. Bernard could write of him to the Bishop of Constance in 1142 or 1143 that he wished " that his doctrine were as sound as his life is strict," that " he is a man who neither eats nor drinks " ; adding, however, that " it is the devil with whom he takes his food and with whom he thirsts for the blood of souls." [3] With more restraint John of Salisbury records him to have been one who " was accustomed to vex his flesh by clothing coarsely and by fasting . . . a vehement preacher of contempt of the world." [4] In the immediate context the same writer describes him as a priest and a canon regular, " keen in intellect, assiduous in study of the Scriptures, eloquent in speech. . . . But reported to have been a seditious person and the promoter of faction who, wherever he might be, prevented the citizens from living at peace with the clergy." Otto of Freising writes of him more severely as " a wolf in sheep's clothing . . . a man certainly not dull in wits but impressive by reason rather of his flow of words, than of the weight of his matter ; a lover of singularity, a seeker after novelty, the kind of person whose mind is apt to invent heresy and to stir up schism. When he returned to Italy from Gaul he became a religious

[1] Otton. Frising. *Gesta Frid. I Imp.*, II. xxviii., Waitz, *Script. Rer. Germ.*

[2] Petr. Abael. *Ep.*, I. 9, Cousin, *Opp.*, I. 19.

[3] *Ep.* 195.

[2] Joann. Sares. *Hist. Pontifical.*, XXXI. 63, *ed.* Poole.

in order that he might the better deceive people, railing at everything, disparaging everything, sparing nobody ; a detractor of clergy and of bishops ; reserving his flattery for the laity alone, for he was wont to say that neither clergy who possessed anything nor bishops who enjoyed *regalia* nor monks who held property could by any means be saved. Everything he held to belong to the secular prince, and by his bounty should be granted only to the laity for their use." With some reserve Otto adds : " In addition to this he is said to have been unsound in his opinions as to the sacrament of the altar and as to the baptism of infants." [1] That this last charge is unfounded is, as Dr. Poole has pointed out, plain from the fact that, had there been any truth in it, it would scarcely have escaped the notice of St. Bernard ; he nowhere refers to it.[2]

The communal spirit which we have recognized at work in France during the years 1138-40 [3] had for long been growing in self-consciousness in the cities of Northern Italy, and not least at Brescia. Allied with it was a reactionary movement, not wholly reprehensible, in the direction of a return to primitive simplicity as regards the clerical life and to disinterested dealing as regards the tenure of ecclesiastical office. Sects like the Arialdists of Milan, or Patarines, so called from their having held their meetings in the ragmen's quarter of the city (*pataria*)—founded by the deacon Arialdus about 1058, strong opponents of clerical marriage on the ground that it tended to promote immersion in mundane affairs, had borne witness to growing feelings against luxury and against simony.[4] Arnald who, after his return to Brescia at a date which in the absence of definite information we may conjecture to have been about 1130, became first a canon regular and subsequently provost of his house, was a personality to which the malcontents would readily rally. His remedies for the prevailing evils would seem to have been the measures to which Otto of Freising refers ; but in their entirety they were by no means acceptable to the clergy. Arnald was a zealous reformer, but he had, we may well think, much of that *amour propre* which so often blinds the theorist to the natural and quite reasonable limitations of the material with which he is called to deal. His proposals that the clerical state should be restored to something more like its evangelical simplicity and that simony should be vigorously suppressed, were doubtless calculated to commend themselves to the high-minded amongst the clergy of all ranks ; but the wholesale abolition of ecclesiastical

[1] Otton. Frising. *op. cit., loc. cit.*

[2] Poole, *Arnold of Brescia and the Establishment of the Roman Senate*; Joann. Sares. *op. cit., ed. cit.,* lix.

[3] Pp. 163 sqq. *supra.*

[4] Alphandéry, *Encycl. Brit., s. tit.* ; Whitney, *Cambr. Med. Hist.,* V. 40 sqq.

21

property, beginning with the *regalia*, was another matter. Opposition on this last score drove Arnald into the ranks of the lay notables who, not, it may be felt, altogether from disinterested motives, received him with open arms. About the year 1138 a crisis arose. Manfred, Bishop of Brescia, was at Rome ; and " during his absence Arnald tried to persuade the citizens not to admit him on his return." [1] Otto's account suggests that he wilfully and maliciously exposed Manfred and his clergy to the contumely of the laity ; in any case the result was that an appeal was lodged with the Apostolic See. At the Lateran Council of April, 1139, Innocent II, " in order that his pernicious teaching might not be more widely diffused, imposed silence upon him " and further deprived him of his office and expelled him from Italy.[2] St. Bernard, in the letter to the Bishop of Constance above cited, refers to these events in terms which make yet plainer his own opinion of Arnald and his doings. " He has left such foul and horrible traces of himself wherever he has been, that he does not dare to return to any place which he has once visited. In a word, he so cruelly embroiled and disturbed his own city that, after having been accused before the lord Pope of the worse kind of schism, he was expelled from it and required to swear that, save only by leave of the Apostolic See, he would never return thither." [3] To St. Bernard Arnald is a " notorious schismatic " rather as being an agitator, a revolutionary, a breaker of the public peace, than as one who sets up altar against altar ; in his view he brings with him social and political strife wherever he goes. And indeed he left behind him at Brescia " such foul and horrible traces of himself " that it was only by means of the expulsion of the two chief magistrates, the consuls, of the commune that peace was ultimately restored to the city.[4]

It would appear that on leaving Italy Arnald went to France, " attached himself to Peter Abélard and zealously promoted his interests with the lord Hyacinth "—who when John wrote was a cardinal—" against the Abbot of Clairvaux." [5] We have already noticed St. Bernard's reference to the part of armour-bearer played by Arnald to Abélard's Goliath, and to the machinations of Hyacinth at Rome in support of Abélard's cause.[6] After the departure of Abélard to Cluny Arnald remained at Paris on the Mont-Ste. Geneviève and taught theology at the Church of St. Hilary, destroyed in the XVIIIth century, where Abélard had lodged. His hearers were scholars, very poor in this world's goods, who

[1] Joann. Sares. *Hist. Pontifical.*, XXXI. 63, *ed. cit.*

[2] Otton. Frising. *op. cit., loc. cit.* ; Joann. Sares. *op. cit., loc. cit.* ; Baron. *Annal., an.* 1140. Cf. Poole, *op. cit.*, lx.

[3] *Ep.* 195.

[4] *Annal. Brix., M.G.H.* XVIII. 812.

[5] Joann. Sares. *op. cit., ed. cit.*, XXXI. 64 ; Poole, *Illustr. of Hist. of Med. Tht.*, 162.

[6] P. 303 *supra*.

lived with him and begged their bread from door to door.
The burden of his message was " that men profess themselves
to be in the fullest agreement with the Christian law, but that
their lives are as fully out of accord with it. He did not spare
bishops for their avarice and love of filthy lucre and especially
for their blemished living, and because they strove to build
the Church of God in blood. The abbot," meaning of course
St. Bernard, " whose name for his many merits was wont
to be held in the highest honour, he reproved as a seeker after
vainglory, who was jealous of all who had any reputation
for learning or for religion, if they were not of his own way of
thinking." John of Salisbury is not a writer who confuses
comment with fact ; we may therefore conclude that Arnald's
strictures were quite as offensive as he reports them to have
been. The personalities reserved for St. Bernard can scarcely
have failed to provoke considerable indignation. These
attacks, however, continued unchecked until St. Bernard
succeeded in persuading Louis le Jeune to expel Arnald
from France,[1] realizing as he did that the danger of his presence consisted rather in the persuasiveness of his address
and in the charm of his manner, than in the violence of his
language. This ascetic figure had great attraction, not only
for the poor and lowly but also for the rich and powerful.
Apparently Arnald's personalities had made it difficult for
an honourable and self-respecting opponent like St. Bernard
to intervene. The Pope had heard of Arnald's doings at
Paris and had written ordering his expulsion, " but there was
nobody who would take that good work in hand." Ultimately St. Bernard had to move in the matter from a sense
of public duty.[2]

Arnald betook himself to Zürich where he does not seem
to have remained for long ; Otto of Freising, who strangely
enough makes no mention of his sojourn on the Mont-Ste.
Geneviève, speaks of " a few days." [3] St. Bernard's letter
addressed to the diocesan Hermann, Bishop of Constance,
giving him the character of this " sower of discord," and
warning him to beware of " the entrance of the thief by
night," had prompt effect.[4] With Italy, France and Germany
now closed to him, where was he to find a refuge ? It was
the autumn of the year 1143, and a certain Cardinal Guy—
not Guy of Castello—had recently arrived in Bohemia on a
legatine mission.[5] To his protection Arnald committed himself, and won his favour to an extent which alarmed St.
Bernard and drew from him without delay a letter of strong
remonstrance. " It is reported," he writes, " that Arnald

[1] Joann. Sares.
op. cit., ed. cit.,
XXXI. 64.

[2] S. Bern. Ep.
195.

[3] Otton. Frising.
op. cit., loc. cit.

[4] Ep. 195.

[5] Jaffé, Regest.,
8238.

of Brescia is with you, the man of honeyed address and poisonous words, with a dove's head and a scorpion's tail : the man vomited up by Brescia, abhorred at Rome, driven forth from France, loathed in Germany, and certainly not desired in Italy. Look to it, I beseech you, that under the shelter of your authority he does not do yet more harm. For he has both the skill and the will to do it ; with the addition of your favour we shall have a rope of three cords difficult to break ; the harm done will, I fear, be quite immeasurable." The report that Guy has received him may not be true ; but if it is, there are only two alternatives ; either he does not know Arnald's character or, as St. Bernard charitably assumes, he has hopes of reforming it. Well ! Let them not prove to be vain. Who will give him " of this stone to raise up a child unto Abraham " ? A satisfactory answer to this question should be found before the cardinal decides to make Arnald an inmate of his house, and thus to give him the credit which must attach to a person who is living on terms of intimacy with a legate of the Apostolic See. The point is : Would the Pope consider that his representative had, without authority, taken the matter out of the hands of his superior, and reversed his judgement ? However, St. Bernard is confident that Guy, now that he knows everything, will give due consideration to the risks involved.[1]

[1] *Ep.* 196.

How far Guy was moved by this letter it is difficult to say. Arnald, " the man of honeyed address," was on the spot, harmless as a dove to all appearances, and certainly apostolic in his personal life, having about him a touch of the old prophets or of the Baptist. Guy might reflect that more than four years had elapsed since his condemnation, not as a heretic but as a turbulent person, by the Lateran Council ; that, beyond the Pope's orders, there seemed to have been no explicit reason for his expulsion from France, which, but for the pressure put upon Louis le Jeune by St. Bernard, might never have taken place and the true explanation of which was possibly the personal affront offered to the Abbot of Clairvaux. And it must be allowed that St. Bernard's charges, albeit they revealed a keen insight into the character of the man, had about them some element of generalization. Finally, the Apostolic See had not banished Arnald from the face of the whole earth.

A few weeks later, on 24th September, 1143, Innocent II died and at some time afterwards Arnald, not improbably by the aid of Cardinal Guy, returned to Italy.[2] John of

[2] Otton. Frising. *op. cit., loc. cit.*; Joann. Sares. *op. cit., ed. cit.,* XXXI. 64.

Salisbury records neither the whereabouts nor the doings of Arnald during the next two years; in view, however, of subsequent events and of his ideals as interpreted by his past history, it is difficult to suppose that his influence was in abeyance. It was, we know, a period of severe testing for the Papacy as a world-power. As Innocent had failed, so also did his successors Celestin II and Lucius II fail, to quell the revolutionary spirit which, generated by the memory of the glories of pagan Rome under the republic, sought to deprive both the Pope of his real and the Emperor of his nominal authority in the city as represented by the Prefect.[1] The root of the mischief was more than superficial and short-lived; it was " deep and perennial ; a momentary calm was preceded and followed by such tempests as had almost sunk the bark of St. Peter." [2] The innate genius of the Roman people, certainly in its force, and perhaps to some extent in its imaginative content, was, as we may infer not only from his letters addressed to Eugenius III, in particular from the treatise *Of Consideration*, but also, as we shall see, from the appeal which he made to its own sense of self-respect,[3] appreciated by St. Bernard. He did not mistake it ; it was a menace to what he considered to be the fulness of the authority of the Apostolic See.

During the brief pontificate of Lucius II from 1144-45 matters came to a head. In order to make it plain that " nothing which concerned the civil government of the city ought to be within the province of the Roman pontiff, but that ecclesiastical authority alone should be reserved to him," the populace appears to have decided " to rebuild the Capitol, to restore the senate and to re-establish the equestrian order," at the cost of considerable destruction of the palaces of the cardinals and of the Roman nobility and of some injury to their persons.[4] The crowning disaster was the death of Lucius on 15th February, 1145, as the result of a blow from a heavy stone sustained while he was taking part, foolishly enough, we may think, in an attack upon the Capitol.[5] The revolutionaries, realizing probably that the terms under which the Prefect of the City held office provided him with an authority by no means derived from the people, had substituted for him an official whom they called the Patrician in the person of Jordanus Leonis, a nephew of the anti-pope Anacletus II.[6] All this meant that " the regalia of Blessed Peter " had passed from the Pope to the newly established senate.[7]

It was impossible for St. Bernard to look on at this un-moved. To whom should he turn for help and for retribution,

[1] Greenaway, *Arnold of Brescia*, 100 sqq.

[2] Gibbon, *Decline and Fall of the Rom. Emp.*, VII. lxix. 351, ed. 1854-55.

[3] *Ep.* 243. Cf. pp. 328 sq. *infra*.

[4] Otton. Frising. *op. cit., loc. cit.*

[5] Otton. Frising. *Chron.*, VII. xxxi, Hofmeister, *Script. Rer. Germ.* ; Watterich, *Pontif. Rom. Vitae*, II. 281 ; Jaffé, *Regest.*, II. 19.

[6] Otton. Frising. *op. cit., loc. cit.* ; Joann. Sares. *op. cit., ed. cit.*, XXVII. 60 ; Gibbon, *op. cit., ed. cit.*, VII. 362.

[7] Joann. Sares. *op. cit., ed. cit., loc. cit.*

if not to the one man who represented what he regarded as the authority divinely commissioned to protect the Church, to Conrad of Hohenstaufen shortly to be entrusted by the Pope with the material sword, the Church's sword to be used at the Church's bidding in the service of the Church ? [1]   Accordingly he addresses to Conrad a letter which in Vacandard's opinion, based upon its position in such primary MSS. as, say, Troyes 852, belongs to the period immediately preceding the pontificate of Eugenius III—an opinion, we may add, supported by such internal evidence as the fact that St. Bernard writes as one suddenly shocked by the divorce between the two swords which the revolutionaries had recently proclaimed as their aim, and in a measure effected. " The kingdom and the priesthood," he writes to Conrad, " could not have been more happily, more amicably, more intimately conjoined or co-established than they are in the person of the Lord, who in respect of both orders was, as incarnate, made for us chief priest and supreme king.   But not only this ; he united them and confederated them in his body ; this body is the Christian people of which he is himself the head."   It is imposssible for the real interests of the Church and of the Empire to clash.   Rome is the Apostolic See ; it is also the head of the Empire ; for the Emperor not to use his own proper sword in defence of Rome is to confess his incapacity to wield it, is to acquiesce in the mutilation of his own proper *imperium*.   " Therefore gird your sword upon your thigh, most potent sir, and let Cæsar render to Cæsar the things which are Cæsar's and to God the things which are God's.   To protect his crown and to defend the Church, both these are Cæsar's interests."   He will have to deal with " an accursed and seditious people which in its folly knows neither the limits of its powers nor the end which it has in view, nor the possible eventualities of its action, but simply in its blind fury has put its hands to this great sacrilege."   It is not for a moment to be supposed that it will face the king without flinching. [2]   Otto of Freising refers to a letter, now lost, written to Conrad by Lucius invoking the help of " the illustrious King of the Romans." [3]

St. Bernard was not the man to allow the mob to rule with impunity ; and he possessed the magnetism which sways masses.   But he had reckoned without his host ; he did not then know Conrad as he would know him a few years later.   The letter seems to have had no immediate effect.   Its value consists in the insight which it gives us into St. Bernard's theory of the constitution of Christendom.   Were we not

[1] S. Bern. *De Consid.*, IV. iii. 7; Joann. Sares. *Policrat.*, IV. iii., *ed.* Webb, I. 239.

[2] *Ep.* 244.

[3] Otton. Frising. *Chron.*, VII. xxxi., *ed. cit.*

in a position to interpret what he writes by the aid of the *De Consideratione* and of various passages in his correspondence, we might be tempted to regard it as tainted with some suspicion of what we now call Erastianism. It has to be remembered that in his view the Apostolic See holds vicariously for Christ both swords. " Peter has two swords, one to be drawn at his command " by the secular power, " the other by his hand so often as is necessary." [1]

In the critical situation created by the tragic end of Lucius II the cardinals lost no time in electing his successor, Eugenius III. As Abbot of San-Paolo-alle-Tre-Fontane the new Pope would have been in close touch with recent events in Rome. It was a politic stroke ; it anticipated any attempt on the part of the senate to dictate to the Sacred College. The further wise step was taken by the cardinals of retiring to the Abbey of Farfa, where the election of Eugenius was duly consummated. This happened on 18th February, 1145, within a few days of the death of Lucius.[2] St. Bernard might well hope for better things as the result of this election than from anything which Conrad might do. He recognizes the great possibilities involved. Much, however, would depend upon the loyal support of the cardinals who had " set up this ragged fellow to direct princes, to command bishops and to dispose of kingdoms and empires." This David taken from the sheepfolds will not fail them, but they must remember that it is in their own interest fervently and faithfully to co-operate in the work which they have initiated by their choice of him as their ruler.[3] To Eugenius he writes : " Placing such confidence in you as we have seen placed in none of your predecessors for many generations past, fitly the whole Church everywhere rejoices and glories in the Lord ; especially that church "—meaning Clairvaux—" whose womb bore you and whose breasts fed you. . . . Strengthen yourself therefore and be firm ; your hands are upon the necks of your enemies." [4]

It was unfortunate that Eugenius was unable to return to Rome immediately after he had been raised to the pontificate at Farfa ; but there was good reason for doubting whether the popular fury would have allowed him to enter the city. After some delay he went to Viterbo, where he remained for more than six months from April to November, 1145. Meanwhile the revolutionaries and their Patrician, Jordanus, finally abolished the office of Prefect of the City, subjected the nobles and the cardinals to the authority of Jordanus, and committed further depredations upon their

[1] S. Bern. *Ep.* 256.

[2] Watterich, *Pontif. Rom. Vitae*, II. 281 sq.; Jaffé, *Regest.*, II. 19 and 21.

[3] S. Bern. *Ep.* 237.

[4] *Ep.* 238.

palaces. They sacrilegiously invaded the Vatican Basilica, ill-treated the pilgrims and robbed them of their offerings; those of them who resisted they murdered in the porch or in the fore-court.[1]

[1] Otton. Frising. Chron., VII. xxxi., ed. cit.

The news that Eugenius was an exile, and that Rome was increasingly at the mercy of infatuated demagogues who had cast responsibility to the four winds would have filled St. Bernard with dismay. Arnald of Brescia was not in the city or in its neighbourhood, and we cannot lay the excesses to his charge except in so far as that the impression might have prevailed that his teaching justified any means taken in pursuit of the end of municipal liberty. Remembering the fate of Lucius II, St Bernard dare not urge Eugenius to take the risk of exposing himself to the popular fury. But there remained something which he could do. There still must be among the Romans some saving remnant, some salt which has not yet lost its savour. To the self-respect, to the native dignity, to the civic pride, of this handful of wise men he would appeal. Permanent recovery would be better assured, were it to represent the free determination of the people than were it to follow the occupation of the city by the forces of Conrad. " To you, exalted and illustrious people, I address myself, although I am but a man of low degree, a mere nobody, scarcely of account of all." This opening passage is far from being the obsequious fawning which, did we not know St. Bernard, it might seem to be ; it is the carefully chosen language of a great diplomatist who never hesitated to make use of quite different language should occasion so require. He will risk the charge of undue forwardness in thus appealing from so far across the Alps to " the glorious people " of Rome. Perhaps they will hearken to the poor man's cry, when they would disregard " the threats of princes and the armed forces of the strong " ; even as once the Babylonians gave heed to the voice of the young Daniel rather than to that of their elders who had seduced them (Dan. xiii, 45. *Vulg.*). And indeed, in the case in point the interest is a common one. The entire Christian world is suffering in its head which is Rome. " What new-born Christian anywhere is there who does not glory in this head ? . . . Are you so mad, O Romans, so ill-advised, so lacking in respect for your honour, as to disfigure that which is at once your own head and the head of the whole Church, that head for which, if needs were, you would not spare your necks ? . . . But what is Rome now better than a truncated corpse, an eyeless brow, a darkened face ? Open your eyes, poor people, and behold your present, your hourly increasing, desolation. How quickly has the fairest of complexions changed and the mistress of the nations, the princess of her provinces, been brought to widowhood!" He warns them that matters are only in their first stage. At enmity, not only with the Pope but also with the secular rulers of Christendom, no end can be expected other than their destruction as a people. Their great danger, however, arises from the enemies within their own household. Against this is to be set the fact that their true friends, their unflinching friends, the apostles and the martyrs, are also of their household. Reconciled to them " the illustrious city, the fatherland of the brave," can have nothing to fear.[1]

[1] *Ep.* 243.

It is a great appeal, an appeal to dignified self-recovery, to *resipiscentia*, to loyalty to their native stock and to the traditions of their race, as the sole sound remedy which can prevent their extinction. For St. Bernard to have made it knowing full well, as he did, their capacity for degeneration meant a surpassing effort of faith on his part. One element in the appeal is perhaps on a lower level. Churches in Rome have been extensively pillaged. Where is all this loot now? " How much of the proceeds is now in your pockets? " St. Bernard pointedly asks. He would remember the cupidity of the Roman people. Later we find him putting, let us hope, hyperbolically, the question to Eugenius : " Can you tell me of one person in the whole of the greatest of all cities who would have received you as Pope, were it not for gain or in the hope of gain? "[2] Even from this mean point of view the Romans were being defrauded by the revolutionaries. The devil was not paying the hush-money.

[2] S. Bern. *De Consid.*, IV. ii. 4. Cf. Joann. Sares. *Hist. Pontifical.*, XXI. 51, *ed.* Poole.

Meanwhile Eugenius was on the look-out for his opportunity. The Romans, proud of the restored senate, signalized their independence by making war upon their ancient enemies the people of Tivoli ;[3] a move which had the effect of enlisting the latter and Campania generally in the cause of the Pope, who was thus enabled to bring the Roman revolutionaries to terms, and to return to the city amid popular acclamation in time to keep there the Feast of the Nativity of 1145. The terms arranged were that the office of Patrician should be suppressed and the Prefect of the City restored ; the senate was to be maintained, but under the sole and undivided authority of the Pope.[4]

[3] Otton. Frising. *Chron.*, VII. xxxi., *ed. cit.*

It is possible that Arnald of Brescia entered Rome with Eugenius, for he had already been received by him at Viterbo, when he undertook to make satisfaction and to obey the orders

[4] *Op. cit.*, VII. xxxiv. ; Jaffé, *Regest.*, 8807 sq.; Watterich, *op. cit.*, II. 283.

of the Apostolic See. "Penance was enjoined upon him which he promised to do by fasting, watching and praying at the holy places in the city; indeed he made solemn oath that he would be faithful in his obedience."[1] He appears to have created a favourable impression by his penitential self-discipline; but, after Eugenius had left Rome for France early in 1146, to have begun to preach, and to have formed a sect which John of Salisbury tells us was in his day still called "the heresy of the Lombards." Not only was his preaching persuasive, if we are to believe Walter Map,[2] but the probity of his conduct and the austerities of his life were attractive, in particular to women. He would preach in the open air, on the Capitoline Hill and in other public places, where it was not long before he began to accuse the cardinals of pride, avarice, hypocrisy and all kinds of foul living, saying that the *Curia* was "not the Church of God but a house of traffic and a den of thieves." Nor did he spare Eugenius. He declared "that the Pope himself was not what he professed to be, an apostolic man and a shepherd of souls, but a man of blood who maintained his authority by fire and by sword, a tormentor of the churches, who blackmailed the innocent and did nothing else in the world than fill his own pockets at the expense of other people. If he was called Apostolic, it was not because he followed the teaching or imitated the life of the apostles, and consequently no obedience or respect was due to him; moreover it was not to be endured that Rome, the seat of empire, the fount of freedom, the mistress of the world, should be held in bondage by him."[3] It is no matter for surprise that Eugenius was again on the safe side of the Tiber in January, 1146. John tells us that he went first to Anagni.[4] He did not return to the city until November, 1149. It is difficult to imagine the state of Rome during the period which elapsed before in 1155 the Englishman, Hadrian IV, at length seized Arnald somewhere on the borders of Tuscany. He was brought to Rome and reserved for the judgement of the Emperor Frederick Barbarossa, then on his way to the city for his coronation. Frederick handed him over to the Prefect; he was hanged, and his remains were burnt and thrown into the Tiber lest they should become an object of popular veneration.[5] It is only fair to Arnald to refer to Walter Map's account of him, derived from an eye-witness of his later exploits in Rome, one Robert of Burnham; although in any matter concerning St. Bernard or the Cistercians Walter is a writer of doubtful authority.[6]

[1] Joann. Sares. Hist. Pontifical., ed. cit., XXXI. 65.

[2] Gault. Map. De Nugis Curial., I. xxiv. 40, ed. James.

[3] Joann. Sares. op. cit., ed. cit., XXXI. 65 sq.

[4] Otton. Frising. Chron., VII. xxxiv., ed. cit.; Joann. Sares. op. cit., ed. cit., XXXII. 66; Jaffé, Regest., 8850.

[5] Otton. Frising. Gesta Frid. I Imp., II. xxviii., ed. cit.

[6] Gault. Map. De Nugis Curial., I. xxiv. 39 sq., ed. James.

It seems possible to detect a certain fundamental affinity between the teaching concerning both Christian practice and ecclesiastical authority associated with Arnald of Brescia and that of various sects, which, however unapostolic their later developments may frequently have been, are sometimes classed under the generic name of Apostolics. Such were the Arialdists or Patarines of Milan to whom reference has already been made.[1] A century and a half later than St. Bernard's day the term was particularly applied to the enthusiasts who followed Segarelli, the weaver of Parma, and his disciple Dolcino. When about the year 1143 St. Bernard in his *Sermons on the Song of Songs* had reached the point at which he was commenting upon the words *Take us the foxes, the little foxes that spoil the vineyards*,[2] by strange coincidence he received from Irwin, Provost of the Premonstratensian house of Steinfeld near Cologne, a letter giving him an account of certain heretics who were causing considerable anxiety in that neighbourhood, and begging him to raise his voice against them. Amongst these people Irwin distinguishes two sects. One declared " that they alone constitute the Church, because they alone tread in the footsteps of Christ and are the true and abiding followers of the apostolic life, seeking not the things of the world ; possessing neither house nor lands nor any other property, even as Christ possessed nothing himself, and forbade his disciples to possess anything. ' But you ' (they say to us) ' add house to house and field to field, and seek the things of this world so that even those amongst you who are regarded as most perfect, such as monks or canons regular, although they do not hold property individually, yet hold it in common ; they really possess all these things.' Of themselves they say : ' We are Christ's poor ; men with no fixed abode, who flee from city to city ; like sheep in the midst of wolves we suffer persecution with the apostles and martyrs ; we live a holy and most strict life of fasting and abstinence ; continuing day and night in prayer and in labour, we seek by these means the necessaries of existence. We are able to endure this because we are not of the world.' " So far the affinity of their teaching to that of Arnald of Brescia is plain. Irwin reports that they disparaged the sacraments generally, deprecated the use of water in baptism, preferring the imposition of hands—and condemned the use of any marriage rite ; adding in regard to this last : " I have not been able to find out their reason, either because they did not dare to give it or, more probably, because they had no reason to give." [3]

[1] P. 321 *supra.*

[2] *In Cant. Cant. Serm.*, LXIV.

[3] Everv. Steinfeld. Praepos. *Ep. ad S. Bern. Ab.* 3.

With regard to the other sectaries, who may easily be recognized as distinct from the first-named by their mutual quarrels, we read that they deny " that the body of Christ is present on the altar, for the simple reason that all the priests are unconsecrated. The Apostolic dignity, they say, is corrupted by immersion in secular affairs ; occupying the chair of Peter, it does not serve God as did Peter, and so has deprived itself of the power of consecration which was given to Peter ; and because it does not possess this power, archbishops and bishops living worldly lives in the Church do not receive this power from it so as to be able to consecrate others." Like the Scribes and Pharisees sitting in the seat of Moses, they can speak and issue commands and nothing more. There is no *sacerdotium* at all in these days, and there are no sacraments except baptism of adults ; of which the real minister is Christ, whoever may happen to be the officiant. Any marriage other than that of virgins is fornication, for God joins together only those who are in the same state as were our first parents. They have no belief in the prayers of the saints or in prayer for the departed. They deny that there is any purgatorial process after death, and maintain that immediately men die they pass either to eternal rest or to eternal punishment.[1] The apostolicism of these latter sectaries led them, we may conclude, a long way farther from the doctrine of the Church than ever Arnald found himself ; indeed, it was Arnald's political rather than his religious doctrine which he developed to the extreme. Unmistakably, however, the insistence upon simplicity of life as an essential Christian ideal, and violent attacks upon the unfaithfulness to such simplicity on the part of the clergy of all ranks, are precisely in Arnald's manner. Alphandéry classifies the former of these two sects as Catharists and the latter as Apostolics ; [2] their mutual opposition indicates some divergence between them but it is a little difficult to say in what it consisted.[3] The latter would appear to have been the more heretical of the two, although it was common to both of them to appeal to the practice of the Church in apostolic days. Referring perhaps rather to the second sect mentioned by Irwin, St. Bernard finds himself unable to classify it under the name of any heresiarch. " Their heresy," he writes, " is not from man nor did they receive it by means of men " ; plainly it is directly diabolical.[4]

We are disposed to think that St. Bernard's strictures in the LXVth Sermon on the Song of Songs apply chiefly to the first sect which Alphandéry, as we have seen, classifies

[1] *Op. cit.*, 4 sq.

[2] Alphandéry, *Encycl. Brit.*, s. tit.

[3] S. Bern. *In Cant. Cant.*, LXV. 8.

[4] *Op. cit.*, LXVI. 2.

as Catharists or Manichæan ascetics. St. Bernard appears
to have obtained further information, in particular as to their
condition and their morals, than had been conveyed by Irwin's
letter. However, the conclusion of this letter does give some
additional interesting details. Speaking probably of them
all as "Satan's apostolics," Irwin tells us that those who
had returned to the Church had confessed that they were
spread throughout almost the whole world in large numbers
and included both clergy and monks; while it had been
elicited from those who had suffered the penalty of burning
that they believed their secret ramifications to have existed
in Greece and elsewhere since the days of the martyrs. He
adds further that they claimed the authority of the apostles
for leading about with them "women who are (as they say)
continent, widows, virgins, their own wives, some of them
among the elect, others of them among believers";[1] the [1] Everv. Stein-
former being the highest, the latter the intermediate, of the feld. Praepos.,
three degrees of perfection into which they were divided; *op. cit.*, 6.
the lowest was that of the hearers.[2]   [2] *Op. cit.*, 3.

St. Bernard confirms the presence in their body of clergy
and of monks who had deserted their cures or their monasteries. For the most part their numbers consisted of weavers,
both men and women—which explains the fact that they were
frequently called *Textores*—who would seem like the rest
of their fellow sectaries to have abjured the married state.[3] [3] *In Cant. Cant.*,
Young and ignorant country girls were peculiarly susceptible LXV. 5.
to the destructive influence of these "little foxes."[4] They [4] *Op. cit.*, LXV.
were bound together by an oath of secrecy which dispensed 8.
them from perjury, were they interrogated as to their doings,
"as though it were not the glory of God to reveal a saying.
Do they," asks St. Bernard, "deny this? I rather believe
that they blush to speak, knowing that what they have to
say is anything but glorious; for they are said to commit in
secret unspeakable obscenities."[5] But he gets closer to the [5] *Op. cit.*, LXV.
point. "Let us return to the question of the women who 2.
consort with them and live in their dwellings; for there
is not one of them who is without such. I ask a man: 'Now,
my friend, who is this woman and what is she here for?
Is she your wife?' 'No,' he says, 'my vow forbids me
to have a wife.' 'I suppose then that she is your daughter.'
'No,' he says. 'Well, who is she? Is she neither your sister,
nor your niece, nor related to you in any degree at all?'
'In no degree,' he replies. 'Then how do you think that you
are going to keep continent? Moreover this sort of thing
is not permitted. Let me tell you (if you do not know it

already) that the Church forbids men and women who have taken a vow of continence to live together. If you wish not to scandalize the Church turn the woman out.' The inference is," St. Bernard adds, "that from this one patent fact all the rest which is not open to the public gaze can readily be believed." [1] The occurrence of a passage like this, of severely judicial tone, in one of the most wonderful mystical studies ever written well illustrates St. Bernard's gift of dealing promptly and suitably with difficult situations, whenever and however unexpectedly they may claim his attention.

The sectary would probably appeal to the gospels, and maintain that they do not forbid in this matter what St. Bernard tells him that the Church forbids. It was characteristic of many of these people not only to treat the requirements of the Church as no better than superstition, but like the Manichæans to reject the Old Testament and even certain epistles of St. Paul. Such evasion, however, does not avail. The New Testament prohibits scandal.[2] But St. Bernard feels that, in spite of the scandal, it is something to have brought these evils to the light of day. "Have we done anything?" he asks. "I think that we have done this. We have caught the fox, in so far as we have discovered his fraud. The false Catholics, the real plunderers, who lay hidden are now manifest." [3] The most dangerous cunning of the fox is displayed in the abolition of marriage. "Take away out of the Church honourable nuptials and the undefiled bed, and do you not fill it with concubinage, incest, self-pollution, effeminacy, sodomy and every kind of uncleanness?" One of two views must be taken, if marriage is to be forbidden to the Christian. Either "all these monsters" are in the way of salvation; or they are not, and it is only the few who practise continence who are. "Neither of these views agrees with the Saviour's purpose. What? Is uncleanness to be crowned? Nothing would less become the author of chastity. Or is the whole world to be condemned for the sake of the few in it who are continent? This would not mean his being the Saviour at all. The continent are rare on earth; and he who is fulness itself did not empty himself only for the advantage of this mere handful." [4]

St. Bernard, considering their condition, is not very hopeful of the recovery of these sectaries. "They are," he writes, "neither convinced by reason because they do not understand it; nor are they corrected by authority because they do not acknowledge it; nor are they moved by persuasion

[1] *Op. cit.*, LXV. 6.

[2] *Op. cit.*, LXV. 3; Everv. Steinfeld. Praepos. *op. cit.*, 5.

[3] *In Cant. Cant.* LXV. 8.

[4] *Op. cit.*, LXVI. 3.

because they are hardened. This has been proved; they prefer to die rather than to be converted. Their end is destruction; the fire awaits them." [1] Irwin had reported to him that some of them had been cited to the bar of the Archbishop of Cologne, who was supported on the occasion by certain clergy and laity, and had been remanded for three days. At the end of which time, they proving to be still obdurate, " the over-zealous people," against the wishes of the authorities, had burnt two or three of them. The victims had " entered the fire and endured its flames, not only with patience but with joy." [2] Apparently this outbreak of popular violence was due to the fact that, " when subjected to the trial by water, they were found to be liars. Whereupon taking, as the saying is, the bit between their teeth they rather professed than confessed their ungodly doings," and willingly accepted martyrdom for their false teaching. St. Bernard does not approve the treatment meted out to them, although he goes so far as to allow that in the last resort severity may sometimes be necessary in the public interest. " We commend," he writes, " the zeal, but we do not recommend what was done; for faith comes by persuasion; it is not imposed by force. Although it is undoubtedly better that men should be coerced by authority which does not bear the sword in vain—than that they should be allowed to lead many into error." In taking such action authority is " God's minister." [3] It should be remembered that some of the excesses, of which St. Bernard hints that these sectaries were guilty, would in many countries to-day render them liable to proceedings under the criminal law. We have noticed that St. Bernard strongly discouraged persecution as a remedy against wrong belief; [4] thus when speaking of the " foxes " in an earlier sermon, he writes, interpreting them to mean heretics: " Let them be caught rather by arguments than by arms." [5] But these Rhineland sectaries were something more than wrong believers; he regarded them as grave offenders against public morals; nor, as he remarks, were they of sufficient intelligence to be open to reason. [6]

What, it may be asked, was his view as to the trial by water? The persons who were subjected to it he reports not to have sunk (*aqua eos non recipiente*), and the test to have been accepted as conclusive by themselves and by the populace. [7] This incident is not mentioned by Irwin, although he states that the action of the crowd in taking the law into its own hands was contrary to the wishes of the authorities. [8] On the whole we are disposed to think that St. Bernard

[1] *Op. cit.*, LXVI. 12.

[2] Everv. Steinfeld. Praepos. *op. cit.*, 2.

[3] *In Cant. Cant.*, LXVI. 12.

[4] Pp. 258 sqq., 266 sq. *supra*.

[5] *In Cant. Cant.*, LXIV. 8.

[6] P. 334 *supra*.

[7] *Op. cit.*, LXVI. 2.

[8] Everv. Steinfeld. Praepos. *op. cit.*, 2.

included the trial by water in his general condemnation of the popular violence ; whether he disapproved of it in itself has been questioned by Vacandard. The common opinion of his day was that it had a juridical value. But then St. Bernard was on many points in advance of contemporary opinion. He certainly regarded sudden illness and sudden death as possible indications of divine judgement. Trial by water was, however, an explicit and direct appeal to divine judgement, founded upon the conviction that God was pledged to answer it. We doubt whether St. Bernard would have shared this conviction. The whole story is told materially to the same effect, both as to the trial by water and as to the burning, in the *Annals of Brauweiler*, an abbey of Black Monks about ten miles from Cologne in the direction of Aix-la-Chapelle, where we might expect it to have been well known.[1]

[1] *Annal. Brun-wilarens., M.G.H.* XIV. 727.

How then would St. Bernard deal with this scandal ? Whether or not the sectaries are left scatheless in their persons, the danger he feels is still there. His keen diagnosis detects the real seat of it. " The lamentable fact is," he writes, " that not only lay princes but also some of the clergy, nay, as I hear, even some of the bishops who ought to have corrected these people, are actually supporting them for the sake of gain, taking bribes from them." [2] The shepherds who feed themselves by blackmailing these people, they it is who are ultimately responsible. It must be made quite plain to the offenders that they have to choose between abjuring their notorious illicit cohabitation and excommunication from the Church, outlawry from the fellowship of decent-minded citizens. This is his last word. May it help them to know better and to protect better the beloved and glorious spouse of Christ !

[2] *In Cant. Cant.,* LXVI. 14.

After referring to these sectaries in the *General Preface* to his folio edition of the *Works of St. Bernard*, published in 1690, Mabillon writes : " There was this in common between the Henrician heretics and the heretics of Cologne, namely, aversion for the ministers of the Church, for the sacraments, for the baptism of infants and for marriage ; there were a few tenets peculiar to each of them which serve to prove, not that they differed generically but that they were both variants of the same sect. In a word they were divers branches growing from one root." [3] Rightly or wrongly he considers this root to have been represented by the teaching of the Flemish layman Tanquelmus whom, together with " the priest Peter in Provence "—of whom presently—Abélard

[3] Mabill., *Oper. S. Bern. Praef. Gen.,* LXXVIII.

reprobates as a dangerous fanatic.[1] This Peter, as Abélard tells us, " had so made void almost every institution of divine, sacred and ecclesiastical authority as to require many people to be re-baptized, to order the abolition of the venerable sign of the Lord's cross, and even to have gone to the extent of forbidding the sacrament of the altar any longer to be celebrated." This account of his teaching is, so far as it goes, confirmed by Peter the Venerable.[2] But Abélard further attributes to him such strange doctrines as that " there are in God three properties by which the three persons are distinguished," which properties are " three essences (*essentiae*), distinct from the persons themselves and from the nature itself of the divinity "; these properties or essences are paternity, filiation and procession. Abélard was no loose thinker who would make such a statement carelessly. Quercetanus of Tours traces here the influence of Roscelinus.[3] Stranger doctrines still are " that the Lord Jesus did not grow in body "—even from infancy—" as do other men," and that monks and nuns who have married, although they have broken their vows, are not to be separated from their spouses (*licet sit voti transgressio, nulla tamen fiet initae copulae separatio*). It is not to be wondered that Abélard should speak of him as " raving like a madman," and of his notions as " muddled." It is the picture of a fanatic, whose vagaries are accentuated by a smattering of bad philosophy. Little more is known of him than that he went by the name of Pierre de Bruys (*Petrus Brusius*), that his followers, gathered chiefly from Provence, Dauphiné and Languedoc, were called Petrobrusians, and that he finally perished by burning at St. Gilles-les-Boucheries, a deliberate retribution for the many crosses at his instigation destroyed by fire.[4]

Of his notorious disciple Henry, whose followers were known as Henricians, we can give fuller particulars. When in 1145 St. Bernard heard of his doings Henry would have been a man of some years ; for we first come across him at Le-Mans, certainly at some date prior to 1125 when Hildebert, Bishop of Le-Mans, became Archbishop of Tours.[5] Hildebert gave him leave to preach in the city, while he himself was absent on a journey to Rome which Vacandard would date in the first decade of the century.[6] There is no record of his birth or of his education, but Mabillon thinks him to have arrived at Le-Mans from Lausanne, whither he had wandered from Northern Italy where, as we have seen, the atmosphere was favourable to the growth of such tenets as he professed.[7] He was essentially a *gyrovagus*, and St. Bernard, in a letter

[1] Abael. *Introd. ad Theol.*, Cousin, *Opp.*, II. 84. Cf. p. 301 *supra*.

[2] Petr. Ven. *Ep. seu Tract. contra Petrobrus.*, P.L. CLXXXIX. 710 sqq.

[3] Quercet. *Notae*, Cousin, *op. cit.*, I. 51.

[4] Petr. Ven. *Tract. contra Petrobrus. Praefat.*, P.L. CLXXXIX. 723.

[5] Mabill., *Opera. S. Bern. Praef. Gen.*, LXXIII.

[6] Vacandard, *Vie de saint Bernard*, II. 225. éd. 1920.

[7] Mabill., *op. cit.*, *loc. cit.* Cf. pp. 321 sq. *supra*.

addressed to Alphonsus, Count of St. Gilles and of Toulouse, refers to his roaming from Lausanne to Le-Mans, to Poitiers and to Bordeaux, and bids the count to inquire with what kind of character he departed from these cities ; for he can tell him that, " owing to the foul traces which he left behind him, no way of return to them is open to him." [1]   In the same letter he describes Henry as " an apostate who has cast off his religious habit (for he was a monk),[2] and returned to the world and to the filthiness of the flesh like a dog to its vomit." The meaning of these wanderings is that people, when they get to know him, cannot endure his presence amongst them. He begs his way and makes some profit out of his preaching ; being personally attractive and a man of education, he can the better practise upon matrons and upon simple folk. The money which he takes, over and above what is necessary for his sustenance, he spends upon gambling and upon yet worse pursuits. " Frequently indeed after a day of popular adulation this distinguished preacher is to be found with prostitutes, sometimes even with married women." [3]   This was written in 1145 [4] when St. Bernard was himself travelling on the spot in Languedoc.   The *Acts* of Hildebert, Bishop of Le-Mans, give him a yet more disreputable character, but describe him as a hermit, not as an apostate monk.[5]   Otto of Freising, we shall remember, speaks of St. Bernard's credulity as to reports reflecting upon the orthodoxy of suspected persons.[6]   Here, however, it is a question of morals ;   and even allowing for some prejudice against Henry, we can scarcely think that so acute an observer would have made a statement, founded probably upon personal investigation, which was altogether wide of the mark.

Henry would appear to have been expelled from the diocese of Le-Mans, and probably from other dioceses ; for St. Bernard writes of him as " a fugitive from the whole of France," who ultimately found open to him no other field than the dominions of the Count of Toulouse in which " to rave with all his fury against the flock of Christ." [7]   In 1135 the Archbishop of Arles had committed him to the judgement of the Apostolic See, and at the Council of Pisa in the same year he had recanted his errors and been required to return to the cloister. St. Bernard offered to receive him at Clairvaux ; but there is no evidence that there or elsewhere did he obey the requirement of the council.[8]

Something of his doctrine may be learned from a tractate addressed by Peter the Venerable to the Archbishops of Arles and Embrun and to the Bishops of Die and Gap, in

[1] *Ep.* 241.

[2] *Vita Prima,* III. vi. 16 ; *Vita Sec.,* xxvi. 72. Cf. *Excerpt. ex Exord. Magn.,* XVII. 26.

[3] *Ep.* 241.
[4] *Gall. Christ.,* II. 814.

[5] *Acta Hild. Cenoman., R.H.G.F.* XII. 547 sqq.
[6] P. 290 *supra.*

[7] *Ep.* 241.

[8] *Gesta Pontif. Cenoman., R.H.G.F.* XII. 554 ; Gaufr. *Ep.* 5, *P.L.* CLXXXV. 412.

which we read : " Henry, the inheritor of his (Peter of Bruys's) iniquity, not so much emended his (Peter's) diabolical doctrine, as changed it in various ways unknown to me and, as I have seen written in the book said to consist of *excerpta* from his own mouth, set it forth not under five, but under more than five heads." [1] Peter himself gives five heads, professing not to be as yet sufficiently sure of his facts to give more. We may take it that what he does give fairly represents the teaching of Henry, whom he would regard as the apostle of Petrobrusianism. The Abbot of Cluny summarizes his doctrine as follows. (1) Infants are not saved by baptism, on the ground that not having attained to the age of reason they cannot exercise faith. (2) All churches and oratories should be destroyed as unnecessary, for Christians can pray to God and be heard by God anywhere. (3) All crosses should be destroyed ; the representation of Christ tortured and dying is no fit object of veneration, but should rather be broken to pieces and burnt by way of taking vengeance on his murderers. (4) The body and blood of the Lord are not really (*in veritate*) offered on the altar ; the sacrament is, in fact, nothing at all (*omnino nihil*), and ought not to be offered to God. Finally, (5) sacrifices, prayers, alms and the like offered for the dead are ridiculous ; they can be of no possible service to them.[2]

It is unnecessary to follow in detail Peter's exposition of the crudities professed by these sectaries. To give, how- ever, two instances. They contended that they could not accept the testimony of the Church because it was not, as is the testimony borne in a court of law, that of actual eye- witnesses ; and they contended that the words spoken at the Last Supper, " this is my body . . . this is my blood," were true only for those then present and for none else.[3] Much of what Peter writes is confirmed by St. Bernard, who is particularly displeased by the refusal of baptism to infants, which, on the sectaries' own showing, deprives them of salvation. They *can* not have faith, and they *may* not have baptism ! Does Henry, " the rapacious wolf "—" think that the little ones have no need of a Saviour, simply because they are so little ? " Manifestly and professedly this heretic is seeking to destroy institutional Christianity, but what he is really doing is promoting a Christianity with no Christ in it.[4] Like the Apostolics and other sectaries of the Rhine- land, Henry and his followers would seem to have rejected what books of the Scriptures it suited them to reject, being, as were they, although probably unaware of it, somewhat

[1] *Petr. Ven. Tract. contra Petrobrus. Praefat., P.L.* CLXXXIX. 723.

[2] *Ap. op. cit.,* 722.

[3] *Petr. Ven. Tract. contra Petrobrus., op. cit.,* 739 and 787.

[4] *Ep.* 241 ; *Vita Prima,* III. vi. 16.

Manichæan in their preference; indeed they went farther, for they professed " to accept from the Church none of its traditions except the gospels but in them to put the firmest faith." [1] This last was the only common ground upon which Peter could reason with them.

After having for long resisted the frequent solicitation of the Church of that region, St. Bernard finally yielded to the pressure of the Cardinal Legate Alberic, Bishop of Ostia, and in 1145 accompanied him to Languedoc.[2] The story of his travels is told by Geoffrey, St. Bernard's biographer, who was, as we gather from the use of the first person plural, himself present throughout. It is in the form of a letter, addressed " to his dearly beloved master Archenfred and to both chapters, his brothers by a common mother," which is given by Mabillon and by Migne at the end of the Sixth Book of the *Vita Prima*, otherwise called the *Liber Miraculorum;* Waitz, in the *Monumenta Germaniae Historica*, places it earlier.[3] It is given also in the Bollandist *Acta* by Pien, who is in doubt as to what is meant by "both chapters," but suggests that the reference is to Clairvaux and to some one of its early foundations, perhaps Troisfontaines.[4]

St. Bernard was evidently in bad health at the time; and when he drew near to Poitiers he began to question whether he had been wise in undertaking the journey. He would seem to have passed two restless nights there, but to have received such divine encouragement as enabled him to set out again by way of Angoulême and Limoges for Bordeaux, where he arrived early in June.[5] He found the metropolitan city disturbed by a contest of now five years' duration between the Archbishop Geoffrey du Loroux and the chapter. An attempt on the part of the former to substitute canons regular for canons secular as the stalls fell vacant was resisted by the chapter; which was so strongly supported by popular sentiment that, during the whole period named, the archbishop had been an exile from his see. The arrival of St. Bernard and Cardinal Alberic was a favourable moment for reconciliation; and the archbishop's appeal to them resulted in his gaining his point.[6]

Here probably were arranged the plans of this great missionary campaign, and here were enrolled such distinguished campaigners as Geoffrey, Bishop of Chartres,[7] and Raymond, Bishop of Agen.[8] The moral support of the civil authorities had, we may think, already been sufficiently enlisted by St. Bernard's letter to the Count of St. Gilles and Toulouse, in which he writes: " Although in great bodily

[1] Petr. Ven. *Tract. contra Petrobrus., op. cit.,* 828.

[2] *Vita Prima,* III. vi. 17.

[3] Gaufr. *Ep., P.L.* CLXXXV. 410 sqq.; *M.G.H.* XXVI. 92.

[4] *Annot. ad Acta SS. Bolland., Aug.* IV. *die* xx. 351.

[5] Gaufr. *Ep.,* 2, *op. cit.,* 410 sq.; *Vita Prima,* IV. iv. 29; *R.H.G.F.* XV. 598, *note* b.

[6] Gaufr. *Ep.,* 3, *op. cit.,* 411; *R.H.G.F.* XV. 599, *note* b. Cf. *Gall. Christ.,* II. 814.

[7] *Vita Prima,* III. vi. 18.

[8] *Gall. Christ.,* II. 814.

weakness, I am on my way to these regions which this beast
of unparalleled savagery is laying waste, so long as there is
no one to resist him or to tame him. . . . I do not come of
myself but drawn by the pitiful call of the Church, if by chance
the thorns and noxious seedlings may be uprooted from the
Lord's field while they are yet tender ; not by my hand, who
am nothing, but by that of the holy bishops who are with
me, your strong right hand working with them." [1] With a
confidence then fortified by the reception which everywhere
was accorded him, St. Bernard made a sweeping movement
in the direction of Toulouse by way of Bergerac, Périgueux,
Sarlat and Cahors, leaving, as it were, no position occupied
by the enemy in his rear or on his flanks.[2] We sometimes,
as here, seem to recognize in him the instinct of a sound
strategist on the field of battle. At Sarlat they brought
him bread to bless. Signing it with the cross he boldly
cried : " If your sick folk eat this and recover, it will be
proof that the truth is with us and error with the heretics."
Geoffrey of Chartres, fearful of the risk, would add : " Yes,
if it is in good faith that they receive it." " No, no," insists
St. Bernard, " I said not that ; in very truth they who eat
will be made whole." It was a psychological stroke and well
calculated ; he would leave nothing to the uncertainty of
their minds. Unconsciously his own faith became theirs ;
many grew better ; the news spread abroad and the whole
neighbourhood was converted.[3]

On their arrival at Toulouse, where they were entertained
by the canons regular who served the Church of St. Sernin,
they found that Henry had fled and lay hidden.[4] We gather
that the sectaries had secret lurking-places in the surrounding
country, for even before St. Bernard arrived the civil authorities had regarded them with suspicion. Nevertheless,
the state of the city was critical. Not a few of the wealthier
inhabitants were on the side of the " weavers (*textores*), who,"
as Geoffrey tells us, " called themselves Arians," in favouring
the prevailing heresy. Probably the weavers were literally
such, the bulk of the artisan class here, as in the Rhineland,
following this trade. But why did they call themselves by
a name of reproach ? Moreover, many of them would never
have heard of Arius. It was probably occasioned by some
remark which fell from Henry's lips ; he might well have
extolled the Arians as the protagonists of revolt against
credal and institutional Christianity. The knightly class,
many of whom hated the clergy and were amused by the
witticisms of Henry and ingratiated by the countenance

[1] *Ep.* 241.

[2] Gaufr. *Ep.*, 3 sq., *op. cit., loc. cit.*

[3] *Vita Prima*, III. vi. 18.

[4] *Vita Prima*, III. vi. 17 ; Gaufr. *Ep.*, 7, *op. cit.*, 413 ; Excerpt. ex Exord. Magn., XVII. 26.

which he openly gave to free living, were of the same mind
as the *bourgeoisie* and the weavers.   However, St. Bernard
bravely set to work.   A remarkable cure effected upon a
certain John, one of the canons regular at St. Sernin, proved
persuasive.   Other similar cures, the success of which was
doubtless promoted by the prevailing atmosphere of confidence in St. Bernard generated thereby, followed in succession—the man of God meanwhile lamenting that things
had come to such a pass, that signs and wonders alone had
any effect upon their obdurate hearts.   Before he left Toulouse
the popular vote overwhelmingly " gave sentence against the
heretics and their supporters, and against all who had any
dealings with them," the people " pledging themselves that
none would either accept their testimony or their judgement,
or even eat with them or trade with them at all." [1]   St.
Bernard did not confine his activities to the city itself, for
we read of him at such places as Daumazan, a little town
beyond Muret and not far from Le-Mas-d'Azil, where the pre-
historic caves would have given convenient shelter to the
Henricians, and later at Verfeil, which Geoffrey stigmatizes
as " the seat of Satan," about twelve miles distant on the
road to Albi. [2]

From Toulouse Cardinal Alberic preceded St. Bernard by
two days to Albi, where the legate was greeted with grotesque
ribaldry, the populace coming out to meet him in mock
procession with asses and with drums.   His Mass on the
following day was attended by scarcely thirty worshippers.
When St. Bernard arrived there was some manifestation of
joy, which he was disposed to regard doubtfully.   It was
28th June, the vigil of " the solemnity of Blessed Peter."
On the feast itself he addressed an overflowing crowd in
the cathedral.   " I had come," he said, " to sow seed, but I
find the ground already sown with noxious weeds.   Yet,
because it is rational ground, for *ye are God's husbandry*, lo,
I show you plainly both seeds in order that you may know
which you ought to choose."   Beginning with the sacrament
of the altar, he took the teaching of Henry point by point,
explaining carefully the Church's faith with regard to each
as it came under review.   To his question as to which they
would choose the answer was unanimous.   They " began to
receive the Word of God with joy."   " Repent then," replied
the preacher, " as many of you as are polluted ; return to the
unity of the Church ; and, that we may know who truly
repents and accepts the word of life, raise your right hands
to heaven in token of Catholic unity."   Every right hand

[1] Gaufr. *Ep.*, 4
sq., 7 and 9,
op. cit., 411 sqq.;
Vita Prima, III.
vi. 19.

[2] Gaufr. *Ep.*, 9,
op. cit., 414.

responded and St. Bernard said no more.   Here too Geoffrey's letter ends.[1]

What are we to say of this outburst of popular enthusiasm ? What would Geoffrey himself have said, had we pressed him for an opinion ?   Earlier in the letter he had remarked : " It is a land so desperately seduced by manifold error as to need a long course of preaching." [2]   He is speaking of Toulouse, but history tells us that his prescient words were truer still of Albi.   Had St. Bernard remained with an army of spiritual occupation on the spot, the result might have been different ;   but pressing letters had been received more than once demanding urgently his presence at Clairvaux, and Geoffrey had replied that he would be there about the Octave of the Assumption, 22nd August.   He would be leaving Languedoc exposed to the influence of the fascinating Henry, who knew only too well how to commend himself to every class in the community.   If we are to believe St. Bernard and Geoffrey, he preached a gospel pleasant to the fleshly appetite of man.   It is not, however, to be supposed that St. Bernard hurried away from the district.   He was not expected at Clairvaux before the third week in August.   There is nothing to suggest that his return was other than direct ; he would have had at least another month in which to continue his missionary labours.

As for Henry, although the tares had been only too sufficiently broadcast and were germinating a hundredfold in favourable soil, the sower was before very long restrained. Hunted from covert to covert, " so that scarcely anywhere was he in safety, he was at last taken and handed over bound to the bishop." [4]   Whether he ever escaped from the episcopal dungeon at Toulouse, or what his end was, we do not know.

It was after St. Bernard had heard of the capture of Henry and probably of other ringleaders of the sect, that he wrote to the Toulousans a letter from Clairvaux.   " I thank God," he tells them, " that my coming to you was not unprofitable and that my stay with you, brief though it was, has not been fruitless.   For by means of the truth which I manifested to you, not in word only but in power, the wolves who, coming to you in sheep's clothing, have devoured your people as bread and as slaughtered sheep, have been taken." [5] This good news had reached him through Bertrand, Abbot of Grand-Selve, and some monks of that house—affiliated to Clairvaux in 1145 [6] — who had also assured him of their " zealous hatred of the heretics."   He longs for an opportunity of visiting them again.   Sick and feeble though

[1] Gaufr. *Ep.*, 9 sq., *op. cit.*, 414 sqq.

[2] Gaufr. *Ep.*, 5, *op. cit.*, 412.

[3] Gaufr. *Ep.*, 6, *op. cit., loc. cit.*

[4] *Vita Prima,* III. vi. 17.

[5] *Ep.* 242.

[6] Pp. 79 sq. *supra.*

he is, it would be no irksome task to him. Let them, however, be steadfast in obedience to their bishop and to all who are set over them, " masters of the Church." And let them show hospitality ; this is the way to please God. Hospitality to the poor, to the naked, to the needy ; the visit paid to the sick ; the redemption of the captive ; all these are really done to the Lord. The stress laid upon good works is noteworthy ; as though he would say : If you want to believe correctly, you will find your end forwarded by a life of good works. Charity is a valuable prophylactic against heresy. But what he has said face to face with them, he will say again by written word. " Receive no strange or unknown preacher, who has not either been sent to you by the Supreme Pontiff or received authority from your own bishop. *How shall they preach*, says the Scripture, *except they be sent ?* " [1]
The bearer of the letter is the Abbot of Grand-Selve. The love and the devotion which they show to him and to his monks will be shown to St. Bernard himself ; and above all, they will be evidence of their sincere acceptance of his admonitions.

Exception may be taken to the association of the sectaries of the Rhineland and of Languedoc with Arnald of Brescia as his congeners. Let us lay aside for the moment the estimate formed of Arnald by Otto of Freising as possibly a little prejudiced, and take account of the record of John of Salisbury. He was, the latter tells us, " reported to have been a seditious person and a promoter of faction, who wherever he might be prevented the citizens from living at peace with the clergy." [2]
John represents the judicial mind. It will be allowed that if Otto represents *parti pris* on one side, Walter Map, so far as he is serious, represents it on the other. Walter, we shall remember, reports the evidence of Robert of Burnham who was in Rome at the time.[3] " Arnald," he writes, " was a man of high standing, of noble birth and of great learning ; distinguished for his religious practices, he indulged himself neither in food nor in attire beyond what the strictest necessity required. He went about preaching, *seeking not his own but the things which are God's.*" This is precisely what Irwin of Steinfeld tells us was a party-cry of one of the two sections of the Rhineland heretics.[4] Walter goes on to state that Arnald made his way into the *Curia*, and in the presence of the Pope rebuked the cardinals for " the gold and silver vessels which adorned their tables and for the delicacies served at their banquets." [5] We shall probably not accept the charge suggested by Otto of Freising's report,

[1] *Ep.* 242.

[2] P. 320 *supra.*

[3] P. 330 *supra.*

[4] P. 331 *supra.*

[5] Gault. Map. *DeNugisCurial.,* I. xxiv. 40, *ed.* James.

that Arnald was " unsound in his opinions as to the sacrament of the altar and as to the baptism of infants " ; [1]
but such were the opinions of the sectaries of Languedoc
on these two points,[2] and the report probably represents
a contemporary view that these sectaries derived their tenets
in some measure from Arnald.   Finally as to Henry, although
we have nothing certain to say about his origin or his early
life, we shall perhaps not be far astray in supposing him
to have been hewn from the same rock and shaped in the
same *atelier* as was Arnald, that is to say, to have come from
some place in Lombardy, a land long notorious for the pro-
duction of disaffected sectaries.

[1] P. 321 *supra.*

[2] P. 339 *supra.*

CHAPTER XV

LAST DAYS

The closing years of St. Bernard's life were saddened by the persistent prevalence of misunderstanding between the Cluniacs and the Cistercians. Not that Peter the Venerable had any part in this; on the contrary, he did his utmost to correct it; but there were old grievances the sense of which was deeply rooted and died hard. We may learn something of the points in dispute, as they presented themselves to a Cistercian living at a little later date when the tension was less strained, by reference to the *Dialogue between a Cluniac and a Cistercian Monk* given by Martène and Durand in their *Thesaurus*.[1] The perusal of this document and of the correspondence between St. Bernard and Peter will probably lead us to conclude that, had every Cluniac been as was Peter and every Cistercian as was St. Bernard, there would have been no controversy at all between the two Orders. Their houses intermingling, as was frequently the case, in comparatively close proximity to one another and their members consisting, as they did, of men drawn from various classes in the community, sons of noble families among the choir-monks, and peasant lads among the Cistercian *conversi*— to say nothing of the artisans regularly employed and of the serfs owned by the Cluniacs, and of the boys in their schools— the material would have been sufficiently inflammable. Both organizations were vast and widespread, and over a large area it is easier to control material observances than spiritual sentiments. Moreover the rapid Cistercian expansion, given even the utmost charity on both sides, might well have seemed to bring reproachful contrast to the very near neighbourhood of one after another house of Black Monks.

That Peter, feeling perhaps the weight of his responsibility as abbot of the mother-house of a congregation of which the rule was practically monarchic, was acutely distressed by all this " mutual rancour "—for so he describes it—is quite plain. In a long letter, replying apparently to one in which

[1] Marten. et Durand. *Thes. Nov. Anecd.*, V. 1569 sqq., Chaumont MS. 78 (121); Williams, *Journ. Theol. Stud.*, 164 sqq., Jan., 1930.

St. Bernard had voiced the general Cistercian strictures, he deals with the subject in a manner which is respectful, even affectionate, and certainly reasonable. The root of the evil he regards as this. " Perhaps," he writes, " the cause of this strife between you "—and he seems to speak both to Cluniacs and to Cistercians—" is the divergence in custom, the variety in observance of monastic rule. Dearly beloved, if this is the cause of so great an evil, then it is quite unreasonable and, if I may say so with due respect to you both, quite childish and silly." [1] He pleads earnestly for the charitable principle of diversity in unity, unity of spirit and unity of aim. " Our father Benedict," he exclaims, " bids the abbot so proportion all things that souls may be saved ; [2] and dost thou doubt the salvation of those who under the same Rule follow different methods (one from the other) ? " [3] Peter illustrates his appeal by reference to the course pursued by St. Maurus, one of St. Benedict's first disciples, who, when by the direction of the founder of the Order establishing Benedictine houses in Gaul, " is reported to have changed certain, nay, many things in the Rule." [4] He had, perhaps twenty-five years earlier, quoted the example of St. Maurus in a letter which may have provoked the *Apology* of St. Bernard.[5] We should not claim it to be material that this particular mission of St. Maurus is historically doubtful.[6]

Peter is anxious that both Cluniacs and Cistercians should realize that they are sons of one father, St. Benedict, to say nothing of the fact that in spite of the black and the white of their fleeces they are the sheep of one divine shepherd.[7] And yet, the very sight of one another's habit is a source of mutual irritation ! " I have seen," he writes, " I cannot say how often, Black Monks laughing at a White Monk whom they have met, as if he were an abortion and as though a centaur or a chimæra or some weird monstrosity had come their way, showing their astonishment by word or by gesture. On the other hand, I have seen White Monks talking together about what was going on around them, when, lo, a Black Monk appeared and they were as silent as if they were protecting themselves against an enemy who was trying to worm out their secrets." [8] All this is very graphically described ; but it is a sad story.

As has been said, Peter had laid before St. Bernard about twenty-five years earlier the Cluniac answer to the Cistercian charges. Many of them he had refuted on such grounds as that the spirit of the Rule is not compulsion but persuasion ; [9] that St. Benedict intended it to be interpreted in its spirit ; [10]

[1] Pet. Ven. *Epp. Lib.*, IV. xvii, *P.L.* CLXXXIX. 325.

[2] *Reg. S.P. Bened.*, II.

[3] *Op. cit.*, 328.

[4] *Op. cit.*, 330.

[5] Pet. Ven. *Epp. Lib.*, I. xxviii, *P.L. tom. cit.*, 129.

[6] Butler, *Western Monachism*, 354.

[7] Pet. Ven. *Epp. Lib.*, IV. xvii, *P.L. tom. cit.*, 333.

[8] *Ep. cit., P.L. tom. cit.*, 331.

[9] Pet. Ven. *Epp. Lib.*, I. xxviii, *P.L. tom. cit.*, 120 sqq., 158.

[10] *Ep. cit., P.L. tom. cit.*, 148 sq., 156 sq.

that there is a valid distinction between immovable and movable commandments, the latter of which are subject to dispensation according to the law of charity.[1]   To this letter of Peter St. Bernard's *Apology*, written about 1125, at the request of his friend William, the Cluniac Abbot of the Cluniac Abbey of St. Thierry-lès-Reims, was, we are disposed to think, a reply, the motive force of which is expressed by its concluding words : " What is praiseworthy in your monks I praise and proclaim as such; if there is anything blameworthy, I am wont to advise you and my other friends to amend it." [2]

The *Apology* is in two parts, the first of which (*Capp.* I-VII) is a rebuke of the offensive detractions of Cistercian pharisaism, being in fact something of an *amende honorable* offered to the " most glorious Order " of Cluny in the person of Peter ; [3]   the second part (*Capp.* VIII-XII) is a scathing condemnation of Cluniac ostentation, luxury and general laxity.   In a Marmoutier MS. the treatise consists of two letters, so Mabillon tells us.[4]   In spite of the kind help of M. Omont, M. Collon of Tours and Dom André Wilmart, the writer has, alas, as yet failed to trace this MS.

It should perhaps be said that St. Bernard's criticism of the decorative features of Cluniac architecture, as we may see them at Vézelay to-day in a form probably more grotesque than anything which has yet been found by Dr. Conant of the Mediæval Academy of America at Cluny itself—was not written from a strictly æsthetic point of view, though doubtless, as would have Plato, St. Bernard would have execrated the Goncourt formula of *l'art pour l'art*.   Nor is there anything in his condemnation of Cluniac self-indulgence which exceeds in severity what Peter himself could write. For example, his remarks as to the use of *pigmenta* in a rich fragrant compound of honey, spices and wine, which he reports to be customary in some houses on great feasts,[5] are in effect mild as compared with Peter's absolute prohibition of it in the Cluniac *Statuta* as edited by him in 1146.[6]   In the same *Statuta* he forbids the wearing of dainty and expensive furs, as " a notable and damnable piece of affectation " on the part of monks.[7]   There is extant a letter upon the whole subject addressed by Peter to the priors of the Order, in which he writes : " Reputable and serious-minded persons report to me—I say so with the deepest regret—that so far as concerns the eating of flesh there is no difference between our brethren and lay folk, between seculars and religious, nay, to put it more pointedly, between rich men's jesters and monks . . . the fleshpots of Egypt alone are acceptable."

[1] *Ep. cit., P.L. tom.cit.,* 148 sqq.

[2] S. Bern. *Apol. ad Guill. S. Theod. Ab.,* I. 1 and XIII. 32. Cf. Mabill. *Admon. in op.,* III.

[3] *Op. cit.,* I. 1, II. 4, V. 10.

[4] Mabill. *Admon. in S. Bern. Apol. ad Guill. S. Theod. Ab.,* VII.

[5] *Op. cit.,* IX. 21.

[6] Pet. Ven. *Stat. Congr. Cluniac.,* XI, *P.L.* CLXXXIX. 1029.

[7] *Op. cit.,* XVII.

He proceeds to particularize. Even well-fed veal, hares, chickens have become insipid to holy monks. Recourse is had to royal and foreign dainties. " By the fowler's art pheasants, partridges, pigeons must be killed lest the servant of God perish of hunger. The utmost pains must be taken to satisfy his every whim, or he is sure to die ! " [1] Before we criticize adversely the *Apology* of St. Bernard, we should learn something of what the sarcasm of Peter the Venerable could amount to when he dealt with the same matter.

We know that in at least two connections Peter emphasizes the distinction between immovable and movable commandments ; once in the apology prefatory to the *Statuta*,[2] and again in a letter already cited.[3] This distinction he explains and illustrates in his preface to the *Statuta*. The immovable commandments are those which are " ordered by the Lord to be unchangeably observed, because in accordance with the eternal law " ; the movable commandments, such as the order to fast or to do manual work or the like, are changeable according to their utility in each case. It is the application of this principle that St. Bernard discusses at length in his treatise *Concerning Precept and Dispensation*, written at their request for the Benedictines of Chartres perhaps about the year 1142.[4] This work was evidently regarded by the Cluniacs as of high authority, for not only did Peter ask St. Bernard to send him a copy of it, if possible by the bearer of his letter, in order that he might read it again,[5] but the Cluniac monk in his *Dialogue* with the Cistercian appeals to it in support of his contention for freedom in bodily observances.[6]

As we might expect, the " mutual rancour " of which Peter complained was only too ready to reveal itself in concrete shapes more disastrous to the maintenance of charity than were frowns and gibes and gestures of disdain. One such sore, which was acute towards the end of St. Bernard's life, remained still unhealed at the time of his death. It was, we may think, unfortunate that, after the Schism in the Papacy was at an end, Innocent II had recognized the eminent services rendered by the Abbot of Clairvaux by exempting all Cistercian houses from the payment of tithe, a privilege which Peter the Venerable declared to the Pope would deprive the Cluniacs of one tenth of their revenue.[7] The grievance came to a head in the case of Gigny in Burgundy, then a Cluniac priory in the diocese of Lyons. Peter had protested in three letters, one to the Pope, another to Cardinal Haimeric, Chancellor of the Apostolic See, and a

[1] Pet. Ven. *Epp. Lib.*, VI. xv, *P.L. tom. cit.*, 418 sq.

[2] Pet. Ven. *Stat. Congr. Cluniac. Apol.*, *P.L. tom. cit.*, 1025.

[3] P. 348 *supra*.

[4] Mabill. *Admon. in S. Bern. Lib. de Praecept. et Disp.*, IV and V.

[5] Pet. Ven. *Epp. Lib.*, IV. xvii, *P.L. tom. cit.*, 343.

[6] *Dial. inter Cluniac. Mon. et Cisterc.*, III. 6 sq., Marten. et Durand. *op. cit.*, *loc. cit.*

[7] Jaffé, *Regest.*, 7544 ; Pet. Ven. *Epp. Lib.*, I. xxiii, *P.L.* CLXXXIX.165.

third to the Abbots of Cîteaux, Clairvaux and Pontigny and
" others assembled in the name of Christ," presumably to the
general chapter.[1] Amongst the tithe-payers of Gigny was
its neighbour the Cistercian Abbey of Miroir, which stood
firmly upon its right to exemption. St. Bernard, after conferring with Peter at Dijon on the Third Sunday after Pentecost
in the year 1151,[2] effected a semblance of concord—but no
more. The situation became critical when soon afterwards
the monks of Gigny took the law into their own hands, and
organized an onslaught upon the property of Miroir, the
damage of which St. Bernard states to have amounted to
"more than 30,000 *solidi*," some thousands of pounds at the
purchasing power of sterling to-day. They endeavoured to
dispense themselves from responsibility for this outrage.
" They said," writes St. Bernard in a letter to Eugenius III,
" ' Some evilly disposed of our people did this wrong.' What
is that to us ? They might have seen what was going on.
Moreover it is a ridiculous excuse. It was notorious throughout the whole neighbourhood that this outrageous crime was
committed by the men of the priory, that some of the monks
were looking on, and that all of them approved of it." [3] In
the letter cited St. Bernard is reporting another conference
of four days' duration held at Cluny by the order of Eugenius,
who required the damage to be assessed and reparation to
be made under pain of censure.[4] Alas, it proved to be entirely abortive and the whole question remained, as we have
said, still unsettled at St. Bernard's death.[5]

It is not to be supposed that Peter the Venerable con-
doned the violence of the monks of Gigny — indeed St.
Bernard's words make it plain that he did not—but he did
regard, we may think, the exemption as a piece of unjust
confiscation ; that it is the duty of the rich to succour the
poor is indisputable ; that the rich monks, if they *are* so
rich as they are said to be—should be robbed for the benefit
of their poorer brethren is quite another matter.[6] A capable
man of business, who had found the finances of Cluny heavily
embarrassed when he became abbot in 1122 and had successfully balanced his budget by retrenchment,[7] Peter looked
to human probability in the matter of ways and means.
As for St. Bernard, God kept his purse and it was not for him
to trouble himself about what was in it.[8] He probably regarded the exemption as literally a godsend, to decline which
would be to affront the sender. And further, it should be
remembered that it meant much to the Cistercians, who were
bound by their constitution to give away three quarters of

[1] *Op. cit.*, xxiii
sqq., *P.L.*
CLXXXIX.
164 sqq.

[2] Pet. Ven. *Epp.
Lib.*, VI. xlvi
sq., *P.L.*
CLXXXIX.
469 and 472 ;
Jaffé, *Regest.*,
9562.

[3] *Ep.* 283.

[4] Jaffé, *Regest.*,
9562 sq.

[5] Horst. et
Mabill. *in S.
Bern. Ep.* 283
Not. Fus. ;
Jaffé, *Regest.*,
9877 ; *Gall.
Christ.*, IV. 297.

[6] Pet. Ven. *Epp.
Lib.*, I. xxxiv,
P.L. tom. cit.,
168 sq.

[7] Pet. Ven.
*Dispos. Rei
Fam. Cluniac.*,
P.L. tom. cit.,
1047 sqq.

[8] P. 25 *supra*.

their tithe in equal parts to their diocesan, to the parish, and
to their guests, widows, orphans and the needy, reserving
only one quarter for the upkeep of the *ecclesia*.[1] We may
note here St. Bernard's view that, whereas secular clergy
live " of the altar," monks live " by their own labour."[2]
But, painfully strained as were the relations between the
two Orders, the appropriate correspondence of St. Bernard
and of Peter is highly edifying reading ; it is most creditable
to them both as revealing the common will of these two men
to raise, each in his own way, the tone of the religious life
of their generation. And, we may add, so generous, so
innocent of party-spirit, was St. Bernard that he would upon
occasion raise his voice in defence of Cluniac rights, as in
a letter written about 1148 to the Countess of Nevers in
behalf of the Abbey of Vézelay.[3]

About the year 1150 [4] St. Bernard was in some anxiety
concerning the vacancy at Troisfontaines, occasioned by the
raising of its abbot Hugh to the Sacred Purple as Cardinal
Bishop of Ostia ; a dignity the bestowal of which was distinctly displeasing to the Abbot of Clairvaux, as he told
Eugenius quite plainly, on the grounds that the whole Order
badly needed Hugh, indeed that he was " the staff of his
old age," and that " a tree bearing good fruit where it stands
may easily bear none at all when transplanted." [5]   There
resulted an unfortunate misunderstanding.   Hugh suggested
for the vacancy a monk of the house by name Nicholas,
who proved to be unacceptable to his brethren.   St. Bernard's
suggestion of another monk, one Robert, failed to please
Hugh.   Thereupon St. Bernard proposed an Englishman then
at Clairvaux, Thorold, formerly fifth Abbot of Fountains,
who had resigned that post owing to some difficulty with
Henry Murdach, Archbishop of York.[6]   But this did not
at once close the incident ; for Hugh seems to have resented
the election of Thorold as a scandal, almost as a personal
affront.   Had his new dignity turned his head ?   St. Bernard
in a letter to Cardinal Hugh insists upon the probity, learning
and general acceptability of Thorold, humbly adding, perhaps
with a touch of irony, " if you wish to remove him you have
the power to do so." [7]   As we may surmise, Thorold remained ;
St. Bernard's right to an interest in the first daughter of
Clairvaux could scarcely have been called in question.

Another sorrow, if possible yet nearer home to St. Bernard,
befell him in these last years.   His first secretary had been
William, subsequently first Abbot of Rievaulx.   We do not
know who filled the office after William's departure until

[1] *Exord. Parv.*, XV., Guignard, *Mon. prim. de la règle Cisterc.*
[2] *Ep.* 397.

[3] *Ep.* 375.
[4] Marten. et Durand. *Thes. Nov. Anecd.*, I. 407 sq. ; Jaffé, *Regest.*, II. 20.

[5] *Ep.* 273.

[6] Dugdale, *Monast. Angl.*, V. 302, xxxix. ed. Caley.

[7] *Ep.* 306.

in 1140 it was undertaken by Geoffrey, a Clairvaux monk and St. Bernard's biographer. In 1145 Geoffrey ceased to be his secretary—although he travelled with him constantly during the following years—and was succeeded by a monk, by name Nicholas, but recently admitted to the community of Clairvaux. It was probably during St. Bernard's absence that he had arrived there from Montier-Ramey, a house of Black Monks about thirteen miles East of Troyes, and professing himself to be desirous of living the stricter Cistercian life had duly been received. Very soon afterwards St. Bernard, apparently impressed by his earnestness and by his capacity, appointed him to be his secretary. For those days the correspondence would have been voluminous and Nicholas had assistants, of one of whom, Gerard of Péronne, we know the name ; for in a letter cited by Mabillon Nicholas describes him as "the inseparable comrade of my secretarial work." [1] Nicholas had the gift of ingratiating himself with persons of distinction ; he would seem to have been specially acceptable to Peter the Venerable, with whom he was in direct correspondence. Peter writes to him : " I loved you when by your colour," that is to say, as a Black Monk, " you belonged to us ; and now, so far as I am concerned, your colour changed but not your heart I love you none the less." [2] Doubtless St. Bernard regarded the friendship between Nicholas and the Abbot of Cluny as a valuable asset. Describing himself once to Peter as interrupted by external calls, he tells him that he tore himself away and shut himself up " with that Nicholas whom your soul loves," in order to be able to attend to his correspondence ; and, unusually in St. Bernard's letters, Nicholas ends on this occasion with his own salutation to Peter and to the community at Cluny.[3] But both these wise abbots were completely hoodwinked ! Within a year's time Nicholas was detected as a clever scoundrel. St. Bernard tells the whole story in a letter to Eugenius III. " The Nicholas you know of *has gone out from us because he was not of us ;* but he has left foul traces behind him. For some time I had been aware of what sort of man he was, but I was waiting to see whether God would convert him or like Judas he would betray himself. And this latter is what has happened. In addition to books, some small coins and much gold, there were found upon him at his departure three seals ; one his own, another the prior's, the third mine. Mine was not the old seal but a quite new one," that is to say, a duplicate which Nicholas had had made. This piece of forgery had not escaped the notice of

[1] Mabill. *Praef. in Tom. III. S. Bern. Opp.,* xlii.

[2] Pet. Ven. *Epp. Lib.,* VI. v, *P.L.* CLXXXIX. 408. Cf. *op. cit.,* VI. xxxiv, xxxvi and xlvii.

[3] *Ep.* 389.

St. Bernard, for he goes on to say : " On account of this treachery and secret theft of his, I had recently been compelled to change my seal. I remember that, without mentioning names, I told you of this before ; because, as I said, we were *in perils among false brethren.* Who can say to how many people he has written whatever he chose in my name, without my knowing anything about it ? " [1] In the earlier letter he had written : " Many letters have been sent to many people under my seal falsely used ; and what I fear more, it is said that such letters have even reached yourself." [2] He proceeds to describe the new seal which he is using as bearing his image and his name. From the later letter it is clear that such forgeries *had* been sent to the Pope, for St. Bernard writes : " It has partly been proved, and partly he has confessed, that not once but several times he has written to you making false use of my seal." [3]

But Nicholas was guilty on a yet graver charge. " As to his uncleanness, which befouls the place and is a warning to all, I refrain from defiling my lips and your ears by speaking of it. If he comes to you—he boasts that he will do so and that he can rely upon friends in the *Curia*—remember Arnald of Brescia, for a worse than Arnald is here. Never was a man more deserving of life-long imprisonment and of condemnation to perpetual silence." [4] He is thinking, doubtless, of Arnald's fascination of Cardinal Guy in Bohemia.

To St. Bernard, " wounded in the house of his friends," the blow would have been staggering. A conscience such as his may perhaps have prompted him to blame himself for his long and frequent absences from Clairvaux, for his immersion in affairs external to the immediate welfare of his sons. But the verdict of to-day, informed by the evidence of successive generations which tells of his services in the edification of Christian character, will acquit the charity which " believeth all things, hopeth all things." In his own day men, not utterly depraved, might well have said of him as the Rugby boy said of Arnold : " You cannot tell the Abbot of Clairvaux a lie, because he believes you."

It was the year 1151 and St. Bernard's old and valued friends, one after another, were passing to their account. Raynald, son of Milo Count of Bar-sur-Seine,[5] was a monk of Clairvaux who in 1133 had become fifth Abbot of Cîteaux. A man of administrative gifts, he had been largely instrumental in the matter of the friendly pact between the Premonstratensians and the Cistercians, to which we have referred above,[6] and had made himself in the main responsible for

[1] *Ep.* 298.

[2] *Ep.* 284.

[3] *Ep.* 298.

[4] *Ep.* 298.

[5] Order. Vital. *Hist. Angl.,* VIII. *P.L.* CLXXXI. 1725, *n.* (2).

[6] *Gall. Christ.,* IV. 985 sq. ; cf. pp. 233 sq. *supra.*

the *Institutes of the General Chapter* issued in 1152 after his death.[1] We shall remember the interview between St. Bernard and Abélard at Cîteaux arranged by him.[2] And now, probably early in 1151, St. Bernard writes to Eugenius : " My lord of Cîteaux has left us desolate ; a sore wound to the whole Order. On me, in very truth, falls a double sorrow who in one man have lost both a father and a son." [3] Raynald had died on 16th December, 1150.[4] Geoffrey tells us that St. Bernard had had some premonition of the nearness of his end.[5]

We may believe that it was on 12th January of this same year, 1151, that Suger died, for an entry in the *Regesta Romanorum Pontificum* under date 19th January, 1152, refers to him as " the late Abbot of St. Denis of venerable memory." [6] To St. Bernard the memory would have been crowded with recollections, first of a great conversion in which he had been privileged to take a human share ; and then of zealous co-operation in monastic reform, of devotion to the highest interests of the Church, of loyal fidelity to the Crown of France under two successive kings, covering a period, stormy and anxious, of little less than thirty years. Although perhaps for a moment at the end of the Second Crusade—and we must remember that he was then a dying man—his patriotism got the better of his judgement, and urged him in the direction of another Crusade to be undertaken primarily in order to punish the treachery of the Greeks ; [7] yet amongst European statesmen of his own, perhaps of any age, he stands in the front rank, at his best far-seeing in outlook, deliberate in action, disinterested in motive. France may well remember that in large measure she owes him to St. Bernard ; and St. Bernard, who after all lacked none of the characteristics of an enthusiast, may have owed something to the moderating influence of Suger ; " a man," he writes to Eugenius, " faithful and prudent in temporal affairs ; in spiritual affairs fervent and humble ; and, what is most difficult, in both conducting himself without reproach." [8]

When the news of his mortal sickness reaches St. Bernard, he at once writes to him in the tenderest terms. After bidding him have no fear of putting off the earthly man, seeing that this must be if he is to be clothed with the heavenly, he continues : " But I deeply yearn, most beloved, to see you before then in order that I may receive your dying blessing. Yet it is not in man to direct his ways, so I do not dare to promise that of which I am not certain. At present I do not see how I can come, but I am doing all I can to come.

[1] Williams, *The First Cistercian Era, Journ. of Theol. Stud.*, Oct., 1930, 56 sqq.

[2] Cf. p. 312 *supra*.

[3] *Ep.* 270.

[4] Manric. *Ann. Cisterc.*, II. 176.

[5] *Vita Prima*, IV. iii. 19.

[6] Jaffé, *Regest.*, 9535. Cf. Vacandard, *Vie de saint Bernard*, II. 516, *n*. (1), *éd.* 1920.

[7] P. 285 *supra*.

[8] *Ep.* 309.

I may or I may not be able to do so. However this may be, I have loved you from the beginning and I shall love you without end. This I can confidently say : It is impossible that I should ever really lose so beloved a friend. A man whose soul is bound to mine by an indissoluble union, by an unbreakable link, I am not losing ; he is going before me. Only, when you reach that place to which you go, remember me, that to me also it may soon be given to follow you and to be with you." And then in a human sort of way, and feeling perhaps that a bare grain of hope may turn the scale, he adds : " Nevertheless God is able even yet to grant your life to those who ask it, to preserve you to those who love you ; that indeed is not to be doubted." [1] From his death-bed Suger was able to dictate a few words in reply, thanking St. Bernard for some little presents sent for his comfort. He knew that his end was near. " Would," he cries, " that, if it were but just once, I might see your angel-face before I pass away ! " [2] Alas, he did not.

In the very next year, 1152, died one, who not only had always known the love and often felt the rebukes of St. Bernard—love and rebukes which had wrought in him an heroic Christian type, not perhaps so marked in any other prince who fell under the influence of the saint—but also during long years on many an occasion had proved himself to be a true friend to the Cistercians, Theobald II, Count of Champagne. [3]

We seem to recognize a decline in St. Bernard's health after his return to Clairvaux from Italy in the summer of 1138 at the end of the Papal Schism. The eight immediately preceding years had probably involved greater physical and mental strain than did any other period of his life ; scarcely for a moment had the effort been relaxed. More than once we have referred to his bodily frailty, to his chronic gastric disorder, to his sensitive temperament. All these were dominated by his self-forgetfulness ; it was as though his sense of his own limitations were concentrated so exclusively upon conscience alone, to the exclusion of all other interests, that his life gave in altruistic service concrete expression to the Pauline formula : *Omnia possum in eo qui me confortat.* [4] " What is stronger," he would ask, " than the strength of men who " deplore their sins ? " " These men have no flesh, because, although in the flesh yet forgetful of the flesh, they hear the apostle say : *Ye then are not in the flesh, but in the spirit.*" [5] But " the guilty conscience is a kind of hell, a very prison of the soul." [6]

[1] *Ep.* 266.

[2] Suger. *Ep. inter S. Bern. Epp.*, 471.

[3] d'Arbois de Jubainville, *Hist. des ducs et comtes de Champ.*, II. 398.

[4] *Phil.*, IV. 13.

[5] *De Divers. Serm.*, XCIII. 2.

[6] *In Assumpt. B.V. Mar. Serm.*, IV. 4.

And yet " the flesh, that good and faithful comrade of the soul," must some day pass from its state of fruitful labour, first to that of rest, and then to that of glory.[1] In this same year of his return from Italy, 1138, he writes to Innocent II : " Lo, as I lie upon my bed it is less the suffering of my body than of my soul which tortures me. For no temporal pain distresses me." [2] The election to the vacant see of Langres was weighing upon his mind ; [3] but we are quite sure that he was also suffering acutely in his body. The sermons on *The Song of Songs*, which date from about the year 1136 and were continued almost until St. Bernard's death, reveal only too plainly his frequent suffering. " That is enough," he remarks regretfully, " my weakness tells me that I must stop. It often does ; so that I am most commonly compelled, as you know, to leave my words unfinished and to postpone the rest until another day." [4] In 1143 or 1144 he writes to Peter the Venerable : " I am broken in health, and I have a legitimate excuse for no longer running about in different directions as I have been accustomed to do." [5] We are not surprised that, at the beginning of his missionary journey in Languedoc so soon afterwards as 1145, he should have been, Geoffrey tells us, in grave doubt concerning the wisdom of his having undertaken it at all.[6] And within less than twelve months he began at Vézelay to preach the Second Crusade ! How he managed to undertake and to survive his travels in Flanders and in the Rhineland during the winter of 1146-47, is only to be accounted for as a miracle of grace. Geoffrey notes that it was characteristic of him that " when any great need claimed him his courage overcame all obstacles, his bodily strength responded and every one was astonished to see him surpassing even strong men in his powers of endurance." [7] To the question as to whether he might have accompanied the Crusaders to the East we have already referred.[8]

Reports as to the increasing gravity of St. Bernard's state began about the year 1151 to cause anxiety in several quarters. The king had heard of it and had written to him ; a visit too from Louis's brother Robert of Dreux had cheered him greatly. " Who am I," he writes, " or what is my father's house that your royal majesty should be thinking about whether I am dead or alive ? However, seeing that I am thus in your esteem, I may tell you that I am just a little better and that, if I can judge by my own feelings, I am for the time out of danger of death, although weak, very weak. But now I particularly want you to know this—that lord

[1] *De Dilig. Deo,* XI. 31.

[2] *Ep.* 166.

[3] Pp. 159 sqq. *supra.*

[4] *In Cant. Cant.,* XLIV. 8.

[5] *Ep.* 228.

[6] P. 340 *supra.*

[7] *Vita Prima,* V. i. 4.

[8] Pp. 286 sq. *supra.*

Robert, your brother, has deigned in the most devoted way to visit me in my sickness, and has spoken to me in such terms as to make me happy and to give me better hope of himself. Love him; because, if his deeds are as good as his words, you will be pleased with him. And if you see fit to do so, let him know that you are gratified that by my advice and that of good men he has promised not to be troublesome in future. My seal is not at hand; but anyone who reads this may recognize that the writing is my own." [1] Robert was, we remember, a terrible fellow whose sword was only too ready to leap from its scabbard. This charming little letter, which we may date either late in 1151 or early in 1152, is interesting as having been St. Bernard's autograph; as we shall notice again, in his last days he seems to have felt that his own handwriting brought him nearer to his friends than did dictation. An earlier letter, that in which he announced the passing of Raynald, Abbot of Cîteaux, would have prepared the Pope to expect at any moment the news of his death. "Your child," he writes, "is more ill than he usually is; he is dying by inches; perhaps he is not counted worthy to die once for all and quickly to enter into life." [2] Evidently something had been heard at Rome from other sources, and there was anxiety for more news; for, in another letter dealing with the difficulties in which Henry, the king's brother, found himself at Beauvais,[3] written to Hugh, Cardinal Bishop of Ostia, probably a little later, we read: "I understand that you are anxious about the state of my health. What you have heard is true; I am sick even unto death, yet I have been called back to death"— meaning that the reprieve is such to him [4]—"but this I feel is not for long; for I am far weaker than can be believed." And then, as though ashamed to have allowed the murmur to escape him, he adds: "I would however say this without prejudice to the divine providence of God, who is able even to raise the dead." [5]

During the winter of 1152-3 he seems to have been so ill that his sons at Clairvaux did not think it possible that he could survive many days, until he reassured them by his conviction that, if "I am to believe myself, the dissolution of my flesh is to be next summer." Perhaps it was thus reassured that Godfrey de la Roche, when one day discussing with him some grave matter, expressed astonishment at his absence of mind; but the saint excused himself. "Do not wonder," he said, "for I no longer belong to this world." [6] Tenderly but firmly he would disengage himself from their

[1] *Ep.* 304.

[2] *Ep.* 270.

[3] Pp. 185 sq. *supra.*

[4] *Vita Prima,* V. i. 3.

[5] *Ep.* 307.

[6] *Vita Prima,* V. ii. 8.

clinging affection, when almost to the very end it prompted them to speak, as he knew, too hopefully of his state. " Why do you detain a wretched man ? You are too brave, too strong, to do that. Refrain, refrain, and let me depart." [1]

Marvellous to relate, there was in the spring of 1153 a great rally, the last of its kind, in response to an external claim which St. Bernard regarded as imperative. On his bed of sickness news reached him of " a very grave disaster " [2] which had befallen the people of Metz. There was open warfare between Stephen, Bishop of Metz, and Matthew, Duke of Lorraine, the latter supported by certain feudatories of the duchy. Caught in a narrow defile of the Moselle under the heights of Froidmont, in the direction of Pont-à-Mousson, and unable to extricate themselves, more than two thousand of the men of Metz perished, some by the sword, others by drowning, on 28th February, 1153.[3] But the spirit of the great city was not broken, and it was preparing itself for revenge, when, foreseeing that the whole province was threatened with devastation, the venerable metropolitan Illin, Archbishop of Trèves, decided to go to Clairvaux and beg the intervention of St. Bernard. Not for a moment did he hesitate, when it was urged that he alone could avail anything with the belligerents. Happily it was one of those brief periods when he was, as he had described it to the Cardinal Bishop of Ostia, " called back to death " ; [4] during the last few days he had been feeling himself to be less weak than usual.[5] To the amazement of all he set out for Metz. He found the opposing forces somewhere on the banks of the Moselle, glaring at one another across the intervening stream. The Messines, their hearts set upon revenge, were obdurate ; and fearing, Geoffrey gives us to understand, lest the magnetism of St. Bernard's presence should turn them from their purpose went their way. Their enemies, blood-lust now stimulated by the slaughter at Froidmont, after declining to listen to the terms proposed by St. Bernard did likewise, in a manner sufficiently discourteous to one who had come so far and at such cost to save their land if possible from internecine strife. " Do not be distressed," he remarked to his companions in despair, " although there are great difficulties to be surmounted, yet the peace which we desire will certainly come." And the influence of the negotiator began to be felt ; for a conference of the leaders of both parties was subsequently held. The matter dragged on for several days ; for long neither belligerent appeared to be willing to do anything else than to leave the issue to the

[1] *Vita Prima,* V. iii. 18.

[2] *Op. cit.,* V. i. 3.

[3] *Chron. Univers. Mettens.,* M.G.H. XXIV. 517.

[4] P. 357 *supra.*

[5] *Vita Prima,* V. i. 3.

arbitrament of war ; finally, however, St. Bernard's conviction that peace would come, his wonderful gift of making peace by willing peace, prevailed and a second conference described circumstantially by Geoffrey was held on a little island in the Moselle above the city—possibly that which lies off the point of St. Symphorian, or another higher up near Vaux—at which such terms were arranged as, at any rate for the time, brought hostilities to an end.[1] But, alas, the peace was not durable ; for we read in a letter written the same year by the Bishop of Metz to Wibald, Abbot of Corbie : " To speak the truth, what seems to have been settled by my lord of Clairvaux in the cause of peace and security not only has brought us no remedy, but has wounded us more severely. For the authors of this great crime," the butchery at Froidmont, " gathering force from the success of their iniquity, have not merely escaped scot-free but have even profited by their wrong-doing." [2] The letter is intended to solicit Wibald's interest with Frederick Barbarossa who had recently in 1152 ascended the imperial throne ; we do not know with what success the appeal met, but it needed a strong hand to restrain the brutal and unscrupulous Matthew of Lorraine.

" This, sweetest father," exclaims Geoffrey, " was the blessed end of thy journeyings and this the last of thy labours ! " We shall measure its merit rather by the conditions which made it difficult than by its material success. St. Bernard's return to Clairvaux, which he was never again to leave, was by way of Toul (*Leuci*) and Gondreville, his footsteps marked by many works of healing.[3]

On 8th July, 1153, died Eugenius III, " a man deeply religious, bountiful in almsgiving, just in judgement, to all comers whether poor or rich easy of approach and courteous in manner." [4] When the news reached St. Bernard he would have been within about a month of his own departure. What it meant to him to hear that his " son of tender age " had been called from that " service of the servants of God," over which during eight critical years he had himself watched with such prayerful solicitude, we cannot know. Nor is this the occasion for an estimate of the work of this great pontiff. John of Salisbury, who was in his service from some date shortly before the Council of Rheims until the day of his death, suggests that he always distrusted his sick and sorry *Curia*—his *latera*, as he called it—and that consequently he would usually act, perhaps a little high-handedly, upon his own judgement alone.[5] We have seen him, in a position

[1] *Vita Prima,* V. i. 4.

[2] *Inter Wibald. Ab. Stabul. Epp.,* 398, P.L. CLXXXIX. 1431.

[3] *Vita Prima,* V. i. 7.

[4] *Annal. de Waverl.,* 235, ed. Luard. *Rolls Series.*

[5] Joann. Sares. *Hist. Pontifical.,* XXI. 51, ed. Poole.

of well-nigh unparalleled yet fully realized responsibility, called to deal with situations both ecclesiastical and civil in which the issue was delicately poised : with the Second Crusade, with anarchy in Rome, with the ambitions and the violences of princes, with the affairs in remote corners of Christendom of the Order of which he was a distinguished ornament. An entirely blameless character, he left to his contemporaries, as he has by their mouths to posterity, a memory of pontifical office upon which St. Bernard in his last days would have dwelt, we cannot doubt, with much gratitude and, surely, with some pardonable pride.

The few remaining weeks were a period of constant suffering, during which his faith and the courage inspired by it rarely if ever failed. He would assure his sons of his abiding presence with them after death, urging them to follow his example and to obey his precepts ; the sense of his re- [1] *Op. cit.*, V. ii. 9. sponsibility for the welfare of their souls grew daily stronger.[1] As they gathered round his bed, " weeping with them that weep " and distraught by their grief he would " raise to heaven his dove-like eyes," and say that he knew not which to choose, whether to remain or to depart, leaving all to the will of God his father. At times he would speak of himself as a barren, fruitless tree, declaring that he could not believe what men said of his services ; then again he would reproach himself for doubting their word ; " such truthful people," [2] *Op. cit.*, V. ii. 12. he would reflect, " could not lie." [2]   Alan of Auxerre records that St. Bernard called to his bedside the brethren who for long had been most intimately related to him, presumably the seniors of the house, and delivered to them a brief, although somewhat formal, charge, the *ipsissima verba* of which it is a little difficult to think of him as having used. He set before them three rules of conduct, subordination of self-opinion, abstinence from retaliation and from vengeance, [3] *Vita Sec.*, xxx. 82. and avoidance and reparation of scandal.[3]   The tone in which he is made to speak of himself, as having always observed these rules, just lacks the touch which we should naturally expect to find in the death-bed exhortation of such a man. There is the faint suggestion of a self-congratulation, of a self-satisfaction, scarcely likely to have been felt by him at the time which is not reflected in what is probably Geoffrey's [4] *Vita Prima*, V. ii. 9. reference to the same episode.[4]

We owe indirectly to Arnald of Bonneval, the writer of the IInd Book of the *Vita Prima*, a record of exceptional [5] Williams, *Studies in St. Bernard of Clairvaux*, I. 11 sq. interest, namely, the last letter which St. Bernard ever wrote, his own autograph throughout.[5]   Arnald had evidently sent some delicacies to tempt his appetite. " I have," he writes, " received your charity in the spirit which prompted it; I cannot say—with pleasure; for what pleasure is there, when bitterness claims everything except the pleasure of eating nothing at all? Sleep has gone from me, lest by the relief of my deadened senses pain should ever leave me. Nearly all my suffering is weakness of the stomach. Frequently by day and by night it craves the solace of a drop of water; for it loathes all solid food. The little which it will take means severe pain; but it fears severer, should it take nothing at all. The least morsel in excess brings terrible suffering. My feet and my legs have swollen as is customary in dropsy. And in all this—to keep nothing from an anxious friend—as regards the inner man—I speak as a fool—the spirit is willing, but the flesh is weak. Pray to the Saviour that he delay no longer the seasonable hour of my departure. Protect by your prayers the heel which is naked of merits, that so he who lies in ambush may have nowhere to fix his teeth and wound. I write myself, such as I am, in order that my handwriting which you know well may tell you something of my state. I wish that I could have written it over again!" [1] This letter, as we learn from Geoffrey, dates from " a very few days " before St. Bernard's death. [2]

As the news of his imminent decease spread abroad, there gathered at Clairvaux neighbouring bishops and many abbots and other religious. At his own request St. Bernard received Extreme Unction and Holy Viaticum; and " at very shortly before the third hour," on Thursday, 20th August, he passed away. [3] His body, clothed in the sacerdotal vestments, lay for two days in the church, where it was venerated with touching demonstrations of affection by crowds of all ranks, both cleric and lay; the women, to whom admission to the cloister was forbidden by the Rule, collected in vast numbers outside lamenting bitterly aloud. [4] On the second day at about noon the crowd was such that it was scarcely possible to restrain it; men besieged the body, touched it with articles of clothing and with coins, kissed effusively the hands and the feet. It was therefore decided to inter it in the morning of the following day, and after due celebration of Mass it was placed in a cavity in the ground specially prepared for it, immediately before the altar of our Lady, that is to say, the high altar of the church. [5] By his own direction he was buried in the tunic taken from St. Malachy's body after his death—which since that day St. Bernard had been accustomed

[1] *Ep.* 310.

[2] *Vita Prima,* V. ii. 9.

[3] *Op. cit.,* V. ii. 13; *Vita Sec.,* xxx. 84 sq.

[4] *Vita Prima.* V. ii. 14.

[5] *Op. cit.,* V. ii. 14 sq. Cf. pp. 58 sq. *supra.*

to wear when saying Mass—even as St. Malachy had been buried in his.[1] On his breast was laid, also by his wish, a casket containing relics of St. Thaddaeus brought to him that same year from Jerusalem.[2] Fittingly may we inscribe on the stone which covers him words which some quarter of a century earlier he had used in a letter to Cardinal Haimeric— for they well express his life—*nulla quae Dei esse constiterit negotia a me duco aliena.*[3]

Less than twenty-one years later he was raised to the altars of the Church by Alexander III, the bull of canonization bearing date 18th January, 1174.[4] It is noticeable that this document makes no reference to any miracle wrought by St. Bernard, for his glorious repute was in the estimate of his contemporaries founded deeper far than that of a thaumaturge ; although, as Bellarmine remarked four centuries afterwards, " he was renowned for more miracles than was any saint, the written record of whose life has come down to us." [5] Many ages passed during which the *mellifluus doctor* was credited by the Christian world with the title of Doctor of the Church before it was formally conferred by a brief of Pius VIII, given in 1830 on 20th August, the feast day of the saint.[6]

[1] *Vita Prima,* V. iii. 23.

[2] *Op. cit.,* V. ii. 15.

[3] *Ep.* 20.

[4] *P.L.* CLXXXV. 622 sq.

[5] Bellarmin. *Controvers.,* II. iv. 14.

[6] *Decreta Authent. C.S.R.,* II. 231 sq.

APPENDIX I

LITERARIA

It would be impossible in a mere note to take stock of St. Bernard's literary qualities. We would simply draw attention to certain aspects of the subject, illustrating from such of his works as are textually most familiar to the present writer.

That St. Bernard was a great master of prose-rhythm cannot be doubted ; above all his *clausulae*, in which frequently he falls into something like a metrical form, call for notice ; in them pre-eminently he is the " mellifluous doctor." A large number of them might be collected ; it would be a pleasant task, for their cadence is very graceful. Let us record a few of them.

" Perambulant in tenebris negotia tenebrarum " (*De Convers.*, VIII. 17), a reminiscence of Ps. xc. 6 (*Vulg.*). How exquisitely balanced is the phrase ! It lingers gratefully upon the ear.

" In levitatem animi, quae secundus gradus est, cito delabitur " (*De Grad. Hum. et Superb.*, X. 38). Here, if we pause for a moment after the word " in," in order to emphasize the answer to an implied question as to whither the *delapsus* leads, the rhythmic phrasing is an almost perfect introduction to the Second Degree of Pride, namely, *levitas animi*.

" Ut sit ipse praemium amantium se, praemium aeternum amantium in aeternum " (*De Dilig. Deo*, XI. 33), where the cadence is infinitely tender and reassuring, precisely what it is meant to be.

" Tam plena in hoc saeculo, quam et in futuro " (*De Grat. et Lib. Arb.*, V. 15). The subject is *libertas arbitrii, quantum in se est ;* and the words are climactic in a statement of its prevalence unimpaired in the reasonable soul.

" Nam finis horum, pretiosa mors est " (*Vita S. Malach.*, XXIX. 66). Here again, the tenderness of the cadence is admirably adapted to the meaning of the words. There is a natural *caesura* after *horum*, and the following clause falls in such a way as to deprive the word " mors " of any suggestion of gloom. " Pretiosa mors est " leaves a glow of joy.

Here and there we find phrases, closing briefer statements and scarcely deserving to be called periodic *clausulae*, which, in spite of their violation of strict prosody, suggest the fourth line of a *sapphicus minor*. Such are " aufert concessum " (*De Grad. Hum. et Superb.*, X. 30) and " corde compungi " (*De Convers.*, XII. 24). In one instance we notice a definitely periodic *clausula* which observes the laws of prosody as the fourth line of a *sapphicus minor*, namely, " membra valerent " (*Vita S. Malach.*, X. 19). On the whole, we may say that there is a kind of sapphic instinct recognizable in St. Bernard's diction, which prompts him to relieve in a melodic fashion the even monotony of long passages, as in a choric *prosa*. The *clausula* above cited, "nam finis horum, pretiosa mors est," is as good a minor sapphic line as may be found, say, in the familiar hymn *Ecce jam noctis tenuatur umbra* (Walpole, *Early Latin Hymns*, pp. 275 sq.), in which there are several lapses from strict prosody.

Occasionally we get a metrical phrase which suggests the reminiscence of a hymn. Such is "Lugendi tempus advenit" (*De Convers.*, XI. 23). The suggestion is almost irresistible, but the hymn has not been traced ; and the reminiscence may really be that of the opening words of a sermon of St. Augustine, "Sollemne tempus advenit" (*Serm.* CCVIII. *In Quadr.* iv.).

This leads us to illustrate St. Bernard's Patristic reminiscences. "Sobria illa ebrietas" (*De Dilig. Deo*, XI. 33) is a striking oxymoron which recalls lines 23 sq. in the *Spendor paternae gloriae* of St. Ambrose,

> "Laeti bibamus sobriam
> Ebrietatem spiritus."

"Eos . . . statuens contra faciem suam" (*De Convers.*, II. 3) may be an echo of St. Augustine's "Constituebas me ante faciem meam" (*Confess.*, VIII. vii.) ; we are speaking, be it remembered, rather of the words than of the thought.

An interesting textual problem is illuminated by an evident reminiscence of a hymn of Sedulius. The reading "praeducem" (*De Convers.*, XII. 24) has strong MS. support against the "praedulcem" of the Benedictine edition. In the immediate context we read "lumen lumine quaerat." We turn to the hymn *A solis ortus cardine*, and we find (lines 34 sq.)

> "Stellam sequentes praeviam ;
> Lumen requirunt lumine."

Can we doubt but that the "praeducem" of St. Bernard is the "praeviam" of Sedulius ?

A reminiscence of St. Jerome's *dictum*, "Monachus non docentis, sed plangentis habet officium" (S. Hier. *Adv. Vigilantium*, VI.), occurs twice. In *Ep.* LXXXIX. 2 we read : "Siquidem vel monachi, quod esse videor, vel peccatoris, quod sum, officium non est docere, sed lugere." And again in *Ep.* CCCLXV. 1 we find : "Monachus non habet docentis, sed plangentis officium." Sometimes St. Bernard quotes explicitly ; for example, from St. Ambrose (*In Psalm.*, I.), when he writes : "Porro occupare locum, et non facere fructum, nec loco expedit, nec vos decet, nec nos. 'Nemo,' ut ait beatus Ambrosius, 'invitus bene facit, etiam si bonum est quod facit : quia nihil prodest spiritus timoris, ubi non est spiritus charitatis '" (*Ep.* CCLVIII.) ; from St. Augustine (*Serm.* LXXXVIII., *De Verbis Dom.*, xviii. 9) in *Ep.* CCCLIII. : "Restitistis quoad potuistis : jam, secundum Augustini sententiam, non vos inquinat alienum malum, quando quidem non consensistis corde, et ore redarguistis. Ait enim : 'Duobus modis non te inquinat alienum malum, si non consentis, et si redarguis.'" Again the "quidam sanctorum" of the *De Praecepto et Dispensatione* (I. 2) is St. Augustine (*Ep. ad Arment.* 127). In *Ep.* LXXVIII. 10 we have a quotation from St. Gregory the Great (*Hom. in Ezech.*, VII.) : "Denique nec cautior sum in verbo, nec circumspectior in sensu, illo qui ait : 'Melius est ut scandalum oriatur, quam veritas relinquatur.'" In *Ep.* XCIV. 1 he twice quotes St. Gregory (*Reg. Pastoral.*, III. xxviii. ; *Hom. in Ezech.*, III).

The quotation from the *Pastoral Rule* occurs again in *Ep*. CCCXIII. 5. The insignificant variations do but serve to emphasize the point. We reproduce it from *Ep*. CCCXIII. " Hoc et beatus Gregorius ait : ' Quisquis,' inquit, ' majus bonum subire proposuit, minus bonum, quod licuit, illicitum fecit. Scriptum quippe est : *Nemo mittens manum suam ad aratrum, et retro respiciens, aptus est regno Dei*. Qui ergo fortiori studio intenderat, retro respicere convincitur, si relictis amplioribus bonis ad minora retorquetur.' " It is the burning question of the seceders from St. Mary of York with which he is concerned (p. 54 *supra*).

St. Jerome (*Ep*. I., *Ad Heliodorum*) he quotes in *Ep*. CCCXXII. 2. Urging a newly converted monk to perseverance he writes : " ' Si prostratus,' ait beatus Hieronymus, ' jaceat in limine pater ; si nudato sinu quibus te lactavit ubera mater ostendat ; si parvulus a collo pendeat nepos ; per calcatum transi patrem, per calcatam perge matrem, et siccis oculis ad vexillum crucis evola. Summum pietatis est genus in hac parte pro Christo esse crudelem.' " The words *per calcatam perge matrem* are not found in the received text of St. Jerome (Pourrat, *La Spirit. Chrétienne*, II. 15) ; but obviously they balance the statement and, moreover, have a characteristically metrical effect when taken with the immediately preceding clause.

As post-Classical, distinguished from Patristic, quotations, two from one whom St. Bernard specially honoured as *par excellence* " the Wise Man " (*Sapiens*), even as later St. Thomas Aquinas would honour Aristotle as the *Philosophus*, are noteworthy. The two passages from Boëthius to which we refer are to be found in two consecutive sections of a treatise in which St. Bernard, whether as an orator or as a writer, is very great indeed, namely, the *De Conversione* (VIII. 13 sq.). The form in which it has come down to us reveals a literary distinction which owes everything to the fact that it was originally both a philippic and a gospel. In the former passage he writes, comparing lust with the intoxicating fumes of sulphur : " Ut ad modicum flagrans sulphureus vapor furentes stimulis agat, et apum par volantum, ubi male grata mella fuderit, nimis tenaci feriat icta corda morsu." Against high MS. authority Mabillon has corrected " volantum " to " volantium." Here is the passage from Boëthius :

> " Habet omni hoc voluptas,
> Stimulis agit fruentes ;
> Apiumque par volantum,
> Ubi grata mella fudit,
> Fugit et nimis tenaci
> Ferit icta corda morsu "

> (*De Consol. Philosophiae*, III. *metrum* 7).

St. Bernard, we note, leaves " volantum," substitutes " furentes " for " fruentes " and, scholar that he was, avails himself of the right to prefer " apum " to " apium." He finds the cadence of " apum par volantum " more congenial—doubtless quite unconsciously, although it would have been impossible had not " apum " been a legitimate alternative ; as for " volantum," " the Wise Man " must be held responsible for that.

The other passage is equally interesting in its own way. " ' O doxa, doxa,' ait sapiens, ' in millibus mortalium nihil aliud quam aurium inflatio vana ' " represents the " O gloria, gloria, fecisti millibus mortalium nullius meriti magnam vitam" of Boëthius (*De Consol. Philosophiae*, III. *prosa* 6). Boëthius is here translating words from the *Andromache* of Euripedes (319 sq.), and the fact that St. Bernard transliterates the Ω δόξα, δόξα of the original is noteworthy. It raises the question as to St. Bernard's knowledge of Greek. We have already (p. 15 *supra*) referred to his translation of two passages from the Septuagint (Gen. iv. 7 and Prov. xviii. 3) in this same treatise (*De Convers.* X. 21 and XI. 23) ; with regard to the former, found also in *Ep.* LXXXVII. 3, it should be said that quotations of it by St. Ambrose, St. Augustine and St. Gregory equally reflect the Greek version, and that therefore St. Bernard may be merely reminiscent of one or more of these writers (Mabillon. *S. Bern. Ep. cit. not. ad loc.*).

A passage occurring in the *De Diligendo Deo* (IV. 12), " dormit inter medios cleros, sortita jam impresentiarum de memoria abundantiae suavitatis tuae," suggests by its treatment of the word " sortita " that he was familiar with the meaning of the Greek κλῆρος ; we may note in passing his use of the Classical *dictio conflata*, " impresentiarum." Again, the words " Terram intuere, ut cognoscas teipsum " (*De Grad. Humil. et Superb.*, X. 28) are reminiscent of the Delphic precept γνῶθι σεαυτόν, although perhaps we should not make too much of this. But his translation of two passages from the Septuagint is certainly stimulating.

To measure the extent of St. Bernard's debt to Classical writers would involve a heavy task. We may, however, illustrate it by a few quotations. Here and there in the text others have been noticed in passing. " Teneo, inquit, longumque tenebo" (*De Convers.*, VI. 10) comes directly from Statius's (*Thebais*, II. 429) :

> " Quae sors justa mihi, quae non indebitus annis
> Sceptra dicavit honos, teneo longumque tenebo."

Caspar Barth, the XVIIth century commentator on Statius, quotes the passage, speaking of the *De Conversione* as " liber aureolus." A few lines earlier in the same treatise St. Bernard represents the disordered will, personified as " vetula furens," exclaiming petulantly : " Atque utinam inter spectandum totum aliquando corpus fieret oculus, aut inter prandendum in fauces membra omnia verterentur." Is not this precisely the thought expressed by Catullus, promising Fabullus some choice unguent :

> " Quod tu cum olfacies, deos rogabis,
> Totum ut te faciant, Fabulle, nasum "
>
> (XIII. 13 sq.) ?

To the authority of Seneca we find St. Bernard appealing directly as that of a great moralist (Senec. *Ep.* XXII.) in a letter to Eugenius III (*Ep.* CCLVI. 1. Cf. p. 286 *supra*) ; " legi," he writes, " apud quemdam sapientem : ' Non est vir fortis, cui non crescit animus in ipsa rerum difficultate,' " having evidently in mind the words of Seneca : " Non est vir fortis et strenuus, qui laborem fugit ; verum ibi crescit illi animus, ipsa rerum difficultate " ; and in his insistence upon the unsatisfying nature of things " quorum solus transitus juvat " (*De Convers.*, VIII. 14) we seem to recognize the implication underlying words of the same writer, " nihil tam utile est ut in transitu prosit " (Senec. *Ep.* II).

Virgil's picture of the Harpies (*Æn.*, III. 244) had evidently captivated St. Bernard's imagination in boyhood ; Arnald of Brescia (*Ep.* CXCV. p. 322 *supra*), Henry the sectary (*Ep.* CCXLI. p. 338 *supra*), the Apostolic Legate, Jordanus de Ursinis (*Ep.* CCXC.), Nicholas of Montier-Ramey (*Ep.* CCXCVIII. p. 352 *supra*), the perpetrator of moral delinquency (*De Convers.*, III. 4), are all disgusting monsters who " vestigia foeda relinquunt." The image remained vivid for him to the end of his life.

Similarly was the Hydra a grim reality as a psychological symbol, of which he seems to surpass Virgil in heightening the horror. Virgil gives it fifty heads (*Æn.*, VI. 576) ; but St. Bernard writes : " Amputata sunt hydrae capita quinque, sed, heu, innumera surrexerunt ! " (*De Convers.* XX. 35), emphasizing thus the contrast with " innumera."

The metrical *clausula*, " vicinamque elementa intentant omnia mortem " (*Vita S. Malach.* XI. 22), cannot fail to recall Virgil's line :

" Praesentemque viris intentant omnia mortem "

(*Æn.*, I. 91) ; as though the whole scene as described by the poet were present to St. Bernard's mind at the time.

The reminiscence of Horace's line,

" Diruit, aedificat, mutat quadrata rotundis "

(Hor. *Epp.* I. i. 10), is unmistakable in the words, " Dirue horrea tua, ut majora aedifices ; muta quadrata rotundis " (*De Convers.*, VIII. 16).

In *Ep.* CXCI. 2 he plainly quotes Ovid : " Necesse est ut huic contagio celeri remedio occurratis.

' Sero (enim) medicina paratur,
Cum mala per longas invaluere moras ' "

(Ovid, *De Remed. Amor.*, I. v. 91 sq.).

In *Ep.* CCCXLII. 3, after the words " Extinguatur ignis, antequam convalescat incendium," he quotes the same passage, reading, for " invaluere," " convaluere," the correct text. And, surely, " nulla mordente cura " (*De Dilig. Deo*, XI. 32) reflects the same poet's " mordet cura medullas " (Ovid, *Amores*, II. v. 43).

Again, the thought that death enters through the windows, derived probably from the " ascendit mors per fenestras nostras " of Jeremiah (ix. 21), which occurs at least twice in the *De Conversione*, is applied in such a way as to suggest that St. Bernard has in mind the " eas partes quae quasi fenestrae sunt animae " of Cicero (*Disput. Tuscul.*, I. 20). " Per fenestras proprias mors ista deprehenditur introisse " he writes (*De Convers.*, VI.), explaining a little later : " singula membra fenestrae singulae, quibus mors intrat ad animam " (*De Convers.*, VI. 11). There are probably hundreds of classical reminiscences in St. Bernard's writings which still remain untraced. We frequently meet with tantalizing phrases like " collecto turgida vento " (*De Grad. Humil. et Superb.*, XII. 40), a touch in the inimitable vignette of the monk obsessed by *inepta laetitia*, which may or may not be entirely original.

The " Heu ! Quaenam miseris tam dira cupido ? " of *Ep.* CCCXXII. 2 evidently reflects the " . . . quae lucis miseris tam dira cupido " of Virgil (*Æn.*, VI. 721). In *Ep.* CCCXLII. 2, in addition to that from Ovid in the same epistle cited above, a quotation of Horace's : "Nam tua res agitur, paries cum proximus ardet" (Hor. *Epp.* I. xviii. 84), occurs in the form : "Vestra enim res agitur, paries cum proximus ardet."

Of Abélard he writes : " Sanctum projicit canibus, et margaritas porcis : fidem corrumpit simplicem, Ecclesiae maculat castitatem. ' Quo semel est imbuta recens servabit odorem testa diu ' " (*Ep.* CCCXXXVIII. 1), the last sentence coming directly from Horace (*Epp.*, I. ii. 69 sq.).

To a young postulant he gives the warning : " Quid dicamus de tenera aetate tua ? Poma saepe ante maturitatem avelluntur de arboribus vel manu vel turbine. Quid de specie et pulchritudine tua ?

> ' O formose puer, nimium ne crede colori :
> Alba ligustra cadunt, vaccinia nigra leguntur ' "

(*Ep.* CCCCXII. 1), quoting Virgil (*Bucolic.*, II. 17 sq.).

" Quanta spe decidit " in *Ep.* CLI. cannot fail to suggest the " Quanta de spe decidi ! " of Terence (*Heautontimor.*, II. iii. 9. Cf. *op. cit.*, IV. viii. 11).

As an illustration of the extent of St. Bernard's Classical reading we should not overlook a passage in the *Apologia* (XII. 28). Persius was perhaps somewhat " caviare to the general " in the XIIth century, but a quotation from the *Satires* (II. 68 sq.) comes readily and not inaptly to St. Bernard's mind. " Illud autem interrogo monachus monachos, quod in gentilibus gentilis arguebat : ' Dicite,' ait ille, ' pontifices : in sancto quid facit aurum ? ' Ego autem dico : Dicite pauperes (non enim attendo versum sed sensum), dicite, inquam, pauperes, si tamen pauperes, in sancto quid facit aurum ? "

Of St. Bernard's Scriptural reminiscences, apart from direct quotation, we need say no more than that they are embedded in his writings like shells in Purbeck marble. The Bible is his chief raw material, both in his treatises and in his sermons, and to some extent in his correspondence ; so it would almost seem. There are certain Scriptural sentences, however, which he treats as epigrammatic, raising them, as it were, to a dignity of their own ; two, in particular. " Corpus enim quod corrumpitur aggravat animam, et terrena inhabitatio deprimit sensum multa cogitantem " (Wisd. ix. 15) is found frequently (*e.g. De Convers.*, XVII. 30 ; *De Grat. et Lib. Arb.*, XI. 37 and XII. 41 ; *In Vigil. Nat. Dom. Serm.* VI. 3 ; *In Ascens. Dom. Serm.* III. 1 ; *De Praecept. et Disp.*, XX. 59). In the last instance he comments on the statement, explaining that what is burdensome is not the *societas* of the body, but its *necessitas* ; " non corpus simpliciter," he remarks, " sed corpus quod corrumpitur ; ut corruptio corporis oneri sit, non natura." The other sentence, derived from Isaiah, xxviii. 19, " sola vexatio intellectum dabit auditui," occurs less frequently. We notice it once in the *De Consideratione* (I. iii. 4) ; and again in the *De Conversione* (VI. 11), where St. Bernard, conformably with the context, substitutes " rationi " for " auditui."

He is, of course, himself strikingly epigrammatic. " Quid vero," he asks, " in rebis humanis certius morte, quid hora mortis incertius invenitur ? " (*De Convers.*, VIII. 16). Again in *Epistle* CV. we read : " Nil mortalibus vel morte certius, vel incertius hora mortis."

Professor Edward Bensly has pointed out to the writer an interesting expression of the same thought in the *Dialogi et Epigrammata* of Joannes Ravisius Textor, p. 116, Rotterdam, 1651 :

" Qui transis igitur fati memor esto supremi,
Certa est mors, mortis te tamen hora latet."

(Jean Tixier Seigneur de Ravisy was a Nivernois of the early XVIth century.) " Quomodo nempe," he exclaims, " stellae in nocte lucent, in die latent, sic vera virtus, quae saepe in prosperis non apparet, eminet in adversis " (*In Cant. Cant.*, XXVII. 8). Many more will be found in a little *florilegium* published by the present writer, entitled *Thoughts of St. Bernard of Clairvaux*. The gift consists in so putting familiar truths that their moral bearing, obscured by their very familiarity, becomes salient. At times St. Bernard's diction invests the thought expressed with an indescribable atmosphere of suitable emotion, complex indeed, but never enervating, as when he writes : " Nec enim opera nostra transeunt, ut videntur ; sed temporalia quaeque velut aeternitatis semina jaciuntur " (*De Convers.*, VIII. 17).

Sometimes we can trace a common proverb, as when he writes : " At difficile, fortassis et impossibile est, ut ex amara radice ambitionis suavis fructus prodeat charitatis " (*De Convers.*, XXI. 38) ; although, be it said, the proverb more usually describes the *fructus* as *dulcis ;* and not only this, but St. Bernard is really, for the purpose in hand, inverting what, when speaking of " litterarum radices amarae, fructus dulces," St. Jerome calls " vetus illa sententia " (*In Iliorem Proph.*, I. vii. 4). The attribution to St. Bernard of the proverb " Love me, love my dog " is incorrect ; he disclaims it himself, prefacing the words with a " dicitur certe vulgari quodam proverbio " (*In Fest. S. Michael. Serm.* I. 3). Another " vulgare proverbium " is quoted in the *De Gradibus Humilitatis et Superbiae* (III. 6), " nescit sanus quid sentiat aeger, aut plenus quid patiatur jejunus," which is very like St. Jerome's " plenus venter facile de jejuniis disputat " (*Ep.* LVIII. 2).

His facility, his felicity, in personification are enthralling. When at his best in this manner, things, forces, habits become alive as he describes them, until suddenly he will turn upon the reader, as doubtless he did upon the hearer face to face, leaving him no escape from responsibility, compelling him to the conviction that all these personalities are summed up in one person—himself. We feel this strongly in the *De Conversione* ; to appreciate it the treatise should be read from cover to cover. In quite a different way the dialogue between Mercy and Truth in the First Sermon for the Feast of the Annunciation is a fine piece of personification, leading to a yet finer still, the eternal embrace of Righteousness and Peace (11 sqq.). But perhaps no personification is more forcible than that of the disordered will, the " vetula furens " of the *De Conversione*. We find it again in the Sermons on the Song of Songs, where the disordered will is a mistress who " vos naturae docet non parcere, rationi non acquiescere, non obtemperare seniorum consilio vel exemplo " (*In Cant. Cant.*, XIX. 7).

St. Bernard's metaphors, which are as a rule somewhat dramatically developed, should not be overlooked. The *sentina* occurs three times in the *De Conversione* ; in each case it is the conscience, the depository of unrepented sin. " In illud siquidem repositorium, velut in sentinam aliquam, tota decurrit abominatio, et immunditia tota defluxit " (III. 4). " Jam sentina redundans domum omnem intolerabili foetore contaminat " (VI. 8). "Nemo ergo sentinam exiens mundatum sese prorsus arbitretur ; quinimmo noverit se multis interim purificationibus egere " (XVII. 30). It will be observed in passing that we read on the best MS. authority " exiens," rather than the " ejiciens " of the Benedictine text. St. Bernard uses *exeo* in the active sense of *avoid*, it would seem.

Another striking metaphor is that of the *stomachus*. The memory is the stomach of the soul. It is perhaps not too fanciful to think that St. Bernard's own gastric suffering would have heightened the realism. " Ita et multa scientia ingesta stomacho animae, quae est memoria, si decocta igne charitatis non fuerit, et sic per quosdam artus animae, mores scilicet atque actus, transfusa atque digesta, quatenus ipsa de bonis quae noverit, vita attestante et moribus, bona efficiatur : nonne illa scientia reputabitur in peccatum, tanquam cibus conversus in pravos noxiosque humores ? " (*In Cant. Cant.*, XXXVI. 4).

Yet, with all this rare pictorial facility, St. Bernard, when he comes to deal scientifically with moral or with psychological problems, is gifted with a delicate *netteté* of expression, corresponding with an almost hard, but nevertheless helpful, clarity of thought. This is best illustrated from the *De Gratia et Libero Arbitrio*, although from time to time it is evident in other treatises. Take the distinction developed in Chapter II. 3 of the *De Gratia et Libero Arbitrio* between *vita, sensus* and *appetitus*, all possessed by man in common with the brute creation, and the unique possessions of man alone. We may exhibit it schematically, a characteristic manner with St. Bernard. What are these unique possessions ?

Consensus { (i) *Nutus voluntatis spontaneus,*
{ (ii) *Habitus animi, liber sui.*

Voluntas { (i) *Motus rationalis,*
{ (ii) *Sensui praesidens et appetitui.*

Ratio { (i) *Comes et quodam modo pedissequa voluntatis—non quod semper voluntas ex ratione, sed quod nunquam absque ratione moveatur, ita ut*
{ (ii) *Multa faciat per ipsam contra ipsam.*

There are many such schematic statements to be found throughout the treatise, some of them worthy of the discriminating *acumen* of St. Thomas. How far they all may be psychologically sound is a question which does not arise. The reader may be referred to Williams, *St. Bernard, Concerning Grace and Freewill, passim.*

The schematic manner may be recognized elsewhere, enforced by the delightful paronomasia, which, however common with St. Bernard, is rarely if ever cloying. Twice at least we get :

Divitiarum { *acquisitio* } *plena* { *laboris*
{ *possessio* } { *timoris*
{ *amissio* } { *doloris*

(*De Convers.*, VIII. 14; *De Divers. Serm.*, XLII. 3). It should be said that the paronomasia of St. Bernard is never a mere *tour de force ;* it is always serious and purposeful. Even when he describes Abélard as the "apis, quae erat in Francia," he is evidently thinking of the "api, quae est in terra Assur" of Isaiah, vii. 18 (*Ep.* CLXXXIX. 3).

Now and then we detect a *ludus in ambiguo*, as when he writes : " Curris per devia, et longe ante moreris quam hoc circuitu pervenias ad optatum " (*De Dilig. Deo*, VII. 18). Reading on the best MS. authority " moreris " for the " morieris " of the Benedictine text, we have here precisely the same play upon the words *mŏror* and *mōror* as is found in Suetonius (*In Neron.*, XXXIII.), " Omnibus contumeliis (Claudium) mortuum insectatus est, modo stultitiae, modo saevitiae arguens. Nam et morari eum inter homines desiisse, producta prima syllaba, jocabatur." Similarly he plays upon the equivocal meaning of the word *deprehendere*. " Latent, inquam, insidiae quas ut deprehendere non potes, sic non potes ipse non deprehendi " (*De Convers.*, IX. 18).

St. Bernard's gift of humour, the edge of which might sometimes seem to us to be a little sharp, as when, laughing " modo illo suo generoso," he describes his physician to William of St. Thierry as an *irrationabilis bestia* (*Vita Prima*, I. vii. 33)—is unmistakable. But it could be pleasantly engaging. " I am sending this boy, the bearer," he writes to Baldwin, Bishop of Noyon, " to eat your bread, in order to see whether it makes you sad, and so to find out how avaricious you are ! Do not grieve ; do not weep. His stomach is small ; he will manage with little. I shall thank you if he comes back, not fatter, but more learned. The way I put this must do for a seal ; my seal is not at hand, for neither is your Geoffrey " (*Ep.* CCCCII.). The letter was evidently autograph and written before 1145, when Geoffrey ceased to be St. Bernard's secretary. The jesting manner was evidently known to be characteristic of the writer, for it would authenticate the letter. The spare, diminutive messenger ; some little unlettered peasant perhaps, destined not too hopefully for the domestic service of the bishop, would irresistibly have elicited it.

Speaking generally, one would perhaps say that St. Bernard's vocabulary and structure are Classical, certainly in the treatises. He had evidently read Cicero's works, some of them at any rate, with discrimination. Here and there, as in Epistle XCII, we recognize military terms familiarized by Caesar (cf. p. 48 *supra*).

As regards the meaning of words, it is interesting to notice that a word like *luxuria* has with him fully acquired the special sense of unchastity which it has not in the writings of St. Augustine (e.g. *Confess.*, II. vi. 13, VIII. x. 24), but which St. Thomas justifies by a reference to Isidore (*Summ. Theol.*, II. (2) cliii. 1 ; Isid. *Etymol.*, X. *ad. lit. L*). The context (*De Convers.*, XX. 34) in which St. Bernard uses the word makes this sufficiently plain.

Finally, we come to the question of the hymns attributed to St. Bernard. Evidently, as Mr. Raby has pointed out (*Hist. of Christian-Latin Poetry*, 329 sq.), St. Bernard did not profess to be a metrical poet. When Guy, Abbot of Montier-Ramey, begged him to write a hymn in honour of St. Victor, the patron of his house, he frankly replied : " Quod ad cantum spectat, hymnum composui, metri negligens, ut sensui non deessem " (*Ep.* CCCXCVIII. 3). We shall read this hymn, " Vita Victoris meritis praeclara," probably with stinted admiration, in the *Officium S. Victoris* (S. Bern. *Opera*, III. *ad fin. ed.* Bened.).

The only other hymn generally accepted as the work of St. Bernard is the *Hymnus de S. Malachia* (*P.L.* CLXXII. 1117 sq.).   To quote one stanza will be sufficient :

> " Signa si quaeris, quis referre queat ?
> Hoc tamen dico ; manifesta satis
> Mortua surgens quantus in hac parte
> Fuit gloriae."

Whether he deliberately disregarded metrical laws, feeling himself bound so to do by the Cistercian tradition, "nos nihil recepimus quod metricis legibus coercetur " (Nicol. Claraevall. *Ep.* XV. *ap. Biblioth. Maxim. Patr.*, XXI.), or was altogether too great a prosepoet to confine himself within the limits of a prescribed framework, we do not presume to say.

As regards the familiar " Jesu, dulcis memoria," or *Jubilus Rhythmicus de Nomine Jesu* (S. Bern. *Opera*, V. 422 sqq., *éd.* 1765), it is no less crowded with St. Bernard's language and instinct with his spirit than are his own writings with those of Scripture.   We have but to read the following passage from a *Sermo de Diversis* (IV) in order to realize this.   " Bonus es, Domine, animae quaerenti te. Si quaerenti, quanto magis invenienti ?   Si tam dulcis est memoria, qualis erit praesentia ?   Si mel et lac dulce est sub lingua, quid erit super linguam ? "   On internal evidence alone could this *Jubilus Rhythmicus* have been written by St. Bernard ?   Not, we may perhaps think, if the hymns in honour of St. Victor and St. Malachy are his work—judging it solely on its metrical merits, which undoubtedly are very high.   For the external evidence we may refer the reader to an able and discriminating article by Mr. Reginald Vaux in the *Church Quarterly Review* (CVIII. 215, April, 1929).   The fact that the *Jubilus Rhythmicus* reflects not only the language, but also the mysticism, of St. Bernard should not be overlooked—what this mysticism was the present writer has sought to set forth in a short study, entitled *The Mysticism of St. Bernard of Clairvaux*.   Nevertheless there remains the alternative, suggested by the evidence offered by Mr. Vaux, that St. Bernard's language, such as is found in the *Sermo de Diversis*, IV, is the reflection of an already existing hymn.

Some MSS. of St. Bernard's works, indeed one of such primary authority as Paris 2565, which is ascribed by M. Henri Omont to the first half of the XIIIth century and bears in a contemporary script an *ex libris* of the Cistercian Abbaye des Escharlis in the archdiocese of Sens near Villefranche-sur-Yonne, contain a *Rhythmus ad singula membra Christi patientis*, as it is entitled in the MS. cited. This is a long poem of seventy stanzas which appears in the Benedictine edition, under the title *Rhythmica oratio ad unumquodlibet membrorum Christi patientis et a cruce pendentis*, amongst *opera supposititia et aliena*.   The concluding ten stanzas of this poem, beginning *Salve, caput cruentatum*, were translated by Paul Gerhardt (*ob.* 1676), and published in the *Praxis Pietatis* (Frankfurt, 1656). This German rendering, *O Haupt voll Blut und Wunden*, appeared in Bunsen's *Versuch eines allgemeinen Gesang und Gebetbuchs* (1833), whence in the form of an English translation by Catherine Winkworth it found its way into *Lyra Germanica* in 1855 ; since which date other English versions of these same stanzas have been made, the most familiar being probably the *O sacred head, surrounded* of Sir Henry W. Baker and the compilers of Hymns Ancient and Modern (1861).   A version by Robert Bridges appeared in the Yattendon

Hymnal (1899) and in the English Hymnal (1906). It is certainly interesting that there should be so early a suggestion of its Bernardine authorship as is indicated by its pressence in the MS. Paris 2565 ; but the argument against it, based upon the metrical quality, would seem to be scarcely less strong than it is in the case of the *Jesu, dulcis memoria ;* moreover we fail to recognize in it the general feeling and the particular expression which afford the sole ground for attributing the latter to St. Bernard.

In the same category the Benedictine editor quotes in their entirety—and rejects (*Admonitio ad loc*), a *Carmen Paraeneticum ad Rainaldum,* a *Rhythmus de Contemptu Mundi,* an *Oratio devota ad Dominum Jesum et B. Mariam matrem ejus,* and even the well-known *Prosa de Nativitate Domini* (*Laetabundus*), as well as the *Jubilus Rhythmicus* to which we have already referred. He further mentions that the *Ave, maris stella* has been ascribed to the same author ; and we know that the *Salve, Regina* has not altogether escaped the uncritical enthusiasm of the saint's devotees. So eager have they shown themselves to be to acclaim him as the Christian Laureate of his age ; but, alas, on such slender evidence.

APPENDIX II

THE CODEX AUREAEVALLENSIS

This is probably our most valuable manuscript authority for the *Life of St. Bernard*. The present writer has given some account of it in the *Dublin Review* for January, 1930 (No. 372, Art. ix.). It originally belonged to the Abbey of Orval in the diocese of Trèves and in the Ardennes, founded as the second daughter of Trois-fontaines on 9th March, 1132. When the abbey was pillaged and burned in 1793 the MS. disappeared, but was recovered by the Trappists in 1841 ; since when it has continuously remained in the hands of Cistercian monks of the Strict Observance. Its recovery was unknown to Vacandard, although he was aware of the existence of two copies of it written on paper, in 1721 and *cir.* 1660, one in the Bibliothèque Nationale at Paris (*fonds latin* 17639), the other in the Collège St. Michel at Brussels (*Collect. Bolland.* 130 [*olim* 30]). The *incipit* of the MS., following the title *Vita sancti BERNARDI*, is : *In territorio lingonis civitatis situm est castellum nobile quondam et inclitum valde cui castellio nomen est.* . . . The word *sancti* in the title is not to be taken as conclusive proof that the MS. was written after the formal canonization in 1174 ; still less has it any bearing upon the date of the original record which it represents. On page 6, after the words *signum fuisse multorum que sibi de eadem postmodum domini nativitate revelata sunt misteriorum*, we read : *Incipit Vita vel Miracula bernardi Abbatis*. On page 80 occurs the *explicit* of this, the first, item of the MS. : *Nichil enim ex omnibus que fecerat seu dixerat potuit deinceps recordari*. Of this *Vita* about one quarter is reproduced in ten sections and six paragraphs printed in the edition of Mabillon of 1690, and reprinted by Migne. The six paragraphs are inserted after the *Vita Quarta*, and are stated to have been *praetermissa* by the Jesuit Chifflet, who had in 1679 published the ten sections in his *Opuscula Quatuor* as *Excerpta singularia ex collectaneis de vita . . . S. Bernardi auctore Gaufrido Abbate* derived from an Orval MS. What MS. furnished Mabillon with this material *postea reperta*, he does not tell us. All that is found in Mabillon's text forms the basis, with other lesser matter, of Pien's work in the *Acta SS. Bollandiana* (Aug. IV. *die* xx. 101 sqq.), being derived from the copy on paper made by his Jesuit *confrère* Alexander Wiltheim, now in the Collège St. Michel at Brussels.

Why Mabillon published no more than what he describes as *Fragmenta ex Tertia Vita S. Bernardi, auctore, ut videtur, Gaufrido monacho Claraevallensi* it is difficult to say. He refers to an Orval MS. as having been collated by him for the Epistles of St. Bernard (*Opera S. Bern. Praefat. Gen. XV. ed.* 1690). We might expect him to have known something of the literary resources of that monastery, if not of the prior copy of our MS. Did he examine this *Vita* and form the opinion that it was not worth publishing in its entirety ? If so, we must think that he was mistaken. The *Vita* is undoubtedly the basis of William of St. Thierry's First Book of the *Vita Prima*, of Arnald of Bonneval's Second Book and of Geoffrey's own Fourth Book. Considering the fact that the *Fragmenta* are not found in Mabillon's earlier and first edition of 1667, it is probable that their existence was unknown to him before the publication in 1679 of Chifflet's *Opuscula Quatuor*. Léopold Delisle, who examined the MS., ascribed it to the XIIth century, and both Hüffer and Vacandard were of opinion that the original record represented by the *Vita* should be dated at 1145. Père Robert Lechat, S.J., who has published the text in full with annotations, together with an able discussion of the whole question, in the *Analecta Bollandiana* (L. 1-2. an. 1932), while he regards the *Vita* in the MS. as the work of one and the same hand throughout, doubts gravely whether this is the hand of Geoffrey or of other than a copyist.

The second item of the MS. consists of Part II of the *Liber Miraculorum*, prefaced by the covering letter to the Clergy of the Church of Cologne, and of Part III so far as the end of Chapter xiii in the capitulation of Mabillon and Migne—but no farther. It will thus be seen that the *Vita* is the more important item of the two, making to our knowledge, as it does, a considerable contribution, unpublished until Père Lechat, at the instance of Dom Alexis Presse, Abbot of Tamié, gave it to us in the *Analecta Bollandiana* so recently as the year 1932. As regards the MS. itself, we may say that it had for nearly a century lain *perdu*, until in 1927 Dom Alexis Presse brought it again to the light of day by means of a paper read before the *Congrès de l'Association Bourguignonne des Sociétés Savantes* at Dijon. If, in illustration of its contribution to our material, we compare the *Vita* with Geoffrey's Fourth Book of the *Vita Prima*, we find that perhaps in only eleven passages is there evidence of similarity of record. That Geoffrey, the Clairvaux monk who had been St. Bernard's notary, was the author of it is plain from the reference on pages 64 sq. of the MS. to his conversion on the occasion of the delivery of the *De Conversione* at Paris in 1140. The MS. has since 1909 been in the possession of the Trappists of the Abbey of Tamié in Savoy. Bound with the *Bernardina*, as a third item in the volume, is a *Vita Sti Hugberti* in four lections, evidently a section from a breviary of probably the XIIth century.

Other documentary material available for constructing the biography of St. Bernard will be found described in the present writer's *Studies in St. Bernard of Clairvaux* (I. 1-40).

APPENDIX III

GEOFFREY THE BIOGRAPHER

THE writer of the *Fragmenta*, commonly called the *Vita Tertia*, as well as of the IIIrd, IVth and Vth Books, and of the larger portion of the 3rd Part of the VIth Book of the *Vita Prima*, the compiler of the *Corpus Epistolarum* of St. Bernard (Hüffer, *Bernard von Clairvaux*, I. 186 ; Vacandard, *Vie de saint Bernard*, I. xiii.) is in these days usually identified as the same person, and known as Geoffrey of Auxerre. Assuming this to be correct, or even qualifying it so far as to discredit his right to any authorship in the VIth Book of the *Vita Prima*, as a biographer of St. Bernard he stands supreme in a class apart ; for not only was he responsible for all, or for nearly all, the above-named works, but what of the *Fragmenta* he did not incorporate in his own IVth Book served in large measure the purpose of William of St. Thierry in writing the Ist Book of the *Vita Prima*, and that of Arnald of Bonneval in writing the IInd (Lechat, *Analect. Bolland.* L. i-ii. 83 sq.; Williams, *Studies in St. Bernard of Clairvaux*, I. *passim*).

We would not depreciate the *Vita Secunda* of Alan of Auxerre ; for this writer probably derived much information from Godfrey de la Roche, St. Bernard's kinsman (Williams, *op. cit.*, I. 25 sq.) ; nor the *Vita Quarta* of John the Hermit, who was privileged to record in his Ist Book certain details concerning the family of St. Bernard for which he was indebted to Robert de Châtillon, cousin-german of the saint (*Vita Quarta*, I. 5). Both these works, however, in spite of the reasonably credible additions which each makes to our knowledge, are on a lower historical level than that of Geoffrey (Williams, *op. cit.*, I. 27 sq.), whose standard of criticism was so high as to prompt him to provide us with a second recension of what he had written, known as Recension B ; which recension is represented by all which is not contained in brackets in the printed editions of Mabillon and Migne, as may be recognized, for example, in the *Vita Prima*, IV. ii. 11 (Williams, *op. cit.*, I. 14 sq.). But who was Geoffrey ?

The common opinion of to-day, which was shared by Vacandard, is that he was a pupil of Abélard who heard from St. Bernard's lips at Paris in 1140 the great *Sermo de Conversione ad Clericos*, and thereupon became a monk of Clairvaux and soon afterwards the abbot's secretary (*Fragmenta ex Tertia Vita*, IX ; *Vita Prima*, III. *Praefat. ed. Bened.*, 1690) ; that he travelled with St. Bernard on the occasion of the latter's missionary journey in Languedoc in 1145, and accompanied him when during the winter of 1146-47 he was preaching the Second Crusade in Flanders, in the Rhineland and elsewhere (pp. 340-343, 269-279 *supra*), having in 1145 been succeeded as St. Bernard's secretary by the notorious Nicholas of Montier-Ramey. Of his further identification Vacandard says nothing ; but the whole question was gravely debated in the XVIIth century.

In 1660 the Jesuit Chifflet published at Dijon the eight items of the Laurentian MS. 1809 (*fonds Libri* 1906) at Florence, all of which were subsequently edited by Delisle. Of these items the fifth is the *Chronicon Clarevallense*, which Delisle ascribes to the XIIIth century, adding that it " nous a conservé la chronique de Clairvaux pour la période comprise entre les années 1147 et 1192 " (Delisle, *Notice sur des manuscrits du fonds Libri conservés à la Laurentienne*, 99. Paris, 1886). Its author was without doubt a monk of Clairvaux, familiar with the archives of his house. The following is its record, so far as it concerns us at the moment.

" Anno Domini 1162, . . . Abbas quoque Igniaci domnus Gaufridus promotus in abbatem Claraevallis quadriennio circiter praefecit. . . . Anno Domini 1165, . . . Eodem anno abbas Claraevallis domnus Gaufridus, videns contra se, sive juste, sive injuste quorumdam odia concitata, abbatiam dimisit. . . . Anno Domini 1174, obiit sanctus Petrus Tharentasiensis archiepiscopus, anno xxiii sui pontificatus. Ejus vitam scripsit domnus Gaufridus, abbas quondam Clarevallensis "—to the MS. of this *Vita* we shall refer later—" Anno Domini 1176, abbas Altaecumbae domnus Henricus, in abbatem Clarevallensem promotus, quatuor circiter praefecit annos. Iste, quam cito filius suus abbas domnus Geraldus de Fossanova factus fuit ante eum abbas Claraevallis, domnum Gaufridum quondam Clarevallensem abbatem, tunc contemplationi vacantem in Fossanova praefecit. Et item quando ipse de Altacumba ad Claramvallem assumptus est, eumdem abbatem Gaufridum ad Altamcumbam loco sui promovere curavit " (Migne, *P.L.* CLXXXV. 1247 sqq.). We notice—and it is interesting in view of statements presently to be recorded—that the Geoffrey of whom the *Chronicon* speaks has no literary work ascribed to him except the *Life of St. Pierre de Tarentaise*. He is said to have been successively Abbot of Igny, of Clairvaux—the fourth in point of fact—of Fossanova and of Hautecombe ; but he is nowhere described as *Autissiodorensis* in any sense of that qualification. Let us take in order the opinions of the chief authorities in the controversy.

1. Carolus de Visch in his *Auctarium ad Bibliothecam Scriptorum S.O. Cisterc.* (32 sqq. *ed. Canivez. Bregenz*, 1927) not only gives us his own view, but also states very fairly those of several other authorities of his time. He remarks that more recent authors have confused Geoffrey of Auxerre with Geoffrey, Fourth Abbot of Clairvaux, " sed antiquiores omnes scriptores "—the statement, be it observed, is not free from a suspicious degree of generalization—" illos distinguunt, nec ulla ex his operibus jam recensitis "—*excerpta* from Patristic and other ancient writers, as well as commentaries upon a considerable number of books of the Bible, the MSS. of which were identified in the library at Cîteaux in 1618 (p. 381 *infra*)—" reperiuntur alibi extare sub nomine Gaufridi Claraevallensis Abbatis." He cites Guillelmus Eisegrenius (*Liber de Scriptoribus Orthodoxis*) as referring to Geoffrey of Auxerre as " virum suae aetatis eloquentissimum, poetam gravem ; theologum sacrarum legum exercitatissimum," terms which, de Visch contends, do not apply, judging from his writings, to Geoffrey, Fourth Abbot of Clairvaux. He cites also the Minorite, Petrus de Alva, as distinguishing Geoffrey of Auxerre from Geoffrey, Abbot of Hautecombe, the latter being, we remember,

on the authority of the *Chronicon Clarevallense* the same person as Geoffrey, Fourth Abbot of Clairvaux.

De Visch himself distinguishes all three Geoffreys, holding the Abbot of Clairvaux to have been St. Bernard's secretary. Under the head : *Gaufridus Claraevallensis Abbas IV, antea S. Bernardi notarius*, he writes : " In Bibliotheca mea tam I^ae editionis quam 2^ae anni 1656 distinxi hunc Gaufridum a Gaufrido Autissiodorensi et Gaufrido Abbate Altae Cumbae, plures egregios secutus scriptores tam Ordinis nostri quam externos, qui ante scripserunt, quorum aliqui etiam nationis Galliae asserebant se praecipuorum monasteriorum Ordinis monumenta illustrasse ; quibus proinde me secure posse fidere credebam." He writes, it will be seen, expressive of an opinion formed before Chifflet had published the *Chronicon Clarevallense* in 1660 ; and he again fails to specify his authorities.

2. In 1658 Claude Maillet, Prior of the Cistercian Abbey of Vauluisant, wrote to de Visch, opposing his view and citing the *Chronicon Clarevallense* which he had evidently examined before Chifflet published it two years later.

3. In 1660 Bertrand Tissier, Prior of Bonne-Fontaine, the learned author of the *Bibliotheca PP. Cisterciensium*, also wrote to de Visch, inclining to the same opinion as that of Maillet, but allowing that, the point being so knotty (*se diu laborasse in enodanda hac difficultate*), " non impedire, quominus, cui aliter visum fuerit, aliter sentiat."

4. Another Cistercian, Philip Seguinus, Prior of Charlieu, claiming to have explored the records of many monasteries in Gaul, including Clairvaux, gave it as his opinion (*De Scriptoribus, Litera G* 2 and 13) that Geoffrey of Auxerre, Geoffrey of Clairvaux and Geoffrey of Hautecombe were three different persons; that Geoffrey of Auxerre wrote the 3rd Part of the VIth Book of the *Vita Prima*, or *Liber Miraculorum*, whereas Geoffrey of Clairvaux, who was St. Bernard's secretary, wrote the IIIrd, IVth and Vth Books.

5. The Jesuit, Antonius Possevinus, author of the *Apparatus Sacer*, followed Seguinus so far as to distinguish three Geoffreys, Geoffrey of Auxerre, Geoffrey of Clairvaux and Geoffrey of Hautecombe.

6. In 1623, however, Chrysostom Henriquez, a Spanish Cistercian of Monte-de-Ramo (cf. p. 92, *supra*), had published his *Fasciculus SS. Ordinis Cisterciensis* in two volumes at Brussels. In this work we find the following entry (*Op. cit.* I. iv. 50). " Gaufridus Notarius sancti Patris Bernardi, postea Abbas Igniacensis, praefuit Claraevallensibus annis quatuor, electusque in Episcopum, dignitatem admittere recusavit : unde tale ipsius tumulo impositum est epitaphium :

> " *Igniaci Pastor Gaufridus legis amator,*
> *Quatuor his annis claruit atque fuit.*
> *Praesulis electus, virtutum nomine clarus,*
> *Noluit hoc fieri, dignus amore Dei.*"

He speaks, we observe, of one Geoffrey only, St. Bernard's secretary, who was Abbot, first of Igny and then of Clairvaux ; he further refers to him as having declined promotion to the episcopate—a statement which Carolus de Visch accepts (p. 381 *infra*)—but he does not specify the see ; nor does he describe him as *Autissiodorensis*, or as ever having been Abbot of Hautecombe. The suggestion is that, after he resigned the Abbacy of Clairvaux, he continued to live there ; was offered, but declined, a bishopric ; and finally died and was buried there. " Aliud implicationis addit elementum," as the Abbot of Tamié, in a letter to the present writer, remarks of this entry.

7. That rare book, the *Cistercienses Annales* of Angelo Manriquez, was published in four volumes at Lyons between 1642 and 1659. Its author was a Cistercian monk of the Abbey of Huerta (*Abbatia Hortensis*) in Old Castile. He writes : " Nec dubitarem Gaufridum eumdem esse, qui sancto Patri, dum vixit, a secretis, post mortem, vitae ipsius scriptor fuit." But, with Seguinus, he distinguishes this Geoffrey from the Geoffrey " qui subscripsit epistolae, quin et tertiam miraculorum partem hominis Dei " ; that is to say, he holds that the writer of Books III, IV and V of the *Vita Prima*, and of the *Fragmenta*, the compiler of the *Corpus Epistolarum*, was a different person from the *signator* of the letter to Hermann, Bishop of Constance, which prefaces Part iii of the *Liber Miraculorum* or VIth Book of the *Vita Prima*, the writer of the larger portion of what immediately follows in this same Part iii (*Op. cit.*, II. v. 13, *an.* 1147 ; II. xi. 6, *an.* 1153). He further distinguishes from both of these the Geoffrey, Abbot of Hautecombe, to whom was entrusted by the Abbots of Cîteaux and Clairvaux, on the authority of Pope Lucius III, the work of writing the *Life* of St. Pierre de Tarentaise (*Op. cit.*, III. iv. 7, *an.* 1174). Thus Manriquez presents to us three different Geoffreys.

8. Mabillon writes (*Admon. in Libr. de Vita et Gest. S. Bern., Opera S. Bern.*, II. 1057 sq., *éd.* 1690) of the Clairvaux monk Geoffrey, the author of Books III-V of the *Vita Prima*, that he was " tertiae partis "—of the *Liber Miraculorum*—" item scriptor, in epistola ad Hermannum episcopum Constantiensem, de miraculis scilicet, quae a Spira usque Leodium, a Bernardo facta viderat." He disagrees with de Visch in the latter's ascription of Books III-V of the *Vita Prima* to Geoffrey the secretary, and of this Part iii of the *Liber Miraculorum* to Geoffrey of Auxerre, " quem a Gaufrido Notario minime distinguendum esse probat Helinandus monachus in *Chronico* his verbis ; *Hujus Petri*, scilicet Abaelardi, *aliquando fuerat discipulus Gaufridus Autissiodorensis, qui multo tempore fuit Notarius sancti Bernardi.*" Helinandus, the writer of this *Chronicon*, was a monk of the Cistercian Abbey of Froidmont who flourished in the first quarter of the XIIIth century (Chevalier, *Répertoire des Sources Historiques du Moyen Âge. Bio-Bibliogr.*, I. 2047). The passage quoted by Mabillon occurs under the year 1142 (Helinand. Chron. xlviii., *P.L.* CCXII. 1035). In addition to identifying Geoffrey the secretary, the Clairvaux monk, with Geoffrey of Auxerre, Helinandus further identifies him with Geoffrey, the author of the *Life* of St. Pierre de Tarentaise (*Chron.* xlviii., *an.* 1100 *op. cit.*, CCXII. 1022 sq). The present writer has examined the XIIIth century MS, of this *Vita* (Dijon 655 [394] p.f.), the *provenance* of which is the Abbey of Cîteaux, and failed to find any reference to its author as *Autissiodorensis*. Fol. 1ro l. 1 reads : " Incipit prefatio domni gaufridi Abbatis in libro de vita et miraculis Scti Petri tarentasiensis Archiepiscopi " ; but there is no indication as to what his abbey was (Helinand. *Chron., op. cit., loc. cit.*). We may cite a few authorities of a date later than the XVIIth century.

1. In the *Mémoires Historiques d'Auxerre* of Lebeuf (II. 488 sq.), published in 1743, we read : " Geoffroi d'Auxerre, appellé par

Jean de Sarisbéri, par Hélinand et autres écrivains aux XIIᵉ et XIIIᵉ siècles, *Gaufridus Autissiodorensis*, avoit étudié sous Abailard, et fut ensuite moine à Clervaux durant treize ans sous saint Bernard, à qui il servit de secrétaire. Il gouverna après la mort de ce saint plusieurs monastères de l'ordre en qualité d'abbé, et même l'abbaye de Clervaux. En fin il quitta le gouvernement pour rester simple religieux ; mais il fut toujours employé en quelques négociations & Henri II, roi d'Angleterre, écrivit au chapitre général de Cîteaux, pour avoir permission de garder auprès de lui Geoffroi d'Auxerre et marqua dans une lettre au Pape Alexandre III, que c'étoit l'un de ceux dont il suivoit les conseils.   Geoffroi s'entremêla dans l'affaire de ce prince avec saint Thomas de Cantorbéri (*Lib.* 3, *Epp. S. Th., Ep.* 20)."

The correspondence concerning this "affaire" contains several references to a Geoffrey, who is variously described as "Geoffrey of Auxerre, formerly Abbot of Clairvaux," as "Geoffrey, who was Abbot of Clairvaux," as "brother Geoffrey of Auxerre," as "brother Geoffrey," and once at least, in the inscription of a letter addressed to him by St. Thomas, as *Gaufridus Autisiodorensis Episcopus* (*Ep.* dcxxxviii. *Materials for the History of Archbp. Th. Becket, R.S.* VII. 225 sq.)—we may remark that the only Bishop of Auxerre who bore the name of Geoffrey was Geoffroi de Champallement (1052-76).   He is represented, as we should expect, as a person devoted on the whole to the interests of the exiled archbishop. The letter written by Henry II of England to the Chapter General of the Cistercians, to which Lebeuf refers, is probably that which the king has in mind when he remarks ; "Praeterea dilectioni vestrae grates uberes exsolvo, quod ad petitionem meam fratrem Gaufridum mihi misistis" (*Henric. Rex Anglor. ad Abbates Cistercienses, Ep.* dlxviii., *op. cit.* VII. 92).

2. An authority of the present century, Ulysse Chevalier, has the following entry in his *Répertoire des Sources Historiques du Moyen Âge* (Bio-Bibliographie, I. 1701. Paris, 1905). "Geoffroy d'Auxerre, cisterc. à Clairvaux 1140, secrét. de St. Bernard, abbé d'Igny, de Clairvaux 1162 (résig. 1165), de Fossanuova 1170, de Hautecombe 1176, † ? nov. 8." Chevalier would thus seem on the whole to follow the *Chronicon Clarevallense ;* but the *Chronicon* says nothing of *Autissiodorensis*.

3. Finally, Dom Paul Séjourné, referring to the Anchin MS. of St. Bernard's works (Douai 372), writes : "Notre manuscrit est certainement postérieur à 1165 "—the date of Geoffrey's resignation of the Abbacy of Clairvaux—" puis qu'il parle de Geoffroy d'Auxerre, *quondam Clarevallensi abbate* " ; a statement on the part of the editor of this MS. which implies that he identifies Geoffrey of Auxerre with the Fourth Abbot of Clairvaux and with the biographer of St. Bernard (*Les inédits Bernardins du manuscrit d'Anchin, Saint Bernard et son Temps,* II. 266. Dijon, 1929).

To the present writer it would seem reasonable to accept, so far as it goes, the evidence of the *Chronicon Clarevallense,* a XIIIth century MS. to which, as we have seen (p. 377 *supra*), so high an authority as Delisle attached great credit as a record of the affairs of Clairvaux from 1147 to 1192, supported, as it is, by an early XIIIth century writer, namely, Helinandus.   Moreover, we recognize a detail in this *Chronicon* which finds confirmation in a letter of John of Salisbury. The *Chronicon* records the resignation of Clairvaux by Abbot Geoffrey

in 1165. In a letter from John of Salisbury to St. Thomas we read :
" Ipse "—namely, the Archbishop of Rheims—" autem ad Claram
Vallem profectus est, accitus, ut aiunt, a majore parte conventus ad
ruinam abbatis." This letter (*Ep.* ccxvii., *op. cit.*, V. 448) the editor
in the Rolls Series (J. C. Robertson) assigns to the July of 1166.
Waiving the question as to whether the date should not be 1165
rather than 1166, it is not improbable that we have here a reference
to the *odia concitata* against Geoffrey which the *Chronicon* records,
and that these *odia* may be connected with his support of the cause of
St. Thomas of Canterbury. The *Chronicon* proceeds to tell us that,
after some few years spent *contemplationi vacans*, Geoffrey became
Abbot of Fossanova, and in 1176 Abbot of Hautecombe ; and further
that he wrote the *Life* of St. Pierre de Tarentaise. St. Pierre died
in 1174 ; and at Hautecombe, not very far distant from the Tarentaise,
Geoffrey would have had every facility for such a purpose. True,
the *Chronicon* does not speak of him either as St. Bernard's secretary
or as his biographer ; but it is a little surprising that, if he were not
such, there is no separate record of so distinguished a monk of
Clairvaux as the secretary and biographer undoubtedly was. His
secretarial and biographical services might well have been a matter
of common knowledge, whereas his authorship of the *Life* of St.
Pierre de Tarentaise, a work done in old age, might not have been.
De Visch (*Op. cit., loc. cit.*) thinks it to be incredible that a man like
Geoffrey, the secretary and biographer, who was so humble as to
decline a bishopric, should have flitted about from Igny to Clairvaux,
to Fossanova and to Hautecombe. But, surely, duty may impose
a wandering life upon the humblest of men ; nor is it quite clear how
in this case the question of advancement, in any worldly sense of the
term, arises.

There is, further, the distinction of the writer of the IIIrd, IVth
and Vth Books of the *Vita Prima*, and of the *Fragmenta*, from the
writer of the larger portion of Part iii of the *Liber Miraculorum*.
This distinction is, as we have seen (pp. 378 sq. *supra*), supported by
various authorities. The last-named work describes the journeying
of St. Bernard from Liège to Clairvaux, from Clairvaux to Étampes,
and thence again to Clairvaux, during which we have good reason for
believing that his biographer Geoffrey accompanied him (*e.g.* " Ipsa
die venimus Barram super Albam." III. xiii. 44) ; this Geoffrey
was certainly the writer of the *Fragmenta ;* moreover Part iii of the
Liber follows immediately the *Fragmenta* in the *Codex Aureaevallensis ;*
although of this last point we should perhaps not make too much.

We have yet to deal with the difficulty presented by the description *Autissiodorensis.*

We need, as we have noticed, take little account of the additional
qualification *Episcopum.* There would seem to be no escaping the
fact that John of Salisbury (*Ep.* cccix, *ad Baldwinum Archidiac.
Exon., op. cit.*, VI. 404) and others knew the Fourth Abbot of Clairvaux
as *Gaufridus Autissiodorensis.* We know that Geoffrey of Auxerre
was a person of great learning (p. 377 *supra*). The MSS. of his various
works were seen by Dom Baldwin Moreau, secretary to Abbot
Nicolas Boucherat, in the library at Cîteaux in 1618 (De Visch,
op. cit., loc. cit.). Is it possible that Geoffrey, the secretary and
biographer, before he was a disciple of Abélard at Ste. Geneviève, had
studied at Auxerre, and that the appellation *Autissiodorensis* had,
for some reason been revived, or perhaps first attached to him,

during the long controversy over the affairs of St. Thomas of Canterbury, persisting in the *Chronicon* of Helinandus written during the first quarter of the XIIIth century ? Here, unfortunately, the Archives de l'Yonne at Auxerre fail us ; the only Geoffrey of this period whom they present to us is a comparatively obscure person who was a member of the Chapter of Sens.

One is sometimes tempted to wonder whether, perhaps, the critical ingenuity of the XVIIth century may not in this instance have over-reached itself ; whether, indeed, after all there ever was more than one Geoffrey in the case—and he *Gaufridus Autissidorensis* simply because he was born at Auxerre. If this be so, the summary given in *Gallia Christiana* (IV. 800 sq. *ed.* Piolin, 1876) may be regarded as in the main sufficiently reliable. Its omissions, however, are noteworthy ; not only is there no such description as *Autissiodorensis,* but there is no suggestion that the Fourth Abbot of Clairvaux ever refused a bishopric. On the other hand, it is significantly stated that when finally he became Abbot of Hautecombe "familiariter usus est S. Petro Stamedii abbate, deinde archiepiscopo Tarentasiensi " ; the difficulty is that, according to the *Chronicon Clarevallense* (p. 377 *supra*), St. Pierre de Tarentaise, who is presumably intended, had died two years earlier, in 1174. This IVth volume of *Gallia Christiana* was issued by the Congrégation de St. Maur in 1738, thirteen years after the death of Dom Denis de Ste Marthe.

APPENDIX IV

THE EPISTLE TO THE CANONS OF LYONS

ABOUT the year 1140 it came to the knowledge of St. Bernard that
what was to him an entirely new feast, namely, that of the Conception
of the B.V. Mary, had been instituted in the Church of Lyons. The
famous Epistle CLXXIV is his remonstrance.   After paying due
tribute to the adherence of this ancient church to the sound traditions
of antiquity, to its abhorrence of novelties lacking the credit of
authority, he writes : " I am indeed surprised that in these days it
has seemed well to some of you to seek to bring discredit upon your
so great reputation by introducing a new solemnity unknown to
the ritual of the Church, unfounded in reason (quam non probat ratio),
unsanctioned by ancient tradition."   It is manifest that in St.
Bernard's view the confirmation of a feast such as this, a feast professedly declaring the Church's interpretation of a fact precedent in the
divine economy to the incarnation of the Son of God, was a matter
for no less an authority than that of the Apostolic See.   However,
he evidently felt it to be open to him, in the absence of any such
authoritative pronouncement, to argue the point on its theological
merits.   He was aware of the story that the doctrine of the immaculate conception of Mary and the command to observe a feast
in its honour had been revealed in a vision to a certain Helsin, Abbot
of Ramsey (Ep. CLXXIV. 6) ; but he was not aware, we may infer,
that in the West the feast is first heard of at Naples in the IXth
century, and had been observed in various churches in England,
perhaps also in Ireland, so early as the middle of the XIth century
(Edmund Bishop, Liturgica Historica, X. 238 sqq.).   It scarcely concerns us to record the history of the observance of the feast in the XIIth
century, or to tell of the controversy which arose between Nicholas,
a monk of the Abbey of St. Alban, and Walter Daniel, the writer of
the Vita Aelredi, in consequence of an attack made by Nicholas upon
St. Bernard's attitude in the matter.   It will be sufficient to refer
the reader to such authorities as Migne, P.L. CCII. 613 sqq., where
is to be found the correspondence on the subject between Nicholas
and Peter de la Celle, Abbot of St. Remi, afterwards Bishop of
Chartres ; E. W. Williamson, The Letters of Osbert of Clare ; Professor
F. M. Powicke, John Rylands Library Bulletin, VI. 318 sqq. ; and
to the Liturgica Historica of Edmund Bishop cited above, which
deals exhaustively with the question, in particular with the correspondence of the above-named Osbert of Clare, a monk of Westminster
who in 1134 became prior of that house, a man who strongly supported Anselm, Abbot of Bury, in the revival of the Feast of the
Conception of Blessed Mary.
    Some ten years before St. Bernard's letter was addressed to the
Canons of Lyons, perhaps in 1129, Osbert had complained to Anselm

of objections raised that " a feast ought not to be celebrated, the origination of which had not been sanctioned by the authority of the Roman Church," and had begged Anselm, as one who " knows by experience the customs of the Roman Church, to inform him if reliable authority can, or at any time shall, be found in that Church for the venerable conception of the Mother of God " (*Ep.* VII, Williamson, *op. cit.* 66 sq.). It is sufficiently plain that in St. Bernard's view no such authority had been found in 1140.

As regards St. Bernard's treatment of the question on its theological merits, it should be said at once that the " santo sene," whom Dante represents to us in the *Paradiso* as confident that the Queen of Heaven would grant them every grace, " perocch' io sono il suo fedel Bernardo " (*Canto* xxxi. 94 sqq., *ed.* Moore, 149), was perhaps the greatest master of devotion to Mary that Christendom has ever known. We need not labour this point. In the letter with which we are dealing he calls upon his correspondents to " magnify the discoverer of grace, the mediator of salvation, the restorer of the ages " (*Ep.* CLXXIV. 2). Elsewhere his sense of the supreme moral greatness of Mary is expressed in such words as " I dare to say that without humility not even the virginity of Mary would have been acceptable " (*Super* Missus est *Hom.* I. 5) ; she is so high because she is so humble,

> " Umile ed alta più che creatura,
> Termine fisso d'eterno consiglio " ;

we are not far astray in taking the beautiful *orazione* with which Dante opens *Canto* xxxiii of the *Paradiso* as expressive of St. Bernard's sense of the glories of Mary. For him as Christ the Lord is the fount of the water of life, so Mary, in a unique sense our Lady, is the aqueduct (*In Nat. B.V. Mar. Serm. de Aquaeductu*, 3 sq.). And yet we find him writing to the Canons of Lyons : " You say that the Lord's mother is worthy of the highest honour. You counsel well ; but the honour of the Queen loveth right judgement " (*Ep.* CLXXIV. 2). What does it mean ?

In his letter to Anselm of Bury (*Ep.* VII, *op. cit.*) Osbert seeks to justify belief in the immaculate conception of Mary on grounds quite apart from the consideration of what authority there may be for the observance of the feast. After quoting the cases of the Baptist and Jeremiah (Jer. i. 5), he proceeds to reason that, even as it was possible for God to form without sin from the rib of Adam our first mother Eve, in order that she might be a helpmate to her husband (*adjutorium viro*), " so we believe that it was not impossible for him to sanctify without infection of sin at her very conception (*sine contagione peccati in ipsa conceptione sanctificaret*) the Blessed Virgin Mary formed from the sinful stock of Adam, through whom he might bestow that helpmate to the human race (*adjutorium humano generi*) eternally predestined to raise it from death unto life." Osbert's meaning is sufficiently plain.

Precisely how the Canons of Lyons reasoned we do not know. We infer however from St. Bernard's words that they instanced the sanctification effected in the cases of Jeremiah and the Baptist. This St. Bernard will allow ; and naturally he will allow no less in the case of Mary. "Without doubt the mother of the Lord was holy before she was born. . . . I hold that a richer blessing of sanctification descended upon her "—than upon Jeremiah or the Baptist—

"which not only sanctified her birth, but from that moment preserved her life free from all sin, a gift which is believed to have been bestowed upon none other born of woman" (*Ep. cit.* 5). He means, of course, "none other born" strictly in the order of nature. But in the case of one not conceived of the Holy Ghost "how," he argues, "was sin excluded, where lust was present?" In attributing the transmission of original sin to *libido actualis* St. Bernard reflects a stage of theological thought which had not yet reached its term. It remained for St. Thomas Aquinas to transmute and complete the theory by a synthesis of the doctrine of St. Anselm and that of St. Augustine. It is *libido habitualis*, "secundum quod appetitus sensitivus non continetur sub ratione, soluto vinculo originalis justitiae," which transmits original sin (*Summa Theol.*, Iᵃ IIᵃᵉ. lxxxii. 4 *ad* 3).

Thus we see (*Ep. cit.* 7) that St. Bernard would allow, indeed maintain, a unique sanctification of the Mother of God effected *in utero*, but not *inter amplexus maritales*, a sanctification which made her birth holy in such a sense that she was born sinless (*excluso peccato*).

Later a clear distinction was drawn between the *conceptio activa*, immediately consequent upon the *amplexus maritales*, and *conceptio passiva* or the *animatio foetus*, a distinction to be recognized, for example, in Albertus Magnus (*In Sent.*, III. viii. 3 sq.), in Alexander of Hales (*Summa Univ. Theol.*, III. ix. 2) and in St. Thomas Aquinas (*Summa Theol.*, III. xxvii. 2). According to this distinction, the *anima* alone being the subject of grace in the sense implied, it alone is receptive of sanctification. We may perhaps quote the *Conclusio* of St. Thomas. "Cum Beata Virgo redemptione et salute, quae per Christum est, indiguerit ; nonnisi post animationem sanctificata fuit." This distinction, whether or not implicit in certain remarks of Osbert of Clare, was not formulated in St. Bernard's day ; in any case we fail to trace it in his Epistle CLXXIV, in which the fundamental point at issue, as he sees it, would rather seem to be whether *quantum ad peccatum originis* Mary was conceived as was Jesus. Nor does a further distinction—which has some bearing upon the subject—that, namely, between what *per se* results *e generatione* and what *per accidens*, appear to have been present to his mind at all.

APPENDIX V

ST. HILDEGARDE

It will be remembered that, after the departure of Louis le Jeune and the Crusaders from St. Denis about the second week in June, 1147, Eugenius III remained in France. Later in the year, on 30th November, he arrived at Trèves, where he consecrated Henry Murdach for the vacant See of York (pp. 167 and 175 *supra*). It was on this occasion that the visions of a certain Hildegarde were brought to the notice of the Pope by her diocesan, Henry Archbishop of Mainz (*Vita S. Hildeg.*, I. 5, *P.L.* CXCVII. 94 sq.).

Hildegarde was a nun, and from 1136 abbess, of the ancient Abbey of St. Disibode, a double Benedictine house in the diocese of Mainz, situated on the Disibodenberg near the right bank of the Nahe some twenty miles above its confluence with the Rhine at Bingen. About the year 1147 or 1148, the number of the nuns increasing, a colony was founded on the Mons-Sancti-Ruperti near Bingen, of which Hildegarde herself became first abbess (Trithem. *Chron. Spanheim. an.* 1148; *Gall. Christ.*, V. 653. *nov. ed.* ; *Acta SS. Bolland.*, *Sept.* V. *die* xvii. 629 sqq., *P.L.* CXCVII. 20 sq.).

History tells us of a most remarkable woman. Her visions, which began when she was of the age of forty-two (S. Hildeg. *Scivias*, I. *Praefat.*, *P.L.* CXCVII. 383), are recorded in considerable number. The work entitled *Scivias*, i.e. *Sci vias Domini*, gives twenty-six. Her other work of the same character, the *Liber Divinorum Operum Simplicis Hominis*, divided into three Parts, contains ten visions, but the points revealed in the more than three hundred *capitula* in which they are presented are innumerable. The concluding words of the *Liber* proclaim at once her motive and her confidence : *Verba autem haec fideles devoto cordis affectu percepiant, quoniam per illum, qui primus et novissimus est, ad utilitatem credentium edita sunt* (*P.L.* CXCVII. 1038).

She was evidently regarded throughout the Rhineland and its neighbouring districts as possessed of genuine prophetic gifts. A very large proportion of the *Epistolae S. Hildegardis* which have come down to us consist of long and careful *responsa* to letters of inquiry and request—which are also given—addressed to her. We have, moreover, her *Solutiones* of thirty-eight difficulties, chiefly Biblical, laid before her by a monk of Gembloux by name Gilbert, as well as *Explanationes* of the Rule of St. Benedict and of the *Symbolum* of St. Athanasius, and another work entitled *Liber Vitae Meritorum* (*Nova Hildeg. Opera, ed.* Pitra). But she was more than a prophetess and a theologian ; she was a keen student of nature, and like Solomon she "spake of trees . . . of fowl . . . and of fishes," nay, even *De Lapidibus* (*Physica*, *P.L.* CXCVII. 1129 sqq.).

She was, however, ignorant of the Latin tongue, for when about the year 1141 she began with much trepidation and in ill-health to commit the *Scivias* to writing she made use of a monk of St. Disibode, who not only acted as her scribe but counselled her generally in the matter (*Scivias*, I. *Praefat.*, *P.L.* CXCVII. 386 ; Trithem. *Chron. Spanheim. an.* 1179; *Acta SS. Bolland.*, *P.L.* CXCVII. 19). It would seem that shortly afterwards Hildegarde consulted St. Bernard. There is a degree of caution about his reply. "Caeterum ubi interior eruditio est, et unctio docens de omnibus," he writes, " quid nos aut docere possumus, aut monere ? Diceris enim coelestia secreta rimari, et ea quae supra homines sunt, Spiritu Sancto illustrante, dignoscere. Unde rogamus magis, et suppliciter postulamus, ut nostri memoriam habeas apud Deum, et eorum pariter qui nobis in spirituali societate juncti sunt " (*Ep.* CCCLXVI).

Eugenius III, when in 1147 the case was submitted to him at Trèves, appointed a commission, consisting of the Bishop of Verdun and others, to visit Hildegarde and report to him, with the result that the Pope accorded his Apostolic recognition to the claims of Hildegarde *multa secreta videre, intelligere et proferre* in a letter addressed to herself (Trithem. *Chron. Hirsaug. an.* 1150; *Acta SS. Bolland.*, *P.L.* CXCVII. 25 ; *Ep. Eugen. Pontif. ad. Hildeg.*, *P.L.* CXCVII. 145) ; but not, it would seem, before he had heard read some or all of such portions of the *Scivias* as were already written— it was not finished until 1151. St. Bernard, although probably he was not a member of the commission which had visited Hildegarde, was present at Trèves to hear its report, and approved the course taken by Eugenius in the matter (*Acta SS. Bolland.*, *P.L.* CXCVII. 19 and 23 ; *Vita S. Hildeg.* I. 5, *P.L.* CXCVII. 95). A letter of John of Salisbury (*Ep.* ccxcvi. *Magistro Girardo Pucelle, Materials for the Hist. of Th. Becket*, VI. 181., *R.S.*), dated 1167 by the editor, is evidence of the high credit which in the opinion of that astute person had been attached to the visions and oracles of Hildegarde by the authority of Eugenius. " Quae," he writes, "mihi ex eo commendata est et venerabilis, quod eam dominus Eugenius speciali caritatis affectu familiarius amplectebatur."

APPENDIX VI

PETER THE VENERABLE

Pierre Maurice de Montboissier, a native of Auvergne, the seventh son of Maurice Seigneur de Montboissier, played a leading part in the world of St. Bernard's day ; his relations with the Abbot of Clairvaux were frequent and intimate. Their correspondence, such of it as is published in the *Patrologia Latina* of Migne (CLXXXIX. 112-475), consists of twenty-two letters which reveal " deux âmes qui veulent le même bien, la parfaite régularité monastique, et qui la poursuivent, l'un par la fermeté, l'autre par la persuasion, méthodes différentes qui se partagent les hommes, les triomphes et les temps " (René Bazin, *Millénaire de Cluny*, I. *Séance d'Ouverture*, 17. Mâcon, 1910). Something like ten more letters, which breathe the same spirit, are to be found in the Benedictine edition and in the *Patrologia* amongst St. Bernard's correspondence.

And in truth it was the possession of a common spirit, rather than the pursuit of a common end, which explained the cordiality of their mutual relations. Peter could write to St. Bernard in 1149 : " Si liceret, si Dei dispositio non obstaret, si in hominis potestate esset via ejus ; maluissem charissimae Beatudini tuae nexu indissolubili adhaerere, quam principari inter mortales alicubi, vel regnare. Quid enim ? Nonne regnis omnibus terrenis praeferri a me deberet grata non solum hominibus, sed et angelis ipsis cohabitatio tua ? . . . Si plane mihi datum fuisset usque ad ultimum spiritum tecum hic esse, daretur fortassis posthac et ubi esses, etiam perpetuo esse " (Petr. Ven. *Ep. ap.* S. Bern. *Epp.* CCLXIV.). These, be it remembered, are the words of a man who was the cautious, level-headed administrator of vast material property—to say nothing else. Of Peter St. Bernard had written in a letter commending him to Eugenius III in 1146 : " Iste est qui manus suas extendit ad pauperes Ordinis nostri ; iste est qui de possessionibus ecclesiae suae, quantum cum pace potest suorum, libenter frequenterque largitur ad victum." He views with anxiety the possibility of Peter's resignation of his abbacy. " In nomine Jesu cur dixerim, audite," he continues. " Si enim petierit (quod suspicor vereorque) dimitti a regimine monasterii, quis illum noscens, in nomine Jesu petere putet ? . . . Quanquam pene ab introitu suo in multis Ordinem illum meliorasse cognoscitur " (*Ep.* CCLXXVII.). We seem to detect here a desire on the part of Peter to become a Clairvaux monk, a desire which St. Bernard regarded with disfavour, albeit on entirely disinterested grounds, and the frustration of which Peter regretted deeply.

Peter paid a formal visit of respect to Eugenius III at Rome in 1146, when he expressed, we gather, this desire to the Pope in person. He describes his reception and the proceedings of the *Curia* in a letter to St. Bernard. " Senatui Romanorum, episcoporum, vel cardinalium, non tantum adjungebar, sed et quandoque adjungi cogebar. Excludebantur universi non Romani a Romanis consiliis : solus aut pene solus ad mysteria jurata vocabar " (*Epp. Lib.* VI. xlvi. *ap. P.L.* CLXXXIX. 466. Cf. Petr. Ven. *De Mirac.* II. 25). He was evidently treated with exceptional honour ; but he is careful to report the almost exclusively Roman influence which prevailed in the *Curia*, a matter of special interest and displeasure to St. Bernard (cf. pp. 249 sq. *supra*). But, like the latter, he was always to be found at the side of the Pope in any difficulty. " Contra spem omnium Innocentio per mare venienti festive occurrit, et sine consilio Gallicanae Ecclesiae, datis sufficienter equitaturis, Cluniacum secum adduxit. Quod reges terrae audientes, mirati sunt quomodo monachum suum in sede positum "—*sc.* Anacletus II—" relinqueret, et extraneum exaltaret : quem tam solemniter suscepit ut orbi universo nota fieret ejus receptio." Peter, as we might say, saw it all through ; " nam usque ad Urbem cum ipso (Innocentio) perrexit, et eum in pace, mortuo antipapa, in sede collocavit " (*Vita Petr. Ven. auctore Rodulpho monacho ejus discipulo*, 4 [Mart. et Dur. *Vet. Script. et Mon. Ampl. Coll.* VI. 1187 sqq. and *P.L.* CLXXXIX. 15 sqq. ex MS. Silviacensis Monast.]). It may be said in passing that this *Vita* is the contemporary work of a monk who was wont to accompany Peter when he visited the *cellae* of the Order ; he is perhaps to be identified with the Rodulphus de Sully, nephew of Henry of Winchester, who was promoted from the Priory of La-Charité-sur-Loire to be XIIth Abbot of Cluny in 1173 ; as such he ruled until 1176 (*Gall. Christ.* IV. 1141 sq.). Another *Vita, ex Chronico Cluniacensi*, is given by Marrier in the *Bibliotheca Cluniacensis*, pp. 589 sqq., Paris, 1614.

A letter to Innocent II (*Epp. Lib.* I. i.) expresses Peter's regret for his failure in adequately supporting the Pope at the Council of Pisa in 1135 and ascribes it to ill-health evidently he found the *elementa* and the *alimenta* of Italy, especially of Rome, grievously *nociva* (*Epp. Lib.* I. iii.). " Doleo quidem, et non parum, teste illo quem fallere non possum, contristor," he writes, " quod sine me labores tantos hoc maxime tempore toleratis, sed fragilitas cerei vasculi mei tanta est ut, sicut saepe expertus sum, ad Italiae soles prius pene cogatur liquescere quam incipiat apparere. Vidistis ipse, qualiter hac de causa, nuper apud Pisas et vobis inutilis, et mihi ipsi importabilis eram, et nisi cito recedere festinassem, vitam simul et negotia terminassem." In this letter he assures the Pope of the fidelity of Cluny to him " sit ubicunque occurrerit habitatio vestra," aptly quoting Lucan (*Phars.* V. 28 sq.) :

> " . . . Veiosque habitante Camillo,
>   Illic Roma fuit . . . "

Evidently the exile of Innocent was seriously prejudicing his cause. Incidentally the letter is a sidelight upon the unwillingness, supposed or real, of French ecclesiastics to be present at the council (cf. pp. 137 sq. *supra*).

A translation of the Koran has been wrongly attributed to Peter —a mistake perchance due to the fact that he wrote a treatise *Contra Saracenos* (*P.L.* CLXXXIX. 661 sq.) ; but there is no doubt but that, when in 1141 he was visiting houses of the Order in Spain, he set others to this task, in particular a certain *Robertus Retenensis* (? *Ketenensis, al. Kertnensis*), a travelled Englishman who settled in Spain and died Archdeacon of Pampeluna. In collaboration with others, but under his own name, Robertus produced *cir.* 1143 a work entitled *Alcoranum in Compendium Redactum Latine*, the preface of which, addressed to Peter, may be found in the *Bibliotheca Cluniacensis* (*Gall. Christ.* IV. 1139; *P.L.* CLXXXIX. 649 sqq., 1073 sqq.).

During his rule of thirty-five years and more, 1122 to 1158, the growth of the Order was phenomenal. The *Bibliotheca Cluniacensis* refers to the aggregation of nearly 314 " ecclesias, collegia et monasteria," including Mount Thabor and a Monastery in the Valley of Jehosaphat ; it speaks of the religious houses and various offices, such as *decanatus* and *praepositurae*, " tam mediate quam immediate eidem subjecta " as " circa duo millia vel amplius."

Peter died on the Feast of the Nativity, as for thirty years he had prayed that he might do (*Vita Petr. Ven. auctore Rodulph.* 17)— 1158, and was buried " juxta altare SS. Jacobi et Philippi " in the Abbey-Church, the rites being performed by Henry of Winchester (*Gall. Christ.* IV. 1139).

APPENDIX VII

PLANS OF THE ABBEY OF CLAIRVAUX

D'Arbois de Jubainville (*Études sur l'état intérieur des abbayes Cisterciennes et principalement de Clairvaux, au xii⁰ et au xiii⁰ siècles.* 36 *n.* 1) refers to Viollet-le-Duc's "réduction du plan général de l'abbaye" (*Dictionnaire d'Architecture,* I. 266 sq.). This gives the plan of the third period subsequent to that of the *Monasterium Vetus,* i.e. of the early fourth quarter of the XIIth century. As a fact, two plans are provided.

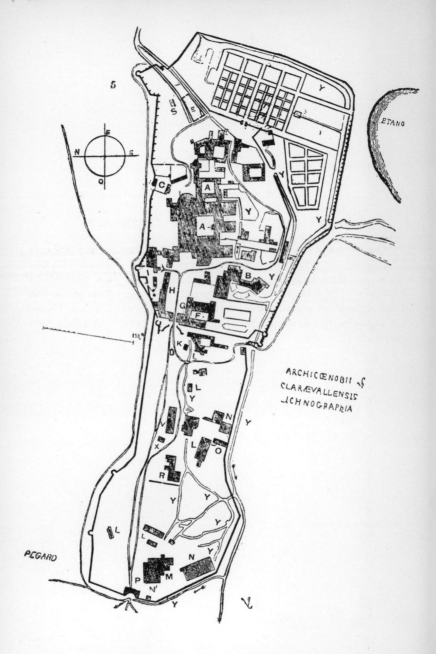

(I), numbered 5, p. 266. Key :—

A, church and two cloisters :

B, bakehouses, flour-mills and oil-mills :

C, cell, oratory and garden of St. Bernard—religiously preserved :

D, principal entrance :

E, fish-pond fed by water-courses :

F, hostelry :

G, abbot's lodging—near principal entrance and hostelry :

H, stables—probably for horses of guests :

I, a *promenoir*—probably so situated for the convenience of guests :

K, *parloir*—for interviewing persons not admitted to the monastery :

LLL, dwellings and workshops of hired artisans :

M, slaughter-house :

NNN, granges and stables :

O, public press-house :

P, great gate to *enceinte* :

R, remains of *Monasterium Vetus* :

S, an oratory :

V, tile-works :

X, kiln of tile-works :

YYY, water-courses.

Note (*a*) watch-towers on walls of *enceinte*, and (*b*) kitchen-gardens to extreme E. watered by trenches.

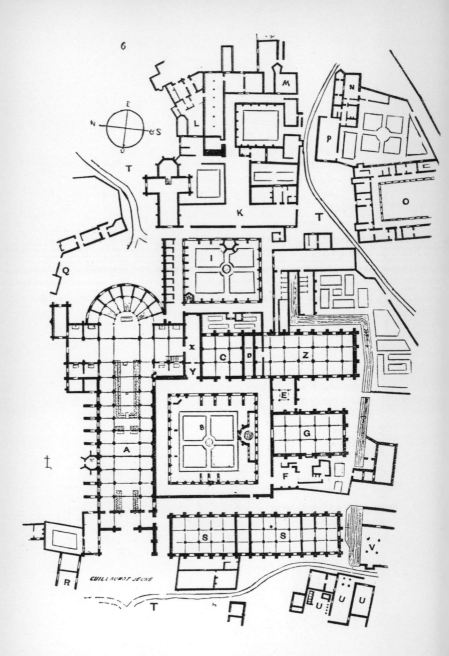

(II), numbered 6, p. 267. Key :—

A, church. Note stalls of (*a*) choir-monks W. of central bay of crossing and of (*b*) *conversi* E. of narthex :

B, greater cloister with covered lavatory :

C, chapter-house with three windows opening to E. on a small garden :

D, monks' *parloir*, with to the S. a passage leading to the staircase to library and dormitory :

E, calefactory, where monks warmed themselves after Lauds, and where they greased their sandals :

F, kitchen, with little yard and running water :

G, refectory, with door opposite lavatory :

I, little cloister, with eight cells for scribes on N. side :

K, infirmary and its offices. The chapel to the N., la-Chapelle-des-Comtes-de-Flandres, was an addition later than 1178 :

L, noviciate :

M, a hostelry additional to Plan I, *F* ; Viollet-le-Duc describes it as *ancien logis des étrangers* :

N, an abbot's lodging additional to Plan I, *G* ; Viollet-le-Duc describes this as *ancien logis abbatial* :

O, cloister of aged and infirm monks :

P, abbot's hall :

Q, cell and oratory of St. Bernard :

R, stables probably for horses, and additional to Plan I, *H* :

S, granges and storehouses :

T, water-courses :

U, sawyers' workshop and oil-mill :

V, tanners' workshop :

X, sacristy :

Y, a small library (*armariolum*) for books in actual use.

The large structure, S. of the chapter-house, monks' *parloir* and adjacent passage, marked *Z*, Viollet-le-Duc does not particularize. Its position suggests that on the ground floor was the fratry and above it an extension of the dormitory. The staircase in the S. transept led to the dormitory, and facilitated attendance at Nocturns. Viollet-le-Duc speaks of the hall S. of the little cloister as used for conferences at which theses were propounded and refuted. The latrines he locates on the edge of the water-course near the little cloister.

As we have suggested (p. 59 *supra*), many of the details of these plans are conjectural. For instance, the juxta-position of library and dormitory is a little difficult to accept without further explanation. The descriptions *ancien logis des étrangers* and *ancien logis abbatial* are even more so. It may be reasonable, considering early Cistercian traditions, to regard the buildings near the principal entrance marked *F* and *G* on Plan I as the original hostelry and abbot's lodging. However conjectural on minor points, the plans in their main features, such as the position and area of the church and adjacent dormitory, the positions of the refectory and two cloisters, give a general impression of the Clairvaux, say, of Petrus Monoculus, the eighth abbot (1179-1186, *Gall. Christ.* IV. 803, *ed.* 1876).

We may compare with Viollet-le-Duc's plans one of Dom Nicolas Milley's plans of 1708, when what Viollet-le-Duc had only read of was in the main still *in situ*. Cf. p. 20 *supra*. It is possible that the latter may be wrong in certain details, e.g. as to the position and number of the *Cellulae Scriptoriae*.

ITINERARIA

Innocent II

Rome (*cir.* Feb. 28th 1130)—Pisa (by sea)—Genoa (by sea)—St. Gilles (by sea)—Cluny (*viâ* the Vivarais)—Roanne—Clermont-en-Auvergne (Nov. 18th)—Orleans and St. Benôit-sur-Loire—Chartres—Abbey of Maurigny (Jan. 1131)—Liège (Ap. 1st)—St. Denis (Holy Week and Easter)—Rouen (May 9th)—Beauvais—Compiègne—Crépy-en-Valois —Auxerre (July 26th-Sept. 24th)—Clairvaux—Rheims (Oct. 18th)— Paris (Nov. 11th)—Auxerre (Nov. 28th-Dec. 30th)—Autun (Jan. 18th 1132)—Cluny (Feb. 2nd)—Lyons—Vienne—Valence—Avignon—Gap (Mar. 30th)—Asti (Ap. 10th)—Piacenza (*cir.* May 31st)—Cremona, Brescia and Modena (July 14th-Nov. 4th)—Piacenza (Nov. 4th)—Roncaglia (*cir.* Nov. 8th)—Bologna (Dec. 13th)—Pisa (*cir.* Jan. 15th 1133)— Grosseto (Mar. 19th)—Calcinaja—Viterbo—Rome (Ap. 30th)—Pisa (by sea, Sept.)—Piacenza (Nov. 5th)—Pisa (Nov. 16th)—Pisa (Jan. 8th 1134)—Pisa (Nov. 8th)—Pisa (May 30th-June 6th 1135)—Viterbo (Mar. 26th-Ap. 8th 1137)—Monte Cassino (May 7th)—Bari (May 30th) —Monte Cassino (July 6th-18th)—Rome (Nov. 1st).

It will be seen that the Pope's exile from Rome falls into two periods. The former and the shorter was for the most part spent in France, and extended from the end of February, 1130, to April, 1133. The longer period began in September, 1133, and ended in October, 1137, during which more than four years Pisa would seem to have been usually the *local* of the Papal Court. The itinerary given is not, however, to be regarded as more than a summary of the story as told in the text.

St. Bernard

The Missionary Journey in Languedoc.—Clairvaux—Poitiers— Angoulême—Limoges—Bordeaux (*cir.* June 1st 1145)—Bergerac— Périgueux—Sarlat—Cahors—Toulouse—Daumazan—Verfeil—Albi (June 28th)—Clairvaux (*cir.* Aug. 22nd).

The Germanicum Iter.—Clairvaux—Arras (*cir.* Sept. 1146)— Abbey of St. Bertin at St. Omer—Ypres—Bruges—Afflighem— Gembloux—Villers (Oct. 18th)—Liège—Worms (*cir.* Nov. 1st)— Mainz (*cir.* Nov. 8th)—Frankfort—Kenzingen (Dec. 1st)—Freiburg (Dec. 3rd)—Krotzingen—Heitersheim—Stieng (? Schliengen)—Basel (Dec. 6th)—Rheinfelden—Schaffhausen (Dec. 8th)—Constance (Dec. 12th)—Winterthur—Zürich—Rheinfelden—Basel—Strassburg (Dec. 22nd)—Spires (Dec. 24th—Jan. 3rd 1147)—Worms—Kreuznach (Jan. 6th)—Pichenbach—Coblenz—Remagen—Cologne—(Jan. 9th) —Abbey of Brauweiler (Jan. 13th)—Jülich—Aix-la-Chapelle (Jan. 15th)—Maëstricht—Liège (Jan. 18th)—Huy—Gembloux (Jan. 22nd)

—Villers (Jan. 23rd)—Fontaine-l'Évêque—Binche—Mons (Jan. 24th)
—Valenciennes (Jan. 25th)—Cambrai (Jan. 26th)—Vaucelles (Jan.
28th)—Gomme (Jan. 29th)—Abbey of Hombleux (Jan. 30th)—St.
Jean-de-Laon (Jan. 31st)—Rheims—Châlons-sur-Marne (Feb. 1st)
—Donnemont (Feb. 4th)—Rosnay—Brienne-le-Château—Bar-sur-
Aube (Feb. 5th)—Clairvaux (Feb. 6th).

The Journey to the Assembly of Étampes.—Clairvaux—Mondeville
—Ville-sur-Arce—Bourguignons—Fouchères—Vaudes—Troyes (*cir.*
Feb. 12th 1147)—Prunay-Belleville—Trainel (Feb. 13th)—Bray—
Montereau-faut-Yonne (Feb. 14th)—Moret-sur-Loing—Étampes (Feb.
15th)—Maisse—Milly—Moret-sur-Loing—Sens (*cir.* Feb. 23rd)—
Joigny—Auxerre—Chablis—Tonnerre (*cir.* Feb. 25th)—Abbey of
Molesme (*cir.* Feb. 26th)—Clairvaux (*cir.* Feb. 27th).

SKETCH-MAP

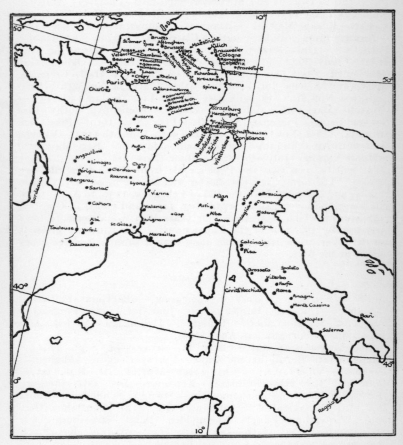

Sketch-map illustrative of the Schism in the Papacy, the Mission in
Languedoc and the Second Crusade.

INDEX OF PERSONS

A

Abélard, Peter, pp. 7, 21, 111, 192, 204, 222, 289 sqq., 318, 320, 322, 336 sq., 354, 368, 376, 381.

Adam, Abbot of Ebrach, p. 274.

Adam, Abbot of St. Denis, pp. 224, 295, 298.

Adam of Petit-Pont, Chancellor of Notre-Dame-de-Paris (subsequently Bishop of St. Asaph), p. 314.

Adela, daughter of William the Conqueror, p. 191.

Adela (or Adelaide), wife of Louis le Gros, pp. 119, 195, 209.

Adelbert I, Count of Saarbrücken and Archbishop of Mainz, Chancellor of Henry V, pp. 45 sq.

Adenulph, Abbot of Farfa, pp. 68 sq.

Aeldred, Abbot of Rievaulx, p. 47.

Agnes, wife of Ebbo of Charenton, p. 61.

Alan (Flandrensis) of Auxerre, biographer of St. Bernard, pp. 2 sq., 66, 188, 360.

Alan of Brittany, founder of the Abbey of St. Mary of York, p. 52.

Alberic, Abbot of La-Bénissons-Dieu, p. 64.

Alberic, 2nd Abbot of Cîteaux, pp. 8, 36.

Alberic (?), Bishop-Elect of Langres, p. 160.

Alberic (formerly Abbot of Vézelay), Cardinal Bishop of Ostia, pp. 208, 315, 340 sqq.

Alberic, Rector of the Cathedral School at Rheims, p. 297.

Albertus Magnus (of Bollstadt), Dominican Provincial in Germany, subsequently Bishop of Regensburg, p. 385.

Albino (formerly Cardinal Deacon of Santa Maria Novella), Cardinal Bishop of Albano, p. 314.

Aldearde, wife's sister to Humbert II, Count of Maurienne, p. 209.

Aleth de Montbard, mother of St. Bernard, pp. 3 sqq., 59.

Alexander, Canon of Cologne, pp. 270, 275.

Alexander de Nagu de Varennes, Prior of St. Marcel-lès-Châlon, p. 313.

Alexander of Hales, a Franciscan, doctor at Paris, p. 385.

Alexander of Scotland, conversus at Foigny, p. 32.

Alexander III, Pope, pp. 362, 380.

Algarda, wife of Oliver de Bessens, p. 79.

Alphandéry, P. D., pp. 332 sq.

Alphonso I, King of Aragon, p. 112.

Alphonso VI, King of Castile, pp. 84, 92.

Alphonso, King of Leon VII and of Castile II, pp. 49, 73 sqq., 78, 83 sqq., 90, 93, 112.

Alphonso I, King of Portugal, pp. 64 sq., 67, 84 sq., 281.

Alphonsus, Count of St. Gilles and of Toulouse, pp. 338, 340 sq.

Alvaro Rodriquez, founder of Meyra, p. 78.

Alvida, Queen of Sweden, foundress of Alfwastra, pp. 77, 89.

Alvisus, Abbot of Anchin (formerly Prior of St. Bertin and subsequently Bishop of Arras), pp. 63, 223, 269, 304, 306.

Amadeus III, Count of Savoy, pp. 55, 61, 265.

Ambrosius, messenger to St. Bernard from Milan, p. 50.

Amelius, Count of Toulouse, p. 79.

Anacletus (or Cletus) I, Pope, p. 68.

Anacletus II (Peter Leonis), Pseudo-Pope, pp. 70, 96, 98 sqq., 115 sq., 121 sq., 126, 134, 138, 145 sqq., 153 sq., 325, 389.

Andrew, brother of St. Bernard, pp. 4, 6, 9 sq., 18, 30.

Andrew of Beaudemont, procurator of Theobald of Champagne, p. 215.

Anseau de Garlande, p. 194.

Anselm, Abbot of Bury, pp. 383 sq.

Anselm, Abbot of Gembloux, the chronicler, pp. 96, 99, 103.

Anselm, Canon of Soignies, founder of Cambron, p. 85.

INDEX OF PLACES

411

INDEX OF MSS. CITED

V

Vatican 3762, XIIth century MS. of the *Liber Pontificalis*, the work in 1142 of " Petrus Guillermus bibliotecarius," identified as a Benedictine monk of the Abbey of St. Gilles. The records, in varying fulness, extend from the days of St. Peter to the death of Honorius II (1130), and are derived from contemporary sources. At the beginning of the XVth century a supplement of twelve leaves has been added, giving records from the pontificate of Innocent II (1130), down to the days—but not to the death in 1285—of Martin IV.
p. 107.

Vatican 663, early XIVth century MS. containing on ff. 3 and 4, between the Epistles of St. Bernard cccxi and ccxli, fourteen *capitula* of the heresies of Abélard. Cf. Vattasso, *Codices Vaticani Latini*, I (1902), pp. 517-522 ; cf. Williams, *Speculum, loc. cit.*
p. 307.

Vatican 1960, *vide* Plans of Mediæval Rome, *note*, pocket.

ABERDEEN : THE UNIVERSITY PRESS